C0-ABX-076

BUREAUCRAT AND INTELLECTUAL IN THE OTTOMAN EMPIRE

PRINCETON STUDIES ON THE NEAR EAST

BUREAUCRAT AND INTELLECTUAL IN THE OTTOMAN EMPIRE

THE HISTORIAN MUSTAFA ÂLİ (1541-1600)

CORNELL H. FLEISCHER

PRINCETON UNIVERSITY PRESS
PRINCETON, NEW JERSEY

Published by Princeton University Press, 41 William Street,
Princeton, New Jersey 08540
In the United Kingdom: Princeton University Press,
Guildford, Surrey

Library of Congress Cataloging in Publication Data will
be found on the last printed page of this book

ISBN 0-691-05464-9

Publication of this book was made possible by a grant from
the Publications Program of the National Endowment
for the Humanities, an independent Federal Agency

This book has been composed in Linotron Times Roman

Clothbound editions of Princeton University Press books
are printed on acid-free paper, and binding materials are chosen
for strength and durability

Printed in the United States of America by Princeton
University Press, Princeton, New Jersey

İTHAFİYE

Çocukluğumu mutlu kılan,
ilim sevgisini uyandıran pederim

Hugh W. Fleischer' in

aziz hatırasına ithaf edilmiştir

To the memory of my father,
a man who loved learning

CONTENTS

List of Illustrations ix
List of Abbreviations xi
Note on Usage xiii
Acknowledgments xvii
Introduction 3

PART I. AN OTTOMAN LIFE

Chapter One. The Making of an Ottoman (1541-63/948-70) 13
Chapter Two. The Poet at the Gates (1563-77/970-84) 41
Chapter Three. To the East (1577-82/984-90) 70
Chapter Four. Toward the Millennium: War, Apocalypse, and History (1583-92/991-1000) 109
Chapter Five. The Final Years (1592-1600/1000-1008) 143

PART II. OTTOMAN LAW, OTTOMAN CAREER

Chapter Six. *Kanun*-Consciousness in the Sixteenth Century 191
Chapter Seven. Âli on the Ottoman Career Paths 201
Chapter Eight. Bureaucracy and Bureaucratic Consciousness 214

PART III. THE MAKING OF OTTOMAN HISTORY

Chapter Nine. Ottoman Historical Writing in the Sixteenth Century 235
Chapter Ten. Muslim and Ottoman 253
Chapter Eleven. The Turkic and Mongol Heritage 273
Chapter Twelve. The Reign of Murad III 293

Appendix A. The Structure of the Ottoman Financial Establishment in the Sixteenth Century 311
Appendix B. Chronology 315

Glossary 319
Bibliography 333
Index 345

LIST OF ILLUSTRATIONS

Page 1: Mustafa Âli. Line drawing by Carolyn Brown, based on detail from NUSRET, 43b. Âli's signature is from the colophon of NADİR, dated December 1568-January 1569/Receb 976.

Following page 142:

Sultan Süleyman the Lawgiver (reg. 1520-66) in 1559; engraving by Melchior Lorichs. From Semavi Eyice, "Avrupalı bir Ressamın Gözü ile Kanunî Sultan Süleyman," in *Kanunî Armağanı* (Ankara, 1970), plate 10.

Grand Vezir Sokollu Mehmed Paşa (1505-79), from life. From Friedrich Kenner, "Die Porträtssammlung des Erzherzogs Ferdinand von Tirol," in *Jahrbuch der Kunsthistorischen Sammlungen des Allerhöchsten Kaiserhauses* 19 (Prague, Vienna, and Leipzig, 1898): 6-146, plate 19, figure 4. Photograph courtesy of Österreichische Nationalbibliothek.

Sultan Selim II (reg. 1566-74) observes an Imperial Council session chaired by Sokollu. From Seyyid Lokman, *Şehname-i Selim Han*, MS TKS A. 3595, 11a.

Sultan Murad III (reg. 1574-95) with Gazanfer Ağa and Hoca Sa'düddin. From NUSRET, 249b.

Comet over Istanbul, November 12, 1577. From NUSRET, 5b.

Sinan Paşa, Koca (d. 1596). From Österreichische Nationalbibliothek, Cod. 8615, fol. 19.

Lala Mustafa Paşa (d. 1580). From Österreichische Nationalbibliothek, Cod. 8615, fol. 20.

Lala Mustafa Paşa's departure from Istanbul to Üsküdar, 5 April 1578/27 Muharrem 986. From NUSRET, 32b.

Lala Mustafa Paşa fêtes the Janissary commanders at İzmid. From NUSRET, 34b.

Âli and Lala Mustafa Paşa at the tomb of Rumi, Konya. From NUSRET, 36a.

Yusuf Beğ, *sancak beği* of Kars, and his Kurds deliver Kızılbaş heads to Lala Mustafa Paşa. From NUSRET, 43b.

Heads arrive at Ardahan. From NUSRET, 62b.

The Ottoman forces before Tiflis. From NUSRET, 80a.

Army encampment. From NUSRET, 93a.

Conquest of Şeki, in Şirvan. From NUSRET, 99b.

Mustafa Paşa, governor-general of Maraş (Zulkadriye), receives imperial treasure for campaign expenses. From NUSRET, 102a.

Ottoman dignitaries perform Friday prayer in newly conquered Ereş, 19 September 1578/16 Receb 986. From NUSRET, 105b.

Campaign council for the disposition of Şirvan. From NUSRET, 106a.

Lala Mustafa Paşa receives the Şamhal, ruler of Dağıstan. From NUSRET, 118b.

Ottoman forces pillage and burn Safavi Iraq. From NUSRET, 154a.

Winter quarters, Erzurum, 1578-79. From NUSRET, 196a.

Sultan Murad III. From Österreichische Nationalbibliothek, Cod. 8615, fol. 15.

İbrahim Paşa, Damad (d. 1601). From Österreichische Nationalbibliothek, Cod. 8615, fol. 23.

Han of the Crimea, Mehmed Giray. From NUSRET, 14b.

Page 309, map: The Ottoman Empire in 1600.

LIST OF ABBREVIATIONS

AB	Nihal Atsız, *Âli Bibliyografyası*
ÂŞIK	Âşık Çelebi, *Meşâʿir üş-şuʿarâ*
BBA	Başbakanlık Arşivi (Başvekâlet Arşivi), Istanbul
BSOAS	*Bulletin of the School of Oriental and African Studies*
CAIRO	Andreas Tietze, *Muṣṭafâ ʿÂlî's Description of Cairo of 1599*
CAMİ'	Âli, *Câmi' ül-buhur der mecâlis-i sûr*. MS Bağdat Köşkü 203
COUNSEL	Andreas Tietze, *Muṣṭafâ ʿÂlî's Counsel for Sultans of 1581*
DİVAN I	Âli, *Divan*. MS Ali Emiri Efendi Türkçe Manzum 275
DİVAN III	Âli, *Divan*. MS İÜ Türkçe 768
DK	Dâr al-kutub al-miṣrîya, Cairo
DKM	Dâr al-kutub al-miṣrîya, Fâḍil Muṣṭafâ Paşa
EI[1]	*Encyclopaedia of Islam*, First Edition
EI[2]	*Encyclopaedia of Islam*, Second Edition
FURSAT	Âli, *Fursatname*. MS Berlin, Preussische Staatsbibliothek ms. or. oct. 2927
FUSUL	Âli, *Fusul-i hall ve akd*. MS Gökbilgin (photocopy)
GAL	Carl Brockelmann, *Geschichte der arabischen Literatur*
GOR	Joseph von Hammer, *Geschichte des osmanischen Reiches*
GOW	Franz Babinger, *Die Geschichtsschreiber der Osmanen und ihre Werke*
İA	*İslâm Ansiklopedisi*
IJMES	*International Journal of Middle East Studies*
İNAL	Mahmud Kemal İbnülemin (İnal), Introduction to *Menakıb-ı hünerveran*
IQD	Ali Mınık, *Al-ʿIqd al-manẓûm fî dhikr afâḍil al-Rûm*
İÜ	İstanbul Üniversitesi Kütüphanesi
İÜİFM	*İstanbul Üniversitesi İktisat Fakültesi Mecmuası*
KA	Âli, *Künh ül-ahbar*
KINALIZADE	Kınalızade Hasan Çelebi, *Tezkeret üş-şu'ara*
KPT	Kâmil Kepeci Tasnifi, Ru'us Defterleri, BBA
LAYİHAT	Âli, *Layihat ül-hakika*. MS DKM Adab Turkî, 21
MD	Mühimme Defterleri, BBA
MENŞE	Âli, *Menşe' ül-inşa*. MS Velieddin 1916
MEVA'İD	Âli, *Mevâ'id ün-nefâ'is fi kavâ'id il-mecâlis*
MH	Âli, *Menakıb-ı hünerveran*
MOG	*Mitteilungen zur osmanischen Geschichte*
NADİR	Âli, *Nadir ül-maharib*. MS DKM Majâmîʿ Turkîya 2
NEVADİR	Âli, *Nevadir ül-hikem*. MS İÜ Türkçe 1846
NUSRET	Âli, *Nusretname*. MS Hazine 1365

Nur	Nuruosmaniye Kütüphanesi
OM	Bursalı Tahir Mehmed, *Osmanlı Mü'ellifleri*
PEÇEVİ	Peçevi (Peçuylu) İbrahim Paşa, *Tarih*
RİYAZ	Âli, *Riyaz üs-sâlikin.* MS Velieddin 1916
SADEF	Âli, *Sadef-i sad güher.* MS Ali Emiri Efendi Türkçe Manzum 978
SBFD	*Ankara Üniversitesi Siyasal Bilgiler Fakültesi Dergisi*
SELANİKİ	Mustafa Selâniki, *Tarih*
SK	Süleymaniye Kütüphanesi, Istanbul
SO	Mehmed Süreyya, *Sicill-i Osmani*
TKS	Topkapı Sarayı Müzesi, Istanbul
TM	*Türkiyat Mecmuası*
TOEM	*Tarih-i Osmani Encümeni Mecmu'ası*
VARİDAT	Âli, *Vâridat ül-enika.* MS Hamidiye 1107
WZKM	*Wiener Zeitschrift für die Kunde des Morgenlandes*
ZDMG	*Zeitschrift der deutschen morgenländischen Gesellschaft*
ZÜBDET	Âli, *Zübdet üt-tevarih.* MS Reşid Efendi 663

NOTE ON USAGE

TRANSLITERATION AND TRANSLATION

ARABIC AND PERSIAN

Arabic and Persian titles, technical terms, and personal names, in appropriate contexts, have been transliterated according to the system now commonly used in most English-language scholarly journals, such as IJMES. In cases in which the context might be either Arabic, Persian, or Turkish, the transliteration system appropriate to the original language has been preferred. In Perso-Turkish contexts Turkish rounded vowels have been retained. Terms familiar to English speakers, such as "Sunni," "Shi'i," "shah," "sultan," and "ulema,' are rendered in their accepted Anglicized form without diacriticals, unless they form part of a transliterated proper name, e.g., "Sulṭân-Ḥusayn Bâyqarâ."

TURKISH

Ottoman Turkish personal names and technical terms have been rendered throughout by means of modern (i.e., post-1928) Turkish orthography, which uses modified Latin script. Modern Turkish transliteration of Arabic and Persian words and constructions used in Ottoman presents some technical problems. The modern system does not distinguish between consonants that are distinct in Arabic script; *ʿeyn* and *hemze* are either ignored or rendered by an apostrophe, and Arabic *dh, z, ẓ*, and *ḍ* are all rendered "z." Readers who wish to know the original, that is, Arabic-script, form of terms may refer to U. Bahadır Alkım, Andreas Tietze, et al., eds., *New Redhouse Turkish-English Dictionary* (Istanbul, 1974), which gives the Arabic orthography of each item, based on late Ottoman usage, following each entry in modern script.

Modern orthography is not entirely consistent in its treatment of Arabic and Persian elements in the language, and the reader will encounter a small number of such inconsistencies in our text. In some cases where Turkish convention might impair recognition of a technical term (e.g., *örf* for Arabic *ʿurf*), both forms will be cited frequently enough to establish their identity. I have attempted to follow Turkish usage in such a way as to at once adhere as closely as possible to current orthography, ease the typesetter's burden, facilitate pronunciation and recognition for the non-Turkish-speaking reader, and still preserve scientific precision.

Long vowels have not been indicated except where it is absolutely essential, either in order to conform to established usage and pronunciation, or to make crucial phonetic and orthographic distinctions; the name Âli (Arabic ʿÂlî) must not be confused with Ali (Ar. ʿAlî, as in ʿAlî b. Abî Ṭâlib). I have been rather more conservative in consistently indicating by means of an apostrophe medial and final (but not initial) *ʿeyn*, medial *hemze*, and final *hemze* when the word in which it occurs is the first part of an Arabic or Persian construct (e.g., *Menşe' ül-inşa*). The medial apostrophe is dropped only when it is common to do so in writing the modern equivalent of the word, and when other orthographic conventions indicate the consonantal ellipsis (e.g., *zeâmet*).

Arabic constructs used as either titles or names in Ottoman Turkish are written, following modern conventions, as a single word. In such constructs, and particularly in the case of patronymics (indicated by the abbreviation "*b.*" for "*ibn*," "son of"), Turkish rather than Arabic grammar and phonetics prevail (e.g., "Şemsüddin Ahmed b. Ebüssu'ud" rather than "Shams al-dîn Aḥmad b. Abî al-Suʿûd"). Readers will find Ottoman names and book titles fully transliterated in the index; in this instance the transliteration system adopted is that generally employed in the *İslâm Ansiklopedisi*, which represents an optimal compromise between recognizability, phonetic accuracy, and scientific transcription.

For readers unfamiliar with Turkish I append a list of those orthographic features that differ from those used in English:

C,c = "j" as in "joy."
Ç,ç = "ch" as in "check."
Ğ,ğ = "soft g," archaically used for a soft gutteral rather like Parisian "r" and Arabic "*ghayn*", now more commonly a soft "g" sound close to "y"; hence I have compromised in transliterating as "*beğ*" ancient "*beg*," modern "*bey*." In medial and final position the consonant is usually pronounced as a lengthening of the preceding vowel.
I,ı = an unrounded back vowel; the first syllable of Turkish "*ırmak*" is much like the first syllable of American English "early."
İ,i = vowel pronounced somewhere between the vocalics of "pill" and "peel."
Ö,ö = "ö" in German "*hören*," "eu" in French "*fleuve*."
Ş,ş = "sh" as in "share."
Ü,ü = "ü" in German "*Müller*," "u" in French "*tu*."
^ = circumflex, used to indicate (1) a lengthened vowel (a, i, or u) in a word of Arabic or Persian origin; (2) palatalization of a preceding g, k, or l.

TRANSLATION

Wherever possible I have established consistent translations for commonly occurring titles and technical terms; in some instances both the Turkish and English terms will be used (e.g., "*beğlerbeği*" and "governor-general," "*kadı*" and "judge"). All fixed translations, as well as terms defined but used in their original form in the text, are listed and defined with reference to the original in the Glossary. English translations have been preferred, wherever possible, in order to render the text more accessible to nonspecialists.

Translations of passages of Âli's poetry and prose are my own, and are based largely on manuscripts. All of the texts translated are cited in full, in Arabic script, in the notes to my 1982 doctoral dissertation (see Bibliography), to which those wishing to examine the Ottoman text may refer. Wherever possible, and this is not often, translations have been made from printed texts. Two of Âli's works have been edited, annotated, and translated into English by Andreas Tietze: *Hâlât ül-Kahire* and *Nushat üs-selâtîn*. I gratefully acknowledge my debt to Professor Tietze's translations, of which I have cheerfully made abundant use; however, in this work I have modified them, both in order to preserve some consistency of translation style and in order to bring out those particular elements in passages which, for thematic reasons, require emphasis. Such emphasis, needless to say, has only been added where it is textually justifiable.

TOPONYMS

Place names are given in their common Anglicized form where these exist (Istanbul, not İstanbul; Bosnia, not Bosna), or in their modern or Ottoman Turkish form (Şirvan, not Shîrvân or Sharvân).

DATES

In the primary sources all dates are given in lunar *hicri* (Anno Hegirae, A.H.) months and years. These have been converted to Common Era (C.E.) equivalents using the conversion tables provided by F.R. Unat in *Hicrî Tarihleri Milâdî Tarihe Çevirme Kılavuzu* (Ankara, 1974). When citation of both dates has been necessary, it takes the form C.E./A.H. The following abbreviations used in citation of dates should be noted:

Rebi' I = Rebi' ül-evvel
Rebi' II = Rebi' ül-ahir
Cümada I = Cümada el-evvel
Cümada II = Cümada el-ahir

CITATION OF SOURCES

A list of abbreviations for frequently cited sources occurs at the beginning of this volume; some of these abbreviations are also used in the Bibliography (e.g., "EI^2," "BBA"). Published materials, except for articles found in alphabetically arranged encyclopedias, are cited by volume and page, with full bibliographical information provided in each first reference. Archival materials are referred to by volume and page or document number. Citations of unpublished sources include manuscript collection name, number, and either folio or page references, with citation of the appropriate chapter or division where the arrangement of the work makes this possible. References to chronicles that utilize annalistic rubrics include citation of the year (*sub anno*).

The Ottoman portion of Âli's *Künh ül-ahbar*, one of my major sources, is arranged by reigns and sequentially numbered Events (*vâkı'a*) within each. Each regnal section, except for that of Murad III, is followed by the biographies of the prominent men of that reign. The biographies, in turn, are grouped according to position or profession (grand vezirs, vezirs and governors-general, chancellors and treasurers, scholars and sheikhs, poets, etc.). References to the *Künh* are made in the following fashion:

1. Name of reigning sultan/
2. Event number, name of section, or biographical category,
3. "Entry,"
4. MS,
5. Folio number.

The following abbreviations used in these references should be noted:

Süleyman = Süleyman I
Selim = Selim II
Murad = Murad III
Mehmed = Mehmed III

ACKNOWLEDGMENTS

EIGHT years have passed since I first began to study Mustafa Âli. To recollect the debts I have accrued in widely different times and places for scholarly advice, moral support, and material aid is to feel not only obligation, but also pride. My studies have led me into association with fine scholars who are also fine people, and I honor their friendship as much as I value the knowledge they have shared.

While I was a student at Princeton University, Norman Itzkowitz initiated me into the mysteries of Ottoman studies, and his critical acumen and imagination have contributed enormously to this work. Martin Dickson first suggested Âli as an ideal research subject for an Islamicist venturing rather timidly into Ottoman learning; much of this study bears the imprint of the teaching, and inspiration, of a man rightly known as the *ustâd-i kâmil*. At an early stage of this project, Andreas Tietze of Vienna, the doyen of Âli studies, befriended and encouraged a young scholar; his example, and the generosity with his time and learning for which he is justly renowned, have been of inestimable value. Bekir Kütükoğlu provided informed and gentle guidance to the manuscripts of Istanbul and to the historiography of the sixteenth century. Three years of research in Istanbul were made both pleasant and productive by those who helped me gain access to important materials: Muammer Ülker, director of the Süleymaniye Library; İbrahim Manav of the Sahaflar; Klaus Kreiser, now of Bamberg; the staffs of the Bayezid, Millet-Genel, Istanbul University, Süleymaniye, and Topkapı Palace Libraries; and the authorities of the Prime Minister's Archives and Topkapı Palace Archives. I express my gratitude to these individuals and institutions, and also to the government of the Republic of Turkey, which repeatedly granted me permission to carry out research in the country I have come to love.

Many colleagues and friends have supplied welcome encouragement, criticism, and suggestions. Norman Itzkowitz, Martin Dickson, Andreas Tietze, and Stephen F. Dale of Ohio State University saw this book through the first phase of its gestation as a doctoral dissertation in 1981-82. The Dissertation Prize Committee of the Middle East Studies Association of North America read the work and awarded it the organization's first dissertation prize in the humanities; for this recognition I am grateful. I must also record my gratitude to those historians who read and criticized my study while it was in this form: Richard Bulliet of Columbia University; Barbara Flemming of the University of Leiden, whose student Jan Schmidt was generous enough to share with me his important discovery of a new piece of ''Âli-ana''; Derek Hirst of Washington University, St. Louis; Halil İnalcık of the University of Chicago; Metin Kunt, New York; Sabine MacCormack of Stanford University; and Marilyn R. Waldman of the Ohio State University. William Hickman of the University of California, Berkeley, and R. Stephen Humphreys of the University of Wisconsin read the final manuscript, and their acute judgment and careful commentary contributed significantly to the improvement of the book. For the quality of the final product I, like so many authors of the Princeton Studies on the Near East, must thank Margaret Case, a scholar and editor of high quality, and a valued friend. Alice Calaprice has been a most capable and patient copyeditor. For such defects as remain, I myself must own responsibility.

I also wish to thank two young colleagues, Gülru and Cemal Kafadar of Harvard and McGill, respectively, for their enthusiasm and much-needed assistance in selecting and procuring illustrations appropriate to Âli and his age. I am further indebted to the authorities of the Topkapı Palace Museum and the Österreichische Nationalbibliothek for granting me permission to publish photographs of materials in their collections.

The initial research upon which this study is based was supported by a Fulbright-Hays Doctoral Dissertation Research Abroad Fellowship during the years 1976-78, which enabled me to work in Turkey, Iran, and Egypt. Further study in Istanbul in 1978-79 was funded by the Program in Near Eastern Studies of Princeton University. Based as it is almost entirely on manuscript and archival material, this study would have been impossible without this support. Parts of the book have also benefited from research I carried out in the summers of 1983 and 1984 in Istanbul with the assistance of Summer Faculty Research Grants from the Graduate School of Washington University and a fellowship from the American Research Institute in Turkey. The Department of History of Washington University, which for the last three years has provided an exceptionally congenial working environment, granted funds and clerical assistance to facilitate typing of the final manuscript. I am grateful to all of these institutions for their generosity, and for the confidence in the value of this research that they have manifested.

Several special debts must be acknowledged, even if they cannot be paid. Hugh and Florence Fleischer gave me a happy childhood in the Middle East and years of moral and material support that helped to form both my scholarly interests and determination. Kay Fleischer weathered years of research and writing with joy and enthusiasm, and tirelessly exercised a critical eye that has saved me from many an infelicity of expression. Finally, I must acknowledge my debt of gratitude to a fine historian who opened for me a new and marvelous world: Mustafa Âli of Gallipoli. *Rûhuna el-fâtiha*.

BUREAUCRAT AND INTELLECTUAL IN THE OTTOMAN EMPIRE

قد وقع الفراغ من هذا التحرير على يد المفتقر المؤلف هذا التسطير

العبد الضعيف عالي خادم الأهالي

Overleaf: Mustafa Âli. Line drawing by Carolyn Brown, based on detail from NUSRET, 43b. Âli's signature is from colophon of NADİR, dated December 1568-January 1569/Receb 976: "The completion of this book took place by the hand of the (poor) author of this work, (the feeble slave) Âli, servant of the community."

INTRODUCTION

DURING the fast month of Ramazan it occurred to Nasreddin Hoca to put a pebble in a jar for each day that passed. This way he would avoid prolonging his suffering and having to rely on the inaccurate and conflicting accounts of his neighbors. After he had done this for a few days his little daughter, who loved to imitate her father, gathered a handful of pebbles and deposited them in the Hoca's jar as he was performing his prayers. That evening the Hoca invited a number of friends to break the fast, and conversation turned to the number of days left in the month. Proud of the scientific method he had invented, the Hoca announced that he could supply the correct answer, and he absented himself to the garden to count his stones. They came to one hundred and twenty, which seemed a large number. "If I tell them the true count," thought Nasreddin, "they will never believe me. I'd better cut it in half." When he announced that the sixtieth day of the month had arrived, his visitors howled with laughter: "Since when does a month have more than thirty days?" they cried.

Nasreddin drew himself up with dignity and said, "You have no right to mock me. For your sakes I cut the number in half; in actual fact it is the one hundred-twentieth day of the sacred month. You had best be satisfied with the answer I gave you."

Ottoman history, in its current state of development as a field of study, is not unlike Nasreddin Hoca's jar. It is certainly one of the richest areas of research open to modern historians. The Ottomans, and their successors in the modern Republic of Turkey, carefully preserved a wealth of manuscript and archival material and a sophisticated historiographical tradition, which render the history of the Empire, in all diverse facets of its economic, political, and cultural life, accessible to scholars from many disciplines. Since the opening of the Prime Minister's Archives to research, the small but growing number of Ottoman specialists have mined the incalculable wealth of raw data offered by innumerable official registers and have, quite understandably, focused their attention on the economic and political institutions and the demographic issues illuminated by these materials. And yet, for all this embarrassment of riches, we do not know all that is there, who put it there, and why. The bits of information we extract are assembled, and a picture appears to emerge; thus the institutional outlines of the Ottoman state have been put together into an intellectually pleasing, apparently comprehensible structure. More citations and more documents require that the picture be altered; but its function, its truth, is still assumed to remain essentially the same, when it may in fact have become something quite different. Our "knowledge" of the structure of the classical Ottoman polity is much like the Hoca's "knowledge" of his jar. We think we understand its purpose and nature, but lack an understanding of circumstances, of context, of the human and intellectual flesh that gives coherence and meaning to the institutional skeleton.

This study attempts to provide sorely needed flesh to the Ottoman skeleton, to delineate not only bones, but organs, veins, emotions, rhythms; to reconstruct the organic reality of which, now, only inanimate relics remain. The focus of this enterprise is the career and thought of Mustafa Âli of Gallipoli, an educated Muslim and Ottoman bureaucrat who stands out as one of the most significant intellectual figures of the sixteenth century. Our basic materials are the voluminous products of his pen, nearly fifty works, about five thousand manuscript folios spanning forty years of creativity over a wide literary spectrum. He wrote poetry, translated works on kingship and sex from Arabic and hagiographies from Persian, collected his personal correspondence, composed a massive universal history, and penned trenchant critiques of Ottoman society and government in his own day. Âli served four Ottoman sultans; he began his career in the heyday of Süleyman the Lawgiver, and died in the reign of Süleyman's great-grandson, Mehmed III, when military reverses and fiscal and social disruption led thoughtful Ottomans to perceive their state as being in decline, relative to the glorious days of only half a century before. The breadth of Âli's experience and acquaintance with the leading cultural and political figures of this crucial era, as well as the scope and volume of his literary activity, make him at once a unique source for the history of the late sixteenth century and an ideal subject for a study of the human realities of the Ottoman Empire. We shall study the Empire from within, as an educated Ottoman experienced it. Furthermore, we shall study why he experienced and described it as he did. My object is to create an *in vivo* portrait of Ottoman intellectual and political life in the sixteenth century against which theory might be tested. There is a gentle polemic embedded in this statement of goals. Modern scholarship on the Ottoman Empire tends to mistrust narrative evidence, especially when it is literary in character, in favor of the depersonalized "hard" data of archival documentation or "factual" narrative. Such a lack of confidence, or fear of the subjectivity inherent in such sources, is not only unjustified but severely limiting. "Soft" evidence, like soft tissues, gives life and significance to the hard structure. Chancery documents and financial records can tell us of administrative actions that were taken, needs that were perceived. But they do not always clarify the background, the implications, the assumptions that underlay a given order or practice, nor do they always record its effects. Historiographical, biographical, even literary sources, by virtue of their nature and purpose, can give intellectual coherence to the dry, terse, and isolated entries that fill the archival registers.

We must perforce dwell for a few moments on the apparent nature of that hard structure as it is commonly described. When Mustafa Âli was born in 1541 the Ottoman state was already over two hundred years old. In the late thirteenth and early fourteenth centuries Turkic tribal freebooters gathered, for plunder and profit, under the leadership of the scions of a minor branch of the Oğuz Turks, Ertuğrul and his son Osman, who became the eponym for the Ottoman (*Osmanlı*) dynasty. The Ottomans and many of their adherents were Muslim, and the location of their principality on the borders of the Christian Byzantine Empire afforded them ample scope for expansion in the form of *gaza*, holy warfare to expand the domains of Islam at the expense of non-Muslim states. In the course of the fourteenth century the Ottomans, who styled themselves *gazi*, "warrior for the faith," extended their dominion in Thrace, the Balkans, and Anatolia by dint of military prowess, mobility, strategy, and the prestige and wealth their success in *gaza* generated. The structure and goals of the Ottoman state were predicated on commitment to continuous conquest.

By 1453 the military strength and sophistication of the Ottomans enabled them to capture Constantinople, a feat about which Muslims had dreamed since the seventh century. Sultan Mehmed the Conqueror, from his new capital of Istanbul, consciously set out to make the *gazi* state an imperial one, creating and consolidating the institutions and high cultural traditions befitting an Islamic empire. As the Empire expanded, old border regions were brought under centralized administration; and as imperial traditions grew, so did high Islam. In 1517 Selim the Grim took possession of the Arab heartlands of Islam, including the holy cities of Mecca and Medina, thereby making himself the most prestigious Muslim sovereign of the time. During the forty-six-year reign of Selim's son Süleyman, Ottoman institutions took definitive form, and the regional and dynastic traditions that had evolved within or were incorporated into the Ottoman state amalgamated with the older religious and cultural traditions to which the Empire had fallen heir. This amalgamation produced a new and distinctive political and cultural synthesis.

In its social structure the Ottoman Empire of the mid-sixteenth century reflected its tribal military origins. The major division in society was that between the *askeri*, "military" class, and the *re'âyâ*, "flock" or subjects. The latter were the taxpayers of the Empire, its primary source of wealth—Muslim, Christian, and Jewish peasants, artisans, and merchants who belonged to the many ethnic and linguistic groups inhabiting the territories ruled by the conquering sultans. The *askeri* class paid no taxes, but protected the *re'âyâ* and formed the military and administrative backbone of the state. Coercive or protective power was the monopoly of the ruling house and its servitors, and anyone who possessed it, or who was allowed to possess it, was by definition *askeri*, whether they were members of the provincial cavalry (*sipahi*s), members of the standing infantry (janissaries), or high-level administrators. By the sixteenth century, in contrast to earlier eras, even the lowest members of the *askeri* class had to be Muslim and conversant with Turkish. It was a cardinal tenet of Ottoman statecraft that the *askeri-re'âyâ* distinction be maintained and the entrance of subjects into the governing class be restricted and controlled.

Not all members of the nontaxpaying elite were military by training or function. All of those associated with government, whether in military, bureaucratic, or judicial capacities, were effectively *askeri*; but within that class, levels of education served to distinguish the true ruling elite from the military rank and file. The well-schooled, whatever their actual function, were the true Ottomans, those versed in Ottoman high culture, whose ability and loyalty to the interests of state and sultan were tried and proven. There were several modes of entry into the restricted ranks of the governing elite. The first was birth into a high-level *askeri* family with a tradition of service to the dynasty. The children of prominent *kul*s, the sultan's slaves and servitors, and those of princely families dispossessed and co-opted by the Ottomans were privileged by birth, and they absorbed education and high culture values in the home.

New members of the ruling elite, whose loyalty could be counted on, were recruited and trained through a system of military slavery centered on the sultan's household. The slaves were Christian in origin, since Islam forbids enslavement of Muslims, and were obtained through warfare and the *devşirme*, a regulated human levy imposed on the rural Christian population. Converted to Islam and taught Turkish, the most promising young slaves were educated for rule in the Imperial Palace. They learned not only the military and administrative arts, but also the arts of civilization—Arabic, Persian, religious science, and literature—that would make them true Ottomans. The bulk of such slaves furnished the Empire's standing forces, such as the Janissary Corps. The elect who reached the highest levels of the Palace system became generals, governors, and eventually the sultan's vezirs, his ministers of state.

Education of a different sort afforded access to an elite career for those who were neither *askeri* aristocrats nor Christians liable to the *devşirme*. The *medrese* universities that dispensed religious and legal learning were open to all Muslims, and it was from the *medrese* ranks that the judges who administered the theoretical law of the land, the *şeri'at* Holy Law, were drawn. Although the *medrese*s were supported by private foundations and were initially independent of government, the Ottomans recognized that the religious and legal institutions necessary to an Islamic state could, in a frontier polity, flourish only with imperial patronage. The Conqueror established a strict hierarchy of schools through which students and professors had to progress in order to qualify for appointment to a judicial or pedagogical post. The sultan himself controlled such appointments and thus coopted and bureaucratized the traditionally independent *ulema*, the specialists in religious science.

In its classical formulation the Ottoman ruling elite was divided into three professional careers. The Men of the Sword (*seyfiye*), who had created the conquering polity, were the military specialists and administrators, and in the mid-sixteenth century were largely, though not exclusively, products of the Palace. The Men of Learning (*ilmiye*) were the legal experts, judges, teachers, and the Islamic conscience of the state, upholders of the Holy Law. Finally, the Men of the Pen (*kalemiye*) dealt with the bureaucratic affairs of the Empire, and combined facets of the functions and training of the first two careers; they were men of some learning and literacy who also performed important administrative tasks. The bureaucracy was also the youngest of the elite career paths, emerging as an independent governmental body only in the mid-sixteenth century as a concomitant of imperial consolidation. In theory, each career was discrete and exclusive, maintaining its own recruitment and training procedures, professional requirements, and hierarchy. Each was ideally based on strict meritocratic principles and implementation of procedures to evaluate individual qualifications. This framework defined social mobility; ambitious *re'âyâ* sought to become *askeri*, and the more ambitious still aspired to become elite Ottomans. These are the broad and highly idealized outlines of Ottoman society in the mid-sixteenth century, and this is the model that Mustafa Âli tested.

At the very start of the year 1000 of the Hijra, Âli began to write a history of the world and of the Ottoman Empire. He titled this *magnum opus* the *Essence of History*. The millennium marked the end of an era, an end that many thought would usher in the apocalypse. But the apocalypse did not arrive, and so the year 1000 also inaugurated a new age. It was a time for retrospection, and perhaps introspection. Âli meditated on the society he had served as a man of learning, a bureaucrat, and a soldier for all of his adult life. He saw it to be in the grip of a moral apocalypse, a cultural and political crisis, a decline from an ideal order that had existed in fact but a few decades before. This retrospective process led Âli to articulate, in his history and social commentaries, the ideals that lay at the heart of Ottoman society at its height; he had to enunciate what he saw as the central, distinguishing features of the Ottoman system in order to analyze their corrosion and failure. Âli thus became perhaps the greatest, if not the first, classicizing formulator of Ottoman tradition. His *Essence of History* is the single most comprehensive source for Ottoman history in the sixteenth century, and it was a literary monument respected and utilized by his historiographical successors.

Âli was an important member of a group of relatively highly placed intellectuals who were gravely concerned over the course their society seemed to be taking in the late sixteenth century, when rapid changes struck economic, political, and social structures all at once; prosperity had turned to famine, the government careers had become confused, venality was rampant, and the military class was being overrun by upstart *re'âyâ*. Âli was able, well educated, and far more outspoken than most of his peers, and he made himself the indefatigable articulator of the values of a generation. His *Counsel for Sultans*, written in 1581, stands at the very head of what in the seventeenth century became a peculiarly Ottoman literary genre, the literature of reform devoted to diagnosis of the causes of Ottoman decline and prescription of measures to reverse it. In this work Âli combined his personal experience with his theoretical view of the state to produce the first pragmatic analysis and critique of Ottoman administrative practice.

With his *Counsel* Âli emerged as the first literary spokesman for *kanun*-consciousness, an awareness of a specific regional and dynastic tradition enshrined in the *kanun* laws issued by the Ottoman house. Intellectuals of Âli's generation elevated *kanun* from the level of mere temporal, "secular" legislation to high symbolic status. *Kanun* embodied the dynasty's commitment to justice, on which its legitimacy rested. The injustice Âli saw around him became a sign of imperial failure to fulfill the dynastic mandate; dissent, in the form of invocation of dynastic ideals, therefore became incumbent upon loyal Ottomans. Justice was defined by the Holy Law as well as *kanun*, and Âli, a *medrese* graduate, was aware of divine as well as human decree. He saw himself as the product of two cultures and civilizational traditions—one Ottoman and regional, the other Islamic, universal, and cosmopolitan. His fascination with history represented an attempt to reconcile these two aspects of his own, and the Ottoman state's, heritage. Âli is an ideal figure for our study because he is at once conventional—in the assumptions and education he shared with many Ottomans—and unconventional—in the directness and outspokenness with which he addresses cultural and historical concerns. He does much to personalize his age because he is unafraid, unlike many of his littérateur colleagues, to inject personal commentary and autobiography into even the most formal of contexts.

This characterization implies a duality mirrored in the several approaches utilized in the following pages. Âli is worthy of study for the strength of his own literary accomplishment, and therefore the intellectual development and changing cultural vision of an important man of letters form one focus of examination. But Âli was also very much a part of the society that spawned him; his works cannot be studied in a vacuum. Âli's biography tells us much about why he wrote, and about the circumstances that transformed a hopeful poet into an embittered bureaucrat who became an historian by avocation. It also furnishes us a window on the society and system within which he lived and allows us to view the ways in which education, politics, and patronage networks functioned within and gave direction to a government and culture that appear, from a distance of four centuries, to be almost monolithic in character. Âli was the child of an age in which the few who were literate and learned could hope, especially if they were blessed with literary talent, for a rewarding career as a judge, teacher, or member of an expanding bureaucracy that needed men of letters. He lived into another age in which the government ranks were crowded, when basic literacy was more commonly available, and when a professionalized bureaucracy trained its own and disdained literary amateurs. Such developments, discerned through Âli's eyes and through his life, illuminate the history of institutional consolidation as much as they explain the emotional and moral distress Ottoman intellectuals experienced in the face of social and institutional transformation.

These two perspectives, individual and institutional, enable us to penetrate beneath the surface of Âli's commentary on Ottoman society. He was a disappointed man who felt that his abilities had gone unrewarded. He had committed himself to the Ottoman meritocratic promise, and it went unfulfilled; but he remained committed to that promise, and he loved the Empire despite his disenchantment. An erudite, determinedly independent historian, he meditated on his polity and compared it with the Islamic states that preceded it, both in order to escape from an intolerable present and to seek a guide for the future. He sought to reconcile conflicts and identify failures that were inherent in the very structure of the state into which he was born and which he served so devotedly. Islamic ideals of government did not always harmonize with those of the Central Asian steppe from which the Ottomans had come; dynastic law provided order and legitimacy, but it overshadowed the Holy Law. Centralization brought efficiency, prosperity, and patronage for the learned; but it also violated the rights of heavily taxed subjects, encouraged venality of office, and degraded the learning and stifled the moral independence of religious scholars. Ottoman absolutism, bounded by dynastic tradition, was the prime guarantor of justice, but produced injustice with the accession of an irresponsible ruler.

These conflicts, these failures, were also Âli's own. Trained for a religious career, he entered government service and embraced the "new learning'' of Ottoman administration. Political realities forced him sometimes to modify, sometimes to violate his own morality and cultural ideals, which yet retained their force. He was both an Ottoman and a Muslim, a scholar and a bureaucrat, identities not always easy to integrate. The golden Empire of his youth disintegrated in his old age. There is here a rhythm, a harmony, between the historian Âli, the course of his life, and the history of his society. And this resonance is central to understanding that vision of the Ottoman Empire that Âli adopted as a youth, altered in middle age, and articulated in the historical works that were, quite literally, the summation of his life. The texts of Ottoman history provide much information; but only by studying who wrote them, and how and why, can we ensure that our science will not be like that of Nasreddin Hoca.

I

AN OTTOMAN LIFE

ONE

THE MAKING OF AN OTTOMAN

(1541-63 / 948-70)

HOMELAND AND FAMILY

My home is the land of Gelibolu;
It is a crossroads, the path to Arabia and Persia.
That marvelous spot, at the edge of the sea!
Its gardens and meadows are like those of pure Heaven.[1]

These were the lines written in 1593 by Mustafa Âli, son of Ahmed, son of Abdullah, when he returned to the city of his birth for the first time since he had left it as a young student thirty-five years before. To commemorate this return to the capital of the Gallipoli peninsula, Âli composed a work in verse which he titled *Sadef-i sad güher, The Lustre of a Hundred Jewels*. He dedicated it to the glories of his homeland, to recollection of family and friends, and to recapitulation of his own literary career. A few lines from this work constitute almost all the information available on the family into which Mustafa Âli was born on 28 April, 1541.[2] Âli writes of his father:

My father Ahmed, son of Abdullah,
Elder [*hoca*] of the people of prosperity, was yet humble,
Constantly giving to the people of learning.

[1] *Sadef-i sad güher*, MS Ali Emiri Türkçe Manzum 978 (hereafter SADEF), p. 236.

[2] Âli, *Nushat üs-selâtin*, published in a model edition with annotated English translation by Andreas Tietze, ed. and trans., *Muṣṭafâ ʿÂlî's Counsel for Sultans of 1581*, 2 vols. (Vienna, 1978-83; hereafter COUNSEL), II, 50 (trans.), 176 (text). Âli states that he was born in "[9]48, the second day of Muharrem, Monday night [i.e., Sunday night], the first hour." 2 Muharrem 948 actually falls on Wednesday-Thursday, a fact that has caused a certain amount of confusion over Âli's birth date, as noted by Babinger, GOW, p. 127. Hammer (GOR, IV, 651-54) incorrectly assigns Âli a 949 birth date on other grounds. Nihal Atsız in his *Âli Bibliyografyası* (Istanbul, 1968; hereafter AB), p. 1, compounds the confusion by accepting the A.H. date but moving the C.E. date back to April 25 (= Monday), without explaining the incorrect A.H.-C.E. correspondence. COUNSEL provided the only date citation for Âli's birth until 1978, when I discovered Âli's second *divan* in the Egyptian National Library. The *Layihat ül-hakika* (MS DKM *Adab Turkî* 21, 1b-156a; hereafter LAYİHAT) had been considered lost. In the introduction (3b) Âli again gives 948 as the year of his birth. This second citation suggests that the year date is correct, and the day wrong. A birth date of 1540/947 would in fact provide a correct correspondence of day, since 2 Muharrem fell on a Sunday (= Monday night).

His generosity and bounty were extraordinary.
Although, like Usâma, he was a slave [*kul*],
He was handsome as Joseph, and blessed with good character.[3]

It is clear that Âli's father Ahmed was not only a merchant but a prosperous one; he had the honorific title of *hoca*, literally "master," which was applied in Ottoman times to both teachers and preeminent men of commerce.[4] The mercantile imagery in which Âli couched the chronogram he composed on the occasion of Ahmed's death in 1565-66 confirms the nature of his father's occupation:

My late father, Hoca Ahmed,
    Exhausted the capital of his life span.
He abandoned completely the goods of Existence,
    And saw thereby that commerce is for nought,
Âli, God inspired this event's chronogram;
    I said at that moment "God rest my father's soul."[5]
[= 1565-66/973]

In what sense Ahmed might be considered a slave, however, is somewhat less clear. In Ottoman usage the word *kul*, "slave," applied to two types of bonded servitude. Anyone could own personal household slaves bought from the slave market. Since Islam forbids the enslavement of freeborn Muslims, most slaves were Christian or other non-Muslim prisoners of war. In Muslim households slaves were frequently converted to Islam and could engage in trade. Manumission was encouraged as a meritorious act, and slaves could also purchase their freedom. Âli usually refers to household slaves of this sort as *müştera kul*, "purchased slave," in order to distinguish them from the more specifically Ottoman *kul*s.[6] These latter were the personal slaves of the sultan recruited primarily, though not exclusively, through the *devşirme* levy on Christian villages in the Balkan and Anatolian provinces of the Empire. The vast majority of these imperial slaves went into the Janissary infantry corps after converting to Islam and learning Turkish. A select few were educated in the Palace to staff the higher levels of the

[3] SADEF, p. 245.

[4] İbnülemin Mahmud Kemal (İnal), Introduction to Âli, *Menakıb-ı hünerveran* (Istanbul, 1926; hereafter İNAL), p. 3. İnal's critical edition of the *Menakıb* is preceded by a lengthy introduction on Âli's life and works (pp. 1-133), which has provided the basis for most later references to the author. Unfortunately İnal, who worked primarily from manuscript sources, provided no folio citations. Henceforth I shall cite the original sources directly, referring to İnal's introduction only when his opinions, or manuscript information unavailable to me, are pertinent.

[5] Quoted İNAL, p. 3.

[6] On the general nature of slavery in the Islamic context, see R. Brunschvig, "ʿAbd," EI[2]. For an instance of Âli's use of the term "*müştera kul*," see *Menşe' ül-inşa*, MS Velieddin 1916 (hereafter MENŞE), 240a.

military governing apparatus. Not all Ottoman administrators, it should be noted, were technically slaves; but even freeborn Muslims in imperial service were considered the sultan's *kul*s or servitors, slaves in the metaphorical rather than the technical sense.[7]

These imperial slaves were by definition members of the *askeri* governing class; Âli's father Ahmed, as a merchant, belonged to the taxpaying subjects (*re'âyâ*). Until the middle of the sixteenth century, strictures on Janissaries' marrying, and a prohibition against their engaging in trade, are thought to have been rigidly observed.[8] It is most likely that Ahmed was a manumitted household slave, or the son of one, rather than an imperial *kul* or *devşirme* product; had he been this sort of "slave" he would have had to have lost his military status relatively early in life. Furthermore, Ahmed was involved in literary life to an extent that suggests a level of education congruent with what a household slave could acquire but well above the learning available to the average *devşirme* recruit who did not enter the Palace. Âli's reference to Usâma and Joseph, two famous slaves who were set free, supports this conclusion.[9] If, however, Âli meant "*kul*" as "*devşirme* slave," his use of the term would have to be understood in the broader sense of "Christian *devşirme* origin." If Âli's grandfather Abdullah were such a *kul*, his son Ahmed would have been born a free Muslim.[10] Âli nowhere de-

[7] H. İnalcık, "Ghulâm," EI²; Halil İnalcık, *The Ottoman Empire: The Classical Age, 1300-1600* (New York, 1973), pp. 76-85; N. Itzkowitz, *Ottoman Empire and Islamic Tradition* (New York, 1973), pp. 49-54. On the multiple meanings of the term *kul* in the sixteenth century, see İ. Metin Kunt, *The Sultan's Servants: The Transformation of Ottoman Provincial Government, 1550-1650* (New York, 1983), pp. 40-44 , and V. L. Ménage, "Some Notes on the Devshirme," BSOAS 29 (1966): 64-78.

[8] İ. H. Uzunçarşılı, *Kapukulu Ocakları*, 2 vols. (Ankara, 1943), I, 306-308. Evidence that has come to light more recently indicates that the sultan's slaves were marrying and producing offspring, and that imperial policy sanctioned the entrance of these children into the *askeri* class, much earlier than has been supposed. For documentation for the early-middle years of the reign of Süleyman, see chapter 8 and my forthcoming study of the Ottoman ruling elite in the age of Süleyman; evidence for still earlier periods will appear in publications by Heath W. Lowry and Cemal Kafadar (oral communications).

[9] Usâma b. Zayd was the child of personal slaves of the Prophet Muḥammad, and was born into slavery. He was one of the first converts to Islam and was distinguished by the Prophet's affection for him. Muḥammad manumitted him when Usâma was nineteen years old, and he became a transmitter of Prophetic Traditions. That he was perhaps something of a proverbial figure in the Ottoman context is suggested by an entry on him in the Ottoman universal encyclopedia of Şemsüddin Sami, *Kamus ül-a'lam*, 6 vols. (Istanbul, 1889-98), II, 854.

[10] Nihal Atsız (AB, p. 1) declares this to be the case, but the available facts do not permit so definite a statement. The name Âli gives his grandfather, Abdullah, is certainly suggestive of a *devşirme* origin, but would indicate that Ahmed rather than his father was the *devşirme* recruit. Upon conversion to Islam the new *kul*s took Muslim names. In addition they adopted Muslim patronymics in formal situations where a father's name would normally be mentioned, and the most common and neutral substitute for a Christian father's name was "Abdullah," meaning simply "Servant of God." In usage such honorific patronymics were interchangeable with equivalent expressions, particularly when the wording of a document or inscription might dictate a change for purposes of rhyme or euphony; Abdülmevla and Abdülmennan, neither of

clares the ethnic origin of his paternal forebears, although circumstantial evidence suggests they were Bosnian; in discussions of the major ethnic groups represented within the Empire, particularly within the ruling establishment, Âli invariably singles out Bosnians and Croatians for exceptional praise.[11]

Whatever the nature of the merchant Ahmed's origins, by the time Mustafa Âli was born his father had achieved some local prominence, particularly as a patron of and participant in cultural life. To attain such a position in Gelibolu, provincial capital though it was, was no mean feat. The city was the first Ottoman conquest in Rumeli, captured in 1354, and it had early become a strategically and culturally important part of the nascent Ottoman state. Since the early fifteenth century Gelibolu had produced a small but significant number of mystics, scholars, and poets, beginning with the brothers Ahmed and Mehmed Yazıcızade.[12] Many of these either lived in Gelibolu or returned to teach there after receiving advanced education at one of the major *medrese* universities of Istanbul.[13] Hence, in addition to native sons who gained repute for scholarship and literary talent outside their homeland, Gelibolu boasted products of local schools who provided basic education in the city. Âli wrote of the ulema of Gelibolu:

> [Gelibolu] produced few great scholars and famous mystics;
> It does not have many orators or commentators of note.
> Its ulema are mostly prayer-leaders and preachers
> Who teach Arabic grammar from morning to night.[14]

Ahmed married into a Gelibolu family which personified the pietistic traditions of the provincial capital and which was also connected with the Ot-

---

them common as actual names, were variants. Hence, the form of Âli's name given on the title page of the *Künh ül-ahbar*, 5 vols. (Istanbul, 1277-85; hereafter KA), "Mustafa b. Ahmed b. Abdülmevla," may reflect the editor's assumption that Ahmed was a *devşirme* recruit and that the name of Âli's grandfather was honorific rather than real. "Abdullah," unlike its variants, also occurred as a real name, and could have been the one taken by Âli's grandfather if he was indeed an imperial *kul*. See also the remarks of V. L. Ménage in "Seven Ottoman Documents from the the Reign of Mehmed II," in *Documents from Islamic Chanceries*, ed. S. M. Stern (Oxford, 1965), pp. 112-18.

[11] For example, see KA, V, 11-12. This pro-Bosnian bias may also reflect ethnic factional rivalry between Albanian and Bosnian *devşirme* elements that became manifest late in the sixteenth century; in describing this conflict Âli emerges as a Bosnian, or anti-Albanian, partisan (see chapter 5).

[12] The Yazıcızade brothers died around the middle of the fifteenth century. They were members of the Bayrami Sufi order, and the authors of two of the earliest mystical religious works in Turkish, the *Muhammedîye* by Mehmed and the *Envâr ül-âşıkin* by Ahmed; see İnalcık, *Empire*, p. 175.

In SADEF (pp. 236-45), Âli lists the most prominent natives of Gelibolu, with particular emphasis on the city's poets, of whom he names the following: Medhi, Sun'i, Tab'i (Şani), Hükmi, Müdami, İbrahim, Genci, Tiraşi, Zuhuri, Sıdki.

[13] For examples see SADEF, p. 240, "Medhi"; KA, V, 185 "Habib-i Hamidi"; KA, Selim/Ulema, "Sinan Halife," Nur 3409, 268b.

[14] SADEF, p. 242.

toman ruling establishment. Âli's mother, whose name is unknown, was the maternal granddaughter of one Şeyh Muslihüddin Mustafa. Şeyh Muslihüddin was a disciple and spiritual successor of the Nakşbendi sheikh Seyyid Ahmed Buhari (d. 1516-17/922). As the deputy (*halife*) of the famous Seyyid Ahmed (also known as Emir-i Buhari), Şeyh Muslihüddin was authorized to propagate the spiritual teachings of the master of the order, and therefore had considerable stature within the Nakşbendi *tarikat*, as well as within the elevated echelons of Ottoman government, among whose representatives the Nakşbendi order gained considerable prominence in the sixteenth century. Şeyh Muslihüddin lived for many years at the mother cloister of the order, the Emir-i Buhari Tekkesi in Istanbul, where he died in 1552-53/960.[15]

For a period beginning between 1520 and 1530 Şeyh Muslihüddin lived in and raised a family in Gelibolu. He had at least two children, one of whom was Âli's maternal grandmother. The other, Âli's great-uncle Derviş Çelebi, received a religious education and embarked on an *ilmiye* career. At some point Derviş Çelebi went to Istanbul, perhaps in company with his father, in order to continue his education and to benefit from his father's connections in the capital. Derviş Çelebi did not reach the upper ranks of the learned establishment occupied by the religious judges (*kadıs*) of important cities and teachers (*müderris*) in major *medrese* universities. Ulema of moderate education who were unwilling or unable to enter the major career tracks of teaching and law had an alternative; they could be appointed to individual mosques as *imam*, "prayer leader," or *hatib*, the official responsible for delivering the sermon and for acting as *imam* at Friday communal prayer in the mosques where Friday prayer was authorized. Positions of this sort, and analogous ones provided by pious endowment (*vakıf*) of many varieties, were often given to people who had some learning and a repute for piety but who, whether by choice or educational level, were not full members of the *ilmiye* who could expect a career as either a judge or a teacher. The greatest number of such figures as Derviş Çelebi were found in the Sufi cloisters of the Ottoman Empire. Adherents of the more fashionable orders would have some degree of religious learning without being required to specialize in the religious sciences of jurisprudence and Qur'ânic exegesis as

[15] KA, Süleyman/Meşayih, "Şeyh Muslihüddin," Nur 3409, 160b; Taşköprüzade, *Al-shaqâ'iq al-nu'mânîya* (Beirut, 1975), p. 324. On the Emir-i Buhari Tekkesi in Istanbul see Ayvansarayi, *Hadikat ül-cevami'*, 2 vols. (Istanbul, 1865), I, 297-98; Âli's reference to the location of the *zaviye*, "Sufi cloister," at which Şeyh Muslihüddin resided, shows it to be identical with the oldest Emir-i Buhari Tekkesi (several *tekke*s had this name) outside of the Edirne Gate. The lists of masters (*post-nişin*) of Istanbul *tekke*s published by Mehmet Tayşi and Klaus Kreiser under the title *Die Istanbuler Derwisch-Konvente und ihre Scheiche (Mecmu'a-ı Tekaya)* (Freiburg, 1980) indicates that Muslihüddin did not become the *şeyh* of the *tekke* (p. 54). On the Nakşbendiye, see Hamid Algar's "The Naqshbandi Order: A Preliminary Survey of its History and Significance," *Studia Islamica* 44 (1976): 123-52.

professional ulema were, but yet had prestige based upon their spiritual accomplishment and ample contact with the ulema and government figures who shared their *tarikat* affiliation.[16]

Some time before 1557/965 Derviş Çelebi attained an important post of this variety, becoming the *hatib* of a royal mosque in Istanbul, the Şehzade Cami'i. It may have been there that Derviş Çelebi attracted the attention of Sultan Süleyman, who had built the mosque to accompany the tomb of his son Prince Mehmed. In 1557-58 Süleyman brought Derviş Çelebi to the Imperial Palace and made him his personal *imam*. He served Süleyman in this capacity until the latter's death in 1566, and appears to have won considerable favor, for the sovereign lavished gifts upon him. Derviş Çelebi did not come from a pedagogical or juridical background, and his post of *imam-ı sultani* would not necessarily lead to anything greater, since it was a special one which depended solely upon the favor of the monarch rather than upon seniority or scholarly output. When Süleyman died, Derviş Çelebi was dismissed from the Palace by the jealous grand vezir Sokollu Mehmed Paşa, and received neither pension nor appointment. In order to live he was forced to sell the gifts he had received from Süleyman. When Süleyman's grandson Sultan Murad III (reg. 1574-95/982-1003) ascended the Ottoman throne, he granted Derviş Çelebi a small retirement stipend, with which he retired to Mecca until his death in about 1583 at the age of sixty or seventy.[17]

CHILDHOOD AND EARLY EDUCATION (1541-56)

IN THE middle of the sixteenth century Ottoman society was still strictly divided into two broad classes: the *re'âyâ*, taxpaying subjects, and the *as-*

[16] On the functional, social, and familial overlap between ulema and Sufis at this time, see H. G. Majer, "Sozialgeschichtliche Probleme um Ulema und Derwische im osmanischen Reich," in *I. Milletler Arası Türkoloji Kongresi (İstanbul, 15-20 x. 1973), Tebliğler* (Istanbul, 1979), I, 218-33, and Hanna Sohrweide, "Gelehrte Scheiche und sufische ʿUlemâ im osmanischen Reich," in *Studien zur Geschichte und Kultur des vorderen Orients (Festschrift für Bertold Spuler)* (Leiden, 1981), pp. 375-86.

[17] KA, Süleyman/Meşayih, "Şeyh Muslihüddin," Nur 3409, 260b. In *Osmanlı Devletinin İlmiye Teşkilatı* (Ankara, 1965), Uzunçarşılı mentions the term *imam-ı sultani* only once (p. 50), and this citation is based upon a late source, Raşid. The position held by Derviş Çelebi, that of personal imam to the sultan, is more commonly known as *hünkâr imamı*; see İ. H. Uzunçarşılı, *Osmanlı Devletinin Saray Teşkilatı* (Ankara, 1945), pp. 373-74. The post did not require the degree of education necessary for the upper levels of mainline *ilmiye* appointments. The *hünkâr imamı* was given a teaching appointment (*müderriskik*), though this might be one of the lowest order, depending upon individual qualifications. Appointment to this office would seem to have been primarily a matter of sultanic favor, which Âli explicitly says to have been the case with his great-uncle; while high-ranking ulema were sometimes appointed to the position, lower-level appointees did not necessarily advance in the regular *ilmiye* hierarchy as a result of holding the office.

keri, people connected with government and the functioning of the state, who did not pay taxes and who received salaries or revenue grants by government appointment. This latter class included bureaucrats and members of the *ilmiye* religious establishment as well as military personnel. The social mobility of the *re'âyâ* was necessarily very restricted, unless they could cross into the *askeri* class, which monopolized the upper echelons of Ottoman society. Such changes of status, however, violated Ottoman ideals of statecraft and social stability, for they deprived the state of revenue and blurred the distinction between the rulers and the ruled.[18]

There were three modes of entry into the *askeri* class. The first, in this period when the Palace slave household dominated the major administrative functions, was through the *devşirme*, which in turn required non-Muslim birth. The second mode of entry was birth into an *askeri* family. At this time the marriage of the rank-and-file *kul*s, the Janissaries, was somewhat restricted; this meant that in order to achieve *askeri* status by birth one's father had to be either a relatively high-ranking *kul*, a scholar, or a member of a family in which military status was or could be hereditary, as was the case with *timar*-holding provincial cavalrymen (*sipahi*s) and established princely families that had accepted Ottoman suzerainty. Other members of military households, such as slaves and freeborn voluntary retainers, could also qualify for low-level *askeri* appointments.[19] The third way into the governing class was education, open to all Muslims, by which means one could enter a religious career that could lead to a judgeship or professorship. This was the avenue most accessible to the children of Muslim *re'âyâ* parents, who were otherwise largely disqualified from *askeri* status at birth. The *ilmiye* hierarchy and the religious educational system upon which it was based allowed such people a means of advancement whereby they would be judged primarily upon accomplishment rather than inherited or *kul* status.

Whatever the specific professional and genealogical requirements of the career tracks within the *askeri* class, one more factor helped to determine individual advancement and both vertical and lateral relationships: *intisab*, "connections." *İntisab* signified a semiofficial patronage system whereby a member of the *askeri* class would help to secure entry into and advancement within the government system for his own protégés, who would in turn support their patron and his interests. *İntisab* was established on the basis of a variety of other sorts of relationships. Blood kinship constituted the most immediate basis for patronage, but friendship, marriage ties, sexual rela-

[18] İnalcık, *Empire*, pp. 68-69.

[19] İnalcık, *Empire*, pp. 104-15; cf. Kunt, *Servants*, pp. 32-47. These various groups within the *askeri* class were not necessarily mutually exclusive. *Kul*s, even of Janissary rank, could and did become *timar*-holders, at which point they became free to marry. The slaves of a high-ranking *kul* were also considered *askeri* and could receive *timar* grants.

tionships, ethnic and geographical origins, household service, and student-teacher bonds also played an important part in the establishment of *intisab* networks.

Mustafa Âli was the firstborn son of Ahmed b. Abdullah, a Muslim merchant. The nature of the status of Âli's immediate family within the structure of Ottoman society was of crucial consequence to his future and to that of his two younger brothers, Mehmed and İbniyamin. In paternalistic Ottoman society the sons of *re'âyâ* fathers were *re'âyâ*. On the maternal side of Âli's family, to be sure, there were connections with the *ilmiye* establishment and with the highest levels of the ruling class. However, neither the kinship status nor the actual positions held by Şeyh Muslihüddin and his son Derviş Çelebi were such as would guarantee *askeri* status for the sons of Ahmed. Neither man was directly involved in either government or the *ilmiye* hierarchy, but both had positions that would enable them to help a relative once the latter qualified for admission to the *askeri* class.[20] It appears that the only way for Ahmed to provide such an opportunity for his sons was to educate them, so that they might assimilate Ottoman high culture and enter state service through the religious or bureaucratic career lines, both of which were open to Muslims conversant with the "Ottoman Way." This is what Ahmed did. As a prosperous merchant he could afford to have his sons well educated, and all of them eventually became not just *askeri* but Ottomans, people whose education and culture made them members of the elite of the ruling class. By 1593 Mustafa had become a provincial governor and director of finance, while his brothers Mehmed and İbniyamin were attached to the Imperial Council (*Divan-ı hümayun*) as a secretary and pursuivant (*çavuş*), respectively.[21]

[20] As suggested above, Muslihüddin may very well have helped his son Derviş Çelebi acquire his appointment as *hatib* of Şehzade Mosque. The fact that Derviş Çelebi both obtained and remained in this post suggests that he did not reach the highest levels of the Ottoman educational system. However, this appointment, and his later attachment to the household of Sultan Süleyman, unquestionably gave him *askeri* status. The question of his father Muslihüddin's standing in terms of the *askeri*/*re'âyâ* split is less clear-cut. The Sufi orders included both groups in their membership, the proportion varying with the nature and fashionableness of the order. Individual lodges (*tekke, hanekah*) were supported by *vakıf* and exempted from taxes, an exemption which usually included those *tarikat* officials who resided at the lodge. However, the appointment of the heads (*post-nişin, şeyh*) of *tekke*s, and of their deputies, was an internal affair in which the government rarely had any direct role. In both institutional and individual terms, important members of the Sufi *tarikat*s who had no other position or occupation (for example, a teaching or administrative post) thus fell outside both of the two major categories into which Ottoman society was divided. Such people, or at least those in the orders popular in government circles, had, if they possessed no inherited distinction of status, a sort of marginal *askeri* standing that was a product of the spiritual prestige they enjoyed and of the pervasiveness of *tarikat* affiliations within the governing class. Distinguished sufis who were taken into important *askeri* households as the spiritual guides (*pir*s) of vezirs or provincial governors-general of course became fully *askeri* and gained opportunities to participate more directly in political life.

[21] SADEF, pp. 245-46, and İNAL, pp. 3, 61, 71, on Âli's brothers. Mehmed knew Arabic

Mustafa Âli's formal education began when he was only six years old. He was sent to an elementary school, a *mekteb*, to begin learning Arabic grammar. These elementary language studies formed the basis of the entire formal Ottoman educational curriculum, which was organized around graduated study of the Qur'ân, religious texts, and scientific works, all in Arabic. Âli did not enjoy his early school days, or at least the discipline imposed on him; he later complained of being frequently and unnecessarily beaten.[22] Even so, he persevered and showed an aptitude for study. When he was twelve years old he was sufficiently well grounded in Arabic and in the rudiments of religious science to read specialized subjects with well-qualified teachers. He studied advanced Arabic grammar with Habib-i Hamidi, whom he describes in the *Künh ül-ahbar, The Essence of History*, as one of the best grammarians of the time, and read logic and theology with Sinan Halife. Sinan Halife had returned to Gelibolu after a period of study with Ebüssu'ud, who was perhaps the foremost Ottoman scholar and legist of the sixteenth century.[23] Âli does not specify the mosque schools to which his teachers were attached, but his description of the subjects he studied shows that at this age he was just beginning at the lowest level of the *medrese* school hierarchy, called "*medrese*s of twenty." A student at this stage had nine more grades of *medrese* training to traverse before achieving the Ottoman equivalent of a full university education.[24]

These subjects were only part of the education necessary for one to become a cultured Ottoman. During these same early years Âli also studied Persian, as did his brother Mehmed. While Arabic was the language of science and scholarship, Persian was the language of courtly society and the vehicle of the works of poetry and prose most important to cultivated Ottomans. Although Âli nowhere states how he learned this language, the mas-

---

and Persian well, and was a skilled calligrapher. İbniyamin was also well educated; in 1592/1000 he calligraphed one of Âli's works, *Mirkat ül-cihad* (MS Reşid Ef. 678), signing his name "İbniyamin Çavuş." It must be admitted that İbniyamin's holding such a position appears somewhat anomalous if my conclusion on Ahmed's *re'âyâ* status is correct. *Çavuş*es of the *Divan* were normally selected from one of the Outside Services of the Palace (on which see İnalcık, *Empire*, pp. 82-83), entrance to which usually required *kul* status (Uzunçarşılı, *Saray*, pp. 408-18); however, it should be noted that neither the Outside Services nor the ranks of the *çavuş*es were staffed exclusively by *devşirme* recruits, as I show in the study referred to in note 8 above. It may be that Ahmed was able to enroll his youngest son, possibly illegally, in the Gelibolu *acemi ocağı*, "novice janissary training center," which was the oldest such institution in the Ottoman Empire, and admission to which was open to the sons of Janissaries as well as *devşirme* recruits (Uzunçarşılı, *Kapukulu*, I, 5-6, 31-34). Explanations for this phenomenon must remain purely speculative. Slightly more information on Âli's brothers is given by İNAL, pp. 61, 71.

22 COUNSEL, II, 50-51 (trans.), 277-78 (text). For an overview of the Ottoman education system and curriculum, see İnalcık, *Empire*, pp. 173-78.

23 KA, V, 185; KA, Selim/Ulema, "Sinan Halife," Nur 3409, 268b. On Ebüssu'ud, who died in 1574 as *şeyhülislam*, "chief jurisconsult," see M. Cavid Baysun, "Ebüssu'ud Efendi," İA.

24 İnalcık, *Empire*, p. 168; Uzunçarşılı, *İlmiye*, pp. 19-23.

tery of it he displays in his earliest works shows that he must have begun to study it at an early age, perhaps with a private tutor.[25]

In the home Âli and his family undoubtedly spoke Turkish, the everyday language of the greater part of the Ottoman dominions. The West Turkish dialect, spoken in Anatolia and Rumeli, had for long remained the language of personal interaction and popular culture, while Arabic and Persian, associated with high Islamic cultural traditions, were the preferred vehicles of science and literature. Only in the late fifteenth century did a specifically Ottoman form of Turkish begin to attain prestige as a literary language. Ottoman Turkish relied heavily upon vocabulary, constructions, and syntactical models taken over from the established languages of Islamic letters, Arabic, Persian, and the Çagatay Turkish, which had gained cultural prominence in Central Asia in the fifteenth century. The corpus of Ottoman Turkish literature grew rapidly in the sixteenth century, as the new form of Turkish increasingly replaced Arabic and Persian as the language of cultured discourse. This literature was largely based on Persian models, and a facility with Ottoman, as opposed to simpler Turkish, came to be one of the hallmarks of membership in the Ottoman ruling class.[26] In the year 1592 Âli described this development:

> The astonishing language current in the state of Rum, composed of four languages [West Turkish, Çagatay, Arabic, and Persian], is a pure gilded tongue which, in the speech of the literati, seems more difficult than any of these. If one were to equate speaking Arabic with a religious obligation [*farz*], and the use of Persian with a sanctioned tradition [*sünnet*], then the speaking of a Turkish made up of these sweetnesses becomes a meritorious act [*müstahabb*], and, in the view of those eloquent in Turkish, the use of simple Turkish should be forbidden.[27]

Poetry was the literary sphere in which this creative combination was first practiced and in which, in the first half of the sixteenth century, it remained most creatively alive. Poetic séances (*meclis*, pl. *mecalis*), in which poets fluent in all three languages recited and criticized verse, were a focal point

[25] See, for example, the opening line of *Mihr u Mah*, a *mesnevi* which represents Âli's first major literary effort, completed in 1561-62/969; it is quoted by Eleazar Birnbaum, "The Date of ʿÂlî's Turkish Mesnevî *Mihr u Mâh*," *BSOAS* 23 (1960): 138. Âli's first historical work, *Nadir ül-maharib*, deals with the conflict of Süleyman's sons, Selim and Bayezid; Âli composed it in both verse and prose in order to display literary versatility, and most of the verse is Persian. Until recently the only known copy of this work was MS Revan 1290, 1b-25a, which gives 1568-69/976 as the date of completion. In 1978 I discovered Âli's autograph of the *Nadir* in the Egyptian National Library (MS DKM *Majâmîʿ Turkîya* 2, 1b-66b; hereafter NADİR). This copy fills some of the lacunae of the Revan MS.

[26] See M. Fuad Köprülü, *Türk Edebiyatı Tarihi* (Istanbul, 1980), pp. 354-407.

[27] KA, I, 11.

of Ottoman cultural and intellectual life. Poetry and the exciting literary and linguistic creativity it embodied formed an important part of Âli's boyhood environment. His father Ahmed cultivated contact with "learned folk" and was a patron of local scholars and poets; one of his close friends was the poet İbadi. Ahmed may have hosted one of Gelibolu's literary salons, for when Mustafa was only twelve he met and conversed with the author of one of the first biographical dictionaries of Ottoman poets, Latifi, when the latter visited Âli's hometown.[28]

For most Ottoman poets at this time adherence to fashionable literary circles entailed more than having a command of Arabic, Persian, and Turkish, exercising a literary flair, and attending poetic salons. Ottoman poetry in the sixteenth century was heavily infused with the mystical ethos of the dervish. The poet was expected to be a mystic, and his imagery was that of the tavern, where love, beauty, and intoxication were to be found. This imagery was, for most poets, not purely metaphorical; extant biographical literature shows that a great many of the premier poets of the time were indeed *rind-meşreb*, people for whom wine parties and the wild life of the tavern were part of their devotion to spiritual ecstasy. This aspect of fashionable literary life too formed part of Âli's early education. As an adolescent he became interested in Sufism, and his spiritual master (*pir*) was Hafiz-ı Leng, who had for years been the boon-companion of the most celebrated poet of Gelibolu, Sun'i. Âli and his *pir* together frequented Sun'i's favorite tavern, where Âli became well acquainted with Sultana, the Greek tavern girl to whom Sun'i had addressed his most passionate love poems and had thereby scandalized all of Gelibolu.[29] Many years later, in a retrospective poem, Âli evoked the heady atmosphere into which he had been plunged at adolescence, when the wine shop was the locus for self-discovery, both spiritual and erotic:

> Childhood departed, Love arrived; debauchery in the taverns became my habit;
> Till my age reached thirty, I was joined to the demon of perdition.
> My heart's desire was The Friend [God], but my soul yearned for others;
> That shameless one inclined now to pretty girls, now to handsome boys.[30]

[28] KA, Selim/Şu'ara, "İbadi"; Süleyman/Şu'ara, "Latifi," Nur 3409, 280b, 204b-205a. Âli dates the meeting to 1552-3/960. On Latifi (d. ca. 1582) and his *Tezkere-i şu'ara*, see Nihad Çetin, "Latifi," İA.

[29] KA, Süleyman/Şu'ara, "Sun'i," Nur 3409, 189-190a; cf. Âşık Çelebi, *Meşa'ir üş-Şu'ara*, ed. G. M. Meredith-Owens (London, 1971; hereafter AŞIK), 220a-b.

[30] LAYİHAT, 47a.

By the time he was fifteen years old, the young Mustafa was proficient in Arabic, Persian, and the new Ottoman Turkish, and deemed himself prepared to enter literary society in his own right. The first requirement for a poet was a *mahlas*, a professional nom de plume with which poets signed their works and by which they were known in literary society. Mustafa adopted the name "Çeşmi," "The Hopeful," and began to compose his own poetry. He soon changed his pen name to "Âli," "The Exalted," by which he was known for the rest of his life. The young poet quickly made a reputation as well as a name for himself; only seven years later he was listed as one of the prominent young poets of Rum in the biographical dictionary of poets of Ahdi.[31]

Âli's choice of a poetic pen name represented a cultural rite of passage into adulthood. At the same time, when he was about fifteen or sixteen years old, he entered a new phase in his formal education. He had already demonstrated his mastery of the elementary skills required to embark on professional training for an *ilmiye* career by composing a number of treatises and commentaries on some of the works he had studied at the *medrese*, and he had exhausted the formal educational resources available in a provincial capital:

> In this fashion I embarked upon the noble career of religious learning, and mastered those sciences that depend upon reason and upon knowledge of religious precepts [*ulum-ı akliye ve fünun-ı nakliye*]. By the time I was sixteen years old I was qualified and prepared to enter the great universities.[32]

Most of the provincial educational institutions of the Ottoman Empire represented only the lowest two ranks of the *medrese* system, the "*medreses* of twenty" and of "thirty," so called because of the daily salary in *akçe* (aspers) that their professors received.[33] In order to receive more advanced

[31] In LAYİHAT, 3b, Âli states that he began to write poetry at the age of sixteen. Common Muslim practice, however, is to assign a child the age of one year at birth; hence, Âli's "sixteen" is probably our "fifteen." The source for Âli's choice and change of his first *mahlas* is Ahdi, *Gülşen üş-şu'ara*, MS Halet Efendi Eki 107, 156a-b (also quoted İNAL, p. 5). Ahdi completed his *tezkere* in 1563-64/971, when Âli was about twenty-two, and commended Âli's command of Arabic and Persian. On Ahdi (d. 1593) and his work see Agâh Sırrı Levend, *Türk Edebiyatı Tarihi*, I (Ankara, 1973), 269-73.

[32] COUNSEL, II, 50-51 (trans.), 177-78 (text).

[33] İnalcık, *Empire*, p. 168. The lower level *medreses* were also called by the names of the primary texts in their curricula, i.e., *haşiye-i tecrid, müftah*, etc. I have utilized the numerical nomenclature for the *medreses* up to the *dahil elli*, "inner fifty," level for the sake of clarity. For *medreses* above that level (*tetimme-i sahn, sahn-ı seman*, etc.) I have not used the numerical terminology, which indeed existed, because it is misleading. The description of *medreses* according to professorial salary ranges served two functions: it differentiated ranks of schools in which future members of the *ilmiye* had to study, and it indicated the status of teachers within the professorial promotion track. Although the two systems were parallel, they were not pre-

training the student had to continue his education at the higher-ranked institutions located in the old capitals of Bursa and Edirne, and in the new capital of Istanbul.

ISTANBUL: THE MEDRESE YEARS (1556-60)

ACADEMIC accomplishment and family connections made it possible for Âli to go to Istanbul, the educational, cultural, and political center of the Ottoman Empire. He made the journey in late 1556 or early 1557 at the age of fifteen.[34] In all likelihood Âli was entrusted to the care of his maternal great-uncle Derviş Çelebi, who was then *hatib* of the Şehzade mosque; Âli later wrote with considerable warmth about his relative, with whom he seems to have been close, and the two could only have had extended contact at this time in Istanbul.[35] Hence, it was probably under the auspices of Derviş Çelebi that Âli came to Istanbul to seek admission to one of the higher *medreses*.

At the time that Âli began his education, in the middle of the sixteenth century, the Ottoman *medrese* system was organized in the following manner. Students had first to receive basic instruction in Arabic grammar, logic, rhetoric, and religious precepts in the *medreses* classified as "outer" (*haric*). These were ranked according to the level of instruction, prestige of the institution, and daily salary of their teachers in *akçe* as the "*medreses* of

cisely equivalent; the terms *ibtida*, "beginning," and *hareket*, "movement," when used in conjunction with the numerical designations, apply only to the professorial promotion system (cf. İnalcık, *Empire*, p. 170).

34 KA, Süleyman/Şu'ara, "Hayali," Nur 3409, 278b-180a. Âli says that he came to Istanbul one year before the death of the famous dervish-poet Hayali, whom he met and who praised the young Âli's poetic efforts. Hayali died in A.H. 964 (1556-57), which would seem to indicate a *hicri* date of 963 for Âli's arrival. All but the first one and a half months of A.H. 963 fall in 1556, when Âli would have been "sixteen" (i.e., fifteen) years old and ready to make the move. It is not known when in 1556-67/964 Hayali died, and Âli's reference to arriving in Istanbul "one year"before Hayali's death should not be taken as precise. Âli often used round figures to express general rather than exact chronology. All of these bits of evidence indicate that Âli probably traveled from Gelibolu to Istanbul in the autumn of 1556/late 963-early 964. In any case, it is extremely hazardous to attempt to establish chronology by counting backwards from fixed dates using the figures for time elapsed that Âli provides. One reason for this is the difference between the manner in which Muslims and non-Muslims calculate age. A second factor is Âli's occasional imprecision in calculating intervals of time. The third complicating element is the concurrent use of two calendar systems, one lunar and one solar. Although in chronicles and archival documents the official lunar (*hicri*) calendar is explicitly maintained, a vernal solar timekeeping system was used for other purposes, as references to certain seasonal landmarks make clear. In Âli's case, several notations show that he also kept time by solar years. Hence, when Âli mentions passage of a number of years, it is often impossible to know whether he means solar or lunar ones.

35 KA, Süleyman/Meşayih, "Şeyh Muslihüddin," Nur 3409, 160b.

twenty," "thirty," "forty," and "fifty." A student had to be certified to have completed the established curriculum of one before he could graduate to the next level. The "*medreses* of fifty," which stood at the pinnacle of this preparatory group of schools, were primarily located in Bursa, Edirne, and Istanbul, being institutions established by members of the royal family other than sultans and by important Ottoman vezirs. After completing instruction in an "outer fifty" *medrese*, a student would enter the "inner" (*dahil*) university system, which provided advanced and specialized training. This track began with the "inner *medreses* of fifty," which were also located in the three major cities of the Empire and were founded by royal and aristocratic Ottomans. Next came the *tetimme*, or preparatory schools for the *Sahn-i seman*, the eight specialized *medreses* founded by the Conqueror, Fatih Sultan Mehmed. The *Sahn-i seman*, the students for which were recruited from those who had completed the preparatory curriculum, represented the apex of the Ottoman university system.

Graduates of the *Sahn* were eligible for designation to fill one of the posts that, although their incumbents were appointed by the central government, fell within the purview of the *ilmiye* hierarchy: teaching positions (*müderrislik*) and judgeships (*kaza, kadılık*). Such designation was known as *mülâzemet*, and its recipient as *mülâzim*. *Mülâzemet* was not appointment to a post as such, but rather a designation to fill a post when it should become vacant through death or promotion of an incumbent, since the number of teaching positions and judgeships was limited by imperial law (*kanun*). Most commonly, *mülâzims* eventually received teaching positions at the "outer twenty" *medrese* level. From there they could be promoted to ever more important *medreses*, essentially following the same order of promotion as professors (*müderris*) as they had as students. At any time teachers could be transferred to a provincial judgeship, the status of which depended upon their professorial rank. From this point they could work for promotion through the judicial ranks. Either one of these *ilmiye* career tracks, pedagogical and juridical, could lead to one of the highest positions available to members of the learned establishment: professorship in the highest-ranked *medreses*, judgeship of one of the nine major cities including Istanbul, the post of chief military judge (*kadıasker*) of Anatolia or Rumeli, or the office of chief jurisconsult of the Empire, the *şeyhülislam*.[36]

Between the years 1552 and 1559 a new apex was added to the *medrese* system as the mosque complex of Sultan Süleyman was completed. The Süleymaniye college included a preparatory school, four general *medreses*, and two specialized institutions devoted to the study of Prophetic tradition (*Darülhadis*) and medicine (*Darüşşifa*). Although the Süleymaniye

[36] Uzunçarşılı, *Ilmiye*, pp. 11-14, 45-48; İnalcık, *Empire*, pp. 168-72.

medreses then replaced the *Sahn* as the pinnacle of the professional ladder for teachers, the latter retained its position as a major educational institution; students who completed the "inner fifty" curriculum could choose to attend either advanced *medrese*, and in either case would become equally eligible for designation to fill a post.[37]

There were strict rules against either students or teachers skipping degrees within this graduated promotional system. An imperial decree (*ferman*) issued in 1576 even specified the minimum amount of time a student had to spend at each level in order to qualify for graduation to the next. Bearing in mind that this decree was issued to counter current abuses of the system, and that it dates from twenty years after Âli's entry into the upper-level *medrese* system, we may take it as something of a guide to ideal practice during Âli's school years. Optimal progress for the exceptional student entailed some three years of constant work at the "outer" level of the "*medreses* of twenty," "thirty," and "forty." This corresponds in Âli's case to the period between the ages of twelve, when he entered the *medrese* system, and fifteen, when he went to Istanbul. Thereafter a student had to spend a year in "outer" and "inner" "*medreses* of fifty," and finally three years as a *danişmend*, i.e., an advanced student in various stages of the *Sahn* system.[38]

Despite the rigidly hierarchical structure of the Ottoman *medrese* system, there was no centralized mechanism for evaluating the qualifications of applicants. Rather, each professor was responsible for personally examining and accepting students, and for assigning them the stipends and accommodations provided for a fixed number of students by the endowment of the *medrese* to which the teacher was attached.[39] The personal bond between student and teacher was fundamental to the *ilmiye* system. When promoted to a higher level teaching post, a professor could take his student with him or, when the student was ready for graduation to a more advanced course of

[37] Uzunçarşılı, *İlmiye*, pp. 33-38.

[38] *Mühimme defteri* (hereafter MD), 27, p. 239, quoted by Uzunçarşılı, *İlmiye*, pp. 13-15. The term *danişmend* must be defined with care, since it is used in both a generic sense to refer to a *medrese* student, and in a technical sense to designate a student in one of the *Sahn medreses*. In this latter sense *danişmend* is used in contrast with *talebe* or *talib-i ilm*, which appears to signify a student at the lower *haric* level. An analogous term that occurs frequently in narrative and archival sources is *müsta'idd*, literally "prepared." As a technical term *müsta'idd* is applied to those who have completed the most advanced educational curriculum and are prepared for *mülâzemet*. More generally, however, *müsta'idd* refers to students at the upper levels of the *medrese* system who are ready to graduate to the next stage. Âli uses the term in this latter sense. For examples, see Uzunçarşılı, *İlmiye*, pp. 15-16, 19, 26, 68. See also a decree, dated 1538/944, which prescribes five years as the minimum period of study of required texts necessary for a student to qualify for admission to the *Sahn* (M. T. Gökbilgin, "Kanuni Sultan Süleyman Devri Müesseseler ve Teşkilatına Işık Tutan Bursa Şer'iye Sicillerinden Örnekler," in *İsmail Hakkı Uzunçarşılı'ya Armağan* [Ankara, 1976], pp. 96-99).

[39] Uzunçarşılı, *İlmiye*, p. 12, citing *Cevdet Tarihi*.

study, would pass him to a trusted colleague at an appropriate institution. This constituted an institutionalized form of the *intisab* system; success within the learned establishment was determined not only by what one studied, but also by whom one studied with, since prominent ulema could secure their pupils' entry into the best schools and best jobs.

In 1557/964, very soon after his arrival in Istanbul, Âli established this crucial relationship, in which Derviş Çelebi may have assisted him. He was accepted as an advanced student by Mevlana Şemsüddin Ahmed, who, although he was then only in his early twenties, was already a professor at the "outer *medrese* of fifty" of Rüstem Paşa in Istanbul.[40] Âli now entered those upper levels of the educational system that could lead to high judgeships and professorships, the most elevated positions to which freeborn Muslims could rise in the Ottoman system. At the time of his initial acceptance by Şemsüddin, Âli was probably assigned a student stipend from the mosque endowment; receipt of a stipend constituted full membership in the Ottoman ruling class.[41]

Şemsüddin Ahmed was the son of the highest-ranking member of the *ilmiye* at that time, Ebüssu'ud Efendi, who as *şeyhülislam* was the supreme authority in the Empire on the Holy Law (*şeri'at*). Şemsüddin's parentage helps to account for his rapid progress through the professional hierarchy at an early age. Between 1557, when he accepted Âli, and 1561, Şemsüddin was promoted from Rüstem Paşa to the "inner *medrese* of fifty" of Haseki Sultan, and then again to one of the *Sahn medrese*s of the Conqueror. For all this, Âli's teacher was not a man in his father's mold; he died at the very beginning of 1563, before his thirtieth birthday, as a result of excessive use of the narcotic substances to which he was addicted.[42]

As a *danişmend* Âli was required to pursue a broad course of study with a variety of teachers of specialized subjects. One year after coming to Istanbul, for example, he was studying with Sürûri, a fellow native of Gelibolu and one of the most renowned experts in grammar and rhetoric of the time,

[40] All of the following information on Şemsüddin is taken from KA, Süleyman/Ulema, "Mevlana Şemsüddin Ahmed b. Ebüssu'ud," Nur 3409, 153a. See also Ali Mınık, *Al-ʿIqd al-manẓûm fî dhikr afâḍil al-Rûm* (Beirut, 1975; hereafter IQD), pp. 354-56. Rüstem Paşa is identified as an "outer fifty" *medrese* by Uzunçarşılı, *İlmiye*, p. 61.

[41] Âli nowhere makes explicit reference to his source of support during his student years, but complains of poverty. In his last work, *Mevâ'id ün-nefâ'is fî ḳavâʿid il-mecâlis*, ed. M. Cavid Baysun (Istanbul, 1956; hereafter MEVA'İD), p. 17, Âli states that he served the sultans Süleyman and Selim II for a total of twenty years. Selim died in 1574/982, a fact which, allowing for some exaggeration in order to provide a round figure, would date the beginning of Âli's "service" to about this time (1557/964). Hence this passage may be an oblique reference to receipt of a stipend.

[42] Şemsüddin died in Cümada I 970/27 December 1562-26 January 1563. His intemperance is said to have caused his father much grief; see C. Baysun, "Ebüssu'ud Efendi," İA. Haseki Sultan is identified as an "inner fifty" *medrese* by Uzunçarşılı, *İlmiye*, p. 61.

at Süruri's own mosque in the Kasım Paşa quarter of Istanbul. Süruri was disaffected from the Ottoman system; he had resigned from a teaching post at Rüstem Paşa in order to teach independently in his own small mosque and thus avoid involvement with either government or *ilmiye* politics. Nevertheless, his scholarship was irreproachable, and his granting of a certification of mastery of a text (*icazet*) still carried considerable weight. He was also a Nakşbendi dervish and an habitué of the Emir-i Buhari Tekkesi, with which Âli had strong family ties through his great-grandfather, Şeyh Muslihüddin.[43] Regional and *tarikat* ties may have played a role in Âli's association with Süruri. The fact that Âli studied with Süruri, even though his courses were not an official part of the *medrese* system, highlights the importance of the personal aspect of Ottoman education. A student's standing was judged not only by the *medrese* to which he might be formally attached, but also by the diplomas of qualification to teach individual texts and subjects he received from recognized authorities, whatever the status of the latter might be. Finally, the case of Süruri, who rebelled against the control which the Ottoman government was establishing over the learned classes, shows that in the mid-sixteenth century the bureaucratization of the *ilmiye* as a branch of the ruling establishment was neither complete nor accepted in principle with equanimity.

No matter with whom else he studied, Âli retained his primary attachment to Şemsüddin Ahmed, who took Âli with him as one of his own advanced students when he was promoted to Haseki Sultan and then to the *Sahn*. In the *Essence of History* Âli wrote of Şemsüddin:

> I became his well-known "advanced student" [*müsta'idd*] in all three of the *medreses* mentioned above, for entry into each of which I was fully qualified. From the year 964 [1556-57] almost until the year 970 [1562] I was occupied with the study of those exalted subjects, theology and Qur'ânic exegesis.[44]

In fact the terminal date which Âli gives for his studies with Şemsüddin Ahmed is very approximate; the true date is 1560, as will be seen below. Âli's progress from "outer fifty" *medrese* student to *Sahn* graduate in a period of time between three and four years in length appears remarkably rapid, although there is little data on other *danişmends* that would establish a basis for comparison; at least it comes close to the optimal progress legislated some twenty years later in the imperial decree cited above. Âli was clearly able and studious; he was also helped along by a teacher who had the best *ilmiye* connections and climbed the professorial ladder quickly.

[43] KA, Süleyman/Ulema, "Sürûri," Nur 3409, 148a-b. See also Ömer Faruk Akün, "Sürûri," İA. Âli studied with Süruri in 1557-58/965.

[44] KA, Süleyman/Ulema, "Mevlana Şemsüddin Ahmed b. Ebüssu'ud," Nur 3409, 153a.

During these university years in Istanbul, Âli maintained the lively interest in belles-lettres that his boyhood in Gelibolu had fostered side by side with his professional studies. He pursued acquaintance with important literary figures of the older generation, such as Hayali Beğ, the celebrated dervish poet of Vardar Yenicesi. Although he met Hayali only one year before the latter's death, Âli later idealized him as the greatest poet of the older generation and as the founder of the new Ottoman "high style" in poetry. Hayali also provided a role model for the young littérateur in a more material sense. He died possessed of tremendous wealth, which he apparently acquired primarily on the basis of his stature as a poet. Âli later in life was to bemoan the fact, as he perceived it, that literary talent no longer brought great material rewards from conscientious patrons, as had been the case in his youth. Throughout his career Âli maintained contact with the family of Hayali in the person of the latter's son Hubbi Ömer Beğ. Both Âli and Hubbi Ömer entered bureaucratic service, and together they edited a selection from Hayali's poetry.[45]

Âli also cultivated Ârifi (Fathullah Ârif Çelebi, d. 1562/969). Ârif Çelebi was an Iranian Türkmen who had come to Istanbul in the early 1540s. His skill in both Persian and Turkish verse, and the high cultural prestige enjoyed by things Persian at the court of Süleyman, led the sultan to appoint Ârif Çelebi the first Ottoman *şehnâmegûy* (or *şehnâmeci*), charged with the composition of a history of the Ottoman dynasty in Persian verse and in the style of Firdawsî's celebrated *Shâhnâmeh*.[46] Âli shared the Persianate cultural orientation of the Ottoman court and prized his contact with Ârif Çelebi, whom he later described in the *Essence* as "the foremost calligrapher of *divani* ['chancery'] script in the Persian style, and a man celebrated for his knowledge of Iranian court practice and protocol."[47]

Despite his youth, Âli also associated with two Ottoman elder statesmen whose influence upon him would prove extremely significant. These were Celalzade Mustafa Çelebi (d. 1567/975) and Ramazanzade Mehmed Paşa (d. 1571/979). Celalzade, also called Koca Nişancı, served Süleyman as chancellor (*nişancı*) for twenty-three years, and established much of what became standard diplomatic usage and chancery practice. Well known for

[45] KA, Süleyman/Şu'ara, "Hayali," Nur 3409, 178b-180a. Hubbi Ömer Beğ died in 1595-96/1004, according to Selaniki, *Tarih*, MS Gökbilgin (hereafter SELANİKİ), *sub anno* 1004, 96a.

[46] On Ârif Çelebi and the *şehnâmegûy* tradition, see Cornell Fleischer, "Alqâs Mîrzâ Ṣafavî," *Encyclopaedia Iranica* (forthcoming); GOW, pp. 87-88; Christine Woodhead, "An Experiment in Official Historiography: The Post of *Şehnameci* in the Ottoman Empire," *Wiener Zeitschrift für die Kunde des Morgenlandes* 75 (1983): 157-82. Despite the assertion of some sources that Ârif Çelebi came to Istanbul in 1547 with the renegade Safavi prince Alqâs Mîrzâ, according to a Palace expenditure register (BBA, Maliyeden Müdevver 17881) entry dated 31 October 1545/24 Şa'ban 952) he was already drawing a stipend at that time.

[47] KA, Süleyman/Şu'ara, "Ârif," Nur 3409, 190b-191b.

his skill in the composition of literary prose (*inşâ*), Celalzade planned, and wrote at least the last portion of, the first comprehensive history of the Ottoman dynasty in Ottoman Turkish, the *Tabakat ül-memalik fi derecat il-mesalik, The Classification of Countries on the Grades of the Ways*.[48] Celalzade's successor as chancellor was Ramazanzade, called Küçük Nişancı, who was also an historian; he authored the *Tarih-i Nişancı*, a digest of world and Ottoman history.[49] Forty years later Âli boasted of his early association with both men, whose spiritual heir and historiographical successor he became when he wrote the *Essence of History*:

> I was frequently together with both [Ramazanzade] and the late Celalzade. Such was the favor they showed me that I was overwhelmed by their desire to have me become their spiritual heir. I became the third, after them, to write a history of the Ottoman house. Finally I acquired the house of Ramazanzade by purchase, and so it seemed as if I had inherited his property as well.[50]

Âli's schoolmates included aspiring poets with whom he participated in literary séances; among his fellow advanced students [*müsta'idd*s] were Baki, Sirri, Ruhi, Rümuzi, Abdi, and Muhibbi (not Sultan Süleyman, who used the same nom de plume). Sirri, like Hayali, was a native of Yenice-i Vardar (Vardar Yenicesi), the poets of which region Âli particularly admired. As students, Sirri and Âli recited poetry to each other, and they maintained contact later in life. Âli also admired Baki, who was to become the premier poet of his generation. Baki, some fourteen years older than Âli, encouraged and helped discipline the younger poet's talents; he became Âli's poetic model, and the two throughout their lives preserved an amicable poetic rivalry tempered by mutual respect and real affection. Much later, when Baki fell into political difficulties, Âli consistently defended his friend and mentor. This special relationship was noted by contemporaries; the two died in the same year, and one chronogram composed on the event was "Âli died and Baki followed him" (1600/1008).[51] It was during these school

[48] GOW, pp. 102-103; M. T. Gökbiligin, "Celâl-zâde," İA. Celalzade's history has been published in facsimile, with introduction and summary, by Petra Kappert, *Geschichte Sulṭân Süleymân Ḳânûnîs von 1520 bis 1557* (Wiesbaden, 1981).

[49] GOW, pp. 103-105; Ş. Turan, "Ramazan-zâde," İA.

[50] KA, Süleyman/Defterdaran, "Mehmed Çelebi Ramazanzade," Nur 3409, 135a-136b, and Nur 3406, 98a (filling a blank left at the end of this passage in 3409).

[51] KA, Selim/Şu'ara, "Ruhi," "Sirri," Nur 3409, 277b, 285a; KA, Süleyman/Şu'ara, "Muhibbi," Nur 3409, 192b-193a. In his last, posthumously compiled *divan* (İÜ Türkçe 768; hereafter DİVAN III) Âli addresses the *kapı ağası* Gazanfer Ağa in a fragmentary poem (f. 86a), which can be dated to 1596-97/1005-1006 on the basis of internal evidence. Âli speaks of himself and Baki, both of whom have been dismissed from their posts, as "the two nightingales amongst the crows" who should be raised to high position despite the slander and jealousy of others. The chronogram is cited by Mustakimzade, *Tuhfe-i Hattatin*, ed. İbnülemin

years in Istanbul that Âli met many of the people who, like himself, were becoming the true Ottomans. In the latter days of the reign of Sultan Süleyman they were on their way to the top of the system, and would form the next generation of Ottoman scholars, judges, bureaucrats, and literary figures under Süleyman's successors.

Âli completed his *medrese* training at the *Sahn* level some time between April and December 1560.[52] He thus became a *müsta'idd* in the technical sense of one qualified for appointment to a teaching or judicial post. Qualification, however, did not ensure employment; in actual fact the career paths open to prospective members of the *ilmiye* were branches of government service. Appointments to judicial posts were made by the military judges of Rumeli and Anatolia, who were in fact officials of the central government. The salary levels of judges were established by dynastic decree, *kanun*, rather than by the Islamic Holy Law they ostensibly served, and salaries were paid by the government as well. The same was true of teaching posts, with the difference that teachers' salaries came from mosque endowments rather than the central treasury.

Admission to candidacy for such positions, the number of which was limited by *kanun*, was governed by a mechanism analogous to the waiting list maintained by the U.S. Foreign Service for those who pass the entrance examinations. Graduates of the eight *Sahn* schools or the Süleymaniye *medrese* complex applied for designation to candidacy for professorship or judgeship. Those lucky graduates who were granted *mülâzemet* then had to wait for an appropriate position at the lower levels of the teaching and judicial lines to fall vacant. *Mülâzim*s were granted actual appointments in order of precedence, according to the date of their admission to the *mülâzemet* list. Only then could young university graduates begin to work their way up within the hierarchy of *ilmiye* posts proper. By 1560, when Âli was ready for employment, the availability of *mülâzemet*s was severely restricted. Their number was limited by *kanun*, and authority to appoint a specified number of *mülâzim*s lay primarily with eleven officials: the two military judges of Anatolia and Rumelia, the judge of Istanbul, and the judges of major provincial capitals with a salary of five hundred *akçe* per day. In the year 1560 restrictions were further tightened by a decree that all *mülâzemet* appointments be registered in the Imperial Records Office (*Ruznamçe-i hümayun*). The purpose of this measure was to curb appointment of unqualified individuals as *mülâzim*s and short-circuiting of the seniority system. Fi-

Mahmud Kemal (Istanbul, 1928), pp. 521-22. See also M. Fuad Köprülü, "Baki," İA. Since Baki was in Aleppo from 1556/963 until July-August 1560/Zulka'de 967, he and Âli must have become acquainted shortly after this latter date, perhaps during one of Âli's trips to Istanbul from Kütahya.

[52] See note 56.

nally, *mülâzemet* appointments were to be made only once every seven years, additional ones only being granted on certain celebratory occasions such as the birth of a prince or a great military victory.[53]

A *medrese* education was therefore only the first step in a lengthy waiting process for ambitious prospective ulema. A graduate could be stopped at the pre-*mülâzemet* level for many years until, whether through seniority, persistence, or connections, he attained designation as a candidate for an *ilmiye* post. After becoming a *mülâzim* he had to wait even longer until he could be appointed to an actual post when an appropriate one fell vacant; *mülâzemet*, at least, carried with it a guarantee of future employment. In the mid-sixteenth century the only viable shortcut through the system was to obtain royal intercession. The poet Baki provides an excellent example of both the personal limitations and the advantages of the system. Baki was about thirty-five years old when, thanks to the efforts of influential friends at court and to Sultan Süleyman's growing admiration for his poetic talent, he was finally designated *mülâzim* by royal fiat. The next year, in May 1564, Baki was given a beginning teaching post at a salary of twenty-five *akçe* per day. One month later he was promoted, again by Süleyman's order and again in violation of the seniority system.[54]

Baki's young friend Âli was only nineteen or twenty years old when he completed his own education and began to seek entry into the *ilmiye* professional system. Like Baki, Âli was ambitious and unwilling to wait for a *mülâzemet*, and hoped to use his skill as a poet to win the favor of those who might help him begin his chosen career. He resolved to try his luck with Prince Selim, Süleyman's designated heir and a renowned patron of poetic talents.

AT THE COURT OF PRINCE SELİM: KONYA AND KÜTAHYA (1561-63)

UNTIL late in the sixteenth century Ottoman princes were given practical administrative training by being assigned to govern a *sancak* (literally, "standard" or "banner"), the second largest unit of Ottoman provincial administration. A number of *sancak* districts together made up a *vilayet*, or province proper. Princes were often "sent to *sancak*," as the Ottomans termed this phenomenon, at a very young age. Consequently, the sultan assigned his sons tutors, called *lala*, from the ranks of his *kul*s who had proven their own administrative abilities at the *sancak* level. The provincial

[53] Uzunçarşılı, *İlmiye*, pp. 45-48.

[54] Köprülü, "Baki"; Uzunçarşılı, *İlmiye*, p. 46.

princely courts mirrored, on a smaller scale, the institutional framework and cultural ethos of the imperial court at Istanbul. However, in the fifteenth and sixteenth centuries no explicit system for regulating succession to the throne, either by primogeniture or by designation, had been worked out. The first two centuries of Ottoman history are punctuated by succession struggles between brother princes which amounted to civil war. The last such conflict in the sixteenth century occurred between Süleyman's sons Selim and Bayezid, who well before their father's death maneuvered for acceptance or outright designation as heir to the throne. The rivalry between the two princes came to a head on 30 May 1559/22 Şa'ban 966, when the forces the two had gathered met in pitched battle on the plain of Konya. Bayezid's forces were routed; the defeated prince fled to Iran and sought the protection of the Safavi Shâh Ṭahmâsb, who was eventually persuaded to allow Bayezid to be executed by Prince Selim's representatives. Selim was left in possession of Konya, which became his *sancak* seat immediately following the battle with Bayezid in the spring of 1559. At some point in the next two and a half years Selim's court was transferred from Konya to Kütahya. The *terminus ante quem* for this move is March 1562, by which time Selim was installed in his new *sancak*.[55]

Prince Selim was almost certainly at Konya when Âli finished his studies at the *Sahn* in 1560. During his student years Âli had been at work on his first major literary composition, a verse work entitled *Mihr u Mah, The Sun and the Moon*. He traveled to Selim's court in order to present the book to the prince. Âli, well aware of Selim's reputation as a connoisseur of poetry, hoped to gain the prince's favor and to secure *mülâzemet* appointment. In this Âli was successful, for Selim was favorably impressed with the young man's talent and designated him *mülâzim*. Âli remained at court; having found princely favor, he wished to press for quick assignment to a judicial or teaching post, which represented the next step in the scholarly career path. Because regular procedures for promotion to the few *ilmiye* posts available were relatively rigidly observed, such an appointment was more difficult for even a prince to make than a simple *mülâzemet* assignment; and Selim had other uses for well-schooled men in need of an income and position. After Âli presented *The Sun and The Moon* (most probably in 1561/968-69), Selim suggested that the young man abandon his *ilmiye* ambitions

[55] On the princely *sancak*s see A. D. Alderson, *The Structure of the Ottoman Dynasty* (Oxford, 1956), pp. 17-24. Alderson gives no source for his date of 1559 for Selim's transfer from Konya to Kütahya (p. 23). The definitive study of the Selim-Bayezid affair is by Şerafettin Turan, *Kanuni'nin Oğlu Şehzade Bayezid Vak'ası* (Ankara, 1961). Turan points out (pp. 151, 178) that Âli's NADİR and KA are the sole sources for the March 1562/Receb 969 date for Selim's change of *sancak*. In the NADİR Âli states that at that time he was already employed as a scribe at Selim's court, and that he composed two chronograms on the occasion of the move to Kütahya (54b-55a).

and instead take service as a chancery secretary (*divan kâtibi, kâtib-i divan*) at the princely court. Âli accepted the offer, which he says was in fact presented as an order, and thus entered bureaucratic service.[56]

Such a change of career was necessarily definitive, for the religious career or ''Path of Learning'' (*tarik-i ilm*) was closed to those who did not enter it in the prescribed fashion and work their way through the ranks. The bureaucratic career or ''Path of Scribal Service'' (*tarik-i kitabet*) in the mid-sixteenth century offered an attractive career alternative to *medrese* graduates. Before the 1530s the Ottomans appear to have possessed little in the way of a professional bureaucracy; such ''scribal'' duties as were required were usually performed by *ilmiye* recruits, who were the most literate people in Ottoman society. Under Sultan Süleyman, one of whose major tasks was to regularize Ottoman administration, the bureaucratic needs of the Empire increased tremendously. A professional bureaucracy, the *kalemiye* (from *kalem*, pen), took form and by midcentury was beginning to establish itself as a career track independent of the religious learned establishment.[57] It is not to be wondered at that the *kalemiye* was so attractive to *medrese* graduates like Âli; the primary requirement for secretarial service was literacy, and young *medrese* graduates could enter the rapidly expanding bu-

[56] The chronology for this period is somewhat confused, and the location of Selim's court at the time of Âli's arrival is unclear. In KA, Selim/Şu'ara, ''Selimşah,'' Nur 3409, 270b, Âli says: ''In 965 I completed the verse work *Mihr u Mah*, which I took to his [Selim's] court with the intention of presenting it, one year after the battle in the plain of Konya [30 May 1559/22 Şa'ban 966]. At the same time [Selim] showed me great favor. He granted my request for a *mülâzemet* and then, out of mercy and compassion, he ordered that I leave the rigors of an *ilmiye* career and exchange my poverty for the rewards of a scribal post.''

The first chronological problem presented by this passage is the completion date of *Mihr u Mah*. According to Birnbaum's description of the British Museum MS, the work was finished in 969 (Birnbaum, ''*Mihr u Mâh*''). Birnbaum, who seems to have been unaware of this passage in the KA, goes on to criticize the statement of Hammer (GOR IV, 652; followed by K. Süssheim, ''ʿÂlî,'' EI[1], and R. Manatran, ''ʿÂlî,'' EI[2]) that Âli presented *Mihr u Mah* in 965, then becoming ''a real secretary instead of an assistant.'' All of these statements in fact stem from a misreading of the passage cited above, which should read as translated. Hammer mistakenly understood *mülâzemet* as scribal rather than *ilmiye* apprenticeship.

This leaves the problem of the date of Âli's arrival at Selim's court. ''One year after the battle of Konya'' would signify late 967 or 968, at which point *Mihr u Mah* had not yet been put in final form. Given Âli's periodic vagueness on dates and other evidence (see below), 968 would seem the most probable date. Âli may have shown Selim a draft of *Mihr u Mah*, which he put into final presentation form a year later.

In the COUNSEL Âli appears to give two different dates for his appointment to scribal duty: on p. 52 (trans.), 179 (text), 968 is cited, while on p. 71 (trans.), 197 (text) he says that the Şehzade's order followed presentation of *Mihr u Mah*, which Birnbaum shows to have been formally completed in 969. The passage from NADİR cited in note 55 shows that Âli was in Selim's scribal service by March 1562/Receb 969.

[57] On this development, see Cornell Fleischer, ''Gelibolulu Mustafa Âli Efendi, 1541-1600: A Study in Ottoman Historical Consciousness (Ph.D. dissertation, Princeton University, 1982), pp. 410-40, and my forthcoming study of the growth of the bureaucracy and dynastic law in the sixteenth century.

reaucracy and advance within it far more easily and quickly than they could hope to do within the rigid *ilmiye* hierarchy. In a society in which entry into state service, as well as education, defined social mobility, the religious career offered the primary mode of access to *askeri* status available to freeborn Muslims; constant attempts by the authorities to reform the *ilmiye* and to weed out unqualified but socially ambitious ulema attest to its popularity. By the middle of the sixteenth century the ranks of ulema and students alike were overcrowded, competition was keen, and progress was slow. Entries in Ottoman biographical dictionaries on Âli and others who made the same career change make it clear that the difficulty of beginning and advancing a religious career at this time was a primary motivating factor for those who exchanged the Path of Learning for that of the Pen.[58] In Âli's case there was also a distinguished precedent for such an action; two of the most important *kalemiye* figures of the preceding generation, the chancellors Celalzade and Ramazanzade, with whom Âli had been close in Istanbul, had begun their careers as *Sahn* students before choosing to enter the bureaucratic service.[59] The *ilmiye* had provided many of the highest-ranking chancery figures before Âli's time, and *medrese* graduates who entered scribal service carried with them the prestige to which their religious education entitled them.[60] When Âli accepted the post of chancery secretary at Selim's court, he was given, in addition to a daily salary of ten *akçe*, the honorific rank of *müteferrika*, "elite," a designation reserved for people of distinguished lineage and for ulema closely associated with the court. Âli received this distinction because he had reached the relatively advanced standing of *mülâzim* within the *ilmiye* system.[61] Although Âli abandoned the religious career, his *medrese* education continued, until the end of his life, to play a central part in his self-image and the image others formed of him.

[58] For example, Kınalızade Hasan Çelebi, Âli's contemporary and author of a *Tezkeret üş-şu'ara* (ed. İbrahim Kutluk, 2 vols. [Ankara, 1978-81]; hereafter KINALIZADE) wrote of Âli: "Though he had been engaged in the constant study of theology, he was unable to bear the difficulties of an *ilmiye* career, nor did he have the patience for it. By his own desire and request he transferred out of the Path of Learning" (KINALIZADE, II, 591-92). Beyani (*Tezkere*, MS İÜ Halis Ef. 2568, 52b) and Riyazi (*Riyaz üş-şu'ara*, MS Millet-Genel 765, 84a) write in a similar vein. For other examples of *medrese* graduates turned bureaucrat, see KINALIZADE, I, 514-15 ("Şahi"), 566 ("Safa'i").

[59] KA, Süleyman/Defterdaran, "Mehmed Çelebi Ramazanzade," Nur 3409, 135a.

[60] See, for example, the career of Tacizade Ca'fer Çelebi, chancellor to Bayezid II and Selim I, analyzed by İsmail E. Erünsal in two publications: "Tâcîzade Ca'fer Çelebi, as Poet and Statesman," *Boğaziçi Üniversitesi Dergisi, Beseri Bilimler* 6 (1978): 123-48; and *The Life and Works of Tâcî-zâde Ca'fer Çelebi, with a Critical Edition of his Dîvân* (Istanbul, 1983).

[61] KA, Selim/Şu'ara, "Hatemi," Nur 3409, 275b. On the designation of *müteferrika*, see M. Z. Pakalın, *Tarih Deyimleri ve Terimleri*, 3 vols. (Istanbul, 1946-54), II, 637-38. While the discussions of Pakalın and Uzunçarşılı (*Saray*, p. 428 f.) deal with *müteferrikalık* as an Istanbul Palace post, the provincial courts mirrored, on a smaller scale, the structure of the central *saray*. *Müteferrikalık*s were of two types: *ulûfeli* (salaried) and *ulûfesiz* (honorific). Ali's was of the second variety.

Âli's interest in poetry and belles-lettres was both personally and professionally congenial to his transfer into secretarial service. The literary skill he displayed in *The Sun and the Moon* won him *mülâzemet*, and then a post as chancery secretary (ca. early 1561), in which capacity he was charged with the composition of elegant correspondence as well as more routine documents. Thereafter he achieved rapid promotion, thanks to his talent for poetry, a commodity highly prized at the princely court. Six months after his initial appointment his salary was increased from ten to sixteen *akçe* per day. Prince Selim's equerry (*mirahur*) Turak Çelebi, himself a poet and patron of poets, granted the increase to Âli and the poet-secretaries Hatemi and Ulvi out of his own salary when Selim promoted him to the post of finance director (*defterdar*). As a chancery secretary Âli accompanied Selim's court to Kütahya when it shifted there, probably in late 1561 or early 1562. There he completed the finished version of *The Sun and The Moon* and, in mid-1562, presented a new work, the *Tuhfet ül-uşşak, Curios of the Lovers*. At this point Âli's literary projects were primarily modeled on older established paradigms; the *Curios*, a treatise on Sufism and Sufi saints, was an imitation (*nazire*) of the Persian *Maṭlaʿ al-anvâr* of Khusraw-i Dihlavî. In his introduction to this work Âli states that it was completed at Selim's court at Kütahya. Certainly his learning and literary activity gained him favor, and he later described himself as having attained the status of head secretary (*başkâtib*) by late 1562 or early 1563. His immediate superior was the secretary-in-chief (*re'isülküttab*) Fazli, who was a noted poet.[62] Professionally, Âli flourished under the patronage of Turak Çelebi, also known by the pen name Nihani, "The Hidden," to whom he addressed a number of odes. Âli was sufficiently highly regarded to be offered the post of secretary-in-chief to Selim's son Prince Murad, then at his own *sancak* seat of Manisa. Âli preferred to remain at the court of Selim, who was next in line for the

[62] Birnbaum, "*Mihr u Mah*"; on the *Hümâyûnnâme*, itself a Turkish translation of *Kalîla wa Dimna*, see Levend, *Türk Edebiyatı Tarihi*, p. 199. The *Tuhfet ül-uşşak* was completed in 969, probably between May and August 1562/Ramazan to Zulhicce, since Âli describes it as an *îdîye*, i.e., a poem intended for presentation on the Feast of Sacrifice, which occurs on 10 Zulhicce (MS Abdullah Çelebi 277, 104a, 105b). Âli describes his change of career by Selim's order and promotion in: SADEF, pp. 246-47; COUNSEL, II, 71 (trans.), 297 (text); KA, Selim/Introduction, and Selim/Şu'ara, "Fazli," Nur 3409, 221a, 282b-283a. The meaning of *başkâtib* is unclear, since it is not a commonly used chancery term. The head of the chancery would have been the *re'isülküttab; başkâtib* may have been "chief scribe" of a subsection, if the term is not merely an invention of Âli's intended to underline his prominence among his peers.

Information on Âli's salary comes from KA, Selim/Şu'ara, "Hatemi," Nur 3409, 275b, in which Âli states that he was appointed *divan kâtibi* six months before Hatemi's arrival at court, at which time he received the increase. This passage would be significant for the chronology of Âli's own career were it not for the fact that all the major manuscripts consulted date Hatemi's arrival at Kütahya to 977. This date is impossible and is probably based on a scribal error for 969, given the orthographic similarity between 69 and 77 in written form.

Ottoman throne, or to be offered a higher position; he appealed to Turak Çelebi to keep him at Kütahya.[63]

Âli's predilection for a literary rather than a pedagogical or legal career was doubtless reinforced by the vibrant poetic milieu within which he found himself at Kütahya. Selim was well known as the son of Süleyman most given to both the literary and bibulous arts of the Ottoman salon. At Kütahya he surrounded himself with a great many boon-companions and poets, most of whom had either district (*sancak*) governorships nearby, or staff and clerical positions at his court. In the *Essence of History* Âli recounts that when he was chancery secretary at Kütahya in 1562-63/970 there were more than twenty poets in attendance on Selim. He goes on to praise Selim's extensive patronage of literary talents, saying that his wine and poetry gatherings were "better than those of Cemşid" and that "his other brothers did not have as many boon-companions and poets."[64] Poetic composition and competition played an important role in court life, and Selim's *musahib*s, "royal companions," were patrons of poetry in their own right. Âli, like many of the other court littérateurs, enjoyed the favor of the finance director Turak Çelebi, who commissioned him to choose the best of the court poets' compositions for submission to Selim. Âli also received a reward from the prince for a poem he composed on the occasion of a royal hunt, which amounted to one hundred gold pieces.[65]

By the age of twenty the ambitious *medrese* graduate had succeeded in gaining a position in the second most important household establishment in the Empire. His status, like that of other courtiers, depended as much upon the nature of his identification with that household, of which government was an extension, as upon the actual position he occupied. The success of his first bid for princely patronage encouraged yet more grandiose ambitions in the young littérateur, who could also see the limitations of his situation. At Kütahya, Âli appears to have been less the protégé of the prince himself than of one of the prince's retainers, Turak Çelebi; and Selim's establishment, though royal, was still a provincial one. Âli nurtured dreams of earning the favor of the sultan himself, so that he might join the premier house-

[63] Âli, *Divan*, Ali Emiri Ef. Türkçe Manzum 271 (hereafter DİVAN I), 16b-17b. Other odes in praise of Turak Çelebi occur on 18a-19a, 19b-20b.

[64] KA, Selim/Introduction, Nur 3409, 220a-221a. Âli lists the prince's *musahib*s as: Celal Beğ (Celali); Turak Çelebi (Nihani); Kurd Beğ (son of Deli Husrev Paşa and nephew of Lala Mustafa Paşa); Gülâbi Beğ; Mirek Çelebi; Sâmi Şeyhzade Mehmed Çelebi; Kassabzade-yi Nabi; Adanalı Tanbur-nevaz Şeyhzade Mustafa Çelebi; Avvad Keşçi Memi; Nakkaş Haydar (Nigâri); Hocazade (Pohyedi/Bokyedi Re'is). Other poets listed in this section (not including those cited separately in KA, Selim/Şu'ara): Fazli (author of *Gül u bülbül* and *re'isülküttab*); Firuz (Münşi Bâli Çelebi, *saray hocası* and later *nişancı*); Fünûni Sami Beğ (*za'im*); Ulvi; Sarı Rami; Hatemi; Kasımi; Va'iz-i Firaki; Makali-yi sani; Merdi (*matbah emini* at *Kütahya*); Âli.

[65] KA, Selim/Şu'ara, "Makali-yi sani," Nur 3409, 286b; COUNSEL, II, 71-72 (trans.), 297-98 (text).

hold of the land and thereby gain entry into a career at the capital. During the year 1562-63/969-70 Âli traveled to Istanbul, perhaps on official business. There he submitted a written request for employment at Süleyman's court. The sultan rejected this petition, saying, "Let his own master care for him. The prince's men should not loiter at my court."[66]

In 1562-63/970 Âli again sought princely favor with a verse work entitled *Mihr u Vefa, Affection and Fidelity*.The poem was unsuccessful, and appeared to duplicate the *Mihr u Vefa* of one Mustafa Çelebi, which even had the same meter as Âli's composition. Âli claims that he was unaware of the earlier work until it was too late; his discovery of Mustafa Çelebi's poem was a setback for an ambitious young poet working in a milieu in which originality was valued.[67] Âli claims that he had a reason other than ambition and disappointment for wanting to leave Selim's court: the enmity of the prince's new tutor, Tütünsüz Hüseyin Beğ, who had been appointed Selim's *lala* at about the same time that Âli acquired his scribal post.[68] Life at Kütahya was becoming uncomfortable.

Âli had somehow made the acquaintance of Selim's previous mentor, Lala Mustafa Paşa. How the two met is unclear; it is possible that Mustafa Paşa, whose dismissal from the tutorship was engineered by the jealous grand vezir Rüstem Paşa in August-November 1560/late 967-early 968, was still at court when Âli joined the prince's entourage.[69] Between the summer of 1562/970 and the summer of 1564/971-72 Lala Mustafa Paşa, after oc-

[66] COUNSEL, II, 70 (trans.), 196 (text). The date of Âli's journey to Istanbul is inferred from his statements on his associations with Baki and Şemsüddin Ahmed b. Ebüssu'ud, cited above. He also refers to having conversed with Celalzade in 970, presumably in Istanbul (KA, Selim I/6, Fatih 4225, 210a). On Ottoman household government, see Kunt, *Servants*, pp. xiii-xxi, 31-40.

[67] The work, of which no MS has been found, is described as a new romance in COUNSEL, II, 52-53 (trans.), 179-80 (text). On the date of composition, see KA, Süleyman/Şu'ara, "Mustafa Çelebi," Nur 3409, 207b. This passage provides evidence against the clichéd view of Ottoman literary ideals as being essentially imitative and opposed to formal innovation.

[68] COUNSEL, II, 71 (trans.), 196 (text).

[69] While İNAL (p. 8) assumes that Âli and Lala Mustafa Paşa met during the latter's tenure as Selim's *lala*, reconstructed chronology indicates that this is barely possible. After having Lala Mustafa Paşa dismissed from the *lalalık*, Rüstem Paşa appointed him first to the *sancak* of Pojega in Bosnia, previously held by Tütünsüz Hüseyin Beğ, and then to the *vilayet* of Tamşvar (between mid-September and mid-October 1560, according to MD 4, docs. 1332, 1481). Selim opposed Rüstem Paşa's attempts to thus separate him from his influential mentor, and interceded with Süleyman. Finally, Lala Mustafa Paşa received the government of Van on 9 November 1560/19 Safer 968, according to MD 3, doc. 2626, cited by Şerafettin Turan, "Lala Mustafa Paşa Hakkında Notlar ve Vesikalar," *Belleten* 22 (1958): 556. Presumably Lala Mustafa Paşa remained with or near Selim as the prince negotiated a suitable appointment. If Âli received his *mülâzemet* in late 967 or early 968, the two could easily have met; at this point Selim's establishment would have been at Konya rather than Kütahya. It is also possible that Kurd Beğ, with whom Âli was on good terms, and who was the son of Lala Mustafa Paşa's older brother, Divane (or Deli) Husrev Paşa, could have established contact between his uncle and Âli.

cupying a number of posts in rapid succession, was made governor-general (*beğlerbeği*) first of Erzurum, then of Aleppo, and finally of Damascus.[70] Before his appointment to Aleppo, Lala Mustafa Paşa invited Âli to accompany him as his confidential secretary.

Âli accepted, and thus established the patronage relationship that was to shape his political future. He also hoped that the threat of losing so valuable a scribe and poet would spur Selim to offer him further blandishments and promotions. However, his departure from Kütahya passed unnoticed, and Âli was forced to fulfill his agreement with Lala Mustafa Paşa. Even at the age of twenty-two Âli, able though he was, had an exaggerated conception of his own worth, or at least of the rewards and respect that a talented and learned young man with few contacts and little experience within the Ottoman system could realistically expect to receive. The bitterness engendered by this incident later led Âli to criticize severely the character of Selim's cultural patronage, which he compared unfavorably with that of Iranian rulers.[71] Throughout his life Âli idealized the tradition of assiduous royal patronage of intellectual and cultural life that he associated with the imperial traditions of the Persian-speaking world. Until his death he dreamed of acquiring a royal protector and high position at the Ottoman court in Istanbul, most particularly when his erstwhile patron Selim succeeded to the Ottoman throne. In this Âli was doomed to frustration; from the time he was twenty-two, when he accepted Lala Mustafa Paşa's invitation to Syria, he was never again to leave provincial service on a permanent or extended basis.

[70] KA, Selim/Beğlerbeğiler, "Lala Mustafa Paşa," Nur 3409, 252b; Turan, "Lala Mustafa Paşa," pp. 556-57. Lala Mustafa Paşa served as governor-general of Erzurum before his appointment to Aleppo, but it is unclear precisely when he took up this post. The epigraphic evidence provided by Lala Mustafa Paşa's endowments in Erzurum (a mosque and adjoining primary school) indicates that he had received the government of the province by July-August 1562/late 969-70, and spent at least part of the year there before his transfer to Aleppo in 1563/971 (Abdurrahim Şerif Beygu, *Erzurum. Tarihi. Anıtları. Kitabeleri* [Istanbul, 1936], p. 149; İ. H. Konyalı, *Abideleri ve Kitabeleri ile Erzurum Tarihi* [Istanbul, 1960], pp. 236, 244, 247, 279). The correct date of Lala Mustafa Paşa's appointment to Aleppo, 27 September 1563/8 Safer 971, is given in KPT 218, p. 23. Ibn Jumʿa's list of the governors and judges of Damascus gives 1564-65/972 as the year that Lala Mustafa Paşa took up that government (Henri Laoust, *Les Gouverneurs de Damas sous les mamlouks et les premiers ottomans (658-1156/1260-1744). Traduction des annales d'Ibn Ṭulûn et d'Ibn Ǧumʿa* [Damascus, 1952], p. 186).

[71] COUNSEL, II, 72 (trans.), 198 (text).

TWO

THE POET AT THE GATES

(1563-77 / 970-84)

DAMASCUS

(1563-68)

IN THE SPRING of 1563 Âli was twenty-two years old. His scholarly promise and ambition had taken him from his provincial home to Istanbul, where he spent four years. His literacy and the poetic skills he had honed in the salons of the capital had further won him three years at the court of the heir to the Ottoman throne, where, however, he found his progress threatened by personal animosities and keen competition. Now he went further afield; in answering Lala Mustafa Paşa's summons to the "Paşa's Gate" (*paşa kapısı*), Âli began a phase of his career that would take him to the extremities of the Ottoman dominions.

Âli traveled overland toward Aleppo. In May he broke his journey in Adana in order to spend part of the fast month of Ramazan with the aged Piri Paşa Ramazanoğlu (d. 1568-69/976), the hereditary governor (*hakim*) of that *sancak*. Piri Paşa was the scion of an old and respected princely family whose aristocratic status and loyalty to the Ottoman house had earned him the rank of paşa, normally granted only to military officials who served as governor-general or vezir, and other epithets of distinction used by the Ottoman sultans in their correspondence with him as a sign of his special standing within the *kul*-dominated Ottoman system. For Âli, Piri Paşa represented a glorious bygone era of Anatolian history, and also the type of prince he idealized: Piri Paşa knew Persian as well as Turkish, was himself a poet, and was deeply interested in literature and history. The young littérateur apparently impressed Piri Paşa as well, for the two spent much time together discussing literature and Anatolian history. Piri Paşa even offered Âli one of his daughters in marriage. Âli refused this honor, not wishing to encumber himself with a family at so young an age, and he later regretted the youthful rashness that had prompted him to reject an alliance with a princely family. Nonetheless, Piri Paşa later became one of Âli's oral sources for his Ottoman history, and also one of that history's heroes.[1]

[1] KA, IV/3, 58, 60; KA, Süleyman/Beğlerbeğiler, Piri Paşa Ramazanoğlu, Nur 3409, 129b;

From Adana, Âli went first to Aleppo, where he joined the newly appointed *beğlerbeği* Lala Mustafa Paşa. Soon after his arrival in 1563 the two moved to Damascus, to the governorship of which province Lala Mustafa Paşa had been transferred. There Âli and his patron remained for five years.[2] Âli served as both chancery and confidential secretary to Lala Mustafa Paşa, and both functions brought him into the central apparatus of provincial government. This was the Paşa's Council (*divan*), modeled on the imperial one (*divan-ı hümayun*) at Istanbul. Its members consisted of both officials appointed by the central government, such as the finance director of the province, and ranking members of the governor-general's household, such as his private secretary. Because of the intimate relationship between the gubernatorial household and provincial government, service to a paşa could eventually lead his retainers to independent careers at the highest levels of Ottoman administration; Lala Mustafa Paşa's steward Köse Mustafa, for example, died in 1594 as governor-general of Maraş.[3]

Âli's official duties left him little time for the literary and mystical pursuits that had been such an important part of his youth. Nearly thirty years later he described how his new responsibilities, and his preoccupation with building a career and a fortune, caused him to abandon his interest in mysticism and to leave unfinished a work on the subject that he had recently begun. In the introduction to this treatise, which he completed in middle age and titled *Riyaz üs-salikin, The Seekers' Bower*, Âli wrote:

Scribal duties and diploma forms
Had become my inspiration day and night.
Then I had many duties and concerns;
Seldom did I seek explanations of [mystical] meaning.
The Way of Poverty [Sufism] had become distasteful;
Gold and silver had become as plentiful as worldly cares.[4]

If nothing else, Âli's secretarial duties gave him a new interest in prose composition and in themes appropriate to it, as Âli himself suggests in an-

---

Faruk Sümer, "Ramazan-oğulları," İA. Âli's first *divan, Varidat ül-enîka (Elegant Inspirations)* (MS Hamidiye 1107; hereafter VARİDAT) contains two odes which Âli addressed to Piri Paşa (ff. 42a-43b). The first identifies the time of their meeting as mid-Ramazan, and the season as spring. The middle of Ramazan 970 fell in early May 1563. One of Piri Paşa's protégés was the Iranian-born poet Zireki, who translated Âli's *Sun and Moon* into Persian for submission to his patron (KA, Süleyman Şu'ara, "Zireki," Nur 3409, 184b-185a).

[2] In COUNSEL, II, 38 (trans.), 159 (text), Âli states that in 970 he lived in both Aleppo and Damascus. A number of other references establish this as the year Âli took up residence in Damascus: KA, Süleyman/Vüzera, "Rüstem Paşa," Nur 3409, 120b; Süleyman/Ümera, "Hacı Beğ," Nur 3409, 136b (this folio actually falls between 136 and 137, having been left out of foliation). The date of Lala Mustafa Paşa's formal appointment to Aleppo (see chapter 1, note 70) suggests that the year was actually 971, though Âli probably left Kütahya in 970.

[3] COUNSEL, II, 12.

[4] *Riyaz üs-sâlikin* (completed 1589-90/998), MS Velieddin 1916 (hereafter RİYAZ), 18a-19a.

other passage of the *Bower*.[5] He was encouraged in this new enthusiasm by one of the most significant Ottoman intellectual figures of the sixteenth century, Kınalızade Ali Çelebi (d. 1572/979). Kınalızade came to Damascus in late summer 1563/970-71 as judge (*kadı*) of the city.[6] His intellectual and literary interests ranged far beyond legal scholarship. Âli later praised Kınalızade's "old fashioned" breadth of learning and his command of the three languages (Arabic, Persian, and Turkish). The two may have arrived in Damascus at about the same time, and Âli hastened to make the acquaintance of and wait upon the renowned scholar. Âli became Kınalızade's literary apprentice, and the two met weekly to criticize their respective works in progress. Indeed, Âli states that he learned the basic premise of criticism from Kınalızade, who said that "true friendship means to look on a friend's work with the eye of an enemy."[7] At that time Kınalızade was writing his *Ahlak-ı Ala'i, The Ala'id Ethics*, which was to become the classic statement of Ottoman social and political morality. It was probably under Kınalızade's guidance that Âli began a prose work of smaller scope but similar theme during his first or second winter in Damascus. This work, the *Enis ül-kulub, The Hearts' Familiar*, remained unfinished. In conception and style it is modeled on the *Hümayunname* of Ali Çelebi (d. 1543/950) and utilizes historical examples to illustrate moral points.[8] This was Âli's first experiment with *inşa*, the elegant, allusive, trilingual form of literary composition in rhymed prose favored by the learned scribal class.

The intellectual and personal bond established between Âli and Kınalızade outlasted the latter's death. Âli was sufficiently intimate with his literary mentor to become acquainted with Kınalızade's young sons, one of whom, Hasan Çelebi, continued to correspond with Âli. Hasan Çelebi much later wrote the last of the four great biographical dictionaries of poets of the sixteenth century, in which he included a long and laudatory entry on his father's pupil. The sons, however, did not impress Âli as much as the father, and in the *Essence* Âli vilified Hasan Çelebi's *Tezkeret üş-şu'ara, Biographies of the Poets*, on stylistic and intellectual grounds. Kınalızade *père*, on the other hand, took a distinguished place in the pantheon of scholars and statesmen of the older generation whom Âli idealized.[9]

[5] RİYAZ, 18b.

[6] Hanna Sohrweide, "Das *Enîs el-Qulûb*, Ein verschollenes Werk des Historikers Muṣṭafâ 'Âlî," in *VIII. Türk Tarih Kongresi (Ankara, 11-15 Ekim 1976). Kongreye Sunulan Bildiriler*, 3 vols. (Ankaka, 1981), II, 985; Nev'izade Ata'i, *Hada'ik ül-haka'ik fi tekmilet iş-şaka'ik* (Bulaq, 1268), p. 165; KINALIZADE, II, 592.

[7] KA, Süleyman/Şu'ara, "Mevlana Ali Çelebi," Nur 3409, 194a; Selim/Ulema, "Mevlana Ala'üddin Emrullah b. Mehmed [Kınalızade]," Nur 3409, 264b-265a. Âli likens Kınalızade to Kemalpaşazade in his breadth of scholarship and catholicity of intellectual interests, saying that these are rare qualities in the ulema of his own time.

[8] Sohrweide, "*Enîs*," 986-87; COUNSEL, II, 52 (trans.), 179 (text).

[9] KINALIZADE, II, 592; much of the entry on Âli is based on information the latter provided in a letter, at Hasan Çelebi's request, before he completed his biographical work in 1586/

Âli must indeed have been occupied, for he did not begin his next major literary project, the *Nadir ül-mahârib* or *Rarity of Warriors*, until the spring of 1567/Ramazan 974. He did not complete this relatively short work (sixty-six folios) until 1568/976. Even so, the *Rarity* marks an important stage in the development of Âli's stylistic and literary preoccupations. Its focus is more topically historical than that of the *Hearts' Familiar*; it deals with the war between the princes Selim and Bayezid. Âli's patron, Lala Mustafa Paşa, was undoubtedly a major source of information, since he had played a central role in the princely conflict. But however historical and topical the work might be, Âli's motivations were literary and professional. He wished to flatter Lala Mustafa Paşa and the victor in the war, Selim, who in 1566 had acceded to the Ottoman throne. And, having entered chancery service, Âli saw the *Rarity* as a vehicle for demonstrating his ability to compose poetry and elegant *inşa* prose in both Persian and Turkish.[10]

While in Damascus Âli continued to write poetry. His output was such that by late 1567 he was able to compile the first recension of a *divan*, a volume of poems arranged in formal fashion in which the major poetic genres of "ode" (*kaside*) and "sonnet" (*gazel*) were represented. The issuance of a *divan*, which required both volume and selectivity in compilation, was an important point in a poet's literary career. It signified reputation, artistic maturity, and the closure of one period of aesthetic activity and beginning of a new one. This particular compilation, Âli's first, was not "published" (put in final form and recopied) for another seven years; only two copies of this version are known to exist. Interestingly enough, one of the two extant copies was made by Âli's brother Mehmed from Âli's own draft in late 1567; Âli himself signed and sealed the colophon. This suggests that Mehmed was with Âli at Damascus, and that the older brother had found employment there for the younger.[11]

Although Âli does not appear to have circulated this *divan*, his compilation of it at the age of twenty-six presents features of interest. In the intro-

---

994. While Hasan Çelebi boasts of his long association with Âli, the latter states in KA that none of Ali Çelebi's sons could match their father in character or ability (Nur 3409, 265b). Âli's criticism of Hasan Çelebi's work ("*tezkere-i İbn ül-muhanna*") occurs in KA, Selim/Şu'ara, "Âşık," Nur 3409, 280a. Âli probably invented this Arabicized form of "Kınalızade" in order to avoid using in a negative context the name by which his respected mentor was known.

The poet and scholar Fehmi (d. late May 1596/late Ramazan 1004) was another of the sons of Ali Çelebi; see SELANİKİ, *sub anno* 1004, 117a; and Andreas Tietze, *Muṣṭafâ 'Âlî's Description of Cairo of 1599* (Vienna, 1975, hereafter CAIRO), p. 75.

[10] NADİR, 5b; COUNSEL, II, 54 (trans.), 181 (text).

[11] The colophon of DİVAN I is photographically reproduced as the frontispiece to İnal's edition of *Menakıb-ı hünerveran* (hereafter MH), and reads: "This volume was calligraphed, with the help of the Eternal King, by the hand of my brother Mehmed (God make him prosper!), copying from my own copy, at the end of *Cümada el-evvel* of the year 975 [Nov.-Dec. 1567]. I am the humble Âli, servitor of the people." I discovered the second copy in Cairo in 1978: MS DKM Majâmī' Turkîya 25.

duction Âli lists the older and contemporary poets he most admired and desired to emulate: first and foremost was Hayali, followed by Hayreti, Necati, Celili, Zati, Mesihi, Celâli, and Fazli, the latter two of whom Âli had known at Selim's court at Kütahya. He also gives voice to some of the bitterness and sense of grievance that so strongly mark his later works. He states that he has compiled this *divan* to silence his critics and enemies who denigrate his poetic talent. Âli describes these latter as people with pretensions to learning and aesthetic sense who in fact do not know enough to appreciate the quality of Âli's poetry, and who have maliciously prevented him from obtaining the recognition due him.[12]

Boastful complaint of this sort was part of the Ottoman poet's stock in trade, and the young Âli's poetry at this time was largely conventional. The *divan* comprises many odes addressed to prominent political figures and love poems inspired by handsome young men, although Âli would later repeatedly express his disapproval of *l'amour grecque*.[13] Âli still saw himself as a poet attempting to make his way in literary circles by following established models and patterns. Even so, the sense of personal grievance that pervades his later writings suggests that he took his complaints seriously, conventional though they might be. Poetic competition at Kütahya had indeed been fierce, and Âli was ambitious, even presumptuous. The two factors combined spurred Âli to assert his stature as a poet ever more arrogantly. It is ironic that he would achieve renown, not as a poet, as he so desperately wished, but rather as an historian and master of *inşa* prose. It is possible to see in the literary efforts of the young secretary in Damascus the seeds of those concerns that would dominate his middle and old age: a fascination with elegant prose, an interest in history, and a desire to be innovative in the creation of new literary types. But such literary ventures were consciously kept within certain broad limits of formal conventionality, and served as stylistic exercises and vehicles for currying favor. Only much later would Âli's obsession with history and with a creativity that ignored or flouted accepted formal models lead him to produce those works of history and social criticism for which he is justly esteemed.

THE EGYPTIAN DÉBACLE: CAIRO (1568)

ÂLI's literary pursuits were interrupted at the beginning of 1568, a year that brought with it a series of momentous political events and personal disasters which were to occupy his attention for some time. Although he was a minor

[12] DİVAN I, 1b-3b.

[13] For example, see MEVA'İD, pp. 44-47; COUNSEL, II, 12-13 (trans.), 125 (text); Fleischer, "Âli," pp. 541-48.

participant in the power struggles that surrounded the Ottoman campaign to the Yemen in 1568, the political alignments and personal hatreds that emerged from the affair seriously affected the rest of Âli's career. Furthermore, these alliances and factional clashes established certain personal paradigms of heroism and villainy that found a prominent place in the Ottoman history written by Âli at the end of his life. Therefore it will be necessary to dwell on the Egyptian prelude to the Yemen campaign in some detail.

Prince Selim's accession to the Ottoman throne in 1566 as Selim II marked an important new stage in the careers of Lala Mustafa Paşa and his faithful confidential secretary. Lala Mustafa Paşa cherished dreams of attaining the highest appointive office in the Ottoman Empire, the grand vezirate (*sadaret-i uzma, sadrazamlık*); these dreams were fueled by the accession of the prince whose tutor he had been, and whose succession he had worked so hard to ensure throughout the struggle with Bayezid. As an important member of Lala Mustafa Paşa's personal household, Âli could reasonably expect to be elevated together with his master, with whose fortunes he identified his own. Âli expressed his deep attachment to his patron, and their mutual hopes, in an ode:

Your noble name is Lala Mustafa Paşa the Just;
You are the flowing torrent that continuously pays homage to the Holy
Law.
Now the grand vezirate awaits you at any moment;
It is near, by God! My Lord, you have almost reached it!
To be a slave [*bende*] at your gate gives glory and joy,
[For] you become the life in the body of whomever you protect.[14]

Sokollu Mehmed Paşa, the incumbent grand vezir at the time when Selim became sultan, presented a formidable obstacle to the realization of Lala Mustafa's ambitions. The two were in fact relatives; Sokollu Mehmed was the most prominent member of the Bosnian Sokolovič clan, which through the *devşirme* provided many of the most distinguished Ottoman *kul*s in the sixteenth century. Sokollu himself, once he had reached a secure position within the Palace system, was assiduous in bringing siblings and cousins into it as well by utilizing the *devşirme* apparatus.[15] Sokollu was grand vezir at the time of Süleyman's death at Sigetvar; he prudently kept the sultan's

[14] DİVAN I, 19b. A similar ode occurs on 17b-18a.

[15] M. Tayyib Gökbilgin, "Mehmed Paşa Sokollu," İA. Although the precise nature of Sokollu Mehmed and Lala Mustafa Paşa's family relationship is unknown, they are stated to have been relatives by both Âli (KA, Murad/17, Nur 3409, 334a) and Peçevi, *Tarih*, 2 vols. (Istanbul, 1283; hereafter PEÇEVİ), II, 20; the latter was himself related to the Sokollu clan. The assertion of J.-L. Bacqué-Grammont in "Notes et documents sur Divane Hüsrev Paşa," *Rocznik Orientalistyczny* 41/4 (1979): 22, that there is no evidence to support a Sokollu affiliation for Lala Mustafa Paşa, is incorrect.

death a secret and maintained order until the formal accession of Selim could be orchestrated. Confirmed in his office by the new sultan, Sokollu was determined to maintain his authority over the Empire and his influence over Selim. Sokollu brooked no opposition or rival, though his iron-handed control of government was resented by other high-ranking servitors, particularly those in Selim's personal retinue. In 1567 the intrigues and palace power struggles centered on the appointment of a field marshal (*serdar*) for a projected campaign of reconquest against the Yemen, where a long period of administrative disorder had prompted a local hereditary ruler displaced by the Ottomans, the Zaydî Shî'î imam Shaykh Muṭahhar, to occupy the province's capital of Ṣan'â and declare independence from Ottoman authority. On 31 December 1567/29 Cümada II 975 Sokollu Mehmed Paşa had Lala Mustafa Paşa appointed field marshal with the rank of vezir, and ordered him to proceed to Cairo, where campaign preparations were to be made.[16]

For Lala Mustafa Paşa the new assignment was extremely important, especially because it gave him veziral rank. The practice of granting this status to selected provincial governors and campaign commanders, then called "outer vezirs," *haric vezirleri*, had only recently begun. A successful campaign would make Lala Mustafa Paşa a war hero and would almost certainly earn him promotion to the ranks of the four "vezirs of the Dome" (*kubbe vezirleri*), who served on the Imperial Council under the grand vezir. In the theory of Süleymanic times a vezir of the Dome (the Dome being that which topped the Council chamber at the Palace) had only to wait his turn to attain the grand vezirate through attrition and seniority.[17] It was therefore crucial to Lala Mustafa Paşa's attainment of his goals that he ensure the success of the expedition.

For Sokollu Mehmed Paşa there were several cogent reasons for choosing Lala Mustafa Paşa as field marshal. Sokollu was in the process of building an *intisab* empire within the upper echelons of Ottoman government through the appointment of protégés and kinsmen to important positions; Lala Mustafa Paşa was a relative and fellow countryman. More impor-

[16] Âli's account of Lala Mustafa Paşa's appointment and the intrigues it engendered occurs in KA, Selim/3, Nur 3409, 223b-227b. Âli's version of the events is the basic source for other Ottoman historians' accounts; it is reexamined in the light of MD material by Turan, "Lala Mustafa Paşa." The dated *hükm-i hümayun* of appointment is transcribed on p. 562. Turan's archival researches also throw new light on the causes and sequence of the Yemeni revolt.

Hammer's statement (GOR, III, 503) that Âli and the historian Selâniki together accompanied the Ottoman forces returning from the 1566 Sigetvar campaign is incorrect. The mistake probably rests on a misreading or copyist's error by which "Gına'i Çelebi" was mistaken for "Âli Çelebi"; see Selâniki, *Tarih* (Istanbul, 1281, repr. Freiburg, 1970; hereafter SELANİKİ), p. 71.

[17] İ. H. Uzunçarşılı, *Osmanlı Devletinin Merkez ve Bahriye Teskilatı* (Ankara, 1948), pp. 188-89, 195-96.

tantly, Lala Mustafa Paşa had close personal ties with Sultan Selim, and Sokollu therefore needed him as an ally in order to maintain his own position. By reason of these same personal ties, the ambitious Lala Mustafa Paşa represented a grave threat to Sokollu should the new sultan choose to assert himself, for Sokollu had been Süleyman's rather than Selim's appointee. Sokollu Mehmed Paşa had therefore to maintain a delicate balance between winning Lala Mustafa Paşa over and keeping him in check. It may be, as Âli later wrote in the *Essence*, that in the instance of the Yemen campaign Sokollu intentionally checked Lala Mustafa Paşa by ordering him to cooperate with a sworn enemy as ambitious as the Lala: the Albanian *kul* Sinan Paşa, later called Koca Sinan. Âli's thesis is that Sokollu knew that the two would come into a conflict that only he could resolve, and thereby assert his authority as grand vezir. The roots of Sinan's enmity for Lala Mustafa Paşa lay in the war of the princes Selim and Bayezid, in which Lala Mustafa had played a central and perfidious part. At the time of Bayezid's flight from the plain of Konya to Iran, Sinan's older brother, Ayas Paşa, had been governor-general of Erzurum, which lay in Bayezid's path. Ayas Paşa had assisted the refugee prince with supplies, for which act he was later dismissed and executed. Sinan Paşa blamed Lala Mustafa for his brother's death.[18] Sinan Paşa himself had succeeded Lala Mustafa Paşa as governor-general of Aleppo (ca. 1563), and shortly before the initiation of plans for the Yemen campaign he had been promoted to the government of Egypt. When Sokollu Mehmed Paşa had Lala Mustafa Paşa appointed field marshal, he also ordered him to obtain the necessary troops and supplies from the governor-general of Egypt, i.e., Sinan Paşa. Lala Mustafa Paşa knew that he could therefore expect little assistance once he arrived in Egypt, but he was anxious to succeed. In the face of repeated orders to proceed to Cairo immediately, he delayed his departure from Damascus for four and a half months, until 13 May 1568/16 Zulka'de 975, while he pleaded for additional troops, supplies, and funds from the Porte, the Gate of Felicity (*der-i sa'âdet*).

Âli, probably acting as his master's agent, was send ahead to Egypt. In March 1568 Âli was in Jerusalem, and by late June he arrived in Cairo. Âli optimistically considered the expedition a turning point in his own career as well as in that of his patron. In both cities he had horoscopes cast, asking about the success of the Yemen campaign and inquiring whether the future

[18] See NADİR, 31a-b; cf, Turan, *Şehzade Bayezid*, pp. 124, 134. Turan is doubtless correct in pointing out that Âli, as an interested party, places what modern historians would view as undue emphasis on the importance of personal animosities between Lala Mustafa Paşa and Sokollu Mehmed on the one hand, and Lala Mustafa and Sinan Paşa on the other. Even so, Âli's analysis of the situation is valuable in that it explores the participants' perceptions of their own and each other's motivations.

held a return to Istanbul and rewards of high posts at the capital. In both cases the answer was that he must be patient and God would grant him his desires.[19]

Immediately after the field marshal's arrival in Cairo a campaign council was convened. Âli, as secretary to Lala Mustafa Paşa, read aloud all the relevant orders issued from Istanbul. These orders were sufficiently vague to appear to be contradictory, at least in the way they were interpreted by the campaign commander and by the governor-general. Lala Mustafa Paşa was told to take what he needed from the treasury and army of Egypt; refusing to proceed without adequate forces and supplies, he demanded four thousand troops and supplies for two years. Sinan Paşa, ordered to give what was necessary, interpreted this in his own fashion and offered only five hundred men and three months' food and fodder. The Yemen campaign preparations became a personal contest between the two enemies, who immediately began reciprocal smear campaigns in the form of letters to the Porte. Sinan Paşa accused Lala Mustafa of disobedience to the sultan in delaying his departure for the Yemen while the situation there worsened. Sinan further charged that Lala Mustafa had organized a plot to poison him (Sinan) and to have given Egypt to his own son, Mehmed Beğ, who through his mother was the great-grandson of the last Mamluk sultan, Kansuh Gavri. Sinan finally argued that Lala Mustafa Paşa wanted additional troops in order to make himself an independent ruler in the Yemen, and sought to emphasize the field marshal's personal disloyalty by claiming that he had insulted the daughters of the sultan who were married to vezirs.

For his own part Lala Mustafa Paşa made common cause with other opponents of Sinan, including Özdemiroğlu Osman Paşa, the newly appointed governor-general of Ṣanʿâ, who was then in Cairo. Other members of the anti-Sinan front were two *sancak beğis* of Egypt, Gazalgüveği Mustafa Beğ and Kuyruklu Yıldız Mehmed Beğ; the supply master (*nüzul emini*) and *müteferrika* of the Porte, Acem Menla Ağa; and the *sancak beği* of Beyşehir, Güllizade Mehmed. In an appeal carried to Istanbul by Güllizade and Lala Mustafa Paşa's steward (*kedhüda*) Köse Mustafa, the group jointly requested that the governorship of Egypt be given to Lala Mustafa Paşa, since Sinan Paşa obstinately refused to obey orders and cooperate with the campaign commander.[20]

Indeed, the size of the original troop allocation and the general financial

[19] The horoscopes and Âli's commentary on them are found in the manuscript of the *Enis* described by Sohrweide, "*Enîs*." It is uncertain whether Âli preceded Lala Mustafa Paşa all the way to Cairo, or whether the latter had also arrived there by the time of the casting of the second horoscope.

[20] The basic account of the prelude to the Yemen campaign and of the campaign itself is given in KA, Selim/3, Nur 3409, 223b-232a; it is repeated by PEÇEVİ, I, 476-82, and confirmed by SELANİKİ, pp. 95-98.

plight of the *sipahi* cavalry forces ordered to participate in the campaign required that the field marshal make supplementary requests. While one thousand Janissaries were to be provided from Damascus, the province held fewer than this on its rosters, and the devaluation of the real worth of *timar* grants in the region necessitated that loans be given to *sipahi*s from the provincial treasuries so that they might provide the required number of armed retainers (*cebelüs*).[21] Whatever the economic and military realities of the situation, the ambition and enmity of the two paşas, and the machinations of the grand vezir Sokollu Mehmed Paşa, determined the outcome of the affair. Although Âli swears solemnly in the *Essence* that Sinan Paşa's accusations had no basis in fact, he hints elsewhere that Lala Mustafa Paşa may indeed have been involved in some sort of plot. In a selection of the *Nushat üs-selatin, Counsel for Sultans*, in which Âli criticizes Lala Mustafa Paşa for consistently allowing irresponsible subordinates to involve him in reprehensible actions, he says:

> The second instance occurred when he had been appointed to quell the rebellion of bedouin Arabs in Yemen and Aden. As soon as he arrived in Cairo the evil propositions of a few intriguing emirs, who rejoiced at the injuries their terrible and insupportable schemes inflicted upon the great men of state, brought about his dismissal before he could perform his duty. The intrigue also caused the execution of one or two *sancak beğ*is who were amongst the group of troublemakers.[22]

At the Porte Sokollu Mehmed Paşa decided in favor of Sinan Paşa, saying of Lala Mustafa Paşa that "a disobedient servant [*kul*] must be killed." As mentioned above, Âli later suggested that Sokollu had engineered the appointments of Sinan Paşa and Lala Mustafa Paşa, knowing full well that they would come into conflict over ambiguous or contradictory orders, in order to discredit the latter and put him out of the running for the grand vezirate.

Özdemiroğlu Osman Paşa sensed trouble, and, recalling his own orders to precede the field marshal to the Yemen, hastily carried them out. Approximately two months after Lala Mustafa arrived in Cairo, an imperial order was issued revoking both his vezirate and his command, which were then bestowed upon Sinan along with all funds allocated for the campaign.[23] Shortly thereafter a delegation of pursuivants (*çavuş*) of the Porte arrived in Cairo to effect the transfer of command and investigate the trouble. According to Âli, they also brought an order for the execution of Özdemiroğlu Os-

[21] Turan, "Lala Mustafa Paşa," pp. 565-66, citing MD 7, docs. 695, 789, 894, 1254, 1256.

[22] COUNSEL, II, 12 (trans.), 123-24 (text).

[23] The *hükm*, dated 15 August 1568/15 Safer 976, is quoted by Turan, "Lala Mustafa Paşa," p. 569.

man Paşa should he still be in Egypt. The two Egyptian *beğs*, Mehmed and Mustafa, were put to death, and Menla Ağa very nearly suffered the same fate.[24]

Sinan Paşa now appropriated the supplies and troops he had denied his rival and departed for the Yemen (December 1568-January 1569/Receb 976). There he attempted to eliminate his other great enemy, Özdemiroğlu Osman Paşa, even going to the extreme of reissuing the imperial order for his execution on one of the blank forms sealed with the *tuğra*, the imperial signature-seal, which at that time were given to campaign commanders. Osman Paşa, however, eluded the new field marshal and took refuge in Mecca, and then proceeded to Istanbul. He, like Lala Mustafa Paşa, suffered from the machinations of Sokollu Mehmed Paşa, who had Özdemiroğlu and his men expelled from Istanbul. Sokollu also supported Sinan Paşa's allegations that Osman Paşa deserved execution for his disobedience. It was only later, through the intercession of his friend and ally Lala Mustafa Paşa, that Özdemiroğlu routed Sokollu and secured appointment to the governor-generalship of Basra and Lahsa. The Yemen campaign fiasco affected the political careers of the participants for the rest of their lives. This held true for Âli as well, who identified closely with his protector, and later in life blamed his frequent dismissal from posts on Sinan Paşa's hatred for Lala Mustafa Paşa and all connected with him. The affair further established one of the major paradigms of Âli's Ottoman history: in the *Essence* Osman Paşa, who later became a great war hero and grand vezir, is praised as the greatest Ottoman *paşazade* (his father was also a paşa) and grand vezir, while Sinan Paşa, who served five terms as grand vezir, is consistently denounced as one of the chief architects of the Empire's ruin.[25]

[24] KA, Nur 3409, 226a-b. These details and the broad lines of Âli's version of the affair are independently confirmed by SELANİKİ, pp. 95-96. Selâniki further states that Sinan Paşa claimed that Lala Mustafa Paşa was indulging in excessive expense and that he, Sinan, could conduct the campaign more cheaply. However, upon receiving the command of the expedition, he happily took all that had been granted his enemy and more.

[25] KA, Selim/3, Nur 3409, 227b-232a; Âli's praise for Osman Paşa occurs on 229b, and the Receb 976 date for Sinan Paşa's arrival in Yemen, copied by PEÇEVİ, is found on 231a. Âli's reference to blank *ferman* forms inscribed with the *tuğra* being given to campaign commanders (227b) is of particular interest. This passage is paraphrased by Peçevi (the first half of whose history is rarely more than a translation of the KA into slightly simpler language), with the additional notation that this practice no longer existed in his own time, ca. 1635 (see GOW, pp. 192-93), when *serdar*s were allowed to inscribe their own *tuğra/pence* on orders (PEÇEVİ, I, 479). Uzunçarşılı (*Merkez*, pp. 184-85, 217), basing himself on SELANİKİ, p. 88, and MD material, attests the issuance of blank forms with the *tuğra* inscribed by the chancellor (*beyaz tuğra, tuğralı ahkâm kâğıdları*) to the *muhafız* or *ka'immakam* (guardian of the city; locum tenens) of Istanbul during the sultan's absence. The first recorded instance of this practice dates from 1566, when Süleyman conducted his last campaign. These forms, which allowed the *muhafız* to issue orders in the sultan's name, were kept locked in the treasury and their use was carefully recorded. Uzunçarşılı's discussion of the issuance of similar forms to *serdars* is largely limited to pre-seventeenth century situations in which grand vezirs on campaign were

One week after his dismissal from the campaign command, Lala Mustafa Paşa was ordered to return to Damascus, where his administration and finances were to be subjected to a comprehensive official investigation (*teftiş-i âmm*). He was accused of injustice, illegal appropriations of property, and of distributing mortmain properties (*vakıf*) as *timar*s.[26] The Lala was in danger of losing his post as governor-general of Damascus, and even his life. He immediately had Âli compose a letter to Sultan Selim in which he denied the charges brought against him and asked for the sultan's personal intercession to save him. This letter was then sent secretly overland to Istanbul, since the paşa's enemies were in control of official courier vessels.[27]

Lala Mustafa Paşa returned to Damascus, where the investigation proceeded for several months, at least until October 1568/Rebi' II 976. Soon thereafter the investigation was moved to Istanbul; once there, Lala Mustafa Paşa was able to enlist the aid of a number of old friends from his days at Selim's court. A small circle of favorites had accompanied Selim from Kütahya to Istanbul at the time of his succession to the throne, and had been established in the Palace as *musahib*s, "royal confidants" or "companions." The companions banded together to maintain their own influence and group affinity against the authority of the grand vezir Sokollu Mehmed, who was after all more a part of Süleyman's regime than of Selim's. Selim's circle of favorites was a heterogeneous group. Celâl Beğ, who later became

---

not accompanied by the chancellor, who remained in Istanbul with the sultan (Uzunçarşılı, *Merkez*, pp. 161-62). Âli's reference to Sinan Paşa's "misuse" of the forms constitutes the first recorded instance of their being given to field marshals who were not of grand-veziral standing. This statement is confirmed by MD 7, p. 283 (cited in *Merkez*, p. 218), which concerns the fifty *beyaz tuğralı kâğıd* sent to Lala Mustafa Paşa as commander of the Yemen campaign. Hence, Josef Matuz is incorrect in stating in *Das Kanzleiwesen Sultan Süleymâns des Prächtigen* (Wiesbaden, 1974), p. 74, that this particular aspect of the practice is first attested in 1584. In fact at least two much earlier instances of issuance of blank *ferman* forms, for very special diplomatic purposes, are attested. When Sultan Süleyman sought to install Devlet Giray as *han* of the Crimea in place of Sahib Giray Han, he gave Devlet Giray *ferman*s with the *tuğra* inscribed; see *Târîh-i Ṣâḥib Giray Han (Histoire de Sahib Giray, Khan de Crimée de 1532 à 1551)*, edited with French translation and notes by D. Özalp Gökbilgin (Ankara, 1973), p. 121 (text), p. 254 (trans.). Earlier still, Selim the Grim, after the battle of Çaldıran in 1514, assigned his advisor İdris-i Bidlisi the task of winning the Kurdish princes and tribal leaders to an Ottoman allegiance, and supplied him with blank *ferman*s, with the *tuğra* inscribed, to use at his discretion for the purpose of confirming new Kurdish vassals and clients in their positions under Ottoman auspices (see Sa'düddin, *Tac üt-tevarih*, 2 vols. [Istanbul, 1863/1280], II, 322). It may be that the forms issued to Lala Mustafa Paşa, and then to Sinan Paşa, had a similar purpose, which would help to account for the chroniclers' implication that Sinan Paşa abused his authority.

[26] The MD document appointing the judges of Medina and Damascus, along with the *sancak beği* of Bursa, to the commission of inquiry is dated 22 August 1568/28 Safer 976 (Turan, "Lala Mustafa Paşa," pp. 570-71). See also KA, Selim/Vüzera, "Lala Mustafa Paşa," Nur 3409, 252b-253a.

[27] KA, Selim/3, Nur 3409, 226b-227b. The full text is reproduced in Âli's correspondence, MENŞE, 192a-194a.

governor-general of Damascus, composed poetry under the pen name Celâli and was noted for his heterodox religious views and interest in Hurufi doctrine. He and Lala Mustafa Paşa had been fellow protégés of Ca'fer Beğ, a major figure at Selim's court. Ata'ullah Efendi was the sultan's religious tutor (*hoca-ı sultani*), and Hubbi Hatun was the widow of Ata'ullah's predecessor Şemsi Efendi. She was a noted poetess and famous beauty who remained at court as a royal confidante and boon-companion after her husband's death; she was rumored to have had love affairs with several of Selim's courtiers. It was through the offices of these Palace allies, who sought to raise one of their own to a position from which Sokollu could be opposed, that Lala Mustafa Paşa was pardoned. More than this, Selim gave his former *lala* a place in the Imperial Council as the sixth vezir in January 1569/Receb 976. This was a special mark of Lala Mustafa's high standing with the sultan, for prior to this appointment there were only five vezirs of the Dome, including the grand vezir, who was considered the first of their number. In the face of Selim's desire to bring his former tutor into the primary policy-making body of the Empire, Sokollu and Lala Mustafa Paşa patched up their differences, primarily on the basis of an understanding that no subordinate vezir, Lala Mustafa included, would ever threaten Sokollu's paramount position and authority. Âli states that after winning this alliance with Lala Mustafa Paşa, Sokollu, whom he describes as "the actual ruler" (*padişah-i ma'nevi*), regretted having given such strong support to the treacherous and ambitious Sinan Paşa.[28]

[28] KA, Süleyman/Sadrazamlar, "Sokollu Mehmed Paşa," Nur 3409, 123b; Selim/3, Nur 3409, 238b; Selim/4, Nur 3409, 239a-b; Selim/Vüzera, "Lala Mustafa Paşa," Nur 3409, 252b; Selim/Vüzera/Introduction, Nur 3409, 251b; Selim/Şu'ara, "Celâl Beğ (Celâli)," Nur 3409, 272b-273b; Selim/Şu'ara, "Hubbi Hatun," Nur 3409, 275a; SELANİKİ, p. 97.

The extraordinary nature and personal importance of Selim's appointment of his former *lala* to the ranks of the vezirs of the Dome is evidenced by the fact that throughout the reign of Süleyman the number of these, including the grand vezir, did not exceed four (Uzunçarşılı, *Merkez*, pp. 188-89). It is therefore probable that Selim established the post of sixth vezir (the fifth vezirate, then held by Zal Mahmud Paşa, was probably created on Selim's accession; according to Mehmed Süreyya, SO, II, 426, it was added in 1567-68/975) largely, if not solely, in order to bring this mentor into the *Divan*.

The statement of M. Tayyib Gökbilgin ("Mehmed Paşa Sokollu," İA) that Tütünsüz Hüseyin Paşa had already been appointed sixth vezir by Selim is based on the rather shaky evidence of Ata's translation of the French version of GOR. The German original (GOR, III, 525) refers only to the appointment of Lala Mustafa Paşa, which Barbaro says Selim made (ca. January 1569) without consulting Sokollu. Âli does indeed state that after Selim's accession Hüseyin Paşa was promoted to the *beğlerbeğilik* of Rumeli and was thereafter given a vezirate (KA, Selim/Vüzera, Nur 3409, 253a). SELANİKİ (pp. 77-78) relates that upon Selim's accession Zal Mahmud Paşa and Piyale Paşa were both made vezirs, and that Lala Hüseyin Paşa received Zal Mahmud's former post, thus becoming *beğlerbeği* of Anatolia. SELANİKİ also refers to Hüseyin Paşa as being a vezir in 1572/980, when the *beğlerbeği* of Rumeli was Siyavuş Paşa (pp. 109-10). According to Bursalı Tahir, OM, II, 184, Hüseyin Paşa became *Anadolu beğlerbeğisi* in 974, *Rumeli beğlerbeğisi* after 976, and finally *kubbe-nişin* shortly before his death in 1572-73/980. Hence he was probably appointed seventh vezir after Lala Mustafa

Precisely how this turn of events affected Âli is uncertain. It is probable that he too returned from Cairo to Damascus with Lala Mustafa Paşa for the investigation. A marginal notation in a manuscript copy of the *Essence* utilized by the historian Peçevi suggests that Âli was responsible for the difficulties in which Lala Mustafa Paşa found himself:

> When the investigation of Lala Kara Mustafa Paşa's affairs was ordered, Âli was his secretary. It was established that all the crimes were his [Âli's] own, and he was in danger of being put to death. Since the late [Ferhad Paşa] was then the beğ of Klis, Âli took refuge with him, and thanks to him was saved from execution.[29]

The specific nature of the charges brought against Lala Mustafa Paşa, and the context in which Peçevi's marginal notation occurs (Peçevi reviles Âli for having insulted Peçevi's uncle, Ferhad Paşa), make it unlikely that this statement is true. Furthermore, Âli did not take immediate refuge with Ferhad, but rather was assigned to Bosnia by Sokollu. Nevertheless, it is noteworthy that Âli seems to have been unable to reestablish his client relationship with Lala Mustafa Paşa for another eight years, despite the latter's political recovery. In a letter he wrote to Lala Mustafa Paşa when his erstwhile patron was in command of the Cyprus campaign (1570-71/977-79), Âli complained that certain individuals had come between them and had usurped Âli's place in the paşa's *divan*. He begged not to be forgotten, and sent his old patron tributary gifts.[30]

MANISA AND ISTANBUL (1568-70)

WHATEVER the reason for their estrangement, Âli did not return to Istanbul with Lala Mustafa Paşa; he made his own way overland to the capital. By December 1568-January 1569/Receb 976 Âli had reached Manisa, the *sancak* seat of Prince Murad, son of Sultan Selim. There Âli once again sought to gain princely favor by means of a literary display; he had *Affection and Fidelity*, written years before at Kütahya, presented to the young prince. He also completed the *Rarity of Warriors*, in which he praised Selim and ex-

Paşa. Sinan Paşa was made seventh vezir of the Dome (ca. May 1573) after Lala Hüseyin Paşa's death. (Ş. Turan, "Sinan Paşa," İA; see also KA, Selim/4, Nur 3409, 238b, and Uzunçarşılı, *Merkez*, p. 190).

[29] İNAL, pp. 10-11. The manuscript is now listed as İÜ 5959; İNAL has identified the author of the marginalia as Peçevi (Peçuyi) İbrahim Paşa (Prof. Bekir Kütükoğlu has established the correct form of the historian's name as "Peçuyi," from his birth at Peçuy; I have continued to use the older and less correct form for the sake of its familiarity). The notation occurs next to a discussion of Ferhad Paşa, about whom Âli makes some less than complimentary remarks.

[30] MENŞE, 198b-200a, partially quoted İNAL, pp. 16-17.

hibited his trilingualism, and he personally signed a presentation copy. Âli sought to repair his shattered career and return to royal service by dedicating the work to both Prince Murad and his father, Sultan Selim.[31]

Although Prince Murad gave him no official appointment, Âli must have received some remuneration and good will in return for his efforts, for he was still a hanger-on at Murad's summer court at Bozdağ six months later in the spring of 1569/Muharrem 977. Âli appears to have taken up temporary residence at Bozdağ in hopes of maintaining high visibility to the prince. Murad there commissioned Âli to write a sex manual (*bahname*) for his young son, Prince Mehmed, who later ascended the throne as Mehmed III. Mehmed had little immediate need of such a work, being only two years old at the time; but in response to this royal request Âli produced the *Rahat ün-nüfus, The Carnal Souls' Comfort*, a rearranged and annotated translation of an Arabic work, Tifâshî's *Rujûʿ al-shaykh ilâ ṣabâh, The Old Man's Restoration to Youth*. Âli's literary flair, *medrese* education in Arabic, and persistence at least gained him this much: soon after the completion of the *Comfort* he was able to depart for Istanbul armed with a letter of recommendation from Prince Murad.[32]

Traveling by way of Bursa, Âli reached Istanbul by September 1569. Lala Mustafa Paşa must by this time have been reinstated at court, since a series of orders commanding him to proceed to Cyprus immediately are dated early December 1569.[33] Nevertheless, Âli was unable to find an influential courtier to present his letter of recommendation either to the sultan or to the man who in fact had virtually total control over appointments, Grand Vezir Sokollu Mehmed Paşa. From this it may be concluded that Âli's relations with his former patron were severely strained. It may also have been the case that Lala Mustafa's position was not yet secure enough to procure

[31] *Varidat ül-enika*, MS Hamidiye 1107 (hereafter VARİDAT), 4b; COUNSEL, II, 76 (trans.), 205 (text); NADİR, 4a (dedication to Murad), 66a-b (dedication to Selim and purpose of work). That Âli probably completed the work at Manisa specifically for Murad is shown by a passage on f. 5a and by the colophon. Incidentally, the work illuminates Âli's Persianate orientation and testifies to the cultural inferiority complex from which the proponents of the nascent Ottoman literary culture suffered; see the verses from NADİR cited in chapter 4, p. 141.

[32] COUNSEL, II, 76 (trans.), 205 (text). *Rahat ün-nüfus*, MS Şehid Ali Paşa, 2014, 4a-6b. Âli refers to his current rootlessness and lack of steady employment, describes the spring at Bozdağ, and states that he remained there so as to constantly display his skills to the prince, who came there to fish in Bozdağ lake. It is also intriguing to note, in view of Âli's later complaints about Murad as a literary patron, that none of the works that Âli presented to the prince at this time seems to have gained any currency, with the possible exception of *Rahat*. *Mihr u Vefa* has not yet been found, and only two copies of the *Nadir* are known to exist. Of the *Rahat*, four exemplars have been located: Şehid Ali Paşa 2014; Esad Efendi 2475; DKM, Funûn Mutanawwiʿa Turkîya 8; and a copy in the Edirne library (oral communication of Prof. Andreas Tietze). On Tifâshî's Arabic work, see GAL, I, 652.

[33] KA, Süleyman/Şu'ara, "Menla Celili," Nur 3409, 174b; Turan, "Lala Mustafa Paşa," p. 575.

a protégé's appointment; Sokollu Mehmed Paşa ruled the court with an iron hand, reserving discretionary appointments for certain relatives and adherents (*mensûbat*). Sokollu was also still suspicious of the Lala, and had intimidated the sultan; the Venetian bailo Barbaro reported that Selim dared to speak openly to his former tutor only while in the company of the other vezirs while riding from Edirne to Istanbul.[34] Âli describes his own predicament in the *Counsel*:

> When Sultan Selim took the throne . . . he quite properly gave free rein to his royal son-in-law Mehmed Paşa, who enjoyed the position of grand vezir and was the refuge of the people in the highest seat of government. Because [Selim] gave him complete independence in matters of administration and government, the generosity of the aforementioned vezir [Sokollu] was reserved for his own protégés, and his lavish kindness in the granting of appointments was spent solely on his relatives and dependents. This being so, one dared not present a case to their [Selim's] Imperial Stirrup; and since it was known that the ropes of rejection and acceptance were in the hands of that advisor, one saw no other possible course [but to approach him].[35]

While searching for a way to have his petition presented to the court, or to an unsympathetic Sokollu Mehmed Paşa, Âli returned to Istanbul literary society, which he had left nine years before. He began to frequent the salon of Kızıl Ahmedlü Şemsi Paşa (d. 1580-81/988). Şemsi Paşa, a former *beğlerbeği* of Rumeli and scion of the princely İsfendiyaroğlu family, had retired from active duty to devote himself to serving as Selim's *musahib*. His home in Üsküdar was an important gathering place for poets, courtiers, and governors returning from the provinces.[36] Âli, himself recently returned to Istanbul, was together with Şemsi Paşa and the poet Kâmi in late September 1569/mid-Rebi' II 977, when a tremendous fire broke out in the Jewish quarter of Istanbul; the flames raged for a week and destroyed thousands of houses. As the three discussed the need for new themes for *inşa*-prose works, Âli suggested the fire as an original topic. He soon thereafter composed a "blaze book" (*harikname*) in the form of a letter to his literary mentor Kınalızade Ali Çelebi, who was then judge (*kadı*) of Edirne. In addition to describing the course and effects of the fire, the letter praised Sokollu Mehmed Paşa for his effective handling of the crisis.[37] Âli sought, through

[34] Barbaro's report, dated 27 January 1569, is cited GOR, III, 525.

[35] COUNSEL, II, 72 (trans.), 198-99 (text).

[36] On Şemsi Paşa's mosque establishment in Üsküdar, completed in the year of his death (1579-80/987), see Ayvansarayi, *Hadikat*, II, 191-94. His career is described by KINALIZADE, I, 521-24. See also COUNSEL, II, 98 (trans.), 228-29 (text), on his reasons for living in Üsküdar rather than Istanbul.

[37] KA, Selim/4 Nur 3409, 238b-241a; MENŞE, 195B-197A. The date of the fire, which is confirmed by a report of Albert de Wyss (GOR, III, 528), is sometimes incorrectly given as

his old teacher, to ingratiate himself with the grand vezir, who had in fact nearly been severely embarrassed by the fire. When the blaze broke out, no immediate attempt was made to contain it because the official responsible for combatting fires in Istanbul, the Janissary commander (*yeniçeri ağası*) Ca'fer Ağa, was ill. Ca'fer Ağa also happened to be the son-in-law of the grand vezir, who was forced to dismiss his relative and to replace him with the chief equerry (*mirahur-i kebir*), Siyavuş Ağa. Sokollu thereafter personally oversaw the organization of the firefighters. The sultan was disturbed at the extent of the damage caused by the blaze, and pointedly asked Sokollu in the Imperial Council why it had not been contained sooner. At this juncture Lala Mustafa Paşa seized the opportunity to save Sokollu's face, and thereby insinuate himself into the good graces of his former enemy; he explained that the density of habitation and height of the wooden houses in the Jewish quarter had made it impossible to put the fire out.

Jobless, Âli remained in Istanbul throughout the winter of 1569-70. Although his family ties, through his great-grandfather Şeyh Muslihüddin, were with the Nakşbendi Sufi order, Âli now affiliated himself with the Halveti *tarikat*, which enjoyed particular prestige in court circles.[38] He became especially close with Sarhoş Bali Efendi, a disciple of Şeyh Ramazan. Bali Efendi enjoyed a wide reputation as an ecstatic mystic, miracle worker (*sahib-keramat*), and poet under the pen name Cevheri. He was also quite wealthy, as became apparent when his personal treasure trove was discovered after his death in 1573/980. Âli visited Bali Efendi frequently at his cloister (*zaviye*), and even received financial assistance from him over the next several years. At the same time Âli formed a relationship with another Halveti sheikh who was Bali Efendi's arch rival: Nurüddinzade Muslihüddin. Nurüddinzade had also been a student of Şeyh Ramazan and, incidentally, was the spiritual master (*pir*) of the grand vezir Sokollu. Nurüddinzade harshly criticized Bali Efendi for his ostentatious display of his spiritual powers and for catering to the popular taste for miracles. Bali Efendi, in turn, ridiculed his critic for his intimate involvement in court affairs. The strife between the two factionalized the Halvetis of Istanbul. Âli

Receb 977 (for example, Turan, "Lala Mustafa Paşa," p. 573). The origin of this error would seem to be the heading that opens this section of the KA, which represents a rhetorical attempt to connect the fire with the news of Sinan Paşa's impending return from the Yemen, which actually took place in 1573/980-81 (see CAIRO, pp. 18, 72-73), in order to emphasize Sinan's inauspicious character. Interestingly, SELANİKİ too makes the two events synchronous, giving the year 976 for both (pp. 98-100); in fact, most of the dates in this section of the printed text of SELANİKİ are off by at least one year.

On Kâmi, a former judge of Edirne and rival of Şemsi Paşa for the position of royal confidant (*musahib*), see COUNSEL, II, 99-100 (trans.), 231-21 (text).

[38] On the prominence of the order in sixteenth-century Istanbul, see H. J. Kissling, "Aus der Geschichte des Chalvetijje-Ordens," ZMDG 103 (1953): 232-89, and Tashin Yazıcı, "Fetih'ten Sonra İstanbul'da İlk Halveti Şeyhleri; Çelebi Muhammed Cemaleddin, Sünbül Sinan ve Merkez Efendi," *İstanbul Enstitüsü Dergisi* 2 (1956): 87-113.

himself, despite the affection and material help Bali Efendi showered upon him, eventually decided for the more politically powerful Nurüddinzade. Âli relates that he saw Bali Efendi in a dream after the latter's death; the sheikh's home appeared to be bare, devoid even of plants. This Âli interpreted to mean that Bali Efendi had not in fact had the power to work miracles. He also claimed to see Bali Efendi's wealth, although Âli himself had benefited from it, as contradictory to a Sufi master's professed disregard for the material world.[39]

It was Şeyh Nurüddinzade Muslihüddin who finally acted for Âli, presenting to Sokollu Mehmed Paşa Âli's latest *inşa* creation, *Heft Meclis, The Seven Scenes*. The work treats the 1566 Sigetvar campaign, the death of Sultan Süleyman, and the accession of Selim; it praises Sokollu Mehmed Paşa lavishly and exhibits a greater concern with style and panegyric than with history. The *Seven Scenes* closes with Âli's description of the hardships he endured as a penniless petitioner in Istanbul in winter, unable to present himself to the Imperial Council even with a letter of recommendation from Prince Murad. Âli thus finally appealed directly to Sokollu to give him a position and an income.[40] Sokollu did not hurry to respond to the request, despite his *pir*'s intercession, and he was certainly not particularly well disposed toward Âli, who hoped for a secretarial post at court. After a lengthy interval Sokollu sent Âli nearly as far from the capital as was possible; he assigned him to serve as chancery secretary to Gazi Ferhad Beğ (later Paşa), yet another member of the Sokollu family, who had just been appointed governor of the *sancak* of Klis in Dalmatia.

[39] KA, Selim/Meşayih, "Şeyh Bali Efendi," Nur 3409, 169a-270a; AŞIK, 69a-b; KINALIZADE, I, 271-74; IQD, pp. 426-29. The location of Bali Efendi's *zaviye* (called "Kurşunlu tekkesi" by M. Süreyya, SO, II, 5), is given neither by Ayvansarayi (*Hadikat*) nor by Zakir (*Mecum'a-ı Tekaya*). On Nurüddinzade Muslihüddin (d. 1574/981), see SO, IV, 494-45, and Kissling, "Chalvetijje," pp. 261, 269-70, and Table 2. He was the student of Şeyh Ramazan through Sofyalı Bali Efendi (d. 1553/960), and according to Kissling played an important role in recruiting adherents to the order in the Balkan region. His dispute with Bali Efendi is detailed in IQD, p. 429. By Süreyya's account he was buried near the Emir-i Buhari Tekkesi, where Âli's great-grandfather Şeyh Muslihüddin had spent many years. Âli also notes that Nurüddinzade was with the party that returned Sultan Süleyman's body from Sigetvar to Istanbul (KA, Süleyman/57, Nur 3409, 115a); Âli, *Heft Meclis* (Istanbul, 1316), p. 48.

[40] COUNSEL, II, 72-73 (trans.), 199-200 (text). *Heft Meclis*, pp. 51-55. The work must have been composed during the winter of 1569-70; the date of 1572-73/980 given by Atsız (AB, pp. 14, 15) is incorrect. Throughout the bibliographical portion of his work on Âli, Atsız, in addition to assigning mistaken dates, expends much energy attempting to reconcile manuscript colophon dates with the "dates" of composition given in COUNSEL, postulating many second recensions. The dates of composition occurring in COUNSEL are given in five- and ten-year blocks that correspond to specific periods of Âli's life. He is in fact listing the ages between which he completed certain works, as he explicitly states on p. 69 (trans.). Âli's reference to the composition of *Heft Meclis* (p. 55 [trans.]) at the age of thirty-five in fact means that he completed it *by* that age. Atsız's confusion on this point also leads him to date the *Nadir* to 978 rather than the correct 976.

BOSNIA

(1570-77)

ELEVEN years after Sokollu appointed him to this post on the Empire's western marches, Âli complained in the *Counsel* that the assignment represented a form of exile for a talented man of letters whose rightful place was in the vibrant literary milieu of Istanbul: "He [Sokollu] thought it permissible that I be sent off to the ends of the earth, implicitly saying 'There is no place in the capital for one of your learning and accomplishment.' "[41] He goes on to relate that a courtier later reproached the grand vezir for treating Âli so badly; Sokollu remonstrated that he had thought Âli to be the calligrapher rather than the author of the work, and had therefore deemed the reward adequate. Âli thus backhandedly exonerates Sokollu of malice, presenting this "betrayal" as a result of the grand vezir's ignorance and disinterest rather than his animosity.[42] Here Âli does Sokollu an injustice; the anecdote reflects the bitterness and chagrin Âli had accumulated by 1581, when he wrote his *Counsel for Sultans*, more than it describes his actual situation in 1570. The evidence of the closing lines of the *Seven Scenes* indicates that Sokollu in fact responded positively to Âli's importunities. Both the letter of recommendation that Prince Murad had given Âli, and the final section of the *Seven Scenes*, requested that Âli be given a *zeâmet*, a *timar*-type land grant valued between 20,000 and 99,999 *akçe* per year, which carried with it military status and military duties. Âli wrote:

I have made the Paşa's name live
  Until the Hour of Resurrection, till the Judgement.
Is it much [to ask] that he should see to my living,
  [With] a *zeâmet* of thirty or forty thousand?[43]

Such appointments were available only in the provinces, and this is precisely the type of assignment Âli received.

Ottoman provincial administration and Ottoman military might rested on the *timar* system. The *timar* was a revenue-producing land unit, the tax income from which, but not its ownership, was granted by the government to a *sipahi*. In return for this usufruct grant the *sipahi*, a cavalryman who of necessity belonged to the *askeri* class, was expected to participate in all military campaigns, to provide additional armed retainers called *cebelü*s, whose number depended on the size of his *timar* grant, and to perform police duty within his assigned area when required. Although land-usufruct

[41] COUNSEL, II, 72-73 (trans.), 199-200 (text).
[42] COUNSEL, II, 73-74 (trans.), 200 (text).
[43] *Heft Meclis*, pp. 53-54.

grants of mounted military personnel were referred to generically as "*timar*," the *timar* proper was a grant that yielded an income of less than 20,000 *akçe* per annum. *Timar*-type grants valued at 20,000 to 99,999 *akçe* were known as *zeâmets*. *Zeâmet* grants also required military and police duty of their holders, (*za'ims*), who also frequently acquired the rank of *subaşı*, head of one of the smaller administrative units (*kaza*) that together constituted a *sancak*. *Timar*-type grants of 100,000 *akçe* or more were called *hass*. *Hass*es were usually granted to high-ranking military administrators such as district governors (*sancak beğis*) and governors-general (*beğlerbeğis*); a few other important provincial officials on the *vilayet* level, such as the finance director (*defterdar*) of an important province, would also receive a *hass*. Unlike the *timar* and *zeâmet*, a *hass* was attached to a specific office and not to its incumbent; it passed in succession to each holder of that office, while a *timar* or *zeâmet* was granted to an individual for life and could even be inherited on the condition that the grantee serve satisfactorily. All over the Empire, as had been the case at Selim's court at Kütahya, the salaries of officials of the central *sancak* or *vilayet* administration were provided for locally in the form of *timar* and *zeâmet* grants.[44] In this context it must be noted that some salary grants of this type, which, being valued at less than 100,000 and more than 20,000 *akçe*, by monetary value fell into the *zeâmet* category, were in fact technically *hass*es in that they were attached to specific administrative offices and passed on to each successive incumbent.

When Âli joined Ferhad Beğ, Sokollu's cousin and the newly appointed governor of Klis, on the Venetian border in the summer of 1570, he did so as the recipient of a *timar* grant.[45] Thus by the age of twenty-nine Âli, after gaining entry into the Ottoman system and *askeri* class in general, had be-

[44] On the *timar* system and its classifications, see İnalcık, *Empire*, pp. 104-18, and Kunt, *Servants*, pp. 9-29.

[45] In an ode he addressed to Sokollu Mehmed soon after his appointment to Bosnia, Âli says that he has come to the border to serve as a secretary-scribe on the grand vezir's orders. He then goes on to request a *zeâmet*, which implies that initially his salary was in the form of a *timar* grant of less than 20,000 *akçe* (VARİDAT, 36a-37a).

Ferhad Beğ's career is outlined by his nephew Peçevi (PEÇEVİ, I, 453-55). Âli makes no explicit mention of the Klis-Bosnia sequence of Ferhad Beğ's appointments, but refers to it obliquely in COUNSEL, I, 71-72 (trans.), 170-71 (text).

Âli seems to refer to the entire region comprising Bosnia proper and the *sancak* of Klis to the south as "Bosnia." When Bosnia was elevated to *eyalet* (province) status in 1580, and Ferhad Beğ to its *paşalık*, the *sancak*s of Klis and Hersek were incorporated into the new unit; see İ. Metin Kunt, *Sancaktan Eyalete* (Istanbul, 1978), pp. 47, 150-51.

Âli probably arrived in Klis in summer 1570/late 977 or early 978, at about the same time that Ferhad Beğ was appointed *sancak beği*. In the conclusion to *Zübdet üt-tevarih* (MS Reşid Efendi 663, 203a; hereafter ZÜBDET), which he completed in April 1575/early Muharrem 983, Âli says that for five years he has served Ferhad Beğ, who came to the region in 1569-70/977. Atsız (AB, p. 3) is incorrect in stating that Âli first went to Bosnia in 980. The fact that Âli wrote to Lala Mustafa Paşa from Bosnia while the latter was in Cyprus proves that he must have been in the region between July 1570 and September 1571/Safer 978 and Cümada II 979.

gun careers in all three of the major Ottoman professional paths: Learning, Pen, and Sword. The precise nature of his duties during the seven years he spent in the Bosnian region is unclear. That he served as Ferhad Beğ's *sancak* secretary is established by Peçevi's marginalia to the *Essence*, cited above, and by a number of official letters he composed for Ferhad and later included in his collected correspondence.[46] As a *timar*-holder in a border province where raiding and combat were a daily fact of life, he must also have performed military duty. Âli served well with both pen and sword, for when Ferhad Beğ was promoted three years later to be *sancak* governor of Bosnia, he took Âli with him to his new post.[47] Further, Âli's service on the border earned him merit increments (*terakki*) and promotions, so that by the end of his stay in Bosnia he commanded a *zeâmet* valued at 60,000 *akçe*.[48]

During his years in Bosnia, Âli must have had duties other than military and secretarial ones, for he made frequent trips between Bosnia and Istanbul and also traveled in Rumeli and the march areas. In the *Counsel* he describes staying at the hospices (*imaret*) founded in Rumeli by Evrenos Beğ (d. 1417/820). Furthermore, he came and went between Istanbul and Rumeli during the period of his association with Şeyh Bali Efendi, whose funeral he attended in the capital in 1573/980.[49] Âli implies that these trips were undertaken in the service of the state; he may have functioned as a liaison between the central and provincial government, or acted as confidential courier for Ferhad Beğ in the course of Ottoman negotiations with Venice and the Hapsburgs.

In none of his works does Âli provide much information about this seven-year period of his life. He would seem to have been content with, or perhaps resigned to, his lot during the early years of his service in Bosnia. Sometime during his first year with Ferhad Beğ he wrote to Lala Mustafa Paşa, who was then commanding the Ottoman conquest of Cyprus, in an attempt to repair their strained relations. In addition to reminding his former master of their closeness and citing the lies of other members of the Paşa's retinue as the cause of their estrangement, Âli submitted a translation of Ghazâlî's *Ayyuhâ al-walad*, a treatise on Sufism. Finally Âli requested, as a token of friendship, the "*defter* of Kobaš" in the *sancak* of Bosnia. In return for this

[46] MENŞE, 200a-201a, 201a-202a, 202a-202b, 203a-204a, 206a-206b.

[47] Ferhad Beğ was dismissed from Klis and appointed to the *sancak* of Bosnia between 13 February 1573/10 Sevval 980 and 23 May 1573/21 Muharrem 981, according to MD 20, docs. 213, 430, and MD 22, doc. 15. This dating is roughly confirmed by a letter (MENŞE, 232b) that Âli addressed to an unidentified figure at court. Âli recalls that, when he was unemployed and poor, the addressee had interceded for him with the grand vezir, who appointed Âli to serve in Klis.

[48] COUNSEL, II, 73 (trans.), 200 (text).

[49] COUNSEL, II, 27-28 (trans.), 145-46 (text); KA Selim/Meşayih, "Şeyh Bali Efendi," Nur 3409, 269b.

favor Âli promised to send Lala Mustafa Paşa three tall, handsome Bosnian pages (*içoğlanı*).[50]

Precisely how "*defter*" is to be understood in this context is unclear. The word itself means "register," and might refer to the registered *harac* income—land tax or head tax paid by non-Muslims, also called *cizye*—of Kobaš, which as a *kaza* represented a substantial administrative unit below the *sancak* level. If this interpretation is correct, Âli must have sought such an assignment of imperial (*miri*) income—revenue collected and controlled by the central government—either as an outright salary grant or as tax-farm (*iltizam*). Presumably Lala Mustafa Paşa, who was now a vezir of the Dome, could arrange for such assignments of imperial revenue. The term may also be bureaucratic jargon for a *timar*-type grant, probably of *zeâmet* status.[51]

Although the result of this petition is not known, it provides an instructive example of the nature of the Ottoman appointment process and patron-client relationships. First, it shows that the line between courtesy and friendly gift giving on the one hand and bribery (*rüşvet*) on the other was in many cases a very fine one. Gift giving was an integral part of the personal and political relationships that joined the Ottoman class, while outright gifts of money between individuals with no other personal or professional ties were considered abnormal. Second, the letter illustrates the way in which the resources provided by official posts could be utilized for both personal and political ends. Lala Mustafa Paşa, as a vezir, could secure favors and supplementary income for his protégés through manipulation of the system, intercession, and exercise of discretionary powers. Âli, posted to a border province that supplied prisoners and slaves, was in a position to offer, at little cost to himself, a more substantial gift than his usual literary efforts. Finally, the letter indicates that, for the moment, Âli's ambitions were largely limited to building a career within the provincial administrative system.

Âli maintained his literary activity as best he could under the conditions of life in the marches. He continued to write poetry, and in 1574/982 put his *divan* into a final recension. He maintained correspondence with fellow littérateurs, as evidenced by a witty epistle he sent from Bosnia to an acquaint-

[50] MENŞE, 198b-200a, where Kobaš is identified as a *kaza* containing "three rivers and three bridges." The district was then within the *sancak* of Bosnia, and is located on the south bank of the Sava, east of the Vrbaš (H. Šabanovič, *Bosanski Pašaluk* [Sarajevo, 1959], p. 179). No MS of Âli's *Ayyuhâ al-walad* has been found; that usually identified as such, Hacı Beşir Ağa 343, is an interlinear translation of *ḥadîth (Hadîs-i erba'în)* with no indication of authorship. On Ghazâlî's original, see GAL, I, 541.

[51] İNAL, p. 15. On the interchangeability of the terms *harac* and *cizye* in the Ottoman period, see H. İnalcık, "Djizya," EI². The granting of *miri* (pertaining to the state) revenues to functionaries of the central government as part of their salary is discussed by Uzunçarşılı in *Merkez*, pp. 326-27, and Pakalın, I, 734-36. Other examples of Âli's requests for a *defter* (MENŞE, 197b-98b, 263a-b) clearly show it to be a source of income. A passage in COUNSEL (II, 21 [trans.], 137 [text]) shows another bureaucratic term, "*kalem*" (pen, or bureau) used to signify "*timar.*" "*Defter*," by analogy, may mean "*zeâmet.*"

ance in Istanbul, and which provides some insight into Âli's social and religious attitudes at this time. Âli's letter is a response to the communication of one Mahmud Çelebi, then posted in Salonika, who had received a request for information from a friend in Istanbul who was a notorious pederast. The Istanbullu had contracted a dangerous fever, and had formally vowed to give up boys if he were cured. He had indeed recovered, but restoration of health had brought a return of desire. The unfortunate man was informed by the ulema of Istanbul that his vow of repentance, once made, could not legally be broken, and therefore he had begged Mahmud Çelebi to inquire of the rabbis of Salonika if they knew of a legal stratagem that would allow him once again to indulge his proclivities. After receiving a negative response from the Jewish scholars, Mahmud Çelebi forwarded the request to Âli so that he might seek the opinions of Catholic and Orthodox priests. Âli in his own letter claims to have posed the problem to Venetian, Serbian, and Croatian religious men, all of whom affirmed that the oath was binding. Âli then goes on to suggest that the man can solve his problem by turning to women, since heterosexual intercourse is more pleasurable and more hygienic, as well as more manly.[52]

In the course of his official travels Âli inevitably sought out prominent literary figures. At some point between 1570/978 and 1572/979, perhaps while on his way to Klis for the first time, Âli stopped at Üsküp (Skopje) for three days to visit the poet and prose stylist Âşık Çelebi, who was then judge of the town. Âşık entertained Âli lavishly, and finally apologized to the young poet for not having read his work and for not including him in his recently completed biographical dictionary of poets. Âli, characteristically, immediately provided Âşık with the requisite biographical and bibliographical information to be added to a revised edition. However, Âşık died soon thereafter (January 1572/Şa'ban 979), and it seems that no notice on Âli made its way into any manuscript of Âşık's *Meşa'ir üş-şu'ara, Stations of the Poets' Pilgrimage*.[53]

Another literary light of the Bosnian marches was Yahya Beğ, one of the most renowned poets of the mid-sixteenth century. Until 1555 Yahya, who was descended from the Albanian Dukagin *beğs*, had enjoyed a promising career in Ottoman financial service as an administrator of royal endowments. Following the execution of Prince Mustafa in 1553, Yahya had composed a bitter elegy to the dead prince which blamed the former grand vezir

[52] MENŞE, 203a-204a.

[53] KA, Selim/Şu'ara, "Menla Âşık," Nur 3409, 279a-b; G. M. Meredith-Owens, introduction to AŞIK, xii-xiii. The 974 date for this meeting given in the KA manuscripts I have examined (also given by Meredith-Owens, AŞIK) is impossible. It is probably a result of an early copyist's error, or Âli's own mistake, which found its way into subsequent MSS; in 974 Âli was in Syria-Palestine. Furthermore, Âli states that he came to Üsküp on official duty, and that Âşık Çelebi was then judge of the city. According to Meredith-Owens's biography of the *tezkere* author, Âşık Çelebi did not occupy this post until after 1568-69/976.

Rüstem Paşa for the entire affair. The elegy became extremely popular, and Rüstem Paşa was enraged. When he again became grand vezir in 1555 Rüstem had Yahya investigated and dismissed from his position. Apparently the charges against Yahya were not sufficiently substantial to warrant his execution, and as a member of the *askeri* class he apparently could not be left to starve. Rüstem Paşa exiled him from the capital to Zvornik in Bosnia, where he was allowed to retain a 30,000-*akçe zeâmet*. It was there that Âli met Yahya in 1574-75/982; he may have had the example of Yahya in mind when he later described himself as a poet too talented to be supported by jealous politicians and subsequently condemned to exile in the border provinces. In any event, Âli's reputation and learning impressed Yahya Beğ, who for all his poetic talent was a professional bureaucrat without a *medrese* education. The year after the two first met in Zvornik, Yahya Beğ sent his son Adem Çelebi to Âli with the draft of the introduction to the most recent recension of his *divan*. He asked that Âli proofread the draft for errors, particularly in Arabic constructions. In fact, the introduction needed no correction.[54]

Yet another poet whom Âli befriended in Bosnia was Şani, a religious scholar resident in Bosnasaray (Sarajevo). Whether or not Âli actually lived in that city after Ferhad Beğ's transfer to the *sancak* of Bosnia, he obviously spent time there, for he and Şani traded poems and Şani composed parallels (*nazir*es) on some of Âli's verse.[55] Though the Bosnian marches did not offer the literary excitement of Istanbul, they did sustain cultural life, and Âli sought it out wherever he could.

Âli's Balkan sojourn represents an intriguing interlude in the course of a career otherwise marked by a commitment to advancement within the chancery service, a yearning for the capital and the court, and a long series of postings to eastern provinces of the Ottoman Empire. Ambitious and highly literate, Âli had achieved rapid advancement at an early age through talent, *intisab*, and recognition of the importance of the expanding bureaucracy. In the wake of the Egyptian débacle, many of his personal ties were severed, and he was thrust into an environment in which learning counted for less than bravery in battle, in which success was measured not in numbers of works authored or distinguished teachers but in service and *timar* grants. In short, in Bosnia Âli entered a new cultural milieu and new professional system, to both of which he appears to have adjusted remarkably well. Some years later, when writing the *Counsel*, Âli described the experience from the point of view of a man of letters thrust into the world of holy warfare on the frontier:

[54] KA, Süleyman/Şu'ara, "Yahya Beğ," Nur 3409, 212a-b; the late addition of an introduction to the work is confirmed by Mehmed Çavuşoğlu in the introduction to his edition of Yahya Beğ's *Divan* (Istanbul, 1977).

[55] KA, Selim/Şu'ara, "Sani," Nur 3409/278b.

> I went off and embarked upon the path followed by ordinary folk, seeking to provide necessities and gain promotion. For eight full years I pitched my tent in the broad plain of battle, and performed my prayers in nine-month campaigns every year. I strove fiercely with the warriors engaged in holy warfare, and sought to cut through the ranks with my blood-thirsty blade; thus I anxiously watched the passage of days and nights. With such attention to duty I attained a 60,000-*akçe zeâmet*, and became noted as one with few equals on the border of the *sancak* of Bosnia for my services with both pen and sword.[56]

Âli goes on in this passage to express his gratitude to Sokollu for having given him the opportunity to become a *gazi* warrior for the faith, which Âli piously says will surely count in his favor on the Day of Judgment.

Even in the second half of the sixteenth century the Rumelian borders of the Ottoman Empire, which directly faced Christian territories, still evoked the *gazi* ethos of the fourteenth and fifteenth centuries. The Ottoman state had been born out of *gaza*, and the first Ottoman rulers had themselves been rude raiders on the marches of the Islamic domains; they had laid the foundations for the uniquely polyethnic and polylingual Ottoman polity by constantly prosecuting the conquest of non-Muslim territories. Âli, with the romanticism of the educated urban Ottoman, absorbed much of this ethos during his Bosnian stay, despite the harshness of life on the borders, where constant raiding and rough frontier justice were the order of the day.[57] Âli constantly connects Bosnia with holy war. For example, in the conclusion to the *Zübdet üt-tevarih, The Choicest of Histories*, he describes the region as "the meeting place of the *gazi*s of the world and the source of the trusty warriors for the faith of [all] the climes." He elsewhere boasts of his intimacy with the *gazi* sons of Malkoç Beğ, whom he visited in 1576-77/984 in their hereditary territory in Klis. Malkoç Beğ was the embodiment of the Rumelian *akıncı* (raider and *gazi* warrior), having risen from the status of a simple *timar*-holding cavalryman to the governorship of the *sancak* of Bosnia.[58]

Until 1574/982 Âli's pleas for assistance were relatively modest and aimed at securing advancement within the provincial administrative system. One such request from this period was addressed to the finance director of Budin (Budun; Buda), the nearest *vilayet* capital. In it Âli asked for a "good *defter*," probably meaning either a grant of imperial revenues from a local source, a *zeâmet*, or a post in the provincial bureaucracy.[59] Âli also sought

[56] COUNSEL, II, 73 (trans.), 200 (text).

[57] For examples, see COUNSEL, I, 72 (trans.), 170-71 (text).

[58] ZÜBDET, 202b; KA, Süleyman/Ümera, "Ali Beğ b. Malkoç," "Malkoç Beğ," Nur 3409, 136a-b. On the *gazi* ideal and its romanticization, see Paul Wittek, *The Rise of the Ottoman Empire* (London, 1938).

[59] MENŞE, 197b-98b; see also note 51 above.

to ingratiate himself with the paşa of Budin, the vezir Mustafa Paşa, who was also a paternal cousin of the grand vezir Sokollu Mehmed Paşa, by sending him a flattering ode.[60] At some point between 1570 and 1573 Âli addressed an appeal in verse to the secretary-in-chief of the Imperial Council, the *re'isülküttab* Feridun Ahmed, Sokollu's protégé and former secretary. In this poem Âli asked to be given a chancery or financial bureau (*kalem*).[61] Âli even petitioned Sokollu himself so that a recently vacated *zeâmet* might be granted to him. Âli was at pains to portray himself in this letter as a loyal supporter of the Sokollu family and its political network; in it he emphasized that he was personally close to the grand vezir's cousin Ferhad Beğ.[62] Indeed, Âli did well in Ferhad Beğ's service, probably heading the chancery section and composing the most important official correspondence, if not all of it.[63] Although Âli in later years criticized Ferhad for his harshness, stubbornness, and disregard for the law, the two appear to have had a good working relationship. Ferhad did well by Âli, and brought him to Bosnia when he became *sancak* governor. By December 1574 Âli was living in Banyaluka, where Ferhad Beğ probably spent the winter, and where his first *sancak* seat may have been located.[64]

Ultimately Âli was not content to remain on "the path followed by ordinary folk," that is, to spend the rest of his life as a landed cavalry officer on the borders of the Empire, where he would be obliged to engage in yearly

[60] VARİDAT, 41a-42a.

[61] VARİDAT, 48b-49a. Feridun Beğ served as *re'isülküttab* from June 1570 to December 1573 (GOW, p. 106).

[62] MENŞE, 206b-208a.

[63] MENŞE, 200a-201a, a victory announcement (*fethname*) dated 8 January 1575/24 Ramazan 982, sent to Istanbul reporting a victory over the Croats; 202a-203b, to the major officials in Bosnia announcing the accession of Sultan Murad, the news officially having reached Bosnia on 12 Sevval 982, nearly five weeks after the event; 203a-204a, from Ferhad Beğ to the Porte, acknowledging the change of ruler.

[64] ZÜBDET, 202b (colophon): "The work was completed, by the grace of God, in the sacred month of Muharrem 983. It was begun in Şevval 982 [January-February 1575], and came to an end at the end of Âşûra week 983 [ca. 26 April 1575]. The composition and copying took place in . . . the *kasaba* of Banaluka [Banyaluka] . . . in the *sancak* of Bosnia. . . ."

On Banyaluka, see Evliya Çelebi, *Seyahatname*, 10 vols. (Istanbul, 1896-1938), V, 504-508, 539-40, and PEÇEVİ, I, 454-55. Banyaluka was first conquered by Ferhad Beğ, who built there a second fortress, a *medrese*, a bath house, a primary school, a hospice, and a personal residence. With the ransom he received from prisoners taken in his Ramazan 982 victory over the Croats (see note 63 above), he built a Friday mosque.

Ferhad Beğ is by no means singled out for the harsh and, frequently, illegal (i.e., in violation of both *şeri'at* and *kanun*) character of his administration. In the COUNSEL Âli notes that at one point Ferhad was investigated by the central government for alleged abuses of authority. At the same time Âli points out that disrespect for law was a phenomenon characteristic of many of the Empire's border provinces, the governors of which tended to rule in absolutist fashion; see COUNSEL, I, 71-75, 80-81 (trans.), 169-74, 180-82 (text). Âli also recounts the extreme measures taken by one of Ferhad Beğ's predecessors in Bosnia, Osmanşah Beğ, in order to establish his authority vis-à-vis both the subjects and the fastidious representatives of the central government (KA, Süleyman/Ümera, "Osmanşah Beğ," Nur 3409, 135b).

campaigns and work his way through the provincial military ranks. Rewarding as such a life might be on a temporary basis, Âli had no wish to end his days like one of his literary colleagues in Rumeli, condemned to provincial life and to awaiting the chance visits of traveling scholars and littérateurs. Âli was ambitious and sought rapid advancement. By the time he was twenty Âli had begun, and abruptly put an end to, a scholarly career, choosing to seek a patron rather than a profession. Over the next ten years he acquired chancery experience in service to individuals—Prince Selim, Lala Mustafa Paşa, and Ferhad Beğ—and learned not only that patrons could be fickle, but also that a protégé fell with his master unless he had a firm position and source of income of his own. Finally, through the generosity of Sokollu Mehmed Paşa, Âli was able to attain a stable situation on his own account in the provincial military administration in Bosnia. He made remarkable progress in the military career, yet he was still dissatisfied; he was certainly aware that, once established in the provinces, most officers of his status (*za'im*) who did not have powerful protectors in the capital tended to stay there.

Âli's appeal to Feridun Beğ suggests that he sought to enter the ranks of the central bureaucracy, a career that offered opportunities for advancement to the highest levels of government service—levels that few, if any, *timar*-holders could hope to attain. Âli's ambitions were intimately bound up with his self-identification as a man of letters and exponent of high culture. He felt that his abilities were wasted in the border provinces, and that his proper place might be in that branch of government service in which letters and learning mattered, the *kalemiye* bureaucracy. Implicit in this attitude, of course, was a consciousness that his literary talent would bring him greater attention and rewards in the central bureaucracy than in the marches. Ultimately, Âli dreamed of leaving behind all three major branches of service—Sword, Pen, and Learning. He saw himself as one day becoming "palace," attached to the Porte itself and to the inner circle of those who served the sultan directly. His earlier experiences with the princes Selim and Murad seemed to show him that the best way for him to gain royal attention and favor was through exercise of his literary talents.

During the first four years on the frontier in Klis and Bosnia, Âli wrote almost nothing but official letters and a bit of poetry. Only the accession of Murad III to the Ottoman throne (22 December 1574/8 Ramazan 982) spurred him to a surge of literary activity. It appears that, after the Egyptian disaster, Âli hoped for little while Selim was still alive; he largely restricted his efforts to ingratiating himself with Sokollu and his relatives in Bosnia. Whatever cloud hung over him at Selim's court would, he felt, disappear with the accession of the new sultan, whose favor he had enjoyed at Bozdağ. Âli once again began to dream of literary glory and of a life at court, and hurriedly revised his *divan* for presentation. He composed a great many new odes congratulating Murad on his accession, and even addressed a number of poems to Murad's young son, Prince Mehmed. Âli added to the work an introduction and dedication to Murad, and called it *Vâridât ül-enîka, Elegant Inspirations.*[65] In the introduction he asks the new sultan to recognize his ability and to alleviate his poverty, and further reminds Murad of his learning and skill in poetry and prose. Finally, he pleads, "Let me not remain a *za'im* in your reign; in your time, may I not [be forced to] even glance at humble posts."[66]

Âli compiled his two formal *divans* (the very first, discussed above, was not circulated, and the third was edited posthumously) at what he considered to be major points in his life. The *Elegant Inspirations* was the first of these, and taken as a whole it provides an indication of Âli's attitudes and preoccupations as of 1574/982. In comparison with his later compilation of verse, the *Inspirations* only occasionally displays the personal bitterness and obsession with a perception of rampant disorder and injustice in Ottoman society that much later came to dominate his poetry. Âli appears at this point in his life to have genuinely felt the personal and social optimism that he expressed in his introductory address to Sultan Murad.

Âli completed and dispatched his *Inspirations* to the court in early February 1575. For the moment he remained at Banyaluka in Bosnia, where he

[65] In his introduction to the VARİDAT, Âli says that he compiled the *divan* in honor of Murad's accession, between early Ramazan and mid-Şevval 982 (3b). If this was in fact the case, unofficial news of the event, which occurred on 22 December 1574/8 Ramazan 982, must have reached Bosnia very quickly. Âli probably did not work continuously, since Ferhad Beğ was engaged in military activities during this period (see note 63 above).

As it now stands in extant manuscripts, VARİDAT represents a later, expanded recension, containing some chronograms and odes datable to at least 1579-80/987, and material may have been added up to 1580-81/988, which Âli says in the introduction to the later LAYİHAT to have been the case (LAYİHAT 3b-4a). Some poems included in the VARİDAT can be identified as belonging to Âli's pre-982 phase, on the basis of subject matter and comparison with the first recension of 975. The introduction and accession odes can be dated more exactly to 1574/982. The remaining poems, with the exception of those dated or datable by internal evidence, cannot be chronologically catalogued with any great precision. The Hạmidiye MS utilized here also contains a small number of poems taken from LAYİHAT and from Âli's last *divan* (İÜ Türkçe 768; hereafter DİVAN III). For example, the odes found on ff. 27b-30a of the VARİDAT were composed at the time of the accession of Mehmed III in 1595/1003. While this may seem a small point, it creates difficulties for the establishment of our author's biography. Such personal material as satirical verses (*hicv*) and odes, which are usually addressed to individuals and contain requests that are often quite specific, provide valuable clues to personal associations and expectations when placed in an historical context. Hence the chronological scope of much of the VARİDAT makes it difficult to trace precisely the growth of Âli's expectations. In one ode (ff. 16a-18a) he asks the sultan to make him *musahib*, while complaining bitterly about lack of recognition for the learned and literary-minded in Murad's time. This is hardly the sort of plea a hopeful provincial scribe would make to a newly enthroned sultan, and one would like to know when and why such a poem was composed.

[66] VARİDAT, 4a-b.

spent the remainder of the winter translating Qâḍî ʿAḍud al-dîn's Arabic *Ishrâq al-tawârîkh, The Illumination of Histories*, into Turkish at the behest of Ferhad Beğ. Âli expanded and reorganized the original work, which deals with the pre-Islamic prophets, Muḥammad, his family, his companions, and subsequent prominent religious figures. Âli called his translation *Zübdet üt-tevarih, The Choicest of Histories*, and dedicated it to both Ferhad Beğ and his cousin Sokollu Mehmed Paşa.[67]

Âli clearly expected that the new sultan would remember his earlier services and recall him to the capital. When this did not occur, Âli went to Istanbul himself to present his accession ode (*cülusiye*) at court.[68] The chronology of his departure from Bosnia is unfortunately somewhat vague. In the *Counsel* Âli says only that, when he received no summons to the court following Murad's enthronement, he "immediately traveled from the border region of Bosnia to the capital, and hurried to present a springtime accession-poem."[69] A fragmentary poem found in Âli's second *divan*, the *Lâyihât ül-hakîka, Visions of Reality*, would seem to be a covering letter accompanying this ode. In it Âli says that when the news of the accession arrived in Bosnia at the end of Ramazan (ca. January 14, 1575), he had been on official duty at the border. Also, vernal New Year (*nevruz*, March 10-11) was near, and therefore he could visit the court only in the spring after that date. Âli seeks to apologize for the lateness of his congratulatory offering, saying that his duties had delayed him.[70]

An ambitious poet from the provinces seeking an appointment could hardly expect to attract much notice at a court in the throes of the palace power struggles that followed the enthronement of a new ruler. Âli's journey to Istanbul in the spring of 1575 proved fruitless, and he returned to Bosnia, where he remained for at least one more year.[71] Âli had not given up his dreams of returning to the capital; he was merely biding his time until the power structure of the new regime took shape.

67 ZÜBDET, 202b-293a. On Qâḍî ʿAḍud al-dîn (d. 1355/756), see GAL, II, 271. For the completion dates of VARİDAT and ZÜBDET, see notes 64, 65 *supra*.

68 COUNSEL, II, 76-85 (trans.), 204-12 (text), provides the basic biographical information on Âli between 1575/983 and 1577/985.

69 COUNSEL, II, 76 (trans.) and 205 (text). The ode in question occurs in VARİDAT, 18a-19b.

70 LAYİHAT, 145b.

71 This chronology is reconstructed from Âli's statements, cited above, that he spent a total of seven to eight years in Bosnia, and from his reference to visiting the sons of Malkoç Beğ in Klis in 1576-77/984 (see note 58 above). In MENŞE (232b) he states that he remained in the capital without a post for "two years" between his departure from Bosnia and his appointment as secretary to the commander of the Şirvan campaign, which took place in about March 1578 (see below).

THREE

TO THE EAST

(1577-82 / 984-90)

ISTANBUL

(1577-78)

ÂLI WAS thirty-six years old in the early spring of 1577/late 984. He had spent seven years in Bosnia, where he had risen through the ranks of the provincial military system to gain a sizable income. As his financial position improved, his personal household grew, he married, and, in 1576-77/984, his son Fazlullah was born.[1] Âli's expectations and optimism must have increased proportionately, particularly after the accession of Murad III, for by early 1577 he had given up his *zeâmet*, left Bosnia for good, and come to Istanbul to seek an appointment at court.

Âli spent the next year trying to bring himself to Murad's attention. When submission of the *Elegant Inspirations* brought no results, he rededicated the *Choicest of Histories* to the sultan and had it presented through an unidentified courtier.[2] Âli sent a flood of laudatory odes to Murad, referring to his own unemployed state and likening himself to such earlier poets as Necati and Hayali, who had received royal patronage. Âli emphasized his high degree of education as well as his literary attainments, complaining that political appointments were given to the unworthy (*erazil*) while the truly learned and able were ignored. He portrayed himself as a latter-day counterpart of the Persian poet Jâmî (d. 1492), and of the scholar-poet and statesman ʿAlî Shîr Navâ'î (d. 1501), both of whom had flourished, together with

[1] MENŞE, 261a-262b, gives the text of a letter Âli wrote to an unidentified worthy asking for his daughter (whom Âli had not yet seen) in marriage. Had the family of the girl been an important one, the status-conscious Âli would surely have identified it. The chronogram Âli composed on the birth of his son Fazlullah, giving the date as 984 (1576-77), is quoted by İNAL, p. 47, citing an undentified *divan*. Although the *tarih* is not found in Hamidiye 1107, it does appear in the DK manuscript of the *Varidat*, DKM Adab Turkî 21, 330b.

[2] COUNSEL, II, 78-79 (trans.), 206-207 (text); MENŞE, 260a-261a. The letter is addressed to the courtier who presented the *Zübdet* at court on Âli's behalf; it summarizes Âli's training and qualifications, and gives the month as Muharrem, probably meaning Muharrem 985/March-April 1577. The new dedication to Murad that Âli added to the *Zübdet* occurs in MS Hazine 1330. This MS has no colophon, but contains the original conclusion referred to above, which may indicate that Âli rededicated the work before leaving Bosnia.

other luminaries, in Timurid Herat of the late fifteenth century.[3] Unlike these, however, Âli did not enjoy the protection of such a prince as Sulṭân-Ḥusayn Bâyqarâ (d. 1506), whose court at Herat he saw as the perfect political and cultural environment, one in which rulers were not only inclined, but duty-bound, to surround themselves with the learned and talented. Over the next twenty years of his life Âli came more and more to judge the cultural and political life of his own times against this nostalgic Persianate ideal. Given his relative failure to achieve the degree of success he felt he deserved, it is hardly surprising that, when at the end of his life he wrote the great historical and moralistic works for which he became famous, Âli found his own society not only wanting but degenerate.

Âli strove to forge new political connections as he sought his fortune in Istanbul. For eight years he had worked hard to ingratiate himself with the powerful grand vezir, Sokollu Mehmed Paşa, and with his relatives and protégés, who increasingly dominated the Ottoman administrative apparatus. However, the accession of Murad provided the catalyst for the formation of a new palace clique, which sought to curb the authority of Sokollu. Some members of this faction had been closely associated with Selim, and had stayed in the Palace after Murad's accession.[4] In the forefront of the anti-Sokollu movement was Şemsi Ahmed Paşa, the old campaigner-turned-courtier, who had served both Selim I and Süleyman before becoming royal confidant to Selim II. He not only retained this position under Sultan Murad, but even gained considerable influence over the new ruler through wit, flattery (he wrote a history in verse of the Ottoman house), and understanding of Murad's weaknesses. The chief of these, Âli states, was cupidity. Murad's first words after becoming sultan were inauspicious: "I am hungry." It was Şemsi Paşa who persuaded the sultan to accept bribes and thus condone administrative corruption and influence-peddling. Şemsi reportedly told Âli that he had corrupted the monarch, knowing that his action would have disastrous consequences for the state. Şemsi Paşa set great store by his

[3] COUNSEL, II, 79-85 (trans.), 207-12 (text). These odes, which Âli lists in order of submission in the COUNSEL, are found in VARİDAT: 16a-18a, on the predominance of the unworthy; 19b-21b, referring to his lack of employment and warning the sultan aganist the lies spread by his detractors (*tîğ*-rhyme); 21a-22b, *sünbül*-rhyme; 22b-23b; 23b-24b, on the occasion of the Feast of Sacrifice 985 (18 February 1578); 24b-25b, on the repair of an imperial caique, dated 1577/985; 30b-31a, *uyur*-rhyme, containing the reference to Jâmî and Sulṭân-Ḥusayn, incorrectly identified in this MS as being addressed to Sultan Mehmed III. For another reference to Âli's Timurid ideal, see COUNSEL, I, 27-28 (trans.), 104-106 (text). On Jâmî and Navâ'î, see Zeki Velidi Togan, "Cami," İA, and Agâh Sırrı Levend, *Ali Şir Nevai*, 4 vols. (Ankara, 1965-68).

[4] The following information on Sultan Murad's Palace personnel is based on KA, Murad/Introduction, Nur 3409, 293a-299b; cf. Gökbilgin, "Mehmed Paşa, Sokollu," İA. On Şemsi Paşa's *Şahname-i Sultan Murad*, see GOW, pp. 105-106.

own princely lineage and sought to take vengeance for the Ottoman dispossession of the house of İsfendiyar.

Gazanfer Ağa had been attached to Selim's princely court, near to which he and his brother Ca'fer Beğ had had *sancak* governorships. At Kütahya Gazanfer had known and befriended both Lala Mustafa Paşa and Âli, and in later years he remained one of Âli's principal patrons and friends at court.[5] When Selim acceded to the throne in 1566, he wished to take the two brothers with him to Istanbul, for he valued their company and loyalty. In order that they might attend him even in his private apartments, and thus increase their opportunities for service, he requested that the two *beğ*s join the ranks of the *ağa*s, the eunuchs. Ca'fer did not survive the operation, but his brother Gazanfer reaped the rewards of his sacrifice by becoming the chief white eunuch and overseer of Palace affairs (*bab üs-sa'âdet ağası*), as well as chief of the Privy Chamber (*hasodabaşı*) to Selim II, Murad III, and the latter's son Mehmed III.[6] In the Harem, Gazanfer Ağa had an important ally in the Mistress Housekeeper (*kedbanu-yi harem, kâhya kadın*), Canfeda Hatun, who under the Queen Mother (*valide sultan*) had charge of the training of the women of the harem.[7] Canfeda Hatun was the sister of Divane ("Crazy") İbrahim Paşa, and an ally of Sultan Murad's strong-willed mother, Nurbanu, whose control of the harem Canfeda assumed on the latter's death.

Under Selim these courtiers had been unable effectively to voice their resentment of the efficient Sokollu Mehmed Paşa, who had easily intimidated a sultan more concerned with pleasure than with politics; the grand vezir was known to have brought about the dismissal, and even execution, of anyone who threatened his own ascendancy over the ruler. The accession of Sultan Murad in 1574 brought new blood into the anti-Sokollu coalition in the persons of his religious tutor, Hoca Sa'düddin, and in his spiritual guide, Şeyh Şüca'üddin. The first was a noted scholar and able politician who, in the reign of his pupil, attained virtual control of the entire *ilmiye* hierarchy. A littérateur as well as a scholar, Sa'düddin later authored one of the best-known histories of the Ottoman house, the *Tac üt-tevarih, The Crown of Histories*. He, too, became one of Âli's most important friends at court.[8] The second man was a religious figure of very different stripe. An illiterate and ostentatiously ecstatic dervish associated with the followers of Ümmi Sinan, Şeyh Şüca' had been a gardener at the court of Prince Murad. Once of Murad's female companions (*musahibe*), Raziye Hatun, brought Şüca' to the prince's attention as a skilled interpreter of dreams. So impressed was

[5] VARİDAT, 45b-46a, is an ode Âli addressed to Gazanfer Beğ at Kütahya.

[6] On these offices, see Uzunçarşılı, *Saray*, pp. 340-42, 354-57.

[7] On this office, see Uzunçarşılı, *Saray*, p. 150.

[8] On Sa'düddin see GOW, pp. 123-26, and Ş. Turan, "Sa'd el-dîn," İA.

Murad with the dervish's understanding of the unseen that he became his disciple; and, despite the notoriety for cupidity and ambisexual lasciviousness Şeyh Şüca' achieved, Sultan Murad refused to heed any complaints about his influential *pir*'s behavior.

Sokollu had good reason to fear the new order. Canfeda Hatun and Gazanfer Ağa were old allies of Sokollu's rival Lala Mustafa Paşa, whom they had rallied around after the Yemen campaign disaster. They were also closely associated with the new Queen Mother, Nurbanu, who wished to exert her own authority from the harem unobstructed by the grand vezir. The fact that the anti-Sokollu faction was composed of those physically and emotionally closest to the sultan threatened Sokollu tremendously, and both sides were eager for a confrontation. Murad's inner circle began to agitate against Sokollu immediately after the accession; Şemsi Paşa, as the sultan's confidant, even suggested that the grand vezir be killed. Barely six weeks after Murad's enthronement, in February 1575/Şevval 982, Sokollu brought the conflict into the open. He ordered an investigation of the affairs of Kara Üveys Çelebi (later Paşa), who had been Prince Murad's finance director (*defterdar*) at Manisa and had accompanied the new sultan to Istanbul. At the urging of Lalezar Mehmed Çelebi, who as treasurer (*başdefterdar*) was the chief financial official of the Empire, Sokollu accused Üveys of allowing illegal disbursal of imperial funds while the royal party journeyed from Manisa to Istanbul. Üveys' friend, Şemsi Paşa, immediately organized the opposition, which included the sultan himself, and encouraged both subjects and servitors to submit complaints about the grand vezir. Üveys was not only exonerated but was appointed to be third financial director of the Empire, in charge of the Second Branch (*şıkk-ı sani*) of the Treasury.[9] About two months later Lalezar Mehmed Çelebi was dismissed from office, and Üveys was promoted to treasurer. From the very beginning of Murad's reign Sokollu Mehmed Paşa lost ground, although he remained grand vezir until his assassination in 1579. Even more devastating for him than Üveys's victory was the purge of Sokollu relatives and protégés that followed. The chancellor, Feridun Ahmed, was dismissed from office, and over thirty Sokollu adherents lost their posts, salaries, and personal property, which was confiscated for the royal treasury. The governor-general of Budin, the grand vezir's cousin Sokollu Mustafa Paşa, was put to death, and his province was given to the treasurer, Üveys Çelebi, who now became Üveys Paşa. In a very short time the anti-Sokollu forces at court permanently curtailed the power of the man who had effectively ruled the Ottoman Empire for eight years.[10]

[9] On the structure of the central financial bureaucracy and the nature of its primary offices, see Appendix A.

[10] KA, Murad/9, 298b-299b; PEÇEVİ, II, 5-10; SELANİKİ, pp. 139-40.

Âli lost no time in changing his allegiance. After coming to Istanbul he addressed odes requesting patronage to almost all of the new powers at court: Hoca Sa'düddin, Şemsi Paşa, Şeyh Şüca', and the chief military judge (*kadıasker*) of Rumeli, Kadızade, who had also played a role in the Sokollu purge.[11] The ode to Şeyh Şüca' very clearly displays the opportunism and hypocritical careerism that were to mark Âli's approach to his professional life until his death. In it he explicitly asks to be made a protégé of the man he later reviled as an imposter whose Sufi garb masked a craving for wealth and extreme debauchery.[12] Âli goes to great lengths to defend Şeyh Şüca' against charges then current that his repute for sanctity was belied by his wealth and concern for worldly power. Âli argues that to the true dervish, wealth and poverty are the same, and that ostentatious poverty is hypocritical. It may be remembered that Âli denied Şeyh Bali Efendi's power to work miracles on the ground that a man as rich as he could not be a true mystic.

Âli's efforts to curry favor with the new Palace powers produced no tangible positive results; indeed, his insistence on recognition probably made him enemies, which may account for some of the bitterness with which he spoke of Şemsi Paşa and Şeyh Şüca' later in life. His relations with Şemsi Paşa were particularly unsatisfactory; this was all the more unfortunate for a littérateur like Âli since Şemsi Paşa held one of the most important literary salons in the capital, graced by important functionaries of state as well as by poets. Âli attended Şemsi Paşa's séances faithfully for some time, until it became clear that Şemsi would do nothing for Âli or his career. In the *Counsel* Âli frankly admits that he frequented Şemsi Paşa's salon expecting to make financial and political gains; he implies that it was Şemsi Paşa's duty as a royal *musahib* to reward talent and enhance the cultural life of the capital by bringing skilled poets to the sultan's attention. Şemsi Paşa was equally frank in admitting to Âli that he would help no one but himself. The tension between the two careerists led to an open falling out. Âli suggested, albeit politely, that Şemsi expected rather a lot from his guests, who had to pay exorbitant boat fares daily in order to come to his house in Üsküdar, on the eastern shore of the Bosphorus, for which investment they received no return. Şemsi in turn ridiculed Âli's choice of pen name, and offered to give him a new one. Âli retorted in a fashion calculated to pique Şemsi Paşa, who

[11] VARİDAT, 31b-34a, 35a-36a, 38a-38b; see also COUNSEL, I, 44-46 (trans.), 132-34 (text); II, 87-89 (trans.), 215-17 (text). These poems are datable by internal evidence to 1574-79. Interestingly enough, VARİDAT contains no odes addressed to Lala Mustafa Paşa, Âli's erstwhile protector, although DİVAN I contains a number of these. This negative evidence corroborates the notion that the VARİDAT represents a primarily political composition, and that Âli remained cautious in his relations with Lala Mustafa Paşa even after their reconciliation in 1585.

[12] KA, Murad/4, Nur 3409, 294a-295a.

jealously guarded his own proximity to Sultan Murad; he suggested that he change "Âli" to "Hakani," meaning both "imperial" and "belonging to the sovereign (*hakan*)," thus implying a close relationship to the monarch.[13] Whether because he was perceived as an ambitious upstart, or because of his difficulties with Şemsi Paşa, or all of these, Âli had serious political problems at court; in a number of odes composed at this time he asks the recipients to pay no heed to the calumnies of his detractors.[14] This situation helps to account for the seemingly endless series of appeals found in Âli's two *divans*, which were directed to Sultan Murad himself and which Âli continued to submit until the sultan's death in 1595. Since Âli could not fully rely on the good offices of courtiers to press his case, he sought the direct intercession of the sovereign.

During this period in Istanbul, Âli was too occupied trying to secure a post to write anything but poems and petitions. Finally, however, his persistence bore fruit in late 1577/985. Sultan Murad was devoted to his *pir*, Şeyh Şüca', and was deeply interested in Sufism, particularly in its more popular manifestations. He commissioned Âli to translate into Turkish a Persian digest of hagiographic lore, the *Faṣl al-khiṭâb, The Final Word*, of the Nakşbendi Khvâjeh Muḥammad Pârsâ (d. 1420). Âli completed this translation in Ramazan of the same year (November-December 1577) and presented it to the sultan under the title *Hilyet ür-rical, The Adornment of Men*.[15]

For two months Âli received no response from the Porte. He tried once more, submitting a poem to Murad on the occasion of the Feast of Sacrifice (18 February 1578/10 Zulhicce 985). Âli mentioned that the Ottoman campaign against Şirvan and Georgia was in preparation and that he had need of employment. He next presented an ode in which he boasted of his skill in Turkish and Persian. Very soon thereafter Âli was appointed campaign secretary by imperial rescript (*hatt-ı hümayun*), and charged with the composition of all official correspondence. The command of Persian and Turkish

[13] COUNSEL, I, 44-46 (trans.), 132-36 (text); II, 97-100 (trans.), 227-32 (text). The context in which both of these anecdotes occur is a discussion of the duties and qualifications of a royal companion (*musahib*), who, being outside of day-to-day political life, is to give truthful reports and disinterested advice to the sultan.

[14] VARİDAT, 16a-18a, 19b-21a, 33b-34a.

[15] COUNSEL, II, 58 (trans.), 185 (text). Âli's statement that the translation was undertaken at Murad's behest should be accepted, since he makes it in the COUNSEL, which was itself submitted directly to the sultan. The *Hilyet* MS found in a collection of Âli's shorter works and identified as an autograph, MS Reşid Efendi 1146, has a colophon (f. 46b) which gives the place and date of completion as Istanbul, Ramazan 985. Âli immediately thereafter made a presentation copy of the work, now MS Revan Köşkü 465, which according to the colophon (f. 64b) was completed a few weeks later, in Şevval (December 1577-January 1578). On Muḥammad Pârsâ's original work, see Yu. E. Bregel', rev. and trans., *Persidskaya Literatura (Persian Literature)*, by C. A. Storey, 3 vols. (Moscow, 1972), I, 118.

that Âli displayed in the *Adornment* very likely contributed to his being appointed to the post. Seeking the allegiance of Safavi vassals was a keystone of Ottoman policy in the Caucasus, and the nature of the campaign required a secretary who could compose elegant, and sometimes delicate, correspondence in both languages. Âli's first assignment was to write letters to the hereditary rulers and Safavi vassals of the Caucasus region, inviting them to declare their allegiance to the sultan and to assist the Ottoman forces. Âli, the inveterate petitioner, still found the time in the midst of his new duties to ask Murad to grant him an income as well as an appointment, and to supply him with personal transport animals.[16]

Âli's superior was none other than his old patron, Lala Mustafa Paşa, now third vezir of the Dome and field marshal of the Şirvan campaign. Lala Mustafa Paşa had secured the imperial order for Âli's appointment through Sultan Murad's tutor, Hoca Sa'düddin.[17] Sa'düddin played a central part in the Ottoman campaign against the Safavis; a great many of the reports sent by the field marshal and others were sent to the sultan indirectly, through Sa'düddin, rather than to Grand Vezir Sokollu Mehmed Paşa.[18] Indeed, the Ottoman decision to launch an attack against the Safavis in 1577/985 provided a new arena for the warring factions in the Palace. Sokollu reportedly opposed the campaign on the grounds that its expense, as had been shown by Sultan Süleyman's numerous offensives against Iran, would be too great to justify the minimal gains that breaking the twenty-year-old peace between the two empires might bring. The anti-Sokollu faction, which once again gathered around Lala Mustafa Paşa, enthusiastically promoted the war in hopes of creating a new hero who could successfully challenge Sokollu's hold on the grand vezirate. Sokollu himself, though he had long favored plans to build an Ottoman presence in the Caucasus and northern Caspian regions, was well aware of the political threat the war party presented. The opposition to the grand vezir won out, and the comet that was seen traveling east over Istanbul on 12 November 1577 was popularly believed to be an augury of Ottoman victory over the Safavis; little did the Ottomans

[16] KA, Murad 10, Nur 3409, 314b; COUNSEL, II, 82-85 (trans.), 210-13 (text); VARİDAT 23b-24b, 30b-31a, 211b; Âli, complaining that he has not yet received a *timar* assignment, asks for two *katar* (transport animals), presumably to carry personal possessions and document files. The relative chronology of this period is provided by COUNSEL, the absolute chronology by Bekir Kütükoğlu, *Osmanlı-İran Siyasi Münasebetleri, 1578-1590* (Istanbul, 1962), p. 37, and M. Fahrettin Kırzıoğlu, *Osmanlıların Kafkas-Ellerini Fethi (1450-1590)* (Ankara, 1976), pp. 278-79. Both of these admirable studies make extensive use of MD material. The letters to the Georgian and Circassian princes were sent in the course of the month of February-March 1578/Zulhicce 985. The inclusion of them in Âli's *Nusretname* (see below) makes it probable that most of them were composed by our historian.

[17] COUNSEL, II, 9 (trans.), 119 (text); KA, Murad/10, Nur 3409, 314b; MENŞE, 220a.

[18] Kütükoğlu, *Osmanlı*, pp. 12, 46, 72, 97; MENŞE, 222b-223a (private report of Husrev Paşa, former governor-general of Van, to Sa'düddin).

know, Âli later wrote, that it rather betokened ten years of war, bankruptcy, and ruination of both the Ottoman and Safavi lands.[19]

BACKGROUND TO THE ŞİRVAN CAMPAIGN OF 1578

ÂLI's factional interpretation of the situation is doubtless somewhat exaggerated. There were in fact powerful incentives for the Ottomans to break the Peace of Amasya, which they had concluded with the Shi'i Safavis in 1555 after forty years of repeated conflict. For twenty years after Amasya, both sides rigidly observed the border demarcation and provisions for the extradition of renegades that the peace had established. However, the death of the Safavi Shâh Ṭahmâsb in 1576 engendered succession disputes and an outbreak of factional strife among the Kızılbaş, the Türkmen tribal groups that formed the administrative and military backbone of the state. For several years Safavi propaganda and the threat of revolt among Shi'i Kızılbaş sympathizers in Ottoman Anatolia had been causing the government considerable anxiety, and propaganda activity seems to have intensified under Ṭahmâsb's successor Ismâʿîl II. Dynastic instability provoked a sharp increase in instances of renegadism among Safavi clients in the border regions, particularly in Kurdistan. In these disturbances on the frontier the Ottomans saw not only a threat to the status quo established by the Peace of Amasya, but also an opportunity to win wavering princes to an Ottoman allegiance.

Finally, Safavi vassals on the western littoral of the Caspian Sea had become restive; the Sunnis of Şirvan had been in open revolt for nearly a year by the time the Ottoman campaign plans were finalized. The Ottomans had longstanding interests in Şirvan, where they had frequently attempted to maintain clients. Only nine years before, the Ottomans had endeavored to counter Russian expansion and maintain the security of their northeastern lines of communication by attempting to construct a canal between the Don and Volga rivers, thus giving their Black Sea fleet access to the Caspian and providing a means of defending the Muslim khanates of the Caspian region from Muscovite depredations. Reasons for declaring war were manifold, and justifications were also at hand. The Ottomans invoked Ismâʿîl's prop-

[19] KA, Murad/10, Nur 3409, 299b-300a; PEÇEVİ, II, 36-37. On Sokollu's Caucasus-Caspian policy and interest in maintaining a secure northern route linking the Ottomans with the Özbek Khanate of Transoxiana, the most spectacular result of which was the Don-Volga canal project, see A. N. Kurat, "The Turkish Expedition to Astrakhan in 1569 and the Problem of the Don-Volga Canal," *Slavonic and East European Review* 40 (1961): 1-23, and Halil Inalcık, "Osmanlı-Rus Rekabetinin Menşei ve Don-Volga Kanali Teşebbüsü," *Belleten* 8 (1944):349-402. See also Kırzıoğlu, *Kafkas*, p. 272, for a letter from Sokollu to Özdemiroğlu Osman Paşa giving instructions for the construction of a small Caspian fleet after the conquest of Derbend.

aganda activities as a breach of the Peace of Amasya, and proclaimed their obligation to free their Sunni brethren of Şirvan from Shi'i domination, despite the fact that before the death of Ṭahmâsb the Porte had so scrupulously observed the terms of the Peace that it refused to give even moral support to vassals seeking independence from Safavi suzerainty.[20]

Yet another important factor in the Ottoman decision—this one of a moral character—emerges implicitly from the narrative sources. From 1555 until his death in 1576, Shâh Ṭahmâsb enjoyed great prestige among the Ottomans. It was he who, at Amasya, had ended a costly succession of wars and who had agreed to define and hold to common borders. By allowing Prince Selim's envoys to execute the renegade Prince Bayezid in 1562, Ṭahmâsb had eliminated the greatest threat to internal Ottoman stability since the fratricidal wars of 1511-12, when Selim the Grim had battled two brothers and a nephew. Most importantly, perhaps, Ṭahmâsb had quashed the independent behavior of the Kızılbaş *oymak*s, which the founder of the Safavi state, Ṭahmâsb's father Shâh Ismâʿil, had relied upon. These same Türkmen tribal groups had friends and sympathizers in Anatolia who represented the dominant factor in the Ottoman perception of a Safavi danger. Shâh Ṭahmâsb, in short, created a stable, centralized state with which the Ottomans could and did deal on a level of parity. Ottoman historians speak of Ṭahmâsb with respect; Âli even composed a brief poem of mourning for the passing of so able a ruler and so prominent a patron of culture.[21] The death of the shah who was in many ways the architect of amicable Ottoman-Safavi relations, and the recrudescence of problems that had led to earlier hostili-

[20] The best accounts of the prelude to the 1578-79 Georgian campaign, from which this summary is drawn, are those of Kütükoğlu (*Osmanlı*, pp. 1-29) and Kırzıoğlu (*Kafkas*, pp. 251-83). The latter work supplements the former, and is particularly valuable for its Caucasian focus. Both Kırzıoğlu (pp. 264-66) and Kütükoğlu (pp. 19-21) establish that preparations for an attack against Safavi territories, small-scale raids, and attempts to attract potential renegades were begun in the spring of 1577, well before the death of Ismâʿîl and before the Ottoman declaration of war at the end of that year. I will treat the problem of renegadism in a future article on the historiography of the Alqâs Mîrzâ revolt.

Şirvan had remained Sunni despite frequent periods of Safavi rule, which was resisted, with periodic success, by the Şirvanşah dynasty, hereditary rulers of the region. Since 1548 the Şirvanşah Burhân ʿAlî (Burhân al-dîn) and his son Abûbakr Mîrzâ had been Ottoman clients. In the spring of 1577, while the pretender Abûbakr Mîrzâ sat in the Crimea awaiting an opportunity to return to Şirvan, his compatriots revolted against the Kızılbaş occupiers and sent a delegation to Istanbul to ask for assistance in the name of Sunni solidarity. Even the ruler of Dağıstan, the Şamhal (Shamkhâl), who had close connections with the Safavi house, had sent out feelers to gauge Ottoman support for a Dağıstani independence movement some years before (MD 24, doc. 510, dated 3 May 1574/11 Muharrem 982). Since the Ottomans were at that point still observing the peace, he was told to do nothing and rule justly. Şirvan also produced a remarkable number of Sunni savants and littérateurs who became prominent in the intellectual life of the Ottoman Empire in the sixteenth century; see Hanna Sohrweide, "Dichter und Gelehrte aus dem Osten im osmanischen Reich," *Der Islam* 46 (1970): 263-302.

[21] VARİDAT, 84a-84b. John Walsh discusses the attitude of Ottoman historians toward the Safavis in "The Historiography of Ottoman-Safavi Relations in the Sixteenth Century," in *Historians of the Middle East*, eds. B. L. Lewis and P. M. Holt (London, 1962), pp. 197-211.

ties, doubtless made it easier for the practical Ottomans to view the Peace of Amasya as something of a personal contract abrogated by the death of one of the parties. The Palace proponents of the Şirvan campaign were bent on war; although Shâh Muḥammad Khudâbandeh, who succeeded his brother Ismâ'îl II in 1578, sent an envoy to try to avert hostilities and re-establish the Peace before the Ottoman armies crossed the frontier, his ambassador was summarily imprisoned. Even so, the Ottomans maintained a semblance of legality, rejecting proposals to attack territories under direct Safavi administration and limiting their initial objectives to those vassal regions where they could claim some political or religious authority.[22]

Initially the war plan called for a two-front attack: the third vezir, Lala Mustafa Paşa, was appointed to lead an Ottoman force through Georgia and Şirvan, and the fourth vezir, Sinan Paşa, would attack the Kızılbaş in the south by way of Baghdad. The two old enemies were appointed joint field marshals on 3 January 1578/22 Şevval 985.[23] Whether or not he actually opposed the war plans, once the decision had been taken Sokollu Mehmed Paşa sought to reenact the scenario of the Yemen campaign. He knew that his two most serious rivals, Lala Mustafa and Sinan Paşa, could be counted on to sabotage each other, if not the entire venture; bickering over the quality and number of troop assignments made to each of the two commanders began almost immediately. Once the conflict had reached unmanageable levels, Sokollu was once again able to establish his ascendancy over his rivals; he decided to limit the first Ottoman effort to the conquest of Transcaucasia and dismissed Sinan Paşa from his command in mid-March 1578/early 986.[24]

THE ŞİRVAN CAMPAIGN OF LALA MUSTAFA PAŞA (1578-79)

ONCE Lala Mustafa Paşa had received sole command of the expedition, campaign preparations proceeded in earnest. Finally, on 27 April 1578/20 Safer 986, the Ottoman army departed for the east. In addition to serving as

[22] Kütükoğlu, *Osmanlı*, pp. 17, 43-44. Qara Valî Beg Ûstâjlû was the Safavi ambassador who was imprisoned in Van and Bitlis for nearly a year. It is of some interest for the state of Ottoman-Safavi cultural relations at this period to note that Valî Beg passed the time by transcribing Latîfî's *tezkere* of Ottoman poets and a section of Mirkhvând's *Rawżat al-ṣafâ* devoted to the history of the Turks. Âli later accorded another Safavi ambassador, İbrâhîm Khân Turkmân, whom Âli may have met in Erzurum in 1582/early 990, a place (albeit a lowly one) in his *tezkere* of calligraphers and book illuminators, the *Menakıb-ı hünerveran* (MH, p. 54).

[23] Kütükoğlu, *Osmanlı*, p. 25. Turan, "Lala Mustafa Paşa," p. 584, incorrectly gives this as the date of Lala Mustafa's appointment as sole commander. Turan is also mistaken in stating that the joint appointment was made in May 1577/Safer 985. His statement is based on a document in MD 32, which he has dated incorrectly. The register actually deals with the last months of 985.

[24] Kütükoğlu, *Osmanlı*, p. 45.

campaign secretary, Âli functioned as Lala Mustafa Paşa's chamberlain and protocol officer, arranging for and advising the commander on the reception of dignitaries and petitioners.[25] Even so, the ambitious Âli still had no regular income-producing post, and he considered this special appointment, by its nature a temporary one outside any established lines of advancement, to be small reward for his abilities and accomplishments. He was particularly dismayed to be exiled from the literary life of the capital and sent to the war-torn extremity of the Empire, and later he complained that Lala Mustafa Paşa had not been sufficiently assiduous in taking care of his protégé.[26]

Conquest of the Caucasus was no light undertaking; it required nearly three months for Lala Mustafa Paşa and his army to reach the border province of Erzurum. From there the army marched to the plain of Çıldır, where it won a costly victory over a major Kızılbaş force which sought to block Ottoman passage through the mountains. Despite the rugged terrain and interminable late summer rainstorms, the Ottoman army reached and occupied Tiflis in late August. The ruler of Tiflis, a Georgian prince called Dâvûd Khân who had converted to Shi'i Islam and held the region as a Safavi vassal, had evacuated the city in the face of the Ottoman advance.[27]

Âli was fascinated by this exotic and largely non-Muslim region, his entry into which stimulated his curiosity and his growing interest in history. During the short time he spent in Georgia, Âli researched the history of the region, of its monarchs, and of the city of Tiflis. Twenty years later he included the results of these efforts in his *Essence of Histories*. Âli also studied the history and folklore of Dağıstan and Şirvan, using as sources both a now-lost history of Darband (Demirkapı) and interviews with knowledgeable inhabitants of the region, including the Şamhal, the ruler of Dağıstan.[28] The pride and anxiety for advancement that stand out so prominently in some of Âli's writings should not obscure the fact that he also possessed a genuinely inquiring mind and a passion for new knowledge.

From Tiflis the Ottoman army crossed over the Kabur river into Şirvan. There Ottoman detachments cooperating with their allies, the Şirvani Sun-

[25] KA, Murad/Third Vezirate of Sinan Paşa. Nur 3409, 409b; COUNSEL, II, 87 (trans.), 214 (text).

[26] COUNSEL, II, 85-87 (trans.), 213-15 (text).

[27] KA, Murad/10, Nur 3409, 308b-309b. The Ottoman army occupied Tiflis on 24 August 1578/20 Cümada II 986, and left five days later.

[28] KA, Murad/10, Nur 3409, 308b-309b (history of Georgia); Murad/10, Nur 3409, 316a-b (interview with Şamhal and outline of tribal structure and history of Dağıstan. The Şamhal's tales from Dağıstani folklore also found their way into Ottoman miniature art; one of them is bizarrely illustrated in the royal edition of Âli's *Nusretname* (MS Hazine 1365, 121a; hereafter NUSRET). The lost history of Darband Âli identifies as the *Risâleh-i Bâbîyeh* of an Iranian scholar named Yûsuf Sinân al-dîn (KA, Murad/10, Nur 3409, 314b). The work, presumably in Persian, must have been completed after early 1583/mid-991, since Âli cites it as a source for events occurring at that time (KA, Murad/20, Nur 3409, 345a-b).

nis, set about destroying the Kızılbaş garrisons in the remaining cities of Şirvan. Lala Mustafa Paşa made provisions for direct Ottoman administration of the newly conquered territories. He appointed his old friend and ally, Özdemiroğlu Osman Paşa, governor-general of Şirvan with the rank of vezir. Osman Paşa was to remain in Şirvan to guard against Safavi attempts at reoccupation, and Mustafa Paşa prepared to return with the main Ottoman force to spend the winter in Erzurum.[29] Before leaving Şirvan with the field marshal, Âli paid a visit to Osman Paşa, whom he had admired since they had first met in Egypt ten years before. Âli also bade farewell to his close friend and apprentice in *inşa* composition, Dal Mehmed Çelebi, also known by the pen name Âsafi. Dal Mehmed was a fellow protégé of Lala Mustafa Paşa and a secretary of the Imperial Council (*divan-ı hümayun kâtibi*), whose subsequent career illustrates the possibilities open to young secretaries in wartime. When Lala Mustafa Paşa left Şirvan he appointed Dal Mehmed Çelebi to the private service of Özdemiroğlu Osman Paşa, to whom he became recording secretary and administrative assistant (*tezkereci*),[30] and also gave him the public charge of carrying out the tax census (*tahrir*) of the new province. Dal Mehmed's salary was in the form of a *timar* assignment, and the military and administrative skill he displayed in a fluid frontier situation, as well as the patronage of Osman Paşa, enabled him quickly to win promotion to the rank of *sancak* governor (*sancak beği*). Lit-

[29] Kütükoğlu, *Osmanlı*, pp. 149-66; NUSRET and KA give meticulously detailed accounts of the division of the new territories into *sancak*s and *vilayet*s, and represent Kütükoğlu's major sources on this topic.

[30] The nature of the office of *tezkereci*, in which capacity Dal Mehmed was appointed to Osman Paşa's service, is somewhat vague. In the central administration the term seems to cover two types of service. In both the Imperial Council and the *divan*s of major state functionaries such as the grand vezir and chief military judges, *tezkereci*s were responsible for reading aloud memos on items of business and for recording the decisions taken on each. However, the term also seems to apply to a rather broad spectrum of scribal functions. Each major section of the financial service, for example, included a *tezkereci* who recorded appointments and complaints, as well as fulfilling a number of other scribal duties under the *defterdar*. He probably also served the *defterdar* in the function of administrative secretary, much as the *tezkereci*s of other high officials did, which would account for the common title. The wide variety of functions performed by *tezkereci*s of all sorts is a reflection of the undifferentiated character of the Ottoman bureaucracy until the mid-sixteenth century. Until this time, many scribal and administrative duties were performed by members of the personal retinues of the chancellor and treasurer, rather than by career bureaucrats or designated functionaries. A *tezkereci* in the financial service could be promoted to the rank of *defterdar*, while the two *tezkereci*s of the *divan-ı hümayun* could be promoted to the office of *re'isülküttab*, chief chancery officer under the *nişancı*. About *tezkereci*s in provincial service we know little beyond the fact that the entourage of a provincial *defterdar* included an official with this title. Âli's statement implies that Dal Mehmed was Osman Paşa's personal *tezkereci*. However, he was also assigned important financial duties, which indicates that he also served under the *defterdar* of Şirvan, Göğüszade Mustafa Çelebi. On the office of *tezkereci*, see Uzunçarşılı, *Merkez*, pp. 137, 236-37, 238, 345; Matuz, *Kanzleiwesen*, pp. 40-43, 45-48, 50-53, 60, 71, 113; İnalcık, *Empire*, pp. 101-102.

erary activity helped Dal Mehmed to consolidate his position; much as Âli later recounted the exploits of Lala Mustafa Paşa in a volume devoted to the Şirvan campaign, Âsafi celebrated the acts of Özdemiroğlu in his *Şecâ'atname*, the *Book of Bravery*. Âsafi was later captured by the Kızılbaş, who finally released him in 1585/993. Âsafi was made governor-general of Kefe (Caffa) in the Crimea, and three years later became governor-general of Şemahı (Şirvan), thus completing a remarkably smooth and rapid progress from scribe, to financial official and member of a paşa's household, to *sancak beği*, to paşa. The example of his former companion-in-arms and student was probably prominent in Âli's mind when he later compared what he saw as his own lack of advancement with the success of his contemporaries.[31]

By early October 1578 Âli had received a real appointment in the financial branch (*maliye*) of the central bureaucracy; he was made registrar of *timars* (*timar defterdarı*) for the province of Aleppo.[32] The post, which entailed responsibility for the records and accounts of all *timar* assignments within the *vilayet*, was a relatively modest one that carried with it a revenue grant of about eighty thousand *akçe*. The registrar of *timars* was the lowest of the three officials who represented the central treasury in the largest and most important Ottoman provinces; above him was the intendant of *zeâmet*-holders (*timar kedhüdası, defter kedhüdası*), who had charge of *zeâmet* accounts, and finally the finance director (*hazine defterdarı, mal defterdarı*), who was the chief representative of the treasury and supervisor of all tax

[31] Selim/7, Nur 3409, 243a; Murad/10, Nur 3409, 314a, and Nur 3406, 225a; MENŞE, 257a (on visiting Osman Paşa). Babinger (GOW, p. 117) is incorrect in identifying this Mehmed Çelebi with Okçuzade Mehmed Paşa, who later served as treasurer and governor of Cyprus and Aleppo. See also KA, Murad/20, Nur 3409, 344a, on Âsafi's capture by the Kızılbaş, and Kütükoğlu, *Osmanlı*, p. 149. According to a chronogram found in LAYİHAT, 149a-b, Dal Mehmed became *beğlerbeği* of Şirvan in 1587-88/996.

[32] In a petition which Âli later submitted to Sultan Murad, published by John R. Walsh, "Müverrih Âli'nin bir Istidânamesi," TM 13 (1958):132, Âli gives 1579/987 as the date of his appointment to this post. However, other evidence makes it clear that this is an error and that the assignment must have occurred by the time of Lala Mustafa Paşa's departure from Ereş, 8 October 1578/6 Şaban 986. In referring to his visit to Osman Paşa at about this time (see preceding footnote) Âli mentions returning from Şirvan "with the *timar defterdarlığı* of Aleppo." Another letter in MENŞE, 231b-232a, reports a conversation between Şeref Han, the Kurdish emir and author of the *Sharafnâmeh*, and Husrev Paşa, governor-general of Van. Şeref Han, who had grown up at the Safavi court, returned to Ottoman service as vassal ruler of his ancestral territory of Bitlis. Husrev Paşa received him at Van on 10 December 1578/10 Şevval 986 (Kütükoğlu, *Osmanlı*), p. 65. According to Âli, who later became close to Husrev Paşa, Şeref Han admired the style of the diploma of investiture (given in full KA, Murad/11, Nur 3409, 319b-320a), which Âli had composed, and asked what position its author held. Husrev replied that Âli was *timar defterdarı* with a salary of 80,000 *akçe*, which purportedly struck Şeref Han as far too little for one of such talent. The stated salary gives the anecdote a ring of authenticity, since thirty-two years later the income for the *timar defterdarı* of Aleppo was given as 81,146 *akçe* by Ayn-ı Ali Efendi, *Kavanin-i Âl-i Osman* (Istanbul, 1863/1280), p. 27. Finally, a third letter (MENŞE, 232b) gives the dates of Âli's tenure in this post as 986-91.

collection and revenue disbursal in the province. The authority of the finance director was independent of that of the governor-general, and while the two lesser provincial financial officers might be appointed from the ranks of local *za'ims*, the director was almost invariably an experienced *maliye* professional sent from Istanbul.[33]

Âli did not take up residence in Aleppo itself for another two years, but since the landed cavalry forces of that province were present on the campaign, he probably assumed his new duties in the field. Hitherto he had occupied positions that essentially constituted personal secretarial service to an individual: scribe to Prince Selim, confidential secretary to Lala Mustafa Paşa, chancery chief to a frontier *beğ*. Such appointments as those Âli had held were by nature somewhat unstable and outside the mainstream careers in the central administrative apparatus, in which seniority, ability, and personal connections enabled one to proceed through a series of hierarchically defined promotions. A great many sixteenth-century Ottoman bureaucrats began their careers in personal service to prominent political figures. The essence of the patronage system, however, was a process analogous to *çıkma*, the graduation procedure whereby the personal slaves of the sultan, after requisite training, were assigned to administrative positions outside the Palace, from which point they would advance through the established military administrative order. Similarly, the protégés, retainers, and slaves of the *kul*s had to make the jump from household to public service, within which latter context they could, if all went well, rise to high rank and benefit their patrons.[34] Entry into a regular administrative career track within the central government apparatus offered greater opportunity for advancement and gain than did personal service, as well as a certain security. A paşa's retainers might easily lose everything with the death or disgrace of their master, while those who reached the middle and upper levels of financial, chancery, or military service were valued for their expertise and rank. As often as not, dismissal from a bureaucratic post was only temporary, and would be followed by reappointment to a post equivalent to or higher than the one lost.[35]

[33] Ayn-ı Ali, p. 27, affirms that Aleppo boasted all three financial offices, on which see Kunt, *Servants*, p. 28. In the conversation referred to above between Husrev Paşa and Şeref Han, Âli refers to his salary as "80,000 *akçe yazar hâss*." This obscure term probably refers to the fact that, although the grant was technically a *zeâmet*, it functioned as a *hass* in that it was income inhering in an office rather than in an individual. Such a *zeâmet* was therefore in a different category from *timar* grants given solely for military service, which could be inherited; cf. Pakalın, I, 420, 750-51.

[34] For a discussion of one aspect of transfer from "private" to "public" service, see İ. Metin Kunt, "Kulların Kulları," *Boğaziçi Üniversitesi Dergisi: Beşeri Bilimler* 3 (1975):27-42, in which the incorporation of the slave retinues of individual *kul*s into the Palace system is discussed. See also Kunt, *Servants*, pp. 44-47.

[35] For documentation, see Fleischer, "Âli," pp. 241-43, and the lists of chancellors and

Âli's appointment to financial office, then, represents the beginning of an important new phase in his career. Professionally, little changed for him, for below the highest levels of the financial and chancery services there was little differentiation of function between scribes who worked in one branch and those who worked in the other. But from this point onward Âli would define and express his career expectations primarily in terms of the pecking order of the central Ottoman bureaucratic establishment. It is necessary only to recall where secretarial and financial office led Âsafi to comprehend how crucial this assignment could be to Âli.

Lala Mustafa Paşa and Âli spent the winter of 1578-79/986-87 in Erzurum. The elements of the main army were dispersed to winter quarters in the border region, in order to prevent a Kızılbaş counteroffensive. The following spring and summer were spent primarily in rebuilding the border fortress of Kars, which had been destroyed in accordance with provisions of the Peace of Amasya, and secondarily in sparring negotiations with the Safavis. Âli continued in his function as chief campaign secretary; he had charge of a protracted correspondence with Ṭoqmaq Khân, the Safavi governor of Erivan (Revan), who had made peace overtures to Lala Mustafa Paşa and hinted that he might offer an Ottoman allegiance. Âli even penned a letter to Shâh Muḥammad Khudâbandeh (who was rumored to be approaching Kars), demanding acceptable peace terms and threatening an Ottoman attack on the Safavi heartlands should these not be forthcoming.[36] Despite such epistolary bravado, the Ottoman occupation of Şirvan was in difficulty. Almost immediately after the withdrawal of the main force in late 1578/986, the Kızılbaş retook most of the region. Özdemiroğlu Osman Paşa, his troops depleted by desertion, had been forced to retreat to the citadel of Darband. Georgia, too, was endangered; it was only with great difficulty that Lala Mustafa Paşa was able to send a relief force to the starving Ottoman garrison of Tiflis, which had been besieged by the Kızılbaş for four months. Osman Paşa was released from his citadel only in October 1579/Şa'ban 987, when Mehmed Giray Han and his Crimean Tatar troops arrived to retake Şirvan for the Ottoman sultan.[37]

---

treasurers of the late sixteenth century given by İ. H. Danişmend, *İzahlı Osmanlı Tarihi Kronolojisi*, 5 vols. (Istanbul, 1971), V, 235-59, 322-30.

[36] Kütükoğlu, *Osmanlı*, pp. 69-76; KA, Murad/12, Nur 3409, 326b-237a. Âli asserts that this letter reached the shah after he had already left Tabriz, and that if frightened him into turning back, a claim not supported by any other sources. Nevertheless, Âli was later to use this "incident" as an example of the power of the pen, particularly his own. He also proclaimed himself, not without some justice, a polylingual master of prose style whose *inşa* was approved by people learned in the Iranian tradition as well as by Ottoman scholars; see MENŞE, 229a-235b, 238a-238b.

[37] Kütükoğlu, *Osmanlı*, pp. 78-103.

THE CHANGING OF THE GUARD: ERZURUM (1579-80)

FOR Lala Mustafa Paşa, reverses in Şirvan were harbingers of a more personal disaster. At the end of August 1579, a freak snowstorm struck Kars, where the field marshal was awaiting news from Şirvan. His troops dispersed in panic and he was forced to return to Erzurum with a tiny retinue for a second winter.[38] Almost immediately thereafter news reached Lala Mustafa Paşa that Grand Vezir Sokollu Mehmed Paşa had been murdered, and his place had been taken by the second vezir, Ahmed Paşa.[39] The news was double-edged, for it meant Lala Mustafa Paşa now became second vezir of the Dome, next in line for the grand vezirate, but it also meant that his most powerful protector against the machinations of Koca Sinan Paşa had disappeared. The latter lost no time in taking advantage of the situation, and almost immediately after Ahmed Paşa's investiture persuaded him to recall Lala Mustafa Paşa and to appoint himself, Sinan, in his place.[40]

Mustafa Paşa received news of his dismissal and recall to Istanbul over two months later; inauspiciously enough, it was delivered to him at Erzurum by Sinan Paşa's personal messenger.[41] A purge of Lala Mustafa's protégés from government service began almost at once. Many of these were charged with corruption and two were imprisoned. Certainly Sinan Paşa's vindictiveness had much to do with the ferocity with which this purge was conducted; for years afterwards he continued to show considerable animosity toward those relatives and friends of Lala Mustafa Paşa who were not dismissed at this point. Even so, the scandals surrounding Lala Mustafa's handling of affairs were quite real. Âli himself speaks quite frankly to this point, saying that Lala Mustafa Paşa was old and less wise than one of his years ought to be. Specifically, the paşa refused to heed Âli's and others' warnings about the depravity and corruption of two of his protégés, Lalezarzade Ahmed Çelebi and Taczade İsma'il Çelebi. The former, the son of the former treasurer Lalezar Mehmed Çelebi, was finance director of Er-

[38] KA, Murad/12, Nur 3409, 329b-330a. This passage provides evidence that Âli used solar as well as lunar *hicri* dating in his history. He incorrectly equates the end of the first week of Receb 987 (29-30 July 1579) with the end of August; he probably meant Şa'ban rather than Receb, which would yield a correct equivalence.

[39] KA, Murad/14, Nur 3409, 331a-b. The news of the assassination, which occurred on 10 September/20 Şa'ban, took only two weeks to reach the frontier (24 September/6 Ramazan).

[40] Kütükoğlu, *Osmanlı*, p. 104, note 140, notes an MD document roughly datable to 20-25 Şa'ban, the days immediately following Sokollu's death, which refers to Koca Sinan Paşa as "*serdar*." Âli (KA, Murad/16, Nur 3409, 332a-b) says that Sinan had intrigued against Lala Mustafa Paşa since the beginning of the campaign, proclaiming himself the abler commander and promising great conquests.

[41] KA, Murad/16, Nur 3409, 332b; the date was 26 December 1579/19 Zulka'de 987.

zurum, and had also gained control of the finances of Aleppo, Damascus, and Diyar Bakır, from the treasuries of which many campaign expenses were met. Lalezarzade, his person and his unprecendented fiscal authority protected by the field marshal, became notorious for office selling and embezzlement. Taczade İsma'il, Lala Mustafa Paşa's confidential secretary, was equally infamous for bribery, incompetence, and addiction to narcotics. These two members of the former field marshal's retinue were arrested by Palace guards (*kapıcı*) when Lala Mustafa Paşa's party reached Tokat, and were immediately transported to prison in Istanbul. Furthermore, Âli charges, Lala Mustafa Paşa relied heavily on the bad advice and unreliable intelligence of Güllizade Mehmed Beğ, the *sancak beği* of Beyşehir and an old ally from Egyptian days, and Mirza-Ali Beğ, the *sancak beği* of Pasin, whom Âli accuses of being a crypto-Kızılbaş traitor. The paşa was disgraced by his most important subordinates, and the Porte almost immediately issued an order that no appointments or *timar* grants made by Lala Mustafa Paşa be honored.[42]

Âli had kept his distance from the field marshal's favorites and from Lala Mustafa Paşa himself, insofar as the latter allowed his subordinates' depradations to continue. Thanks to his caution and a reputation for genuine honesty, Âli avoided any guilt by association; the frequency with which he repeats this in his letters suggests that there was indeed such a danger. "While those criminals who were intimate with the field marshal were bound and fettered [for their crimes], I did not demolish the edifice of my honor and sense of shame."[43] He also preserved his political independence; immediately after the news of Ahmed Paşa's appointment as grand vezir reached Erzurum, Âli addressed an ode of congratulations to him in which he offered his services and decried the nepotistic practice of the recently deceased Sokollu Mehmed Paşa. In a covering letter Âli expressed his hope that the new grand vezir would honor people of learning for their accomplishments rather than their connections, and requested that he be made chancellor, or at least promoted from his post as *timar* registrar to the finance directorship (*mal defterdarlığı*) of a major province.[44] Having entered

[42] COUNSEL, II, 12-19 (trans.), 125-34 (text); Âli suggests that Lalezarzade came by his propensity for malfeasance and sexual depravity honestly, insofar as his father had gained a considerable reputation in both areas. The *ru'us* document revoking Lala Mustafa Paşa's appointments (KPT 236, p. 221) is dated 1580/early 988.

[43] MENŞE, 233a.

[44] MENŞE, 268a-270b; VARİDAT 37a-38a. This ode represents Âli's first presentation of this theme, which he later harped on in the COUNSEL; Sokollu's death allowed him to speak freely. Nepotism is in fact the only major complaint Âli lodges against Sokollu, whose genuine abilities he admits. Given the role that Sokollu had played in limiting Lala Mustafa Paşa's advancement and in hampering Âli's own career (at least as he saw it), this accusation is hardly surprising. At the same time Âli was on good terms with Sokollu's son Hasan Paşa, the *beğlerbeği* of Damascus during the Şirvan campaign, who undertook a heroic relief mission to Tiflis (KA, Murad/12, Nur 3409, 329a-b).

the lower ranks of the central bureaucracy of the Empire, Âli now framed his requests for advancement in terms of those posts that represented the upper reaches of the chancery and financial career lines.

When Lala Mustafa Paşa departed for Istanbul, Husrev Paşa, the governor-general of Van, was appointed garrison commander and guardian (*muhafız*) of Erzurum. He was also ordered to depute (as *ka'immakam*) for the new field marshal until the latter should reach the front. Âli was instructed to continue to serve as campaign secretary and to assist Husrev Paşa. These arrangements were complicated by Husrev Paşa's sudden dismissal from the governor-generalship of Van soon after the departure of Lala Mustafa Paşa; he had Âli compose a letter to Hoca Sa'düddin, in which he complained of his unexpected dismissal and of the disorganization wrought by the change of command. Âli was prevented from taking up his post in Aleppo that winter of 1579-80, at the end of which he was sent to Trabzon to supervise the unloading and storage of grain supplies for the coming spring campaign.[45] At the Black Sea port he became acquainted with its *sancak beği*, Ömer Beğ, a longtime Sokollu protégé. This experience later provided the basis for some of Âli's pithier observations on the abuses of authority that occurred in the Ottoman provinces. He was particularly struck by the greed, coarseness, and voracious sexual appetite of the government's chief representative in Trabzon, who, despite his seventy years, required a temporary wife—usually an unwilling village maid—each night when traveling for purposes of carrying out a tax census.[46]

Back in Istanbul the second vezir Lala Mustafa Paşa worked furiously to recoup his own influence and combat that of Sinan. Early in 1580/988 the grand vezir, Ahmed Paşa, died, leaving the field to the two old rivals, who were now the senior members of the Imperial Council. Although Lala Mustafa Paşa should have succeeded to the post, according to the customary usage established in Sultan Süleyman's time, the third vezir, Sinan Paşa, argued that Lala Mustafa would only sabotage the campaign of which he, Sinan, was now commander. For a period the seal of office was given to neither, and Lala Mustafa performed the administrative duties of grand vezir without confirmation. Sinan Paşa, maneuvering for position, delayed his departure from Istanbul as long as he could; shortly after he was forced to leave for Erzurum on 25 April 1580/10 Rebi' II 988, the grand vezir's seal of office (*mühr*) was sent to him.[47]

Âli had good reason to fear Sinan Paşa's arrival at Erzurum, for he was

[45] KA, Murad/16, Nur 3409, 332a-b; COUNSEL, II, 86 (trans.), 213-14 (text). Two letters which Âli wrote for the *ka'immakam* Husrev Paşa are included in the *Nusretname* (Kütükoğlu, *Osmanlı*, p. 104), and show that he indeed served as Husrev Paşa's secretary. The letter of complaint occurs in MENŞE, 222b-223a; Husrev Paşa learned of his dismissal on 21 February 1580/5 Muharrem 988.

[46] COUNSEL, II, 22-25 (trans.), 137-41 (text).

[47] Kütükoğlu, *Osmanlı*, p. 105; Turan, "Lala Mustafa Paşa," pp. 591-93.

identified as a member of the Lala Mustafa Paşa camp. Sinan Paşa, as campaign commander, could now operate freely in the field and he set about having his old rival's allies removed from their posts; just as quickly, he had his own family members and adherents appointed to recently vacated positions. Apparently the new field marshal did indeed try to have Âli dismissed after he arrived at the frontier capital of Erzurum in June-July 1580; but Sinan Paşa, unable to find any valid charges against him such as those that had brought about the fall of other Lala Mustafa Paşa protégés, was forced to confirm Âli in his post. Âli, though bitter at his lack of promotion, felt lucky to escape with his job.[48] Spared the greater torment of dismissal, Âli was subjected to the lesser one of trying to survive and advance under a commander personally hostile to him. About a year after these events Âli voiced his feelings in the *Counsel for Sultans*:

> Those allegations of extortion and rumors and complaints of oppression which were brought against the other protégés [of Lala Mustafa Paşa] were not directed at or circulated [about me]. [Sinan Paşa] perceived that the skirt of my honor was unsullied by the dust of unlawful aggression, and that the hem of [my garment of] truth and sincerity was free of the soil of injustice and oppression, like a shining mirror. Knowing this, he should have encouraged me and rewarded me with deserved promotions, or given even more than was expected, in accordance with his own claims to justice and equity. Instead he contented himself with not dismissing me, and thus made me distinguished among the great, as if I had been given a new post.[49]

For the remainder of the year Âli, solely in his capacity as *timar* registrar of Aleppo, accompanied the Aleppine forces on what amounted to a poorly orchestrated and unsuccessful tour of Georgia conducted by Sinan Paşa. The field marshal left Erzurum in mid-July 1580 and received the seal of office that made him the second most powerful man in the Empire around the end of August 1580, while still on his tour of inspection. Some time thereafter the news reached the army that Lala Mustafa Paşa was dead.[50] As

[48] COUNSEL, II, 86-87 (trans.), 214-15 (text); MENŞE, 220b; LAYİHAT, 138a, contains two short poems reviling a vezir, most probably Sinan, who has accused Âli of financial impropriety and who has sent *çavuş*es to investigate him; see also Kütükoğlu, *Osmanlı*, pp. 105-106. Before his return to Erzurum, Sinan Paşa investigated and dimissed the governor-general of Erzurum, Mehmed Paşa, a relative of Lala Mustafa, and replaced him with his (Sinan's) own elder brother Mahmud Paşa (KA, Murad/18, Nur 3409, 335b). Âli notes in FURSAT, 24b-25b, that as soon as he received confirmation of his appointment to the grand vezirate, Sinan Paşa secured other appointments for relatives. His son Mehmed was given the *sancak* of Kastamonu with a 500,000-*akçe hass*, and another relative named Ahmed Beğ received the *sancak* of Maʿarra in Syria with 300,000 *akçe*.

[49] COUNSEL, II, 87 (trans.), 214-15 (text).

[50] Kütükoğlu, *Osmanlı*, pp. 106-109.

welcome as this communication must have been to Sinan Paşa, it was a bitter blow to Âli, who was compiling the letters he had composed during his tenure as campaign secretary into an historical work celebrating Lala Mustafa Paşa's conquests in Şirvan, the *Nusretname, The Book of Victory*. Âli had to write a new ending to the work, describing the death of his longtime patron.

Âli thus lost his most powerful protector and his hopes for appointment to high office.[51] More than this, the deaths of Sokollu Mehmed and Lala Mustafa Paşas signified the passing of an era, for they had come to political prominence under Sultan Süleyman and presented living links with a monarch whom Âli and later writers would idealize for his sagacity and administrative rectitude. The attrition of the old guard paralleled momentous changes in the character of political life that came about under the successors of Süleyman and Selim; only Koca Sinan Paşa, portrayed by most Ottoman historians as one of the most villainous figures in Ottoman history, survived his peers to live into the reign of Mehmed III, wreaking political havoc all the while. In November 1580/early Şevval 988 Sinan Paşa returned to Erzurum to begin preparations for the following spring's campaign. Âli was finally able to go to Aleppo for the winter, but before he did so Sinan Paşa ordered him to compose a sequel to the *The Book of Victory*. Sinan wished Âli to describe his own Georgian excursion and the conquests he hoped to make the following year, and the irony of Âli's situation was certainly not lost on the grand vezir. Âli entitled the work *Fursatname, The Book of Opportunity*, and only abandoned it when Sinan Paşa suddenly returned to Istanbul in July 1581, leaving his projected conquests unmade.[52]

[51] KA, Murad/17, Nur 3409, 333b-334b; COUNSEL, II, 85-86 (trans.), 212-13 (text), according to which Lala Mustafa Paşa supported Âli's request to be made chancellor or finance director, but with less persistence than was desirable. Âli's obituary for his patron is quite frank, noting his excessive ambition, cupidity, and poor judgment in choosing some of his subordinates. These defects were balanced by bravery, piety, and military ability. Âli credits Lala Mustafa Paşa with having had a premonition of his death seventeen days before the event, which took place on 7 August 1580/25 Cümada II 988, when Lala Mustafa was more than seventy years old. The premonition took the form of buying a burial plot next to the shrine of Ebu Eyyub el-Ensari in Istanbul, where Lala Mustafa Paşa's gravestone is still one of the more prominent monuments in the area.

[52] Kütükoğlu, *Osmanlı*, pp. 108-10. The unique manuscript of the *Fursatname* was only recently discovered in Berlin by Manfred Götz (*Die türkische Handschriften in Deutschland*, IV [Wiesbaden, 1979], 214-18); I am grateful to the Preussische Staatsbibliothek for providing me with a photocopy of the work. The manuscript is almost certainly either an autograph or a copy made for Âli's own use; the handwriting and certain misspellings are identical with those in the MS Husrev Paşa 311, which was copied either by or for Âli. The work is incomplete; many dates are blank, and the narrative breaks off abruptly on f. 53b. On 4a-b the *Nusretname* is referred to as already completed, and in the COUNSEL, which was largely completed by Zulka'de 989 (I, 10), Âli lists the *Fursatname* as one of his works (II, 59-60 [trans.], 187 [text]). Âli clearly had little enthusiasm for his subject, for the work is uninspired as well as incomplete. He most probably dropped work on it at the first opportunity, i.e., when Sinan

THE "POISON YEARS": ALEPPO (1581-83)

THE YEAR 1581 marked the beginning of a new phase in Âli's life, as he himself was keenly aware. It was his third year in the same post, and his third year on a campaign from which the future held little promise of respite; in the spring he accompanied the newly appointed governor-general of Aleppo, Ahmed Paşa b. Çerkes İskender Paşa, and the rest of the Aleppine forces to guard the Van frontier during the campaign season. Âli only returned to Aleppo in November after helping to organize the repair of the fortress of Van.[53] The personal traumas of the preceding months, the hardships imposed by constant campaigning on the frontier, and professional disappointment wrought a significant transformation in Âli's outlook; the hopeful careerist became a bitter man with an almost obsessive concern with the functioning and malfunctioning of the Ottoman state. At the age of forty-one, Âli later wrote, he found that his youthful hopes had faded, and that his life had become poisonous. To symbolize this psychological moment Âli, the man of letters, closed his first *divan* of poetry, *The Elegant Inspirations*, and began a new one, which he would call *Intimations of Truth (Layihat ül-hakika)*.[54]

Life on the frontier in wartime was hard, and Âli experienced constant financial as well as psychological problems. From his 80,000-*akçe* grant as

---

Paşa departed. Sinan Paşa's commissioning of the work to cover his activities in both 988 and 989 is described in a passage on ff. 7a-b, in which Âli says that he is *timar* registrar of Aleppo and that he has been in Sinan Paşa's service. FURSAT adds almost nothing to the KA account of these events. However, it does provide the text of the Turkish translation of Khudâbandeh's offer of peace, which Maqṣûd Khân, governor of Tabriz, carried to Istanbul in 1580 (ff. 10b-13b). This may be the original of the copy cited by Kütükoğlu, *Osmanlı*, p. 106. Âli also refers to a special friend and pupil called Sâfi, who was with Âli on this second Georgian expedition (f. 25b-26b, also noted KA, Murad/18, Nur 3409, 335b-336a). This Sâfi is probably the author of a *Cihadname* (*Book of Holy War*), a history of the exploits of Hayreddin Paşa Barbaros. Charles Rieu mistakenly identifies him with the slightly later Mustafa Sâfi who authored a continuation of the *Tac üt-tevarih* (C. Rieu, *Catalogue of the Turkish Manuscripts in the British Museum* [London, 1888], p. 61; GOW, p. 146).

A *ru'us* document dated 30 November 1580/22 Şevval 988, KPT 237, p. 211, supports the supposition that Âli went to Aleppo at this time. It authorizes increases (*terakki*) and initial *timar* grants (*ibtida*) for eleven men of "Mustafa Efendi, registrar of *timar*s, in Aleppo."

[53] COUNSEL, II, 70 (trans.), 195-196 (text), and the colophon of MS Husrev Paşa 311, which states that the work was completed 29 November 1581/3 Zulka'de 989 in Aleppo; MENŞE, 257a, referring to the repair of Van. According to KPT 238, p. 308, Ahmed Paşa (son of Çerkes İskender Paşa) replaced an aged Ahmed as governor of Aleppo on 25 March 1581/19 Safer 989.

[54] COUNSEL, II, 70 (trans.), 195-196 (text). According to LAYİHAT (3b-4a), the first *divan* (VARİDAT) contains poetry composed between 964 and 988, while the second comprises verses dating from the period 988-1000. Âli's characterization of this period occurs in an autobiographical ode in LAYİHAT, 147b.

timar registrar of Aleppo, he had to meet his administrative and personal expenses, which included providing for a family, a personal retinue, and armed retainers. In fact, his salary covered only two-thirds of his obligations, and he was forced into debt in order to meet the remainder. Whether these difficulties were the result of inflation, prodigality, or of Âli's honesty and reluctance to supplement his income by graft, or all of these, Âli complained vociferously about the inadequacy of his salary.[55]

Indeed, Âli had already resolved, by the autumn of 1580, to somehow have himself promoted out of his "valueless post," as he called it. He addressed appeals to anyone who might help to have him appointed chancellor, or at least finance director of a major province. He sought to curry favor with two acquaintances who had recently gained importance in Istanbul, Azmi Efendi and Nişancı Mehmed Paşa. The first had just been named religious tutor to the Crown Prince, Mehmed, while the second was a distinguished former treasurer and chancellor who was promoted from the latter post to a vezirate at just this time. Professing himself an old well-wisher of Mehmed Paşa, who had previously served as governor-general of Aleppo, Âli asked the vezir to designate him as his successor in the chancellorship in place of the "ignorant" Hamze Çelebi, who had been appointed to the position after Mehmed Paşa's promotion.[56] Soon after dispatching pleas to these luminaries, in the winter of 1580-81, Âli completed his *Nusretname, The Book of Victory*. He submitted his work to the Porte, together with a covering letter signed by a governor-general. Âli himself composed the letter, which sings Âli's praises as a stylist, endorses the *Book*, and then requests that he, instead of Hamze Çelebi, be appointed chancellor.[57]

[55] MENŞE, 270b-272b, to Nişancı Mehmed Paşa after his promotion to vezirate (ca. August 1580). See also 229a-232b, a letter of recommendation for Âli sent to Sultan Murad by an unidentified *beğlerbeği* at this time, and 218a-219a, a letter sent to Hoca Sa'düddin by Âli a year later. Yet another letter, datable to 1581/late 989, contains a request for a loan so that Âli can redeem the collateral he gave for a 500 gold-piece (*altun*) loan he had taken out the previous year (225a-256a). Shortly after this, Âli submitted two petitions in verse to the grand vezir and Sultan Murad (257a-258a 258a-258b). In still another message (232b-233b), Âli complains that while his salary yields 2,000 *altun* for his expenses, 3,000 are necessary to enable him to live.

[56] MENŞE, 265a-266a, 274b-275b, are letters of congratulations to Azmi, who was appointed tutor to Şehzade Mehmed on 26 November 1580/18 Sevval 988 (KPT 238, p. 161); MENŞE, 270b-272a, a congratulatory epistle to Nişancı Mehmed Paşa on his promotion from the *nişancılık* to a vezirate. SELANİKİ, p. 161, dates Nişancı Mehmed Paşa's promotion to some time soon after July-August 1580/Cümada II 988. Selâniki was in Mehmed Paşa's service for four years, and praises him highly, especially for his knowledge of *kanun* and his insistence upon following "the ways of the predecessors without deviation." It is of particular interest that Selâniki, who admired Âli and was his exact contemporary, should voice such a preoccupation, and that Âli should apply directly to Mehmed Paşa.

[57] MENŞE, 229a-232b. The letter states that the *Nusretname* has been completed and is being presented. It also recites Âli's virtues, qualifications for the post of *nişancı*, his fifteen published literary works up to the (current) age of forty, and the injustice of his present circum-

Âli summarized his problems and aspirations in a message he sent at this time to an unidentified vezir: after three years in office he has spent all that he had saved from his previous *timar* and *zeâmet* assignments, and he has been forced into debt simply in order to live and perform his duties. Such a post, he elaborates, is little reward for his services, but he is unable to secure a promotion under Sinan Paşa due to his identification as an adherent of Lala Mustafa Paşa. His situation is so difficult that it can only be properly explained by the bearer of the letter, the (Bektaşi) sheikh of the Janissary Corps, Şeyh Husrev. Finally, Âli complains that the newly appointed chancellor, Hamze Çelebi, is an ignoramus who should not have the post. He explains that, while the chancellorship is in the chancery scribal career line (*kitâbet*) in which he (Âli) has been involved for many years, the post is one given on the basis of ability and *not* seniority (*eskilik*). Therefore the addressee can and should have Âli appointed chancellor, since his ability has been demonstrated and his lack of seniority will not be an obstacle. Failing this, Âli asks for any post in the capital, or even dismissal and recall so that he can get out of Aleppo.[58]

These same requests and complaints recur throughout Âli's correspondence over the next two years, during which period another theme gradually gains prominence. Why, Âli asks, are all those around him being promoted in accordance with the hierarchy of posts stipulated by imperial law (*kanun*), while he remains a lowly *timar* registrar? In a plea to Hoca Sa'düddin penned by Âli in 1582-83, he complains that after four years on campaign he is still a financial official in Aleppo:

> Since I came to Aleppo the governorship has changed hands five times, and a number of deputy *defterdar*s [*defter kedhüdası*] have had their assignments changed. As for this insignificant servant, I have thus far been unable to secure any advancement, remaining where I am. Apart from this, since I have no connection with powerful people, a few deputies of low status have been promoted over me, against imperial law [*kanun-ı padişahi*]; my debasement and misery have been made complete with such betrayal.[59]

Âli's perception of his own professional situation emerges quite clearly from his plaints. A learned and able man, he had spent twenty years trying to build a career, only to have it blocked by the death of his patron and the

stances. It asks that the sultan not allow Âli, who has no veziral patron, to remain in peripheral provincial posts (*kenar menasıbı*). The dating of the letter is provided by the reference to the recent appointment of Hamze Çelebi (see preceding and following footnotes).

[58] MENŞE, 220a-222a. According to Danişmend, V, 324, Hamze Çelebi (Paşa) held the post of *nişancı* for the first time between August 1580 and February 1581 (26 Cümada II 988-Muharrem 989).

[59] MENŞE, 218b.

animosity of the grand vezir. The chancellorship had long been Âli's heart's desire, and his longing for this office betokened more than a mere craving for high position. It was, rather, closely related to the other major concern that Âli's writings of this period manifest: a preoccupation with articulating and examining the ideals and realities of the "Ottoman Way" embodied in *kanun*. These imperial "customary" (*urfi*) laws, derived from both established usage and royal decree, operated parallel to and supplemented the *şeri'at*, the Islamic law that was theoretically paramount in any Muslim state. The dynastic codes, written and unwritten, were promulgated as law and codified primarily between the reigns of the Conqueror Mehmed and Sultan Süleyman.[60] The *kanun-ı osmani*, the Ottoman Code, governed matters ranging from taxation to court ceremonial, from officials' salaries to the paths by which they might be promoted. For Âli *kanun* was prescriptive as well as descriptive; insofar as it defined the structure of government and the nature of Ottoman society, it was *kanun* that made the Empire distinctively Ottoman and enshrined its ideals. The very nature of a dynastic law that was mutable, based on precedent and imperial discretion, and was to some extent unwritten, required that a specialized authority be appointed to oversee and interpret it. This was the chancellor, to the history of whose office Âli devoted much thought and ink at this time. While the chancellor had originally been charged with affixing the sultan's signature-seal (*tuğra*) to imperial orders and other documents, he came to be the supreme expert on imperial law. Âli characterized him as the "*müfti* of *kanun*," who pronounced on matters of secular law just as the Chief Jurisconsult (*şeyhülislam, müfti*) made all final decisions on *şeri'at*.[61] Âli's analogy, which was repeated by later commentators on Ottoman government, is a telling one. It points up the degree to which *kanun* gained importance and prestige in the sixteenth century—so much so that it could be likened to the Holy Law—and its supreme authority to the premier religious figure in the land. It also hints at an important aspect of the chancellor's duties; not only was *kanun* functionally analogous to the *şeri'at*, but its strictures theoretically had to be in accord with the provisions of the superior law. Therefore, the chancellor ought to

[60] The most lucid explanation of the nature and development of *kanun* is that of Halil İnalcık, "Suleiman the Lawgiver and Ottoman Law," *Archivum Ottomanicum* I (1969):105-38. A more detailed account of the functioning of penal aspects of Ottoman law and of the relationship between *kanun* and *şeri'at* is given by Uriel Heyd, *Studies in Old Ottoman Criminal Law*, ed. V. L. Ménage (Oxford, 1973), pp. 167-207. See also H. İnalcık, "Ḳânûn," "Kânûnnâme," EI².

[61] COUNSEL, I, 50 (trans.), 140 (text); MENŞE, 221b, 229a, 234a. Âli later included an account of the history of the *nişancılık* in the KA (MS Fatih 4225, 184a). This aspect of the chancellor's duties is also described by İnalcık, "Suleiman the Lawgiver," pp. 115-16: "Originally arranged by the *nişancı*, the highest authority in the matter of *ʿurfî* laws, it [the *Kanunname* of the Conqueror] was modified by the sultan and ratified by his personal hand-written order (*hatt-i şerif*)."

be educated both in legal reasoning and in the details of *şer'i* practice—that is, educated in the *medrese*.

Âli himself, of course, was a *medrese* graduate as well as an experienced bureaucrat. He idolized and strove to emulate two of the most eminent chancellors of the sixteenth century, Celalzade and Ramazanzade, both of whom had also begun their careers by training for the religious profession. These two men personified Âli's highest cultural as well as professional ideals. They were fully educated, worldly, preeminent littérateurs who distinguished themselves in the service of the state by virtue of their learning and devotion to codifying and creating the "Ottoman Way." In emulating them Âli took upon himself the role of Ottoman Conscience. In the course of years of service on the frontier, Âli again and again saw his personal and administrative ideals violated. Also, he saw in his own failure to advance, and in his inability to achieve recognition for his learning and willingness to serve the state, an unjust distortion of his vision of the meritocratic society founded on commitment to justice that was expressed in *kanun*. Âli sought to restore this vision by focusing his own, and others', attention on the prescriptive character of dynastic law and on the importance of appointing the best-qualified and most historically minded person to the office of chancellor. Hence, for example, he was at pains in his appeals for appointment to demonstrate his knowledge of *kanun* by pointing out that the chancellorship, historically, was not given on the basis of seniority; even on the basis of seniority within the financial bureaucratic hierarchy, however, he should have received a promotion of some sort.[62]

Âli's insistence on these points illuminates his own career pattern as well as the character of his new concerns. Although he had been involved in chancery service since his days as a secretary at Selim's court, he had entered the central bureaucratic service only when he was appointed to the *timar* registry of Aleppo, which came after seven years of provincial military service. Âli had something of the parvenue's consciousness of rank and eye for professional opportunity, and therefore insisted that the seniority principle, which he saw to be fundamental to Ottoman government service, be observed in his favor. Ultimately, however, both his ambition and his predilection moved him to seek to circumvent the normal promotion processes by asking to be made chancellor. Âli's statement that seniority within the chancery service was not applicable to the choice of a chancellor is quite

[62] In several of the letters referred to above, and in another addressed to a vezir (MENŞE, 233b-235a), Âli outlines the history of the *nişancılık* in terms of its most distinguished incumbents, the last of these being Celalzade. After comparing himself to his idol, Âli declares that all of those he has mentioned were promoted to the post by grand vezirs; however, Celalzade was dismissed by one such, Rüstem Paşa, after the execution of his protector, İbrahim Paşa. Âli himself has had no luck with grand vezirs, so he places his hopes in either the addressee or the sultan himself.

accurate. Although he headed the chancery branch of the *kalemiye* bureaucracy, the chancellor was personally responsible to the sultan; chancellors were commonly appointed from outside the body of professional bureaucrats, and frequently from the ranks of senior *medrese* professors. The office, then, retained its ties to the learned establishment from which the Ottoman bureaucracy had sprung, and learning was the primary criterion dictating appointment. Âli viewed the chancellorship as more prestigious, and morally more important, than the office of the other major bureaucratic official of the Empire, the treasurer, who by the late sixteenth century was almost invariably an appointee with no formal *medrese* education who had worked his way through the ranks of the more highly specialized and professionalized financial bureaucracy.[63] To return to Âli's analogy, the chancellor was similar to the *seyhülislam* in more respects than educational background. Both officials were appointed by and directly attached to the sultan, both symbolized in their functions Ottoman ideals of sacred and secular justice, and both were "Palace" rather than professional, representing special appointments of highly qualified individuals rather than the product of hierarchically defined promotions. Âli still dreamed of a Palace position that would remove him from the trials and sordid politicking of normal career advancement.

THE *Counsel for Sultans*

Âli's passionate interest in dynastic law and in displaying his knowledge of it was not limited to those aspects of *kanun* that determined order of precedence, salary, and promotion in government service. He was also concerned with actual administrative practice, and with what he perceived as a general decline in the standards of justice, administrative efficiency, and morality maintained in the Ottoman Empire. In the summer and autumn of 1581, while he was in Van, Âli began to broach these concerns in an organized fashion in a new work, which he called *Nushat üs-selatin, Counsel for Sultans*.[64] The work would appear, from its title, to hark back to the old Perso-Islamic genre of "mirrors for princes" literature, and the association was doubtless intentional. In content, however, the *Counsel* differs rather dramatically from its generic predecessors. Although Âli does indeed deal with some of the topics traditional to "morals-and-manners" literature,

[63] This development will be treated more fully in chapter 8.

[64] Na'ima's description of the COUNSEL as a translation of an advice work written for the Ayyubid Ṣalâḥ al-dîn by one "ʿAbd al-raḥmân al-Shîrâzî" is incorrect (Na'ima, *Tarih*, 6 vols. [Istanbul, 1281-83], I, 43-44); the work is completely original, and Âli never translated the treatise in question, properly the *Nahj al-maslûk fî siyâsat al-mulûk* of ʿAbd al-raḥmân al-Shayzarî (GOW, suppl. I, p. 832). The description of the COUNSEL given by Klaus Röhrborn, *Untersuchungen zur osmanischen Verwaltungsgeschichte* (Berlin, 1973), p. 10, must be corrected accordingly.

such as the ruler's choice of companions and vezirs, regal responsibility, the use of spies, and the like, he does so from a very personal point of view and draws examples from both contemporary history and his own experiences. Much of the *Counsel* is devoted to a recounting of current abuses of Ottoman law or other practices invidious to the Empire, all of which Âli has observed or heard about. Dismissing the sultan's vezirs and companions as too concerned with their own interests to tell him about the declining state of the Empire and the abuses of justice running riot in his dominions, Âli explains in the introduction that he wrote the work so that the sultan, who had withdrawn from day-to-day affairs and neglected his supervisory duties, might know the extent to which bribery, corruption, and ignorance had taken over his realm. Âli completed the basic manuscript at the end of December 1581 and prepared to submit it directly to Murad, declaring himself to be unafraid of the wrath of vezirs. He stated that the *Counsel* was completely original in type, and that he had intentionally chosen contemporary examples in order to display his knowledge of Ottoman *kanun* (doubtless in pursuit of the chancellorship); Âli sought to represent the work as a testimonial to his own loyalty and sense of responsibility to the dynasty.[65]

For Âli, justice and law were the foundations of the Ottoman state, and while he wished these for the entire Empire he also wished them for himself; he devoted the fourth chapter of the *Counsel* to a rehearsal of the injuries he had suffered in the course of his career. What Âli desired was recognition for his honesty and ability in the form of a high post and regular promotion through the government system. Âli perceived the Ottoman system to function, ideally, on the basis of impersonal meritocracy and regularity. Given merit, one should be able to plug into the system and receive regular promotions, with one's peers, as related parts of the apparatus shifted; hence Âli's insistence upon the injustice of nepotism, however much he tried to acquire a protector, and on the impropriety of his being passed over for promotion when personnel shifts occurred in Aleppo. Unfortunately for Âli, the machine did not function this neatly, and he did not operate well as a cog. Nevertheless, Âli stressed the themes of justice, meritocracy, and administrative regularity throughout the *Counsel*. A few selections from portions of the work will serve to illustrate the constancy of these principles in Âli's exposition, and will also convey something of the tone of the original.

In the course of a discussion of *kalemiye* service Âli writes in the *Counsel*:

> So, it is necessary for the sovereign [lit., "the caliph of God"], and seemly for his watchful deputies, that they concern themselves with this group [as closely] as one would examine a pen-case, and that they

[65] COUNSEL, I, 17-22 (trans.), 89-96 (text); II, 115-16 (trans.), 254-56 (text).

> undertake to ensure their advancement [as regularly] as one advances a reed pen [on the cutting-board]. They should employ those of them that are straight as pens, and put to service those that work with an honesty that is like the [whiteness of] paper.[66]

On the effects of nepotism on the military class Âli says:

> The sixteenth requirement [of just rule]: Office-holders should not be dismissed on pretext of slight evidence; and, after people in official positions have been dismissed and relieved of their duties, they should not be appointed again to another office at the behest of one of the great men of state. Such unsuitable grants [of office] harm the entire military class, and such deleterious actions in our day are one of the causes of the oceanic disturbances of the whole victorious army. It is manifest injustice to dismiss a person who discharges his office honorably, and it is most improper to give a person a post, because of personal intercession, after he has been dismissed on accusations of having committed a sin or crime.[67]

Finally, Âli sums up the situation of Ottoman officials thus:

> In short . . . it is one of the essentials of religion and state [*dîn u devlet*], and a necessary [requirement] of sovereignty and generosity, that the ranks of those servitors [of the state] who have proved their worth gradually increase, and that their positions rise with time.[68]

There is indeed statistical substance to Âli's observations on the insecurity of government service and the irresponsible, or at least increasingly unpredictable, character of the appointment process during the latter part of the sixteenth century. While the top bureaucratic posts, for example, tended to be filled by the same individuals, many of these remained in office only for a few months or a year at most. Between the years of 1573 and 1596 the position of treasurer was held twice each by Lalezar Mehmed Çelebi (despite his notoriety for despoiling the public treasury and for pederasty) and Şerif Mehmed Paşa; three times by Kara Üveys Çelebi, whose integrity Sokollu Mehmed Paşa had impugned; and four times by Hacı İbrahim Paşa. Between 1576 and 1601 the chancellor's office was given twice to Feridun Ahmed, twice to Muhyi Çelebi, three times to Boyalı Mehmed Paşa, and four times to Hamze Çelebi (Paşa). Okçuzade Şah Mehmed was chancellor five times between 1599 and 1624, though his father, as treasurer,

[66] COUNSEL, I, 49 (trans.), 138 (text).

[67] COUNSEL, I, 63 (trans.), 159 (text).

[68] COUNSEL, I, 64 (trans.), 160 (text). Âli repeats his complaints about improper promotion procedures in an ode addressed about this time to İskender Paşa, *beğlerbeği* of Van (LAYİHAT, 29b-30b).

had been imprisoned for embezzlement.[69] Thus the incidence of dismissal and reappointment, in part at least a function of increased factionalism among major court figures, increased dramatically during the reigns of Murad III and Mehmed III. A scan of the appointment notices given by Selaniki, and of order (*mühimme*) and appointment (*ru'us*) registers for the years 1585-99/993-1007, reveals that this pattern was mirrored on those levels of the financial service immediately below the treasurer (*Anadolu defterdarı, şıkk-ı sani defterdarı, defter emini*), with the same personnel shifting back and forth between these positions. The major provincial financial bureaus were similarly subjected to frequent shakeups, with the finance directors of such important provinces as Aleppo and Erzurum often being appointed to positions at the capital. At the upper reaches of the bureaucratic service, however, it seems that there was much motion but little mobility.

Several factors help to explain this phenomenon, which to some extent occurs during this same period on the level of provincial governorships as well. One is that most frequently cited by Ottoman historians, namely, the pervasive influence of factionalism, nepotism, and bribery, which appear (or were perceived) to have increased markedly after Murad III's accession. The other and perhaps more significant factors are military and economic. The Ottoman Empire, from the beginning of Murad's reign, faced a grave economic threat in the form of a glut of American silver that led to a near 100 percent devaluation of that metal. At the same time, the Empire embarked on two long and costly wars that yielded no new permanent conquests or sources of revenue—against the Safavis between 1578 and 1590, and against the Hapsburgs between 1593 and 1606. The dire economic plight of the Empire, which needed more and more cash in an inflationary situation to prosecute its military ventures and keep internal order, has been so well documented as to require little space here. However, it is worthwhile noting that the archival materials cited above, particularly the *mühimme* registers of orders sent from the Porte to the provinces, reveal that economic and military concerns had a considerable effect on the appointment process and on administration. Relative to earlier years, the registers from this period show an increasing concern with collection of back taxes (*bakaya*); ever larger numbers of provincial appointments to both financial and military positions were made by contract (*iltizam*), a process whereby the hopeful appointee guaranteed to remit to the central treasury a fixed amount of cash from provincial revenues. In some cases the stipulated amount had to be delivered before the appointee took office, after which he was to recompense himself, as well as perform his administrative duties, from such revenues as he was able to collect. This process, which amounted

[69] Danişmend, *Kronoloji*, V, 235-59, 322-30).

to legalized job selling, encouraged frequent changes of personnel for economic ends. Finally, this somewhat chaotic system of fiscal practice, combined with the frequent absence of provincial governors and other officials on campaign, gave financial officers who were left ''minding the store'' ample opportunity for corruption and theft, usually by means of ''creative accounting.'' Hence, there were frequent scandals and dismissals.

Âli probably did not actually submit the *Counsel* for at least another five years. For four years after he completed the bulk of the work, he added sections; he may very well have been afraid of the effect ''publication'' might have on his own career.[70] Nevertheless, the fact that he conceived and completed most of the *Counsel* at this time is a significant indicator of his state of mind. Âli, without a protector, was determined to bring himself to the sultan's attention as an honest and fearless fighter for justice. For example in 1582/990 the oppressive Ahmed Paşa b. Çerkes İskender Paşa was dismissed from the government of Aleppo, but remained there for some time awaiting his replacement, Üveys Paşa. Although the *timar* registers had been sealed as a matter of course at the time of his dismissal, Ahmed Paşa, in concert with the registrar (*defter emini*) and council secretary (*tezkereci*) of Aleppo, revoked some forty *timar* assignments without cause and sold them. Âli immediately wrote to the Porte to expose the entire matter.[71]

THE *Counsel for Sultans* in Retrospect

Âli's composition of the *Counsel* in 1581 marks a critical stage in the intellectual development of Âli the historian. It also represents a landmark in the history of Ottoman letters and political thought. Earlier exemplars of advice literature tended to fall into two broad types. ''Mirrors for princes,''

[70] COUNSEL, I, 10. The presence of a copy in the Imperial Treasury Library (MS Hazine 1601), and a verse Âli composed for its presentation (LAYİHAT, 150a-b) indicate that the completed COUNSEL was actually submitted, probably in 1585-86/994-95.

[71] MENŞE, 253a-254b. The identities of Ahmed Paşa and Üveys Paşa are established by: LAYİHAT, 15a-16a, in which Âli praises the new governor-general (Kara) Üveys Paşa, and reviles his predecessor, Ahmed Paşa b. Çerkes İskender, for graft and oppression; MD 50, doc. 203, which probably dates from 1582/990 and lists Üveys as *beğlerbeği* of Aleppo. Üveys was certainly there at the end of the year, when he had Âli write a letter of congratulations to the new vezir, İbrahim Paşa (MENŞE, 277a-277b; SELANİKİ, p. 170). Üveys Paşa served in Aleppo until he was appointed governor-general of Damascus shortly before 13 July 1586/15 Receb 993 (KPT 246, p. 15). Üveys was again appointed governor of Aleppo for a brief period, and then was ordered back to Istanbul to serve a second term as treasurer, this time with the rank and pay of a *beğlerbeği*, on 26 February 1586/7 Rebi' I 994, according to KPT 246, p. 167, and SELANİKİ, p. 204. SELANİKİ dates this latter appointment to the following month, probably referring to the time of Üveys Paşa's arrival in Istanbul.

It was probably Âli who provided most of the content for a report that Üveys Paşa had him send to the Porte concerning the depredations of a Turkish-Arabic court translator named Osman. Osman had become wealthy and powerful through abuse of his office, and had bribed most of the previous governors and finance directors of Aleppo to keep silent about his activities (MENŞE, 227b-229a).

works of advice to rulers on matters of court etiquette and government, were based on Persian models and usually originated in court circles. In the sixteenth-century Ottoman context, the *Âsafname* of Lutfi Paşa is perhaps the best example of this sort of political literature.[72] *Ahlak* works, treatises on manners and morals, represented the second type of advice literature. These were usually authored by ulema, and were informed both by the religious-legal perspective of the *medrese* and by the philosophical ethics tradition from which they ultimately derived. The most important Ottoman "ethics" book of the sixteenth century was the *Ahlak-ı Ala'i* of Âli's mentor, Kınalızade Ali Çelebi.[73] The works of Lutfi Paşa and Kınalızade represent significant new developments in themselves. Lutfi Paşa drew on his experience as a grand vezir to comment on Ottoman government and make certain specific recommendations, and Kınalızade included in his work commentary on Ottoman administrative practice and recent history. Nevertheless, both authors maintained a detached and largely theoretical perspective and mode of expression. When they utilized historical examples, these tended to be drawn from the past rather than the immediate present. In the *Counsel* Âli departed from these established models in that he detailed contemporary administrative practices and problems, and made specific recommendations for reform of the Ottoman system.

In several senses Âli, in his person as well as in his work, combined and built upon the works of his predecessors. Like Lutfi Paşa, he was a government functionary, albeit a much lower-ranking one, and the *Counsel* displays many features of the "mirrors for princes" genre. Âli was also an *ilmiye* product like Kınalızade; his constant concern for the principles of justice, morality, and law embodied in both the Islamic *şeri'at* and Ottoman *kanun* shows many reflexes of his *medrese* background and of the "ethics" literature with which he was familiar. At the same time, Âli was neither a judge committed to a legalistic mode of expression, nor a vezir concerned with the highest levels of the operation of government, but a middle-ranking bureaucrat and intellectual whose preoccupations were the day-to-day functioning of the administrative apparatus. Âli brought to his own advice work a wealth of detail based on observation and experience, and a level of specificity and practicality unmatched in the works of his predecessors. Andreas Tietze has observed that Âli's practical concerns with specific evils override

[72] Rudolf Tschudi, ed. and trans., *Das Âṣafnâme des Lutfî Pascha* (Berlin, 1910).

[73] Kınalızade Ali Çelebi, *Ahlak-ı Ala'i* (Bulaq, 1248). The work is an expanded adaptation of the earlier *Akhlâq-i Jalâlî* of Jalâl al-dîn Davânî (d. 1502), which is itself based on the *Akhlâq-i Nâṣirî* of Naṣîr al-dîn Ṭûsî (d. 1274); see my "Royal Authority, Dynastic Cyclism, and 'Ibn Khaldûnism' in Sixteenth-Century Ottoman Letters," *Journal of Asian and African Studies* 18/3-4 (1983): 198-220, and "From Şehzade Korkud to Mustafa Âli: Cultural Origins of the Ottoman *Nasihatname*," *Proceedings of the Third International Congress on the Economic and Social History of Turkey* (forthcoming).

organizational priorities; although Âli in his introduction outlined an overall conceptual framework, he paid little attention to his comprehensive scheme in his anxiety to point out institutional and social problems.[74] This phenomenon is partially explicable by Âli's professional status; in contrast to Lutfi Paşa and Kınalızade, he was not committed to a specific generic mode of presentation, nor was he in a position to view an overall pattern.

Several other factors must also be taken into account in any consideration of the structure and significance of the *Counsel*. Âli was the first Ottoman political commentator to treat the problems of economic, social, and political change and institutional disruption so explicitly and extensively. Furthermore, Âli wrote the *Counsel* at a time when the negative effects of protracted warfare, economic crisis provoked by inflation and other factors, institutional transformation, and changes in the character of political life were just beginning to make themselves felt. Âli viewed these changes, and the problems they created, as evidence of a decline in the order of the state, relative to more orderly and more glorious phases of Ottoman history such as the time of Sultan Süleyman, in the latter half of whose reign Âli had grown up. To the extent that Âli saw the various facets of change as stemming from deviation from established law and custom (*şeri' at* and *kanun*), or from the failure of the sovereign and his ministers to exercise their moral responsibilities, he was able to conceptualize and generalize his perception of decline. For the most part, however, this perception was too new and amorphous, at least in Ottoman letters, for Âli to do more than grapple with the multifarious manifestations of social and political malaise. In different sections of the work he variously attacks individuals, decline in public and private morality, faults in the Ottoman system, ignorance of history and law, and economic disorder as causes of the Empire's difficulties. The ideology of Ottoman decline and Ottoman reform had not yet developed; the *Counsel* displays little of the nostalgia for the "golden age" of Süleyman's time, or of the theoretical models of state and society, which characterize the writings of later reform-minded Ottomans. For Âli in 1581 the "golden age," when the Empire was seen to have functioned successfully, had not yet receded into an irretrievable past; he appears to have felt that good government and orderly society could be restored through the reform or restoration of specific institutions and moral principles.

Âli's *Counsel for Sultans* may fairly be considered the pioneering work of a new genre of political reform literature, the *nasihatname*. In the seventeenth century a comparatively large number of Ottoman writers turned their hand to treatises devoted to elaborating proposals for restoration of the Empire's glory, which was held to be exemplified by the reign of Süleyman.

[74] COUNSEL, I, 8-9.

The authors of these works—the anonymous writer of the *Kitab-i müstetab*, Koçi Beğ, Kâtib Çelebi, and Na'ima, to name only a few—shared Âli's practical approach to problem solving through the examination of contemporary history and specific key institutions.[75] Much research remains to be done on the development of the *nasihatname* genre. In a few instances connections between Âli and his successors can be verified; Na'ima cites the *Counsel*, and Kâtib Çelebi at least saw the work.[76] The *Counsel for Sultans*, on the basis of chronology and methodological similarity, would appear to be the forerunner and prototype of later commentaries. While Âli did write the first *nasihatname* of the new type, however, he did not work in isolation. In his concern for justice, he had intellectual links with earlier Ottoman thinkers, and the critical approaches adopted by his contemporaries Selâniki and Akhisari strongly suggest that "*kanun*-consciousness," a concern for preservation of Ottoman ideals and practice in the face of rapid changes in the political, economic, and social spheres, became increasingly important in Ottoman intellectual circles in the second half of the sixteenth century.[77] Original though the *Counsel* was, its author may have been as much a spokesman for a group of like-minded people as a literary innovator.

One final comment must be made on Âli's composition of the *Counsel*. A large proportion of its entries deal with imperial finance, methods for curbing waste, and ways to save money. At this time the central government

[75] *Kitab-ı Müstetab*, ed. Yaşar Yücel (Ankara, 1974); Kâtib Çelebi, *Destur ül-amel li ıslah il-halel* (Istanbul, 1280); Kâtib Çelebi, *Mizan ül-hakk*, translated by Geoffrey Lewis as *The Balance of Truth* (London, 1957); Koçi Beğ, *Risale*, ed. Ali Kemali Aksüt (Istanbul, 1939); Na'ima, *Tarih*, I, 2-65; *Kitâbü Mesalihi' l-Müslimin ve Menafi' i' l-Mü' minin*, ed. Yaşar Yücel, 2 vols. (Ankara, 1980-81).

[76] Na'ima, *Tarih*, I, 43-44; Kâtib Çelebi, *Keşf el-zunûn*, eds. Şerafettin Yaltkaya and Rifat Bilge, 2 vols. (Istanbul, 1941-43), II, 1958.

[77] On the scope of Ottoman advice literature, see Bernard Lewis, "Ottoman Observers of Ottoman Decline," *Islamic Studies* 1 (1962):71-87; Röhrborn, *Verwaltungsgeschichte*, pp. 6-11; Hans Georg Majer, "Die Kritik an den Ulema in den osmanischen politischen Traktaten des 16.-18. Jahrhunderts," in *Social and Economic History of Turkey (1071-1920)*, eds. Osman Okyar and Halil İnalcık (Ankara, 1980), pp. 147-55; Halil İnalcık, "Military and Fiscal Transformation in the Ottoman Empire, 1600-1700," *Archivum Ottomanicum* 6 (1980): 283-84.

A preliminary attempt to trace the connections between *nasihatname* writers has been made by Rhoads Murphey, "The Veliüddin Telhis: Notes on the Sources and Interrelations between Koçi Bey and Contemporary Writers of Advice to Kings," *Belleten* 43 (1979): 547-71. Murphey has applied the methodology utilized by Bekir Kütükoğlu in a study of Kâtib Çelebi's use of sources: *Katib Çelebi "Fezleke" sinin Kaynakları* (Istanbul, 1974).

I have outlined precedents for Âli's style of frank criticism in "From Şehzade Korkud to Mustafa Âli," utilizing an Arabic critique of Ottoman administration authored by Prince Korkud, son of Bayezid II. On parallels between Âli and Selaniki, see, pp. 130-31, 156. The advice work of Akhisari (Hasan el-Kâfi) is the *Usul ül-hikem fi nizâm il-âlem* (MS Düğümlü Baba 438, ff. 1-67), which dates from 1595 (cf. GOW, pp. 144-45). Akhisari's Turkish translation of the Arabic original has been published by Mehmet İpşirli as "Hasan Kâfî el-Akhisarî ve Devlet Düzenine ait Eseri *Usûlü' l-Hikem fî Nizâmi' l-Âlem*," *Tarih Enstitüsü Dergisi* 10-11 (1979-80): 239-78.

was very immediately concerned to maintain a ready supply of cash; inflation, the exigencies of protracted warfare, the loss of revenue through cessation of conquest and peasant flight from the land, disruption of the *timar* system, expansion of the standing military establishment, and social disorder all combined to give fiscal matters a high priority. While the *Counsel* clearly reflects this orientation, it also represents something of an impartial outsider's perspective. In 1581 Âli had but newly entered the financial service and did not approach fiscal matters with the eye of a career financial official. He was, however, determined to make a success of his new career. The *Counsel*, insofar as Âli planned to present it to Sultan Murad, was intended to display his honesty (in addressing matters of corruption and maladministration directly) and loyalty to the state; it was also a vehicle for demonstrating his financial initiative and usefulness in the immediate crisis. To put the case more crudely, Âli's previous literary efforts along accepted lines had earned him neither great rewards nor a stable patronage relationship. He therefore saw fit to apply directly to the sultan, and to appeal to Murad's monetary instincts rather than his cultural ones. In his commentary on Murad's character in the *Essence of History*, Âli stresses that the sultan's interest in acquiring and saving money predominated even over his passion for Sufism, to which Âli had earlier catered.[78]

VERACITY OF THE *Counsel for Sultans*

Âli's careerist tendencies, his personal bitterness, his concern with appointment practices that he felt hindered his own progress, and the petitionary character of the *Counsel* might suggest that Âli exaggerated the nature and scale of those abuses of the Ottoman system he observed in the provinces and in the capital. It is also true that the "decline" which Âli was one of the first to treat was in some senses more a literary than an objective reality.[79] However, narrative and archival materials confirm many of the contentions put forth by Âli in the *Counsel* and in his correspondence at this time, and show that the problems he perceived were not merely personal peeves, but were also of real concern to the central government. A number of examples will clarify this point.

In the course of a discussion of his later experiences as finance director of Baghdad (1585-86/993-94), Âli comments that governors-general, by virtue of their supervisory authority (*nezaret*) and greater coercive power, can do as they wish with tax income, although this is actually the province of

[78] KA Murad/Introduction, Nur 3409, 289b; according to this passage, Murad's only fault of character was his greed for money, which Âli explains (facetiously?) as a product of the sultan's desire to fill the treasury against the great disorders that astrologers had predicted for the Muslim millennium (1591-92/1000).

[79] Fleischer, "From Şehzade Korkud to Mustafa Âli."

the independent finance director, who is responsible directly to the central government. *Beğlerbeği*s are thus able to embezzle or use income illegally, according to Âli. A *mühimme* document dated August-September 1585/Ramazan 993 orders the governor-general of Aleppo to cease interfering with imperial (*miri*) income and to leave its disbursal to the independent finance director.[80]

Elsewhere in the *Counsel* Âli complains that governors-general, particularly those of frontier provinces, support their own establishments by giving their personal retainers *timar* grants, thus depriving the Empire of fighting men and deserving *sipahis* of a living. One such *beğlerbeği* of Aleppo, almost certainly the Ahmed Paşa b. Çerkes İskender Paşa referred to above, distributed four-fifths of the available *timar*s in this fashion in his first year of office. An appointment register records very large grants to men of the new governor-general of Aleppo, Ahmed Paşa, in August 1580, while an order issued five years later requires that all letters of patent for *timar*-holders (*berat*) in the eastern provinces be reviewed and their system of issue reformed because of rampant irregularities.[81]

In 1582-83 Âli and the governor-general of Aleppo, Üveys Paşa, submitted to Istanbul a report on the misdeeds of the Turkish-Arabic *şeri'at* court translator, Osman. Two orders preserved in the *mühimme* registers and dated 20 October 1583/3 Şevval 991 were addressed to the *beğlerbeği*s of Damascus and Aleppo. The orders recite complaints that had reached Istanbul about the excessive power and corruption of such court translators and require that they be kept under control.[82]

In several passages of the *Counsel* Âli rails against the sale of posts, particularly finance directorships and governor-generalships; against the corruption and incompetence of financial clerks and officials; and against finance directors and *beğlerbeği*s who, particularly in the eastern border provinces, regularly conspire to rob the state treasury. A *ru'us* document dated 5 February 1585/15 Safer 994 concerns the appointment of a new governor-general to Diyar Bakır. For several years the central treasury had received no tax remittance (*irsaliye*) from that province because the *defterdar*, one Ahmed, had been able to embezzle all remittance funds and had bribed the incumbent governor-general to ignore the matter. Ahmed, very possibly identical with the Lalezarzade Ahmed of whom Âli speaks so harshly, had previously held the finance directorships of Erzurum, Damascus, and Baghdad, all of which posts he had purchased. The new governor is appointed to Diyar Bakır on condition that he remit 20,000 florins per year for three

80 COUNSEL, I, 65 (trans.), 161-62 (text); MD 58, doc. 389.
81 COUNSEL, I, 85 (trans.), 186 (text); KPT 237, pp. 65-66; MD 59, doc. 326.
82 MD 51, docs. 230, 249. On Osman, see note 71 above.

years, that he allow no tax arrears (*bakaya*) to accrue, and that he not interfere with designated financial officials.[83]

ALEPPO EPILOGUE

Âli's efforts to bring himself to the attention of Sultan Murad did not end with the *Counsel for Sultans*. In 1581 he commissioned local painters of miniatures and gilders to produce a special illustrated edition of the *Book of Victory*; a presentation poem contained in Âli's second *divan* establishes that he presented the monarch with a copy of the work, illuminated at his own expense, well before the production of the well-known royal edition (MS Hazine 1365). The copy that Âli had made is very likely the British Museum manuscript of the *Nusretname*, which contains five miniatures executed in a rather crude (or provincial) style, the calligraphy having been completed in April-May 1582/Rebi' I 990.[84] This is the first indication of Âli's interest in book production and illumination, an interest that bore fruit five years later when Âli wrote his famous historical and biographical study of calligraphers and painters, *Menakıb-ı hünerveran, The Artists' Exploits*.

Illustration of historical works had become something of a fashion at the court of Murad, a fact of which Âli must have been aware.[85] The court *şehname*-writer (*şehnameci*), Seyyid Lokman of Urmiye (like all of the first holders of the post, he was an Iranian Turkman), was just coming into his own at this time; in 1584/992 he produced the *Mücmil üt-tûmâr, The Gatherer of Records*, the first of a series of works lavishly illustrated at the imperial atelier. Seyyid Lokman gained considerable wealth and influence in this position, and in presenting an illuminated *Book of Victory* Âli doubtless sought to compete with the *şehnameci*, whose versifying ability he ridiculed.[86] Âli's efforts to gain acceptance for his work also show that there

[83] COUNSEL, I, 48-49, 65 (trans.), 149, 159-60 (text); KPT 246, p. 147.

[84] LAYİHAT, 137b-138a; Âli apologizes for the condition of the manuscript, pleading that if it is dirty it is because he has been at war and on the road. He then asks that painters be supplied from the palace atelier so that a royal edition might be produced. On the British Museum MS, see Rieu, *Turkish Manuscripts*, p. 61. Âli probably did not present the volume until he went to Istanbul in 1583/991.

[85] Of the twenty-one sixteenth-century illustrated historical manuscripts preserved in the Topkapı Sarayı Museum, over half are datable to the reign of Murad III. Of these nearly half are the work of Seyyid Lokman; see Fehmi Edhem Karatay, *Topkapı Sarayı Müzesi Kütüphanesi, Türkçe Yazmalar Kataloğu*, 2 vols. (Istanbul, 1961).

[86] On Seyyid Lokman, see GOW, pp. 164-67, where further bibliographical references are given. Âli's criticism of Lokman and other Iranian (Türkmen) *şehnamecis* occurs at the end of Murad's reign, KA, Nur 3409, 419b-422a. Âli declares that the *şehnamecilik*, which had originally called for the composition of Persian verse in the style of Firdawsi's *Shâhnâmeh*, celebrating the exploits of the Ottoman house, had become the monopoly of Iranian-born Türkmen who emigrated to the Ottoman realms. Despite his birth, however, Lokman was seemingly incapable of producing Persian verse, and his Turkish poetry, Âli declared, left much to be desired. The *ru'us* registers KPT 236, 238, and 246, covering the years 1580-86, contain frequent references to Lokman, who was able to obtain many grants for his relatives and for his

were artisans resident in the provincial capital of Aleppo who were capable of producing illuminated manuscripts; in fact, Aleppo even boasted an Iranian painter and gilder, Valîjân Tabrîzî, who lived there at precisely this time.[87]

In the spring of the year 1582/990 Âli received a letter from the Porte announcing the impending ceremonies celebrating the circumcision (*sûr*) of Prince Mehmed. Âli was asked to write a letter of congratulations, which he did in the name of the dignitaries of Aleppo.[88] The fact that he was ordered to compose such a letter shows that Âli had some literary standing in the capital. The circumcision celebrations and entertainments were a consciously planned cultural event that lasted for nearly two months, longer than any previous ceremonies of this type. Something of a publicity event for the dynasty, the *sûr* provided littérateurs with an opportunity to gain attention. At least four examples of a new literary genre, the *sûrname*, came out on this occasion.[89] One of these, *Cami' ül-buhûr der mecâlis-i sûr, The Gathering of the Seas* [or *Meters*] *on the Scenes of the Celebration*, was written by Âli over the last six months of 1583/991.[90] Âli once again proclaimed his own creative initiative in inventing new literary forms. It is difficult to establish whether his *Gathering* was indeed the prototype for other

---

protégés in the royal atelier. These records confirm Âli's assessment of Lokman's excessive wealth and dominance in the imperial atelier. KPT 246, p. 68, refers to Lokman's famous *Hünername*, an historical work commissioned by Sultan Murad, as still incomplete in mid-October 1585/mid-Şevval 993. Lokman was dismissed from his post, which he had held since 1569, shortly after the accession of Mehmed III, the reason being that he had written nothing since the accession (SELANİKİ, *sub anno* 1003, 84b). Selâniki gives the date of dismissal as September 1596/mid-Muharrem; cf. Necib Asım, "Osmanlı tarih-nüvisleri ve müverrihleri," TOEM, II (1329), 430-32.

87 MH, pp. 68, 73.

88 KA, Murad/19, Nur 3409, 340a-343a; Âli, *Câmi' ül-buhur der mecâlis-i sûr*, MS Bağdat Köşkü 203 (hereafter CAMİ'), 7a-10b. Âli gives the text of the order and of his response. The same two letters occur in a *mecmua* found in Berlin, Staatsbibliothek, MS or. fol. 3332, Teil 14, 193a-b (Götz, IV, no. 305, p. 292). Âli's letter also occurs in MENŞE, 275b-276b. The *sûr* began on 29 May 1582/6 Cümada I, and continued for nearly sixty days. Atsız (AB, p. 18) is mistaken in saying that Âli was invited to attend the ceremonies; on the contrary, he was ordered to remain in his post.

89 Levend, *Türk Edebiyatı Tarihi*, I, 158-159, lists only one prototype for the *sûrnames* which appeared on this occasion, the *sûriye kasidesi* of Figani, written on the occasion of the circumcision of Süleyman's sons Mustafa, Mehmed, and Selim.

90 CAMİ' (MS Bağdat Köşkü 203) is a presentation copy, which Âli had made in 1585-86/994, when he was finance director in Baghdad. Nine empty spaces have been left for illumination. It is impossible to know whether Âli intended to have miniatures painted in Baghdad, where he was quite involved with calligraphy and illumination, or whether he hoped to have the blanks filled in Istanbul. An illustrated copy of the COUNSEL (MS Revan 406) may have been prepared at the same time.

At the end of the work Âli states that, inspired by his compatriot Yazıcızade, the author of the *Muhammediye*, he composed the *Câmi'* in six months, and that the like of the work has not been seen. The *terminus ante quem* for composition is 1583/991; a letter written in that year (dated on the basis of internal evidence) by Üveys Paşa cites the work as already completed (MENŞE, 236a-237a).

"circumcision books" or whether Âli was simply closely attuned to cultural currents in the capital, even at a distance. Be this as it may, the work is of interest for other reasons. In a letter of recommendation for Âli, which Üveys Paşa, governor of Aleppo, sent to Prince Mehmed in 1583/991 after the *Gatherer* had been submitted to the Porte, the work is praised for preserving a "record of events that earlier generations failed to keep."[91] Âli somehow indeed obtained a very careful record of these events. In the *Gatherer* he lists the gifts that dignitaries and foreign monarchs sent to the prince and sultan. This list, which is remarkably detailed, is very close to the official register of presents received on the occasion preserved in the Topkapı Palace Archives.[92] The coincidence is tantalizing; it appears that Âli must have had access to information basically archival in nature. Copies of such documents may have circulated among members of the scribal service, much as state letters and *kanunname*s found their way, via successive copies, into individual correspondence collections (*münşe'at*) and literary scrapbooks (*mecmu'a*). It is also possible that Üveys Paşa, who came to Aleppo as governor-general some time in 1582/990, provided Âli with a copy of the list. Immediately before his appointment to Aleppo, Üveys Paşa had served his second term as treasurer, in which capacity he would certainly have had access to the gift register.[93] This is an intriguing hint at the nature of current information available to Âli in his bureaucratic capacity.

At the time of the circumcision celebration itself (summer 1582) Âli submitted an ode to the court, asking once again, in vain, for a better appointment.[94] Despite his poor connections in Istanbul, Âli cultivated a number of friendships on the frontier. Üveys Paşa, the *beğlerbeği* of Aleppo, seems to have thought highly of him, and Âli was also on very good terms with Husrev Paşa, the reinstated governor-general of Erzurum. Âli sent several poems of praise to Özdemiroğlu Osman Paşa in Şirvan, reminding him of their long relationship and common friendship with the late Lala Mustafa Paşa.[95]

[91] See preceding footnote.

[92] CAMİ', 24b-29a; TKS Arşivi, D 9614.

[93] It is not known precisely when during this year Üveys Paşa was appointed governor-general of Aleppo and was succeeded as *başdefterdar* by Okçuzade Mehmed Efendi. Üveys was certainly in Aleppo at the end of A.H. 990 (see note 71 above). The fact that in the TKS gift list a blank space is left for the name of the governor of Aleppo, while other gubernatorial contributors are named, suggests that at the time the register was compiled Üveys Paşa had not yet been definitely appointed, and was probably still in Istanbul. Cf. Danişmend, *Kronoloji* V, 254.

[94] LAYİHAT, 39b-41a; MENŞE, 236a-237a.

[95] LAYİHAT, 24b-25b, an ode (*cenk*-rhyme) in praise of Osman Paşa, which Âli sent to him at Demir Kapı together with a covering letter (MENŞE, 257a). In the letter Âli asks to be made *sancak beği* of Kefe (Caffa). Another letter in verse (LAYİHAT, 42a-43a) refers to a new ode called *Gûy u çevgân, Ball and Mallet*, and requests the finance directorship in Aleppo. *Gûy u çevgân* itself occurs in LAYİHAT, 35b-36b, and asks that Osman Paşa give Âli a *sancak* in Rumeli. The precise date of these compositions is ambiguous; they were composed either at

Suddenly, at the end of 1582/990, developments in Istanbul gave Âli new hope. A dwarf of the Harem, Nasuh Ağa, who had tremendous influence at the highest levels of government, was denounced for corruption and extortion. The scandals that attended exposure of Nasuh Ağa's affairs led to a major shakeup of the central government apparatus as many of his partners in crime, including the treasurer, Okçuzade Mehmed Paşa, were investigated and imprisoned. Soon after these events the hated Sinan Paşa was dismissed from the grand vezirate, was banished to Malkara, and his adherents were purged from government posts (December 1582).[96] Âli rushed to send congratulations to the new grand vezir, Siyavuş Paşa. In the ode he composed for the occasion, Âli reviled Sinan as an incompetent vezir and vicious bully whom all had feared, and asked Siyavuş Paşa to give him a Council post. Such an appointment, Âli suggested, would only be just recompense for Sinan's ill-treatment of him, and for the financial losses he had suffered in the course of the past four years.[97] Âli expected to be promoted as a matter of course in the administrative shakeup; his own superior, the finance director of Aleppo, Hacı İbrahim Efendi, was made treasurer in Istanbul. Âli also hoped that İbrahim Paşa, who was made vezir at just this time, would help him. When he received no new directives from the capital, Âli wrote a letter of protest to Hoca Sa'düddin, whom he asked to intercede with the sultan so that he might be transferred. To remain *timar* registrar of Aleppo for five years, to be constantly passed over for promotion, Âli wrote, was an unthinkable and anomalous violation of established Ottoman practice, *kanun*.[98] Faced with the possibility of remaining in the provinces for the rest of his career, Âli prepared to take desperate action.

---

this time or two or three years later, when Âli had established a close relationship with Özdemiroğlu.

It is very likely that a number of letters from MENŞE described as being from "a dignitary" were sent by Husrev Paşa, and Âli's letter of congratulations to a reinstated *beğlerbeği* is almost certainly addressed to Husrev (MENŞE, 272b-273b).

[96] SELANİKİ, pp. 168-69. Sinan was dismissed and Siyavuş appointed in December 1582/ late Zulka'de 990.

[97] MENŞE, 276b-277a; LAYİHAT, 26b-38a. The ode is extremely harsh in tone, and suggests that Âli hoped that Siyavuş would approve of one who so frankly expressed his hatred for Sinan.

[98] SELANİKİ, pp. 168-70; MENŞE, 277a-278b, is Üveys Paşa's letter of congratulations to İbrahim Paşa, composed by Âli. İbrahim became vezir in late December 1582. See also MENŞE, 241a-243a, a letter Âli wrote to İbrahim Paşa some years later. The letter to Sa'düddin occurs in MENŞE, 218a-219a.

FOUR

TOWARD THE MILLENNIUM: WAR, APOCALYPSE, AND HISTORY

(1583-92 / 991-1000)

ISTANBUL

(1583-84)

ÂLI PREPARED to take action in the early spring of 1583, as soon as travel was possible. He had armed himself with letters of recommendation, signed by Üveys Paşa and other frontier dignitaries and addressed to Sultan Murad, Prince Mehmed, and Hoca Sa'düddin. With these in hand Âli resigned his post, gathered up his illuminated *Book of Victory*, and traveled to Istanbul.[1]

Âli traveled in company with the former finance director of Aleppo, Cübni Sinan, and the two reached the capital together in the middle of spring. Cübni Sinan's efforts were rewarded with a posting as finance director of Erzurum. Âli, however, was less fortunate; he found on his arrival in Istanbul that İbrahim Paşa, from whom he had expected much assistance in obtaining a new post, had just departed the city in order to assume the government of Egypt.[2] Âli used his letters of recommendation and wrote new appeals that he be made chancellor or given another position at court. He no

[1] MENŞE, 235a, to Sa'düddin, commending Âli for his service and literary works, particularly the *Câmi'* and *Nusretname*, which Âli wished to present at court in illuminated editions. The Hoca is requested to assist him in presentation and in obtaining a suitable post. The letter also makes it clear that Âli has voluntarily given up his post and, putting his trust in God (*tevekkül*), has set off for Istanbul in hopes of attaining his desires. See also MENŞE, 236a-237a, Üveys Paşa to Prince Mehmed; 237a-238a, Üveys Paşa to Sultan Murad, again referring to Âli's illustrated *Nusretname*. In other letters Âli refers to himself as "*Haleb timar defterdarlığından fâriğ*," meaning that he gave up his post voluntarily. Since Âli is quite frank about later instances of dismissal, there is no reason not to accept his statement on this affair; there is no documentation for Atsız's hostile assertion that Âli was dismissed (AB, p. 5).

[2] MENŞE, 238a-239, Âli to Özdemiroğlu Osman Paşa, 1584/992; 241a-243a, Âli to İbrahim Paşa, governor of Egypt. Âli continued to write to him, asking to be given a *sancak* in Egypt, but without success. Since İbrahim Paşa arrived in Egypt on 2 June 1583/11 Cümada I 991 (CAIRO, p. 18), he likely left Istanbul in early May. This date of Âli's arrival in Istanbul is supported by a BBA document, *Maliyeden Müdevver* 7164, pp. 96-101, which lists the *defterdars* of Aleppo as of 13 July 1583/4 Receb 991; Âli is not among them. Two other references, MENŞE, 232b, and John R. Walsh, "İstidâname" 132, give 991 as the terminal date for Âli's service in Aleppo.

longer wished, he said, to remain in financial service, particularly in times of fiscal chaos: "My greatest wish is to become chancellor, for I do not like being a financial officer, and I don't wish to interfere with the public treasury (*beyt ül-mâl il-müslimin*)."[3] Since the power structure of the court had changed in the wake of Sinan Paşa's disgrace, Âli could once again stress in his appeals the high esteem in which the late Lala Mustafa Paşa had held him, and the probity that had kept him out of the scandals that attended the Lala's dismissal.[4]

Âli renewed his friendship with the *kapı ağası*, Gazanfer Ağa, whom he had known at Kütahya as Gazanfer Beğ. Gazanfer was now chief white eunuch of the Harem and overseer of the Palace, and he came to Âli's rescue by arranging for the illustrated *Book of Victory* to be presented to the sultan. Murad was very impressed with the work, and ordered that a new and more lavish edition be prepared in the royal workshops. Âli himself was assigned to oversee the production of the manuscript, and this task occupied him and the artists under his supervision for nearly a year, until mid-July 1584/Receb 992.[5] The final product, now MS Hazine 1365, was extravagantly beautiful, and it was kept in the Palace treasury. The *Book* was clearly composed in order to be illustrated, for Âli divided it into *mecâlis*, which may be understood as both "séances" and "miniatures, depictions." The Hazine manuscript contains forty-eight illustrations, some of which are double pages. These miniatures are remarkable not only for their quality, but also for their consistent realism. As both supervisor of the production and an eyewitness to many of the events recounted in his book, Âli would appear to have been

[3] MENŞE, 233b-235a, to a vezir. Âli gives a brief history of the office of *nişancı* and connects the institution with the establishment of a formal educational structure under the Conqueror, saying that the graduates of the *semaniye medrese*s became increasingly responsible for the Empire's administration. On the term *beyt ül-mal il-müslimin*, and on the public (or state) treasury, see B. Lewis, "Bayt al-mâl," EI[2], and C. Orhonlu, "Khazîne," EI[2].

[4] MENŞE, 257a-258a, a verse appeal to the grand vezir, which cites Âli's learning, service, and the low quality of current appointees to high posts; 258a-258b, a verse appeal to the sultan in which Âli calls himself the polylingual scribe of the age, fluent in four languages (Arabic, Persian, Ottoman Turkish, Çagatay Turkish), and asks to be made either *nişancı* or *Rumeli defterdarı* so that his vast experience might not be wasted; 232b-233b is addressed to an unidentified courtier who had previously helped Âli obtain his Bosnian posting, and whom Âli had last seen in Erzurum. Âli stresses the addressee's respect for people of learning and, after reciting his troubles of the past five years, asks for either the *nişancılık* or, if the incumbent cannot be dislodged, a *sancak beğliği* in Cairo. Âli's attempts to have the current chancellor dismissed are at odds with his declared stand against nepotistic appointment practices, although he justifies this on the basis of his greater qualification for the post.

[5] MENŞE, 241a-243a, addressed to İbrahim Paşa, states that Âli presented the *Nusretname* and a few small treatises through the good offices of Gazanfer Ağa; 256a-256b, from a field marshal (probably Osman Paşa) to the Porte, refers to Âli's special imperial appointment to oversee the production of the *Nusretname* as having lasted nearly a year: the colophon of MS Hazine 1365 gives the date of completion as mid-July 1584/mid-Receb 992, and the name of the copyist as Mustafa b. Abdülcelil, one of the private scribes of the Porte (264a).

fastidious on this count. In a few miniatures, for example, the major participants in the Şirvan campaign are identified by labels, and the same figures are recognizable throughout the manuscript by the consistency with which they are portrayed. Âli appears several times as a short, round-faced figure clutching a bound volume and writing implements.

Ironically, this appointment gave Âli new insight into the ways of the Palace. In giving details on the making of the splendid volume in the *Counsel*, Âli cites the excessive fees paid to the twenty calligraphers, gilders, and painters who were assigned to the project as an example of a waste of treasury funds. He also notes that the gold beaters augmented their income by selling the gold foil provided for atelier use.[6]

By his own decision Âli was once again deprived of a regular post, his appointment to the royal atelier being a special one. He spent the year in Istanbul trying to obtain a position from which to advance his career along one of the established employment tracks. Although he must have realized that his chances for a post at court were slim, Âli did not lower the level of his expectations. His request to be made a provincial finance director was reasonable in view of his previous service as a *timar* registrar; however, his simultaneous pleas for appointment as governor-general of a major province were considerably less reasonable, for neither his rank nor his experience would render such an appointment plausible.[7] Âli was not deterred by the enormity of his demands for recognition, for he still believed he could gain royal intercession. He attempted to parlay Murad's favorable reception of the *Book of Victory* into something more tangible by pandering shamelessly to Murad's keen interest in popular esotericism. In early 1584/992 Âli presented a series of short treatises designed to appeal to Murad's fascination with Sufism. In the first of these, entitled *Câmi' ül-kemâlât, Gatherer of Perfections*, Âli explained the secrets of the number twelve, and stated that Sultan Murad would live for one hundred and twenty years. Âli explicated the numerological principles (*ilm-i cefr*) behind this assertion in a companion piece called *Tali' üs-selâtin, The Sultans' Ascendant*; Âli offered to compose more treatises on numerology if the sultan would allow him to utilize the royal library. Finally, Âli submitted a commentary on five of Murad's mystical verses, to which he gave the title *Nükât ül-kal fi tazmîn il-makal, Subtleties of Discourse on the Quotation of Speech*.[8]

[6] COUNSEL, I, 61 (trans.), 156-57 (text). The sale of gold foil by Palace artisans is confirmed by MD 23, doc. 174, which records the appointment of a new supervisor to the Palace workshops so that such practices might be halted.

[7] For more detailed discussion of the Ottoman career paths, see chapter 6.

[8] MS Reşid Efendi 1146, 50b-78b (*Câmi' ül-kemâlât*); 102b-108b (*Tali' üs-sel-âtin*); 113b-116b (*Nükât ül-kal*). The presentation copy of *Câmi' ül-kemalat*, now located in The Scottish National Library, is dated February-March 1584/Safer 992, and contains two miniature portraits of Murad (Walsh, "İstidâname," p. 131). Two other short treatises addressed to Murad

Âli also expressed more material concerns in these *opera minora*; the *Subtleties*, for example, contains yet another request that Âli be made chancellor. Âli had a special presentation copy of the *Gatherer of Perfections* adorned with two portraits of Sultan Murad, which were probably executed by moonlighting court artists. He also appended a personal petition to the monarch, in which he requested that Murad send him back to Aleppo, this time as finance director rather than as a lowly *timar* registrar. In the text of this document Âli justifies his request by citing his extensive experience in the area and intimate knowledge of local conditions and procedures. The province is in sore need of a reforming administrator, Âli states, and he goes on to recount instances of anarchy and administrative corruption in Aleppo, which the constituted authorities are afraid to report to the sultan. This petition contains many echoes of the *Counsel* in its condemnation of official irresponsibility, discussion of specific administrative problems, and emphasis on the need for officials, like Âli of course, who have local expertise and who will be answerable only to the sultan, who is ultimately responsible for the state's welfare. Stylistically the document is skillfully structured, for Âli introduces his comments with a numerological discussion. According to an apocalyptic tradition, he says, the destruction of Aleppo is to be one of the signs of the Last Days, and by 999, one year before the millennium, there will be no Arabs left on earth. Âli then turns the prophecy on its head, saying that it would be shameful for the sultan, through negligence, to allow the prophecy to come true before its time. Âli asks to be sent to Aleppo to put the situation right, and then to return to a post at court as Murad's ʿAlî Shîr Navâ'i, his counselor and court poet.[9]

Âli may have overestimated Murad's gullibility and passion for the arcane; his efforts to curry favor with eunuchs of the Harem and to attract the sultan's attention brought no results.[10] Frustration and desperation gripped Âli ever more strongly, and he supplemented literary offerings to Murad with verse petitions that became increasingly strident in tone. In these three

may also date from this period: İÜ Türkçe Mecmua 3543, 36b-39a (untitled), and 40b-47a (*Daka'ik üt-tevhid*).

[9] Walsh, "İstidâname." Âli may have been trying out some of the ideas for administrative reform which he presented in fuller form in the *Counsel*. The *istidâname* again demonstrates the nature of the unofficial information network of the Empire. In it Ali refers to a bedouin raid on the environs of Aleppo during the preceding Ramazan, which no official had communicated to the Porte. Ali was in Istanbul in Ramazan 991, so he must have learned of the affair from old friends in Aleppo.

[10] Apart from Gazanfer Ağa, Âli had close connections with another eunuch of the harem, Zirek Ağa, to whom Âli wrote (addressing him as "my son") while he was at work on the *Nusretname* (MENŞE, 240a-241a). A rumor of Murad's death had thrown Âli, his assignment for the sultan not yet completed, into a panic, but it was happily dispelled when his slave informed him of the rumor's falsehood. In his joy Âli set the slave free and performed a sacrificce at Eyüp.

odes Âli couches his demands in terms of posts at the upper level of the financial bureaucratic hierarchy. These are, in descending order, the offices of treasurer (*başdefterdarlık*); secretary-in-chief of the Imperial Council (*re'isülküttab*); finance director of either Egypt or Aleppo; or, at the very least, the post of deputy finance director (*defter kedhüdası*) in one of these two provinces. Âli gives two reasons why he should be granted his requests. The first is literacy: he should be promoted within the bureaucracy because his skill in *inşa* composition, demonstrated in his handling of international correspondence in the course of the Şirvan campaign, has been certified by Ottoman, Iranian, and Arab scholars. The second reason Âli gives echoes the thrust of the *Counsel*; his probity in administrative matters has been demonstrated, and Lala Mustafa Paşa, whose memory had been vindicated by the disgrace of Sinan Paşa, had cherished him. For all of this, Âli complains, he has been unable to attain even his minimal expectations because he has no vezir to promote his interests, no money to purchase an appointment, and because jealous courtiers and bureaucrats have slandered him and poisoned his repute. Âli suggests that, since the established bureaucratic career paths are thus closed to him, the sultan should recognize him by giving him a Palace appointment as a companion.[11]

In the composition of the *Counsel for Sultans*, which he had not yet completed at this time, Âli began to exhibit a preoccupation with *kanun* as a body of customary practice and a legal spirit pervading Ottoman administrative procedure. In these poetic petitions Âli shows a keen sense of *kanun* as customary law defining the promotional hierarchy within the established governmental career tracks. Having spent five years in what he considered a dead-end post, and being possessed of a very high opinion of his own worth, Âli was seeking any appointment that he considered worthy of him and which would lead him to yet higher office. In terms of late sixteenth-century promotion practice within the financial bureaucracy, which Âli had entered with his appointment to Aleppo, his requests make perfect sense for a man who had declared his desire to become either chancellor or treasurer (despite his avowed distaste for finance). The office of secretary-in-chief could lead to either of the two higher bureaucratic posts. Within the financial track alone, the finance directors of Aleppo and Egypt, two of the most important and prestigious provinces in the Empire, frequently attained the treasury immediately after their provincial posting. The position of deputy finance director in either Aleppo or Egypt could be a steppingstone to the provincial *defterdarlık*.[12] Ambitious as Âli was, he was extremely con-

[11] LAYİHAT, 10b-12a (probably composed mid-December 1583/early Zulhicce 991), 12a-14a, 152b-53a.

[12] Aleppo, formerly the seat of the old *Arab ve Acem defterdarlığı*, in the late sixteenth century retained its prestige as one of the oldest parts of the central financial system. Egypt was a

scious of the restrictions imposed on the mode, if not the extent, of his advancement by what he called *kanun*. Âli's vision and representation of dynastic law will be a theme that will recur frequently in the following pages.

An opportunity for advancement arrived in May 1584/Cümada I 992 with the news that the second vezir, Özdemiroğlu Osman Paşa, had quelled the rebellion of the Crimean Mehmed Giray Han. Âli requested, and was granted, the task of composing the official victory announcement. He performed this task for Sultan Murad, and also asked to be assigned to Osman Paşa's service.[13] Osman Paşa arrived in the capital two months later, acting on Gazanfer Ağa's advice that he come to Istanbul in order to capitalize on his victory. The hero of Şirvan, after six years of campaigning, had to face the hostility and intrigues of his fellow vezirs, particularly those of the incumbent chief minister, Siyavuş Paşa. The harem contingent, headed by Gazanfer Ağa, favored the appointment of the outsider Özdemiroğlu as grand vezir, and on 18 July 1584/20 Receb 992 the seal of office was presented to him in front of the assembled Council.[14]

Âli petitioned the new grand vezir for a suitable post, citing again the well-attested rectitude he had displayed in his years on campaign and in Aleppo. In attempting to secure an appointment from Özdemiroğlu, Âli appears to have invoked a new twist on the seniority principle. A letter preserved in Âli's correspondence was very probably sent by Özdemiroğlu Osman Paşa to the sultan in response to Âli's plea. The letter cites not only Âli's "two years" of service in the capital in preparation of the royal *Book of Victory*, but also the length of his service in all capacities as a consideration in reviewing his request for an appointment. His contemporaries in the religious career, the letter states, are now at the level of *mevleviyet*, judgeship of a major provincial capital, while those in financial service receive choice provincial finance directorships.[15] The implication of these state-

salyane province, its governor receiving a salary rather than a *hass* grant; it was extraordinarily rich and hence one of the most important sources of imperial revenue. For examples of *defterdar*s from these provinces being promoted to the capital, see above on Cübni Sinan, and CAIRO, p. 18.

[13] KA, Murad/26, Nur 3409, 258b-259b; the news of Osman Paşa's victory reached Istanbul 23 May 1584/13 Cümada I 992, and Âli composed the *fethname*. Âli also composed a personal letter of congratulations to Osman Paşa from Gazanfer Ağa, who portentously suggested that Osman come to court because great things might emerge for him from this victory (MENŞE, 279a-280b). Gazanfer may have secured the *fethname* commission for Âli.

[14] KA, Murad/27, Nur 3409, 259b-261. Osman Paşa arrived in Istanbul in mid-July 1584/ early Receb 992, and was appointed grand vezir on 28 July/20 Receb. Osman Paşa himself related to Âli his adventures with the *han* of the Crimea, and the tale of the reception he received in Istanbul (260b).

[15] MENŞE, 238a-239a, addressed to Sadrazam Osman Paşa. Âli says that all the *beğlerbeğis* of the east have written letters praising him, and that he has never been dismissed from a post. Özdemiroğlu himself may have responded to this by writing a letter to the sultan; MENŞE, 256a-256b, is "from the *serdar*," and dates from this time.

ments is clear; the regular character of the stratified Ottoman system and promotional procedure within career lines implies preservation of an approximate parity between the members of a peer group who enter the system at the same time. If Âli has not progressed as much as his peers, according to this schema, it must be because he has been unjustly hampered in his career. While seniority did actually function as one of the factors that determined individual career patterns, it did so within career tracks; Âli in fact had left the *ilmiye* and thus had given up any expectations such a career might foster, and he had spent only five years within the central bureaucracy. Âli's appeal to considerations of putative seniority, based on the fact that he had entered *ilmiye* training proper at about the age of fifteen, was spurious, for he had changed careers several times; he demanded seniority merely as a *kul*, a servant of the state.

Âli had good relations with Özdemiroğlu Osman Paşa, and this relationship finally brought him success in his efforts to secure a good position within the financial establishment. Through the new grand vezir's intercession, Âli was given a very important finance directorship, that of Erzurum, on 9 September 1584/4 Ramazan 992.[16] Özdemiroğlu himself volunteered to conduct a new campaign against the fractious Nogays and the Safavis; this expedition resulted in a twenty-year Ottoman occupation of the former Safavi capital of Tabriz. In mid-October 1584 Özdemiroğlu and his forces left Istanbul. Âli accompanied his new protector as far as Bolu, and then traveled on to Erzurum.[17]

ERZURUM
(1584-85)

ÂLI'S promotion to an important provincial capital improved his situation considerably. Instead of the 80,000 *akçe zeâmet* grant he had held in Aleppo, he now had a yearly *hass* income of 140,000 *akçe* at his disposal. Âli was determined to make a success of this posting, which could easily lead to an appointment as finance director of either Aleppo or Egypt, and he set out to demonstrate his fiscal acumen. He collected three years' worth of unpaid taxes amounting to some 7,100,000 *akçe* in revenue. By skillful management of local financial resources, the precise nature of which Âli does not specify, he had the fortress of Van, which had been severely damaged by the explosion of a powder magazine the year before, repaired with-

[16] KA, Murad/27, Nur 3409, 262a.

[17] See preceding note and Kütükoğlu, *Osmanlı*, p. 143.

out any cost to the treasury, although repair costs had been estimated at 800,000-1,000,000 *akçe*.[18]

Âli's responsibilities were weighty. Osman Paşa spent the winter in Kastamonu, and in the spring he began a leisurely progress toward the frontier capital of Erzurum, gathering forces. Âli had been sent ahead to prepare for the field marshal's arrival. The governor-general of Erzurum, Hasan Paşa b. Sokollu Mehmed, was away guarding Tomanis, on the Georgian border, and therefore Âli had to depute for the absent governor as well as for the field marshal. In this capacity he was charged with caring for the Safavi envoy Ibrâhîm Khân Turkmân, who had been held secretly in Erzurum since the autumn of 1584, pending a decision on what should be done with him.[19] Âli's preparatory tasks were made all the more difficult by food shortages and high prices engendered by the approach of the army. Even so, he managed to supply the Erzurum forces by personally subsidizing their food, buying on the market at higher prices and selling to the soldiery at lower ones.[20]

Âli's eight months in Erzurum were very nearly the height of his career in the financial service. His literary career prospered, too; it was during this period that Kınalızade Hasan Çelebi wrote to Âli asking for his bibliography for inclusion in his biographical dictionary of poets. Âli was sufficiently politically influential to help an old friend, the poet Sırri, to regain his post as judge of Trabzon after being dismissed. This is yet another indication that Âli did not necessarily practice the high principles he propounded in the *Counsel*, in which he decried nepotism. However, in the *Essence* Âli suggests that he personally took care to ensure Sırri's reform.[21] Âli's relations with his subordinates and colleagues were not always good, both because of his diligence and, it is clear, his pride. Osman Paşa arrived in Erzurum on 2 August 1585/5 Şa'ban 993, and Âli hoped to be rewarded for his services with a more important assignment. Unfortunately for Âli, Özdemiroğlu was

[18] MENŞE, 210b-211b (to Doğancı Mehmed Paşa); 211b-213a (to a vezir). The due revenues Âli collected were *mukata'a* taxes that had been left in *emanet*, or, more accurately, neglected due to bureaucratic confusion. Âli states that by *kanun* he should have gone to Aleppo, Egypt, or the capital after this post. Ayn-ı Ali, p. 24, gives the value of the *hass* of the *defterdar* of Erzurum as 142,985 *akçe*.

On the repair of the fortress, see KA, Murad/30, Nur 3409, 362a, and Kütükoğlu, *Osmanlı*, p. 140. Âli gives no details on how he financed the repair, saying only that he spared the treasury any expense by skillful management (*ahsen-i tedarükle*) and by being just. He himself paid for the forty sheep sacrificed at the completion of the repairs.

[19] KA, Murad/30, Nur 3409, 362a. MD 59, doc. 29, dated 30 March 1585/28 Rebi' I 993, is an order to Âli as *defterdar* of Erzurum to prepare personally supplies and war materiel for the impending arrival of Osman Paşa; MD 59, docs. 270, 271, dated 24 July 1585/26 Receb 993, are addressed to Hasan Paşa, *beğlerbeği* of Erzurum, in *muhafaza* of Tomanis. See Kütükoğlu, *Osmanlı*, pp. 140-41, on Ibrâhîm Khân Turkmân's second Ottoman mission.

[20] MENŞE, 212b, 242a.

[21] Âli had known Sırri since his student days; see KA Selim/Şu'ara, Nur 3409, 277b.

accompanied by the secretary-in-chief (*re'isülküttab*) Hamze Çelebi. This was the same Hamze who had briefly served as chancellor, and whom Âli had sought to displace. Hamze Çelebi was doubtless aware that Âli had publicly expressed contempt for his abilities and qualifications, and he was now in a position to avenge himself. At the time that Özdemiroğlu Osman Paşa arrived in Erzurum, the central financial bureaus were undergoing an administrative shakeup, which provided a real opportunity for the grand vezir to secure Âli's promotion; but Hamze Çelebi persuaded Osman Paşa to appoint Âli finance director of Baghdad, a relative backwater. Âli was outraged, and he vented his spleen against the "ignorant" Hamze in a letter to İbrahim Paşa, governor-general of Egypt. He described the secretary of the Imperial Council as

> the one who had control of appointments to all posts, who in relationship to the virtual monarch of that army [i.e., Osman Paşa] was the vezir to whom no gratitude is due, the minister of manifold faults; [he is] a lecher without shame, leader of the debauched ones who take pride in lewdness, the evil-working chief of pederasts who is called secretary-in-chief.[22]

This characterization is mere prologue to a detailed rehearsal of the seamier details of the behavior of the bibulous, boy-chasing Hamze, whom Âli calls a dishonor to the state. Such invective, of course, however morally satisfying, could do Âli little good. Chagrined, he left Erzurum in mid-August 1585, and made his way to Baghdad by way of Konya.[23]

[22] MENŞE, 242a-b. The identity of the secretary-in-chief present on this campaign with Hamze is established by SELANİKİ, p. 186.

[23] Kütükoğlu, *Osmanlı*, p. 149; Osman Paşa left Erzurum on 11 August 1585/15 Şa'ban 993, by which time Âli must have been dismissed from the finance directorship of Erzurum. This supposition is confirmed by archival evidence: *Maliyeden Müdevver* 426, p. 2, is the beginning of a financial summary of the state of the Erzurum treasury during the tenure of a *defterdar* named Yusuf, covering the period 26 Şa'ban to end Zulhicce 993. In fact, because of frequent shifts of personnel and sometimes long delays in the arrival of appointees at their new posts, such appointments are difficult to trace precisely. For example, MD 59, doc. 165, and MD 60, doc. 165, both of which are dated 22 November 1585/28 Zulka'de 993, are orders to "Erzurum *defterdarı* Sinan." This appears to conflict with the *Maliyeden Müdevver* document. Yusuf may have been doing interim duty until Sinan's arrival and may have stayed on for some time. It should also be noted that the unqualified term "*defterdar*" in archival documents may apply to either the *hazine* or *timar defterdarı* of a province. The second of these MD orders may cast some light on how Âli saved money, and on why he was dismissed. It inquires why there are no wages for the garrison troops (*neferat*), and why the salary budgets are in a shambles.

Âli may not have received the Baghdad appointment immediately, though this is what he says. KPT 246, p. 88, dated 12 November 1585/18 Zulka'de 993, states that the incumbent *defterdar* of Baghdad has died, that the finances of the provinces are in extreme disorder, and that a replacement for the deceased and a new governor-general must be found at once. This news may have reached Erzurum before it got to Istanbul, and Âli may simply have been appointed directly from Erzurum by Osman Paşa before the details of the incumbent's dismissal

It is possible that Âli's Baghdad appointment was a reward for his assiduous service rather than a punishment. The province was to be on the southern front of the impending struggle with the Safavis; furthermore, its finances were in disorder after the sudden death of the incumbent finance director, and had to be put right. In at least one poem, admittedly one suppressed from his second *divan*, Âli expressed joy at the appointment.[24] However, by the time he arrived in Baghdad in late 1585/993, his affairs had taken a distinctly inauspicious turn. Immediately after the Ottoman armies occupied Tabriz, Âli's new patron, Özdemiroğlu Osman Paşa, died.[25] Âli also learned upon reaching Baghdad that his position had been given to another who had contracted for it; all that remained for him was to perform interim duty as finance director until his replacement arrived to take over. The desperate Âli had no recourse but to seek, once again, the help of influential people in Istanbul. He wrote immediately to the governor-general of Rumeli, Doğancı Mehmed Paşa, saying:

> Although I had been sent to Baghdad, the news of my dismissal entered the city with me, for the post had been given to another in contract [*iltizam*] by an act of the Porte. Plagued with such disaster, I have remained in the wastes of Baghdad and have hastened to make my case known to you.[26]

EXCURSUS: CHAOS IN THE WARTIME APPOINTMENT PROCESS

GRAND vezirs and field marshals on campaign had the authority to make appointments in the field on the sultan's behalf. In wartime, posting decisions made in the field could conflict with those made at the Porte. This problem was compounded by communication lags and by the late sixteenth-century financial crisis, which resulted in an increase in the practice of appointment by contract as a means of dealing with the ever greater deficits produced by inflation, military expenditure, and disruption of the finances

---

were worked out. Clearly some interim arrangement was made since Âli not only had to travel to Baghdad but did so in a very roundabout fashion, through Konya, where he planned to visit the tomb of Rumi (MENŞE, 259b-260a).

In the middle of August 1585/Şa'ban 993, the three ranking financial officers of the Empire (Rumeli, Anadolu, and *şıkk-ı sani defterdarları*) were dismissed and replaced (SELANİKİ, p. 192, dated 15 Şa'ban; KPT 246, p. 29, dated 14 Şa'ban). The new *şıkk-ı sani* appointee was Köse (Köseç) Mustafa, the steward of the late Lala Mustafa Paşa and an old enemy of Âli (COUNSEL, II, 12 (trans.), 123 (text).

24 VARİDAT, 64a-b.

25 Osman Paşa died on 28 October 1585/4 Zulka'de 993, according to Kütükoğlu, *Osmanlı*, p. 159.

26 MENŞE, 211b.

of border provinces.[27] The growth of *iltizam* and protracted warfare had a direct impact upon administrative processes and gave the Ottoman financial crisis something of the character of a vicious cycle. The governors and other officials of border provinces, far removed from central supervision, had ample opportunity for extortion and financial malfeasance in the constant state of emergency that existed in the frontier regions. Therefore an already strained financial situation became worse. The more officials were dismissed for maladministration or corruption, or due to the appointment of contract officials (*mültezims*), the shorter the terms in office became. Therefore officeholders, deprived of any assurance of extended tenure, took maximum advantage of their brief terms in office for personal financial gain, and the situation became worse still.

At the same time that Âli was traveling from Erzurum to Baghdad to take up the post given to him by Özdemiroğlu Osman Paşa, the Porte appointed Sührab, the Kurdish *sançak beği* of Derteng, to be the new finance director of Baghdad. Sührab had written to the Porte saying that the treasury of Baghdad was suffering great losses due to the recent death of the *defterdar* and the venality of the incumbent governor-general, Süleyman Paşa (b. Kubad Paşa). Sührab suggested that Husrev Paşa, who was known to be honest, be appointed governor-general of Baghdad. He further requested that he himself be given the finance directorship of the province, together with the rank of pursuivant (*çavuş*) of the Porte and the post of *sancak* governor of Mosul. These measures, he said, would solve the problems of Baghdad and would yield greatly increased revenues for the central treasury. An imperial rescript (*hatt-ı hümayun*) was issued, granting all of Sührab's requests on condition that he send to Istanbul 26,666 *akçe* each year above the usual Baghdad remittance (*irsaliye*).[28]

In theory the military administration of a province and its finances were in charge of independent appointees—the governor-general and finance director, respectively—each of whom was responsible directly to the Porte. This separation of powers was deliberate and intended to prevent abuse. However, in certain extraordinary situations, and particularly in wartime, an individual could attain both military and financial control of all or part of a province, as was the case with Sührab. Conversely, greater numbers of financial experts began to be appointed to *sancak* and *vilayet* governorships. As the importance of the financial bureaucracy grew in the late sixteenth century, financial authority presented functionaries with the greatest opportunities for personal enrichment under legal cover. In some provinces *beğ-*

[27] See Röhrborn, *Verwaltungsgeschichte*, pp. 125-44, on the nature and growth of *iltizam*, which his data suggests began to become relatively common practice on the *sancak* and *vilayet* level at precisely this time (1585/993).

[28] KPT 246, p. 88, dated 11 November 1585/18 Zulka'de 993.

lerbeğis had the right of *nezaret*, supervision of the financial affairs of the province, although such matters were actually handled by the finance director in those provinces that had a full complement of financial officials. For governors-general, *nezaret* involved not only theoretical supervision of financial matters, as the administrative head of a province, but also actual assumption of fiscal control when the finance director was absent, dismissed, or incompetent. In a wartime situation in which dismissals, absences of officials on campaign, and administrative changes and discontinuity became increasingly frequent, so the governor-general's right of supervision came to be exercised more and more.[29] All of these factors combined to produce the sort of administrative situation Âli found at Baghdad when he arrived there in 1585. In a section of the *Counsel* in which he argues for the abolition of *nezaret*, Âli writes:

> This humble one became finance director of Baghdad, the abode of the caliphate, in the year 992 [sic]. During my time there I found that governors-general who had been dismissed from their posts were each bidding 40,000 gold pieces for the government of Baghdad. As much as I calculated what they received from the treasury in cash each year, I reached the conclusion that this did not amount to more than 30,000 gold pieces. Why then should they give so much money and be so desirous of the government of Baghdad? Wondering about this, I investigated the receipts of one of them; I learned that, by virtue of being the agent of the finance directors, in one year he collected 11,000,000 *akçe* for the imperial treasury, and 24,000,000 *akçe* for that devastated ruin that was his own treasury.
>
> If their right of supervision was abolished, and [financial] matters entrusted solely to the finance directors, there can be no doubt that [the revenues of] the imperial treasury would increase day by day, and that the market of graft which arises from them [i.e., the governors] would suffer a decline. I swear by God and His glory that, for that government for which they now pay 40,000 gold pieces with supervision [of finances], they would not give even 5,000 florins without the supervision.[30]

Âli's reference to "bidding" here is a reference to the late sixteenth-century practice of appointees' giving appointment gifts (*pişkeş*) to the grand vezir upon being assigned to a post. Such payments were outright gifts; they were not part of the official *iltizam* process, nor were they bribes, at least in theory, although they came to be viewed as such by Ottoman commentators

[29] See chapters 5 and 7, and Appendix A.
[30] COUNSEL, I, 65 (trans.), 161-62 (text).

who decried the growing prevalence of the practice and the abuse of a courteous custom to the point that it became an institutionalized form of corruption.[31] The grand vezir's acceptance of *pişkeş* bids amounted to post-selling, as did *iltizam* in the final analysis, and introduced yet another variable into the chaotic appointment process that shaped the careers of sixteenth-century Ottomans.

Contract appointment, bidding for posts, war, and the existence of two independent centers of authority, one in Istanbul and one in the field, wrought havoc with the Ottoman appointment system. The disorganization that resulted affected the highest levels of provincial service, as well as those lower echelons that were at least in part made up of the protégés of the great paşas. The situation that led up to and followed Âli's assignment to the finance directorship of Baghdad provides an excellent example of how the system did and did not function. Happily, a surviving appointment register enables us to trace the administrative history of Baghdad in 1585-86. In autumn 1585 the government of Damascus was assigned by the vezir İbrahim Paşa, then in Istanbul, to Elvendoğlu Ali Paşa; at the same time the grand vezir and field marshal Osman Paşa, then in the east, gave Damascus to Husrev Paşa.[32] The Porte decided to resolve the problem of having two *beğlerbeği*s by appointing Ali Paşa to replace Üveys Paşa as governor of Damascus. Husrev Paşa had to be compensated; two weeks later (late October 1585) Süleyman Paşa, the governor-general of Baghdad, was dismissed, and his post was given to Husrev Paşa, possibly at the instigation of Sührab, *sancak beği* of Derteng.[33]

Further administrative developments in Baghdad can be followed with the aid of the same register. The accompanying table summarizes the information this register provides on the *beğlerbeği*s and *defterdar*s of the province Between October 1585 and April 1586 the finance directorship of Baghdad changed hands five or six times. The first finance director died, and he was replaced by Âli, who was simultaneously dislodged by Sührab, who was appointed by the Porte rather than by the grand vezir. According to the register, Sührab had been replaced by, or perhaps was appointed as deputy for, one Süleyman. In April 1586 Ahmed took Süleyman's place, perhaps only for a few days, if the final entry is not a scribal error. During this same seven-month period the governorship of Baghdad passed from Süleyman Paşa, to Husrev Paşa, to (Elvendoğlu) Ali Paşa, and finally back to Süleyman Paşa, who is listed as governor-general of the province in orders

[31] On the development of this institution and its perception by Âli and his successors in the *nasihatname* genre as a form of bribery, see Röhrborn, *Verwaltungsgeschichte*, pp. 114-25.

[32] KPT 246, p. 69, dated 15 October 1585/20 Şevval 993.

[33] KPT 246, p. 73, dated 27 October 1585/3 Zulka'de 993.

DATE	NAME, TITLE
27 January 1586/6 Safer 994	Süleyman, *defterdar* of Baghdad[1]
22 April 1586/3 Cümada I 994	Süleyman, *defterdar* of Baghdad[2]
26 April 1586/7 Cümada I 994	Ali Paşa, *beğlerbeği* of Baghdad[3]
27 April 1586/8 Cümada I 994	Ahmed Efendi, *defterdar* of Baghdad[4]
28 April 1586/9 Cümada I 994	Ali Paşa, former *beğlerbeği* of Baghdad Süleyman, former *defterdar* of Baghdad[5]
28 April 1586/9 Cümada I 994	Ahmed, *defterdar* of Baghdad[6]
30 April 1586/11 Cümada I 994	Süleyman, *hazine defterdarı* of Baghdad[7]

[1] KPT 246, p. 138. [2] KPT 246, p. 228. [3] KPT 246, p. 228. [4] KPT 246, p. 232. [5] KPT 246, p. 234. [6] KPT 246, p. 235. [7] KPT 246, p. 238.

dated 17 June 1586/28 Cümada II 994.[34] It should be noted that changes at the top of the provincial system were sometimes accompanied by broader administrative changes; the example utilized here shows that the governor-general Âli Paşa and the finance director Süleyman were replaced within a few days of one another.

A caveat must be appended to this examination of wartime appointment practice in the eastern provinces of the Ottoman Empire through archival notations. It is difficult to judge the extent to which personnel changes made on paper were carried out in practice. It is probable that, unless new appointees were on the spot, administrative changes may sometimes have taken months to effect, particularly when conflicting appointments were issued or when the same office changed hands in a matter of weeks. It is also probable that the administrative confusion that these documents portray is exacerbated, from the historian's point of view, by periodic scribal carelessness; dismissed officials were ranked according to the last post they had held, and in some cases scribes, whether through neglect or inability to keep up with the most recent developments, failed to precede the names and titles of such officials with the word *sabık*, "former." Despite these reservations, a clear picture of administrative disorganization and irresponsibility at the upper levels of provincial government emerges, and this picture is of immediate relevance to this study of Âli's career. Âli was not alone in the difficulties he experienced in trying to establish himself within the financial service. Short tenure in office and frequent dismissal were facts of life for a great many Ottoman administrators and bureaucrats in the late sixteenth century. The violent fluctuations the provincial government of the province of Baghdad underwent in 1585 and 1586 also help to explain how Âli, al-

[34] MD 60, docs. 655-57, 660, 662-66.

though he learned of his dismissal upon his arrival, could remain in Baghdad performing interim duty as finance director for so long; he was the man on the spot.

BAGHDAD
(1585-86)

ALTHOUGH Âli's Baghdad sojourn was a political disaster, the provincial capital offered substantial cultural compensations. Âli found some thirty poets in residence there, all of whom turned out to greet him upon his arrival. Among these were Tarzi, Ruhi, and Ahdi.[35] In Baghdad Âli had a rare opportunity to immerse himself in a largely Persianate milieu and to learn firsthand about Safavi cultural affairs. In addition to such Iranian poets as Ahdi and the celebrated trilingual *divan* poet Ruhi, Âli met and conversed frequently with Quṭb al-dîn Yazdî, who had served as storyteller (*qiṣṣeh-khvân*) and calligrapher at the court of Shâh Ṭahmâsb. Quṭb al-dîn had long before composed for the shah a biographical treatise on calligraphers and painters, a copy of which Âli acquired in Baghdad. This work, and his friendship with Quṭb al-dîn, spurred Âli's already well-developed interest in calligraphy and book illumination, and led him to compose the *Artists' Exploits* (*Menakıb-ı hünerveran*) the next year. The *Exploits* utilizes oral communications from Quṭb al-dîn as well as his biographical treatise, and it contains a number of references to contemporary Iranian practitioners of the calligraphic arts.[36]

Jobless in Baghdad, Âli must have felt that his career was permanently stalled. In one letter that he wrote to a vezir at this time, he asked to be retired, or to be given an assignment that would enable him to make the pilgrimage to Mecca and Medina. Failing this, he said, he would quit govern-

[35] KA, Selim/Şu'ara, "Ahdi," Nur 3409, 282b, Nur 3406, 201a. Ahdi, of Iranian origin, was born in Baghdad. After spending ten years in Istanbul he completed a *tezkere* of poets, the *Gülşen üs-şu'ara*, in 1563-64/971, and retired to his native city, where he died in 1593/1002 (Levend, *Türk Edebiyatı Tarihi*, I, 269-70).

[36] Âli refers to his acquisition of the *Risâleh* of Quṭb al-dîn in Baghdad on p. 7, and on the following page cites as his second oral source Abdullah Kırimî (*kâtib-i tâtâr*), one of the foremost calligraphers at the Ottoman court. For references to contemporary Safavi calligraphers, see pp. 51-52 (Muḥammad Raḥîm-i Mashhadî); p. 52 (Menlâ ʿAyshî, a *qûrchî* of the shah); p. 55 (Menlâ Muḥammad Rizâ Tabrîzî, who came to Istanbul in 994); p. 73 (Menlâ Qâsim ʿAlî Tabrîzî, who came to Istanbul in 995). Quṭb al-dîn's Persian *Risâleh*, completed in 1556-57/964, has been published in abridged form by Khadîv-Jam, "Risâleh-i dar târîkh-i khaṭṭ va naqqâshî," *Sukhan* 17, nos. 6-7 (1967/1346): 666-76. The uniqueness of Âli's *Exploits* as a source for Safavi as well as Ottoman painters and calligraphers has been appreciated, and the work extensively utilized, by Martin Dickson and Stuart Cary Welch, *The Houghton Shahnameh*, 2 vols. (Cambridge, 1981), I, *passim*, esp. 242a-243b.

ment service and become a hermit.[37] Âli consoled himself with culture, pious contemplation, and pilgrimages to the holy places of Iraq. Despite his lack of employment, he had enough in savings to endow and build a fountain at Kerbela, the site of Imâm Ḥusayn's martyrdom.[38]

Good news arrived in early spring 1586. Üveys Paşa, Âli's old friend who served successively as governor-general of Aleppo, Damascus, and again Aleppo, was appointed to a second term as treasurer.[39] Âli wrote to Üveys to congratulate him as soon as he received the news. Dismissed from his post, Âli said, he was still in Baghdad, but would leave by mid-July/end of Receb. He pleaded with Üveys to have him made director of the "second branch," third-ranking financial official of the Empire, before his arrival in Istanbul. Âli clearly trusted the strength of his relationship with Üveys Paşa, for he left Baghdad that summer. Âli's itinerary took him first to Mosul. There the inhabitants complained to him of the behavior of the *sancak beği*, Sührab, whom they described as a Kurdish brigand. They further accused Sührab, the same man who had displaced Âli as finance director of Baghdad, of harboring Shi'i sympathies and of collecting illegal taxes. Âli assisted the dignitaries of Mosul, and avenged himself, by writing a letter on their behalf to the Porte, in which he exposed Sührab's depradations.[40]

ISTANBUL
(1586-88)

ÂLI continued his journey through Diyar Bakır and Konya to Istanbul, where he arrived in November 1586. Üveys Paşa may never have received Âli's letter, or may have been unable to help him, for Âli found no post waiting for him in Istanbul.[41] In any event, Üveys, who had been brought to the capital to rectify the chaotic financial situation of the central treasury, was soon thereafter (February 1587/Rebi' I 995) appointed governor-gen-

[37] MENŞE, 213a.

[38] The documents of appointment of the administrator of the *vakıf* endowment (*mütevelli*) and the caretaker of the *sebilhane* (*müsebbil*) are found in MENŞE, 243a-244a, 244a-244b, and in İÜ Türkçe Mecmua 3543, 90b-105a. They are dated 9-19 May 1586/early Cümada II 994, and name the Baghdad poet Derviş Kelâmi/Cihan Dede and the dervish Zahir Abdal as *mütevelli* and *müsebbil*, respectively, effective 1 Ramazan 994. Âli's special attachment to the Holy Imams appears clearly in his *divans*, all of which include numerous *mersiyes*, elegies traditionally composed for Aşura, 10 Muharrem, the anniversary of Ḥusayn's martyrdom.

[39] SELANİKİ, p. 204, gives March-April 1586/Rebi' II 994 as the date of the appointment. However, KPT 246, p. 153, dates it to 26 February/7 Rebi' I of that year. SELANİKİ probably refers to the date of Üveys's arrival in Istanbul.

[40] MENŞE, 254a-255a.

[41] MENŞE, 278b-279b, to Üveys Paşa; 261a-262b, from Âli, in Konya, to Su'udi Efendi, saying he intends to arrive in Istanbul before the *id-i şerif*, 10 Zulhicce, which in A.H. 994 fell on 22 November 1586.

eral of Egypt so that he could do the same there; he could no longer be of much assistance to Âli.[42]

After a short period of rest, Âli once again began the now familiar round of pleading. While he continued to address appeals to the sultan, Âli spent much time and energy cultivating Gazanfer Ağa, Hoca Sa'düddin, and a friend of long standing, the governor-general of Rumeli, Doğancı Mehmed Paşa. Soon after Âli's arrival in Istanbul, Mehmed Paşa, who was also a good friend of Üveys Paşa, was made vezir and royal companion (1 February 1587/22 Safer).[43] Far from admitting desperation, Âli raised the level of his demands in the appeals he made to these dignitaries; in addition to the posts of chancellor, secretary-in-chief, and finance director of Aleppo, he asked for a finance directorship of the Porte, the finance directorship of Egypt, and the government of either Basra or Aleppo.[44]

In terms of his rank (the highest post he had held was that of finance director of Erzurum) and promotion practice, Âli could not be considered eligible for any of these posts except for a provincial finance directorship, or possibly either the "second branch" (*şıkk-ı sani defterdarlığı*) or secretariat (*riyaset*). His dream of attaining the chancellorship, for which professional seniority was not a necessity, was of long standing. It appears that Âli the careerist was at this point trying to take advantage of the administrative disorder, nepotistic practice, and contract system that he deplored in the *Counsel*. For example, in asking Sultan Murad to make him governor-general of either Aleppo or Basra, Âli states that a large number of appointments to such posts have been made by contract (*iltizam*) and he promises to reform provincial finances and bring in new revenues if his request is granted.[45] Âli's argument, of course, evades the issue of his professional eligibility for

[42] SELANİKİ, p. 318; KA, Murad/38, Nur 3409, 397a-397b; Cairo, p. 74 (trans.), pp. 164-65 (text). Üveys was appointed *beğlerbeği* of Egypt in mid-February 1587/Rebi' I 995, and arrived there in May-June/Cümada II. He remained there until he died in 1591/999, and was given the rank of vezir a year before his death. Âli praises Üveys as both a sound financial administrator and a just and firm governor, and finds no fault with him.

[43] The date of Mehmed Paşa's appointment is given by SELANİKİ, p. 218. His career is outlined in KA, Murad/35, Nur 3409, 391b-393b. Âli does not give him high marks for effectiveness, and in particular castigates him for working against his former ally, Damad İbrahim Paşa. This judgment may reflect Âli's friendly relationship with İbrahim Paşa, about whom, however, he did not hesitate to speak frankly.

[44] LAYİHAT, 144b-145a, to Sultan Murad, asking to be made *beğlerbeği* of Aleppo or Basra; 134a, saying that two good positions in the Imperial Council have just fallen vacant, and that one of them should be given to Âli rather than to the ignorant ones (*edani*) who have received them. Though this request is impossible to date with absolute certainty, it probably refers to the administrative changes that followed Üveys Paşa's appointment to Egypt. LAYİHAT, 44a-45a, to Doğancı Mehmed Paşa, complaining of dismissal and asking for the *beğlerbeğilik* of Basra; 142a, to Gazanfer Ağa and Zirek Ağa, asking for the *nişancılık, riyaset*, or *defterdarlık* of the Porte; 38a-39a, 39a-b, to Gazanfer Ağa, datable to autumn 1587/mid-late 995; 19b-20b, asking for a *beğlerbeğilik* and promising to be of use to Gazanfer.

[45] MENŞE, 145a-b.

appointment as a governor-general, before even serving as a district (*sancak*) governor.[46] In two odes Âli addressed to Gazanfer Ağa in the spring of 1587, he requested that the Ağa use his influence to have Âli appointed finance director of Egypt under the new governor-general Üveys Paşa. The incumbent finance director, Âli says, is a protégé of Hoca Sa'düddin who has held successive important financial posts for the previous seven years; if he is dismissed so that Âli, who has been jobless for over a year, might be appointed in his place, he will not remain without a post for long.[47] The gentle and somewhat shame-faced tone of these odes suggests that Âli was uncomfortable with the ethical impropriety of his request, and that he meant to play upon Gazanfer Ağa's vanity as a patron rather than upon any animosity for Sa'düddin. This appeal also suggests the possibility that a sort of "share the wealth" ethic may have counterbalanced the fierce competition operative within the upper ranks of the expanding bureaucracy. The number of posts available to financial officials was limited, while the number of candidates for positions who had bureaucratic expertise was growing, although a relatively small number of functionaries dominated and exchanged the highest posts. It is possible that bureaucratic expansion produced a limited overpopulation of the financial service in particular, and that an abundance of candidates subject to periodic promotions combined with patronage-network operations to contribute to the increasingly rapid turnover in bureaucratic and even military appointments that became so pronounced toward the end of the sixteenth century.

Âli's appeals went unanswered, and for the first year back in Istanbul he compensated for unemployment with furious literary activity. When a new prince was born in February 1587/mid-Rebi' I 995, Âli hastened to compose and submit to Sultan Murad a short work on the auspicious astrological aspects of the event, entitled *Ferâ'id ül-vilâde, Unique Pearls on the Birth*.[48] The *Counsel* was most likely presented at this time too, since the work contains no additions after 1586/994.[49] Soon thereafter, at the request of Doğancı Mehmed Paşa, he completed yet another work designed to appeal to Murad's interest in popular esotericism. This treatise, called *Mir'at ül-avâlim, Mirror of the Worlds*, explicates popular cosmology, the major calendar systems used in historical (Islamic and pre-Islamic) times, and gives an account of the signs of the Apocalypse, which in popular thought was expected at the Muslim millennium, then only five years away. Âli dedi-

[46] On the eligibility of financial officials for *beğlerbeğilik*, see chapter 6.

[47] MENŞE, 38a-39a, 39a-b.

[48] *Ferâ'id ül-vilâde*, İÜ Türkçe Mecmua 3543, 28b-32a. The colophon gives the date and place as mid-Rebi' I 995, Istanbul, and refers to the author's extreme haste.

[49] See above, p. 99. If the illustrated *Cami'ül-buhur* (see p. 106 above) was actually prepared by Âli, he would have presented it soon after his return from Baghdad.

cated the *Mirror*, which in later centuries became extremely popular, to Doğancı Mehmed Paşa and Sultan Murad.[50]

Within two months of presenting the *Pearls*, Âli signed completed copies of two more extensive and more significant works. The first of these, the *Artists' Exploits*, he dedicated to Hoca Sa'düddin in early April 1587/late Rebi' II 995.[51] The contrast between the popular treatises Âli wrote for Murad, and the learned, polished style of the *Exploits*, is striking. Âli was far more successful when he exercised his learning, training, and intellectual and social interests than when he wrote to flatter or to please what to him was an alien taste. Âli, the man of culture and observer of society, gave his inclinations full rein in his next composition, the *Kavâ'id ül-mecâlis, The Etiquette of Salons*.[52] Sultan Murad had asked his companion, Doğancı Mehmed Paşa, questions on polite manners and social mores (*mecâlis ve âdâb*); Mehmed Paşa, in turn, suggesed that Âli write a treatise on the subject. The result was a semisatirical examination of types of social gatherings, sexual mores, and other matters. Âli included in it verses that a host could use to avert an embarrassing situation, such as when the arrival of young boys in search of wine and amusement aroused desires that might threaten to lower the tone of the party.[53] Âli also used the work as a vehicle to express his growing sense of social degeneration. Although the literary gatherings of twenty years before had been serious affairs devoted to the cultivation of learning and friendship, Âli says, they have become, among those wealthy enough to invite people to their homes, pretexts for drink and ostentation. Therefore there is a need for a manual explaining the rules of social propriety and the true character of the lost art of social intercourse. Âli went so far as to prescribe the size of house and degree of luxury appropriate to various ranks within the class of Ottoman servitors.[54]

If Âli may be believed, the *Etiquette of Salons* became instantly popular. Hoca Sa'düddin was particularly impressed, and asked him to expand the work.[55] In the *Etiquette* we see, for the first time, Âli writing for himself

[50] *Mir'at ül-avâlim*, MS Reşid Efendi 1146, 80b-101b. The dedication to Mehmed Paşa, whose salons Âli attended, occurs on 81a-82a, and the date of composition is given on 98b; Âli slyly remarks that in fact no Signs of the Hour have as yet appeared. Not all manuscripts of the work (of which there are many; see AB, pp. 19-21, for a partial list) contain the dedication to Mehmed Paşa. Âli certainly deleted this portion after Mehmed Paşa's disgrace and death.

[51] MH, pp. 5-7. One of the texts utilized by İnal in his edition gives the end of Rebi' II as the final date of composition (İNAL, p. 133).

[52] A number of manuscripts of the work exist. MS Reşid Efendi 1146, 119b-142a, probably an autograph, gives a colophon date of 7-16 June 1587/early Receb 995.

[53] MS İÜ Türkçe 3951, 7b-9b.

[54] MS İÜ Türkçe 3951, 1b-4a. Âli's observations on luxury and rank have been studied by Andreas Tietze, "Muṣṭafâ ʿÂlî on Luxury and the Status Symbols of Ottoman Gentlemen," *Studia Turcologica Memoriae Alexii Bombaci Dicata* (Naples, 1982), pp. 577-90.

[55] MEVA'İD, pp. 4-7. This facsimile edition of the *Mevâ'id*, which Âli undertook twelve

with the directness, honesty, and racy sense of humor and style that would mark most of his later works. Thematically, too, the work was original, and it marked a new phase in Âli's intellectual career; his subsequent fame rests very largely upon this personal fascination with his society, its people, and its history, which Âli began to display in this work and developed in subsequent writings.

Âli does not seem to have exaggerated the impression made by this treatise, and perhaps by other literary efforts. He actually put a copy of the *Etiquette* in mortmain (*vakıf*), restricting its circulation outside of Istanbul and stipulating the conditions (quality, accuracy, etc.) under which it might be copied. The practice of putting copies of new compositions in endowment, to which Âli refers elsewhere in his writings, would appear to have constituted a form of copyright. The deed of endowment was signed by eight of the most prominent ulema of the time. Each of these preceded his signature with a testimonial to Âli's superlative learning, eloquence, and rhetorical skill in three languages.[56] In addition to gaining recommendations, Âli, now approaching the age of fifty, was reestablishing contact with his intellectual and cultural roots in the *medrese*. This is a theme that appears with increasing frequency during this period. Nearly thirty years earlier he had left the *ilmiye* for a literary scribal career and, by his own lights, had failed to achieve the status he felt he deserved. His friend Baki, by contrast, had recently held the posts of judge of Istanbul and military judge of Anatolia.[57] Âli was very conscious of the extent to which he and his schoolmates had parted company in rank as well as in profession. Three of the latest letters found in

years later as a continuation of the *Kavâ'id*, is now supplemented by a modern Turkish translation and commentary by Orhan Şaik Gökyay: *Görgü ve Toplum Kuralları üzerinde Ziyafet Sofraları*, 2 vols. (Istanbul, 1978). The earlier Turkish translation of Cemil Yener, *Mevâ'idü'nnefâ'is fi kavâ'idi'l-mecâlis* (Istanbul, 1975), is worthless.

[56] İnal refers to these recommendations, and quotes some of them, without giving manuscript details (İNAL, pp. 116-18). In 1977 I discovered a full copy in *Mecmua* 231 of the Türk Tarih Kurumu Library in Ankara. This manuscript is a copy of the original, and its folios are largely unnumbered. The *vakıf* document (f. 81a) occurs near the end (f. 86b) of a copy of the *Kavâ'id*. The testimonials and signatures fall on 88a-88b, an intervening page being misbound. The signatories are: Şeyhülislam Çivizade; Şeyhülislam Şeyhi Efendi; Bustanzade Efendi, military judge of Rumeli; Baha'üddin Efendi, military judge of Rumeli; Abdülgani b. Emirşah, military judge of Anatolia; Menla Çelebi Mehmed, military judge of Rumeli; Menla Ahmed b. Ruhullah el-Ensari, military judge of Rumeli, judge of Edirne; and Lutfi Beğzade, judge of Edirne. The deed of endowment is dated 26 July 1587/28 Sa'ban 995. Since Çivizade died on 6 May 1587/28 Cümada I 995, according to Mustakimzade, *Devhat ül-Meşayih* (reprint, Istanbul 1978), p. 40, it is possible that the testimonials were collected separately or before the *vakıf* copy of the work was completed.

Âli made reference to this event ten years later in the KA. The text of this passage is quoted by İNAL (p. 116), and translated by Atsız (AB, p. 93; "12" in this text should be emended to "10").

[57] Baki became judge of Istanbul twice, in 1584/992 and 1586/994, and was made military judge of Anatolia soon after Âli's arrival in Istanbul in 1587/995 (Köprülü, "Baki," İA).

his correspondence, datable to the period 1582-86/992-94, attest to this new preoccupation. In one of these, addressed to a vezir, Âli states that he spent fifteen years studying to enter the *ilmiye*, and that had he remained in that career he would now be one of the highest-ranking professors or judges.[58] In a second letter devoted to a request to be appointed chancellor, Âli stresses the connection between *medrese* training and a successful chancery career in a discussion of the history of the chancellor's office.[59] A third epistle, probably sent to the sultan on Âli's behalf by Özdemiroğlu Osman Paşa, declares that while Âli's position is relatively humble, his contemporaries in the *ilmiye* are now at the level of *mevleviyet*, the judgeship of a major provincial capital.[60] The more preoccupied Âli became with the hopes and ideals of his youth, the more these colored his perceptions of the world around him. He became bitter, to be sure; his poems and letters from this period repeat ad nauseam that in his time the learned and able are not appreciated or patronized, and that only the dishonest and ignorant can make their way in the world. Âli was almost obsessed with the notion that a society's success could be measured by the accomplishments of, and regard shown to, its exponents of high culture. He withdrew into an inner world dominated by poetry and the past, and the bitter bureaucrat became an historian. It is intriguing to note in this connection that Âli's correspondence collection, *Menşe' ül-inşâ, The Fountainhead of Composition*, contains no material dated later than 1586/994; only a very few isolated examples of correspondence composed by Âli after that date exist, and his later works make no mention of any later correspondence compilation. In closing the *Fountainhead*, Âli gave up or rejected, to some extent, the official life and career building that his letters documented and symbolized. His presentation of the *Counsel* to Sultan Murad at about the same time, after years of work and hesitation, represented much the same thing: a break with the immediate past and present, and a casting aside of fear.

Âli's withdrawal from society and service was not entirely voluntary. During the next several years he had ample time to devote to history because his official career went into a decline marked more by stops than by starts. Despite his high standing with the ulema, he did not receive another post until late in February of 1588, when he was made finance director of the province of Rum (Sivas).[61] In comparison to the highest post he had previ-

[58] MENŞE, 211b-213a.

[59] MENŞE, 233b-235a.

[60] MENŞE, 256a-b.

[61] SELANİKİ, p. 238, gives the date of appointment as late February 1588/late Rebi' I 996. İNAL, pp. 30-32, disputes Selâniki's date for Âli's appointment on the basis of a partially quoted passage from the *Nevâdir ül-hikem*, which Âli wrote in winter 1588-89/997 while *defterdar* of Sivas. The apparent chronological conflict is easily resolved by the passage immediately following that quoted by İnal, in which Âli recounts a retreat (*çihil*) he took at the shrine

ously held, that of finance director of Erzurum, the position was a low one. He asked the sultan, through Gazanfer Ağa, to make him either finance director of Damascus or trustee (*emin*) and governor of Jidda, so that he might go on the pilgrimage. Âli's plea, once again, went unanswered, and in any event this assignment did not last long; by April of 1589 his post was purchased by another through an *iltizam* contract.[62]

EXCURSUS: ÂLİ AND SELÂNİKİ

MUSTAFA Selâniki's Ottoman chronicle is the source for the precise date of Âli's appointment to Sivas, a fact which requires a short digression. Selâniki does not normally record such low-level appointments. The fact that he does so in the case of Âli, whom he describes as "the former finance director and outstanding man of learning," is indicative of the great admiration he felt for Âli and of the close attention with which he followed the latter's career. The two historians, Âli and Selâniki, present many striking parallels. Both men were bureaucrats, and both became historians who wrote the recent and contemporary history of the Ottoman Empire. Their respective histories were compiled at exactly the same time, and they even died within a few years of each other.[63] While Âli was an educated *medrese* graduate, Selâniki was a bureaucratic professional who had learned his trade on the job. Âli's high level of education helps to explain the esteem in which Selâniki held him, and the difference in the two men's background is apparent in their prose; Âli's is highly stylized and literary, while Selâniki's is simpler and less subtle.

The two men probably knew each other, and this probability becomes all the more intriguing in the light of the extent to which the content and spirit of Selâniki's *History* and Âli's *Essence of History* parallel each other, beginning with the year 1588/997. In the same year that Âli lost his post as finance director of Rum (1589/997) because of contract and patronage appointments, Selâniki lost his own position, that of secretary of the Silahdar (weapon-bearer) Corps (*silahdar kâtibi*) in precisely the same manner. At this point in his history, Selâniki breaks his usual factual tone to decry the decay of the system that allows a man with money and connections to obtain effortlessly a post that he, Selâniki, had worked all his life to attain through

of Şeyh Ahmed Ensari near Tokat during the winter *erba'in* of 997 (MS İÜ Türkçe 1846, 4b; hereafter NEVADİR). The *erba'in* are the forty days of midwinter, 21 December-30 January (Redhouse, *Turkish-English Lexicon* (Istanbul, 1890), p. 60, and the *erba'in* of 997 covers the first months of the *hicri* year, 21 December 1588-30 January 1589/2 Safer-12 Rebi' I. Âli would have arrived the preceding spring, since he served less than a year in office and was dismissed in the spring of 1589/997.

62 NEVADİR, Introduction, 3b-5b.

63 On SELANİKİ, see GOW, pp. 136, 37.

merit and skill.[64] After recording Âli's first appointment (1592/1000) as secretary of the Janissary Corps (*yeniçeri kâtibi*), Selâniki remarks that it is shameful that high-ranking financial officials of Âli's caliber should be appointed to lower-level secretarial positions, a sentiment with which Âli fervently concurred.[65] Under the *sub anno* rubric A.H. 1000, Selâniki complains that the seniority system does not really function in the bureaucratic career track, echoing observations made by Âli.[66] The list of similarities could be considerably extended. It is of course possible that Âli influenced Selâniki. At the same time, the degree of parallelism and the precise synchronity of Âli's *Essence* and Selâniki's *History* bespeak a shared intellectual milieu and orientation. Financial bureaucrats in the late sixteenth century faced problems common to the entire profession, and it is not surprising that two of these at least should voice similar views of the situation. Observed in this context, Âli, for all his careerism and vociferous complaining, appears to have been simply more outspoken than many of his contemporaries, rather than having been a complete eccentric.

SIVAS AND CENTRAL ANATOLIA (1588-89)

IN THE Anatolian heartland the embittered Âli developed two new passions: Sufi contemplation and Anatolian Turkish folk traditions. He explains his state of mind in the introduction to *Nevâdir ül-hikem, Curious Bits of Wisdom*, a collection of essays he wrote during the winter of 1588-89.[67] Nearly fifty years of age, Âli felt old and near to death. He was ever more disgusted with financial service and the exigencies of supervising incompetent and corrupt officials. He did his utmost to withdraw from society and his duties; he wished only to make the pilgrimage and to spend his days in mystical contemplation. In retreat at the shrine of a local saint, near Tokat, Âli was inspired to present his case to the sultan, along with a synopsis of his thoughts on his life and his times. The result of this inspiration was the *Curious Bits*, itself something of a testament to Âli's new mood. The work is a series of seven essays, which range from bitter comments on the nature of the times and the self-fulfilling character of current apocalyptic expectation, to a solution to the doctrinal and political split between Sunnis and Shi'is that would put an end to the ceaseless Ottoman-Safavi wars, and finally to a whimsical fantasy on the professions that various classes of gov-

[64] SELANİKİ, p. 258.
[65] SELANİKİ, p. 327, and chapter 6 below.
[66] SELANİKİ, *sub anno* 1001, 11a.
[67] NEVADİR, Introduction, 3b-5b.

ernment officials would occupy if they were to be brought down in the world.[68]

During a sojourn in Niksar in 1588 Âli acquired a fourteenth-century Turkish *Danişmendname, The Book of Melik Danişmend*, which was the composition of one Ârif Ali. Ârif's work itself was based upon the thirteenth-century *Danişmendname* of İbn Alâ.[69] Âli's imagination was fired by this folk epic, which recounted the exploits of Melik Danişmend, the eleventh-century *gazi* who founded in northern Anatolia the Danişmendid principality, which rivaled the Seljuk state. The *gazi*-epic genre had a well established place in the folk-mystical traditions of Anatolia.[70] For this reason alone *The Book of Melik Danişmend* would have appealed to Âli, but it also offered, or so he thought, a glimpse of the non-Ottoman Turkish past with which Âli was becoming ever more fascinated. In late winter or early spring of 1589/997, Âli received the news that he had been dismissed from the finance directorship of Rum because the post had been given to a contract appointee who had promised to produce more revenue. Âli had earlier submitted to the sultan his recently completed *Curious Bits*, which included an appeal to be posted to either Damascus or Jidda so that he might perform the pilgrimage. Now, dismissed even from the poor post that had been allotted to him, Âli retired to the vicinity of Çorum to await an answer to his request for a new assignment.[71] To console himself, he reworked Ârif Ali's linguistically primitive work into more elegant Ottoman Turkish, and entitled his

[68] On the work and its significance for Âli's conception of "decline," see my "Muṣṭafâ ʿÂlî's *Curious Bits of Wisdom*," *Wiener Zeitschrift für die Kunde des Morgenlandes*, 1984 (forthcoming). In the last article (ff. 27b-28b), Âli says that a poet should become a painter (*nakkaş, nakşbend*). His use of the term *nakşbend* in several punning contexts may be a hint at his formal *tarikat* affiliation at the time.

[69] Ârif Ali's *Danişmendname* has been edited, translated, and exhaustively studied by Irène Mélikoff, *La Geste de Melik Dânişmend*, 2 vols. (Paris, 1960). The genesis of the successive *Danişmendnames*, for which Âli is a major source, is discussed in vol. I, pp. 53-70. Âli did not retire to Niksar after his dismissal, as Mélikoff states on p. 63; he had acquired the manuscript during a visit to the tomb of Melik Danişmend, and only later paraphrased it while camped near Çorum (İNAL, pp. 60-61).

[70] Mélikoff, *Geste*, I, 49-52.

[71] NEVADİR, 4b; Âli wrote the *Nevadir* in the winter of 1588-89 and submitted it to the sultan in order to request this change of assignment. The following spring (1589) he was dismissed and remained in the vicinity of Çorum, awaiting a reply to his petition. During this interval of fifty days he wrote the *Mirkat ül-cihad*, the introduction to which gives an account of the affair (MS Revan Köşkü 364, 2b-9b). Âli complains that although he is a favorite protégé of Gazanfer Ağa, he has received an unworthy post, upon which all the vezirs agree. Even this then was taken from him when the *defterdarlık* of Sivas was given to another in *iltizam*, and no vezir lifted a finger to help him. The approximate date for his dismissal, March 1589, is provided by his composition of the *Mirkat* in forty days. Âli's brother, İbniyamin Çavuş, began copying a clean version in 16-25 May 1589/early Receb 997, according to the colophon of MS Millet Genel, Reşid Efendi 678 (quoted by İNAL, p. 61). İbniyamin copied the work in Istanbul, after Âli's arrival there. Allowing for Âli's fifty days near Çorum and traveling time to the capital, mid-March in the latest possible date for Âli's dismissal.

translation *Mirkat ül-cihad, The Ascending Stair of Holy War*. Ever the scholar, Âli added an introduction and philological observations.[72]

ISTANBUL: THE APPROACH OF THE MILLENNIUM (1589-91)

ÂLI returned from Anatolia to Istanbul in the spring, his pleas and requests having met no response. He must have arrived in the capital when the city was still reeling from the shock of the *Beğlerbeği* Incident of early April 1589. The Janissaries had rioted in protest over their payment in the debased silver coinage that was then flooding the Empire. They demanded, and got, the heads of those whom they believed responsible for the payment policy: the *beğlerbeği* of Rumeli Doğancı Mehmed Paşa, and the treasurer Mahmud Efendi. Âli had been close to both men; the *Beğlerbeği* Incident deprived him of two friends at once. Âli was particularly bitter over the death of Mahmud Efendi, whom he admired and felt to be an innocent sacrifice. Nine years later, in writing the *Essence*, Âli described this affair as a new landmark in imperial decline. The Janissary uprising and sacrifice of the two men had been orchestrated by Âli's erstwhile friend Damad İbrahim Paşa, who wished to be rid of Doğancı Mehmed. By using the Janissary Corps to attain personal political ends, İbrahim Paşa had perverted the Ottoman system to a new extreme, and the sultan, through his negligence, had allowed a dangerous precedent to be set. The Janissaries were henceforth to attack the Imperial Council frequently. Finally, the *Beğlerbeği* Incident symbolized, in particularly brutal fashion, the economic deterioration and attendant social malaise of the Ottoman Empire.[73]

Shocking as it was in itself, the *Beğlerbeği* Incident had more immediate effects. Sultan Murad, angered by the affair and his ministers' irresponsibility, dismissed Siyavuş, İbrahim, and Cerrah Mehmed Paşas. The grand vezir Siyavuş Paşa was replaced by Âli's old nemesis, Koca Sinan. The political disorder in the capital was matched by rebellions in the provinces, and

[72] *Mirkat ül-cihad*, MS Revan Köşkü 364. Âli completed the translation in forty days; see preceding note and Mélikoff, *Geste*, I, 63, 64.

[73] SELANİKİ, pp. 252-55, gives the date of 2 April 1589/17 Cümada I (in the printed text "996" is an error for "997"). Âli wrote his version of the affair, and his analysis of its political and economic significance, in KA, Murad/35, Nur 3409, 391a-394b. Mahmud Efendi, of whom Âli speaks so highly, was a fellow devotee of Şeyh Bali Efendi. Âli's treatment of İbrahim Paşa's role in the incident is remarkable for its evenhandedness.

Though Âli was friendly with İbrahim Paşa, and remarks that he had legitimate grievances against Doğancı Mehmed, he also clearly spells out the terrible implications of his action. Two poems from the LAYİHAT are evidence of Âli's ongoing and friendly association with İbrahim Paşa: f. 143a, a poem composed on the occasion of İbrahim Paşa's visit to Âli's home, and ff. 16b-17a, a *kaside* asking İbrahim for a horse and a *timar* assignment (*bir at ve berat*).

two great fires ravaged several quarters of Istanbul in the weeks that followed the Janissary riot. Istanbul was reminded that the Muslim millennium, the *hicri* year 1000, was only two years away, and apocalyptic expectation ran high. Âli himself did not believe that the end of the world was approaching, as he stated in the *Mirror of the Worlds*. However, he shared the millennial mood of Istanbul, a mood heightened by a plague that ravaged the city in 1590.[74] Âli's poetry from the years 1589-91 is dominated by imagery of disease, want, and personal and public apocalypse. The substance of Âli's abundant apocalyptic verse is the following. In the social sphere, the world is upside down; the ulema are no longer learned or pious, the pillars of the state are fiends and liars; the truly learned are disdained and dismissed, and government service now brings pain and poverty rather than pride and wealth. The plague destroying the world is moral as well as physical, for bribery and corruption are the order of the day, and the world has become an idiot old crone.[75]

These themes in Âli's poetry did not emerge solely from a generalization of apocalyptic expectation; they began to appear during the Aleppo period, when Âli started to confront his professional disappointment and disillusionment, and grew steadily in intensity. Âli's millennial descriptions of a world turned upside down are prefigured most clearly in his *Curious Bits of Wisdom* of 1589, written before he returned to Istanbul, in which he expatiates on the viciousness of a society in which all are seeking advancement at any cost to themselves and their colleagues, and in which careerism has infected even the ulema—the guardians of moral and intellectual standards—to the extent that they are no longer truly committed to learning.[76] Âli suggested, therefore, that ulema be given appointments on the basis of examination and proven merit. Appointment by examination for his ability was something Âli had proposed to the sultan several times, since he felt himself to be learned and qualified. Âli's lack of advancement in the face of his perception of himself, as well as the increasingly violent and factional character of political life in Istanbul, had much to do with his sense of apoc-

[74] On these fires, which broke out in the Jewish quarter of Galata and in Tahta Kale, and which were popularly seen as divine retribution for the Janissary disturbance, see SELANİKİ, pp. 255-56. The plague is mentioned on p. 273.

[75] These themes are developed in LAYİHAT, 20b-23b ("On the Perversity of Fate and the Disruption of the World"); 45b-46a, on the state of Istanbul; 14a-b, to Sultan Murad, *mansıb*-rhyme; 135a-137b, to Sinan Paşa, on the apocalyptic character of the time. A long *terci'-bend* in which Âli describes Ottoman society in a similarly pessimistic fashion, the *Hulasat ül-ahval, Summary of Circumstances*, has been published by Andreas Tietze, "The Poet as Critique of Society: A 16th Century Ottoman Poem," *Turcica* 9/1 (1977): 120-60, with a postscript in *Turcica* 11 (1978): 205-209. Since the poem occurs in the LAYİHAT, is must have been composed between A.H. 988 and 1000. On the basis of thematic considerations and an examination of the entire *divan*, I would put its probable date closer to 1589-90/998.

[76] NEVADİR, 8a-9a.

alypse. Âli had no hope of obtaining a position while Sinan Paşa was in power. He complained openly to Sultan Murad about the grand vezir's slanders, and suggested that if he continued to suffer such indignities he would have to emigrate to India, where men of learning were valued. Âli was so bitter that he abandoned his accustomed fulsome courtesy in addressing the sultan; he submitted to Murad a long ode in which he asked to be made a companion (*musahib*), after bluntly describing the injustice that prevailed in Ottoman domains.[77]

At the end of the longest of the apocalyptic odes, Âli describes Sinan Paşa as something of an anti-Christ figure, reviling him as the enemy of the state and religion, and of poets. Âli goes on to pray that God will give him the strength to forget and put aside the worldly concerns that have obsessed him for so long. He says that he has turned to pious contemplation of the Prophet and imams, and to Sufism, as the only means of salvation left to him.[78] During these years Âli did indeed maintain the preoccupation with Sufism that he first evinced in *Curious Bits*. In 1589-90/998 he returned to, and completed, the *Seekers' Bower, Riyaz üs-salikin*, a treatise on mysticism that he had begun and then abandoned at the very beginning of his career in 1562.[79] At the age of fifty, Âli was poor and out of work, and he sought solace in religion, as he states in the introduction to the *Bower*. The evidence of the *Bower* provides valuable clues to the nature of Âli's attitude toward religion, Sufism, and himself.

In at least one of his works, the *Hulasat ül-ahval, Summary of Circumstances*, Âli expressed a cynical hostility toward Sufi orders.[80] In fact, a thorough examination of his works reveals conflicting attitudes toward Sufism and its practitioners. These attitudes changed over time, and his interest in the subject was periodic, being most pronounced first in his early youth, and again in middle age. During the intervening years Âli had devoted himself to career building and to the more material realities of daily life. In turning to mystical piety immediately before the millennium, Âli was not being hypocritical or merely indulging his sense of personal failure; he was in the grip of a midlife crisis. In turning to Sufism he returned, psychologically, to his youth, when the world had been in order and when mysticism had been an integral part of the exciting literary and social life of Ot-

[77] LAYİHAT, 138a, 155b, 12a-14a; cf. 14a-b, 154a-155a.

[78] LAYİHAT, 20b-23b. Âli accuses Sinan Paşa of gross ignorance, impiety, and disloyalty to the sultan. The entire poem is remarkable for a sincerely pietistic tone rarely found in Âli's verse.

[79] On RİYAZ, see chapter 2. The introductory material utilized below occurs in RİYAZ, 18a-19a; the date of composition is found on ff. 18a-b. Âli later submitted the work to Sultan Murad with a request that he be given the post of *defter emini* or *yeniçeri kâtibi* (LAYİHAT, 149b-150a).

[80] Tietze, "Poet," p. 124.

toman culture. The pietistic Sufi stance of the fifty-year-old Âli was part and parcel of the retrospective process upon which he was then engaged, and idealization of the cultural and spiritual values of his youth was an important concomitant of this process. Âli's social stance at this time represented a second major factor in his seeming ambivalence toward Sufism. Highly intelligent and ambitious, he was a thwarted man and increasingly adopted the posture of a detached, cynical social critic and perpetual outsider. His most frequently voiced criticisms of Sufi sheikhs and orders center on their external moral and social aspects. Âli is particularly hard, for example, on the sheikhs of fashionable orders who use their prestige and position to gain, and sometimes abuse, wealth and power. He is also cynically critical of those who style themselves as dervishes and then use the designation as an excuse for debauchery and moral laxity. Such criticisms may be contrasted with the respect with which Âli speaks of other mystics, in whose sanctity he sincerely believed.[81] Particularly instructive in this context is a remark Âli makes in the *Essence* about the renowned *şeyhülislam* Ebüssu'ud Efendi, whose only fault, he says, had been his lack of sympathy for the mystical orientation.[82] However much he may have criticized its practice, Âli endorsed and believed in Sufism as an ideal and as a necessary part of religious life.

Âli himself had no exclusive *tarikat* affiliations. As we have seen above, he consorted with Halvetis, Nakşbendis, and Bektaşis. He later became intrigued with the Melâmi-Bayramis, particularly the more involved he became with Anatolian and early Ottoman history, in which these played a significant part. In fact, the antisocial Melâmi tradition appealed most strongly of all to the loner Âli. In one mystical poem, probably written around 1590-91/999, he expressed himself in the best Melâmi fashion, saying that he has no mystic master and no order affiliation, and that his sole spiritual guide has been wine.[83] Despite his lack of either a *pir* or a *tarikat*, Âli wanted very much to believe in the power of holy men and in the possibility of enlightenment, as his poetry and visits to saints' shrines show.[84] Only thus, he felt, might he resolve the conflicts he himself perceived between his hopes and reality, between Âli the scholar and Âli the political animal, between his moral sense and his ambition. While Âli was never quite able to quell his ambition and sense of personal grievance, he became

[81] See above, on Şeyh Şüca', and chapter 2, note 38, on Bali Efendi. For examples of sheikhs of whom Âli thought highly, see KA, Selim/Ulema-Meşayih, "Mevlana Tacüddin," "Hekim Efendi," Nur 3409, 258b-259b, 268a.

[82] KA, Selim/Ulema, "Ebüsu'ud," Nur 3409, 266b-267a.

[83] LAYİHAT, 26a-29b. In the introduction to the *Layihat*, composed in October-November 1591/Muharrem 1000, Âli repeats that he had never had a *pir*. Cf. a *melâmi gazel* found in DİVAN III, 59b.

[84] In 1596/1004-1005 Âli visited the tombs of Akşemsüddin, Hacı Bayram, Hacı Bektaş, and other Anatolian saints; see DİVAN III, 25a-25b, 25b-26a, 52b, 58a, 71a.

increasingly aware that he ought to do so. Just before the millennium, Âli contemplated his life and summarized it in the following manner in a long ode. Until he reached the age of thirty, life had been full of excitement, and he had spent his days and nights in carousal. By the time he was forty life had become poisonous, and by fifty there was no joy left in it. The world was topsy-turvy, and he saw that he had wasted his years in the search for worldly glory and wealth. He repented of his actions, swore to conquer his appetites, and gave himself up to pious contemplation; only thus had beauty been restored to his existence.[85] Just as Âli became increasingly critical of an Ottoman society that he saw as crassly materialistic and corrupt, he perceived and rejected similar characteristics in himself, whether these were innate or acquired through years of dedication to being an Ottoman.

However piously Âli attempted to ignore or reject the world, he still had to support himself and his household in a manner befitting his status as a finance director. He nowhere mentions the source of his income during these years (1589-92) of unemployment. Presumably he had some savings from his previous postings, which he may have invested in trade. It is more probable that he received help from his brothers Mehmed and İbniyamin, both of whom had government posts in Istanbul. Whether this was the case or not, Âli's needs were considerable; his statement in the *Essence* that in 1591/1000 he had a household of one hundred relatives and retainers to maintain suggests both pretension and severe want. In order to support this establishment, Âli writes bitterly, he was forced to sell his dearest possessions, his books.[86] In the face of desperate need for income-producing employment, Âli, in the years before the millennium, swallowed his pride and grudgingly attempted to make a necessary, if hypocritical, peace with the grand vezir Sinan Paşa. Sinan appears to have been unimpressed, for Âli received nothing. This is hardly surprising, since Âli could not keep a grudging tone out of his verse appeal to Sinan; he prefaced his request for a reconciliation with a scolding discourse on the wretched state of the Empire and on the dishonor heaped upon the most distinguished poets of the time through Sinan's disinterest in culture and learning.[87]

[85] LAYİHAT, 46a-50a.

[86] KA, I, 31.

[87] LAYİHAT, 135a-137b, is an ode addressed to Sinan Paşa during the plague. After reciting the horrors of rampant disease and dearth which marked the approach of the Apocalypse, Âli asks the grant vezir why distinguished poets are not honored in his time. Apart from himself, he cites Baki, Nev'i, Ehli, Mecdi, Hatemi, Sa'i, and Misali as being unemployed, and decries the corruption of bureaucratic officeholders (*ehl-i kalem*). He finally apologizes for his own poor service to Sinan in the past, and requests the grand vezir's favor. In addition to this ode, Âli composed chronograms on the construction of Sinan Paşa's new palace and on the appointment of his son, the cowardly Mehmed Paşa, to the government of Damascus, both of which events took place in 1590-91/999 (LAYİHAT, 148a; *Mecmu'a*, Esad Efendi 3436, 20b; Laoust, *Gouverneurs*, p. 191).

ISTANBUL AT THE MILLENNIUM

A.H. 1000 (1591-92)

YEAR 1000 of the Hijra ushered in a new era for the Muslim world, and brought Âli to a psychological turning point. While he may have intellectually rejected the notion that the world would come to an end, he had at least subconsciously participated in popular expectation that great events and calamitous changes would come about in the year 1000. But the calendar turned quietly, the world was still intact, and decisions had to be made about how to go on with life. He signaled this psychic moment in the first month of the new millennium by closing his second *divan*, the *Intimations of Truth*, which memorialized his verse from the "poison years."[88] Âli wrote an introduction to the *Intimations* in which he summarized his situation at the time, and also exposed the frame of mind that dominated his last years. The essence of Âli's exposition is as follows. After a life spent in government service and literary endeavor, Âli had recently remained without a post and salary for some years. He had a large household and, because he was by rank a finance director, was obligated to maintain the appearance of prosperity. For several years he had withdrawn from the world and attempted to find peace by devoting himself to the inner spiritual life. In this he was only partially successful. He still felt that those who wielded political and economic power had an obligation to promote learning and culture; it was his misfortune to live in a time when knowledge was prized less than money, when a man's greatness was judged by his wealth and power rather than by his prominence as a scholar or patron of the arts. Ignorance was rampant, and the powerful were uninterested in or even hostile to learning. Because of this cultural and moral decline, Âli had been condemned to poverty while his contemporaries prospered, despite universal acclamation of his writings and scholarship:

> In sum, the evil father, Fate, and serpent-tempered mother, treacherous Fortune, brought forth this perplexed and disappointed child in a happy age filled with hope; [but it became a time when] great and small desired not meaning, but money, and the exalted [of society] favored not learning and mystical knowledge, but only chatter and gossip.[89]

There are, of course, obvious self-serving aspects to Âli's summary of his situation at the turn of the millennium. While certain of Âli's misfortunes may be attributed to bad luck and to the animosity of Sinan Paşa, it is clear

[88] LAYİHAT, 3a-b, gives the date of composition as October-November 1591/Muharrem 1000.

[89] LAYİHAT, 3b-7a, quote, 5a.

that his must have been an abrasive personality; he may simply not have been very well liked. The actual degree of his poverty is difficult to judge, since he insisted on keeping up appearances and maintaining a large establishment in the prestigious Fatih section of Istanbul.[90] That Âli should have kept up appearances in this fashion is hardly surprising, for he rejected the idea of becoming a hermit or dervish. In returning to Ottoman society and reaffirming his own vision of its ideals, he necessarily had to maintain at least the image of an Ottoman identity, an image largely defined by his place in the system. Being unemployed, Âli was not even eligible for retirement, and apart from allowing Ottoman officials to become dervishes or to retire to Sufi convents, the Ottoman system provided no genteel avenue of descent or exit for a man on his way down or out.

Questions of Âli's pretensions, or of the justice or injustice of his complaints, are of less importance than the final transformation in Âli's point of view which his remarks in the *Intimations* reveal. They convey a grudging recognition of the changes wrought by time, and a resignation to them. The enthusiastic proposals for practical fiscal and administrative reform propounded by Âli in the *Counsel* embodied a hope that change and deterioration could be reversed by a return to Ottoman ideals and by strict observance of *kanun* in letter and spirit. In the year A.H. 1000 these hopes were replaced by a nostalgia for a past that could never come again, a golden era embodied by the reigns of the Conqueror, Bayezid II, and Selim I. Âli's topical and practical outlook on Ottoman affairs gave way to a larger, more abstract view of history, a view that judged a society by its ideals and the extent to which it fulfilled them. For Âli, promulgation of a cosmopolitan high culture went hand-in-hand with political success and adherence to religion. Patronage and justice were the touchstones by which he judged the life of his own and other times. Measured by this scale, the Ottoman Empire of his own time was not only lacking, but degenerate; intellectual, moral, and political decline were inextricably intertwined.[91] As well as he could, Âli accepted the conclusion that he had been born at the wrong time in the wrong place, that his ideals were not those of his own age. His only resort was to

[90] See chapter 1, note 50, and LAYİHAT, 139b-140a, a poem praising and describing his home near Fatih. The location is confirmed by one of Peçevi's marginal notations in the KA, and by another note found in a manuscript of Kınalızade's *Tezkere*, both quoted by İNAL, pp. 34-35. The house faced the dwelling of the *şeyhülislam* Çivizade, and later passed to the military judge, Aziz Efendi b. Hoca Sa'düddin. The neighborhood was thus a prestigious one. The marginalia in Kınalızade's *Tezkere* suggest that Âli built the house when he served as *yeniçeri kâtibi* in 1592. The inclusion of the poem cited above in LAYİHAT makes this unlikely, unless Âli either sold or moved out of his original Fatih dwelling, a house formerly owned by Ramazanzade.

[91] See, for example, Âli's complaint to Sinan Paşa on the condition of the poets of Rum (note 87 above), and an ode from the same period and in a similar vein in LAYİHAT, 9a-10b. See also my "Royal Authority."

resign himself to his lack of success and devote himself to his own inner world, to an explication and celebration of the heritage and culture with which he had grown up, which had excited him, and to which he had devoted himself so wholeheartedly. Two months after he closed his second *divan*, on a Friday in the early winter of 1591-92/1000, Âli began his monumental history of the world, to which he gave the title *Künh ül-ahbar, The Essence of History*.[92]

In his long introduction to the work, Âli says that he began it as a long-wished-for labor of love, which his unemployed state and consequent leisure allowed him to undertake. He also wished to perform a meritorious act which would atone for all his misdeeds and serve as a memorial to his name.[93] For the last eight years of his life Âli dedicated himself almost exclusively to the *Essence*. Indeed, his devotion to the composition of his great history represents a very personal act; the work was not commissioned, it contains no dedication to a monarch or statesman, and over the following years Âli repeatedly requested posts that would help and allow him to complete it. Âli's last *divan*, untitled and posthumously compiled, was begun at the same time as the *Essence*, and it testifies to Âli's new frame of mind. While the *divan* still resounds with complaints and poems in praise of his own ability, in comparison to Âli's previous poetry collections it contains fewer odes to dignitaries and more poetry of a purely personal nature.[94]

Âli's nostagia for the past, however, was not the conventional one traditionally associated with the Islamic domains, whereby history is seen as a process of decline proceeding inevitably as the ''perfect'' era of the Prophet's lifetime and the days of the primal Muslim community recede further into the past.[95] Âli brought to his historiography a critical faculty and determined independence of thought that set him apart from run-of-the-mill chroniclers. One of the most pertinent and striking examples of this self-

[92] Âli is to blame for the imprecision in the date on which he began to write the *Essence*. In the introduction he gives the year as A.H. 1000 (KA, I, 8) and the date as ''autumn, at the appearance of December, 14 Rebi' II, Friday'' (KA, I, 5). 14 Rebi' II 1000 is actually equivalent to Wednesday, 30 January 1592. If the references to ''autumn'' and ''December'' are more descriptive than chronologically precise, it is possible that Âli simply made a mistake of one or two days, and that the true date was 15 or 16 Rebi' II. It is also possible that ''Rebi' II'' is an error for Rebi' I, which would yield a C.E. date of December 30, 1591. However, this day was a Monday, and it is more likely that the day is correct and the date wrong. The size of the work, considering that it is the result of only seven years' work, is staggering. The printed portion of the *Essence* comprises 1,647 pages in five volumes, and ends with the conquest of Istanbul. The unpublished remainder of the work, carrying Ottoman history down to 1597, contains 500-600 large manuscript folios.

[93] KA, I, 6-8.

[94] DİVAN III. This *divan* was compiled by one Hisali, whom I have been unable to identify. Hisali provided dates and notations of occasions for many of the poems.

[95] See M.G.S. Hodgson, *The Venture of Islam*, 3 vols. (Chicago, 1974), II, 452-55, for discussion of this phenomenon.

conscious independence occurs in the *Curious Bits*, in the course of a discussion of the great ulema of each age. Âli states that the commonly accepted view of cultural history holds that there had been a decline and gradual extinction (*inkıraz*) of the learned and saintly since the time of the Prophet. While it is true that the current age represents a decline in comparison to earlier periods, Âli admits, the view that the further one moves from the time of Muhammad, the more knowledge decreases is incorrect. Were it true, he says, there would have been more great scholars and saints (judging both by their numbers and their productivity) in the first through the fourth *hicri* centuries than in the fifth through the seventh. However, the reverse is true, for there were more prominent scholars and Sufi masters in the later period.[96]

Âli's own yearning was for the more immediate past, the fourteenth and fifteenth centuries of the Common Era, which represented for him the heyday of patronage and the flowering of the cosmopolitan literary and political culture of the post-Mongol Islamic world. This is made abundantly evident by Âli's constant references to the courts of Fatih Sultan Mehmed and Sulṭân-Ḥusayn Bâyqarâ as the paradigmatic models of statecraft and literary patronage. A particularly significant and psychologically intriguing aspect of the nostalgia that overcame Âli late in his life is his renewed identification with the prestigious Persianate Islamic literary tradition that had dominated the courts of both rulers. Early in his literary career, Âli, in describing the *Rarity of Warriors* (*Nadir ül-maharib*), had given expression to the sense of cultural inferiority, vis-à-vis the older Persian tradition, which plagued proponents of the nascent Ottoman literary culture in the days of Süleyman:

> Many are its Persian *mesnevi*s, each revolving round a poetic pearl.
> Though I am a Rumi, I have poetic power joined to the Inspirer's
> inspiration.
> I am not like the poets of Rum; my heart flows with God-given verse.[97]

When Âli turned to meditation on things Persian at the turn of the millennium, he did so not only to relive his youth, but also to escape, psychologically, from Rum and from the Ottoman present. In 1591-92/1000 Âli composed a series of fifty-three parallel poems (*nazire*) in Persian on the "sonnets" (*gazel*) of Ḥâfiẓ (d. 1390/792). His pupil Nef'i, who was later to become one of the most famous of Ottoman poets, persuaded Âli to gather them into a volume for publication. He added a Persian introduction and appropriately entitled the volume *Majmaʿ al-baḥreyn, The Confluence of the*

[96] NEVADİR, 9a-10b, and Fleischer, "*Curious Bits*."
[97] NADİR, 65b.

Two Seas.[98] Two years later, in a state of depression engendered by unemployment, a sense of failure, and exhaustion from overwork on the *Essence*, Âli wrote another Persian work entitled *Badîʿ al-ruqûm, The Embellishment of Inscriptions*.[99] Âli prefaced this collection of parallel compositions on the verses of famous Persian poets with an examination of his own place in the world of letters. After comparing himself to his more successful Ottoman contemporaries Baki, Nev'i, Rahmi, and Yahya, Âli goes on to express his identification with great figures of the Iranian poetic tradition: Firdawsî, Hâtifî, Salmân-i Sâvajî, Kâtibî, and Ẓahîr-i Faryâbî. Indeed, Âli had never lost his admiration for things Persian, although it was more apparent in his youth and old age. He relates in the *Embellishment* that he had assiduously cultivated modern exponents of the tradition well before his Baghdad sojourn. During the Georgian campaign he had met and conversed with Mawlânâ Sharaf al-dîn Shîrvânî at Ereş, and before the outbreak of the Ottoman-Safavi wars in 1578 he had corresponded with the celebrated Muḥtasham-i Kâshânî, whom he viewed as one of the greatest poets of his own time.[100] Âli no longer composed much original poetry; he became preoccupied with studying and imitating the great poets of the past on the one hand, and with the *Essence of History* on the other. Âli would seem to have recognized that he would never achieve lasting fame as a poet, in spite of the dreams of his youth. Instead, he would be remembered as an historian.

[98] The work and its contents have been described by the owner of the sole manuscript, Abdülkadir Karahan, in "Âli'nin bilinmeyen bir Eseri: *Mecma' ül-bahreyn*," *V. Türk Tarih Kongresi, Tebliğler* (Ankara, 1960), pp. 329-30. The introduction to the work provides yet another clue that Âli kept time by vernal rather than lunar years, which would account for some of the anomalies in his dates. After discussing Ḥâfiẓ's death and burial in 1390/792 (H. Ritter, "Ḥâfiẓ," EI²), Âli says that "after 151 years I came into the world at Gelibolu in Rum" (Karahan, p. 332). Âli's accounting for the date of his birth will only come close to his actual birth date in 1541/948 if the reckoning is made in vernal years.

[99] *Badî' al-ruqûm*, MS Kadızade Mehmed 429, 82b-123a. Âli began the work in 1593-94/1002; he says that he had given up writing poetry for some time, and had devoted himself exclusively to his history and to the study of Ḥâfiẓ. He composed *nazire*s on the poetry of authors he admired, wrote an introduction, and completed the volume in 1594-95/1003 (92a).

[100] *Badîʿ al-ruqûm*, MS Kadızade Mehmed 429, 86b-95b. In the course of a discussion of his own career (90b-92a), Âli gives Sultan Selim II a positive evaluation as a generous patron of literature. This contrasts markedly with the views he expressed on that sultan years before in the COUNSEL, where he criticized Selim for not knowing the worth of Âli. On Muḥtasham-i Kâshânî, see E. G. Browne, *A Literary History of Persia*, 4 vols. (Cambridge, 1969; reprint), IV, 172-77. The theme of a distinction between Ottoman and Iranian cultural as well as political spheres (Rum, Acem) recurs frequently in Âli's later writings. In the *Exploits*, for example, Âli distinguishes between Rumi and Acemi styles in calligraphy and bookbinding, and in the *Curious Bits* he lists separately Ottoman and Iranian poets and Sufi sheikhs (NEVADİR, 7b-9a).

Kanuni Sultan Süleyman, the Lawgiver (reg. 1520-66) in 1559; engraving by Melchior Lorichs.

Grand Vezir Sokollu Mehmed Paşa (1505-79), from life.

Facing page: Sokollu Mehmed Paşa presides over a meeting of the Imperial Council in the Chamber of the Dome at the Palace; Sultan Selim II (reg. 1566-74) looks on from his private observation chamber above. To Sokollu's right sit the five subordinate vezirs, while the chancellor makes written record of the proceedings. The two chief military judges and the three finance directors of the Porte sit to Sokollu's left.

بشرایط تعظیم و تشریف گذاشته و بیت مناسب را که بخط تعلیق نوشته بوده برخوانده
هر یکی را بترغیب غریب و تحسین دلفریب میل و مبادرت فزوده
گویان باتفاق همگنان از شفقت و عنایتش مستفید گشته بالجمله
بخدمات مرجوعه در کوشیدیم و بفحوای
از همت مردان بهره مند گشتیم
کار زین گنبد گردان نکند هرچه کند همت مردان کند

عساکر ظفر مآثرده مسرت و شادی آثارلری نمایان اولدوغی حینده بوابان
خاصه‌دن ایکی جوانمرد عتبهٔ علیادن ارضروم سرحدینه طوغرو راه نورد
اولوب جناب پادشاهیدن فاضل‌لردن دانا وکامل سعادت نشان اعنی به
حضرت پادشاه هفت اقلیم
خان مراد بن شهریار سلیم
غضنفر آغا
سعد الدین زمان خواجهٔ پادشاه جهان حضرتلرینک خط شریفلری و انشاء
منیفلریله سردار خدمتکذاره بو کونه استمالت نامه و قشلادقی عساکر ظفر
قرینه مواعظ لطیفه ایله بویوردن موهبت نامه ایراد ایلدیلرکه صورتی نقل اولندی

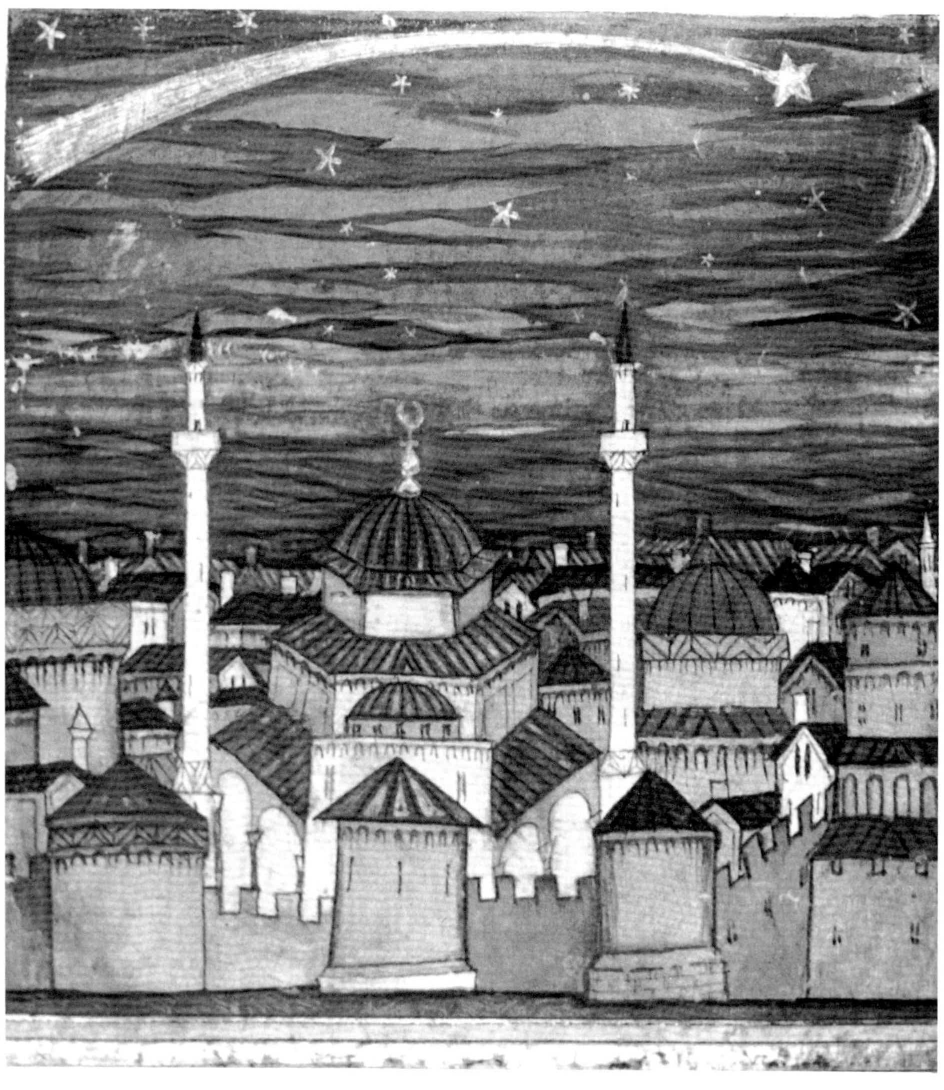

The comet seen over Istanbul on November 12, 1577, here over Aya Sofya. Its eastward path was popularly assumed to presage Ottoman victory over the Safavis.

Facing page: Sultan Murad III (reg. 1574-95), the chief white eunuch Gazanfer Ağa (to Murad's right), and the royal tutor Hoca Sa'düddin discuss the letter of approval Sa'düddin has composed for the field marshal Lala Mustafa Paşa.

Sinan Paşa (d. 1596), called Koca, "the ancient," who served five times as grand vezir.

Lala Mustafa Paşa (d. 1580), Âli's longtime patron, who died at over seventy years of age without ever attaining the grand vezirate.

Lala Mustafa Paşa takes leave of Sultan Murad (upper right) and then leaves the Palace to cross the Bosphorus to Üsküdar, staging area for the first leg of the march to Şirvan (5 April 1578/27 Muharrem 986).

At İzmid (İznikbend) Lala Mustafa Paşa fêtes the Janissary commanders before sending his troops to the frontier, where he will rendezvous with them.

Following their own path to the East, Âli (upper left) and Lala Mustafa Paşa (facing Âli) visit the tomb (seen at top) of Mevlana Celalüddin Rumi at Konya and attend a Mevlevi ceremony.

Yusuf Beğ, *sancak beği* of Kars, and his Kurds meet Lala Mustafa Paşa at Çermik and present heads taken in a recent encounter with the Kızılbaş. Âli stands to the right of Lala Mustafa Paşa, holding his book.

At Ardahan Lala Mustafa Paşa receives a letter, Kızılbaş prisoners, and heads from Husrev Paşa, governor-general of Van. Âli stands to the right of the field marshal.

The Ottoman army arrives before Tiflis (24 August 1578/20 Cümada II 986). Özdemiroğlu Osman Paşa (d. 1585) rides before the walls, while in the foreground Lala Mustafa Paşa approaches with the Janissary infantry and the *sipahi*s of the Porte.

Purchase, preparation, and distribution of food in the camp of the imperial army (*ordu-yı hümayun*).

Şeki, western capital of Şirvan, is taken by Mirza Ali Beğ, *sancak beği* of Pasin (middle ground), and Georgians under Aleksandr Han II (Levendoğlu), prince of Kaheti (foreground).

Cash boxes containing imperial treasure for campaign expenses are delivered to Mustafa Paşa, governor-general of Maraş (Zulkadriye).

In the great mosque of Ereş, in Sunni Şirvan, Ottoman dignitaries and Şirvanis perform Friday prayer, forbidden for the previous half century of Safavi rule (19 September 1578/16 Receb 986).

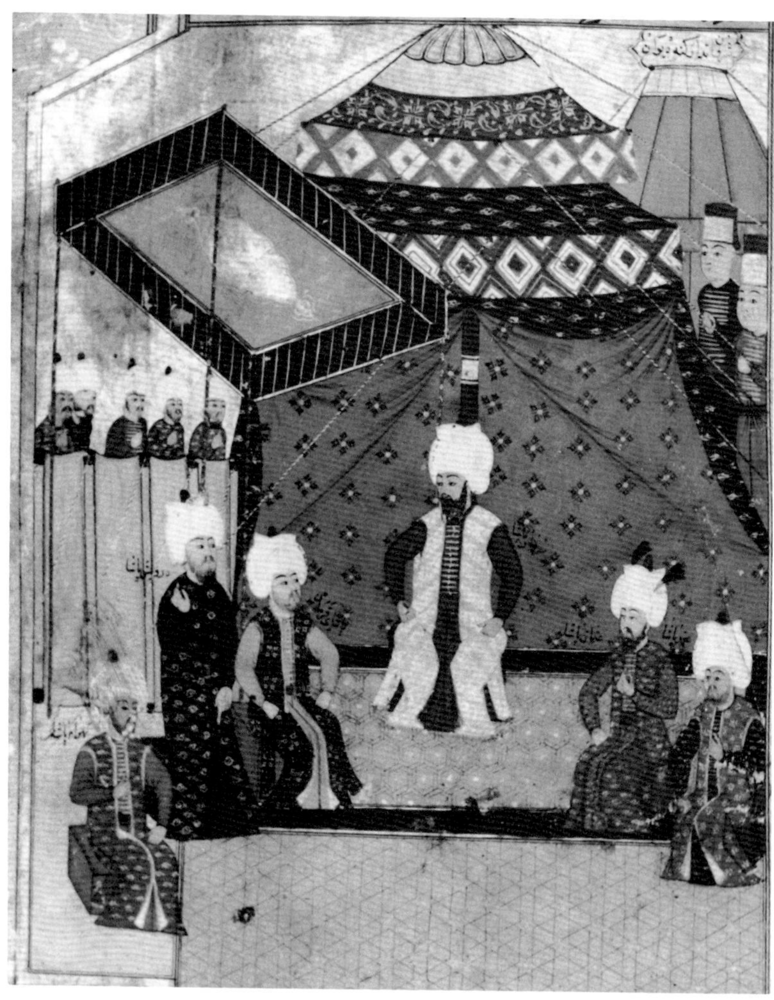

Lala Mustafa Paşa convenes a council for the disposition of Şirvan as an Ottoman province. In attendance are (left to right): Behram Paşa, governor-general of Erzurum; Derviş Paşa of Diyar Bakır; Mehmed Paşa of Karaman; Lala Mustafa Paşa, vezir and field marshal; Özdemiroğlu Osman Paşa, formerly governor-general of Diyar Bakır, now to be appointed that of Şirvan; and Mehmed Paşa, governor-general of Aleppo, a relative of Lala Mustafa Paşa.

Facing page: On the night of *bera'et* (16-17 October 1578/14-15 Şa'ban 986), Lala Mustafa Paşa receives the Şamhal, the Kımık-Kaytak ruler of Dağıstan, who comes to tender his allegiance after years of alliance with the Safavis.

Ottoman forces pillage and burn Safavi Iraq.

Erzurum, winter quarters for Lala Mustafa Paşa and his forces in 1578-79. In the upper left stands the citadel. Mehmed Paşa, governor-general of the province, is in the middle right behind the imperial mosque and to the left of the governor's residence. Also identified (clockwise, from top) are: Mahmud Paşa, governor-general of Rum (Sivas); Behram Paşa of Diyar Bakır; Hasan Paşa, son of Sokollu Mehmed Paşa and governor-general of Damascus; Mehmed Paşa of Karaman; and the commander of the *sipahi*s of the Porte.

Sultan Murad III.

İbrahim Paşa (d. 1601), Âli's erstwhile patron and friend and author of the *Beğlerbeği* Incident.

Mehmed II Giray, Cengizid *han* of the Crimea (reg. 1577-84).

FIVE

THE FINAL YEARS

(1592-1600 / 1000-1008)

ISTANBUL

(1592-93)

AT THE turn of the millennium Âli's inner life was dominated by an overwhelming sense of dislocation and social alienation. He voiced this feeling in poetry that decried the times, which allowed him no honorable place in society and subordinated him to lesser folk.[1] This very discontent, however, spurred him to his greatest and most personal creative effort, a monumental history of the world from Creation to his own day. His feverish work on the *Essence of History* enabled him both to escape into the more orderly and happier world of his youth and to document, with the jaundiced eye of the social critic, his personal disenchantment with Ottoman society. The *Essence* is littered with such asides as that which occurs in the biography of the poet Rahiki, who died in the middle of the reign of Süleyman. Rahiki had enriched himself by compounding and selling *ma'cun*, a popular narcotic mixture. Âli goes on to say that in his own time addiction to narcotics had grown to the point that thirty slaves working day and night could not meet the Istanbul demand for *ma'cun*. To this moral observation Âli the bureaucrat added that the situation was all the more scandalous in that the government did not tax the tremendous profits realized by the producers.[2]

Although Âli was fully absorbed by his historiographical labors, he still had to live and support his household. When Siyavuş Paşa replaced Ferhad Paşa as grand vezir in early April 1592, Âli wrote a fulsome chronogram on the occasion.[3] It must have been Siyavuş Paşa who several months later (mid-July 1592) gave Âli the first post he had held in three years. Âli was appointed secretary of the Janissary Corps (*yeniçeri kâtibi*). Though the post was an important one within the context of the Janissary organization, within the bureaucratic framework it constituted a substantial demotion for

[1] For examples of complaints made in the year 1000, see DİVAN III, 28b, 72b.

[2] KA, Süleyman/Şu'ara, "Rahiki," Nur 3409, 182b.

[3] DİVAN, III, 93a. Âli's date for Siyavuş Paşa's appointment, 9 May 1592/25 Cümada II 1000, is at odds with Selâniki's date of 21 Cümada II (SELANİKİ, pp. 310-12).

a finance director like Âli; normally Janissary secretaries were promoted from that office to a provincial finance directorship, and not the other way around.[4] Âli was conscious of the slight, but was nevertheless grateful for any form of employment. In a poem that he probably addressed to Siyavuş Paşa at this time, Âli declared his satisfaction with the post, despite its low salary.[5]

Âli's joy was short-lived, for he was dismissed after less than four months in office. Âli explains this event as the result of a slander campaign directed against him, but he nowhere specifies what accusations were made.[6] The historian Peçevi, in one of his marginal notations to the *Essence*, says that Sultan Murad, while passing through the city, had caught Âli employing a large number of Janissaries to construct his home. This display seems to have aroused envy at court, or at least suspicion about the source of Âli's wealth, for the sultan dismissed Âli at once.[7] If this story is true, and not one of Peçevi's embroideries, it would appear that Âli repudiated his millennial morality along with his pietistic posture when he was given the opportunity to reenter the official life. It is also possible that the story is either untrue or exaggerated, for Âli succeeded to the far more prestigious post of registrar of the Imperial Council (*defter emini*) within a few days or weeks of his dismissal from the Janissary secretariat.[8]

[4] SELANİKİ, p. 327, gives the date of Âli's appointment as Janissary secretary as Şevval 1000; the chronological position of this entry suggests that the event occurred between the sixth and tenth of that month, which period corresponds to mid-July 1592. The nature of the position is discussed by Uzunçarşılı, *Kapukulu Ocakları*, I, 384-89. The secretary of the Janissary Corps (also known as *yeniçeri efendisi*) headed the office that maintained the Corps' registers of enrollment, promotion, pay, and death. In contrast to other Corps functionaries, who were promoted from the ranks, the secretary was independently appointed by the grand vezir from the professional scribal class (*küttab*), and the appointment was renewed yearly. This was done in order to provide external control over the crucial matters of enrollment and pay, since group solidarity among the Janissaries was exceptionally strong, and illegal registration of family members had become a major financial and military problem.

Normally, secretaries who were promoted would be given a provincial financial post, such as Âli had held previously. Âli's appointment to the position hence represented an unusual phenomenon in the Ottoman bureaucratic service. The unsuccessful career tended to be halted through lack of promotion, dismissal, or retirement, rather than reversed. Selâniki comments that this instance of a finance director being sent back to a purely scribal post is symptomatic of the confusion of the times and of the distintegration of moral and social order.

[5] DİVAN III, 22b. This poem is of some interest for Âli's psychological state; he says that he will no longer be burdened with financial cares, and that he has given up his pious attempts to resign himself to his lot.

[6] SELANİKİ, p. 340: Âli was dismissed in early November 1592/Muharrem 1001. DİVAN III, 60b, contains a poem said on the occasion, in which Âli says that plotters have poisoned the sultan's mind against him although he is innocent of all charges.

[7] Cited by İNAL, pp. 34-35: "Âli was a high liver. He would, if he could, have spent 100,000 *akçe* a day. The late Sultan Murad had given him the secretaryship of the Janissaries. . . . One day the late sultan was passing by Âli's house and saw as many as three hundred Janissary trainees [*acemi oğlan*] and Janissaries building the house. He asked whose the house was. As soon as he was told it belonged to Âli, he dismissed him."

[8] SELANİKİ, *sub anno* 1001, 4b; Âli lost this post in February-March 1593/end of Cümada

With this appointment Âli finally succeeded in finding a significant place in the central administration. As registrar he attended meetings of the Imperial Council and, under the supervision of the chancellor, had charge of the bureau that controlled the records of all provincial revenue sources and grants. The registrar was only slightly lower in rank, if at all, than the chief officers of the central financial service, and was eligible for promotion to either a finance directorship of the Porte or the chancellorship.[9]

Two *gazel*s from Âli's third *divan* indicate that Âli reverted to his old careerist behavior pattern after he reentered official life. In one of these, which he wrote while still serving as Janissary secretary, Âli asked Sultan Murad to bring him to court with the poet Baki, who had retired, so that the sultan might test and compare the two. He requested that he be made registrar and then chancellor.[10] Âli clearly wished to use his office as registrar as a steppingstone to the post he had dreamed of for so many years. The second "sonnet" suggests that Âli's plea worked, and that he finally obtained royal intercession; Âli celebrates his appointment as registrar and describes himself as the protégé (*mensub*) of the sultan and no other. Ever conscious of status and the hierarchy of posts established by *kanun*, Âli noted in the same poem that as registrar he was not lower in rank than a finance director.[11]

For a time after this appointment Âli was able to maintain the patronage relationship he had established with the sultan, perhaps with the help of the royal teacher, Sa'düddin. Murad sent Âli requests for explanations of riddles and Prophetic traditions, to which Âli joyfully responded.[12] Eventually Âli, characteristically, presumed upon the relationship. He sent Sultan Murad a poem in which he complained that his subordinates in the registry (*defterhane*) could not live on their salaries, while much of the revenue they col-

---

I 1001. The printed text of SELANİKİ, p. 241, cites the appointment of "Ali Efendi" as *defter emini* in early November/late Muharrem. This is very likely a scribal or printer's error for "Âli Efendi," since the careful Selâniki records no other changes in this post until Âli's dismissal. That Âli abandoned his vows of temperance is shown by a short poem in DİVAN III, 92a-b, in which Âli rejoices at the arrival of the *îd* at the end of Ramazan, since he can then once again indulge his passion for wine and "beauties" (*hûbân*).

9 Mehmed Ârif, ed., *Kanunname-i Âl-i Osman, TOEM*, suppl. 3 (Istanbul, 1330), pp. 14, 16-18, 22; Uzunçarşılı, *Merkez*, pp. 95-98.

10 DİVAN III, 67b; İNAL, p. 36. The poem is addressed to Sultan Murad and is dated "The Feast of Sacrifice," i.e., 10 Zulhicce. The year must therefore be 1592/1000. Âli probably meant no disrespect to Baki, to whose poetic standards he aspired. Rather, Âli's constant linking of their names, particularly during this last period of his life, is a manifestation of his oft-repeated conviction that the foremost men of learning should be honored and given high posts. In certain respects the two poets were very similar; Baki, too, was extremely ambitious, had begun his career in the *ilmiye* through his literary talent, and had retired from the post of chief military judge of Rumeli two years before in disappointment over his inability to secure further advancement; see Köprülü, "Baki."

11 DİVAN III, 40a-b.

12 DİVAN III, 80a-b.

lected went to the Imperial Kitchen (*matbah*). In this poem Âli played his old role of informer, attempting to show himself as one of the monarch's few honest servitors; he implied that Kitchen officials, such as the keeper of Kitchen accounts (*matbah emini*), were illegally diverting funds and supplies.[13] In his new position Âli undoubtedly made new enemies. He also had to contend with old ones, for Koca Sinan Paşa was appointed to his third term as grand vezir on 29 January 1593. About one month later Âli was dismissed from the registrarship, charged with financial malfeasance.[14] It is probable that Âli's downfall was a result of both his zeal for exposing corruption and the enmity of Sinan Paşa. Âli took the event to heart, having lost, then regained, and again lost hope of advancement. He protested his innocence of any wrongdoing to Sultan Murad, and at the same time told himself and his peers, in a poem that appears to have gained some topical currency, that the post had been a burden from which he was glad to be relieved.[15] In these verses Âli described himself as a man interested in higher things, who could return to the contemplation of spiritual mysteries after being freed from noisome obligations:

> Worldly cares I've left behind, the master of secrets have I become.
> The *simurg* bird on the mystic mount of peace, that wondrous being
> have I become.
> Praise to God, I've put aside the bonds of the Registry;
> Freed from the cage, a bird flying like the phoenix [*hüma*] have I
> become.[16]

Âli's sour grapes did not impress some of his fellow poets, who composed satirical parodies of Âli's "bird" poem. The most scathing of these was penned by Ma'ruf Efendi, the teacher of Sinan Paşa, who insulted Âli as well as accused him of bribery and corruption:

> Don't think yourself a flying phoenix, don't liken yourself to the
> *simurg*!
> With that vain flight of fancy, a tale-bearing crow have you become.
> Your account has been called and closed, you've escaped the cage;
> A goose caught in the falcon's claw have you become.[17]

[13] DİVAN III, 79b-80a. SELANİKİ, *sub anno* 1004, 84a, mentions a false scandal over Imperial Kitchen supplies, which surfaced a few years later.

[14] SELANİKİ, *sub anno* 1000, 3a, gives the date of Sinan Paşa's appointment as 29 January 1593/25 Rebi' II 1001. According to the same source (4b) Âli was dismissed from the *defterhane* in the last week of February or first week of March 1593/late Cümada I 1001.

[15] DİVAN III, 44b. İNAL, p. 38, gives an excerpt from this plaint to Murad; 54b is a private lament that his worth is not recognized, despite his four *divans* in four languages. The "release poem" and another in a similar vein occur in DİVAN III, 60a-b (excerpt İNAL, pp. 36-37).

[16] DİVAN, III, 60a-b.

[17] SELANİKİ, *sub anno* 1001, 4a-b, gives the full text of the satire, and refers to the general amusement Âli's poem provoked. İNAL, p. 37, quotes a shorter version of the parody and

Âli composed this "swan song" in the spring of 1593. He closed the poem with these lines:

> Away Âli! From vengeful foes' calumnies. A Ḥâfiẓ of Shiraz seeking to leave his homeland have I become.
> To the ruler who holds the world, true service did I offer;
> A tale-bearer, who reveals others' faults, have I become.[18]

Âli here displays, implicitly, many of the conflicts and reflexes that marked his final years. He did indeed turn to Ḥâfiẓ of Shiraz, in order to escape the realities of his own world and time. He rejected worldly glory in favor of pious contentment, although, or perhaps because, he desired the world so. Âli's ambition, as well as his convictions on the value of learning and justice, drove him to criticize loudly and thereby make enemies. Though he rationalized such behavior as "true service," he was sufficiently self-conscious to be aware of the self-serving aspect of his verbal paranoia, and of his own inner conflicts. True, Âli spent most of his remaining years "revealing others' faults" in his new role as social critic. He also sometimes saw himself as others did—as a tale-bearer—and admonished himself to reform. In a series of short poetic pieces composed during these last years, Âli commented on his own ugliness, saying he was shunned by all except in the tavern. He chided himself for having made himself a pagan by serving worldly kings so slavishly, and told himself not to speak so harshly of others, as such words could not be taken back.[19] In fragments such as these, Âli shows himself to have been a man trapped in a body, in a psyche, and in a society he longed to change or escape but could not.

RETREAT IN GELIBOLU (1593)

ÂLI sought solace for his disappointment, and perhaps solitude and reorientation, in a return to the childhood home he had left as an adolescent. He traveled to Gelibolu in the spring of 1593. There he began a series of retrospective literary exercises that consisted largely of compiling excerpts from his two *divans* and other poetry not included in them. The first of these, *Sadef-i sad güher, Lustre of a Hundred Jewels*, was written in Gelibolu. The text is preceded by a long celebration in verse of Âli's birthplace, its poets,

identifies the author as Ma'ruf Efendi on the basis of a *mecmua* entry in his private collection. SO, IV, 502, lists Ma'ruf Efendi, who died in 1593-94/1002, as the teacher of Sinan Paşa.

[18] DİVAN III, 60b; İNAL, p. 37.

[19] DİVAN III, 91a-92a.

its ulema and saints, and his own family.[20] The journey, as well as the *Lustre*, represented a return and rejuvenation. Âli, plagued by years of disappointment, reaffirmed his own worth and ideals, as evidenced by a section of the introduction in which he gives his autobiography, lists all his literary works, and praises his own accomplishments.[21]

Âli quickly produced several more modest anthologies of this type, which presumably gave him a rest from his labors on the *Essence*, as well as provided therapeutic assistance in his positive reevaluation of himself and his life. The *Gül-i sad berg, Blossoms of a Hundred Leaves*, was probably composed in Gelibolu, and consists of one hundred opening verses (*matla'*) selected from his two poetry collections.[22] In the *Sübhat ül-ebdal, The Saints' Rosary*, completed in 1593-94/1002, Âli collected elegies for Ḥusayn that he had written on the Âşûrâs of years ranging from 1585/993 to 1591/1000.[23]

ISTANBUL: THE LAST YEARS OF SULTAN MURAD (1593-95)

AFTER a few months' rest and psychological recuperation in Gelibolu, Âli returned to Istanbul and gave his energies to two projects. The first was completion of the *Essence of History*, on which he concentrated to the exclusion of virtually any other literary activity. By 1593-94/1002 Âli had already written much of the work, and in that year he composed the lengthy (48 pages) introduction to his history.[24]

Âli's second goal was reinstatement to some sort of official position. During this period of unemployment in Istanbul, Âli doubtless maintained contact with literary circles. He had also reaffirmed for himself the notion that had dominated his youth—that the learned and literary were the primary pillars of Ottoman society. In a poem sent to Sultan Murad about this time, Âli

[20] SADEF (see chapter 1, note 1). The introduction ends on p. 252, and on p. 250 the time of composition is given as 1593/1001, after his return to his homeland following years of travel and travail. The remainder of the work consists of excerpts from the *Varidat* and *Layihat*.

[21] SADEF, pp. 245-50. This autobiography and list of works are heavily utilized by İNAL.

[22] *Gül-i sad berg*, MS Ali Emiri Türkçe Manzum 978, pp. 286-90.

[23] *Sübhat ül-ebdal*, MS Ali Emiri Türkçe Manzum 978, pp. 292-303. The date of composition occurs on p. 293.

[24] Âli was in Istanbul for part, and probably all of, the years 1593-94/1002. He composed a chronogram on the completion of the Cerrah Mehmed Paşa Mosque, which occurred in that year (DİVAN, III, 93b; Ayvansarayi, *Hadikat*, I, 71). He was certainly at his home in Istanbul toward the end of the year, when he began the *Badî' al-ruqûm*. The extent of Âli's industry on the *Essence* is illustrated by the number and diverse character of sections of it that are explicitly dated to the year 1002: General Introduction (KA, I, 36); Süleyman/Ulema, "Arabzade Muhyiddin," Nur 3409, 213b; Süleyman/Beğlerbeğiler, "Şemsi Ahmed Paşa," Nur 3409, 131a (probable).

recommended that Murad give the foremost poets of the time positions in the Imperial Council. In this group Âli associated his own name with those of two slightly older and more successful members of his own generation who, unlike Âli, had remained in the *ilmiye*.[25] Baki, a friend of long standing, was retired and in disfavor. Nev'i, a distinguished poet and teacher, was the tutor of the older Ottoman princes. Âli's designation of these two, together with himself, as major intellectual figures who ought to be rewarded certainly reflects his good personal relationship with them. It also shows whom he identified with and measured himself against within what he considered his peer group; Âli remained a *medrese* product at heart. In their deaths, at least, these three figures, together with Sultan Murad's teacher Hoca Sa'düddin, constituted an almost mathematically precise generation; all four died within a year of each other, between 1599 and 1600.[26]

The personal connections and intellectual similarities between these men are suggestive of the cultural and professional world within which Âli had lived since his early youth. The three older members of the group had all been schoolmates, and had been particularly influenced by the *Sahn* teacher Karamani Mehmed Efendi, whose circle of students produced an unusually large number of poets. When Âli first came to Istanbul as a student, they formed the younger segment of the literary milieu in which Âli was caught up. Nev'i, like Âli, had been a close associate of Sarhoş Bali Efendi. Hoca Sa'düddin periodically assisted Âli, and like him became interested in producing a comprehensive and organized Ottoman history. All four men were trilingual in Turkish, Persian, and Arabic, and were fascinated with the combined potential that Ottoman Turkish represented. All were concerned to make Turkish a literary language, either through translation from the established vehicles of polite letters or through the creation of new works. Baki's description of Turkish as "a tongue of sweet expression, scattering sugar" mirrored the enthusiasm Âli expressed for it in the *Essence*, saying that Turkish provided great scope and excitement for a user educated in all three languages.[27] Finally, all of these men shared an admiration for Persian literary models and, with the exception of Sa'düddin, subscribed at least nominally to the dervish orientation and profligate ways that had dominated educated Ottoman society in the mid-sixteenth century.

[25] DİVAN III, 67a-68a.

[26] Köprülü, "Baki, "İA; Abdülkadir Karahan, "Nev'i," İA; Turan, "Sa'd-ed-din," İA. Baki was the eldest of the lot, born in 1526; Nev'i was born in 1533 and Sa'düddin in 1536. Âli was the youngest, born in 1541. Âli's relations with Baki and Sa'düddin have already been alluded to. He mentions Nev'i only twice (KA, Murad/End, Mehmed/Cülus, Nur 3409, 419a-b, 428a-b), but promises to give a biography of him in the biographical section on dignitaries of Murad's reign, which was to follow the events. This portion of the *Essence* was never completed or, in fact, started.

[27] Köprülü, "Baki"; KA, I, 11.

Âli, too, began training for a religious career and reached a level which, had he continued, would theoretically have allowed him to reach similar professional stature. Baki, Nev'i, and Sa'düddin remained in the *ilmiye*, and to some extent subordinated their literary interests to professional ones. The impatient Âli left the *ilmiye* to make his way primarily as a littérateur and protégé of the powerful, thereby embarking on an erratic and independent progress that left him with no firm professional standing in any career line. In late middle age, as he psychologically returned to the beginning of his life and tried to come to terms with the world, Âli sought to identify and establish his own parity with those of his "peers" who had succeeded where he had failed. This he did, in the passage cited above, by comparing his literary accomplishments to those of Baki and Nev'i. While admitting the poetic preeminence of these two, Âli states that, although he is younger than either, he is by far the more prolific writer of poetry and prose; while Baki and Nev'i have gained fame on the basis of a single *divan* and single prose work each, Âli lays claim to nearly fifty works, including "four *divan*s in Persian and Turkish." In fact, Baki and Nev'i wrote more than one book each, but most of their prose efforts, unlike those of Âli, consisted of translations from Arabic and Persian into Turkish.

Âli's political position at this time was a delicate one. His primary supporters at court were the Palace overseer Gazanfer Ağa and the royal tutor, Sa'düddin. These two also cooperated with Âli's old enemy, the grand vezir Sinan Paşa, who was the last of the old guard of vezirs who had begun their careers under Süleyman.[28] Gazanfer and Sa'düddin probably counseled Âli to try once again to ingratiate himself with the man he had reviled for decades. In the autumn of 1593 Sinan Paşa left Istanbul to begin organizing a campaign against the Hapsburgs. When about a year later the capital received the news that the Ottoman forces had taken the fortress of Raab (Turkish: Yanık) in Austrian Hungary, Âli dispatched a personal letter of congratulations and entreaty to the grand vezir. Âli declared his devotion to Sinan, blaming their poor relations on the intrigues of malefactors, the worst of whom had fortunately just died. Out of work, Âli said that he was so poor that only by selling his books could he live from week to week. His sole activity at the time was writing the *Essence of History*, which Âli declared to have been endorsed in writing by the chief jurisconsult Bustanzade and other prominent ulema as the abrogator of all earlier histories. This great work, Âli said, was the product of his idleness and depression.[29] Hoca

[28] KA, Mehmed/Fourth Vezirate of Sinan Paşa, Halet Efendi 598, 436b; Turan, "Sa'd-ed-Din."

[29] On the Hungarian campaign of this year, see C. Max Kortepeter, *Ottoman Imperialism during the Reformation, Europe and the Caucasus* (New York, 1972), pp. 136-43. Raab fell on 27 September 1594/12 Muharrem 1003, and the news reached Istanbul nearly a month later;

Sa'düddin later secured for Âli the commission to compose Sinan Paşa's official account of the conquest.[30]

Âli's patent hypocrisy in fawning on Sinan Paşa at precisely this period emerges clearly from his account of Sinan Paşa's attack on Raab in the *Essence*, where he accuses the grand vezir of irrationality and of wasting men and money through poor planning. To this Âli adds that Sinan's son Mehmed Paşa disgraced himself through abject cowardice during the attack.[31] Such hypocrisy was a necessary expedient in an increasingly factionalized political environment. In any event, Âli seems to have profited either from Sinan Paşa's favor or from his absence, for in early December 1594/late Rebi' I 1003 Sultan Murad personally reappointed him secretary of the Janissary Corps, although most of these were still in the field.[32]

This was the last favor Âli would receive from Sultan Murad, whom he had known for twenty-five years. Shortly after he made the appointment, Murad fell ill with a gastrointestinal ailment. In the *Essence* Âli records the anxiety that overcame the court as Murad's illness progressed. Courtiers began to have ominous dreams in which they saw great trees downed in the Palace grounds, or witnessed the destruction of the mosque of Aya Sofya (Hagia Sophia), symbol of Istanbul and of Ottoman dynastic prestige. Even before the sultan's illness manifested itself, Sa'atçi Hasan Paşa, who had previously served as the sultan's sword bearer (*silahdar*) and who was also noted for his skill as an astrologer, had a particularly disturbing dream. Hasan Paşa had but recently returned to Istanbul after being dismissed from the government of Diyar Bakır by Sinan Paşa; he recounted his dream to his close friend Âli, who interpreted it to mean that the sultan would fall gravely ill. Hasan Paşa sent an account of his dream, and of Âli's interpretation, to the then healthy Sultan Murad. Three days later he was stricken, and he wrote to Hasan Paşa to inform him of the truth of the augury. About one month later, on January 16, 1595, Sultan Murad III died, and eleven days later his son Mehmed ascended the Ottoman throne as Mehmed III.[33]

---

see SELANİKİ, *sub anno* 1003; KA, Murad/Yanık, Nur 3409, 412b. Âli's letter is found in an album, Halet Efendi Eki 245, 7b-8b. Atsız (AB, p. 51) mistakenly dates it to 1598-99/1007-1008.

[30] Halet Efendi Eki 245, 4b-5b. The heading reads: "The *fethname* on the occasion of the conquest of Yanık, for Serdar Sinan Paşa, by Gelibolulu Âli Çelebi, at the behest of Hoca Sa'düddin Efendi." The date of composition given at the end (27-29 Cümada II) seems somewhat anomalous, since by this time Sinan Paşa had been dismissed from the grand vezirate.

[31] KA Murad/Yanık, Nur 3409, 410b-413b.

[32] SELANİKİ, *sub anno* 1003, 47a. Selâniki gives the date of appointment as late Rebi' I 1003, and says pointedly that it was made by imperial rescript. Selâniki also emphasizes that Âli was made full secretary, the office having been temporarily divided between an official in the field and one in the capital who had charge of payment of those Janissaries who remained in Istanbul.

[33] KA, Murad/ End, Nur 3409, 417a-419a; B. Kütükoğlu, "Murad III," İA; T. Gökbilgin, "Mehmed III," İA.

Âli's *Essence* account of Sultan Murad's last days provides a fascinating glimpse of the psychic life of a court that revolved around a monarch who was manifestly intrigued with popular occultism. The apocalyptic air generated by the turn of the millennium carried over to the end of a reign that marked a particularly troubled period of Ottoman history; in his account of the transition from Murad to Mehmed, Âli, whether consciously or not, evokes the atmosphere by constant reference to astrology, numerology, and to the dying Sultan Murad's periodic clairvoyance. The placement of this passage in the *Essence* reinforces a sense of momentous, even apocalyptic change; it is sandwiched between a long account of the wasteful and bloody Austrian wars, and a description of the universal mourning that attended the newly enthroned Sultan Mehmed's execution of his nineteen younger brothers, in accordance with established Ottoman dynastic practice. In Istanbul expectation of great change ran high; it was still too early to predict whether the new era of Sultan Mehmed would be better or worse than the reign of his father.

ISTANBUL: THE ACCESSION OF MEHMED III (1595)

WHEN Murad died, his son Prince Mehmed was summoned from his *sancak* at Manisa to assume the throne. This he did formally on January 27, 1595. An important part of the Ottoman accession ceremonial was the distribution of gifts of money and objects to Palace servitors and, in particular, to the members of the Palace military units, including the Janissaries. As Janissary secretary, Âli recorded all the accession gifts distributed by the sultan to the members of the Corps. Âli himself, however, as a self-appointed authority on *kanun*, refused the cloak of honor and the nine thousand-*akçe* gift to which his post entitled him. Âli asserted that, inasmuch as his real rank was that of finance director, he should receive much more; and indeed, the next day he was granted a new cloak and fifty thousand *akçe*.[34]

Âli seems to have felt himself to be in good position vis-à-vis the new sultan. Besides having written a celebration of Mehmed's circumcision cer-

[34] KA, Mehmed/Cülus, Nur 3409 427b. Âli also records that he directly or indirectly interceded with the sultan in order to have an accession gift made to the thousand "Janissaries" of the Bread Kitchens (*fodladaki yeniçeriyan*), something which had never been done before. On the Janissary Bread Kitchens (*fodla, fürun-ı segbanan*), see Uzunçarşılı, *Kapukulu Ocakları*, I, 260-62, 308. The precise meaning of Âli's use of "Janissaries" is imprecise, since the Bread Kitchens, which produced bread for free distribution to certain members of the Corps and to the orphaned children of Janissaries, employed only fifty or sixty bakers. The number cited makes it clear that Âli in fact means the children of aged or dead Janissaries who were registered to receive daily bread from the *fodla*, and eventually to enter the Janissary ranks themselves.

emonies, Âli could claim great experience and knowledge of the Ottoman house, since he had served the new ruler's father, grandfather, and great-grandfather. Mehmed's accession brought a flood of congratulatory odes, and those of Baki, Nev'i, and Âli were judged the best of those submitted. Baki, in reward, was reappointed chief military judge of Rumeli; and Nev'i, who had lost his position through the death of his pupils, Sultan Mehmed's brothers, was retired on full pay. Âli was offered permanent tenure as Janissary secretary and retirement with two hundred thousand *akçe* per year. Âli once again pointed out that he was actually a finance director by rank, and that furthermore the work load of the Janissary secretaryship had severely hindered his work on the *Essence*. Therefore, he resigned his post and asked to be given the finance directorship of Egypt, which better befitted his rank and was presumably less onerous, as well as providing him access to the book markets of Cairo. If Âli may be believed, his bold request was granted immediately.[35]

In discussing his own accession ode, Âli claims that the *seyhülislam* Bustanzade, as well as others able to appreciate its subleties, were delighted with its originality of both style and content.[36] It is the content of this ode that shows the extent of Âli's temerity and self-confidence.[37] He counsels Mehmed to emulate the greatest of his ancestors, Mehmed II, Selim I, and Süleyman, in their zeal for justice, for it is by justice that kings are known. He must root out corruption and bribery, and prevent infiltration of unworthy people, particularly newcomers from the eastern regions of the Empire, into the Ottoman system.[38] Âli finally asks to be appointed companion so that he might continue to advise the sultan. Âli states his thesis even more directly in another poem addressed to Mehmed, in which he celebrates the enthronement of the new ruler who will rectify the evils of the preceding regime, which he then proceeds to enumerate.[39] Under Murad the subjects were oppressed because the sultan paid little heed to law and justice. Appointments were effectively made, not by the sultan, but by those in control of his harem, and undue preference had been given in government and Palace service to "foreigners" (*ecnebi*) from the east, who since the Ottoman conquest of Şirvan and Tabriz had come westward to seek their fortunes.

[35] KA, Mehmed/Cülus, Nur 3409, 428a-429a. Âli was careful to make himself known to the sultan's mother, Safiye Hatun, who was the new ruler of the women's harem. He sent her an ode on the occasion of Mehmed's accession, in which he reminded her of his earlier services (DİVAN III, 13a-b).

[36] KA, Mehmed/Cülus, Nur 3409, 428a; Âli also notes that the scholar and poet Tab'i deemed his ode superior to those of Baki and Nev'i.

[37] In the KA passage cited in the preceding footnote, Âli cites only the first line of the poem. Its full text occurs in DİVAN III, 11a-12b.

[38] DİVAN III, 12b ("Persian cooks and scoundrelly Kurds").

[39] DİVAN III, 10b-11a.

In still another poem, Âli makes it clear that he was sincerely optimistic that Mehmed would, in apocalyptic terms, put right the order of the state, which he saw as having been destroyed under Murad through the sultan's irresponsibility, greed, and lack of concern for justice. Âli hoped that in the new order the educated and worthy would once again be elevated to high position.[40] That Âli should have couched his optimism in the terms he did, and broadcast it so openly, suggests that his feelings were indeed shared by others, and that the problems that plagued Murad's reign were a common topic of conversation among the intelligentsia. Otherwise, it is unlikely that even the brash Âli could have addressed the newly enthroned Mehmed so baldly.[41]

The Legacy of Murad III: The Eastern Problem

During the period immediately following Mehmed's accession, Âli was much concerned with the role of "eastern foreigners" in the Empire's troubles, and his preoccupation deserves discussion.[42] Âli asserts that in Murad's time people coming from the former Safavi territories of Şirvan and Azerbaycan were favored over Palace-trained *devşirme* slaves, and that this preferment was based on ethnic origin:

> The suitability and merit [of the Palace recruits] were disregarded. The sultan preferred "Iranians" [*acemler*, including Kurds, Arabs, and Türkmens from the border provinces] from abroad to novice *devşirme* recruits [*acemiler*]. Thus the home products were driven out and the foreigners were deemed worthy of power and position.[43]

If preferred treatment for Iranians did indeed occur under Murad (for the most part we only have Âli's word that this was so), it may be viewed as

[40] DİVAN III, 23b-24b. Âli develops these poetic evaluations of Murad's reign in the KA, where he stresses the sultan's abdication of responsibility for administration and his compulsion to gather money as primary factors in the confusion, corruption, and institutional erosion that plagued the state; KA, Murad/End, Nur 3409, 292b, 417a, 419a-420a, 425b. Murad's shortsightedness is epitomized, Âli says, by his devotion to the delights of the harem, from which issued nineteen male offspring who then had to be killed, cruelly and wastefully, at tender ages on their father's death. Had Murad been more conscious of *kanun* and of the nature of his position, Âli says, he would not have left so many children.

[41] For an analog, see the account of Mehmed's accession composed by Âli's contemporary Ta'likizade for inclusion in an official history of the Hungarian campaign, in Christine Woodhead, *Ta'lîkî-zâde's Şehnâme-i Hümâyûn: A History of the Ottoman Campaign into Hungary, 1593-94* (Freiburg, 1983), pp. 372-403.

[42] Apart from the harsh criticism of "*ecnebiler*" found in the two accession poems cited above, Âli devoted considerable space to the problem in those sections of the KA that cover the end of Murad's reign and the beginning of Mehmed's: KA Murad/Şehnameguyan, Nur 3409, 419b-422a; Murad/Acemiler, 424a-427a; Mehmed/Bölük Halkı, 431a-b. Such dates as Âli provides, and internal evidence, indicate that this portion of the KA was composed between late 1595/1004 and early 1598/1006.

[43] KA, Murad/Acemiler, Nur 3409, 424b.

both a cultural and a political phenomenon. In the literary sphere it reflects a continuation of the Persianate orientation of the Ottoman court, and the cultural prestige enjoyed by the hinterland regions of Şirvan and Tabriz in the sixteenth century. Three of the four Ottoman court historians (*şehnameci*) of the sixteenth century were Türkmens from Şirvan or Azerbaycan. It is understandable that native speakers of Persian would have the edge over other contenders for the post of *şehname* writer, since the office was initially established in order to provide for the composition of an Ottoman history in Persian verse. This aspect of "Iranian preferment" was a particularly sore point with Âli, who prided himself on his versifying ability in both Persian and Turkish. Âli ridiculed the verse of Eflatun-ı Şirvani, Seyyid Lokman, and Ta'likizade, giving only the first *şehnameci*, Ârif Çelebi, a positive evaluation.[44] In this context, Âli's complaints become comprehensible and their self-serving aspect becomes apparent; Âli's own stock-in-trade was his education and self-identification as a major literary figure.

There is also a political and institutional dimension to the "eastern problem" that is somewhat more broadly attested in Ottoman sources than its cultural aspect: the influx of Muslim natives of the newly conquered eastern provinces into the *kul*-dominated Ottoman military establishment. Âli elaborates on the ramifications of the Ottoman acquisition of Şirvan and Azerbaycan in a discussion of the growing insubordination of the mounted troops of the Porte (*bölük halkı*).[45] In order to hold the new conquests, a great many local people had been enrolled for garrison duty. As these duties were normally performed by Palace (*kapıkulu*) troops or *timar* holders, this meant that the newcomers acquired *askeri* or quasi-*kul* status. After a few years of service, they came west and were assigned to Palace military units, despite their lack of training as military slaves. Consequently, the ranks of the Palace forces were swelled with untrained, undisciplined, and rapacious newcomers from the east. Âli lays much of the blame for the successive revolts of the Palace units (in 1588, 1593, and 1595) in Istanbul on the influx of these insubordinate elements, and on Sultan Murad's failure to adhere to established Ottoman practice, whereby the Palace military units had been filled primarily with *devşirme* products or their children. According to Âli, the slave system was part of Ottoman *kanun*; it had preserved order and made the Empire great, and should be upheld. Selâniki's analysis of the reasons for repeated Palace unit rebellions is essentially the same; he states that

[44] In what may be a later version of the introduction to the *Essence*, now preserved in a unique recension in Leiden (MS Cod. Warner 288, 3a-10a), Âli expresses a more positive evaluation of Ta'likizade's abilities (7a). Mr. Jan Schmidt drew my attention to this passage, which he is now editing for publication.

[45] KA, Mehmed/Grand Vezirate of Ferhad Paşa, Nur 3409, 430b-431b. The structure of the *bölük* units is outlined, and their revolts discussed, by Uzunçarşılı, *Kapukulu Ocakları*, II, 138-41, 196-201.

they were the product of the infiltration of unworthy and unauthorized "foreigners" into all sectors of government service, an infiltration that Sultan Murad allowed and encouraged.[46] It is interesting to note, parenthetically, that Selâniki's placement of this discussion, as well as his judgment, precisely parallels Âli's treatment of the subject. Both historians use their accounts of the 1595 *bölük* revolt against the grand vezir Ferhad Paşa as a vehicle for review of the previous rebellions and for discussion of the eastern problem.

Swelling of the ranks of the Palace forces by such unauthorized "foreigners" during the late sixteenth and early seventeenth centuries is also attested by the anonymous author of the *Kitab-i müstetab, The Approved Book*, who wrote only a few years after Âli and Selâniki. He cites as a particular cause of the disruption of the military establishment the intrusion of "Türkmens, Kurds, Gypsies, Tats, and Iranians."[47] The evidence provided thus far might suggest that the problem of "eastern foreigners" was exaggerated by writers in the *nasihatname* mode, or at least that they may have given an ethnic slant to a fundamentally instututional problem. An order dated late December 1585 and addressed to the governor-general of Baghdad shows that the central government, too, was aware of the special institutional problems created by the conquest of Muslim territories not subject to the *devşirme*, and that Istanbul also viewed the situation in ethnic or, at least, geographical terms.[48] The document notes that local Baghdad military units have been infiltrated by "Tats, Çepni Türkmens, and Safavi Türkmen" who have purchased appointment or *gedük*s, a designation to fill a post when it should fall vacant.[49] The governor-general is ordered to halt such practices, for they go against established usage, which has been to fill local military positions in the provinces with "Rumi warriors and the sons of imperial servants of Rumi origin." Unauthorized military personnel are to be removed and their places filled with "men who are not from the east . . . *timars* are to be given to able Rumi warriors and sons of [illegible] and sons of *za'im*s and *sipahi*s. As long as the candidate is not a Rumi warrior, no *timar* will be offered him." The content of this document clarifies the nature of the "eastern problem" described by historians writing some ten years later. The first concern of the government was to preserve the *askeri-re'âyâ* distinction, and to restrict entrance into the provincial military system to the

[46] SELANİKİ, *sub anno* 1003, cited by Uzunçarşılı, *Kapukulu Ocaklari*, II, 200-201.

[47] *Kitab-i müstetab*, pp. 3-4, 7-10; see p. 4; "*Etrâk ve ekrâd ve çingâne ve tat ve a'câm.*" On the term "Tat," which in this instance signifies either a particular Iranian ethnic group or people of Iranian origin living under Ottoman rule, presumably to be distinguished from "native born" Iranians (*a'câm*), see V. Minorsky, "Tât," EI[1].

[48] MD 60, doc. 312, dated early Muharrem 994.

[49] On the Çepni *oymak* of the Oğuz, see Faruk Sümer, *Oğuzlar (Türkmenler)* (Istanbul, 1980), pp. 327-35.

members of established *askeri* families from the Ottoman hinterland. To allow new elements from the eastern border reaches to cross the *askeri-re'âyâ* line would deprive the government of tax revenues and disrupt the military establishment. Apart from the fact that, for *timar* holders, membership in the *askeri* class was largely a function of heredity and proven family loyalty to the dynasty, the inhabitants of the Ottoman-Safavi border regions, whether Kurdish or Türkmen, posed a particular threat to Ottoman security in that their loyalty was neither well established nor certain. For this reason, it would be unwise to push too far the notion that "anti-eastern" prejudice, defined ethnically or geographically, was a major factor in Ottoman perception of an eastern problem, although in certain circles such prejudice was certainly a byproduct of the situation. In the *Essence*, for example, Âli excoriates Şerif Mehmed Paşa, an Iranian of indeterminate origin who served twice as treasurer and was appointed governor-general of Egypt in 1596. Âli casts doubt on the Paşa's claim to descent from the Prophet, accuses him of harboring heretical Shi'i beliefs, and then quotes a poem that the poet Akli composed by way of comment on the appointment. These verses illustrate the negative side of Ottoman polyethnicity, as well as showing that Âli was not alone in his feelings about the impropriety of "Iranian predominance" in official life:

> Albanian, Bosnian, and Hungarian slaves have been governors.
> Until now, has the sultan ever made an *acemi* [Iranian or tyro] governor of Egypt?
> In the old days a black-faced Arab ruled it, now a Persian red-head [*kızılbaş*] has become governor.[50]

It is of considerable interest to note, in light of the archival evidence cited above, that the central government, as well as Ottoman historians, to some extent identified Ottomanism and Ottoman loyalty with the geographical hinterland of Rum, and viewed with suspicion those who, Muslim Turks though they might be, were not themselves identifiable as Rumi.

Ottoman perception of a "foreign problem" was very real; Âli devoted an entire section of his discussion of Murad's last years in the *Essence* to an

[50] KA, Murad/End, Nur 3409, 426b. The date of Şerif Mehmed Paşa's appointment is given in CAIRO, p. 18. For another instance of literary expression of ethnic prejudice, see a poem by Fehmi quoted in CAIRO, pp. 75-76 (trans.), 166-67 (text). Âli must have written this KA passage shortly before 4 March 1596/4 Receb 1004, when Kurd Paşa was deposed as governor of Egypt and Şerif Mehmed Paşa appointed in his place (SELANİKİ, *sub anno* 1004, 106b). Âli refers to Kurd Paşa as the incumbent, and describes Şerif Mehmed's supporters' attempts to have him replace Kurd Paşa as unsuccessful. Âli later moderated his views on Şerif Mehmed Paşa and gave him high marks for administrative ability; his earlier disparagement of Şerif Mehmed may in part have been occasioned by the latter's standing as a favorite protégé of Sinan Paşa (CAIRO, pp. 74-76 [trans.], 164-67 [text]).

analysis of the historical role and recent prominence of *Acemler*, ''Iranians, easterners,'' in the Ottoman Empire.[51] In his exposition Âli makes it clear that his, and others', objections to the ''Iranian'' influx are neither purely personal nor primarily ethnic in origin. The ''foreign upstarts'' were not only *Acem*, ''Iranians,'' but also *acemi*, ''novice.'' They were, finally, also *ecnebi*, ''foreign,'' in the sense that they had no place within the established Ottoman system.[52] Âli and his contemporaries had spent lifetimes building careers within the parameters of certain career tracks, only to see outsiders who were neither born into nor trained within these tracks suddenly raised to positions of prominence, or attaining posts formerly reserved for the products of the Palace education system. The personal chagrin of those who saw themselves and others born into the Ottoman system displaced by ''foreign upstarts,'' however small their actual number may have been, translated into ''*kanun*-consciousness.'' *Kanun*-consciousness sprang from a concern for the integrity of the Ottoman system, as the historian-bureaucrat envisioned it, and from an Ottoman chauvinism centered on the history and distinctive culture of the Ottoman Empire as these developed through the reign of Süleyman. In this discussion of the eastern problem, Âli differentiates between those Iranians who settled in Rum in earlier times and who had gained deserved promienence by virtue of their descent and learning, such as Ali Kuşçi (d. 1474/879) and Muslihüddin Lari (d. 1572/979), and those recent immigrants with no genealogical or educational qualifications for service apart from their ''Iranian'' origins.[53]

Âli says that all rulers have trained servitors upon whom they can rely, and that the descendants of these propagate the tradition of service generation after generation. The Ottomans, due to a scarcity of manpower, developed the practice of recruiting and training slaves to fill the most important positions in the state, their selection being based solely on merit. The children of devoted servitors are protected by their master and should be brought into service as well. In other words, merit, training within the Ottoman system, and proven loyalty to the dynasty are the primary criteria for service and advancement. The slave system and polyethnicity, in Âli's view, are fundamental characteristics of Ottomanism and Ottoman government. In the introduction to the *Essence*, Âli states proudly that ''most of the inhabitants of the land of Rum are of mixed origin. Amongst the more

[51] KA, Murad/End, Nur 3409, 424a-426b.

[52] For an example of this use of *ecnebi*, see KA, Selim/Vüzera, ''Kapudan Ali Paşa,'' Nur 3409, 253b. Ali Paşa is specifically termed *ecnebi* because he was not a *devşirme*-Palace product; he is also described as ''better than the other *ecnebi*s of this time.'' It must be noted, however, that there was also a regional definition of the term ''foreigner''; Sultan Süleyman rejected the notion that anyone living within his domains, subject or government servant, could be called *ecnebi* (see Kunt, *Servants*, p. 35).

[53] KA, Murad/End, Nur 3409, 424b-425a.

prominent there are few whose genealogies do not go back to a convert to Islam; or whose ethnic origins, either on their mother or father's side, do not go back to a filthy infidel, despite the fact that they themselves have grown up as upright and outstanding Muslims.''[54] Âli saw, or at least portrayed, the entry of Muslims from territories other than those parts of Rumeli and Anatolia that had been part of the "classical" (i.e., 1453-1566) Ottoman state into the Ottoman system as a disruption and betrayal of what was most essential in it. The foreigners were neither slaves nor scholars, and hence they had no right to enter the system, much less to receive preferential treatment.[55] The logic of Âli's argument is, to be sure, somewhat strained and heavily informed by his personal sense of grievance. Nevertheless, the strain was to some extent inherent in the Ottoman system, and began to manifest itself as the system changed and intellectuals such as Âli sought to define immutable Ottoman ideals and an Ottoman identity.[56]

Factional Realignment at the Accession of Mehmed III

Âli and his fellow intellectuals were soon disabused of any notions that the new sultan would inaugurate a restoration of Ottoman justice and glory. Mehmed III showed good intentions at the outset of his reign; a few weeks after his accession he dismissed Sinan Paşa from the grand vezirate and replaced him with another Albanian, Ferhad Paşa. Mehmed also tried to curb abuses that his father had allowed to go unchecked, and in particular made efforts to rid the Harem of "dwarves, eunuchs, and mutes," whom he found to have acquired many protégés and much influence in administrative matters. Nevertheless, the major power centers among the old guard of Palace and government functionaries remained in place, and these jockeyed for postion in the new administration.[57] The two most important ulema of the time, Sa'düddin, who retained his position as royal tutor under Mehmed, and the chief jurisconsult Bustanzade, had hated each other since their stu-

[54] KA, I, 16.

[55] Additional evidence in support of the notion that Ottomans such as Âli viewed with distaste the entry into the highest government circles of freeborn Muslims from the eastern reaches of the Empire is found in MEVA'İD, pp. 37-42. In a discussion of the office of *musahib*, Âli says that the function of the royal companion was to act as a control on spies and vezirs, and that the *musahib* should not seek a regular government office. Furthermore, he should be chosen from the ulema, poets, or dervishes, and should not be a black eunuch, Arab, or "Iranian" (*Acem*). Klaus Röhrborn, basing himself largely on Âli, has also noted the ethnic element (i.e., influx of freeborn Turks) in the late sixteenth-century burgeoning of the *maliye* service in "Die Emanzipation der Finanzbürokratie im osmanischen Reich (Ende 16. Jahrhundert)," ZDMG 122 (1972): 133-37.

[56] These topics will be dealt with more extensively in chapters 6 and 7.

[57] KA, Mehmed/Grand Vezirate of Ferhad, Nur 3409, 430a-b. Sinan Paşa had returned to Istanbul from his winter campaign quarters. On 16 February 1595/6 Cümada II 1003 the seal of office was taken from him and given to Ferhad Paşa, and Sinan was once again exiled to his farm in Malkara.

dent days, when both had competed for the favor of their common teacher, Ebüssu'ud. Murad had despaired of making peace between the two, and they pursued their rivalry under Murad's son Mehmed with renewed vigor. Sa'düddin and Bustanzade made the *ilmiye* hierarchy a battleground in their struggle to gain influence and moral authority over the new sultan. The rivalry had wider implications, for each man sought to secure control of the *ilmiye* establishment for himself, and a monopoly of its highest positions for his own family; each demanded from Mehmed, and received, ever more important posts for sons and brothers who were in fact either too young or too ignorant to be eligible for such appointments. Sa'düddin eventually won the contest, but not before the prestige and morale of the learned establishment had been severely damaged. The ulema were shocked and revolted by the deformation of the *ilmiye* hierarchical structure that attended the conflict, for the appointments over which Sa'düddin and Bustanzade fought were properly the province of the chief military judges of Rumeli and Anatolia, not of the chief jurisconsult or royal tutor, who were in theory extrapolitical officials attached directly to the Palace.[58] Âli thus saw his beloved *ilmiye*, the last bastion of moral authority in a rapidly changing Ottoman world, go the way of other institutions, whose deformation and fall from ideal purity he had decried.

Âli's personal political situation was doubtless complicated by the ensuing factional struggles. Both Hoca Sa'düddin and Bustanzade had given him some measure of assistance, but he could hardly become too closely identified with either, and clearly did not wish to be. The two ulema later became involved in Palace rivalries over the grand vezirate that raged between the vezirs Sinan Paşa, Damad İbrahim Paşa, and Hadim Hasan Paşa. The ambitious Baki, who had always coveted the position of chief jurisconsult, joined the melée. In the course of these intrigues, which persisted until

[58] KA, Murad/End, Nur 3409, 422a-423a. Âli credits this rivalry with having devastating effects on the morale and prestige, as well as career expectations, of the *ilmiye* establishment. He links this development, if only by juxtaposition, with the moral and administrative chaos which the irresponsible, self-interested, and ignorant Sinan Paşa wrought in his last three terms as grand vezir (KA, Nur 3409, 423a-424a).

MD 73, doc. 740, is an order issued sometime soon after Mehmed's accession, which takes note of prevalent abuses of the *mülâzemet* system. It orders that unqualified applicants not be registered as *mülâzims*, and that the *mülâzim* quotas established by *kanun* be strictly enforced. SELANİKİ, *sub anno* 1004, 83b, states that this return to *kanun* norms for the *ilmiye* was actually carried out, with one change: the *hoca-ı sultani* was to be allowed twenty-five *mülâzims*, and the *şeyhülislam* thirty. Selâniki goes on to meticulously record the victory of Sa'düddin over Bustanzade in their contest. In his discussion of the first year of Mehmed's reign (*sub anno* 1003), Selâniki again parallels Âli, complaining that the major figures of state were so busy intriguing against each other that they paid no attention to affairs of state (70a). Selâniki also attacks Sinan Paşa and decries his pernicious influence (78b), and comments bitterly on the widespread practice of post-selling and on the incompetence and low quality of those who have bought their offices out from under more worthy candidates (80a-b).

his death in 1600, Baki first joined his old enemy Bustanzade, then turned on his protector Ferhad Paşa in order to gain Sinan Paşa's favor, and ended by becoming the rival and enemy of his old friend and patron Sa'düddin.[59] Such was the human political environment within which Âli was to live the last years of his life, as he began his career once again.

AMASYA AND KAYSERİ
(1595-96)

IT IS hardly surprising that Âli should have been unable to preserve his new position within these shifting factional currents. Powerful members of the inner core of Palace retainers opposed his posting as finance director of Egypt, and he had to be satisfied with a dual appointment as district governor of Amasya and finance director of Sivas (Rum).[60] Even this postion may have been difficult to retain; in one poem addressed to Sultan Mehmed, Âli complained that although he had been given a post, the intrigues of his detractors delayed implementation of the order for a month, which he spent in Üsküdar waiting to depart.[61] By early August 1595 Âli was in Amasya, and he remained in Anatolia for something over a year in a variety of capacities. The bulk of the regular forces of the province of Rum were engaged in the Hungarian wars, and therefore Âli had to add guardianship of areas outside of Amasya to his duties as *sancak beği* and director of finance. Provincial uprisings by Celâli rebels, acute food shortages, and an epidemic that particularly affected cattle, which were used both as draught animals and food, compounded Âli's difficulties. Âli interpreted these natural and political disasters as divine retribution for the moral decrepitude of the Empire and the erosion of its basic institutions: the peasants had lost their piety, impoverished *timar*-holders squeezed the peasantry unjustly, the Janissaries had entered trade, and tradesmen gouged unmercifully and refused to observe official price ceilings.[62]

Unpleasant as the post may have been, Âli was mindful of the potential

[59] For details of these intrigues, see Köprülü, "Baki," and Turan, "Sa'd-el-Din." Âli refers to Baki's dismissal from the *kadıaskerlik* of Rumeli soon after his retirement (dismissed July 1595) as a result of complaints lodged against him by members of the *ilmiye* (KA, Mehmed/Cülus, Nur 3409, 429a). According to Köprülü, this was the result of Bustanzade's plotting; having used Baki to help unseat Ferhad Paşa and bring about Sinan Paşa's return to office, the *şeyhülislam* wished to rid himself of a dangerous rival.

[60] KA, Mehmed/Cülus, Nur 3409 429a.

[61] DİVAN III, 61b. Although this *gazel* is not dated, Âli's reference to Üsküdar, and to being made *sahib-i tabl u alem, "sancak beği,"* suggests he had been given a *sancak* post in Anatolia, which could only refer to this appointment.

[62] KA, Mehmed/Fourth Vezirate of Sinan Paşa, Nur 3409, 437a-b. By September-October 1595/Muharrem 1004, Âli was in Rum as *sancak beği* of Amasya and *defterdar* of Sivas.

benefits of his dual status. Having established himself within the financial bureaucracy, with his appointment to a *sancak* post Âli made the jump into the military administration, as did other financial figures in the late sixteenth century.[63] The rank of *sancak beği* opened new career possibilities to Âli. He began to petition Sultan Mehmed to elevate him to the rank of governor-general, for which he was now eligible as a *sancak beği*. In an ode most likely submitted in late 1595, Âli suggested that Mehmed show him personal favor, as the monarch's father and grandfather had done, by making him a governor-general, even vezir. He suggested that in return for such favor he would dedicate the *Essence of History*, then still in progress, to the sultan. Finally, Âli stated that in light of recent promotions to governor-generalships of figures inferior to him in ability and probity, his current position was too low. Should Âli be made vezir, he would tell Mehmed secrets of just administration that no one else would dare to divulge—i.e., he would inform on malefactors. Claiming to have authored thirty works, Âli tried once again to convince a ruler of the wisdom of literary patronage.[64] Later that same year he pressed another well-worn theme on the sultan; he asked to be given a post at court worthy of him, decrying the fact that he was still a district governor while most of his contemporaries were governors-general.[65] Just as he had earlier attempted to convince Murad of his worth and seniority in the financial career line, he now sought similar recognition in military-administrative service, though he had actually spent very little time as a *sancak beği*. As much as Âli decried changes in the Ottoman system that led to abandonment of seniority principles and a blurring of distinctions between the military and bureaucratic career tracks, he also tried to profit from them.

In any event, Âli's dual appointment did not last long, for protracted warfare on the Empire's western front and constant unrest in Anatolia did much to further destabilize the situation of administrative appointees. Soon after Âli's arrival in central Anatolia in the late summer of 1595, the finance directorship of Rum was abolished, and supervision of financial matters was given to the governor-general of the province.[66] It seems clear that there was

[63] On this phenomenon, see Röhrborn, "Emanzipation," and chapter 8 below.

[64] DİVAN III, 20a-b. In this poem, as well as another on f. 55a, Âli boasts of the honor his dual appointment confers, indicating that he is mighty with both sword and pen.

[65] DİVAN III, 31b, a *gazel* composed on the occasion of Mehmed's departure on the Egri campaign in June 1596/Şevval 1004.

[66] That Âli was officially relieved of his financial duties soon after his arrival is made clear by a number of documents in MD 73. Doc. 650, which probably dates from late August 1595/mid-Zulhicce 1003, refers to a letter sent by "Mustafa, *sancak beği* of Amasya and former *defterdar* of Erzurum," informing the Porte of Celâli activities in Çorum. Doc. 1155, probably dated a few days later (doc. 1164 is dated 18 Zulhicce 1003) is addressed to "*Defterdar* of Rum and *sancak beği* of Amasya Âli." He was dismissed from the *defterdarlık* and the post itself was abolished, being replaced by *nezaret*. Financial supervision of Sivas was then given to the

a shortage of administrative personnel in central Anatolia because preparations were underway to launch a new offensive against Austria in the following spring.

In the course of the year 1596/1004-1005, Âli was transferred to the governorship of the *sancak* of Kayseri, dismissed after a month, and then reappointed to the same *sancak*. In a poem that Âli composed on the lot of a district governor, he suggests that these rapid changes of appointment occurred because his post was being bought and sold, on paper at least, in Istanbul. Âli adds that the frequent dismissal of high-level appointees is a sign of Ottoman degeneration, for this practice was not allowed in Iran or India.[67] The date of the first of these appointments is not absolutely clear, but Âli was definitely *sancak beği* of Kayseri by June of 1596, immediately before Mehmed III left Istanbul to lead the Egri campaign. At this time Âli was given responsibility for keeping order in the *sancak*s of Niğde, Aksaray, and Kırşehir in the *vilayet* of Karaman, and Bozok in the *vilayet* of Rum, all of which had been depleted of peace-keeping forces and were therefore vulnerable to Celâli threats.[68]

This new posting followed two other events that gladdened Âli's heart and restored his hopes of achieving glory as a master of the pen rather than the sword. While Âli was in central Anatolia, Koca Sinan Paşa had twice become grand vezir, for the fourth and fifth times. Suddenly he died, on

---

newly appointed *beğlerbeği* (doc. 1173).

MD 73 and 74 are rather difficult to use for purposes of establishing chronology. A great many entries in both are undated, and individual documents do not necessarily follow each other chronologically. Despite the initial and terminal dates given by Midhat Sertoğlu in *Muhteva Bakımından/Başvekâlet Arşivi* (Ankara, 1955), p. 18, MD 73 contains a number of documents dated December 1590/Safer 999. MD 74 appears to contain entries only up to December 1596/Rebi' II 1005, rather than Şevval as Sertoğlu has it.

[67] DİVAN III, 73a-74a. Âli complains that he was twice appointed *sancak beği* of Kayseri, once for twenty-eight days and then again for forty-two, and rails against the system of post-selling. Another poem, DİVAN III, 72b-73a, is dated 1004, "while emir of Kayseri." Âli also refers to this appointment in KA, Süleyman/Şu'ara, "Şekeri," Nur 3409, 189a, where he relates that he had contact with an emir of the Dulkadır family while in Kayseri.

[68] MD 74, doc. 140, is an order addressed to Âli as *sancak beği* of Kayseri, informing him of preparations for the impending Egri campaign. He is instructed to enforce the call to arms of all *bölük halkı* and to prevent them from marauding. The order also lists the *sancak*s of which he was appointed guardian. Doc. 170 is dated 12 July 1596/17 Zulka'de 1004, and is addressed to "Kayseriye *sancaği beği* Âli." It revokes his *muhafaza* authoritry, since it conflicts with that of the newly appointed *muhafiz* of the entire province of Karaman, Nuh Paşa. This was undoubtedly disappointing to Âli, who was informed at the end of doc. 140 that "if you perform your duties well, you will be granted recompense by promotion." In the same *defter*, docs. 136, 331 (probably 27 August 1596/3 Muharrem 1005), 371, 486, 586 (24 June 1586/27 Şevval) and 591 (24 June 1586/27 Şevval 1004) deal with Celâli disturbances and local problems which Âli had reported to the Porte. Âli is identified by name in doc. 486 ("Kayseriye *sancaği beği* Âli Mustafa"). The identity of subject matter between this and the other documents cited make it clear that these latter, too, are addressed to him, though in these he is called only "Kayseriye *sancaği beği*." The dating of these documents indicates that Âli was appointed to Kayseri by late June, and did not leave before the end of August 1596.

April 3, 1596/4 Şa'ban 1004, and his office was bestowed on Damad İbrahim Paşa, whom Âli had previously cultivated.[69] Âli rejoiced on both counts. He was unable to contain his glee at the death of the nemesis who had stalked him throughout his career, and who had notoriously little brief for literary folk. Âli sent an ode to Sultan Mehmed congratulating him on the departure of so evil a servant. He further recommended that Sinan's son, Mehmed Paşa, be sent to join his father, and that the bribes and ill-gotten treasures these two had collected be confiscated for the treasury.[70] Both Âli and Selâniki report that a majority of Ottoman poets, all of whom had suffered at Sinan Paşa's hands, rejoiced at his death, and many composed joyous chronograms on the occasion.[71] In the final pages of the *Essence of History*, Âli rehearsed the misdeeds of the man he considered the single most pernicious influence in the Empire. Sinan Paşa had placed his personal political goals over matters of state to the extent of plotting and engineering the dismissal and, in the case of Ferhad Paşa, execution of other men of state. He had been cowardly, ignorant, corrupt, and hated learning. He had destroyed the state and betrayed religion by embroiling the Ottomans in a long series of Hungarian wars; this he had done to aggrandize his own position as sole commander, but he had ended by draining the Ottoman state of men and bankrupting its treasury. The precedent for violent factional conflict within the ruling elite that Sinan Paşa had established, Âli noted, contributed to the increasing incidence of internal political disaster within the preceding decade. Sinan Paşa was also an Albanian and, according to Âli, personified the worst character traits of that undesirable race: rebelliousness, cowardice, stubbornness, ignorance, violence, and physical ugliness. Âli furthermore claimed that Sinan Paşa betrayed the ideals of the Ottoman elite by fostering and utilizing Albanian group solidarity (as opposed to dynastic loyalty) among the Palace units in order to consolidate his own position and threaten his non-Albanian rivals.[72] The ever-increasing

[69] KA Mehmed/Grand Vezirate of Damad İbrahim Paşa, Halet Efendi 598, 438b. Âli gives the date of death as Wednesday, 5 Şa'ban 1004 (4 April 1596). April 4 was actually a Thursday rather than Wednesday, so the date of death may actually have been 3 April. However, SELANİKİ (*sub anno* 1004, 111a) agrees with Âli's date down to the name of the day. The disparity may be accounted for by the difference in beginning points of days between the Muslim and Christian systems; the former begins a new day at sundown. Atsız (AB, p. 91) as usual preserves the *hicri* date given by Âli, but following Danişmend (*Kronoloji*, III, 161) gives an incorrectly adjusted C.E. equivalent.

[70] DİVAN III, 21a-22a. Âli also expresses the pious hope that those who helped bring him to power will soon receive their desserts.

[71] KA, Mehmed/Fifth Vezirate of Sinan Paşa, Halet 538, 437b-438b; SELANİKİ, *sub anno* 1004, 110b-112a. Selâniki notes that Sinan Paşa's treasures and funds were indeed confiscated for the state by Damad İbrahim Paşa.

[72] KA, Murad 37, and Murad/Third Vezirate of Sinan Paşa, Nur 3409, 395-397a, 399b-400b; Mehmed/Grand Vezirate of Ferhad Paşa, Fourth and Fifth Vezirates of Sinan Paşa, Nur 3409, 432a-436b; Halet Efendi 598, 434a-437b. SELANİKİ (*sub anno* 1004, 110b-112a) agrees with Âli's assessment of Sinan's character, though he does not put the case quite as

power of the irresponsible, self-centered, and factious Koca Sinan Paşa, acquired through successive terms of office as grand vezir under Murad and Mehmed, had been intimately bound up with Âli's apocalyptic vision of a state rapidly succumbing to chaos.

Âli hastened to congratulate Damad İbrahim Paşa in a letter in which he expressed his faith that the new grand vezir would restore the fortunes of the Ottoman house by reestablishing justice and strict observance of *kanun*. He likened the state to a ship manned by the members of the Imperial Council. After referring to the endorsement of his learning and literary ability made ten years earlier by leading ulema, he asked to be made a member of the crew, thus suggesting indirectly that he be made chancellor.[73] Others, too,

---

strongly. Âli adds that even in death Sinan Paşa showed that he was no pious Muslim; the workers digging the foundation for Sinan's tomb struck a Christian graveyard, and Sinan Paşa was buried next to a Greek priest.

In general, Âli frequently expresses a profound dislike for Albanians. For example, in the MEVA'İD (pp. 65-68), in the course of a discussion of the insults suffered by the learned at the hands of the ignorant, Âli identifies Lutfi Paşa, who at least had pretensions to learning, and Sinan Paşa as particular offenders, and remarks pointedly on their common Albanian origin. For other examples of this ethnic bias see KA, Süleyman/Sadrazamlar, "Ayas Paşa," "Lutfi Paşa," Faith 4225, 318b. On the Ottoman view of Albanians, see Bedriye Atsız, "Das Albanerbild der Türken nach osmanischen Chroniken des 15.-16. Jahrhunderts," *Münchner Zeitschrift für Balkankunde* I (1978): 15-25.

In discussing Sinan Paşa, Âli constantly refers to his ethnic identity, saying, for example, that only Albanians mourned his death. He also cites several instances of an Albanian group solidarity operative within the Ottoman military establishment and exploited by Sinan Paşa (KA, Murad/Third Vezirate of Sinan Paşa, Nur 3409, 399b; Mehmed/Fourth Vezirate of Sinan Paşa, Halet Efendi 598, 430b). Âli also says that during his third term in office Sinan brought about the dismissal of the *yeniçeri ağası* Mehmed Ağa because the latter was a Bosnian, and then replaced him with a fellow Albanian, Yemişçi Hasan Ağa (KA, Nur 3409, 408b). While these statements may be somewhat exaggerated, an extension of Âli's hatred for Sinan Paşa, they provide some evidence to support the general thesis propounded by Metin Kunt in "Ethnic-Regional (*Cins*) Solidarity in the Seventeenth-Century Ottoman Establishment," IJMES 5 (1974): 233-39. Kunt suggests that ethnic solidarity amongst *devşirme* recruits who reached positions of power within the Ottoman establishment led, in the seventeenth century, to a rivalry between "western" Albanians and Bosnians on the one hand, and "eastern" Georgians and Circassians on the other, from which the former emerged as the dominant faction. The evidence that Âli provides, and his general tendency to praise Bosnians (see, for example, his praise of Damad İbrahim Paşa, KA, Halet Efendi 598, 439b-440a), while execrating Albanians, indicates that in the sixteenth century at least the two major "western" factions were pitted against each other, and that Sinan Paşa utilized Albanian solidarity to dismantle the Bosnian ascendancy established by Sokollu Mehmed Paşa and his family. Such ethnic considerations, of course, should not be viewed as constituting more than one of many factors (kinship, education and training, *intisab*, etc.) determining relationships within the Ottoman power elite.

[73] Âli gives the text of this letter in KA, Mehmed/ Grand vezirate of Damad İbrahim Paşa, Halet Efendi 598, 438b-439b.Âli says that the ship of state is piloted by five officers: the sultan, the grand vezir, the treasurer, the secretary-in-chief, and the head of the Janissary Corps. He then asks to be taken on as the sixth, without specifying the office but probably meaning the chancellorship.

Âli may well have considered dedicating the *Essence* to his friend İbrahim Paşa at about this point, or slightly later. This letter introduces the very last section of the Ottoman portion of the *Essence*, which consists of some ten folios. This final portion has much the air of a hastily composed appendix to the work. In style it differs drastically from the preceding portion, be-hoped that a restoration of Ottoman traditions, along with elimination of old evils, would revive the state and restore royal authority. Soon after İbrahim Paşa became grand vezir, Hoca Sa'düdin prevailed upon Sultan Mehmed personally to lead his troops into the field on the Egri (Erlau) campaign, something no Ottoman sultan had done since the death of Süleyman at Sigetvar.[74] In this new atmosphere Âli's youthful dreams of gaining the chancellorship as a leading exponent of the Ottoman high-cultural tradition (and as a protégé of the new grand vezir) were reborn.

In the early days of preparation for the Egri campaign, Âli had been appointed *sancak beği* of Kayseri with additional duties of guardianship. Âli proceeded to Bozok, probably to deal with Celâli disturbances, at the same time that the sultan and İbrahim Paşa left Istanbul. There he began a new literary work, the *Mahâsin ül-âdâb, Beauties of Polite Observance*. The *Beauties* was an adapted translation of a work attributed to Jâḥiẓ known as *Kitâb al-tâj, The Book of the Crown*, which is one of the earliest exemplars of Islamic "mirrors for princes" literature. Âli reorganized the work, updating it to describe Ottoman usages and giving it a topical arrangement. Once again he saw himself as a cultured advisor to kings and statesmen; he dedicated the *Beauties* to Sultan Mehmed and the new grand vezir İbrahim Paşa. Âli also asked Sultan Mehmed to show him personal favor and promote him to the rank of governor-general.[75]

Âli's second Anatolian sojourn was marked by a resurgence, if that is the proper term, of his fascination with Anatolian Sufism. He was particularly attached to those saints of Melâmi-Bayrami stripe whose names were closely associated with early Anatolian history. It was probably on his way to Amasya, in 1595, that Âli stopped at Göynük to make a pilgrimage to the

---

coming extremely ornate and self-consciously literary. In content it deals primarily with the virtues of Damad İbrahim Paşa and the Egri campaign, which ended with the conquest of Egri on 12 October 1596/19 Safer 1005 (SELANİKİ, *sub anno* 1005, 130a). The concluding two folios are in praise of Cağaloğlu Yusuf Sinan Paşa, who became grand vezir on the field of battle shortly after the victory. Âli addressed Cağaloğlu in these pages, asking that his learning and knowledge of *kanun* be honored by appointment to a position in the Imperial Council. It appears that Âli began this section hoping to curry favor with İbrahim Paşa by dedicating the *Essence* to him, and then hastily had to adjust his plans when Cağaloğlu became grand vezir. Since Cağaloğlu was dismissed after serving only forty days, this final portion of the KA must have been written in late October or early November 1596 (cf. Gökbilgin, "Mehmed III"). Âli continued, of course, to fill in sections of the work until his death.

[74] Gökbilgin, "Mehmed III."

[75] *Mahâsin ül-âdâb*, MS Nuruosmaniye 3668. The dedication occurs on ff. 1b-2b, and criticism of Jâḥiẓ's haphazard arrangement of material on ff. 2b-3a. Âli had a passion for order and topical presentation of themes. The circumstances and date of composition are found on ff. 3a-4b. The form of the title of the work is established on f. 5b, and ff. 5b-6b comprise discussions of the ideal qualities of a sultan, and of the Ottoman dual treasury system. These are typical of the sorts of emendations Âli made in his "translation"; Âli left his Ottoman mark even when appearing to invoke a classical tradition of statecraft. On the original *Kitâb al-tâj* attributed to Jâḥiẓ, see the French translation of Charles Pellat, *Le Livre de la Couronne* (Paris, 1954).

tomb of Akşemsüddin, arriving on 16 August 1595/10 Zulhicce 1003. There he promised to spend the Feast of Sacrifice at the tomb of Hacı Bayram, the founder of the order, in Ankara. This Âli did, and while there he declared his faith in Hacı Bayram and in his disciple Yazıcızade Mehmed, who had done so much to propagate Bayrami teachings in Âli's native Gelibolu. Âli described Hacı Bayram as "the spiritual guide of all Rum."[76] Once he arrived in Amasya, the old seat of Ottoman princes and a major provincial center of culture, Âli was inspired by nostalgia for pre-Ottoman glories and a yearning to throw himself into Sufism.[77] On the way to Kayseri, Âli made a visit to the tomb of Hacı Bektaş, one of the most famous and popular of Anatolian saints. Âli felt a special bond with the patron of the Janissary Corps, to which he had twice been appointed secretary, and he asked the saint for intercession so that he might secure a position close to the sultan.[78] Âli also requested protection on his travels from one Hasan Baba, a saint of the Amasya area, and in the spring visited the shrine of Şeyh Parmak.[79] In the late spring of 1596, at Kayseri, Âli addressed the folk-saints Hızır and İlyas, crediting them (or him, since the two are often confused) with affording him protection and with securing his appointment as *sancak beği*.[80] Finally, Âli addressed Hızır and a certain Şeyh Abdürrahman as "the two poles of the world, the two protectors of Rum, who make the candle of my aspirations burn brightly."[81]

Âli's immersion in popular Anatolian Sufism bears notice on both intellectual and psychological grounds. While it reflects trends in Âli's development noted previously, it also highlights his susceptibility to environment, as witnessed by Amasya's evocation of past glories. Thrust into a world in which folk traditions were alive, Âli embraced them and became a participant. As an historian Âli was increasingly conscious of being the

[76] DİVAN III, 52b, 58a. On Akşemsüddin, Yazıcızade, and Hacı Bayram, see H. J. Kissling, "Zur Geschichte des Derwischordens der Bajramijje," *Südostforschungen* 15 (1956): 251-58.

[77] DİVAN III, 24b-25a.

[78] DİVAN III, 83b; in this poem Âli states his aspiration to become a member of the Council or a companion. Âli also lists Hacı Bektaş among the great spiritual leaders of the world in a *kaside* found on 2b-4b.

[79] DİVAN III, 25b-26a (to Hasan Baba); 25a-25b (said at the tomb of Şeyh Parmak). I have been unable to further identify these two *abdal*s.

[80] DİVAN III, 92b. In Islamic lore Hızır is the spiritual master and succorer of those who have no living master, and of those who are in need. In popular Anatolian (as well as general Islamic) belief, he is often identified with the Old Testament İlyas; both are held to have gained immortality by drinking the Water of Life (*Âb-ı hayat*). The day the two met to do this is celebrated in Anatolia as Hızır-İlyas Day (Hıdrellez), equivalent to May 6. Âli most probably wrote these lines to Hızır-İlyas at that season in 1596, declaring himself to be the protégé of the saint-prophet. By this time Âli would have been in or near Kayseri. On Hızır and Hızır-İlyas, see A. J. Wensinck, "Hızır," and Pertev Naili Boratav, "Türklerde Hızır," İA.

[81] DİVAN III, 93a.

product of a specific cultural, historical, and geographical complex. He was a Rumi as well as an Ottoman. Once in the Anatolian heartland, Âli, on the level of popular piety or in his Sufi persona, could identify with the popular culture specific to his "homeland," as well as with the cosmopolitan high culture within which he had been trained in Istanbul.

To be sure, there is an element of nostalgic romanticism in all of this. Âli the Anatolian saint-worshipper no longer engages in the intense dissection of conscience and soul that had preoccupied the Sufi Âli during the millennial years. The doubts are gone, and self-examination has been replaced by a culturally inspired belief in the power of the *rical ül-gayb*—unseen figures, long-dead holy men who can yet intervene in the affairs of this world to set it right. With hope that it might yet come again, or that it had not disappeared, Âli in Anatolia took another step into an idealized past which he adopted as his own world, and which he could still find alive in the Rumi heartland.

In the world of 1596, however, Âli was doomed to disappointment. İbrahim Paşa did nothing for him, and in the late summer or autumn of that year Âli, for the second time, was dismissed from his post as *sancak beği* of Kayseri.

ISTANBUL
(1596-97)

Âli was dismissed because complaints had been lodged about his administration. Âli, who remained unemployed for at least two years thereafter, denied these unspecified charges and called them the work of slanderous enemies.[82] He returned to Istanbul and continued his work on the *Essence* while waiting for the sultan and the major figures of state to return from the

[82] Âli nowhere states precisely how or when he was dismissed from the *sancak* of Kayseri. If his statement that he served in this post twice, for twenty-eight and then forty-two days, may be taken as accurate, it must be reconciled with other evidence. Archival material presented above (note 68) suggests that Âli held the post between mid-June and late August 1596. Finally, the shorter term in office may have followed this one.

The circumstances of Âli's dismissal are hinted at in the following poems in DİVAN III: 51a-b, to the sultan, pleading that he (Âli) is in fact a righteous man, and asking that the sultan pay no heed to the whisperings of his detractors; 49b-50a, to the sultan, complaining of the injustice of his dismissal when there are so few righteous administrators (*gayr-i zâlim*); 7b-10b, an autumn (1597) *kaside* to the newly appointed grand vezir, Hadim Hasan Paşa, proclaiming that his government (*hükûmet*) had been just, and that those who say otherwise are slanderous; 86a-b, to Gazanfer Ağa, asking him to intercede with the sultan for him because his position has been endangered by those who claim that he is *hod-füruş*, boastful beyond his abilities, which charge he denies. With the exception of the third poem listed above, none of these pieces is precisely dated. They are cited here because, on the grounds of internal evidence, they appear likely to apply to this situation.

Austrian campaign.[83] When the news reached the capital that Damad İbrahim Paşa had been replaced as grand vezir by Cağaloğlu Sinan Paşa, Âli hastily added a few appropriately laudatory pages to the final portion of the *Essence* and sent a poem of congratulation to Cağaloğlu. In his history Âli asked Cağaloğlu to restore the golden days of the Ottoman state and to give him a post in the Imperial Council, since he was an expert on *kanun*, as the *Essence* showed. In his poem Âli made a more modest request for a *sancak* or provincial governorship. Cağaloğlu, he said, was a man who knew the worth of men of learning. By contrast, the two previous grand vezirs whom he had petitioned had done nothing for him; Sinan Paşa had hated him as a Lala Mustafa Paşa adherent, and İbrahim Paşa, whom Âli had considered a friend, had been unresponsive. By his own account Âli was the Firdawsî and Jâmî of the Ottoman realms, and asked to be Mîr Alî Shîr to Cağaloğlu's Bâyqarâ.[84]

Âli was undoubtedly encouraged to cultivate the new grand vezir by the knowledge that Cağaloğlu was favored by two old patrons, Hoca Sa'düddin and Gazanfer Ağa; both men had accompanied the sultan on the Egri campaign and had supported Cağaloğlu's specious claim to full credit for the victory at Haçova (Mezőkeresztes) following that at Egri. Due to his incompetence, Cağaloğlu was dismissed in disgrace after forty days in office, and his partisans, too, suffered the sultan's disfavor.[85] Though his hopes were dashed, the now hardened Âli had sufficient conscience, and political sense,

[83] It is unclear just when Âli returned to the capital; he was certainly there during 1596-97/1005, when he composed a chronogram on the completion of a fountain built by Gazanfer Ağa near Topkapı Sarayı (DİVAN III, 16b), and presented an ode to Sultan Mehmed on the Feast of Sacrifice at the end of the *hicri* year (DİVAN III, 16b). It is probable that he actually arrived in the capital around early Rebi' I 1005/late October 1596, since he had word of Cağaloğlu Sinan Paşa's promotion to the grand vezirate in time to send him a letter of congratulation (see below). Cağaloğlu's promotion was made in the field, and his appointment lasted only forty days; Âli must have been close enough to get the news quickly.

[84] KA, Halet Efendi 598, 448b-449a; DİVAN III, 85a-b.

[85] M. Tayyib Gökbilgin, "Ciğala-zâde," "Mehmed III," İA; İsmet Parmaksızoğlu, İbrahim Paşa, Damad," İA. The dates given for Cağaloğlu's appointment to the office vary from 26-27 October 1596/5 Rebi' I 1005 to 27-28 October/6 Rebi' I. The reason for this variation is that, immediately following the battle at Haçova, Cağaloğlu was the first to enter the sultan's pavilion. He unjustly claimed full credit for the victory and, with the help of his allies, secured the grand vezirate as a reward. However, İbrahim Paşa continued to act as grand vezir until the seal of office was taken from him sometime later. Sultan Mehmed dismissed and exiled Cağaloğlu forty days later on orders from his mother, the *valide sultan*.

Na'ima (*Tarih*, I, 169) states that although Gazanfer Ağa was not on bad terms with İbrahim Paşa, he was persuaded to support Cağaloğlu because, being of Italian origin, he was a fellow Frank (*Firenk*). Among late sixteenth-century sources I have encountered no references to such ethnic solidarity (particularly among slaves of Western European origin) outside of Âli's works. It would be interesting to know whether this was indeed a social dynamic of the time, or whether Na'ima was simply reading seventeenth-century concerns (cf. Kunt, "*Cins*") back into the late sixteenth century.

to admonish in verse both the exiled Cağaloğlu and Damad İbrahim Paşa, who was restored to office:

> The grand vezirate, in one year, has seen three chief ministers;
> This state of affairs has cowed the bullying spirits of every vezir.[86]

In early winter the court returned to Istanbul. Âli retired under the wing of Gazanfer Ağa, to whose virtues as a patron he devoted a section of the *Essence*:

> By the date of this writing, the year 1005 [1596-97], I, who truthfully praise [Gazanfer Ağa], had composed thirty collections of writing, more than twenty treatises, and four eloquent *divans* in Persian and Turkish. All people of quality know that I have always gained endless opportunities and renewal of life through that most generous one's kindness, generosity, and boundless energy in seeking for me high appointments. He always gave full value to my learning and ability, and took pride in me as a product of his patronage. I received purse after purse from that noble person, and carried off to storage the cloaks and valuable gifts he bestowed on me.[87]

Âli appears to have been dependent upon his patron to some extent for income as well as political favor, as this passage makes quite clear. A number of short poems found in Âli's third *divan* illuminate the material side of a patronage relationship. One of these, in which Âli asked Gazanfer Ağa to supply him with firewood for the winter, suggests poverty.[88] Others, which are not specifically addressed but may very well have been directed to Gazanfer, indicate that Âli supported a lively life style and a well-appointed establishment. From "great ones" he variously requested a bookcase and cabinet, an Egyptian carpet, a stove, a store of wine, an Abyssinian slave boy, and an Egyptian mattress.[89] Indeed, in his last years Âli seems to have delighted in wine and revelry, which he had sworn off during his "repentance period" around the turn of the millennium. There are also suggestions in these and a few other poetic pieces from this time that Âli may have disregarded his own expressed disapproval of pederasty.[90]

When İbrahim Paşa was briefly deposed from the grand vezirate in favor of Cağaloğlu Sinan Paşa, Âli quickly rededicated the *Beauties of Polite Observance* to Gazanfer Ağa, obliterating all mention of the man Âli had de-

[86] DİVAN III, 85a, incorrectly described as referring to the dismissal of İbrahim Paşa.

[87] KA, Murad/Introduction, Nur 3409, 291a; text published by İNAL, pp. 126-27.

[88] DİVAN III, 87b.

[89] DİVAN III, 84a-b, 88b-89a.

[90] See, for example, DİVAN III, 52a-b, dated the end of Ramazan 1005, expressing joy that he can then return to wine, forbidden during the month of fast; 36b-37a, to beautiful tavern boys; 37a-b, 88a, to beloved beauties (*hûbân*); 50b, to a young lover (*mahbub*).

scribed as one who would put right the affairs of the Empire, and whom Gazanfer Ağa had worked to dislodge.[91] Âli also began to bombard the Palace overseer with pleas for help, full patronage, and intercession with the sultan, and expatiated on Gazanfer's reputation as a patron and upholder of both scholarly and administrative standards. Âli declared Baki and himself to be the ablest poets and men of culture of the age. That these two should be brought low by slander and condemned to unemployment and impotence—that all posts should go to the base and ignorant—was a scandal that Âli urged Gazanfer Ağa to rectify.[92] Âli certainly wished to help his friend Baki, with whom he had shared both poetry and professional disappointment. He also wished to be considered Baki's peer in literary and political standing. Gazanfer Ağa was probably unable to provide very much intercessory assistance at this point; he was still suffering the effects of his implication in the disastrous appointment of Cağaloğlu Sinan Paşa to the grand vezirate. Âli's next appeal to him struck a decidedly plaintive note. He reminded Gazanfer Ağa of all the poetry he had dedicated to him, and asked whether the *kapı ağası* could not plead his case to the sultan, all in a poem rhyming in, "Have you forgotten?"[93]

Âli also sent pleas to the grand vezir, İbrahim Paşa, protesting his loyalty and stressing his qualifications for high position.[94] Finally, in exasperation, he began to make poetic overtures to the sultan himself. These began, probably around the summer of 1597, as gentle reminders of his past service and admonitions to ignore the slanders of Âli's enemies. The times were indeed strange when one of the few honest men in the realm should be left jobless, particularly when his abilities, literary and administrative, should guarantee him either a Council post or a provincial governorship.[95]

Increasingly frustrated and discontented with his lot, Âli soon began to make more specific demands. In doing so he utilized all the tactics he had employed so often before. He cited his literary corpus of some forty to fifty works, and submitted new ones: a translation of *kırk hadis*, "forty Prophetic

[91] MS Nur 4224 of the *Mahâsin* contains a new dedication to Gazanfer Ağa.

[92] DİVAN III, 17a-b, is an ode addressed to Gazanfer Ağa, pleading for patronage. The poem is dated winter, probably that of 1596-97, when Gazanfer returned to Istanbul with the sultan. The poem in which Âli pleads his own and Baki's case and decries the evil of the times occurs on ff. 86a-b. Âli also defends himself against calumnies that he is *hod-füruş*. Another piece in praise of Gazanfer as a patron is found on f. 87b; Âli claims the eunuch as his special protector.

[93] DİVAN III, 70a-b.

[94] DİVAN III, 41a; a *gazel* to a grand vezir, stating that an unworthy person has just become a governor-general, while Âli goes jobless; see also ff. 65b, 66a. None of these poems names the addressee, but internal evidence makes it likely that they were written to İbrahim Paşa or to his successor, Hadim Hasan Paşa, during the years 1597-98/1005-1006.

[95] DİVAN III, 16b, dated 25 July 1597/10 Zulhicce, in which Âli claims to be the greatest poet in the three languages; poems on 48a, 49b-50a, 51a-b are all addressed to "the sultan."

traditions,'' and an ode on divine unity, the latter being presented to the sultan on Âli's behalf by Gazanfer Ağa. Âli stated that while others made their way professionally through connections with the powerful, he was loyal only to the sultan, and therefore dependent upon him. Although he had been frequently dismissed from his posts, Âli was comparable in qualifications to Tacizade Ca'fer Çelebi, the prominent chancellor of the early sixteenth century. Finally, Âli implied that he had certain rights of seniority; he had served four sultans, and had reached the rank of both *sancak beği* and finance director. On this basis he should be given either a governorship or the office of chancellor. The sultan, he implied, had an obligation to staff the central government with his own retainers, and not leave all matters of appointment to self-interested vezirs.[96]

Âli made his requests, and criticisms, still more specific. He asked to be made governor-general of Aleppo, with the stipulation that the position not be taken away from him in a few days. This condition reflected Âli's own experience as a *sancak beği*, as well as the more general situation generated by political instability at the highest levels of the central government, and by the contract appointment system. Also, insecurity of tenure encouraged governors to collect excessive taxes and squeeze the population to the limit, in order to profit from what might well be a short period in office followed by years of unemployment. Âli generalized his observations into a blanket evaluation of the Ottoman Empire of his time; nowhere else, neither in India nor in Iran, was there such corruption and disorder, which condemned the worthy to poverty and elevated the base. Âli cited his own case as an example; while his peers were governors-general, he was still a mere *sancak beği*.[97]

Âli advanced an appointment to the chancellorship as an alternative to a provincial government, asking the sultan not to deem him less than ''Hamze and Ali,'' two recent appointees to that position.[98] Âli had long since made an enemy of Hamze Paşa, whom he viewed as an ignorant upstart. ''Ali'' was Lam Ali Çelebi, a former finance director of Anatolia who had replaced Hamze as chancellor in the course of the Egri campaign. Lam Ali Çelebi was removed after only three months in office for his participation in the plot that had brought Cağaloğlu Sinan Paşa to the grand vezirate; he had written the official victory announcement for the battle of Haçova, falsely assigning all credit for the victory to Cağaloğlu. Âli had written satirical verse on Lam Ali as well as on Hamze, calling him ignorant and corrupt.[99]

[96] DİVAN III, 74b-75a, 77a, all dated January-February 1598/Cümada II 1006.

[97] DİVAN III, 73a-74a, 74a-b, on the state of being a *sancak beği*; 75b-76a, a general condemnation of the professional conditions in Rum.

[98] DİVAN III, 82a.

[99] DİVAN III, 78a. On Lam Ali Çelebi, see Na'ima, *Tarih*, I, 173.

These two were undoubtedly among the enemies Âli had at court who wished to block any appointments he might be given, particularly since he wished to displace them and, to this end, used satire to publicize their incompetence and his own superior qualifications.

EXCURSUS: CAREERISM AND HISTORICISM

ÂLI also suggested that he could accept an appointment as secretary-in-chief, and asked that the sultan give him an examination at the same time that he requested the chancellorship, so that his qualifications might be evaluated.[100] This proposal is a reflex of an *idée fixe* that preoccupied Âli during his last years, particularly as he worked to complete the Ottoman portion of the *Essence* and developed a comprehensive vision of Ottoman history.[101] During this period, beginning in about 1596, Âli frequently expressed his conviction that, ideally, Ottoman government was based upon meritocratic principles, which were implicit in the slave-household system, the notion of seniority, *kanun*, and implementation of examination procedures. Âli had first broached this notion in practical fashion in the *Counsel*, where he suggested that periodic examinations of the ulema and scrutiny of their scholarly work be instituted as a means of upholding standards and determining qualification for promotion.[102] At the end of his life, when Âli incorporated much of the spirit of the *Counsel* into the broader context of his historical and social writings, he presented meritocracy and seniority as intrinsic to classical Ottoman institutions. In the *Essence*, for example, he stated that Sultan Süleyman applied these principles even to the grand vezirate, establishing it as an office given to the most senior vezir on the theory that the office represented a craft that could be learned in thirty years by any slave able enough to make his way through the ranks of service by way of merit promotion.[103] In his last work, Âli declared that the institutes of the Conqueror required that *devşirme* recruits be examined individually for intrinsic qualities.[104] In a very real sense, the historiographical labors that dominated Âli's final years must be seen as an attempt to give coherence and definition to the Ottoman experience and Ottoman ideals, which were a product of history and encapsulated in ideal form in *kanun*.

[100] DİVAN III, 36b, 82a.

[101] That Âli was still at work on the *Essence* at this time is shown by two references. KA, Murad/Introduction, Nur 3409, 289a, refers to a plague of 1597-98/1006, which carried off two-thirds of the royal princesses (daughters of Murad) lodged in the Old Palace. The entry on Ayas Paşa (Süleyman/Sadrazamlar, Fatih 4225, 318b) is dated 1598-99/1007.

[102] COUNSEL, I, 77 (trans.), 177 (text).

[103] KA, Süleyman/Introduction, Nur 3409, 2b-4a (also quoted by Röhrborn, "Emanzipation," p. 132).

[104] MEVA'ID, pp. 20-21.

Âli's frequent references to Fatih Sultan Mehmed and Sultan Süleyman are indicative of his major preoccupation during his last years. He viewed these two monarchs as the real architects of the Ottoman state, not only because they were great conquerors, but also because they promulgated, or their names were associated with, the *kanun* codes that regularized and regulated Ottoman administrative, financial, and penal practice. The importance that Âli, as both a bureaucrat and an historian, attached to *kanun*, is indicated by the fact that he was the first Ottoman chronicler to utilize and quote extensively the *kanunname* of the Conqueror, which theoretically regulated all matters of function, rank, and promotion for all of Ottoman officialdom.[105] Âli's obsession with becoming chancellor was a function of his conviction, which became stronger and more coherent as he increasingly devoted himself to history, that *kanun* as both custom and legislation was central to Ottoman state and society. We have seen how Âli's career expectations and disappointments molded his view of recent Ottoman history. The reverse is also true—that Âli's dedication to history helped to establish and formulate his career goals and self-image.

Âli's request to be made governor-general is perfectly consonant with his career situation; this was the next step for a district governor. It is curious, however, that the careerist Âli, at this late stage in his life, should not have also played upon his financial background as well by asking for a finance directorship of the Porte. Rather, he wished for the chancellorship or, as a steppingstone to that office, the office of secretary-in-chief, neither of which was on a par with either a provincial governorship or finance directorship of the Porte.[106] Even so, in terms of Âli's historical vision and his own background, the chancellorship possessed tremendous moral significance. If *kanun* was central to the Ottoman Empire as a symbol of secular justice and order analogous to the *şeri'at* religious law, then the chancellor, the "*müfti* of *kanun*," represented half of the moral conscience of the state, the other half being the chief jurisconsult. The symbolic importance Âli attached to *kanun* and its watchdog, the chancellor, cannot be exaggerated. It is striking that, as often as the analogy between the chief jurisconsult and the chancellor has been repeated by later commentators, Âli is the sole sixteenth-century source for this analysis of the chancellor's functions.[107] Historically, too, the chancellorship showed a development that clearly appealed to Âli, who believed that education and culture were as integral to

[105] Ârif, *Kanunname*, pp. 7-8. Âli's discussion of the *Kanunname* of the Conqueror occurs in KA, Fatih/Conquest of Constantinople, Fatih 4225, 96b-106b.

[106] Fleischer, "Âli," pp. 370-76, 420.

[107] For examples in modern scholarship, see M. Tayyıb Gökbilgin, "Nişancı," İA; Matuz, *Kanzleiswesen*, p. 23; Uzunçarşılı, *Merkez*, pp. 215, 219, also citing the late seventeenth- to early eighteenth-century *Kanunname* of Abdurrahman Paşa, which confirms the view of the *nişancı* as the premier interpreter of *kanun*.

the life of a polity as political success, and that the learned should rightfully have prominent positions at court. In the middle of the sixteenth century the Ottoman bureaucracy, which until then had been dominated by *medrese* graduates, began to split into a chancery branch, headed by the chancellor, and financial section, presided over by the treasurer. By the end of the sixteenth century, the financial service had expanded tremendously and had become highly professionalized. Those who rose to its highest ranks were no longer former ulema or university graduates, but professional bureaucrats who had learned their skills on the job. The chancellorship, by contrast, had preserved its early *ilmiye* connections, and the chancery service retained an aura of learning; in Âli's view, *defterdar*s were professional financial clerks, while *nişancı*s, by and large, tended to be *medrese* graduates like Âli himself, who retained the prestige and intellectual breadth that such an education bestowed. The chancery, therefore, even in the late sixteenth century, embodied the world of Âli's youth, when the learned and cultivated had received both respect and rewards, and when bureaucratic service had offered an exciting and prestigious political career to ambitious young men who had received the finest education available in the Ottoman Empire. Âli desired the chancellorship not only as a reward for his oft-proclaimed personal virtues and services, but also as a vindication of the cultural ideals to which he had committed himself as a young man and now explicated as an historian.

ISTANBUL: THE LAST TWO YEARS (1597-99)

APART from Sultan Mehmed and Gazanfer Ağa, Âli approached only one other person for help after his return from Kayseri. When Hadim Hasan Paşa succeeded to the grand vezirate in early November 1597, Âli sent him an ode in which he praised the new grand vezir's repute as a patron of poets, and asked to be made his protégé. Âli was apparently still struggling against unpopularity at court, for he warned Hasan Paşa that the rumors current about his mismanagement of his last *sancak* posts were completely untrue.[108] The times were not propitious, nor was Âli's choice of a potential patron. Hadim Hasan Paşa was dismissed after five months in office, during which the inner circle of the court was wracked with intrigue and scandal. The new grand vezir brought favor-selling to a new level of blatancy, and himself fueled the rumor that he had bought his own position from the Queen Mother. He attempted to secure the execution of Gazanfer Ağa and,

108 DİVAN III, 7b-10b, dated Autumn. Hadim Hasan Paşa served as grand vezir from 4 November 1597/23 Rebi' I 1006 to 9 April 1598/2 Ramazan 1006 (Na'ima, *Tarih*, I, 185-87).

after the death of the *şeyhülislam* Bustanzade, sought to curb the influence of Sa'düddin by pressing for the installation of Baki as chief jurisconsult. Sa'düddin, the sultan's preferred candidate, won out, but he and Baki were definitely set at odds. The major result of the affair was to strengthen the Palace coalition of Sa'düddin, Ganzanfer Ağa, and the sultan's mother, Safiye.[109]

In the midst of the factional strife that preceded the dismissal of Hadim Hasan Paşa, Âli realized that he could hope for nothing from the corrupt grand vezir, or from a political atmosphere so violent that even old friends became enemies. After over forty years of service and literary activity, Âli was exceedingly bitter. If he could not obtain the position he desired, or at least achieve parity with his contemporaries by being given a provincial government (he specifically requested Aleppo), Âli preferred to withdraw altogether from official life and from the Ottoman heartlands of Rum. He asked for permission to retire to Mecca, where he could devote himself to piety and learning away from the temptations and frustrations of the capital. He wished to reject the land that had rejected him, and console himself with religion and history. To this end he asked the sultan to grant him a modest retirement of 100,000 *akçe* in *timar* assignments.[110]

Even honorable retirement was not allowed Âli; his request drew no response. His continuing work on the *Essence* was his sole consolation. At the age of fifty-seven he was ever more aware of growing old, of running out of time, and of what he perceived as an irrevocable spiritual and moral decline in the Ottoman world. In August 1598/Muharrem 1007 Âli wrote:

No chance is there to embrace the beloved's beauty;
Everywhere there is much talk, but no meaning.
Crafty bastards are the race of the age,
No longer is there a pure seed like the daughter of the vine.
The Sufi hopes for understanding in auguries;
There is no true mystic to guide that fool.
Though none can resist the burden of love for God,
In that asinine Sufi there is no such possibility.
Âli, your worth was not known in this your time,
As if the world contained no men of worth.[111]

At this time, the beginning of a new *hicri* year, Âli began a new type of moralistic work that combined the fruits of his extensive historical studies with

[109] Na'ima, *Tarih*, I, 185-87.

[110] DİVAN III, 15a-16b, 401, 74b-75b, 76a-77a. The latter two pieces, addressed to Sultan Mehmed and Gazanfer Ağa, respectively, are dated January-February 1598/Cümada II 1006. The other two poems are datable to the same period on thematic and internal grounds.

[111] DİVAN III, 46a, dated Muharrem 1007.

his millennial sense of a world gone wrong. The *Fusul-i hall ve akd fi usul-i harc ve nakd, The Seasons of Sovereignty on the Principles of Critical Expenditure*, was a spinoff from the *Essence of History* that Âli undertook for presentation to the sultan and his mother Safiye Hatun, at the request of members of the Queen Mother's circle, probably Gazanfer Ağa and Hoca Sa'düddin.[112] In the introduction to the *Seasons* Âli explained the occasion of its composition:

> The year 1007 has begun, and order has disappeared from the earth. Rulers no longer rule, nor do they value things at their real worth. The upright are dismissed, and only sly sharpers have come to prominence. . . . Though the sultan does not condone oppression, his vezirs . . . bring unworthy ones into service and destroy the order of the world by bribe-taking. They do not tell the sultan the truth, excusing themselves by saying they cannot tell him such things out of fear. However, they contradict themselves. Do they imagine it will be easier for them if, fearing his anger, they tell the *valide sultan*? She would never allow such disruption of order, or such affairs to besmirch the reputation of her dear son.[113]

The delicacy of this reference to Safiye Hatun's prominent role in government during the reign of Mehmed sets the tone for the entire work, in which Âli approaches the subject of political decline more subtly and indirectly than previously. Rather than expound on contemporary problems, Âli sets out, in thirty-two chapters (*fasl*, pl. *fusul*), a capsule moralistic history of previous Islamic dynasties, the material for which he extracted from the *Essence*. For each dynasty he pointed out the causes of the success and eventual decline of the states under discussion, and he referred to the current Ottoman situation only in a brief appendix. The moral of this arrangement of material is clear: the Ottoman state, placed in a comparative historical context, was subject to the same historical cycles as other states, and could

[112] The *Fusul* was completed between September 1598 and mid-February 1599. MS Ali Emiri Efendi, Tarih 245, calligraphed in 1744-45/1157, contains what may be a copy of the original colophon of the text from which it was copied. This remnant dates the composition of the work to 3 September-1 October 1598/Safer 1007. The oldest extant MS, Nur 3300, is dated 7-17 February 1600/mid-Receb 1007.

My references are to a photocopy of a manuscript formerly in the possession of M. Tayyıb Gökbilgin, dated 1 April 1735/7 Zulka'de 1147 (hereafter FUSUL). It was copied by Derviş Mehmed b. Ahmed, *tezkereci* of the treasury of Erzurum, and contains 105 folios written in clear *ta'lik*. The *Fusul* contains an introduction, thirty-two chapters, an appendix (*tezyil*), and a conclusion. In the introduction Âli refers to the year of composition as 1007 (4b), and identifies the recipient of the work (5a). In the appendix, which deals with the Ottomans, Âli says that he was urged to write the book by one who had achieved great power in the state through the good offices of both the *valide sultan* and the sultan, and by one of the great scholars of the time (94b).

[113] FUSUL, Introduction, 4b-5a.

fall apart as quickly as it had risen. Therefore its rulers should learn from history to avoid the errors of omission or commission that had brought about the demise of earlier dynasties.

Âli's capsule analysis of the Ottoman situation within a broader historical context emerges from a passage that illuminates the importance of *kanun* as at once a tangible sign of dynastic mandate and a means whereby the dynasty can protect itself from decline. Âli takes as his setting the conquest of Istanbul, the historical moment when the Ottoman principality took imperial form:

> The Conqueror of Istanbul, Sultan Mehmed, together with his wise vezir Mahmud Paşa, planned well for the future by establishing a venerable law [*kanun-ı kadim*]. The previous rulers had not done such a thing, and had perhaps not even imagined it. When the *kanun* had been arranged, and order established in accordance with it, the late sultan asked his vezir, "Once this law is observed, how can the state be destroyed, heaven forbid?"
>
> Mahmud Paşa answered, "Only the Eternal King does not pass away. However, among poor earthly rulers there is no path surer or firmer than this *kanun* we have established. Despite its strength, there are still two ways in which the kingdom and state could be destroyed. One is the case in which one of your noble descendants might not observe the *kanun*, saying that *kanun* is whatever he decrees. The second way [of destruction] is the entry of unauthorized [*ecnebi*] people into the military, which will destroy the order of the servitors [*kul*] of the state.[114]

Âli elaborates on these themes in the following manner. Since 1582, when Janissary discipline was temporarily relaxed, the military had become unruly and lawless and had plundered the people. Officially sanctioned bribery and post buying had bcome customary in the bureaucracy, and in their anxiety to recoup their graft expenses, officials pressed the taxpayers and those lower down on the bureaucratic scale. After the year A.H. 1000 they no longer made a pretense of decorum, and they came to expect bribes as the *sipahi* expected his lawful tithes.[115]

Âli also voiced stylistic concerns in the *Seasons*, which are in marked contrast with those that had occupied the young littérateur: "So that this work might be easily understandable to both the select and the masses, I have not written in rhymed prose nor used complex Arabic and Persian constructions."[116] Âli wrote this very statement in rhymed prose. Nevertheless,

[114] FUSUL, Appendix, 93b-94a.
[115] FUSUL, Appendix, 94a-b.
[116] FUSUL, Introduction, 5b.

the language of the *Seasons* is indeed far less ornate than that of such earlier works as *The Rarity of Warriors*. A similar verbal commitment to simplicity of language in the interests of expanded communication appears in the introductions to the *Essence* and his two last works, *Hâlât ül-Kahire, The Conditions of Cairo*, and *Mevâ'id ün-nefâ'is, Tables of Delicacies*.[117] The *Tables*, which Âli completed slightly over a year after the *Seasons*, is written in a style approaching the colloquial. All of these writings are historical or social in content, and are either concerned with or informed by the situation of contemporary Ottoman society. In his youth and middle age, Âli had experienced the excitement of the linguistic flowering of Ottoman Turkish, and had been keen to show his mastery of it in works of largely literary character. Âli the old man had seen much, endured much, and cared much. The literary standards, tastes, and possibilities of his youth were no longer applicable. He had become obsessed with the decline of his society, and was concerned with communicating his knowledge, insights, fears, and warnings to the widest possible audience, even including those whose education had not been as complete as his own. It may be that Âli's explanation of the genesis of the *Seasons* should be taken seriously. Others, he said, had urged him not to keep quiet, to expose all of the wrongdoing he had seen, and to use his profound knowledge of history to explain the troubles that had beset the Empire: "Being one who has been nourished by the beneficence of the Ottoman state, I deemed it improper to be silent on this subject."[118] Late in his life, because of both personal despair and an anguished social conscience, Âli came to feel that he had a mission to analyze, articulate, and publicize the disappointment and fear experienced by older sectors of the Ottoman intelligentsia. Frustrated in his attempts to build a career, faced with the reality of a world changed drastically, and confronted by old age and death, Âli had little to lose in appointing himself the outspoken conscience of a generation. Whether because of its content or its accessibility, the *Seasons* became one of Âli's most popular works; it was recopied time after time for at least two centuries after his death.[119]

Âli had yet another reason for modifying his prose style. He had heard from Harem officials and others in the royal confidence that Sultan Mehmed did not like to read long, embroidered literary works. He preferred stories that were simple, immediately comprehensible, and to the point. Therefore Âli, when he later wrote the *Tables of Delicacies* for submission to the sul-

[117] KA, I, pp. 9, 11; CAIRO, p. 28 (trans.), p. 95 (text); MEVA'İD, p. 9. On Âli's use of language and prose style, see Andreas Tietze, "Muṣṭafâ ʿÂlî of Gallipoli's Prose Style," *Archivum Ottomanicum* 5 (1973): 297-319.

[118] FUSUL, Introduction, 5a-b.

[119] Atsız (AB, pp. 28-30), whose lists are far from complete, lists twenty-nine manuscripts of the work in Istanbul alone.

tan, used simple language and divided that work, like the *Seasons*, into short sections, the point of each of which was clearly summarized.[120]

Âli's new literary attempts to ingratiate himself with the Queen Mother, and the support of Sa'düddin and Gazanfer Ağa, finally yielded positive results. In the spring of 1599/Şa'ban-Zulhicce 1007, Âli was appointed governor-general of Damascus. This was indeed a fine post; the governorship of Damascus carried a revenue of about one million *akçe* per annum, and the potential for promotion to as important a government as that of Egypt.[121] Âli appeared to have finally received the recognition he desired. He never actually took up the post, however; he was dismissed either before his departure or during the journey.[122] The aging Âli had wished to delay his arrival in Damascus so that he might first make the pilgrimage to Mecca and Medina, and in the *Tables* he cites this pious desire as the reason for his loss of the post.[123] Other factors undoubtedly contributed to Âli's dismissal, for the Ottoman appointment process was in great disorder. Between the years 1597/1006 and 1599/1007, the new governor-general of Damascus, Cağaloğlu Sinan Paşa, was replaced by Ahmed Paşa, who was himself dismissed after a month in office and replaced by Husrev Paşa.[124] Âli's appointment was probably made and unmade in the course of this rapid administrative shuffle, to which his desire to delay his arrival in Damascus added yet more confusion.

Âli was compensated for the loss of his governor-generalship, which he had held on paper only, with another, albeit less exalted, post. He was made *sancak beği* and trustee (*emin*) of Jidda, the port of Mecca.[125] As trustee, Âli was charged with the management of this important commercial and military port, and with the collection of imperial customs revenues. The post, though not a governor-generalship, was becoming an extremely important one; soon after this time Jidda became the *sancak* seat of the gov-

[120] MEVA'İD, pp. 14-15. Âli goes on to congratulate himself for the originality of the style and format of the work.

[121] In the MEVA'İD, which he completed in 1599/1008, Âli twice mentions having recently been appointed *beğlerbeği* of Damascus (pp. 16, 17); see also Cavid Baysun, "Müverrih Âli'nin *Mevâ'id ün-nefâ'is fî kavâ'id il mecâlis*'i Hakkında," *Tarih Dergisi* 2/1 (1950): 396-98. Âli makes no reference to such an appointment in the *Seasons*, completed by March 1599, and he left Istanbul for Egypt in another capacity by some time in June 1599/Zulhicce 1007. Therefore, the appointment must have taken place between these dates. Mustakimzade, *Tuhfe-i hattatin*, pp. 521-22, confirms Âli's appointment to the government of Damascus. Ayn-ı Ali, p. 26, gives the stipend of the *beğlerbeği* of Damascus in his own time as 1,000,000 *akçe*.

[122] Baysun, "Müverrih," p. 398.

[123] MEVA'İD, p. 17. This passage supports the spring 1599 dating for this appointment. Âli probably wished to perform the *hacc* during its proper season, Zulhicce, which fell between 25 June and 23 July in that year.

[124] Laoust, *Gouverneurs*, p. 196; Baysun, "Müverrih," p. 398, citing the *Sûriye Salnamesi*, 25.

[125] MEVA'İD, p. 234; CAIRO, p. 25 (trans.), p. 91 (text); DİVAN III, 88b.

ernor of the expanded province of Habeş, made up of the Sudan, Ottoman East Africa, and the western Hijaz.[126]

CAIRO
(1599)

IT IS unclear whether Âli's appointment to Jidda was made before or after he set out to make the pilgrimage. In any event, he left Istanbul by July of 1599. He traveled by sea, a mode of transport he abominated and feared; he had only journeyed on open water twice before, going to and from Gallipoli. By late July 1599/early Muharrem 1008 he was in Cairo for the second time in his life. His new appointment had been confirmed by the time he arrived.[127]

Âli was in no hurry to reach Jidda. He remained in Egypt for five months, observing its people and customs and comparing the Cairo of 1599 with that of 1568. A difficult and dangerous journey, a new post, and the success of his literary endeavors all put an end to Âli's work on the *Essence*. Âli may have been largely satisfied with the work's state of completion, despite considerable gaps; renewed optimism probably prompted him to set aside the life-work that had in many ways been the product and the symbol of his years of failure and disappointment. In any event, no sections of the *Essence* are dated later than 1599/1007. Âli also enjoyed his new role as social observer and creator of original and topical literary models, and he longed to pursue these new directions. This is the clear implication of a passage in the introduction to the *Tables of Delicacies*, which Âli began as an expansion of his earlier *Etiquette of Salons*: "From the beginning of the *hicri* year 1000 until 1008 [I was occupied] with writing and making additions to the *Essence of History*. The enormity of that task, and the composition of [other] books and treatises in the course of writing the *Essence*, prevented fulfillment of that goal [i.e., expansion of the earlier work]."[128]

Âli's faith in his youthful notion that literary ability and originality would

[126] Cengiz Orhonlu, *Habeş Eyaleti* (Istanbul, 1974), pp. 10, 96, 127; İ. H. Uzunçarşılı, *Mekke-i Mükerreme Emirleri* (Ankara, 1972), pp. 23, 26-27, 75. The *sancak* of Jidda was a *salyane* post; incumbents drew salaries directly from the *sancak* customs revenues rather than receive *hass*-land grants. *Salyane* provinces ordinarily supported no local *sipahi* forces, but provided revenues for administration and for the pay of imperial forces. Jidda received its military forces, when needed, from Egypt.

[127] MEVA'İD, p. 234. Âli had long wished to return to Cairo because of the city's prominence as a book market. The *terminus ante quem* for his arrival there, mid-Muharrem 1008, emerges from a passage in CAIRO, pp. 7, 27 (introduction and trans.), p. 93 (text). An *âşûrâ*-poem, which Âli composed in Cairo in Muharrem 1008, confirms this dating (DİVAN III, 34b).

[128] MEVA'İD, p. 7.

necessarily bring concrete rewards—albeit he was now interested in very different themes than in his youth—was restored. Throughout his later career he sought to create new forms, to bring new subjects and new stylistic and analytical skills into literature. Even in the introduction to the *Essence*, for example, he touted the originality and clarity of his organizational scheme, and appended a long discourse on the theory of historiography.[129] He considered himself a ''master author'' who had composed ''forty or fifty'' works, which he had put in mortmain.[130]

Now in Egypt, Âli embarked on a new literary venture. He wrote the *Hâlât ül-Kahire mine 'l-âdât iz-zâhire, The Conditions of Cairo Concerning Her Actual Customs*, during his first three months in Cairo.[131] In this work he described the life, customs, and character of the people of the country, and the nature of its social and political institutions. In an appendix, Âli the historian discussed Egypt under Ottoman administration. Specifically, he compared the overall state of the province in 1599 with its condition thirty years earlier. He concluded that the interval had produced a ruinous decline, which he analyzed through the use of specific examples and graphic description, as he had done in the *Counsel*.[132] Âli also related the negative aspects of Ottoman government in Egypt to the problems afflicting the Empire as a whole: moral laxity, corruption, relaxation of *kanun* observance, and the bad administration of governors-general and *sancak beğis* whom he named by name. In the *Conditions* Âli fused the traveler's curiosity with the moral critic's eye for fault and the historian's passion for causes and patterns. Âli had a clean copy made for his patron Gazanfer Ağa, to whom he dedicated and then dispatched the work.[133] That Âli would present a work containing so frank and direct a critique of Ottoman administration to one of the most influential figures in the Palace shows that his serious concerns about ''decline'' and the chaotic state of the Empire must have been shared by at least a portion of the Ottoman intelligentsia and ruling elite.[134]

[129] KA, I, 13-17, 47.

[130] MEVA'İD, p. 18.

[131] Âli completed the work in October 1599/Rebi' I 1008; see CAIRO, pp. 7-8, p. 83 (text), plate 89. The translation of the title given here is that of Professor Tietze.

[132] For Âli's general statement on the vile state of Egypt (''a place more fiery and abject than the depths of Hell''), see CAIRO, pp. 27-28 (trans.), pp. 93-94 (text). Âli also made many comparisons between Egyptians and hinterland Turks, and found the former strange; for examples, see CAIRO, pp. 40-41 (trans.), pp. 113-15 (text).

[133] CAIRO, pp. 25, 28 (trans.), pp. 91, 95-96 (text).

[134] In a review of Tietze's edition of the *Hâlât* published in BSOAS 40/2 (1977): 392-95, Colin Heywood has offered an alternative stemma of the extant MSS of the work (CAIRO, pp. 8-9). He also plausibly suggests that Âli deleted from Gazanfer Ağa's presentation copy the most directly critical section of the work, paragraph 5, found in CAIRO, pp. 57-66 (trans.), 138-51 (text). Absolute confirmation of this thesis must await further manuscript evidence. (In 1978 I discovered the ''lost'' Cairo copy in the Egyptian National Library. It appeared to be a very late and defective manuscript; unfortunately, I did not then have access to a copy of the

Âli had yet another motive in composing the *Conditions* and in delaying his departure to the Hijaz; he was trying to secure appointment as governor-general of Egypt. He clearly wished to capitalize on his brief appointment to Damascus and his effective elevation to governor-general's rank. When Âli took up the government and trusteeship of Jidda, he thanked the sultan for the posting, which had put an end to years of unemployment and disappointment. He expressed these same sentiments in a companion piece to which he added that, welcome as the dual appointment was, a higher post would in fact be much more suitable.[135] In the introduction to the *Tables*, written soon after he left Cairo for Jidda, Âli asked outright for the governor-generalship; since he had been made a governor-general once, he said, it would be easy for the sultan to give him the government of Egypt.[136] Âli probably hoped that, by showing his knowledge of and concern about local Egyptian conditions and administrative problems, he could convince Gazanfer Ağa of the wisdom of securing the government for him. The detailed and critical appraisal of the policies and characters of the Ottoman governors of the province, which Âli appended to the *Conditions*, was in fact a broad hint, an invitation to Gazanfer Ağa to compare Âli's wisdom and ability with the qualities of both previous and current administrators of the province.[137] Âli had no success and was finally obliged to proceed to the Hijaz. He ended his stay in Egypt depressed over both his own situation and that of the province:

Egypt's distress, like the river Nile,
Has muddied the sweet stream of life beyond endurance.
Stop going door to door in hope of help!
The doors of generosity are all closed for good.
Don't brood, Âli, over those that envy you;
See what, out of envy, Joseph's brothers did to him!
[To be] ruler of Egypt, for a man of talent in Joseph's image,
Brings only empty pomp and calamity for all time.[138]

THE HIJAZ

(1599-1600)

ÂLI still wished to perform the pilgrimage before taking up his duties in Jidda. He at last left Cairo at the beginning of the winter of 1599, when the

Tietze edition for comparison.) Even if this is the case, the remaining paragraphs contain sufficient critical material to support the idea that a certain concern over "decline" was generalized.

135 DİVAN III, 88b.
136 MEVA'İD, pp. 16-17.
137 CAIRO, pp. 69-80 (trans.), 156-72 (text).
138 DİVAN III, 27b.

weather had cooled enough for comfortable travel. He crossed overland to Suez, and from there took sea passage to Jidda, having sent a copy of the *Conditions of Cairo* to Gazanfer Ağa about a month earlier.[139] The sea voyage threw him into intimate contact with social and professional groups, such as sailors and boatmen, with whom he had previously had little to do. The coarseness and novelty of their behavior inspired him to take advantage of the leisure afforded him by the exigencies of travel and his completion of other literary projects. He began an expanded version of his earlier commentary on contemporary manners and mores, the *Etiquette of Salons*, which the recently deceased Hoca Sa'düddin had suggested when Âli first "published" the *Etiquette*. The project, which Âli compiled as a series of 104 short articles, was to result in his last literary work, the *Mevâ'id ün-nefâ'is fi kavâ'id il-mecâlis, Tables of Delicacies on the Etiquette of Salons*.[140] According to Âli's introduction to this book, the impetus for writing the *Etiquette* had come from the late Sultan Murad, who had asked his vezir Doğancı Mehmed Paşa whether informal, rotating salons like those that were popular in Murad's time had been a social custom in his ancestor's days as well.[141] The spirit of comparison of contemporary social and political practices with those of earlier times that is implicit in this question pervades the wide-ranging articles of the *Tables*, if not the entries in its more restricted predecessor, which is concisely prescriptive in tone and content.

Âli rejoiced when he finally arrived at Jidda in December 1599, if only because the unpleasant sea voyages were at an end and because he was finally able to assume a post without being recalled. Two poems from his last *divan* attest to Âli's continued anxiety for his career. The first is a poem of thanks addressed to Sultan Mehmed, sent from Jidda, in which Âli expressed his gratitude for his appointment and asked for promotion.[142] The second appears to have been composed after a meeting in Cairo with Hızır Paşa, the governor-general of Egypt. Perhaps because of his past experiences, or because he was maneuvering to be appointed governor himself, Âli had approached Hızır Paşa with considerable trepidation. However, their meeting appears to have been amicable, and Âli was reassured that all would go well for him in his new post.[143]

Even before his arrival in Jidda, Âli had planned to make the pilgrimage as soon as possible, the opportunity to do so being one of the principal ben-

[139] MEVA'İD, p. 8; CAIRO, p. 8, pp. 25, 28 (trans.) 91, 96 (text). On the somewhat murky chronology of these events, see Fleischer, "Âli," pp. 364-65.

[140] MEVA'İD, pp. 6, 11-13. Hoca Sa'düddin died on 30 September or 2 October 1599/10 or 12 Rebi' I 1008 (Gökbilgin, "Sa'd-ed-Din,"), and is referred to as *merhum*, "the late," on p. 66 of the MEVA'İD.

[141] MEVA'İD, pp. 5-6.

[142] DİVAN III, 88b.

[143] DİVAN III, 81b.

efits of his current posting.[144] After several months, he set out for Mecca. While he may have wished to wait for the pilgrimage season at the end of the *hicri* year, Âli almost certainly departed before that date.[145] Once in Mecca, Âli had much to occupy him, apart from the visitation of the Holy Places he had so long dreamed of accomplishing. He had to establish relations with the *şerif* of Mecca, the dynastic ruler of the holy city under Ottoman suzerainty, who received half of the customs revenues collected at the port of Jidda. Âli took advantage of these meetings to show the *Tables*, which he was just then completing, to the incumbent *şerif*, Ḥasan b. Abî Numayy.[146] By Âli's account, Şerif Ḥasan was enthusiastic about the work and endorsed various articles in his own hand.[147] Encouraged by the approval of so prestigious a figure, and once again hopeful, Âli wrote an introduction to the work in which he explained its genesis and purpose. He then dedicated the *Tables of Delicacies* to Sultan Mehmed, to whom he hoped to have it submitted.[148]

In his introduction Âli boasted that the work was completely original in type, that "no one, Arab, Iranian, Turk, Greek, or Deylemi, has produced its like in the world."[149] Indeed, Âli did not exaggerate greatly. The *Tables* are a unique commentary on the social and political life of the Ottoman Empire in the sixteenth century. Focusing on a wide variety of institutions, social groups, and contemporary problems, Âli traced what he saw as a pervasive moral and material decline, progressing from the days of his youth in mid-century until the opening years of the second Islamic millennium, which affected all segments of society. The *Tables of Delicacies* goes far beyond the parameters of an essay on manners to give a vivid picture of late

144 DİVAN III, 52a, a *gazel* on performance of the *hacc* and *umre* (the lesser pilgrimage performed at any time of the year), composed at sea before Âli's arrival in Jidda.

145 DİVAN III, 81a, two poems on the *hacc*, which Âli says he is about to perform. Baysun opines that Âli must have remained in Jidda for two to three months; this he estimates to be the minimum time required to complete so lengthy a work as the *Mevâ'id*, which was finished in Mecca ("Müverrih," p. 400). Despite the work's completion in the holy city, Âli does not style himself *hâcc* or *hacı*, which he certainly would have done had he been in Mecca during the pilgrimage season (cf. CAIRO, p. 8). Finally, Âli died in Jidda during the *hicri* year 1008 (see below); it is unlikely that he could have both performed the pilgrimage in the last month of the year and returned to his post before his death. Most probably he arrived in Mecca sometime before the beginning of Ramazan (16 March 1600).

146 MEVA'İD, pp. 19-20. On the administrative situation of the *şerifs* of Mecca under the Ottomans, and on Ḥasan b. Abî Numayy, see Uzunçarşılı, *Mekke-i Mükerreme Emirleri*, pp. 19, 23-27, 77. Âli considered the *şerifs* of Mecca a legitimate sovereign dynasty, despite their vassalage to the Ottomans; see KA, MS Leiden, Cod. Warner 288, 4a, edited by Jan Schmidt in an unpublished *doctoraal-scriptie* for the University of Leiden, "De 'Verantwoording' in het Leidse Handschrift van de *Künhü'l-ahbar*" (April, 1983).

147 MEVA'İD, p. 20.

148 MEVA'İD, pp. 2-20.

149 MEVA'İD, p. 9.

sixteenth-century Ottoman life, albeit one highly colored by a bitter pessimism and sense of loss.[150]

In his introduction to the work, Âli expanded on the old theme of the utility of a royal confidant unafraid to tell the sultan the unvarnished truth, as Âli claimed to do in the *Tables*:

He [the sultan] is rich in heart, he likes not corruption,
And his wrath is death to the graft-taker.
[Yet] no one can tell him this secret [i.e., of graft],
Even so many intimates cannot inform him.
Such intimates are criminals to kings!
They sin by concealing the truth.[151]

Âli proceeded to recite his own long history of service to the Ottoman house and his literary accomplishments, in recognition of which he requested that the government of Egypt be conferred upon him. He suggested that Sultan Mehmed would gain prestige from having so distinguished an author and scholar as a governor-general, and averred that none of the forty *beğlerbeği*s of the Empire could match himself in culture and learning. Once again, Âli pressed his case by citing distinguished precedent; he could be to Sultan Mehmed what the poet and vezir Ahmed Paşa had been to the Conqueror, or Mîr ʿAlî Shîr to Sulṭân-Ḥusayn Bâyqarâ. Thus, Âli implied, the sultan could turn back the clock for the Empire and restore it to the glory it had known in the late fifteenth century, when rulers had known the worth of their advisors.[152]

In presenting to the sultan this last literary work, Âli, despite the pervasive gloom with which he imbued it, struck an optimistic note. Until the end of his life he remained firmly committed to the value and validity of the cultural ideals of his youth, which dictated that learning, merit, originality, and integrity be honored and rewarded in the public sphere as in the private. As Âli saw it, the life of the mind, of society as a whole, and of government were based on the same basic ideals, and were inextricably intertwined. This, for Âli, had been the Ottoman promise.

Soon after completing the *Tables of Delicacies* at Mecca, Âli returned to Jidda to throw himself, with renewed hope of promotion, into his new duties. In Jidda he fell ill. Unable to work or write because of the severity of his illness, he composed what were probably his last verses. Appropriately, he wrote them in Persian and Arabic;

[150] Cf. Baysun's introduction to MEVA'ID, pp. viii-ix.
[151] MEVA'İD, pp. 13-14.
[152] MEVA'İD, pp. 16-18.

The unworthy dream, while the learned wish to write and compose.
The first remains in the pit of fear, the second is higher than Venus's apogee.
From the signs of Fate I read the lesson, the difference of these two states;
Wherever perpetuity lies, take it! Work is sweeter than honey.[153]

In the first part of the year 1600, in his fifty-eighth year, Mustafa Âli died.[154]

153 DİVAN III, 89a.

154 For the *tezkere* citations that establish that Âli died at Jidda during the year 1599-1600/1008, see İNAL, p. 45. That he must have lived into the year 1600 is established by the chronology of his movements after his departure from Cairo, discussed above. A possible *terminus ante quem* for his death is provided by the chronogram on his death cited by Mustakimzade, *Tuhfe-i-Hattatin*, p. 522: "Âli died and Baki followed him." According to Köprülü, Baki died in Istanbul on 8 April 1600/23 Ramazan 1008, two months before the end of the *hicri* year (Köprülü, "Baki"). This evidence is of questionable chronological value. While Âli may have died sometime before Baki, it may also have been the case that the two events occurred closely enough together that the anonymous chronogram writer could conveniently use these words to form a double chronogram. The length of time required, beginning from late December 1599/early Cümada II 1008 onwards to travel to Jidda, Mecca, back to Jidda, and meanwhile complete the *Mevâ'id*, suggests that Âli probably did not die before February-March 1600/mid-Şa'ban 1008 at the earliest.

Documentary evidence still extant in the early part of this century showed that a tomb (*türbe*) for Âli had existed in his native city of Gelibolu, though it is unlikely that he was actually buried there, since he died at Jidda; see İNAL, p. 45.

II

OTTOMAN LAW, OTTOMAN CAREER

SIX

KANUN-CONSCIOUSNESS IN THE SIXTEENTH CENTURY

INTRODUCTION

MUSTAFA ÂLI'S life and times have occupied us for many pages. His education, professional advancements and trials, and the evolution of his literary interests and production have provided a focus for the study of a major Ottoman intellectual. Âli's biography has also furnished us a window on his society and a means to examine the transformations it underwent in the second half of the sixteenth century. Now it is only fitting that this focus itself be examined, that we study Âli from within as well as without. Âli's own perception and representation of Ottoman history, carefully analyzed, can tell us as much about his society and Ottoman intellectualism as does his *curriculum vitae*. There is a subtle rhythm, a resonance, between the triumphs and tribulations of Mustafa Âli and the waxing and waning of Ottoman imperial glory; between Âli's disappointments and his growing sense that Ottoman ideals, whether these were explicitly articulated or not, had been betrayed by the whole of society; and between Âli's increasing awareness of the approach of death and his perception of an Ottoman world in decline. This rhythm, of course, had a profound effect on the way in which Âli portrayed his polity and its history, and it was this very resonance that helped to transform an embittered careerist, as ashamed of his own moral slackness as of his lack of success, into a great historian. The extent to which Âli identified with the Ottoman Empire cannot be overestimated. He saw himself and his career as an example, or even a symbol, of the successes and failures of the Ottoman experiment; and this identification does much to illuminate Âli's curious love-hate relationship with the Ottoman Empire of his time.

With these considerations in mind, we shall now turn to those ideas, images, and patterns that informed Âli's inner vision of the Ottoman world. And, because we have thus far been concerned with the course of Âli's professional life, we shall begin with a subject close to his professional heart: the Ottoman government career paths and the legal mechanisms that governed them. In those sociopolitical writings that were the major product of the last nineteen years of his life, Âli elaborated the notion that the decline he perceived in the state of the Ottoman Empire stemmed in large measure from a progressive abandonment of respect for the standards and strictures embodied in Ottoman dynastic law, *kanun*, which was at once a symbol of the Ottoman commitment to justice, a corpus of secular legislation, and accepted customary practice. Âli's preoccupation with the *kanun* concept permeates such works as the *Counsel* and *Tables*, and had a direct impact on later Ottoman political commentators. More than this, there is ample evidence to suggest that Âli's concerns were shared by other Ottomans in the late sixteenth century. The character of the relationship between *kanun* and the *şeri'at* religious law will be dealt with in a later chapter. Here we shall focus on Âli's conception of *kanun*, the theory and reality of *kanun* in the sixteenth century, and on the historical context within which *kanun*-consciousness developed among the Ottoman intelligentsia.

In fact, the majority of Âli's complaints about neglect of *kanun* center on matters of the admission to the ranks of government officials of "unworthy" people and on patterns of promotion to high position that he considered to be illegal from the standpoint of institutionalized Ottoman practice. Âli's sense of *kanun* was tightly bound to his self-identity and his professional expectations. During the last eight years of his life he repeatedly asked to be made either chancellor or governor-general, and he carefully framed these requests in terms of lines of promotion that he described as permissible by law. At this same time Âli was writing the *Essence of History*, in which he made extensive use of the dynastic code (*kanunname*) of the Conqueror, the document that theoretically regulated all matters of function, rank, and promotion for Ottoman officialdom. In order to evaluate Âli's conception of the meaning of career and *kanun*, on which he sought to demonstrate his expertise, we must briefly study the structure of the central government services and the theoretical organization that dictated the patterns of employment and professional expectations of government servants.

PALACE SERVICE AND PROMOTION

THE general dynastic code promulgated by Mehmed II, the Conqueror, in the late fifteenth century was the document that defined and identified the key institutions and personnel of a border principality turned Ottoman Empire. On the subject of eligibility for promotion to the ranks of district governor (*sancak beği*) and governor-general (*beglerbegi*) the *Kanunname* states:

> Governor-generalship [*beğlerbeğilik*] is open to four officials: finance directors [*mal defterdarları*], chancellors [*nişancı*] with the rank

> of [*sancak*] *beğ*, judges [*kadı*] of 500-*akçe* [per day] rank, and *sancak beğis* who have reached the level of 400,000 *akçe* [per year]. *Sancak beğis* remain above all the commanders of the Outer services [*ağas*].
>
> Chancellorship is open to professors of Inner [*dahil*] and *Sahn* rank. If a finance director becomes chancellor, he does so with the rank of governor-general. If a secretary-in-chief [*re'is ül-küttab*] becomes chancellor, he does so with the rank of *sancak* [*beği*].
>
> When finance directors accept a *sancak*, it is given in the value of 450,000 [*akçe*]. The Janissary commander and other commanders of the Stirrup [*üzengi ağaları*] are given [*sancaks*] with 430,000. *Sancak beğis* of less than 400,000 cannot become governors-general. If the Porte commanders [*kapı ağaları*] of my Palace go to a *sancak*, they do so with 400,000. . . . By my law [*kanun*] it is possible for finance directors and chancellors with the rank of *beğ* to become vezirs directly.[1]

An early seventeenth-century digest of *kanun* compiled by Ayn-ı Ali Efendi shows that much the same system was in effect over a century after the Conqueror issued his code, despite some differences in the size of grants and relative ranks of appointees. In a section of his treatise dealing with *çıkma*, the graduation procedure whereby Palace personnel were given military commands or provincial assignments, Ayn-ı Ali writes:

> When commanders of the Porte are promoted to a *sancak* post they begin with a post of more than 200,000 *akçe*. The rules for each [official of the Porte] are different. For example, the Janissary commander is promoted [to a *sancak*] of 500,000 *akçe*, and the chancellor, finance directors of the Porte [*kapı defterdarları*], and the standard-bearer [*mir-i alem*] are sent to 450,000-*akçe* posts.[2]

The purpose of quoting these documents is not to extrapolate changes in the relative ranks of high Ottoman officials, although the evidence suggests that this occurred, but rather to point out certain theoretical features of the Ottoman career system. Only when this theory is understood, and its practice examined, will Âli's criticisms of changes in the Ottoman professional system become comprehensible in their proper context.

Çıkma, as a technical term, refers to the graduation process to which those *kuls* who were part of the Palace system were periodically subjected. These *kuls* were largely, but by no means exclusively, of *devşirme* origin.[3] At graduation those members of the Inner Palace (*enderun*) service deemed

[1] Ârif, *Kanunname*, pp. 14-15.

[2] Ayn-ı Ali, p. 38. For chronologically intermediate confirmation of these rules of advancement from the *Kanunname* of Selim II, see Röhrborn, *Verwaltungsgeschichte*, pp. 107-108.

[3] Kunt, *Servants*, pp. 32-56; see also İnalcık, "Ghulâm," EI², and *Empire*, pp. 76-88, on *çıkma*.

worthy were promoted to a higher position within that sector; those at the highest levels of the Inner Palace were then sent out to the provinces as district governors or governors-general. Those who did not reach the highest levels of Inner service were given posts in the Outer Palace (*birun*). Outside officers could work their way through the Outer Palace ranks, and were eligible for a provincial assignment at a subsequent graduation. The nature of their provincial grant depended upon the level at which they left the Outer Service.

''Graduation'' was the theoretical goal of the Ottoman *kul*s, the members of the military career (*seyfiye*) who were associated with the Palace as slaves, *devşirme* recruits, or freeborn members of one of the Palace units, such as the Elite Corps (*müteferrika*) or the Palace Cavalry. The evidence of the documents cited above shows that *çıkma*, in the general sense of promotion to a provincial governorship, was also a possible career goal of other members of the central administrative apparatus who were not members of the strictly military elite trained in the Palace. This has important implications for our understanding of Ottoman career paths. Even the highest positions within the central bureaucracy, the offices of chancellor and treasurer, did not necessarily represent the pinnacle or terminal point of a career line. The superiority in rank of a governor-general to a treasurer, despite the latter's status as a member of the Imperial Council, is neatly illustrated by the case of Üveys Paşa, Âli's one-time patron. Üveys began his career as a judge, became treasurer under Sultan Murad, and was eventually made governor-general of Budin, Aleppo, Damascus, and Aleppo again. When he was recalled to Istanbul to resume the post of treasurer in order to cope with pressing financial difficulties, he was pointedly given the office with the rank and salary of governor-general of Damascus. Thereafter he was made governor of Egypt with a vezirate, a rank that was the career goal of governors-general. Having attained the rank of vezir, one could become a vezir of the Dome and then, theoretically, grand vezir.[4]

Further, these passages illuminate the process whereby Ottoman career lines usually considered distinct—the ways of the Sword, Pen, and Learning—intertwined at the upper reaches of government. The first and most common mode of promotion to governor-general's rank was through the Palace military career, i.e., working one's way from the Inner Service to the Outer Service, and then through provincial governorships. However, a variety of personnel from the Palace and central bureaucratic services, both military and nonmilitary, also had access to this career line. The second avenue of direct promotion to governor-generalship was through the bureau-

[4] On the career of Üveys Paşa, see chapter 3, and Röhrborn, *Verwaltungsgeschichte*, pp. 20-21, 147.

cracy, in either the financial or the chancery services; insofar as these two wings of the bureaucratic service became distinct from each other, they appear to have done so in the mid-to late sixteenth century, and then by virtue of the increasing importance of financial specialization.[5] This branch of government service, in turn, was accessible to members of the *ilmiye*; professors could become chancellors, judges could become finance directors.[6] Finally, high-ranking *ilmiye* professionals, judges of 500 *akçe*, were eligible for direct promotion to a provincial governorship.

In theory, then, the three major career lines were permeable at the uppermost levels of government service. Such a notion appears to contradict the commonly held view that each was discrete and self-contained, a view that Âli and his immediate successors among Ottoman political commentators seem to have been largely responsible for propagating. We shall see that these divisions, for Âli and his contemporaries, were less categorical than modern scholars have supposed. This is so both because of differences between theory and actual practice, and because the theory of Ottoman state organization has been imperfectly understood. To take an example from the case at hand, we may note that the statement of the *Kanunname* that judges of 500 *akçe*, members of the religious career, could attain high military position appears particularly anomalous in view of the rigid functional and ideological barriers that divided Men of the Sword from Men of Learning. The fact that 500-*akçe* judges were eligible for such appointment, however, does not mean that such appointments would normally, or perhaps ever, take place. Why then should it be legislated as possible? Leaving aside (for the moment) the question of "hidden" mechanisms affecting the appointment process, such as family and patronage relationships, we can state that the evidence of the *Kanunname* suggests that our views on who was eligible for promotion to provincial governorship are too narrow.

Modern scholarship, by and large, holds that in the sixteenth century such posts were the preserve of Palace military specialists primarily of *devşirme* origin. Freeborn Muslims from the other careers (Pen and Learning) who, like Âli, increasingly toward the end of the century came to attain military positions, tend to be viewed as "illegal infiltrators" of the slave-dominated military-administrative establishment. This argument has been summarized and criticized by Metin Kunt, who points out that the *kul*s who were sent to *sancak* posts after serving in the Palace were not all *devşirme* slaves. The ranks of those affiliated with one or another of the Palace services included freeborn Muslims, the scions of princely families, sons of high-ranking

[5] See below and Röhrborn, "Emanzipation," 118-26, 132-35. See also Matuz, *Kanzleiwesen*, 18-45, 57-61, on these career lines in the immediately preceding period.

[6] Above and *Kanunname*, p. 17, which states that a *kadı* who has reached the salary of 300 *akçe* may become a *defterdar*.

*kul*s, and the retainers of *kul*s.[7] This, taken together with the evidence of the *Kanunname*, shows that a new categorization of Ottoman functionaries eligible for promotion to provincial government, at once broader and more exclusive, is required to reconcile theory and actual patterns of appointment. The designation "Palace" will cover not only the slave products of the Harem education system (and here again not all of those associated with the Harem were slaves), but also freeborn members of the Outer services and nonmilitary officials who served in or were associated with the Imperial Council, which was both the central administrative and decision-making body of Ottoman government and a part of the Palace system. The notion of a Palace class, which includes high-ranking administrators of differing family and professional backgrounds, helps to account for the theoretical eligibility for governorship of 500-*akçe* judges. These were the judges of the most important provincial capitals; they had important administrative as well as legal duties and were, within the *ilmiye* system, only one step below the military judges of Rumeli and Anatolia, who served on the Imperial Council. The Palace class of servitors to which the *Kanunname* gave order was in fact the patrimonial household made government, enlarged, rationalized, bureaucratized, and refined.

An important feature of the system of promotion operative within the central government was a horizontal cross-referencing of ranks between the professional branches. Hierarchies of rank within a given career track were clearly established, but the central government comprised functionaries from all three careers. Their relative standing was determined according to a scale based on military categories (reflecting the military origins of the state), but which in the case of bureaucratic figures had little or nothing to do with their actual function. A secretary-in-chief promoted to the chancellorship did so with the rank of *sancak beği*, while a finance director who became chancellor acquired the rank of governor-general (*paşa*). There are many examples of important bureaucratic officials who received honorific rank (in later terminology, *pâye*) without exercising the actual function (*rütbe*) which that rank implied. For instance, of the chancellors of Selim II and Murad III, Feridun Ahmed became *sancak beği* of Semendre with the rank of *paşa*, and Muhyi Çelebi and Hamze Çelebi were given the rank, but not the office, of governor-general of Anatolia.[8]

One effect of this mechanism was clearly to distinguish between the professional backgrounds of various incumbents of a single position, and thus refine categories of promotion eligibility. Finance directors, for example, would appear to have received *beğ* status upon appointment, and attained honorific governor-generalship upon removal to the chancellorship,

[7] See above, note 3, and Kunt, *Sancaktan Eyalete*, pp. 65-71, 112-20.

[8] Danişmend, *Kronoloji*, V, 322-26.

while a chancellor who had prior to his appointment served as secretary-in-chief remained at a lower honorific rank. The statement that only chancellors with the rank of *beğ*, that is, appointees from the post of secretary-in-chief or finance director, could be made governor-general, is of interest because it precludes such promotion for chancellors without the rank of *beğ*, i.e., those appointed from the ranks of distinguished *medrese* professors. In this refined form *kanun* provided for the exclusion from military-administrative service of members of the *ilmiye* who, unlike ranking judges, did not have extensive administrative experience, although they could be appointed to bureaucratic positions within the central government, which at first glance would seem to give them access to a provincial governorship.

Other refinements of the system allowed for the extraordinary promotion of exceptionally well-qualified individuals. Treasurers and chancellors with the rank of *beğ* could be made vezirs without going through the usual preliminary service as provincial governors-general. The number of people with which this portion of the *Kanunname* of the Conqueror deals is perforce very small. At these elevated levels of government service, proven administrative ability, professional experience, personal connections, and demonstrated loyalty to the dynasty were as important in the development of an individual career as functional or technical rank, for all of the system's theoretical subtleties. Therefore it must be considered whether, within the central administration, there was indeed a norm or typical mode of professional progress despite, or perhaps in light of, the strictures of the *Kanunname*. It is clear that, in examining the relative status of particular positions within the central government of the Ottoman Empire, we cannot assume that the hierarchy of ranks was absolutely fixed. In a certain sense the importance of an office, and where that office could lead its incumbent, depended upon the individual, what he brought to his post in terms of professional background, and the relative standing of other major functionaries.

THE *KANUNNAME* OF MEHMED II

THE nature of the Code of the Conqueror deserves attention at this juncture, for it is the document upon which Âli based his expertise in *kanun*. Mehmed II, after his conquest of Constantinople in 1453, followed the tradition of the great Central Asian conquerors who proclaimed their establishment of nomadic empires with the issuance of a new dynastic law. He had the customary practice of his forebears codified by his chancellor, personally made additions and revisions, and issued the *Kanunname*, which was to guide his successors in ruling in the "Ottoman Way."[9]

[9] See Halil İnalcık, "Osmanlı Hukukuna Giriş," SBFD 13/2 (1958): 111-12, 116. For other

That portion of the Conqueror's institutes dealing with the structure of the central government (as opposed to his tax legislation), which formed the effective constitution of the Empire, was thus a mixture of description of actual practice, acknowledgment of precedent, and prescription emanating from the ruler's discretionary authority, all given canonical force. The *Kanunname* legislated *possible* as well as normal or desirable practice, and hence does not necessarily indicate which of several paths of promotion was most common. The Code of the Conqueror is best seen as an outline of the broad lines within which deviations from the effective norms of promotion might be tolerated. The direct appointment of treasurers or chancellors to a vezirate, for example, was not typical, but merely allowable.

Kanun was an accretive and, within limits, mutable phenomenon. The institutes of the "founding father" were to be binding on his descendants, for they expressed the dynastic mandate. But Mehmed also enjoined his successors to amend usage as necessary.[10] *Kanun* was not to be changed willfully, however, but only in accordance with the spirit of impersonal justice and dynastic honor that informed the primal promulgation. This is why Âli had Mahmud Paşa state in the *Seasons of Sovereignty* that a sultan who ignored the ancestral law, declaring law to be whatever he might decree, would destroy the Empire.[11] Imperial custom, as *kanun*, had prescriptive force even when unwritten; it could be, and was, added to or modified only by a specific declaration of the dynastic representative. Hence successive sultans built upon and adjusted, but never fully abrogated, the laws of their fathers by issuing their own supplemental codes, reaffirmations, and revisions of standing legislation (*adaletname*).[12] The cumulative character of dynastic law was such that ascription of a *kanunname* to a particular sultan did not affect its legality; the two greatest lawgivers of the Empire, Mehmed II and Süleyman, were compilers of custom as much as promulgators of new regulations required by new circumstances.[13] Dynastic law, though cumulative, allowed for innovation and variation as need arose. Failure to comprehend this aspect of *kanun* has lead some scholars to misunderstand the concept of "legality" at the heart of late sixteenth-century intellectuals' complaints about violation of *kanun* norms. One Turcologist, for example, basing himself in part on statements made by Âli, found the increasing incidence of crossing of career lines in the late sixteenth century, as more and

---

examples of Ottoman adherence to Central Asian political traditions, see the same author's "Osmanlılarda Saltanat Veraseti," SBFD 14/1 (1959): 69-94.

[10] *Kanunname*, pp. 11, 23; İnalcık, "Hukuk," p. 116.

[11] See above, p. 178.

[12] For an example of change of protocol in the Imperial Council which required abrogation of a standing rule, see KA, Süleyman/Ümera, "Nevbaharzade Beğ," Nur 3409, 136a.

[13] İnalcık, "Suleiman the Lawgiver." The *Kanunname* of Süleyman was published by Mehmed Ârif in TOEM, suppl. 2, 1329/1911.

more financial officers gained military appointment, to represent an "abnormal" or "illegal" development.[14] He also assumed, following the work of a scholar who had documented anachronistic elements in the *Kanunname* of the Conqueror, that the "so-called lawbook of the Conqueror" was a benign forgery of the late sixteenth century compiled to legitimize practice current at that time, and that therefore it did not reflect the intentions of the Conqueror or the governmental structure of the fifteenth century.[15] This view of the document as "unauthentic" because of anachronistic elements has been shown to be untenable,[16] and happily so, for it distorts the significance that the *idea* of *kanun*, as well as its specific provisions, held for intellectuals of Âli's generation.

The circulation in the late sixteenth century of *kanun* compilations associated with the names of Fatih Mehmed and Süleyman is, to be sure, a significant phenomenon. Âli himself must have been aware of anachronistic elements when he utilized the document; in that section of the *Essence* in which he quotes the institutes of the Conqueror, he describes the "Arab and Iranian directorate" (*Arab ve Acem defterdarlığı*) as part of the financial institution Sultan Mehmed established, although he elsewhere recounts the conquests of Selim I which necessitated creation of the office. Even so, Âli consistently emphasizes the importance of the role of Mehmed and Süleyman as lawgivers.[17] A partial solution to this apparent anomaly, if Âli is not merely to be accused of historiographical carelessness, may be found in the nature of the *kanunname*s of these two rulers. Both are general codes comprising legislation affecting the entire Empire, be it the organization of the upper echelons of the central government (Fatih), or general matters of provincial military organization, penal justice, taxation, and the position of certain minorities within the Empire (Süleyman). These were the guiding documents of the Ottoman system that were in a class of *kanun* separate from, and higher than, more specific regional legislation. They derived legality and legitimacy from (reasonable) ascription to or association with the most prestigious builders and law codifiers of the state. Changes in the bodies of legislation collected around the names of Süleyman and Mehmed could be accepted as need arose, provided that these additions did not violate the spirit of the original codes.

Whatever the relative "authenticity" of various portions of the *Kanun-*

[14] Röhrborn, "Emanzipation."

[15] Konrad Dilger, *Untersuchungen zur Geschichte des osmanischen Hofzeremoniells im 15. und 16. Jahrhundert* (Munich, 1967), pp. 14-36, 113-16.

[16] Matuz, *Kanzleiwesen*, p. 35; Richard Repp, "Some Observations on the Development of the Ottoman Learned Hierarchy," in *Scholars, Saints, and Sufis*, ed. Nikki R. Keddie (Berkeley, 1972), p. 19; Fleischer, "Âli," pp. 380-82, 405-407.

[17] KA, Fatih/Conquest of Istanbul, MS Fatih 4225, 96b-106b (*Kanunname*); KA, Süleyman/Introduction, Nur 3409, 2b-4b (Süleyman); Röhrborn, "Emanzipation," p. 132.

name of the Conqueror, the evidence of anachronism and Âli's utilization of the document show that in its extant form it must have been compiled in the late sixteenth century. Other contemporary historians, notably Selâniki, were also very concerned with *kanun*; Selâniki precedes many descriptions of ceremonial with the phrase *kanun-ı kadim üzre*, "in accordance with ancient custom [or *kanun*]." Other instances of Selâniki's admiration for those who knew *kanun*, and disgust for perversions of established practice, have been cited above. This evidence suggests that interest in "constitutionality" was a relatively widespread phenomenon during the traumatic late sixteenth century, a period of Ottoman history that required adjustment to altered circumstances and saw significant change in administrative practice and individual career patterns. The "Golden Age" of the state was still within living memory, and the past and its ways were idealized in the face of calamitous transformation. It is a curious coincidence, and symbolically appropriate, that the earliest extant manuscript of the *Kanunname* of the Conqueror used by Mehmed Ârif for his edition should have been copied in the same year, 1620/1029, in which the earliest dated manuscript of the *Essence of History* was copied at the mosque of the Conqueror in Istanbul.[18] We shall now study Âli's statements on the nature of the government career paths in his time in order to determine why and how the concept of *kanun* became so important, symbolically and practically, to intellectual bureaucrats in the late sixteenth century.

[18] *Kanunname*, p. 2; KA, MS Fatih 4225.

SEVEN

ÂLİ ON THE OTTOMAN CAREER PATHS

WRITING about the year 1581, Âli opened the second chapter of his *Counsel for Sultans* with a capsule description of its contents. It deals with "the pervasive decline that has appeared in our time, [due to] contravention of customary laws." He elaborates that each functionary covets the position of those above him; judges seek to become district governors, the latter long to become governors-general, and the great governors fight for vezirate.

> If they are not told, "This is not your career path," but rather, "It has been given, therefore it has become your [professional] path," and these officials are deemed suitable for high position in violation of custom [*kanun*], then the strictures of the law become completely null and void. The intrusion of various classes [of official] into the different careers, and the permissiveness and laxity of the vezirs of high standing in [allowing] such developments, have caused total disruption and dispersal of the people. Of necessity the food of the table of state becomes mixed like *aşura* [a sweet of many ingredients], and the sustenance of those who live perfectly becomes vile and confused like (God forbid!) vomit.[1]

Âli's first example of this phenomenon is the increasingly frequent appointment of judges to finance directorships, which they often as not gained through bribery. Many of these judges then proceeded, in the manner prescribed for finance directors, to attain district and provincial governorships. Because of their corruption and lack of professional training in either finance or military administration, Âli says, the results of such appointments were disastrous for the state.[2] Klaus Röhrborn has utilized these passages to show that Âli decried the crossing of rigid career lines as a violation of *kanun*, a complaint that appears to contradict the evidence of the *kanunname* of the Conqueror.[3] Âli's statement, however, viewed in its proper context, is susceptible of a less categorical interpretation.

[1] COUNSEL, I, 66 (trans.), 163 (text).
[2] COUNSEL, I, 66-70 (trans.), 163-69 (text).
[3] Röhrborn, "Emanzipation," pp. 134-36.

Âli does not elaborate on the nature of "classes" and "careers," except by way of negative implication. In this particular passage his specific objections to the entry of judges into other career lines boil down to two. First, judges were famed for corruption and cupidity, accustomed as they were to receiving fees for their services. They were also considered ignorant, for they suffered from the same decline in educational standards which, according to Âli, plagued the *ilmiye* as a whole at this time.[4] Second, Âli faulted judges who left the judicial career for their lack of training in and unprofessional approach to financial and military service. In the passage cited above, Âli caustically describes the demeanor of ambitious judges who have attained military command (*beğlik*) from a finance directorship, or who seek such a promotion. Though they take on military clothing and affect martial behavior, they can neither sit a horse nor cope with military administration. Âli's objections emerge as both emotional and practical; judges are untrustworthy, and the appointment of unqualified and unsuitable personnel to administrative positions is inefficient and harmful.

Âli's complaints about the admission of judges to financial service can also be reconciled with the evidence of the *Kanunname* of the Conqueror. The *Kanunname* states that judges of 300 *akçe* may become finance directors, meaning *defterdar*s below the rank of treasurer.[5] In the *Essence*, Âli comments that Sokollu Mehmed Paşa dominated the government by filling all available posts with his relatives and protégés. Since most of these appointees were in fact able, Âli says, Sokollu might be excused for his nepotism, which did no actual harm. The one negative aspect of this nepotistic practice was that Sokollu appointed a number of small-town judges (*kuzat-ı kasabat*) to finance directorships. This was generally disapproved of because small-town judges were particularly used to surviving on fees, and abused their new power by collecting bribes.[6] Small-town judges had a maximum salary of 150 *akçe*, and were hence considerably lower in rank than the 300- and 500-*akçe* judges (i.e., those of major provincial capitals) whose promotion to finance director the *Kanunname* authorizes.[7] Thus Âli's comments in the *Counsel* cannot be taken as contradicting the *kanunname* or as evidence of its being a late sixteenth-century invention.

In a sense this evidence is negative, for while it establishes certain parameters to Âli's complaints, it does not tell what his objections really were or what they were based on. Nor does it make clear how frequently judges became finance directors and then perhaps *sancak beği*s; Âli says only that

[4] For an example of this prejudicial view of the judicial establishment, see COUNSEL, I, 77-79 (trans.), 177-80 (text).

[5] *Kanunname*, pp. 16-17.

[6] KA, Selim/Vüzera, Nur 3409, 251b.

[7] İnalcık, *Empire*, pp. 170-71.

some ten finance directors had attained their positions from judicial posts, and gives but one specific example in the *Counsel*.[8] In the *Conditions of Cairo* Âli mentions two *sancak beği*s of Egypt, notorious libertines and incompetents, who had formerly served as judges.[9] Since Âli repeated this complaint for nearly twenty years, between his writing of the *Counsel* and *Cairo*, it is likely that there is some substance to his assertions. Statistical corroboration for such a development is extremely difficult to gather; extant Ottoman biographical literature on administrative personnel does not normally record the careers of functionaries below the rank of governor-general, treasurer, chancellor, or secretary-in-chief. Nevertheless, when Âli cites the Cairene judges-turned-*beğ* as examples of the disorder and decline overtaking the Empire, he also gives an important clue to the cause of his unhappiness. Egypt was a *salyane* province in which the *timar* system as such was not applied; many of those who held *sancak beği* rank in Egypt were actually garrison commanders (*muhafaza beğleri*) of the Cairo citadel. Egypt was a very important province, and its *beğ*s and *beğlerbeği*s had a very different status from officials of the same title serving elsewhere in the Empire. Âli says of the post of garrison commander of Cairo:

> [In former times it] used to be given to men of long service, to members of the corps of Royal Tasters who had done long service as janissary commanders in Egypt, or to those who, as scribes of the Imperial Council, had distinguished themselves as finance directors of Aleppo and Damascus and Diyar Bakr. It was even deemed appropriate for those high-ranking ones who served long in the Palace as chancellors . . . or finance directors in the Imperial Council. Since it was regarded as equivalent to the retirement pay given to the great vezirs, it was granted only to those who in all respects merited such reward. It was not deemed appropriate for judges who had made their way with registration and certification fees. . . . As judgeship was an assignment to be made by the military judges, such parasites were not allowed to become military officers. Today, however, that blessed [professional] system has been destroyed.[10]

The most significant points that emerge from this passage are the following. First, Âli objected to the granting of positions traditionally reserved for the select, those who had distinguished themselves in Palace service, to those who fell short of his criteria. Second, he did not see the assignment of bureaucratic personnel to military positions as abnormal, which is hardly surprising in light of his own experience. Third, Âli did object strenuously to

[8] COUNSEL, I, 66-69 (trans.), 163-67 (text).
[9] CAIRO, p. 60 (trans.), 143-44 (text).
[10] CAIRO, pp. 57-58 (trans.), pp. 138-39 (text).

the granting of military posts to people identified as belonging to the *ilmiye*, although he does not, and probably could not, specify how long a former judge had to serve as a finance director in order to qualify for promotion to a military post. Âli's old friend Üveys Paşa, for example, began his career as a judge, but had so long and distinguished a career in financial service that no complaints appear to have been voiced about his elevation to governor-generalship and vezirate. Âli's complaint in the *Conditions of Cairo* passage echoes his earlier one: professional ulema were neither qualified for nor inclined to military service. As we have seen, the *Kanunname* of the Conqueror also incorporated a mechanism that militated against the promotion to *sancak* or *vilayet* posts of members of the *ilmiye* who were still identified as such, i.e., appointees to the chancellorship who came from outside the established apparatus of the central government. The prejudice voiced by Âli had an institutional counterpart, the ramifications of which we shall explore later.

Âli's unhappiness with the system of his time sprang less from a concern for maintaining the integrity of career lines per se than from disgust with a decline in the quality of administrative personnel. A section of the *Tables of Delicacies* in which Âli discusses the scribal bureaucratic career line illuminates the nature of his concerns, and may be summarized as follows.[11] In recent times, ignorant people with no concept of literature or literary style have become bureaucrats (*ehl-i kalem*). In particular, the bureaucracy has been invaded by lowly products of the Palace slave system (*içerüden çıkma süfeha*) who are not trained for such duties and who band together with other unqualified people (*na-mahall*) to pack the ranks of the bureaucracy. Within the scribal class, groups are to some extent differentiated by title; professional bureaucrats (largely of freeborn Muslim origin) are called *efendi*, while those of Palace slave origin (*köle kısmı*) are called *beğ*, presumably because of their military training and status.[12] In the old days the bureaucratic system was under the control of the chancellor and secretary-in-chief, who gathered *ilmiye* trainees and candidates and appointed scribes from among the judges and professors. From this group of ulema-turned-bureaucrats came the most competent and notable chancery chiefs of the century, such as Celalzade, Ramazanzade, and Egri Abdizade. In those times (i.e., the reigns of Bayezid II, Selim I, and Süleyman), the chancellorship was a post of the highest importance, since the holder of the office was "*müfti* of

[11] MEVA'İD, pp. 33-37.

[12] For independent confirmation of this distinction between officials of slave-military origin and freeborn Muslims, see SELANİKİ, *sub anno* 1006 (cited Röhrborn, "Emanzipation," p. 127). According to this entry, *kalemiye* figures who were given the honorific rank of *beğlerbeği* were usually called *efendi* rather than *paşa*, the latter designation being reserved for those who actually performed military-administrative service.

kanun.'' Therefore, if no suitable candidates for the position were found within the ranks of the bureaucratic service itself, a chancellor would be chosen from the teachers of the Outer, Inner, or *Sahn medrese*s. These were selected on the basis of their learning and ability. By contrast, in recent times, and especially since the reign of Murad III, unqualified folk of ''slave'' origin have entered the bureaucracy as scribes, and have then proceeded through the hierarchy to become secretary-in-chief and chancellor, despite their fundamental ignorance of the requisite skills. In comparison to the well-educated chancery figures of earlier times, Âli declares in the *Essence*, contemporary chancellors are mere artisans (*ehl-i hiref*), uneducated folk who have mechanically learned a trade, and are corrupt as well. Of the reign of Bayezid II, who before appointing Tac Beğ as chancellor preferred to leave the post empty rather than fill it with one who was unqualified, Âli writes:

> What a beautiful age was that fine era,
> [For] the clean and the dirty were clear to people.
> Now we have come to a time
> When neither the incapable nor the noble is distinct.
> No one rewards the people of dignity;
> Rather, they are mocked and betrayed.[13]

A number of significant points emerge from these passages. Âli's discussions of suitability for promotion show that the customary practice governing professional advancement was a more complex phenomenon than has been supposed. Âli did not view the entry of *ilmiye*-trained people into the central government in itself as harmful; on the contrary, the bureaucratic class should ideally recruit its most prominent representatives from the ulema, who were especially well qualified by virtue of their literary and legal training. Âli does, however, appear to object strongly to the intrusion of Palace slaves into the bureaucracy. Who these people were is obscure; Âli probably means here slaves who left the Palace at a relatively low level, before receiving advanced training. In the *Conditions of Cairo* Âli cites one example of a notoriously ignorant chancery official in Egypt who had become a scribe after leaving the Inner Palace. This reference occurs in the context of a diatribe on the poor quality of the staff of the Egyptian chancery, of whom Âli says:

> Among the secretaries of the Council of Egypt there are few whose literacy is sound. Truly, they exemplify the proverb ''every scribe is ignorant.'' At the time of writing [1599], within the chancery building filled with clerks there are but three or four well-educated ones able to

[13] KA, Bayezid II/Nişancılar, Introduction, Fatih 4225, 183b.

comprehend the opening lines of a register. They are obviously very few.[14]

Here again, Âli's complaints are based on professional and educational concerns, on a sense of standards, rather than on an insistence upon maintaining career-track distinctions. It is of course also possible that Âli felt Palace products, by virtue of their connections, to have an unfair advantage over freeborn Muslims, just as judges were better able to raise the money to buy administrative posts than were honest bureaucrats. Although Âli decries the elevation of judges to financial directorship and thence to military command, he nowhere voices opposition to the promotion of finance directors of the Porte or chancellors to provincial governorships, which the *Kanunname* states to be a legitimate professional path. Such a complaint might be expected if Âli were voicing a blanket condemnation of the crossing of career lines. In light of his positive evaluation of certain bureaucratic figures, some of them of *ilmiye* background, who eventually became district governors, governors-general, or even vezirs (Feridun Ahmed, Egri Abdizade, Üveys Paşa. and Piri Paşa, grand vezir to Selim I), and of his own requests for military appointment, it may be safely assumed that Âli accepted career-line permeability at the upper levels of government as legal practice sanctioned by tradition. In the *Counsel* Âli states this explicitly, making the point that the ultimate criterion for promotion is ability, and that in the case of exceptional individuals the customary norm is not prescriptive:

> Let no one object to the selection of the learned and employment of wise men [for government service] saying, "This is not the old custom [*kanun-ı kadim*]." Among those of equal seniority in different career paths let the well-known principle be applied that their trading capital is the coin of intelligence, and that the capital of [beneficial] plans and hopes is the jewel of a penetrating mind. The words of the uncaused Creator, "Are those who know the equal of those who do not?" are scriptural proof of the complete superiority of the learned [*ulema*] and of the precedence of the wise, which must be respected.[15]

Âli then cites with approbation the example of Piri Paşa, a judge whom Selim I appointed treasurer, then vezir, and finally grand vezir. Of course, high-level bureaucrats had an advantage in this situation, at least in Âli's *ilmiye*-oriented view. It was more likely that a chancellor or treasurer of *ilmiye* background could acquire the administrative skills required to rule a province than that a *devşirme* recruit at a lower level, trained for essentially

[14] CAIRO, p. 64 (trans.), p. 148 (text).
[15] COUNSEL, I, 50 (trans.), 140 (text).

military service, could gain the literary and bureaucratic knowledge demanded by the scribal career.

Distinctions were of course made between Ottoman officials which were based on the career they followed, their heredity, education, and status as slaves or free men; the difference in titles applied to slave and freeborn scribes shows this clearly. Elsewhere in the *Counsel*, Âli inveighs against the crossing of career lines, and stresses that the example of Piri Paşa should not be used as a justification for such practice.[16] We must ask what the truth of the situation was. Was Âli merely contradicting himself in an access of spleen and frustration over his own lack of success, or were the distinctions expressed in terms of integral career lines real ones? If they were real, were they theoretically categorical or actually part of a larger and more complex system determining status, rank, and function, which actually accommodated promotions that *appear* anomalous in light of the theory that the Ottoman career tracks were mutually exclusive? Fortunately Âli himself answers these questions fairly succinctly in a section of the *Conditions of Cairo*:

> The reason for the breakdown in the order of the Egyptian army is that all career paths have been subverted by those who do not belong in them [*ecnebiler*]; and the cause of the disordered state of the province is that its great officers, even its finance director and garrison commanders, are unsuitable people [*na-mahaller*] who have yet, each in his own way, infiltrated those positions. In earlier times, appointment as finance director of Egypt was given to those who were either bookkeepers for the Imperial Council, or accountants in the capital of the same rank, or other officials of the same standing.[17]

Âli goes on to state that garrison commanderships (*muhafaza beğliği*) used not to be given, as they were in his time, to judges, financial trustees (*emin*), tax farmers, and *mıklacı*s (people who do not serve one of the great statesmen) nor to

> those wretches who, going door to door, have become pensioners of the *beğ*s and governors-general. . . . Now, however, that blessed order has been ruined. At this time, of the thirty or forty noted *sancak beği*s and janissary commanders found in the Council of Egypt, there are few who have come out from the royal Palace or, if they came from outside [the Palace], had served the high officers of state and attained the rank of *beğ* through merit. In any case, there are none who have advanced by distinguishing themselves with the sword or cultivating that learn-

[16] COUNSEL, I, 67 (trans.), 165 (text).

[17] CAIRO, p. 57 (trans.), pp. 138-39 (text).

ing and wisdom which elevates the personality. But there are many "foreigners" [*ecnebiler*] and incapable upstarts and wealthy men, who, having become salaried retainers to the *paşa*s and *beğ*s of Yemen and Egypt and Syria, have in some fashion gained a military appointment and stipend [*dirlük*].

[This is harmful] because the foundation of the edifice of the Ottoman state, and the basis for the pillars of kingdom and sovereignty, are those military administrators who have come forth from the noble Palace and have reached the rank of governor. The fact that they have been trained in the elevated Inner Services makes it appropriate to liken them to the unseen, hidden foundation. In the same manner, one may compare those who have become military administrators [*rütbe-i emarete yetişenler*] through service to the great men of state to the walls of the building. Therefore, those other than the products of the noble Palace or the men trained in the service of high statesmen, who have somehow come from outside and attained *timar*-grants or appointments, are similar to the scaffolding, the shingles, and the tiles of the structure, that is, to some of its superficial, extraneous elements. In other words, whether in the eyes of the sovereign or the regard of the famous vezirs, these are not accounted to be basic to the structure; because they are a kind of gift, they are not considered to be either of the foundation or of the four walls of the building. For this reason, they are unable to cope with [lit., digest] wealth and station; being ravenous wretches, they do not understand the wrongness of gorging on the repast of bribes.[18]

These passages are very rich for our purposes. They clarify the career path question in that they demonstrate that Âli, the self-designated expert on *kanun*, considered appointment to high military-administrative rank (*beğlik*) equally appropriate for Men of the Sword and Men of the Pen, provided these attained sufficiently advanced standing within either the Palace service or the central administration. The determining factor in such appointments was not career so much as seniority and status in terms of the horizontal ranking system that cut across the established professional paths. Âli's statements give form and substance to the concept of a "Palace" identity, rather than "slave" identity, as the primary factor determining the composition and career expectations of the Ottoman governing class in the sixteenth century. Âli lists two classes of servitors as worthy of promotion to high office: products of the Harem system; and those who, while not slaves themselves, were associated with the Palace and with high-ranking Palace "graduates" in any of several ways. In discussing the *sancak beği*s

[18] CAIRO, pp. 57-58 (trans.), pp. 139-40 (text).

of Egypt, Âli cites four examples of officials of the second category of whom he approved.[19] One was a professional financial officer who had begun his professional life in service to a high statesman and had reached the top of the financial career; the other three were the children of prominent Ottomans (only one of them a slave) who had a history of service to the Ottoman house. What these four figures had in common was service at high levels, meaning the Palace or Imperial Council, or association with those who so served, and a high level of education of the broad humanistic variety provided by the Palace and, analogously, by the household establishments of the great. Education and full literacy, whether in the *medrese* or the Palace fashion, were Âli's *sine qua non*s for admission to the Ottoman class.

Slave status and blood connections were not the only means of entry into the "Palace" class of true Ottomans, those whose identity was centered on the Palace system, though not necessarily of it. What Âli means by "those who have become military administrators through service to the great men of state" is *intisab*. *İntisab* was something more formal than establishment of connections; it implied incorporation into the household of a statesman (*paşa kapısı*) and, in terms of loyalty and identification, had many of the overtones and obligations, as well as the benefits, of a family relationship. Hence, Âli decries those who make their way by changing their allegiance from *beğ* to *beğ* and *paşa* to *paşa* in the interests of self-advancement. The loyalties and familial bonds implied by household service could be extended, as the interlocking of the household establishment of the sovereign with those of his primary supporters shows; the paşa's servitor was indirectly the sultan's, and could attain a more direct relationship by being given a formal government appointment. The practical utility of this "networking" household system is illustrated by the career of Âli, who, with his appointment as *timar* registrar of Aleppo, made the jump from "the *paşa*'s gate" to the central financial service.

The nature of this, Âli's first central administrative appointment, is instructive. A relatively low post, the registry of *timar*s carried with it military duties, and so represents a low-level convergence of military and bureaucratic careers. It was also equally accessible to people who had served in the Outer Services of the Palace, and to provincial officers of at least *za'im* status. Metin Kunt, in a study of sixteenth and seventeenth-century Ottoman provincial administrative personnel, has demonstrated that within the military career, identification with the central administration, based on professional and family background, was a significant determinant of promotion prospects.[20] The highest levels of provincial administration, in the sixteenth

[19] CAIRO, p. 59 (trans.), pp. 141-42 (text).

[20] Kunt, *Servants*, pp. 57-58, and *Sancak*, pp. 65-71.

century, appear to have been largely reserved for those identified with the Palace; it was much more difficult for those who began their careers at low levels of the provincial system (i.e., *timar* and *zeâmet* holders), and were hence identified as provincial rather than central personnel, to attain such posts, than for those who had a higher-level or longer-standing association with the Palace or the Imperial Council.[21] There was an effective limit on how high those identified as "outside" could rise within the system, and they largely remained in the provinces unless they could somehow attain a post, like the *timar* registry of a province, which was identified as part of the central administrative apparatus. Only in border provinces of the Empire could men of local military origin rise as high as district governor. This was because the frontier provinces were sensitive regions in which local expertise, experience, and influence counted for much.[22] For the same reasons, however, such officials tended to remain in their home territories.

Kunt's distinction between "central" and "provincial" personnel illustrates one facet of our "Palace" category, which comprehends high-level bureaucrats and religious functionaries as well as military administrators. Many of Âli's complaints about disruption of the Ottoman professional stem from his perception of a breakdown of the rules of the patrimonial household system; he saw a blurring of the lines between central and provincial personnel, between those of the Palace system and those "foreigners" who did not belong to it. Specifically, he objected to a trend toward allowing those who began their careers in the provinces, and particularly in the border provinces where the niceties of protocol and *kanun* counted for far less than coercive power and influence, to obtain positions traditionally reserved for Palace people. This could happen in many ways; contract appointment, the need to garrison frontier forts, bribery, and local connections all played a part in this process, and Âli rails against it constantly.[23] The case of the Kurdish *sancak beği* Sührab, who took Âli's post of finance director of Baghdad, illustrates how a provincial official could take advantage of circumstances to gain Palace standing and so enhance his future prospects, in this case by "purchasing" appointment as pursuivant of the Porte.[24] A similar phenomenon occurred at even lower levels of provincial service. Âli cites examples of provincial "outsiders" who were able to enter the military class, in both scribal and military careers, by parlaying one position into another. The fact that many of these took service with the military commanders of border provinces, and moved from one household to another, seems to have violated Âli's definition of a true *intisab* relationship

[21] Kunt, *Servants*, pp. 57-75.

[22] Kunt, *Servants*, pp. 63-65.

[23] For examples, see COUNSEL, I, 68-71 (trans.), 165-69 (text); CAIRO, pp. 59-63 (trans.), pp. 142-48 (text).

[24] See above, p. 119.

with one of the great men of state. Such upstarts were precluded from "Palace" status, both because of their lack of education or qualification, and because their origins and mode of advancement did not display the loyalty and achievement expected of true members of a household network.

Âli's premise is that merit and service were the primary criteria determining an individual's qualification for appointment to high office, and that there were definite, if complex, approved modes, collectively known as *kanun*, for demonstrating accomplishment and loyalty. Âli saw Ottoman "decline" in the late sixteenth century largely as a breakdown of the established standards whereby personnel decisions were made, but not solely as a function of confusion of career lines. The perception that this was the case is a product of the peculiar nature of *kanun*, and of the tremendous numerical growth, even congestion, of the Ottoman government careers in the sixteenth century.

We must now return briefly to the question of *kanun* as legislation, in the form of the *Kanunname*, and *kanun* as practice. To a great extent legislation grew out of practice. Formally promulgated *kanun* could reflect either common or occasional practice, and prescribe it in general terms without necessarily restricting it. *Kanun* could also legislate modifications of practice so as to bring it into line with religious and practical ideals. Finally, it could legitimize exceptional practice. The *Kanunname* of the Conqueror, even if it was partially codified under one of his two or three immediate successors, may indeed have declared high-ranking judges eligible for a finance directorship of the Porte or a governor-generalship. This does not mean, however, that such appointments were made as a rule. Rather, only exceptionally well-qualified individuals, if any, received such promotions. Merit, experience, efficiency, and loyalty were the guiding principles behind the institutes governing Ottoman rules of promotion and advancement. Actual practice, particularly as the Empire expanded and centralized, necessitated greater emphasis on specialized professional competence.

At the beginning of the sixteenth century practical exigencies militated against the appointment of judges, for example, to *sancak*s. The pool of experienced and qualified administrators, and the pool of available provincial posts, were considerably smaller through the first quarter of the century than thereafter, when Süleyman embarked on a program of conquest and administrative consolidation. Until the middle of the sixteenth century, for example, there were only three finance directorships in the entire Empire (Rumeli, Anadolu, Arab ve Acem), as opposed to four central ones and a shifting number of perhaps fifteen or twenty provincial treasuries by the early seventeenth century.[25] Consequently, during the early part of the sixteenth century, assignments had to be made with great care, since individual

[25] Uzunçarşılı, *Merkez*, pp. 328-31; Matuz, *Kanzleiwesen*, p. 58, and Appendix A, below.

responsibility was greater and the candidates, before the bureaucracy fully developed, were fewer. Thereafter, imperial manpower needs increased tremendously, a development that doubtless encouraged changes of career; Âli was only one of many who abandoned the mosque for the bureau. At the same time, the need to regularize Empirewide administrative practice and to cope with growing financial problems led not only to the growth of central government, but also to the formation of an increasingly professionalized bureaucratic establishment, within which the financial service was especially important. Certainly, the expanded Ottoman government of the late sixteenth century was more heavily bureaucratized, and in this sense perhaps less selective of individuals, than the "nuclear" one of the early sixteenth century. *Kanun*, whether as general legislation or usage based on precedent, could not keep up with the rapid expansion of government or comprehend quickly the development of a new professional path. In speaking of violations of Ottoman law in the appointment practices of the late 1500's, Âli and other intellectuals who endowed *kanun* with high symbolic value were to some extent applying the standards of the early sixteenth century to an institutional structure in the midst of tremendous change.

To summarize: Within the *askeri* class as a whole during the sixteenth century, the primary operative distinction between career lines was a vertical one between the military and religious paths. Horizontally, the *askeri* class was broadly, if somewhat nebulously, divided into Palace and non-Palace sectors. Palace status was conferred by an amalgam of factors that could vary from individual to individual: family background, education, patronage, and high rank within any one of the three career lines. The lateral ranking system to which the *Kanunname* of the Conqueror gives expression served to establish equivalencies of rank for senior Men of the Sword, the Pen, and Learning, and to introduce refinements into the promotion process that gave recognition to differences in family and professional background. Honorific titles and wage increments given for merit also helped to define the relative status of officials, even within a single career line. This is not to say that professional distinctions were not made between functionaries at even the most elevated levels of government, for they certainly were; the question is how normative these distinctions were held to be, given that the number of high-level administrators was really very small. Within this system the position of the bureaucracy, the initially undifferentiated chancery and financial organization of the Men of the Pen, was a curious one; it fell somewhere between the Sword and Learning, and shared certain characteristics (administrative responsibilities and literacy, respectively) with both. In terms of promotion potential, high-ranking bureaucratic officials had access to positions that were traditionally considered the preserve, from one perspective, of military administrative specialists, and that of Palace servitors from another viewpoint. Âli's statements suggest that in this respect some bureaucrats were considered to be in the same category as ranking Men of the Sword; indeed, provincial financial officers often served in the military. *İlmiye* figures, on the other hand, only had access to military administrative posts (except, in theory only, for the most exalted judges) through an intervening bureaucratic career. Furthermore, within the bureaucracy as a whole, financial specialists had the advantage over purely chancery functionaries; in general terms, finance directors had a higher military rank than chancellors (who might not achieve even honorific *beğ* rank), and therefore in theory as well as statistical fact approximated more closely to Men of the Sword. Some of the seeming anomalies presented (when viewed from a presumed ideal of career-line purity) by the careers of sixteenth-century bureaucrats, the blurring of career lines of which such commentators as Âli complain, and the transitional character of the bureaucratic career between the Sword and Learning, were direct products of the birth and rapid development in the sixteenth century of a professional bureaucracy that did not exist in the time of the Conqueror. The emergence of an independent bureaucratic career track had immediate effects upon the professional expectations of members of the *askeri* class, and played a significant role in the growth of *kanun* consciousness.

EIGHT

BUREAUCRACY AND BUREAUCRATIC CONSCIOUSNESS

THE GROWTH OF THE BUREAUCRATIC CAREER

IN THE TIME of Sultan Süleyman Kanuni (The Lawgiver), the central bureaucracy of the Ottoman Empire had none of the institutional complexity it developed in the seventeenth century. Rather, it was a loose structure dominated by the personal offices of its two premier officeholders: the chancellor, who oversaw chancery affairs, and the treasurer, who managed the Empire's finances.[1] The secretary-in-chief assisted the chancellor in his chancery duties and in the meetings of the Imperial Council, but was of much lower rank than his superior. These three officials, together with the Council secretary (*tezkereci*) and registrar (*defter emini*), were the most important bureaucratic officials of the Empire, insofar as they all served on the Imperial Council. Only the chancellor and treasurer were full members of the Council with a voice in deliberations; the others served in purely functionary capacities.[2] A prosopographic analysis of the holders of these major bureaucratic offices in the fifteenth and sixteenth centuries, from the reign of the Conqueror until the death of Murad III in 1595, affords significant insights into the history of the birth and growth of the Ottoman bureaucratic institution, and also provides important clues to the meaning of the *Kanunname* of the Conqueror.[3] In order to understand Mustafa Âli's perception of professional life and *kanun* practice in his own time, it is necessary to study the institution within which he spent most of his career, and the historical

[1] Matuz, *Kanzleiwesen*, pp. 18-22.

[2] Matuz, *Kanzleiwesen*, pp. 33-41, 45-47. The *tezkereci* appears to have been yet another subordinate of the chancellor. I disagree with Matuz's interpretation of Âli's statement in MEVA'İD, pp. 32-37. Matuz states that by the end of the sixteenth century the office of *re'isülküttab* had gained considerable importance vis-à-vis the mid-sixteenth century, and then accuses Âli of anachronism: "When the historian Âli, perhaps speaking of his own time, asserts that the office of *re'isülküttab* is not highly valued, this judgment can without doubt be seen to stem from the time of Süleyman" (pp. 37-38). In fact, Âli makes the opposite point: both the *nişancılık* and *riyaset* are high posts, the value of which has been degraded through the practice of appointing ignorant and unworthy people to them.

[3] The prosopographical analysis summarized here is detailed in my "Âli," pp. 410-23. This material forms part of a forthcoming monograph on the rise of the Ottoman bureaucracy and the consolidation of dynastic law in the sixteenth century.

perspective within which he viewed it. The purpose of this brief exposition is to outline the manner in which the Ottoman bureaucracy, comprising both chancery and financial services, was born out of the ranks of *medrese*-trained scholars, consolidated into a relatively discrete professional body, and further divided into chancery and financial specializations in the mid-late sixteenth century. By examining over time the professional backgrounds and career patterns of the chiefs of the bureaucracy, we can gain an idea of the evolution of bureaucratic ideals and of the extent to which internal recruitment, supported by a professionalized training system and bureaucratized organization, came to be favored.

We may begin with a general observation on the period, in a sense a caveat, suggested by the preceding analysis of the Ottoman career problem. To what extent were career tracks considered to be distinct from one another at the elevated levels at which they intertwined, and how important was the ranking of Council functionaries prescribed in the *Kanunname* in determining the specific career expectations of individuals? When did rank and status within a career path become a more significant determinant of promotion than individual merit and function? The *Kanunname* of the Conqueror cites as a possible career path transfer from a finance directorship of the Porte, including the post of treasurer (*Rumeli defterdarı*), to the chancellorship. It also makes clear that a finance director has precedence over a chancellor in Council protocol, and by the late sixteenth century no treasurers became chancellors. This entry in the *Kanunname*, which does not prescribe demotions, takes on the air of an anomaly. The law actually reflects occasional practice of the late fifteenth and early sixteenth centuries, and precedents which were only rarely repeated later, but which are also instructive. During the reigns of Mehmed II and Bayezid II, two ranking bureaucrats, Fenarizade Ahmed Çelebi and Feylesufzade Ahmed Çelebi, were appointed chancellor after serving as treasurer. Two more important chancery officials of Bayezid and his son Selim I, Cezerizade Safi Çelebi and Hocazade Mehmed Çelebi, became chancellor, then treasurer, and again chancellor. In the reign of Süleyman, Egri Abdizade was successively appointed finance director of the East (*Arab ve Acem*), director of the second branch, chancellor, treasurer, again chancellor, and finally *sancak beği*, while Ramazanzade served as chancellor, finance director of the east, *sancak beği* of Egypt, and again chancellor.[4]

[4] Danişmend, *Kronoloji*, V, 242-43, 246-48, 314-18, 322-26; Matuz, *Kanzleiwesen*, pp. 31-33 (corrected by Âli, KA, Süleyman/Defterdaran, "Ramazanzade," Nur 3409, 135a-b; Ramazanzade did not serve as governor-general of Egypt). Matuz discounts the statement of Danişmend (followed by Röhrborn, "Emanzipation") that Ramazanzade served as treasurer before becoming chancellor. Note, too, that according to MD 2, docs. 1590-91, Celalzade retired from the chancellorship as a *müteferrika*, with a retirement pension provided by *timar*s and the *kâğıd emini*, on 21 Zulhicce 963/26 October 1556. He was succeeded immediately by

It can hardly be the case that such individuals suffered demotion late in their careers. The conclusion to be drawn is that such transfers, whatever the guidelines provided or implied by the *Kanunname*, could be and were made on the basis of individual merit and imperial need. *Kanun* could pronounce on exceptional situations for which there was precedent, and ignore, while allowing, those for which there was none. These few examples are sufficient to indicate that through the first half of the sixteenth century, at the top of the bureaucratic career the position was not as important as the individual who filled it. For exceptional individuals, questions of the relative rank a given post conferred meant less than imperial recognition and need, and the niceties of Divan protocol or theoretical distinctions between career specializations had little actual effect upon the real world of administration. It may be countered that the examples cited above are atypical. This is true, but the importance of the chief chancery and financial officers in the Empire was such that appointees were chosen because they were atypical. Only in the latter part of the sixteenth century, when a professionalized bureaucracy had been established, did career specialization and adherence to a prescribed professional path come to play a dominant role in the promotion process. This was a development, like the increasing incidence of appointment of financial officers to military positions, for which *kanun* allowed but, because of its general nature, did not specifically provide.

The accessible history of the Ottoman bureaucratic establishment begins with the age of the Conqueror and his legislation; although at least two citations confirm that a treasurer and chancellor were active at the Ottoman court in the twelve years preceding the conquest of Constantinople, we know nothing more about these offices or who filled them before 1453.[5] Certainly, the archival record shows that tax censuses were taken, records were kept, and official correspondence was composed in the preconquest era. But study of the major bureaucrats of the reigns of Fatih Mehmed, Bayezid II, and Selim I shows that between 1453 and 1520 the Ottoman bureaucracy was rudimentary and its branches were relatively undifferentiated.[6] Even later the chancellor, for example, had certain supervisory concerns with financial matters insofar as he was the theoretical superior of the imperial registrar (*defter emini*).[7] More importantly, the two officials whose

the *şıkk-ı sani defterdarı* (Egri Abdizade) Mehmed Çelebi who was assigned a living (*dirlük*) of 200,000 *akçe*.

[5] Halil İnalcık has noted the presence of Chancellor (*Nişancı*) İbrahim Paşa in 1444 (*Fatih Devri Üzerinde Tetkikler*, I [Ankara, 1954], p. 87), and a document referring to a "treasurer" (*defterdar*) named Murad b. Yahya Beğ in 1444 has been published by Klaus Schwarz, "Eine Herrscherurkunde Sultan Murâd II für den Wesir Fazlullâh," *Journal of Turkish Studies* 5 (1981): 53.

[6] For sources see note 3 above.

[7] Matuz, *Kanzleiwesen*, p. 24.

personal offices constituted such bureaucracy as the state possessed were almost invariably drawn directly from the professionally undifferentiated pool of religious scholars and teachers. Most of the chancellors were appointed to the post directly from the *medrese*. The frequency of instances of individuals' shifting back and forth between the posts of treasurer and chancellor indicates that this was possible (a) because personal and educational qualifications for either position were essentially the same; (b) both the need for bureaucratic functionaries and the pool of suitable candidates for such positions were small; and (c) the bureaucratic career line, which later divided so sharply into scribal and financial branches, was as yet a single line within which little distinction was made between chancery and financial functions. We may now begin to answer the question posed above: When did function become more important than status? The answer for this early period is that very probably function defined status or was more significant. Little distinction of rank seems to have been made between chancellors and treasurers. They were nearly all, after all, ulema. Indeed, the Path of the Pen did not yet constitute a real career, being little more than a small number of learned men "seconded" to the Imperial Council.[8] Although it is possible, or even likely, that such distinctions in rank as that between the chancellor and the treasurer were legislated in the Conqueror's time, it is doubtful that they were rigidly observed, given the small pool of candidates and the small, or undifferentiated, number of scribal and bureaucratic functions involved.

Süleyman's reign brought changes to this fluid structure. To be sure, several individuals did shift back and forth between chancery and financial service, although only one served as both chancellor and treasurer. The order of appointments in individual cases, particularly to financial posts, suggests that the later hierarchy of bureaucratic assignments to which Âli paid such attention had not yet solidified (*vide* the careers of Ramazanzade and Egri Abdizade). Even so, a definite professionalization of both bureaucratic services is evident. Although the chancellors retained their familial and educational ties to the *ilmiye*, they also had to undergo scribal training and

[8] An early example of this phenomenon is Tursun Beğ, a member of a high-ranking military family who also wrote a history of the reign of Mehmed the Conqueror. Under the Conqueror Tursun, who had held a *timar* but had also received a *medrese* education, served as secretary of the Imperial Council, finance director and then registrar of the *timar*s and *zeâmet*s of Anatolia, and finally treasurer (see Tursun Bey, *Târıh-i Ebü'l-Feth*, ed. Mertol Tulum [Istanbul, 1977], pp. xvii-xviii, 6-8; and Tursun Beg, *The History of Mehmed the Conqueror*, ed. and trans. Halil İnalcık and Rhoads Murphey [Minneapolis and Chicago, 1978], pp. 11-13). Tursun Beğ does not occur in the standard lists of the treasurers of this period, and to be sure he never became chancellor; but the number and variety of "bureaucratic" positions he says himself to have held reinforces our conclusion that the number of such posts was small, that qualified applicants were few, and that the sultans utilized the expertise at hand during this early period.

work their way to the office through the office of secretary-in-chief, which appears to have been established early in the reign of Süleyman in order to provide the chancellor with assistance.[9] From this point in time onward, only one outside appointment (i.e., from the *medrese*) to the chancellorship occurred, that of Mu'allimzade Mahmud Efendi, who served for only one year under Murad III. A key figure in this process of bureaucratic consolidation was Mustafa Celalzade, who served as chancellor from 1534 until 1556. Celalzade established the document forms and diplomatic formulae used for the remainder of the sixteenth century. He also played a leading role in the codification and standardization of *kanun*, the project that won for Sultan Süleyman the sobriquet "Lawgiver."[10] It was the *medrese*-trained Celalzade, working in concert with the chief jurisconsult Ebüssu'ud, who not only helped to legitimize the *kanun* principle and rationalize its specifics with the demands of the Holy Law, but also established the position of the chancellor as the preeminent *kanun* authority, secular counterpart to the *şeyhülislam*. The legitimation of dynastic law, which the bureaucracy administered and lived by, was a central element in the consolidation of both state and bureaucracy.

This trend to regularization of bureaucratic procedures is even more striking in the case of the treasurers of Süleyman's time. A relatively small proportion of these (four of fifteen) had *ilmiye* connections, and those who did also had extensive bureaucratic experience. The remainder of the appointees seem to have been internal products of the financial service with no other claim to distinction, i.e., *ilmiye* training or family.

Finally, Süleyman's time saw the beginnings of specialization within the bureaucratic establishment in the form of a split into financial and bureaucratic lines, with decreasing crossover between the two at the upper levels. Early in Süleyman's reign the Imperial Secretarial Corps (*cema'at-i kâtiban-ı divan*), which dealt with all bureaucratic matters, was divided into two groups attached to the chancellor and treasurer, respectively. Even so, the body was apparently a rather small one, comprising a total of eighteen to twenty-five salaried scribes, in addition to such assistants as the chief bureaucrats may have had in their personal retinues.[11] Âli relates an anecdote

[9] İnalcık, "Reis-ül-küttab," İA; Matuz, *Kanzleiwesen*, pp. 34-38.

[10] KA, Süleyman/Defterdaran, "Celalzade," Nur 3409, 135a; Matuz (p. 31) cites this same information via PEÇEVİ.

[11] Matuz, *Kanzleiwesen*, pp. 48-49. Matuz here relies upon the salary list (TKS Arşivi D. 3442) published by Ömer Lutfi Barkan, "H. 933-934 (M. 1527-1528) Mali Yılına ait bir Bütçe Örneği," İÜİFM 15 (1953-54): 251-329. It is worthwhile to note here that there exist several such lists of salaried functionaries and stipendiaries who received monthly payments (*müşâhere-horan*) for the reign of Süleyman, in addition to those published by Barkan (see also Ö. L. Barkan, "954-955 (1547-1548) Mali Yılına ait bir Osmanlı Bütçesi," İÜİFM 19 [1957-58]: 219-76); Maliyeden Müdevver 559 (1536-37/942-43) and Maliyeden Müdevver 7118 (1548-49/955-56). These salary lists can only be used with some caution for purposes of determining

that suggests how restricted the bureaucratic circle was in Süleyman's time. When Celalzade's ink-keeper (*devatdar*), Nevbaharzade, was suddenly appointed to the newly created finance directorship of the second branch, he refused to take precedence in Council seating over his former master. The sultan therefore abrogated the established *kanun* that gave preferred status to finance directors, and replaced it with a rule of precedence by seniority.[12] This story reveals that below the highest administrative levels the two bureaucratic services were still connected by common personnel and training requirements; candidates for both were drawn from the same pool. Although preference for *ilmiye* candidates, indicated by higher pay and status, was operative throughout the bureaucratic service, the financial line began earlier to emphasize professional training and establish itself as a career track independent of its *ilmiye* background. The chancery branch, by contrast, was more conservative in that it clung to the *medrese* and its broad educational ideals, at least in the person of the chancellor.[13]

After the death of Süleyman these tendencies became yet more marked. In only one case did a financial figure become chancellor; and even the chancellorship was affected by the trend to professionalism, in that for the first (verifiable) time two scribal functionaries with no *ilmiye* connections were appointed to that office directly from the post of secretary-in-chief. This office appears to have become the watershed for professional bureau-

---

empirically the size of the Ottoman bureaucratic establishment, for they name only those paid in cash by the Porte. Many secretaries and clerks, however, were given *timar* assignments in recompense for their services, and so they are not named in the salary lists (see, for example, KPT 285 [1551/958], pp. 33, 85). Appointment registers for this period contain many references to *timar*-holding scribes of the Imperial Council, and thus indicate that the body of those performing clerical functions that would now be identified as bureaucratic was somewhat larger than has been supposed.

[12] KA, Süleyman/Ümera, "Nevbaharzade Beğ," Nur 3409, 136a. According to Uzunçarşılı, *Merkez*, pp. 327-28, the third *defterdarlık* of the Porte was established between 1540 and 1560; but see Appendix A.

[13] Âli refers to this in his discussion of the appointment of "Mehmed Çelebi" (Boyalı Mehmed) to the chancellorship because of his distinguished background; he was the nephew (on his mother's side) of Celalzade. Âli says that despite his genealogy he was not a learned man, and hence a poor chancellor. According to KA, Selim/Defterdaran, "Mehmed Çelebi," Nur 3409, 257a, Boyalı Mehmed was the son of a judge of Aleppo, Pir Ahmed, who married the sister of Celalzade.

The bureaucratic split into chancery and financial specializations was common to earlier Muslim polities as well; see R. Stephen Humphreys, *From Saladin to the Mongols: The Ayyubids of Damascus, 1193-1260* (Albany, 1977), pp. 377-80, and Carl F. Petry, *The Civilian Elite of Cairo in the Later Middle Ages* (Princeton, 1981), pp. 313-25. Humphreys notes that under the Ayyubids, as under the Ottomans, a judicial career, with its administrative responsibilities, was particularly likely to lead a member of the ulema to the sort of bureaucratic or administrative post to which such people might not otherwise have access. The difference between the context within which bureaucratic development took place in the Ottoman domains and that obtaining under the Ayyubids or Mamluks, of course, is that the Ottomans initially had little in the way of established bureaucratic practice, or of bureaucratic families in the newly conquered regions, upon which to draw.

crats; *re'isülküttab*s tended either to be promoted directly to the chancellorship, and thus become professional chancery officers, or to enter the ranks of the finance directors. As the effective gateway to the chancellorship or to high financial office, the office of secretary-in-chief gained considerable importance by the late sixteenth century.

A glance at the relative number of officeholders in these two branches of the bureaucracy during the sixteenth century is also instructive. Many more individuals became treasurer than chancellor. This might be evidence of the relative instability of a financial as opposed to chancery career, particularly when finance became a pressing problem in Murad III's time. It is more accurately viewed as a result of the enhanced importance and tremendous numerical expansion of the financial service in the second half of the century. That a service in which internal appointment to its chief offices began to be favored very early could provide so many officers is evidence of the development of the financial bureaucracy. Specialization undoubtedly helped to alter the relative standing and career expectations of chancellors and treasurers. The latter became more powerful as fiscal problems grew and financial administration was regularized and brought under their supervision. Chancellors, on the other hand, were increasingly restricted to supervision of the chancery, to inscribing the imperial signature, and to codifying and pronouncing upon questions of *kanun*. The chancellor was not only the Empire's premier authority on and codifier of *örfi* law, he had also to ensure that it did not conflict with the theoretically paramount *şeri'at*. This facet of the chancellor's functions helps to explain the pro-*ilmiye* bias manifested in appointments to the position.

By the late sixteenth century, within the bureaucracy as a whole a financial specialization offered a more active and promising career than a chancery one, though it must be noted that specialization per se does not appear to have taken place, or cannot be perceived, below the highest levels of the bureaucracy. From the mid-sixteenth century there were more important financial posts in the Empire, especially as provincial treasuries proliferated, than there were for chancery specialists, who could hope only to work under or succeed the secretary-in-chief. For this reason, and perhaps also because of the closer identification of finance directors with the military-administrative establishment implied by the *Kanunname*, a financial career provided many more avenues of mobility and advancement than the chancery. Röhrborn has listed eight major finance directors who received actual appointments as governor-general between 1573 and 1597.[14] Of the chancellors of

[14] Röhrborn, ''Emanzipation,'' pp. 129-30. Röhrborn, as has been mentioned, treats the entry of financial officials into the military-administrative path as anomalous. However, there exists solid historical evidence, which I shall present in my forthcoming study of bureaucratic development, to show that the upper levels of the financial and military careers were closely

the same period, only Boyalı Mehmed Paşa achieved such an appointment, although Feridun Beğ, Hamze Beğ, and Muhyi Çelebi retired from office with honorific governor-general's rank.

When the bureaucracy as a whole began in Süleyman's time to establish itself as a career path in its own right, independent of the *ilmiye* from which it had originated, it provided a means of entry into government service and social advancement for many who could not have hoped for such under the old system. These were the freeborn Muslims, of whatever ethnic and social origin, for whom nearly the only path of mobility was an *ilmiye* career as teacher or judge. The number of such positions was limited by *kanun* and by a well-established hierarchy. The expanding scribal service, by contrast, had need of qualified, literate secretaries, and represented an alternative career made all the more attractive to frustrated *ilmiye* trainees, in that *ilmiye* recruits to scribal service were shown particular honor in comparison to professional scribes, in the form of honorific titles and increased salaries.[15]

By the same token, and by virtue of the growing importance of professional training, the expanding bureaucracy offered career opportunities to elements of Ottoman society for whom—being neither highborn, nor Christians liable to the *devşirme*, nor ulema—social mobility had previously been restricted. In the fifteenth and early sixteenth centuries the Ottoman governing class was essentially composed of Men of the Sword and Men of Learning, between whom there was a sharp division. Bureaucratic service, when more manpower was needed, seems to have been open to Muslims of all walks of life. Candidates for scribal service needed only literacy and ability; *ilmiye* training, membership in ulema families, or even descent from *devşirme* forebears were not sine qua nons for aspiring scribes, although such factors could help an individual to begin a career. In the late sixteenth century the financial bureaucracy not only became the preserve of freeborn Muslims (as opposed to Palace products), as has been argued by Röhrborn;[16] it also tended to become the preserve of non-*ilmiye* Muslims. The

linked from an early date (Tursun Beğ is perhaps the earliest example of this phenomenon). Specifically, as provincial treasuries were first established in the middle of the sixteenth century, their chiefs (*defterdar*s) were often selected from the scions of established military families and from the ranks of Palace-trained personnel who had served as administrators of endowments, as well as from those employed more directly by the central treasury.

[15] Matuz, *Kanzleiwesen*, pp. 49-54, making use of the salary list for scribes of 1527-28 published by Barkan (see note 11 above). Since scribes from *ilmiye* families are specified as such, Matuz deduces that those not so designated have no blood ties to the *ilmiye*. The sons of judges received salaries that were considerably higher than those of other scribes, which suggests that *ilmiye*-trained personnel (as the sons of judges would certainly have been) who changed career lines to enter the scribal service enjoyed particular prestige compared to their purely professionally trained colleagues. Âli, it may be recalled, received the honorary designation "elite" when he entered Prince Selim's service as a scribe, in recognition of his standing as a candidate for an *ilmiye* post.

[16] Röhrborn, "Emanzipation," pp. 131-35.

reason for this is clear. Once into the system, an apprentice learned specific skills on the job. As the financial service became professionalized and bureaucratic processes became more complex, he would be promoted on the basis of his mastery of them. An advanced *medrese* student entering the bureaucracy had the edge, in terms of prestige and broad literacy, over a less well-educated scribe, but only a slight one, for the professional mastery required of both was specific. The literate and able Muslim boy could achieve job parity with a university graduate without investing the same time in a *medrese* education.

Once these two hypothetical scribes reached the middle-upper levels of the scribal service, their paths might diverge. The former student might well choose, or be forced, to pursue a chancery specialization because of that branch's residual ties to the *ilmiye*, its prejudice in favor of *medrese* products at its upper levels, and the greater literacy and literary ability required of chancery officials. The other scribe could look forward to a profitable career in the financial service, which offered greater opportunities for advancement and emphasized professional skill, particularly in a time of economic crisis, over family status or educational background.

Who these non-*ilmiye* recruits to the bureaucracy were is difficult to establish through Ottoman biographical literature, which records the careers of the distinguished rather than the average, and also tends to pass over in polite silence the preprofessional background of those major bureaucratic officials who were not associated by blood or education with the *ilmiye*. Therefore the evidence that some worked their way through the scribal ranks to become finance directors and treasurers is of a negative character. There are more positive indications, admittedly few, of how such people made their way. Âli states in his biography of the poet Yahya Beğ that Yahya's father, a Janissary, enrolled his son in the Corps as an apprentice in the office of the Janissary secretary (*yeniçeri kâtibi*). From there Yahya was appointed administrator of a number of endowments (*evkaf*), following a career path "that would have led to a finance directorship" had not the anger of the grand vezir Rüstem Paşa over Yahya's elegy for the murdered Prince Mustafa cut short his career.[17] This entry is of interest from a number of standpoints. It shows that Janissaries were not only marrying, but also enrolling their sons in the Corps, early in the reign of Süleyman when Yahya must have begun his apprenticeship. It also demonstrates that the military and bureaucratic careers overlapped at low levels as well as high, but in this instance at least in the opposite direction. Such Janissary infiltration of the bureaucratic ranks sheds light on Âli's complaints about "Palace slave" appointments to scribal positions. Most importantly, this passage indicates

[17] KA, Süleyman/Şu'ara, "Yahya Beğ," Nur 3409, 212a.

that professional bureaucratic apprenticeships, a phenomenon otherwise poorly attested in sixteenth-century sources, functioned even early in that century as an alternative (i.e., non-*medrese*) means of educating scribes and clerks.[18]

It was presumably easier for men with connections, like Yahya's father (besides being a Janissary, he was from the family of the Albanian Dukakin *beğ*s), to secure apprenticeships for their sons. Even so, it does not appear to be the case that all professional scribes or bureaucrats were from low-level *kul* families. It is also possible that people of some wealth were able to buy entry for their children into the growing bureaucracy, which had neither the traditions nor the strict requirements of either the military or the religious careers. The most basic requirement for entry into a scribal career, and perhaps scribal apprenticeship as well, was a certain literacy in Ottoman Turkish. How "ordinary" people acquired such literacy, outside of the *medrese* or the Palace, is something of a mystery. Certainly the scribal career was open to ulema and their children, who would be educated at home as well as in the *mekteb* primary schools. Indeed, Âli makes it clear that he considered the scribal service the proper preserve of the *ilmiye*-trained. Even so, a relatively high degree of literacy seems to have been accessible to even the lowest-ranking members of the *askeri* class. Ottoman biographies of poets of the sixteenth century contain numerous notices of poets who were the sons of Janissaries, garrison soldiers (*hisar eri*), and *sipahi*s. Urban residents in particular appear to have been able to attain some degree of education, for the sons of shopkeepers also occur as poets of note in these works. Âli frequently refers, usually unflatteringly, to "city boys" (*şehir oğlanı*), who were noted for their linguistic prowess and witty tongues.[19] It is probable that such people as these, who were literate at a certain level but did not have enough education to be identified as *ilmiye* products, also provided recruits for the burgeoning bureaucracy, and saw in it a hitherto unavailable means of entry into the military-administrative class. That this was the case is suggested by Âli's discussion, in the *Conditions of Cairo*, of a *sancak beği* of Egypt named Küçük Sinan Beğ. Sinan Beğ was of Anatolian peasant origin. In his youth he traveled to the Yemen, and there began his career in

[18] Among sixteenth-century narrative sources I have encountered only one other reference to scribal apprenticeship. It occurs in MEVA'ID, p. 36, in the context of Âli's complaints about the quality of the *kalemiye*; Âli states that unworthy people "who could not even become apprentices" were obtaining scribal posts. However, appointment registers and salary lists for the reign of Süleyman (which I shall study in detail elsewhere) confirm that apprenticeship was a common feature of many scribal offices during this period. These records also show that the administration of imperial endowments, to which Palace graduates were often appointed, was an important training and recruiting ground for ranking financial officials and an alternative to service in the central bureaux as a path to high office.

[19] For examples, see MEVA'İD, p. 225, and Tietze, "Prose Style," p. 312.

the service of a retainer of the governor-general. Âli writes, "Since he was more or less literate, he was able to obtain the post of secretary to the salaried men." Küçük Sinan eventually became Council secretary for the province; through this post he was able to obtain a military designation, which he gradually parlayed into an important garrison commandership (*sancak beğilik*) in Egypt.[20]

ÂLİ AND THE BUREAUCRACY OF HIS TIME

MANY of Âli's complaints now become more comprehensible and take on substance. He makes frequent reference to the prevalence in government of people whom he describes as "ignorant," "vile," and "unworthy," particularly in the financial service, which he often characterizes as filled with "pernicious financial officers" (*ummal-i bed-a'mal*). These, according to Âli, filled the ranks of government by the end of the century, and through their ignorance and rapacity brought disaster to the Empire. Âli clearly had a high opinion of himself, but it would be simplistic to assume that he reviled anyone who had a higher position as a matter of principle. His own lineage was not distinguished; what set him apart from many of his fellow bureaucrats was his *medrese* training. His wrath was directed against professional bureaucrats who were able to reach high office without the broad education enjoyed by him and important bureaucratic figures of earlier times. His chagrin was analogous to that of a Harvard graduate who finds that secretarial school alumni get more and better jobs. Âli singled out the chancellors Hamze Paşa and Lam Ali Çelebi for opprobrium; both were professional bureaucrats. At the same time, he admired Feridun Beğ, who also belonged to this category, showing that cultural quality was the fundamental criterion by which he measured his contemporaries; in contrast to Hamze Paşa and Lam Ali Çelebi, Feridun Beğ was a littérateur and noted *inşa* stylist.

It appears that the expansion and centralization of the Empire, together with the growth of the financial bureaucracy, gave rise to new expectations within certain segments of Ottoman society. In the case of the military organization, the exigencies of border warfare required that the ranks be opened to people previously excluded, or at least that entrance be made con-

[20] CAIRO, pp. 61-62 (trans.), pp. 144-45 (text). The archival materials referred to in note 18 above confirm the likelihood that such a case could have occurred, and that for some of the "lower orders" literacy was available. In the provinces as well as in the capital, each military unit had a secretary who was selected from the ranks on the basis of his ability to read and write. He could thus win promotion to a higher military rank, transfer to another unit, or possibly enter the provincial financial service. Also, each endowment and tax concession (*mukata'a*) had a scribe who was recruited from the provincial ranks.

tingent on less stringent conditions. Similarly, a dramatic rise in the need for scribal and financial expertise, and professionalization of the bureaucracy, allowed many who were literate, if not learned in the *medrese* sense, to hope for a government career that promised profit and advancement. This development encouraged career changes which were uncommon, if not unthinkable, in the early sixteenth century. Under the pre-Süleymanic system, judges, for example, had to rise to a very high level within the *ilmiye* career line before they might begin to hope for a transfer to a high administrative post, a phenomenon that would only occur in the case of an unusual individual. Later in the century, however, they had access from a much lower level to a financial career that potentially offered more money and power than following the prescribed stages of the *ilmiye* path.

Blurring of career lines and social roles that in the time of Süleyman and earlier had been held to be effectively discrete—i.e., the ways of Sword and Learning—was produced and exacerbated by expansion, new manpower requirements, and financial crisis. The establishment of a new government career line, which shared certain characteristics as well as personnel with the established and distinct military and religious careers, was a major contributing factor in the restructuring of the Ottoman class that took place in the sixteenth century. The dislocations these changes engendered were exacerbated by the growth of the central government; crowding of the Ottoman ranks, a result of both the effective cessation of expansion in the last quarter of the sixteenth century, and of increased recruitment of officials from previously untapped, or rarely utilized, sources, such as the families and households of *kul*s of high and low rank;[21] the practice of contract appointment, which increased competition for posts and helped to shorten tenure in office; the growing autonomy and factionalism of the pillars of state, particularly the vezirs, whose large households took on new importance; the increasingly disorganized character of the appointment process; and the sultan's abdication of authority. Although the beginnings of this process of internal change, in both negative and positive aspects, may be seen in the last years of Süleyman, it came into full bloom under Murad and progressed rapidly. It is doubtful that *kanun*, particularly in its legislative function, could keep up with these changes. *Kanun* was based upon precedent, custom, and the sultan's discretionary powers, and in the latter case presumed a sultan like Fatih Mehmed or Süleyman who was cognizant of his own legislative responsibility. In Murad's reign the times were too exceptional, the crises too immediate, and the changes in administrative organization too rapid for decisions to be made on other than an ad hoc basis. In Âli's case

[21] This development, which I have traced in terms of bureaucratic growth, also occurred in the military career; see Kunt, *Servants*, p. 76.

alone there are two examples of abrupt change in the provincial financial structure: the reorganization of the finance directorship of Baghdad, and the abolition of that of Sivas. We have also seen that the proliferation of provincial financial centers and concomitant restructuring of ranking and promotion procedures does not seem to be reflected in *kanun* until these stabilized in the early seventeenth century. From this point on, provincial treasuries were probably ranked in the same manner as provinces, i.e., by order of precedence of establishment.[22] By the same token, the ever larger numbers of financial officials who attained military governorships reflects not a disregard for *kanun*, which allowed such promotion even if it was not common earlier in the century, but the increased size and prominence of the financial establishment.

In the late sixteenth century existing *kanun* legislation, by its nature, made no provision for the explosion of the financial bureaucracy, or for the garrisoning of fortresses on expanded but unexpanding frontiers. Circumstances required immediate actions, and there ensued a period of organizational instability until problems were perceived and legislation could catch up with the situation. What then becomes of the implicit and explicit complaints of such writers as Selâniki and Âli that *kanun*, either as law or as practice, was being violated? Their statements reflect a yearning for an order that existed in theory in their own times, but not in actuality. The last time such a thing had existed in fact, or so it seemed to them, had been in the early to middle years of Süleyman's reign, when the Ottoman Empire underwent growth and consolidation. These authors were in fact interpreting *kanun* much as legists interpreted the *şeri'at*. They felt that a regular system of promotion by merit and seniority, such as they perceived to have been in effect in earlier times (whether or not this was actually so), should likewise be the rule for the expanded bureaucratic service. Under Süleyman's successors this, of course, was very often not the case; the bureaucracy was too new, grew too quickly, and corruption was too common for it to be so. Âli and Selâniki, and their successors in the *nasihatname* genre who were more explicitly nostalgic for the "golden age" of Süleyman, posited the notion of *kanun* as the primary legitimate ordering mechanism for political life. However, its specifics did not always cover actual circumstances, and the *kanun*-minded, who were numerous in this period, had to extrapolate from more orderly periods of history. Nostalgia for Süleyman represented not just a desire for order but also a yearning for simpler times.[23]

[22] See Ayn-ı Ali, p. 10.

[23] On the nostalgia for Süleyman among Ottoman political commentators of the seventeenth century, see Röhrborn, *Verwaltungsgeschichte*, pp. 6-11; Majer, "Kritik"; Fleischer, "Şehzade Korkud to Mustafa Âli." In the COUNSEL, a relatively practically oriented advice work written before the Ottoman ideology of decline was fully developed, Âli largely reserved his nostalgia for the courts of Sulṭân-Ḥusayn Bâyqarâ and the Conqueror. Only toward the end of his life did Âli begin to evince a longing for more recent "good old days," and an overwhelm-

The division of Ottoman society into discrete segments and career lines was a fact of life in the stable society of the first half of the sixteenth century. In the second half, such a division became a theory and an ideal. In the section of the *Tables of Delicacies* in which he discusses appointment to the scribal career line in earlier and in modern times, Âli interprets older practice as canonical and more recent usage as harmful innovation, even though there was no specific legislation on this point. From this interpretation proceed a number of implicit ramifications. In Âli's view, the bureaucratic career line theoretically had an *ilmiye* backbone, it was distinct from other career tracks, and the military hierarchy should be discrete from other branches of service. While such was the de facto situation in earlier times, thinkers like Âli, who contemplated *kanun* practice in light of altered circumstances, began to elaborate both the theoretical and specific aspects of customary law. This interpretative tendency of late sixteenth-century intellectuals illuminates the function of the chancellor as the "*müfti* of *kanun*." The metaphor is apt, for the function of the chief jurisconsult was to adjudicate the religious legality of actions in situations for which there was no legal precedent, basing his decision on interpretation of the existing body of *şeri'at* law. As the background of such chancellors as Celalzade and the latter's close cooperation with the *şeyhulislam* Ebüssu'ud show, the head of the chancery was both intellectually and professionally part of the *medrese*. Ottoman *kanun*, analogously, was rationalized by one of Âli's teachers, the judge Kınalızade, as a set of dynastic institutes supportive of the *şeri'at* and derived, with the help of religious scholars, from *şer'i* principles.[24] Sultanic or dynastic law was also the proper sphere of scholarship for bureaucrats, the chancery official's badge of learning analogous to the *şeri'at* of the ulema.[25] In light of these institutional and theoretical aspects of the sixteenth-century legitimation of secular dynastic law, it is significant that Âli,

---

ing preoccupation with old customs (*kavanin*). This is apparent in the *Tables*, in which Âli prescribes such things as proper administration of the Palace through a comparison of specific late sixteenth-century practices with those established by custom in earlier times (for examples, see MEVA'İD, pp. 20-47). The point of such discussions is that the old ways, dating from a time of stability and success, should be the model for practice, which Âli saw in his own time to have allowed so many innovations that society and state were disrupted. Even given this premise, however, Âli takes a more critical view of recent history than some of his successors. Because he is concerned with the historical disruption of specific institutions, Âli even faults Süleyman for introducing practices that later produced difficulties (see, for example, MEVA'İD, p. 26).

[24] Kınalızade, *Ahlak-ı Alâ'i*, Book II, pp. 75-76.

[25] This vision of *kanun* appears to have had deep roots in Ottoman bureaucratic culture. It is attested, by implication, in the late fifteenth-century history of the bureaucrat-scholar and historian Tursun Beğ, who in his introduction on statecraft stresses the central importance of dynastic law (*siyaset-i sultani, yasağ-ı padişahi, örf*) as an expression of the principle of universal justice upon which the state must be founded. Tursun Beğ's formulations, like those of Kınalızade Ali Çelebi, are ultimately based on the *Nasirean Ethics* of Naṣîr al-dîn Ṭûsî (see *Tarih-i Ebü'l-Feth*, ed. M. Tulum, pp. 12-18).

only a few years after demonstrating his knowledge of *kanun* in the *Counsel*, occupied himself with editing and writing an introduction to a collection of the legal opinions (*fetvâ*, pl. *fetâvâ*) of the great Ebüssu'ud.[26]

Âli's obsession with the chancellorship becomes comprehensible in view of his, and others', preoccupation with *kanun* at a time when it was in dire need of interpretation. Âli's desire is also explicable in terms of the office's historical position within the Ottoman administrative structure. Finance directors were mere professional accountants and clerks, while chancellors maintained the prestige, learning, and *ilmiye* connections of a *medrese* education. Âli himself certainly subscribed to this view of the major bureaucratic officials of the Empire, as he states in the *Counsel*:

> The chancellors of the Council are the jurisconsults of the imperial law. Therefore they are to be given more respect and shown more kindness than other high officials [*ümera*]. It is particularly necessary to give them honor and precedence over the directors of the financial services. The latter are in the service of money and property, the vain foolishness of this world, while the chancellors are those who guard the secrets of the varieties of imperial edicts which concern justice and equity, and matters of public jurisdiction. In the cage of the imperial cypher [*tuğra*] is the peerless phoenix of the [the chancellor's] dedication ever apparent, and the consolidation of the laws of [Ottoman] sovereignty is manifested in the prose composition which issues from them [i.e., the chancellors].[27]

The chancellor's office, in the late sixteenth century, symbolized Âli's Ottoman ideals and embodied the world of Âli's youth, when the learned and cultured had received enormous respect, and when bureaucratic service had offered an exciting and prestigious career to ambitious young men who had received the best education available. In his desire to be given this post, in symbolic recognition of his personal values as well as his virtues, Âli was willing to accept the post of secretary-in-chief, the last steppingstone within the chancery service, which he hoped would automatically lead to his goal. This willingness is probably also indicative of the enhanced importance of the office in the late sixteenth century, since Âli would hardly request a post

[26] Âli worked on the *Resâ'il ül-mesâ'il* while in Sivas in 1588. The work (Staatsbibliothek Berlin, MS or. quart. 1741, Teil 8, ff. 54b-113b) was begun by Mahmud Bezenzade, a scholar and student of Ebüsu'ud who died only one year after his teacher, in 1575-76. See Hanna Sohrweide, *Türkische Handschriften, Teil 5 (Verzeichnis der orientalischen Handschriften in Deutschland)*, ed. Wolfgang Voigt, vol. XIII, 5 (Wiesbaden, 1981), no. 102, 91-93.

[27] COUNSEL, I, 50 (trans.), 140 (text).

he considered beneath him.[28] Those appeals for entry into the numerically limited upper echelons of the chancery service that Âli repeated during the last two years of his life are evidence not only of his ambition, but also of his vocation. Âli had for twenty years served only in financial and, latterly, military posts, which provided greater opportunities for advancement and profit than a chancery career. He yet wished to leave the financial service, which he viewed as unpleasant and somewhat demeaning, for a post that embodied those personal and cultural ideals with which he had grown up. The ethical and administrative climate of his age, Âli felt, violated those ideals. In the *Essence* he wrote that, while the rectitude and conscientiousness with which he had discharged his fiscal duties ought to be rewarded by a state that was based on justice, even the sultan thought differently: "He [the sultan] said, 'What you call justice produces a lack of revenue, and what you consider compassion for the subjects prevents the increase of *dinars* and *dirhems*.' "[29]

Such a career change, in the Ottoman world of 1596, was probably unrealistic in an increasingly professionalized and bureaucratized system; Âli himself recognized that, regrettably, the day of the talented littérateur in government service had passed. His alternative request to be made a governor-general was rather tendentious from the standpoint of legislated practice, since none of his *sancak* posts had carried the income necessary to qualify him for such a promotion, nor was he a finance director of the Porte who might reasonably expect such an appointment.[30] Âli clearly felt that if he were forced to remain in military-financial service he should properly receive a governor-generalship by virtue of his rank, literary ability, learning, and generational standing. Even so, he made clear his distaste for the military-financial career in verses in which he complained of the duties and the greedy, crude, disloyal subordinates who fell to the lot of the provincial governor. He closed this poem, composed in 1596 in Kayseri, with the lines:

Listen to me, elder brother, for I've experienced this!
The wail of pipe and drum [of a governor] is a great headache.

[28] Further evidence for this is provided by Hamze Paşa, who several times was removed from the chancellorship to the post of *re'isülküttab*, only to become chancellor once more. This suggests that there were in fact few posts within the chancery service which ranking bureaucrats could hold if they were not deemed suitable for a *sancak* appointment. See SELANİKİ, pp. 161-62, 186, 326.

[29] KA, I, 32.

[30] Fleischer, "Âli," p. 437; Ayn-ı Ali, pp. 16, 23 (salaries of the *sancak beğis* and *defterdars* of Amasya and Kayseri). A very few (three) provincial finance directors of the last quarter of the sixteenth century were promoted directly to governor-generalship without doing intermediate service in Istanbul; such promotion appears to be the exception rather than the rule (see Röhrborn, "Emanzipation," pp. 129-30).

Is not the state of wisdom enough for you, Âli?
Why should lowly people humiliate you?
Try to become worthy of a post from which there is no dismissal;
Make yourself suited to seating on a throne.[31]

In another poem, this one a plaint on the sorry state of the Empire, Âli refers directly to what he saw as the intellectual and moral damage wrought by generalized Ottoman bureaucratization, particularly in the learned and bureaucratic careers:

Temporal power and secular law [*örf*] have become the scholars' badge of learning;
All that remains of knowledge are the names of [calligraphic] lines and taxes [*rüsum*].
Previously, the lands of Rum were built upon justice;
Now they are destroyed with curses sparked by the flame of injustice.[32]

Âli, as we have seen, saw high culture and political success as inextricably linked. These lines demonstrate the way in which this same concept informed Âli's view of professional life and the life of the state. They also illustrate the extent to which Âli was a product of the nascent bureaucracy of the mid-sixteenth century, composed as it was of elements of both the administrative and scholarly careers. Âli himself was torn between Palace and *medrese*, and found himself trying to reconcile things that for him were irreconcilable opposites. The *kanun* that preserved an ideal order was also the law of decree and coercion, *örf*, which overshadowed the *şeri'at* and degraded true learning. The state, which supported the Holy Law by fostering the religious establishment, also made judges into administrators of human as well as divine law, and created a body of scholars more concerned with advancement within a bureaucratized system than with learning and its propagation.

As Âli saw it, the more the growing ranks of government officials moved toward narrow professional specialization and away from a broad *medrese* education, the lower became their moral and intellectual capacity to fulfill their responsibilities properly. Poorly educated and ethically illiterate people made bad administrators. Âli associates this trend toward professionalization of government and moral laxity, in a manner that is at least partly causal, with the other phenomena characteristic of the general decline he perceived: rapacity of administrators, official irresponsibility, generalized ambition and greed, and lack of respect for either religious law or customary

[31] DİVAN III, 82b-83a.
[32] DİVAN III, 58b.

social values. While to some degree Âli was describing symptoms rather than causes of "decline," it must be noted that this is but one aspect of a "decline" that Âli also treated in political and economic terms. Himself a part of the history of this turbulent period, Âli was necessarily concerned with immediate manifestations and their causes, and proved himself an exceedingly perceptive observer and analyst. The foregoing discussion of the history of the Ottoman bureaucracy in the sixteenth century suggests that there is indeed more substance to some of Âli's complaints than might at first be thought. To take but one example, Âli in his later years decried what he saw as a lack of recognition of or concern for poetic talent, a recent development relative to his youth. The courts of Süleyman and Selim had set a high standard of patronage unmatched by those of their successors. Âli's own early career, and the careers of the many other poet-scribes gathered at the court of Selim, bear witness that in the mid-sixteenth century literary talent and education could provide the primary means of advancement for those who chose to enter the understaffed bureaucracy. By the time of Murad, on the other hand, bureaucratic procedures and skills were well established, and creative talent ceased to be a criterion by which candidates for office might be judged. Allowing for some hyperbole engendered by Âli's personal bitterness, it is very probable that this situation, in combination with diminution of financial resources, political crisis, and the particular cultural orientation of Sultan Murad, did in fact significantly change patterns of imperial patronage. Able historian though he was, Âli, *medrese* student, self-confident littérateur, and ambitious man of the Pen who had begun his career in the reign of Süleyman the Lawgiver, was unable either to accept such changes, or to reconcile his youth and his old age.

III

THE MAKING OF OTTOMAN HISTORY

NINE

OTTOMAN HISTORICAL WRITING IN THE SIXTEENTH CENTURY

OFFICIAL AND UNOFFICIAL HISTORIOGRAPHY

MUSTAFA ÂLI achieved posthumous fame largely by virtue of his tremendous historiographical output and his outspoken social and political critiques. To these works Âli brought great learning and an acute critical intelligence, as well as a strong sense of personal grievance that is never far beneath the surface of his prose. The analytical account of Âli's career, intellectual development, and social milieu embarked on here must take some account of this prominent facet of his life and work. Certain aspects of Âli's historical orientation have been discussed, and his veracity examined, in the preceding chapters where they were chronologically or thematically appropriate. It is now in order that we view specifically those intellectual products which, in terms of both the chronology of Âli's development and his legacy to his own culture, represent in some sense the summation of his life. A thorough evaluation of the massive *Essence of History*, or even of its Ottoman portion, would require a volume unto itself, and such a study is outside the parameters of this work. Rather, a few judiciously chosen examples will serve to elucidate and define Âli's intellectual orientation and his approach to history. Although a writer, and particularly an historian, cannot be separated from his cultural context, the examples chosen will help to distinguish between the man Âli, bitter and hypercritical, and the historian Âli, who sought to assess the development and character of the civilization into which he was born, and with which he identified.

Only three of Âli's works truly fit generically into the category of historiographical literature: the early *Rarity of Warriors*, the *Book of Victory*, and the later and far more extensive *Essence of History*. The question of the definition of historical genre in sixteenth-century Ottoman letters is a complex one. Earlier chroniclers, such as Neşri (d. reign of Selim I) and Âşıkpaşazade (fl. 1484), had contented themselves with a bald recounting of events in simple language and in annalistic format.[1] The educated elite of

[1] GOW, pp. 35-39; V. L. Ménage, *Neshrî's History of the Ottomans* (London, 1964), pp. 1-5; idem, "The Beginnings of Ottoman Historiography," in *Historians of the Middle East*, eds. B. L. Lewis and P. M. Holt (London, 1962), pp. 168-79.

the middle and late sixteenth century, however, attempted to make the writing of history the province of polite literature. Inspired to a great extent by the mature Persian literary-historical tradition, such writers as Celalzade, Sa'düddin, and Âli tried to integrate the writing of historical prose with the high Ottoman Turkish literary tradition that burgeoned and matured, with all its stylistic complexity and polylingualism, precisely during this period. For such writers, the composition of a chronicle was as much an exercise in literary creation as in historiography. The tradition of straightforward chronicling also persisted; a comparison between the elegant phraseology of Âli or Celalzade and the unadorned prose of Selâniki or Peçevi immediately reveals the difference between the littérateur-historian and the humble chronicler.

Other formal considerations must come into play in any effort to narrow down the concept of historiography in a context in which it is not clearly distinguishable from literature. These are formal organizational structure and the author's intent, whether stated or implicit. In very general terms, one might accept as historiography any work that has an historical event, or a series of events, as its main focus, and certainly most such works can yield basic historical information of greater or lesser factual value. Here a comparison between the *Rarity* and the *Essence* is instructive. The former has an historical focus, the conflict between the princes Bayezid and Selim. Based largely on contemporary oral reports, the work is also a unique source for the events it recounts. However, its purpose, as stated by the author, was to display stylistic and linguistic skill and versatility. Less explicitly, the *Rarity* was written to flatter the reigning Sultan Selim and his son Murad with an elegant description of the events that constituted Selim's victory over his rival. The *Essence*, by contrast, was dedicated to no one (although Âli did not shrink from seeking a patron when the work had neared completion) and was a purely personal product. The *Essence* also contains a long introduction on the virtues and necessity of historical and historiographical science, and in this introduction Âli claims that he has not succumbed to literary temptations in the composition of the work, so that its significance as a work of history might not be obscured by gratuitous displays of linguistic virtuosity. Although a man as thoroughly imbued with the traditions of belles-lettres as Âli could hardly be expected completely to refrain from expressing himself in high-cultural style, it is clear that his intent was to write a coherent history rather than to create a literary display.

Whatever the validity of such a distinction between literature and historiography, Âli himself perceived the presence of one. Formally, the *Essence* adheres to the canons of the chronicle (*tarih*) format. Although it contains asides, occasional personal commentary, and innovative organizational features, the work follows a chronological, regnal sequence within each geographical region and historical period that it treats. While the range and nature of pertinent material was largely dictated by his sources, Âli was critical as well as comprehensive, selecting the most correct or reasonable account, or synthesizing variant versions of an event, from the mass of reports available to him.[2] By and large, Âli strove to adhere to an ideal of flat, seemingly objective presentation of major, pertinent events and historical facts, with relatively few intrusions of opinion or subjective tone. A comparison between the *Essence*, which Âli described as a work of history, and the *Seasons of Sovereignty* reveals the extent to which this was indeed the case. While this latter work was derived from the *Essence* and utilized precisely the same material, its purpose was very different. In the interest of conveying a moral lesson appropriate to the *Seasons*, but not to the *Essence*, Âli both ignored information included in his formal history and emphasized elements presented as incidental in the *Essence*. In the latter work, for example, Âli gives a standard Sunni account of the Mongol destruction of the Abbasid caliphate that stresses the negative role played by two Shi'is, the caliph's vezir al-ʿAlqamî and the scholar Naṣîr al-dîn Ṭûsî, advisor to Hülegü. But in the *Seasons* Âli wishes to show that the caliph prepared his own fate by alienating his scholars and ministers; he makes no mention of the Shi'ism of ʿAlqamî or Ṭusî.[3] The *Essence of History*, then, was intended by its author to be a work of history and part of a particular historiographical genre, even though the canons of that genre might not be explicitly articulated.

Official Ottoman historiography as such did not come into being until the late seventeenth century, when the office of court chronicler (*vak'anüvis*) appears to have been established.[4] The Ottoman court chroniclers, the first

[2] Âli claims to have made two major organizational and methodological innovations relative to other works in the *tarih* genre. The first is that he has appended the biographies of each of the major classes of notables to the end of the reign of each Ottoman sultan under whom these flourished or died (KA, I, 16). The other is that, rather than present all accounts (*rivayet*) pertinent to a given topic, he has chosen only the most reliable or correct ones (*asahh-ı rivayat*) for inclusion in the *Künh* (KA, I, 10). While such "improvements" had long been standard features of earlier Islamicate historiography, especially in the Ayyubid and Mamluk literary traditions, the first did indeed represent an important innovation in Ottoman historical writing.

The question of genre in Islamicate literary works generally classified as historical, in both pre- and post-Mongol times, is a topic still requiring a great deal of research; it is as yet impossible to attempt a comprehensive discussion of the problem. For other perspectives on Muslim historiography in various periods, see Franz Rosenthal, *A History of Muslim Historiography* (Leiden, 1952); Marilyn Waldman, *Toward a Theory of Historical Narrative: A Case Study in Perso-Islamicate Historiography* (Columbus, Ohio, 1980); M.G.S. Hodgson, *The Venture of Islam*, I, 350-58; III, 73-80; H.A.R. Gibb, "Târîkh," in *Studies of the Civilization of Islam*, eds. Stanford Shaw and William Polk (Boston, 1962), pp. 108-37; Peter Hardy, *Historians of Medieval India* (London, 1960 [repr. Westport, 1982]).

[3] KA, IV, 210-18; FUSUL, 12b-15a (*fasl* 4).

[4] This paragraph is based on Lewis V. Thomas, *A Study of Naima* (New York, 1972), pp. 36-42, 66-73, and Necib Âsım, "Osmanlı tarihnüvisleri ve müverrihleri," TOEM, II, 425-35.

of whom was Na'ima, were given access to archival materials and were charged with compiling a record of the major events in the history of the Ottoman Empire and of the Ottoman house. This record was thereafter kept up to date by successive appointees. It is of interest to note the nature of Na'ima's charge when he began his history, usually known as *Tarih-i Na'ima*. He was to compose an Ottoman history detailing events occurring subsequent to the *hicri* year 1000, a fact that underlines the significance of the millennium in Ottoman historical thinking. Na'ima's task was also didactic and propagandistic; his history opens with an attempt to rationalize and make palatable the "disgraceful" Treaty of Karlowitz of 1699 by comparing it to the Prophet's tactical Peace of Ḥudaybîya. The *vak'anüvis*, then, was to present the court-approved, official version of Ottoman history. It must be noted that, in the case of Na'ima, "court-approved" did not mean "sanitized"; Na'ima incorporated into his history much of the *nasihatname* style of political criticism that had begun with Âli's *Counsel*, and which by Na'ima's time was an accepted part of historical lore.

Whether the appointment of an official court historian at the end of the seventeenth century can be seen as the product of an evolutionary process is questionable. In the mid-fifteenth century the conquest of Constantinople greatly enhanced Ottoman prestige and brought to the new court Persian poets who vied with one another to produce panegyric and historical verse on the exploits of the Conqueror. The vigorous cultural life of the new capital, as well as the social and ideological tensions generated by the Conqueror's autocratic methods of consolidating his empire, generated an interest in history and an imperial cognizance of its political utility. The reign of the Conqueror's son, Bayezid II, saw the first flowering of indigenous historiography, both popular and courtly. Bayezid was keenly aware of a need to bolster his own image as the most prestigious (and pious) Muslim sovereign of his day, as well as to give cultural legitimacy to the state his father had founded by force.

To be sure, there already existed an indigenous Turkish-language historiographical tradition. The stylistically straightforward *Tevarih-i Âl-i Osman (Chronicles of the Ottoman House)* genre, based in part on popular tales and anonymous compilations, was carried on through the late fifteenth and early sixteenth centuries by such historians as Âşıkpaşazade and Neşri.[5] Although the works of these authors were respected as sources by later historians, the literati of the sixteenth century found distasteful the popular

[5] On the *şehnamecilik*, see Âsım, "Müverrihler"; GOW, pp. 87-88, 163-69; Woodhead, "*Şehnameci*." On the beginnings of indigenous Ottoman historiography, see H. İnalcık, "The Rise of Ottoman Historiography," in *Historians of the Middle East*, eds. B. L. Lewis and P. M. Holt (London, 1962), pp. 152-67; Ménage, "Beginnings"; idem, *Neshrî's History of the Ottomans*; Fr. Taeschner, "Âshıḳ-Pasha-zâde," EI².

character of such *Chronicles*, a character manifested as much by a frontier-campfire storytelling style as by an unsophisticated use of language. Too, they sometimes expressed a nostalgia for the freedom of the early days of border warfare that ill accorded with the centralizing policies of the new imperial state. It was Bayezid II who commissioned the first comprehensive histories of the Ottoman dynasty in learned style. At the sultan's behest İdrîs-i Bidlîsî (d. 1520/926), an experienced chancery official who had served as chancellor at the Akkoyunlu court before fleeing the Safavi conquest, composed the *Eight Paradises (Hasht Bihisht)* in elaborate Persian. Slightly later Bayezid was persuaded to ask the scholar and teacher Kemalpaşazade (d. 1534/940) to apply his learning to producing an Ottoman history in a Turkish prose that would equal the stylistic elegance of Bidlîsî's Persian version. Kemalpaşazade's *History of the Ottoman House*, though sometimes described as a translation of the *Eight Paradises*, was in fact an independent work. Kemalpaşazade used earlier chronicles but attempted to present a more historically analytical, as well as more linguistically elegant, history of the dynasty than had his annalistic predecessors.[6]

Under Bayezid's immediate successors there appear to have been no imperial commissions for full-blown dynastic histories until the mid-1550s, when Süleyman created the post of royal *şehname*-writer. The *şehnameci* was charged with composing a dynastic history in Persian verse and panegyric style; indeed, until Seyyid Lokman in the late sixteenth century began to write in Turkish prose and poetry (retaining the "heroic" [*mütekarib*] meter of Firdawsî), court-commissioned historiography, and courtly literature in general, remained tied to Persianate literary forms. The function of the *şehnameci*, in particular, was at least as much literary as historical. This view is confirmed by Âli's criticism of the first four (or five) incumbents on purely stylistic and literary grounds.[7] Elegant dynastic propaganda rather than justification of action or presentation of an officially sanctioned version of events was the purpose of the imperial *şehname*-writer. In the early seventeenth century the office effectively died out, and few instances of imperial commissioning of historical works appear until the end of that century.[8]

Initially the office was not terribly successful; only in the 1580s did the

[6] İnalcık, "Rise," pp. 165-67; Ménage, "Beginnings," pp. 176-77; idem, "Bidlîsî, Idrîs," EI²; idem, "Kemâl Pasha-zâde," EI²; Fleischer, "Bedlîsî, Edrîs," *Encyclopaedia Iranica*.

[7] KA Murad/Şehnameguyan, Nur 3409, 419b-422a, KA, Süleyman/Şuara, "Ârif," "Eflâtûn," Nur 3409, 190b-191b, 169b; and KA, MS Leiden, 6b-8b. Âli cites Ârif, Eflâtûn, Lokman, Ta'likizade, and the otherwise unknown Nutki (who may not have been formally appointed) as the successive holders of the position, all except Ta'likizade being of Iranian origin. Âli's observations, some of which are contradictory (in the *şehnameguyan* discussion he praises Nutki over Ta'likizade but reverses his judgment in the Leiden MS introduction), are analyzed by Jan Schmidt, "Verantwoording," pp. 40-45. See also Sohrweide, "Dichter und Gelehrte," pp. 89-92.

[8] Âsım, "Müverrihler."

şehnameci's atelier begin to bear fruit. Of course, works of more or less historical nature continued to be written throughout the sixteenth century, despite the relative dearth, or occasional character, of royal patronage. These tended to be of three types. A great many of these works, both in verse and in prose, were devoted to a single event or campaign or to the reign of a single sultan (*fethnames*, *gazavatnames*, *Selimnames*, *Sigetvarnames*, for example). Âli composed three such works—the *Rarity of Warriors*, the *Seven Scenes*, and the *Book of Victory*. Historiography of this type was largely literary in character, and the authors of these works generally hoped to win favor from those they praised. The second historiographical strain is represented by histories of the Ottoman house, written in simple Turkish, which continued the *Tevarih-i Âl-i Osman* genre. Two examples of this type of historical writing are the Ottoman chronicle of the grand vezir Lutfi Paşa and that attributed to Rüstem Paşa (it is actually the work of Rüstem Paşa's client, Matrakçı Nasuh), both of which date from the mid-sixteenth century.[9]

Finally, there were universal histories that included accounts, which varied in length and level of detail, of Ottoman history. The models for universal history were the highly respected works of authors of the Mongol and post-Mongol era—Rashîd al-dîn, Ibn al-Athîr, and Mîrkhvând—and the elaborate chancery style of the Mongol dynastic histories of Juveynî and Vaṣṣâf was admired and emulated. This type of historical writing remained tied to the established languages of Islamic discourse, particularly Persian, until Ramazanzade composed his short Ottoman Turkish digest of world history in the mid-1560s. The Anatolian scholar and teacher Şükrullah was the first to write a universal history in the Ottoman domains; he completed his Persian-language *Splendor of Histories (Bahjat al-tavârîkh)*, which included a short account of Ottoman rule, in about 1458 and dedicated it to the Conqueror's grand vezir, Mahmud Paşa.[10] As the first genuinely Ottoman "high-culture" history, the *Splendor* enjoyed considerable prestige and remained a favorite source for later historians on cosmology and pre-Ottoman as well as Ottoman history. Even in the second half of the sixteenth century, Ottoman historians adhered to this cultural and linguistic conven-

[9] GOW, pp. 39-42, 80-82. The proper identification of the history of Rüstem Paşa was made in light of new manuscript evidence by Hüseyin G. Yurdaydın in the introduction to Naṣûḥü's-Silâḥî (Maṭrâḳçî), *Beyan-ı Menâzil-i Sefer-i ʿIrâḳeyn-i Sulṭân Süleymân Hân* (Ankara, 1976), pp. 20-25. See also Friedrich Giese, "Einleitung zu meiner Textausgabe der altosmanischen anonymen Chroniken tewârîh-i âl-i ʿosmân," MOG I/2-3 (1922): 49-75; İnalcık, "Rise"; Ménage, "Beginnings."

[10] Theodor Seif, "Der Abschnitt über die Osmanen in Şükrüllâh's persischer Universalgeschichte," MOG II/1-2 (1952): 63-128, esp. 63-72; GOW, pp. 19-20; Nihal Atsız, *Osmanlı Tarihleri* (Istanbul, 1949), pp. 39-44 (introduction to Atsız's modern Turkish translation of the Ottoman portion of the *Splendor*).

tion; the scholars Muslihüddin Lari (d. 1572/979) and Mustafa Cenabi (d. 1590-91/999) used Persian and Arabic as the vehicles for their respective histories of the world, although Cenabi also made a Turkish translation of his work.[11]

There were a number of possible solutions to the problems posed by such cultural bilingualism (or trilingualism), which virtually required that certain types of prose work intended to be accepted as part of a high-culture tradition be written in Persian or Arabic rather than Turkish. In an historiographical tradition composed of as many disparate elements as that of the nascent Ottoman state, this situation also contributed to a sense that the sources of dynastic history were scattered, that there was no comprehensive account extant in a garb culturally appropriate to the established imperial entity of the sixteenth century. One solution was that adopted by Hoca Sa'düddin, who translated much of Lari's history into elegant Ottoman Turkish and expanded it with his *Crown of Histories (Tac üt-tevarih)*, a detailed, comprehensive, and to some extent self-consciously critical, history of the Ottoman state until 1520.[12] Others, predecessors of Sa'düddin such as Celalzade and Ramazanzade, and contemporaries like Âli, attempted a more creative solution. These authors composed new histories, purely dynastic (Celalzade) or universal, in the blossoming Ottoman Turkish literary language, heavily imbued with vocabulary and constructions taken directly from Persian and Arabic. Utilizing this new language, they cast their works into the stylistic and organizational form of Arabic and Persian histories. While these innovators depended heavily upon older Arabic and Persian sources for pre-Ottoman history, in the composition of the Ottoman portion of their chronicles they made use of available biographical sources in Persian or Arabic, the *Tevarih-i Âl-i Osman* works, their own memories, and oral sources. Celalzade, Ramazanzade, and Âli sought a cultural amalgamation in both language and literary form, which incorporated that which was unique and vital in the new Ottoman regional culture while yet paying honest obeisance to the prestige of the Muslim Arabicate and Persianate cultural hinterlands that had bequeathed their high-cultural values to the Ottoman Empire. The compilation of the great Ottoman histories of the sixteenth century constituted a statement, and a hope, that the Ottomans had achieved cultural as well as political legitimacy.

Âli's great world history, uncommissioned by any statesman or monarch, had no affiliation with any sort of official historiography. Âli's mission in

[11] GOW, pp. 94-95, 108-109.

[12] GOW, pp. 123-26. See *Tac üt-tevarih*, I, 159, for a critical discussion of the Tîmûrid and Ottoman sources on the conflict between Bayezid I and Tîmûr. This critique is a striking parallel to that introduced by Âli into the *Essence* (see chapter 11), although Âli's is somewhat more sophisticated.

composing the *Essence of History* was cultural and intellectual rather than political; he designated himself, it will be remembered, the continuator of the historiographical tradition established by his mentors Celalzade and Ramazanzade. Furthermore, he took seriously the notion that history was a branch of learning in and of itself, separate from literary endeavour, and sought to view events critically and analytically. Commitment to the literary mode of historiography, despite Âli's use of requisite formulaic elements, did not preclude intrusion of the analytic historian's voice to criticize either accepted historical interpretations or the acts of individual monarchs or statesmen, particularly when these had been his contemporaries.

In placing his account of the Ottoman Empire within the context of world history, and particularly that of Islamic history, Âli did two things. First, he attempted to establish his own political, religious, and literary culture as a part of an ongoing historical continuum and as the inheritor of older and more prestigious Islamic traditions. He complained in the introduction to the *Essence*, for example, that there were few or no historians of the Ottomans as prominent or well known as those of the Arabs and Iranians.[13] Second, Âli invited and essayed judgment of his own civilization in terms of comparison with the historically dominant political and cultural traditions within that continuum. Âli looked to the present at least as much as to the past, seeking patterns and analogies in the latter which could explain developments in his own time. As we shall see, Âli also looked at certain aspects of past history in light of the experience of his own time, as is of course the wont of any historian, medieval or modern.

Âli's personal motivations for writing history have been dealt with in some detail in preceding pages. He was disillusioned by his own society as well as fascinated by its development, and was deeply committed to the Ottoman cultural ideals of his youth. In order to put Âli's intellectual interests into perspective, we may note that the reign of Murad III witnessed something of an historiographical explosion. Indeed, a tremendous interest in the documentation of events seems to have been a relatively generalized phenomenon in the last quarter of the sixteenth century. During this reign royal patronage for works of historical content, and for their lavish illumination, increased dramatically relative to the preceding and succeeding periods. Furthermore, this period produced a tremendous number of less "official" historical works, in the form of general histories, Ottoman chronicles, and accounts of individual campaigns to such an extent that the reigns of Murad and his predecessor Selim II remain one of the best-documented segments of Ottoman history. While a relatively widespread interest in history may be noted as an aspect of *Zeitgeist*, an explanation for the phenomenon cannot

[13] KA, I, 38.

be precisely documented. However, analysis of Âli's writings provides some hints.

Awareness that by mid-century the Ottoman state had developed a unique imperial tradition—that it was indeed the most extensive and powerful political entity west of China—probably encouraged documentation of its history. Consciousness of the enhanced prestige of Ottoman Islamic cultural traditions—the legacy of Selim I's conquest of the Arab heartlands of Islam and assumption of responsibility for protection of the Holy Places—also played a role. Further expansion and institutional consolidation under Süleyman the Lawgiver reinforced Ottoman perceptions that an imperial peak had been reached. This is certainly the sense of Âli's introduction to the Ottoman portion of the *Essence*. There he traces the growth in territory and authority of the Ottoman state, which in the time of the founder Osman comprised but a single province (*beğlerbeğilik*). It became a far larger entity of twenty provinces under Süleyman, who ruled "with justice for forty-eight [= forty-six] years and cherished and fostered the scholars, poets, bureaucrats, and military"; then, in the reign of Murad III, the Empire totaled "forty provinces" and commanded tribute and obeisance from independent monarchs of east and west.[14]

On the negative side, the second half of the sixteenth century saw tremendous social and economic upheaval, almost continuous warfare without conquest on the Süleymanic scale, and great changes in patterns of government. All of these developments served to initiate a malaise among intellectuals that eventually produced, among other things, a nostalgia for more orderly and glorious times. It may also be that the Empire's changed circumstances indirectly fueled the court's interest in the documentation of contemporary events and dynastic history as a means of propagandistic compensation for sad realities. Too, the occurrence of such tremendous changes within a single generation was a phenomenon which, at least for Âli, required analysis within an historical perspective. This impulse was an important component of Âli's motivation for writing history. In the Ottoman introduction to the *Essence*, Âli, after outlining the growth of the Empire to the year 1000, comments extensively on its current disorder. In addition to describing the spread of corruption and irresponsibility in government, the injustice destroying the realm, and the growing political influence of women and eunuchs of the Harem, Âli gives a chronological synopsis of the symbolic and effective causes of disruption: Süleyman's execution of his son Mustafa in 1553, Selim II's abdication of absolute authority to Sokollu Mehmed Paşa, and Sultan Murad's acquiescence to the graft system. We shall return to the specifics of Âli's analysis; here it is

[14] KA, MS Leiden, 4b-5a.

enough to note that he goes on to liken the sovereign to a physician who, charged with caring for the diseased body politic, has himself fallen ill and is therefore incapable of prescribing the proper remedy, justice.[15] Âli then articulates his own historiographical mission by quoting a verse by Fehmi, the son of Kınalızade Ali Çelebi. This quotation illuminates the degree to which Âli was driven to the composition of a universal history by contemporary problems, by a fascination with their nature and genesis, and by a learned man's desire to awaken his fellow Ottomans, the well- and poorly educated alike, to the urgent need to deal with disorder before it became irreversible decline:

There is no one who will tell of the state of the world!
The sovereign remains withdrawn in seclusion,
[And] the ministers are one and all preoccupied with gathering wealth,
While all others are tormented by the fire of poverty.
Neither jurisconsult nor sheikh will tell the secret to the ruler of the world;
[Or] if they are told to reveal it, no one will write it down, in a book.[16]

Finally, the fact that the Islamic millennium was only sixteen years away when Murad ascended the Ottoman throne must not be forgotten. Apocalyptic expectations and millennial anxieties, the enhanced significance of events in what might be the last years, and also the fact that the end did not come, undoubtedly contributed to the upsurge of historical composition and concern for recordkeeping.[17] The supposition that Murad's court viewed the year A.H. 1000 as a significant turning point is supported by the historian Selâniki. In an entry dated Muharrem 1001 (October 1592), Selâniki writes that at this time the sultan ordered that a record be kept, in register form, of all communications of provincial governors to the Porte, so that an organized and continuous record of events might be kept, beginning with that year, for which later generations would be grateful.[18] Other literary evidence shows that eschatological hopes and fears were relatively common throughout the sixteenth century, the tenth of the Muslim era, and that such expectations stimulated historiographical experimentation and the production of new forms of historical writing.[19] Âli himself, although he wrote his

[15] KA, MS Leiden, 5b; Fleischer, "Royal Authority," pp. 212-13.

[16] KA, MS Leiden, 5b.

[17] See chapters 4 and 5, and Fleischer, "*Curious Bits*."

[18] SELANİKİ, p. 338.

[19] Barbara Flemming, "Der *Ğâmi*ʿ *ül-meknûnât*: Eine Quelle ʿÂlî's aus der Zeit Sultan Süleymâns," *Studien zur Geschichte und Kultur des vorderen Orients* (Leiden, 1981), pp. 81, 89-92. Another of the great universal histories of the age is the *History of the Millennium, Târîkh-i alfî*, composed in India between A.H. 993 and 1000 by order of the Emperor Akbar (Bregel', *Persidskaya Literatura*, I, 419-21). The Ottoman historiographical florescence of the late sixteenth and early seventeenth centuries had its counterparts in Safavi Iran and Mughal India.

general and Ottoman introductions to the *Essence* between 1000 and 1006 (1591-98), constantly refers to the millennium as the watershed date, that in which he began his massive effort, and that against which civilizational progress and decline was to be measured.[20]

THE *ESSENCE OF HISTORY*

ÂLI conceived of his masterpiece as an integrated structure resting on four ''Pillars'' (*rükn*), each one a volume. The first Pillar is devoted to cosmology, geography, and the creation of man. The second deals with the pre-Islamic prophets and Islamic history until the Mongol invasions, and the third with the Mongol and Turkic dynasties. The fourth Pillar, which constitutes about a third of the entire work, recounts the history of the Ottoman house.[21] Despite this conceptual unity, or perhaps because of it, Âli composed the *Essence* in piecemeal fashion, working on different portions at the same time and adding to them later. Parts of the fourth Pillar are dated as early as 1592-93/1001, others as late as 1598-99/1007, and even entries under the same chronological or biographical section were sometimes written years apart.[22] Nevertheless, Âli must have completed much of the work and given it its basic form very quickly. Only two years after he began the *Essence* in early 1592/1000, he composed an elaborate introduction explaining his motivations, his historiographical methods and theories, and the structure of the work, and listing all of his major Arabic, Persian, and Turkish sources.[23]

Each Pillar differs somewhat in format according to the subject and source materials available. Volume I is primarily a geography sandwiched between accounts of the Creation and of Adam and Eve in the Garden. The second Pillar proceeds chronologically by prophetic era or, in the Islamic period, caliphal reign. The history of the Turco-Mongol states is divided first into geographical regions, then into dynasties within those regions, and finally into individual dynasts. The last Pillar is arranged chronologically by reigns, each of which in turn is treated not strictly annalistically, but in terms of major ''events,'' which are numbered. Âli was not content simply to recount political developments and military operations. In order to give a

[20] KA, I, 8, 36; V, 6.

[21] KA, I, 13-15.

[22] Some sample dates: 1001: KA, Selim/7, Nur 3409, 245b; 1002: Süleyman/54, Nur 3409, 94b; Süleyman/Ulema, ''Arabzade Muslihüddin,'' Nur 3409, 151a; 1005: Selim/Şu'ara, ''Hatemi,'' ''Muhibbi,'' Nur 3409, 275b, 285a; Murad/Introduction, Nur 3409, 291a; Mehmed/Grand Vezirate of Damad İbrahim Paşa, Halet Ef. 598, 438b-439b; 1006: Murad/32, Nur 3409, 375b; 1007: Murad/Introduction, Nur 3409, 292a; Süleyman/Ümera, ''Canpulad Beğ,'' Esad Ef. 2162, 396a.

[23] KA, I, 2-47. The date of 1593-94/1002 is given on p. 36.

complete picture of the times and regnal style of each Ottoman sultan, he placed at the end of each reign systematic biographies of the great political and cultural figures of that age. These biographical sections are arranged by professional classification—vezirs, governors, chancellors and treasurers, scholars, sheikhs, and poets—and become richer as Âli moves toward his own time. This inclusion of extensive biographical materials within the body of a formal history was an important structural innovation within the Ottoman historiographical context; it reflected Âli's keen interest in the individuals who had helped to shape his society, and made him a major source for study of the human and social dimensions of sixteenth-century Ottoman life, dimensions which biography, unlike formal history, can illuminate in profuse and colorful detail. That Âli was not able to complete the *Essence* as he hoped is shown by the absence of biographies for the reign of Murad III, although he intended to write this section. But by 1597-98/1006 the Ottoman volume was in full enough form for Âli to compose a special introduction to it.[24]

The wide variety of sources that Âli cites in his general introduction (in fact he used many more, citing them where appropriate) testifies to his industry.[25] Indeed, he saw his *Essence* as a critical encyclopedia of historical knowledge, a vehicle for his own erudition that would benefit both the learned and those who were basically literate but not fully educated:

> One should follow the [Arabic] dictum, "The best of speech is that adorned with completeness, which [both] the elite and the commonality comprehend." That is, its benefit should be for all, and both the elite and the commonality should profit from it, such that each derives benefit from the concern shown for his [own] comprehension and understanding.[26]

Âli goes on to extol the value of his encyclopedic history;

> This collection of stories and historical accounts is a pleasing book marked with eloquence. It is the quintessence [*zübde*] of one hundred thirty books, and each of those is the choice extract of other volumes of tales; if these latter are also counted, [the *Essence*] is the essence of six hundred books. True, it is difficult for the empty-handed [i.e., the impoverished] to possess it, since the difficulty of copying four such volumes, and the amount of the expenditures necessary are as evident as the full moon. But it is not an easy thing to lay hands on a hidden treasure, nor does anyone obtain the essence [*cevahir*] of Elixir easily

[24] KA, V, 2-18, and MS Leiden, 3a-10a.
[25] KA, I, 17-20.
[26] KA, I, 9.

> or without great expense. [My work is particularly valuable because by owning it] one is saved from the weighty burden of carrying many tomes, and one can [therefore sell them to] defray the cost of acquiring a fine compilation.[27]

Âli's imagined audience consisted of scholars, educated statesmen, and the growing body of Ottomans, such as professional bureaucrats and merchants, who were literate in Ottoman Turkish but might not have the knowledge of Persian and Arabic, or the wealth and leisure, to build or use large libraries. In his introduction Âli complains of what he saw as a general decline of education in his time. In using his learning to compose a vast epitome of Islamic and Ottoman historical knowledge, Âli in a sense acknowledged the force of this perception and the growth of a nonelite literate class, at the same time that he sought to remedy deficiencies of education. The result was a comprehensive, thoughtful representation of the Ottoman experience within its proper context, the literary molding and casting of a relatively new cultural tradition.

Âli's Ottoman history is, of course, the most important portion of the *Essence*, and this fourth Pillar, like the other three, forms a truly independent volume. Its value lies not only in its detailed presentation of the second half of the sixteenth century, for which Âli drew heavily on his own experience and eyewitness reports from the many Ottomans, of high and low rank, with whom he was acquainted, but also in its comprehensive and often original treatment of earlier periods based on nearly all the sources then available. We have already noted, for example, that Âli was the sole sixteenth-century historian to make use of and quote from the *Kanunname* of the Conqueror. Âli included in his introduction a brief bibliographical essay on the major Ottoman histories he utilized. This passage is an abbreviated history of the development of Ottoman historiography, and it shows which works Âli saw as forming a part of a culturally approved historiographical chain. This was the chain leading up to his own *magnum opus*, which he hoped would give classical form to a nascent literary tradition, one that Âli feared was in danger of being disrupted or degraded by a growing lack of concern for "good" historical writing.

Âli first names four chroniclers identified as "those who first wrote the history of the Ottoman house, up through the time of Sultan Bayezid."[28] These are Âşıkpaşazade, Ruhi (fl. 1511),[29] Neşri, and "Mevlana İsa, the praiseworthy man of Hamid-ili, author of the *Collector of the Concealed*

[27] KA, I, 13.

[28] The following discussion of Âli's source list is based on KA, MS Leiden, 6a-8b.

[29] Ruhi's history actually ends with the year 1511; see V. L. Ménage "Edirneli Rûhî'ye Atfedilen Osmanlı Tarihinden İki Parça," in *Ord. Prof. İsmail Hakkı Uzunçarşılı'ya Armağan* (Ankara, 1976), pp. 311-15; M. K. Özergin, "Ruhi," İA.

[Câmi' ül-meknunat]."[30] All of these works belong to the popular *Chronicles* tradition, and Âli pointedly states that they are just that: basic annalistic works and collections of tales valuable for the record they provide but devoid of any literary or conceptual elegance. Their worthy authors, "it is known, were not authors and stylists such as befit [the subject]."[31]

Âli next enumerates those more scholarly and linguistically conscious authors who wrote comprehensive dynastic histories, the form and content of which combined the highest historical acumen with the best of learned literary style. The first of these is the *Eight Paradises* of Idrîs-i Bidlîsî, the only fault of which, Âli says, is its excessively complex rhetoric, which apparently impeded even Âli's comprehension.[32] Because Bidlîsî's Persian posed difficulties for Rumi readers, Âli states, prominent Ottomans persuaded Sultan Bayezid to commission a Turkish version from Kemalpaşazade, "who wrote well, with the clear form of expression used at that time."[33] Next came Chancellor Celalzade, "who described the ways and institutions of the Ottoman house."[34] Celalzade's successor in office, Ramazanzade, wrote a summary of world and Ottoman history "thinking that it was the necessary task of chancellors to write a history of the Ottomans."[35] Finally, the distinguished scholar, professor, and author Sa'düddin wrote his *Crown of Histories*, and "he truly surpassed all of his predecessors who wrote in Turkish; he cut the die in marble."[36]

Âli was personally acquainted with three of the five historians he praises here so highly; and all five were either ulema or bureaucrats of chancellor status. Although the histories of Bidlîsî and Kemalpaşazade were the product of royal patronage, none of these authors was an "official" historian in the sense of one employed or patronized specifically for that purpose. For Âli, they were above all loyal Ottomans and learned men respected for the knowledge and skill they displayed in dynastic service, literary or otherwise. In the continuation of his bibliographical essay, Âli contrasts them with his more immediate contemporaries, the official *şehname* writers. He first notes important changes in the character of cultural life: the great administrators are obsessed with money, the ulema are unproductive and concerned only with earning and advancement, Sufi sheikhs are mere time-servers making a living. Âli implies that the dearth of independent scholar-

30 This work, previously considered anonymous, actually extends to 1529; see Flemming, "*Ğâmi' ül-meknûnât*," pp. 81-85, and Schmidt, "Verantwoording," p. 24.

31 KA, MS Leiden, 6a.

32 KA, MS Leiden, 6a; Âli mistakenly states that Idrîs came to Rum in the days of the Conqueror, and that he wrote his history by that Sultan's order.

33 KA, MS Leiden, 6a.

34 KA, MS Leiden, 6b.

35 KA, MS Leiden, 6b.

36 KA, MS Leiden, 6b.

ship, a product of the decline in patronage and appreciation for learning and talent, reinforced the imperial need to bureaucratize the position of court historiographer. He explicitly states that, "When the state of the times reached this pass, shameful men who [happened to be] literate made claims to honor and came to be called men of talent."[37] These were the *şehnameci*s Seyyid Lokman, Nutki, and Ta'likizade. Âli was familiar with even the most recent of their works (he quotes from Ta'likizade's verse history of the Egri campaign, completed in 1597-98/1006),[38] but in general, or perhaps on principle, he held no very high opinion of these professional writers of heroic verse: "In our time there is no difference between the *şehname*-writer and the teller of [popular] tales."[39] It may have been for political reasons that Âli singled out the incumbent *şehnameci* Ta'likizade, a member of the scholastically distinguished Fenari family, as the only one of the lot who had a genuine talent for poetry and prose.[40] Âli's extended criticism of the *şehnameci*s, who were professional scribes rather than scholars, is based entirely on considerations of style, especially poetic. Âli was particularly hard on Seyyid Lokman, whom he considered incompetent in both Persian and Turkish, despite the fact that he used at least one, and probably all, of Lokman's works as sources.[41]

Âli self-consciously cast himself in the role of continuator of a tradition of formal, if not official, history writing. This was a tradition established by scholar-littérateurs who were as concerned with giving imperial history a high-culture form, in Ottoman Turkish, as with presenting facts. Âli judged the importance and standing of a work of history by its quality as a literary and cultural artifact as much as by the quality of its information, assuming the basic integrity and veracity of earlier scholar-historians. Given this assumption, in cultural terms the form of a history, which necessarily displayed the author's critical as well as stylistic capacities, was in a sense just as important as the basic information it provided, if not in fact more so.

This does not mean that Âli was uncritical in his use of the works of ad-

[37] KA, MS Leiden, 6b.

[38] KA, MS Leiden, 8a; Christine Woodhead, "From Scribe to Littérateur: The Career of a Sixteenth-Century Ottoman *Kâtib*," *Bulletin of the British Society for Middle East Studies* 9 (1982): 67.

[39] KA, Murad/Şehnameguyan, Nur 3409, 422a.

[40] KA, MS Leiden, 6b-8b. For the bibliography of Ta'likizade see Woodhead, "Scribe"; for that of Seyyid Lokman, see GOW, pp. 164-67. Âli's expressed sympathy for Ta'likizade is particularly interesting in light of the similarity of the views of the state of the Empire that each articulated at the time of the accession of Mehmed III (see chapter 5); this suggests that the two knew each other, or at least belonged to the same circle of intellectuals in the capital who were concerned with the drastic need for reform. But compare Âli's harsh criticism of Ta'likizade in KA, Murad/Şehnameguyan, Nur 3409, 422a.

[41] KA, MS Leiden, 7a-b; KA, Murad/Şehnameguyan, Nur 3409, 421a-422a; KA, V, 25 (citing an unidentified work by Seyyid Lokman), 38 (citing his *Kıyâfet ül-insânîye fî şemâyil il-Osmânîye*).

mired predecessors, for he felt free to disagree with both their facts and their interpretations. Nor does it mean that he applied such restrictive criteria to his selection of source material. While Âli the littérateur might identify those works with which he wished his *Essence* to be compared, Âli the conscientious historian (the two personae are not, of course, dichotomous) made a point of knowing about, and where necessary comparing and citing, every source relevant to his Ottoman history. In addition to those histories listed in his introduction, Âli referred, for example, to the earliest Ottoman historical works, those of Ahmedi (d. 1413/815), his brother Hamzavi, and their contemporary Ahmed-i Da'i.[42] Of Persian and Arabic sources touching on or dealing with the Ottomans Âli cited Şükrullah's *Splendor of Histories*, the Tîmûrid histories of Ibn ʿArabshâh (d. 1450/854), Sharaf al-dîn Yazdî (d. 1454/858) and Niẓâm al-dîn Shâmî (fl. 1404) and the universal histories of Khvândamîr (d. 1535/942) and Lari;[43] and this list is by no means complete. Of more specific relevance to the history of Rum in the Ottoman period, if less immediately identifiable to modern scholars, are an anonymous Ottoman chronicle written in the time of Bayezid II;[44] a work entitled the *Hidden Pearl*, which covers material at least as late as the reign of Bayezid but has yet to be identified;[45] one of the three historical works of the treasurer Ebülfazl Mehmed (d. ca. 1579-80/987), son of Idrîs-i Bidlîsî;[46] and popular histories of pre-Conquest Constantinople and Aya Sofya.[47]

Some works Âli appears to have been reluctant to use explicitly, although he admitted familiarity with them. One such was the *Tevarih-i Âl-i Osman* of Lutfi Paşa (d. 1564/971); Âli had read at least part of the work, but he disapproved of its style and found Lutfi Paşa's pretensions to the scholarship immoderate and ill-founded.[48] Despite such apparent idiosyncrasies, Âli was assiduous in collecting, or taking advantage of, the works of his contemporaries and official documents to which he had access, or which found their way into private collections. He used, for instance, the official account of Sinan Paşa's reconquest of the Yemen, the product of Menla Şihabi, son

[42] KA, V, 94, 129-30; GOW, pp. 11-14. On Ahmedi and Hamzavi, see Tunca Kortantamer, *Leben und Weltbild des altosmanischen Dichters Ahmedi unter besonderer Berücksichtigung seines Dîwâns* (Freiburg, 1973), pp. 1-32.

[43] KA, I, 19, 50-51; V, 103; GAL, II, 36-37 (Ibn ʿArabshâh); C. A. Storey, *Persian Literature: A Bio-Bibliographical Survey*, 2 vols. (London, 1970; repr.), I, 101-109 (Khvândamîr), 92-101 (Mîrkhvând), 278-79 (Shâmî), 283-87 (Yazdî).

[44] KA, V, 24.

[45] KA, Bayezid/36, Fatih 4225, 171b-173a. Ménage (''Ruhi,'' p. 314) suggests that the title may refer to the *Câmi' ül-meknûnât*, while Flemming (''*Ǧami' ül-meknûnât*,'' p. 82) seems to incline to the view that it is yet a different work. The *Dürr-i meknûn* in question cannot be Yazıcıoğlu's (Yazıcızade) work of that title, since it extends into the early sixteenth century.

[46] KA, IV/3, 33; cf. GOW, pp. 95-97.

[47] See GOW, pp. 27-31.

[48] KA, Süleyman/Sadrazamlar, ''Lutfi Paşa,'' Fatih 4225, 318b-319a. For the death date of Lutfi Paşa, see Röhrborn, *Verwaltungsgeschichte*, p. 7.

of Menla Şükri, himself the author of a *Selimname*.[49] Âli also praised the *Book of Bravery*, his friend Âsafi's history of the conquest of Şirvan.[50] With his passion for human detail, Âli obtained, and later quoted, a list of the possessions left by the grand vezir Rüstem Paşa at his death (1561/968); a copy of the official audit list had been put into Sokollu Mehmed Paşa's own memorabilia album (*cönk*), from which Sinan Paşa, who died as governor-general of Cyprus, had had a copy made for his own scrapbook, and it was there that Âli saw the document.[51]

Âli devoted much space to the biographies of prominent Ottomans. For information on the scholars and mystics of the Empire since its inception he relied heavily upon the *Crimson Peonies (Al-Shaqâ'iq al-nuʿmânîya)* of Taşköprüzade (d. 1561/968) and upon the continuations of that work authored by Âşık Çelebi and Ali Mınık (d. 1584/992).[52] Âli studied and evaluated all four of the Ottoman biographical compendia of poets then available: the *tezkeres* of Sehi (d. 1548/955), Latifi (d. 1582/990), Âşık Çelebi, and Kınalızade Hasan Çelebi.[53] He also knew of the anthology of Ahdi, completed in 1563 and in which Âli himself was mentioned, but he discounted the work as a product of the Iranian Ahdi's naiveté about Rumi poetry.[54] Historical biography was Âli's special passion. He supplemented his extensive, and usually careful, use of written materials with personal knowledge, the oral traditions and reports he seems to have tirelessly solicited, and a judicious exploitation of gossip, another of his passions.[55] The narrative portion of his history, particularly that covering his own lifetime, for which there were no truly comprehensive sources for him to draw upon, benefited in like manner from Âli's enthusiasm for collecting and describing the historical lineaments of his society.

This survey of the resources Âli brought to bear on the writing of the *Es-*

[49] KA, Selim/3, Nur 3409, 229b.

[50] KA, Selim/7, Nur 3409, 243b.

[51] KA, Süleyman/Sadrazamlar, "Rüstem Paşa," Nur 3409, 121b.

[52] KA, Süleyman/Ulema, "Taşköprüzade," Nur 3409, 145b-146b, where Âli states that up to this point he has relied upon Taşköprüzade verbatim, then goes on to praise Ali Mınık's continuation (*zeyl*), as well as comment on the utility of some of the contributions made by Âşık Çelebi, Cf. GOW, pp. 69, 84-87, 112-13.

[53] KA, Selim/Şu'ara, "*tezyil*" following "Âşık," Nur 3409, 270b-280a. In Süleyman/Şu'ara, "Hayali Beğ," Nur 3409, 179a-b, Âli praises Âşık Çelebi, upon whom he relies heavily for the poets of Süleyman's time, but cites several areas in which he disagrees with him. Âli's biographies of poets are the subject of a doctoral dissertation by Mustafa İsen, Lecturer in Ottoman at Atatürk University, Erzurum; this work is unfortunately not available to me.

Sehi's *Heşt Bihişt* has been published by Günay Kut (Cambridge, 1978). Latifi's *Tezkere* was printed in Istanbul, 1314; for analysis of its contents, see Levend, *Edebiyat*, I, 261-69.

[54] KA, Selim/Şu'ara, "Ahdi," Nur 3409, 201a.

[55] For example, Âli cites as sources for his account of the reign of Selim I direct oral communications from Piri Paşa Ramazanoğlu (KA, Selim I/10, Fatih 4225, 220b) and Celalzade (KA, Selim I/ Vüzera, "Mustafa Paşa," Fatih 4225, 228b).

sence of History cannot pretend to exhaustiveness; but the focus of this section of our study remains Âli the historian, rather than the specifics of his text. Our purpose has been to outline Âli's vision of the Ottoman historiographical heritage and then to illuminate the dedication to completeness, the erudition, and the imaginative use of very disparate source materials—some of them formal histories, some not—with which Âli attempted to carry out his self-appointed task. It now remains to study, if only within the context of a few important examples, what Âli wrought with his resources and his vision.

TEN

MUSLIM AND OTTOMAN

ÂLİ'S VIEW OF RUM

MUSTAFA ÂLI'S perception of history was oriented by the two cultural traditions of which he was a product. As a Rumi, one born and raised in the Ottoman domains, he identified with the distinctive regional culture that had developed in Anatolia and Rumeli. As a graduate of the *ilmiye* educational system, he also identified with the universalist religious tradition of the *medrese* and the cosmopolitan Arabo-Persianate high culture to which the Ottoman Empire was heir. The two orientations were not absolutely distinct from one another; but certainly, important facets of the Ottoman experiment made the Empire a unique, if not aberrant, phenomenon within the context of Islamicate history. In large measure it was this unique character of the Empire, which in the sixteenth century emerged as a vital and creatively syncretic cultural and political entity, that gave Âli his enthusiasm for its literature and its history.

Âli articulates his passion for things Ottoman in the general introduction to the *Essence*, in the course of a discussion of his own use of language:

The volumes of books of history are endless;
What a mine is language, that it still provides jewels!
Though in Turkish and Arabic and Persian speech
Books have been written, and literary works have strung their pearls,
Some are closed [by language], and some give no pleasure;
Some are in foul Turkish, and do not console.
Incomprehensible books will not enlighten the people of Rum,
Nor do the enlightened find good fortune in reading Turkish.

In fact the astonishing language current in the state of Rum, composed of four languages [West Turkish, Çagatay, Arabic, and Persian], is a pure gilded tongue which, in the speech of the literati, seems more difficult than any of these. If one were to equate speaking Arabic with a religious obligation [*farz*], and the use of Persian with a sanctioned tradition [*sünnet*], then the speaking of a Turkish made up of these sweetnesses [Arabic and Persian] becomes a meritorious act [*müsta-*

> *habb*], and, in the view of those eloquent in Turkish, the use of simple Turkish should be forbidden.[1]

Âli goes on to explicate those factors of origin, ethnic constitution, and culture that give the Ottoman state a distinctive place in the history of the Islamic world:

> Those varied peoples and different types of Rumis living in the glorious days of the Ottoman dynasty, who are not [generically] separate from those tribes of Turks and Tatars dealt with in the third Pillar, are a select community and pure, pleasing people who, just as they are distinguished in the origins of their state, are singled out for their piety [*diyanet*], cleanliness [*nazafet*], and faith [*akidet*]. Apart from this, most of the inhabitants of Rum are of confused ethnic origins. Among its notables there are few whose lineage does not go back to a convert to Islam . . . either on their father or their mother's side, the genealogy is traced to a filthy infidel. It is as if two different species of fruitbearing tree mingled and mated, with leaves and fruits; and the fruit of this union was large and filled with liquid, like a princely pearl. The best qualities of the progenitors were then manifested and gave distinction, either in physical beauty, or in spiritual wisdom.[2]

Âli develops this latter theme in a delineation of the cultural and religious history of Rum. In speaking of "Rum" in a cultural context, Âli means the Anatolian and Rumelian heartlands of the Ottoman state, the regions in which the Ottomans had first established themselves and then expanded through *gaza* in the fourteenth and fifteenth centuries; Âli expresses his schema of cultural development in terms of a racial metaphor. Until the beginning of the formation of the Ottoman state in 1300/700, the Muslim inhabitants of Anatolia were a mixed lot—Arabs, Turks, and Iranians who mingled with the non-Muslim population and produced a yet more mixed race with no interest in culture, fit only for eating and drinking. Then, from Transoxiana came "the Ottoman tribes," who were very close to the resident Selcuks, "as if they had both descended from a single lineage." Thirty or forty years later the Ottomans began their conquest of Rumeli and mated with the non-Muslim inhabitants of those regions. Gradually, Arab, Iranian, and Tatar ulema mingled with these, the products of their unions being more fit for and inclined to religious learning. Finally, non-Muslim subjects, such as Serbs, began to convert to Islam and "in the second or third generation cast off the stigma of unbelief." These produced physically beautiful children who were capable of receiving the enlightenment of knowledge and civilized culture. Rum thus became a breeding ground for

[1] KA, I, 11 (also quoted above, chapter 1, note 27).
[2] KA, I, 16.

exceptionally fine, able, pious people; it was through the cultivation and encouragement of these, and by attracting learned men to Rum, that the Ottoman sultans had built up their state and made it "the envy of the Arabs and Iranians."[3]

Here, at the beginning of his world history, Âli introduces several motifs that permeate the remainder of the work. One of these, on the emotional level, is the sheer adventure and excitement of the development of a frontier society which, while coping with ethnic and linguistic diversity, made itself the inheritor of one high cultural tradition and then elaborated another of its own. By Âli's time Ottoman literary and political culture had emerged from humble beginnings to achieve, at the very least, rough or potential parity with the older established traditions that had found their expression in Arabic and Persian; and that blossoming had just begun in its full force when Âli was young. Âli, in short, was proud of his Rumi origins, excited and enlivened by the Ottoman experiment. His expressions of enthusiasm for the regional culture for which "Rum" stood extend beyond his comments on language and race to his use of sources. For example, in the cosmological portion of the *Essence* Âli pointedly describes one of his major sources, İbn Melekzade Mehmed (d. 1450-51/854), as "one of the scholars of Rum," and he also makes frequent reference to the *Splendor of Histories* of Şükrüllah.[4] Âli's "Rumi chauvinism," of course, is intimately bound up with, and perhaps a form of compensation for, a sense of cultural inferiority vis-à-vis the older civilizational traditions of the Islamic world.[5]

A second theme that Âli introduces is that of ethnic heterogeneity as a primary characteristic of the Ottoman state. By implication, he also extols the importance and efficacy of the *devşirme* slave system that institutionalized and perpetuated that heterogeneity. Not only does Âli view the Arabic and Iranian cultural spheres as separate from his own; he also sees the distinctive identity of the Ottoman cultural nexus as directly related to that mixing of ethnic and confessional groups the *locus classicus* of which was Rumeli, the western portion of the Ottoman Empire. When he discusses in detail the primary constituent ethnic groups of the Empire, Âli almost invariably focuses on the *kul cinsi*, those non-Muslim groups eligible for *devşirme* recruitment. In his Ottoman introduction to the *Essence*, Âli examines the major positive and negative characteristics of each group, and concludes with a discussion of the importance of physiognomy in the determination of a *devşirme* recruit's innate abilities.[6]

[3] KA, I, 33-34; V, 8-9.

[4] KA, I, 48-55. Âli cites specifically İbn Melekzade's *Rawḍat al-muttaqîn, The Garden of the Pious*; see OM, I, 220. Âli also calls his author "İbn Firişte," the designation usually reserved for his uncle, the Hurufi author Abdülmecid; see "Firişte-oğlu," İA, and Abdülbaki Gölpınarlı, *Hurufilik Metinleri Kataloğu* (Ankara, 1973), pp. 12-16.

[5] See chapter 4, note 104, and chapter 9, note 13.

[6] KA, V, 9-15; here Âli lists the constituent groups as Arabs, Circassians, Abaza, Albani-

Âli's point in these discussions is the following. By virtue of its geographical location and origins as a Muslim *gazi* state, the Ottoman Empire acquired unique human resources. Mingling of constituent ethnic groups potentially allowed for optimal combinations of physical, moral, and intellectual characteristics within that heterogeneous population; physical strength and beauty came from the non-Muslims, intellectual prowess and piety from representatives of the heartlands of Islamic civilization. The Ottoman sultans, by understanding the nature and quality of each group, by institution of the *devşirme* system, and by judicious selection, were able to mold an especially able governing class composed of those most loyal to the Ottoman dynasty and its ideals, and of those best qualified, by virtue of both innate characteristics and training, to rule, create, and teach. It was this aspect of Ottoman heterogeneity, nurtured and institutionalized by the ruling house, which had brought the Empire to its peak of political and cultural greatness, and had facilitated the establishment of a centralized, well-ordered, just state. In large measure it was these products of conversion and of the slave system whom Âli considered to be the most genuine Ottomans, trained for military service and rule within the Ottoman tradition. While Âli did identify Turkish language with Ottomanism, Turkish ethnicity had nothing to do with the Ottoman state except in the origins of its founders. In the *Counsel* he advised the sultan against giving excessive authority to indigenous Muslim military elements, namely Kurdish and Turkish tribal leaders from Anatolia, who were not part of what he viewed as the fundamental process in the creation of the centralized state and the *askeri* class: the deracination, education, and Ottomanization of the subject peoples.[7] Here it must be remembered that Âli himself, who came from a *kul* family background, had something of a vested interest in implicitly portraying the human backbone of the Ottoman state as a product of the *devşirme*, of education, and of several generations of breeding among the sultan's servitors.

---

ans, Croats (Bosnians), Franks, Hungarians, Georgians, Russians, Germans, Wallachians, and Moldavians. Such discussions of racial characteristics seem to have been part of common Ottoman intellectual lore in the sixteenth century; Kınalızade Ali Çelebi, for example, devoted a chapter of his *Ahlak-ı Ala'i* to the subject (Book II, pp. 58-65). See also V. L. Ménage, "Devshirme," EI², and H. İnalcık, "Ghulâm," EI². A curious variation on this theme is a passage in MEVA'İD (pp. 44-47) in which Âli discusses the virtues and special amorous talents of boys of the various ethnic groups found in the Empire, at the same time decrying pederasty as unmanly and ostentatiously using the dubitative "*miş*" suffix to show that he had no firsthand knowledge of such practices.

[7] COUNSEL, I, 62-63 (trans.), 157-59 (text). Nihal Atsız, an extreme Turkish nationalist, seized upon this passage as proof of anti-Turkish prejudice and historical ignorance in an historian of non-Turkish *devşirme* origin. In fact, Âli's objection to the inclusion of Kurds and "Turks" (i.e., Türkmen tribesmen) in government has less to do with ethnicity than with their tribal character. Established tribal groups in the Empire could, and frequently did, take an independent and resistant attitude toward the central government in order to serve their own interests, something that converted, deracinated *devşirme* products could not do.

Âli's family did not belong to the *askeri* class, but came from one of the ethnic groups that had come to supply much of that class, and Âli gained his own credentials through education. He was not a born Ottoman, but a self-made one.

Polyethnicity also had less positive aspects, in that it could produce or exacerbate certain types of conflict. According to Âli, for example, Sinan Paşa utilized Albanian solidarity for his own purposes, and new arrivals from freshly conquered eastern territories were viewed with suspicion. Âli also saw the lighter side of Ottoman ethnic diversity. In a poem composed during one of his provincial postings, Âli bemoaned the lot of the finance director, whose fate was to listen to rude demands for pay made by troops of various origins, each in his own language. Âli reproduced the speech of the Arab, Iranian, Kurd, Bosnian, Albanian, Greek, Frank, Serb, Eastern Turk (*Çagatay adamı*), and crude Anatolian (*manav*).[8]

Âli's third major theme in the passages cited above is the overriding importance of Islamic religion and civilization in the genesis of the Ottoman state. In terms of his racial imagery, it was the advent of Muslim scholars from Iran and the Arab lands (which from the Ottoman perspective constituted the hinterland), bringing with them a high cultural tradition, which raised the Muslims of Rum above the level of beings fit only for basic physical activity. Islam, broadly considered as a legal and cultural system, provided the means whereby members of the diverse communities who inhabited the frontier between Muslim and non-Muslim domains were incorporated into the Ottoman state and then into the Ottoman class. Clearly, in Âli's view, Muslim identity was not enough to create and ensure the success of a state; a polity also had to cultivate the mature universalistic intellectual and spiritual traditions associated with Islamic religious culture. Âli draws a dichotomy between body and soul; the Ottoman frontier populace provided strong bodies and warriors, while soul and mind came from the *medreses* of the hinterland. By bringing high culture to the marches, the ulema bequeathed to future generations a propensity and respect for learning that enabled the Ottoman state to attain cultural greatness. This is a direct expression of Âli's conviction that broad learning in the high Islamic mold was as fundamental to the life of a polity as military achievement.[9]

ISLAM IN RUM

IN ÂLI'S introductory discussions of the history of his own time, these two types of self-identification—Ottoman regionalism and Islamic universal-

[8] *Divan (Vâridât ül-enîka)*, MS İÜ Türkçe 695, 232b-233a. I am grateful to Professor Andreas Tietze for drawing my attention to this partial ode addressed to Sultan Murad.

[9] See Fleischer, "Royal Authority," pp. 213-14.

ism—appear as the two poles of his world view. Âli was attracted more strongly now to one, now to the other, particularly the more realities diverged from ideals. One of the most striking examples of this phenomenon occurs in the course of a complaint that learning and its exponents are no longer respected. While the "people of the Prophet" (*ehl-i resûl*) and the educated receive no rewards, Âli says, the great statesmen responsible for the ruin of the state are Bosnians, Albanians, and Franks, and the majority of the governors and vezirs are of Christian origin.[10] Admittedly, this passage occurs in the context of a somewhat rhetorical poem. Nevertheless, it is worthy of attention, for its content sits poorly with Âli's stated enthusiasm for Ottoman ecumenism, and raises questions about Âli's self-identification. Âli's own lineage was very similar to that of those vezirs he reviled and who, by virtue of their *devşirme* origin and high status, were those same "real Ottomans" whom he considered to be the greatest asset of the state. Âli clearly identifies here with the "*ehl-i resûl*," which would normally be translated as "descendants of the Prophet." Âli could hardly have claimed such descent. Rather, the phrase should be taken metaphorically to refer to those who preserve Muḥammad's heritage, i.e., those learned in the Islamic tradition. Why then should Âli in this context consider himself more a Muslim than an Ottoman, or a better Muslim or better person than other Ottomans? The answer is, quite simply, his education. For Âli, the good of the state is directly connected with the rectitude of its religion, and those who uphold and maintain religion are the most able scholars, teachers, and the generally well educated, in which group Âli of course includes himself. Âli's concept of the importance of Islam goes far beyond narrow scholasticism or rigid personal piety to include a broad, if somewhat nebulous, notion of a complete moral and political culture. A summary of Âli's discussions of the moral and cultural history of the Ottoman Empire will clarify this point.[11]

Until about the year 1553 the Ottoman state was the envy of the Muslim world. Then Sultan Süleyman made his first great mistake in having his son Mustafa executed as a result of the plottings of the grand vezir Rüstem Paşa and the "harem women," meaning Süleyman's consort Hurrem Sultan. Mustafa was the Ottoman prince most favored as successor to the throne by the ulema and other educated people. From this point on the Empire went into extreme disorder and decline; the unworthy began to dominate government, plagues (a sign of divine retribution and apocalypse) became frequent, and the change in the Empire's material circumstances destroyed the

[10] KA, I, 31.

[11] The following, except where noted, is a summary of KA, I, 34-39.

moral character of most of the inhabitants of Rum, who abandoned generosity, sincerity, and rectitude for greed and opportunism.

Âli returns to this symbolic moment again and again in the *Essence*, enumerating the other major events in the moral disintegration of the Empire that followed the execution of Prince Mustafa. Süleyman's harem women, eager to have their collaborator Rüstem Paşa restored to office, engineered the killing of his successor Ahmed Paşa; Prince Bayezid, Süleyman's rebel son, declared after his flight to Iran that this had been the sultan's second major error, which had contributed significantly to the outbreak of civil war.[12] Decline became yet more apparent in the reign of Selim, who, "although he did not allow developments that were contrary to the ancestral law [*kanun-ı kadim*]," devoted himself to pleasure and gave over all his authority to the nepotistic Sokollu Mehmed Paşa, who filled the government with his relatives and retainers, regardless of their suitability for office. The last watershed in imperial decline, for Âli, came when Şemsi Ahmed Paşa persuaded Sultan Murad to accept a bribe, thereby inflicting moral degradation on the sovereign and forcing him to acquiesce, by participation, to the graft which was becoming rampant in the state.[13]

Âli, having established the importance of the moral bond between the sovereign and the men of religion, goes on in his general introduction to delineate a religious typology of the people of Rum, and particularly the inhabitants of Istanbul, at the end of the sixteenth/tenth century:

1. The masses, who are either blind believers in Islam, or are secret adherents of heretical religious doctrines.

2. The "middle classes" (*evâsit-ı nâs*), the people of trades and crafts, who are given to enjoyment and to thinking themselves better than is in fact the case. Of cultural life they know poetry best, but even in this know less than they pretend. They insist upon recitation of the works of old, famous poets, but refuse to recognize new poets of quality if they have never heard their names.

3. The ulema, who also fall into three categories:

   a. The great ulema, who are able to distinguish all degrees of truth and quality, though they have a tendency to avoid admitting the virtues of others.

   b. The middle range of ulema, who will not admit of new truths for fear of demeaning their own position.

   c. The lowest group, fundamentalists who hold so firmly to the words of the oldest authorities that they refuse to consider that new insights or new works are possible. These sin in the direction of fanaticism and

[12] KA, Süleyman/Sadrazamlar, "Ahmed Paşa," Nur 3409, 122a-b.

[13] KA, MS Leiden, 5a-b.

blindness, like the Jews and Christians who refused to acknowledge the authority of the Prophet, and are primarily "infamous Turks" (*Türkân-ı bednâm*), ulema who wear the trappings of learning but have none.

Sayyid Şharîf Jurjânî (1340-1413/740-816) had once traveled from Iran to Rum and had praised the determination of the frontier scholars to acquire knowledge; but he also wrote verses saying that religious learning arose in Arabia, found maturity and stability in Iran, and found its end in Rum because of the prevalence of customary or non-*şer'i* legal usage (*örf*). The Conqueror and his immediate successors through Süleyman had done their best to remedy the low level of religious learning and culture by attracting prominent scholars from hinterland areas to the capital, and by establishing universities so that Ottoman students need no longer travel abroad in search of education. After Süleyman, however, the situation changed and observance of the *şeri'at* gave way to customary or arbitrary practice (*örf*). Ulema, and judges in particular, became corrupt, wealthy, and ostentatious, doffing their clerical garments in favor of military (*sipahi*) attire, such as large turbans. The vezirs no longer respect or patronize learning, and there are few left who are able to interpret the works of the old authorities. Rum has few or no historians of the stature of those of the Arabs or Iranians. Âli concludes this discourse on a personal note; he has withdrawn from a world that is far from ideal, has consoled himself with contemplation of the verses of the old masters Ḥâfiẓ and ʿUmar Khayyâm, and has decided to write his world history.

Some of Âli's argument here is admittedly self-serving and self-aggrandizing. He implies a causal link between what he perceived (doubtlessly in somewhat exaggerated fashion) as moral decline and apocalyptic chaos on the one hand, and rejection of the *medrese* and its legal and scholastic values, symbolized by Süleyman's rejection of the *ilmiye* candidate for the Ottoman throne, on the other. Âli identified himself with the *medrese* and its values, though he was not a professional *âlim*. His frequently proferred observations and advice were not accepted, his solutions to the Empire's problems were not acted upon, and he had great difficulty obtaining what he saw as suitable rewards. Ergo, the learned were not respected and those best qualified to bring order to chaos were not sought out. In fact, this passage follows a somewhat more impassioned statement on the absolute necessity for royal patronage of members of the educated elite, like himself. Âli's complaints about the failure of certain groups to recognize the validity of new poetic and intellectual products can be taken in a similar light, as a reference to the lack of recognition from which he suffered. The congruence between the causes of Âli's personal bitterness and his analysis, however, does not vitiate the value of the latter. His complaints were formed by the ideals and expectations, and the historical situation, of the educated elite to which he belonged, and they are therefore instructive. It is extremely significant for our understanding of Ottoman religiosity, for example, that Âli's typology of "Islamic" classes is based as much upon cultural criteria associated with but not, strictly speaking, part of, styles of piety or Islamic scholarship, as upon moral and doctrinal considerations.

RELIGION AND STATE IN THE OTTOMAN EMPIRE

ÂLI'S observations on the religious and political culture of Rum are indicative of far more than personal peeve and chagrin. The two poles of Âli's historical orientation, regional Ottomanism and Islamic universalism, correspond precisely to the two legal institutions that together constituted the basis of Ottoman legitimacy and identity: *kanun* and *şeri'at*. *Kanun*, promulgated by the sultans on the basis of dynastic prestige and the conditions peculiar to Rum, was the very embodiment of regional Ottomanism. In the introduction to the *Essence* Âli also displays the universalistic *şeri'at*-consciousness of the *medrese* graduate, and he shows clearly that these two poles of self-identity can come into conflict. Âli's own inability, as an historian of the Ottoman Empire, to establish a single stance mirrors the greater Ottoman dilemma, which sprang from the inherently contradictory nature of the relationship between dynastic and divine law.

In theory, the sole valid legal system for any Islamic state was the *şeri'at*, revealed by God through the Prophet and the Community and predicated upon the universalistic egalitarian principle that only God can make laws and legislate public or private morality. Man-made law, like *kanun*, was based on a hierarchical principle of legislative authority inhering in a human monarch, and was by definition illegal from the *şer'i* standpoint. *Kanun*, to be sure, was technically assimilated to *örf* (*ʿurf*), a legal principle of last resort admitted by the jurists that could sanction, within broader or narrower limits depending upon the legal rite, action based upon customary usage or discretionary political authority exercised in the public interest, provided that these did not contravene the Holy Law. To be sure, the problem of defining the boundaries between the discretionary authority of the ruler and the province of the Holy Law had confronted all Muslim polities since Abbasid times, when legists first sanctioned implementation of *ʿurf* in public matters; but the difficulties it posed were particularly acute for Ottomans in the sixteenth century. Ottoman theoreticians justified *kanun* as an aid to effective government that only supplemented and, ideally, supported the *şeri'at* without encroaching on it. In actual practice, however, the Ottomans utilized and promoted *kanun* as an instrument of government to an extent that it did encroach; in certain domains of public life, such as taxation, and organization of the *ilmiye* hierarchy, *kanun* became as important as the *şeri'at*, if not in fact more so. The one was divinely ordained, eternal, and by definition denied the moral power of men or governments to establish any legislation; the other was secular, mutable, and based upon the need of the government to maintain order and collect taxes efficiently.[14]

Ottoman intellectuals rationalized the system by appealing to philosophical principles to show that the Holy Law could not be maintained without the strong central authority that utilized *kanun*. The classical expression of this rationalization is the Circle of Equity, an ancient piece of political wisdom attributed to Aristotle (among others), which was systematized and Islamicized by Davânî and his Ottoman adaptor Kınalızade:

> There can be no royal authority without the military
> There can be no military without wealth
> The subjects produce the wealth
> Justice preserves the subjects' loyalty to the sovereign
> Justice requires harmony in the world
> The world is a garden, its walls are the state
> The Holy Law orders the state
> There is no support for the Holy Law except through royal authority.[15]

Despite the reconciliatory efforts of intellectual ulema, the coexistence of *kanun* and *şeri'at* was uncomfortable, particularly when Islamic moral ideals and administrative expediency collided. Âli was keenly aware of the problem, but was never able to define precisely the nature of the relationship between the two forms of law, and his floundering with the issue is very much a reflection of his own life and time, during which certain institutional implications of the legitimization of *kanun* began to become apparent. Early in the sixteenth century *şeri'at* and *kanun* had been in more or less open conflict, the battle being waged by two essentially antagonistic groups: the Men of Learning and the Men of the Sword. The Lawgiver's efforts to integrate sacred and dynastic law ran parallel to the rapid growth of a bureaucracy which, while devoted to implementation of revised *örfi* law, mediated between the military and religious establishments. For intellectual bureaucrats of Âli's generation the process of reconciliation was not yet complete; the old duality, based, for the *medrese*-educated, on the primacy of the Holy Law, could no longer be maintained, but neither had a complete fusion, institutional or ideological, taken place. In Âli's perceptions the demands of *kanun* and *şeri'at* were both present, neither wholly distinct from one another nor wholly compatible.[16]

[14] For a concise discussion of *örf* in the Ottoman context, see H. İnalcık, "Örf," İA.

[15] Kınalızade, *Ahlak-ı Ala'i*, Book III, p. 49; Fleischer, "Royal Authority," p. 201.

[16] See my "Şehzade Korkud to Mustafa Âli," and my forthcoming study of *kanun* and the bureaucracy.

We may now return to Âli's summary of the development of the Ottoman state in order to examine the way in which he deals, as an historian, with the conflicts between Ottoman and Islamic identity, and between *kanun* and *şeri'at*. Âli's first point is that, in his view, until the middle of the century high Islamic traditions and Ottomanism were coterminous and mutually compatible, if not identical. This was a product of the zeal of the sultans from Fatih to Süleyman for learning, their respect for *şer'i* norms, and support for the *ilmiye* establishment. Âli's references to the importance of open-minded recognition of intellectual, spiritual, and legal creativity suggest that, in addition to desiring reward for his own originality, he associated the "Golden Age" of culture with such creativity. He himself was born and grew up at the very end of the "Golden Age"; much of what he found admirable in his state and culture rested upon its newness, and upon the creativity of both rulers and scholars in forging a new political, social, and intellectual amalgam, based at once on Islamic tradition and on the "Ottoman Way" embodied in *kanun*. It was when rulers and scholars ceased to prize and foster cultural creativity, when *şer'i* norms, even in the slightly attenuated form in which they were incorporated into *kanun*, were replaced by *örfi* ones based on administrative and immediate practical needs, when the ulema ceased to be model scholars and Muslims and became government functionaries interested in advancement, that Âli began to differentiate between Islam and Ottomanism.

Âli in this fashion establishes *şer'i* rectitude as a fundamental principle of the state. He goes on to make the second point that the Ottoman system, for all its virtues, carried within it the seeds of its own destruction. The Ottoman Empire emerged out of a border warfare situation in which, for both Muslims and non-Muslims, military prowess was of greater immediate value than the arts of a civilization whose centers were far away from the western Anatolian and Rumelian fronts. Coercion, observance of local administrative usage, and immediate practical methods necessarily played a greater role in the establishment of the Empire than rapid Islamicization of the state and *şer'i* consciousness.[17] According to Âli's schema, the work of putting the state on a firm Islamic footing, of transforming it from a border state into a Muslim empire that upheld and nurtured the high cultural traditions of the Islamic hinterland to the east, began with the Conqueror. Fatih Mehmed's wholesale importation of scholars from around the Islamic world, and his establishment of new imperial *medrese*s that served both to encourage and centralize the development of an indigenous Ottoman educational system, initiated a process of wide-scale implementation of both

[17] The Ottomans' accommodation with local non-Muslim military groups and their partial observance of regional administrative practice based on non-*şer'i (örfi)* norms have been well documented. See H. İnalcık, "Ottoman Methods of Conquest," *Studia Islamica* 2 (1954): 104-29.

şeri'at and *kanun* and established an imperial tradition of cultural patronage.[18] It should be noted here that, for all his attention to learning and institutional innovation, Fatih Mehmed was hardly a rigidly *şeri'at*-minded ruler. While he was manifestly interested in a great range of intellectual and spiritual endeavors, his own leanings were toward the esoteric philosophical and mystical side of Islam (*irfan*) rather than to its legalistic and scholastic facet, for which he had little patience except insofar as it aided in the establishment of a centralized state.[19] He sought to be a philosopher-king or absolute ruler of the philosophers, the Perfect Man of the Sufis, rather than the humble servant of the Holy Law, and indeed such theorists as Davânî and Kınalızade portrayed the ideal sovereigns of their own times as fulfilling both roles. The founding of the *Sahn medrese*s in Istanbul, which became the training ground for the highest religious and legal functionaries in the Ottoman domains, represented a means of controlling and curbing the independent power of the *ilmiye* establishment. Âli's view of Islam was similar; he had little brief for rigid conservatism and legalism, and was oriented toward the mystical traditions associated with Islam that had dominated the intellectual and cultural life of the milieu in which he grew up. This is not to say that Âli was himself a mystic, but rather that the esoteric trends that had to some extent seen their greatest development in Anatolia in the Mongol period, and which by the sixteenth century had come to play a dominant role in Islamic literary culture, formed part of the intellectual baggage that the young Ottoman Âli had inherited. As we have seen, Âli's religious views were rather latitudinarian, tolerant of certain sorts of innovation, and defined more by broad intellectual and aesthetic parameters than by pietistic ones.

What is Âli's historical view of the function of Islamic traditions within the Ottoman context? His citation of the examples of Fatih Mehmed, Bayezid II, Selim I, and Süleyman shows that, in his view, Islamic institutions and morality could flourish and grow only through the attentiveness to such matters of the state's central figure, the sultan. Since the frontier and the frontier state necessarily lacked the high-culture institutions of the hinterland, and of course the scholars, judges, and teachers to establish them, it

[18] Certainly earlier Ottoman sultans had founded imperial mosques and schools; the scale and breadth of the Conqueror's cultural and centralizing activities, however, went far beyond those of any of his predecessors. The wide scope and catholicity of the Conqueror's intellectual interests have been documented by Dr. Julian Raby (Magdalen College, Oxford) in his recently completed Ph.D. dissertation, which exhaustively studies the Conqueror's collection at Topkapı Palace. Although I have not yet seen Dr. Raby's dissertation, we held frequent conversations on the subject in Istanbul in 1978-79.

[19] Franz Babinger, *Mehmed the Conqueror and his Time*, trans. Ralph Manheim, ed. William Hickman (Princeton, 1978), pp. 410-16, 447. For examples of the Conqueror's commissioning of copies of works on *irfan*, see William C. Chittick, "Sulṭân Burhân al-Dîn's Sufi Correspondence," WZKM 73 (1981): 37-38.

rested with the sultans to fill these gaps through importation, legislation, and institutional innovation. This means that the ideal Ottoman ruler had to be (a) cognizant of the inherent importance of establishing an Islamic identity for the state and promoting observance of *şer'i* norms, and (b) responsible for overseeing, guiding, and maintaining such a development. By its very nature such a situation is tenuous, if not fragile, depending as it does upon the authority and conscience of a single individual. According to Âli's schema, breakdown of the system occurred when accord was broken between the sultan, the upholder of the *şeri'at*, and the ulema who interpret and represent it. Thereafter, rulers who were either irresponsible or insufficiently cognizant of their duty to religion as well as state, which ideally were inseparable, exacerbated the problem by allowing the quality of the religious establishment to decline and putting interests of state before those of religion. The result was a generalized disruption of morality. Âli felt that *örf* and low standards of culture and morality were the natural norm of Rum, and that only the vigilance of the ruler could raise the standard.[20]

There is a conflict inherent in the ideals which Âli espouses, and to which he gives direct voice. This conflict is the product of the creative solution the Ottomans adopted to solve the problem of fostering high Islamic traditions in a frontier environment. The centralization of the *ilmiye* education and employment system under government patronage, and the development of *kanun* to regulate the hierarchy and promotion of these protectors of the *şeri'at*, made the *ilmiye* a branch of government subordinate, in practice, to the will of the ruler, although he, too, as a Muslim monarch, was theoretically subject to the strictures of Islamic law. In practice this aspect of the Ottoman Way made it very difficult for the ulema to fulfill their traditional functions of being model Muslims within the Islamic community and opposing actions, even those taken by the government or its representatives, which contravened the letter or spirit of Islamic morality embodied in the *şeri'at*. In most other Islamic polities a certain amount of tension had existed between government, itself theoretically subordinate to the *şeri'at* but actually oriented toward practical concerns, and the essentially discrete scholarly establishment, which tended to distance itself from politics in the direction of insistence upon *şer'i* observance uncontaminated by the ethical and moral difficulties presented by administration. The ulema hence represented a potential, and sometimes actual, locus of opposition to government. The authoritarian Fatih Mehmed attempted to solve this problem, which was inherent in the very nature of a high Islamic state, by co-opting the entire learned establishment.[21]

[20] For fuller discussion, see "Şehzade Korkud to Mustafa Âli."
[21] Cf. Repp, "Observations."

Âli shows that, Ottoman though he was, he subscribed implicitly to the older ideal of the *âlim*, a figure representing and embodying disinterested learning and morality, endowed with a universalistic conscience transcending local political and administrative considerations. Âli objects strenuously to those ulema who abandon the scholar's (traditionally) ideal humility and pietistic stance in favor of wealth, glory, and political advancement. In describing ulema who put off their turbans to don military habits, Âli in fact shows what happened to ulema who became government functionaries. They became ambitious in spheres outside that of scholarship and morality, and their advancement depended less upon their Islamic rectitude than upon their ability to function politically within the Ottoman system. They thus betrayed what for Âli constituted one of the ideals of Islamic society, that the true arbiters of public and private morality were the scholars most learned in the sciences and traditions of Islam. In the *Essence* Âli expressed his objections in a poetic evocation of the decline of religious life and political morality at the end of the sixteenth century:

The vezirs are well off, they gain much from bribe-taking;
Each protects his position and squeezes all.
The ulema too do well, they've reaped the great rewards of hush-money;
Each one stands dumb-struck, as if his mouth were bound shut.[22]

Before examining the validity of Âli's standpoint, we must take note that there existed considerable precedent for Âli's concern over institutional and moral dimensions of the relationship between government and ulema in a frontier state. The centralizing policies of the Conqueror and his strengthening of royal authority vis-à-vis the religious law were vigorously resisted by the *şeri'at*-minded, thus provoking a struggle in the legal field between *şeri'at* and *kanun*. The reign of his successor, Bayezid II, saw something of an official restoration of *şer'i* values and acknowledgment by the Palace of the supremacy of the Holy Law. Even so, the tug-of-war between sultans and ulema continued until the time of Süleyman, who resolved the problem by incorporating the *şer'i* insistence on justice into *kanun* legislation, and by patronizing the learned establishment.[23] Âli in a sense perpetuated the stance of his teachers, the ulema of the late fifteenth and early sixteenth centuries who had sought at once to accept the benefits of political patronage, to influence government and to maintain moral purity and independence. The dilemma confronting these men was given its most extreme and striking expression by Prince Korkud, the most scholarly of the sons of Bayezid,

[22] KA, I, 33.
[23] İnalcık, "Suleiman the Lawgiver," pp. 108-10.

who in 1508 asked to be excused from candidacy for the throne because, in a land like Rum, where there was little respect for religion, it was impossible to be both a good ruler, committed to *örf*, and a good Muslim, committed to the Holy Law. Even the justice for which the Ottoman state was renowned, Korkud complained, was not true justice because it was based on the will of the sovereign rather than on that of God; and the ulema, who as judges were charged to uphold the *şeri'at*, as government officials became administrators of *örf*.[24]

EVALUATION

Âli's statements on the topic of Ottoman and Islamic identity are somewhat difficult to evaluate objectively because they are general and abstract. That his observations also strongly reflect an inner conflict from which Âli himself suffered, as well as a more general social dilemma, further complicates the issue. For analytical purposes, the emotionalism of Âli's stated views might be tempered by recalling features of the historical context within which they were written. Leaving aside Âli's personal career frustrations and the social and political turmoil that plagued this period of Ottoman history, a number of factors more historical than moral might account for some of the phenomena he cites as evidence of a decline in *şer'i* moral standards. The Ottoman Empire, due to war and inflation, was faced with severe financial crises. These crises necessitated extraordinary measures that were often of very dubious legality from a *şer'i* standpoint. As Ottoman government expanded in size, adequate supervision of functionaries undoubtedly became more difficult. On a broader level, the (outward) Sunni Muslim orthodoxy and cultural prestige of the Ottoman sultans was well-established by the second half of the sixteenth century; they did not have to display it as aggressively as had their empire-building forebears, since the Islamic character of the Ottoman state was by then taken for granted. Similarly, the politicization of *ilmiye* life may be seen as a natural product of the institutionalization of the learned hierarchy as a fixed part of the state apparatus organized on bureaucratic lines.

Such observations do not invalidate, but rather mitigate, the harshness of Âli's criticisms. The fundamental question is, was Âli really documenting a change in the life of the Empire, and if so, what was the nature of that change? To cast the question into other terms, was Âli in fact utilizing the touchstone of a vaguely defined Islamic consciousness to describe social turmoil and change, which necessarily possessed a moral dimension, or did a decline in educational and moral standards actually accompany politici-

[24] See my forthcoming "Islamic Ideals and Ottoman Realities."

zation of the scholarly profession and the sultan's abdication of supervisory responsibilities? Âli idealized the Ottoman civilization of his youth and execrated the present. Were then things really better in the areas of morality and educational standards before mid-century than after? It may be that Âli simply perceived more, and more critically, as an old man than as a young one.

In answer one must say that there was indeed change, and that in all probability many of the phenomena Âli refers to as being associated with these changes did occur. Some of these are documentable insofar as they affected institutional structure and operation: by the end of the sixteenth century political violence had become commonplace within the upper echelons of the ruling class, investigations of corrupt financial officials had become frequent, and the leading ulema battled each other for control of the available posts. Even some of the more general transformations Âli describes may be at least partially documented. There appears to have occurred, for example, a marked change in the cultural outlook of members of the Ottoman house. The Conqueror had books copied for him in a variety of languages, Korkud b. Bayezid could compose learned quasi-legal treatises in Arabic, and Selim I wrote Persian verse. Murad III, by contrast, favored translations of Arabic books into Ottoman Turkish and works on popular esotericism, and his son Mehmed III did not like linguistically ornate and lengthy stories. Such variation in the cultural orientation of individual monarchs must to some degree reflect education as well as personal taste, and would also have affected their stance as patrons and supervisors of learning.

Modern historians striving for "objectivity" necessarily have some difficulty in weighing and evaluating the historical evidence provided by premodern historians, such as Âli, who present their arguments in explicitly moral and ethical terms, entering judgments that appear to color and distort the nature and degree of social and political change. The use made by Ottoman commentators of such moral-historical schema as the Circle of Equity and the Medical Analogy reinforces the perception that Ottoman historians were to some extent bound by established models for the analysis of historical development.[25] The ideal of the "Golden Age" and the notion of decline, which recur throughout that political literature, were rhetorical devices that served more to express dissatisfaction with the present than to portray an historical reality.[26] This suggests that historians were poorly equipped to perceive the causes, rather than the mere manifestations, of contemporary problems. There is some justice to such an analysis in that it properly addresses the importance, for the premodern historian, of repre-

[25] Itzkowitz, *Ottoman Empire*, pp. 100-103; Fleischer, "Royal Authority," pp. 199-201.
[26] Fleischer, "Şehzade Korkud to Mustafa Âli."

sentation of moral truth side by side with presentation of facts; but pushed to an extreme it does injustice to historians of Âli's caliber. For him, the history of an Islamic polity explicitly possessed a moral and ethical dimension; state and religion should ideally be combined in the person of the monarch, and secondarily in his servitors. Therefore history was susceptible of interpretation in the moral terms dictated by the *şeri'at*, the absolute gauge against which the moral worth of acts must be measured. Most broadly considered, these are the standards Âli used in passing judgment on the moral quality of the Empire. Even in the course of such an evaluation, however, Âli pointedly refers to the specific historical factors that made Ottoman Islam and the Ottoman religious establishment special within the context of Islamic history. He did not apply his standards ahistorically. Taking a quasi-*şer'i* stance on historical development in the introduction to the *Essence* did not preclude Âli's using other analytical frameworks—philosophical, economic, political, cultural, and literary—in other portions of the work. While it is possible to perceive certain fundamental ideals that informed his viewpoint and thus defined the parameters of his stance, Âli combined a number of personae in his approach to history, as he did in his personal and professional life. His historiographical ability, perceptivity, and veracity must be judged as the sum of these approaches, and not by the limitations that any one of them might impose.

Âli's primary value systems, those which informed much, but not all, of his historiographical activity, must be extracted from the context of those ideals with which he grew up. He was first an Ottoman, by training and by self-designation. This aspect of Âli's identity shows most clearly in his enthusiasm for the Ottoman political and cultural experiment, and in his insistence that the letter and principle of an idealized Ottoman *kanun* be upheld. Âli's Ottoman value system was, or could be, distinct from his Islamic one, although to a certain degree the former presupposed the existence of the latter. Second, Âli's education was that of a prospective member of the *ilmiye*. As such he partook of and identified with the wider and older religio-cultural heritage of the Islamic world which the *medrese* represented and perpetuated. These two broad modes of identification were, at least in the world of Âli's youth, compatible and complementary; political figures were learned or interested in learning, scholars were given governmental functions, and all Ottomans met in the sphere of letters, poetry, and in the Sufi cloister, all of them fundamental parts of the emergent Ottoman-Islamic cultural synthesis. The ideal Ottoman, like the sultan, should combine the two orientations. Âli saw himself in a similar light, as the product of both a regional and a universal heritage. His obsession with obtaining the chancellorship is again instructive in this regard. The chancellor had the background and prestige of a member of the *ilmiye*, but he was also an important member of Ottoman government whose proper sphere of activity was application of his knowledge and intellect to the "new learning" of Ottoman statecraft and administration.

It would be both unfair and inaccurate to dichotomize fully Ottoman and Islamic identity. Âli possessed and utilized both in varying degrees in different contexts and at different periods throughout his life. In discussing matters of administrative practice or *kanun*, Âli could ignore the obvious *şer'i* implications of a question. For example, in the *Counsel*, after expounding on the illegality of oppressive acts committed by appointed administrators, Âli admits that unfortunately governors of frontier provinces might have to use coercive measures to a degree unthinkable and improper in more civilized or stable heartland regions.[27] Such an admission of the existence, unlaudable as it might be, of an administrative double standard runs counter to a strict *şer'i* ideal of universal application of moral standards. Indeed, Âli indicates in this passage that his conscience is troubled. This does not necessarily make Âli a hypocrite; it rather shows, at best, a sense of appropriateness of context, and at worst a disinclination fully to confront the *şeri'at-kanun* dilemma. For Âli, as for many Ottomans, administrative questions came down to matters of royal authority and the *kanun* that expressed it. Theoretically, royal authority both presumed and supported supremacy of the *şeri'at*, which therefore need not be discussed, or perhaps even considered in detail in an administrative context. It was this concept of two interrelated modes of justice, expressed theoretically in the Circle of Equity, and more concretely in *kanun*, which allowed the Ottomans to take a very liberal stance on the letter of *şer'i* law. When Âli does stress the importance of *şer'i* standards, he nearly always does so in a general sense and context, as in the passages cited above. For him Islamic ideals incorporated and symbolized a moral social order and a high cultural and spiritual standard that had little to do with narrow legalism. Ottomanism and the commitment to justice proclaimed by *kanun* could, if not too closely scrutinized, be assimilated to such a broad definition of Islamic consciousness. Of course, Âli's *ilmiye* background and identification also obtrude themselves in appropriate contexts, such as literary or scholarly work intended to form part of the older Islamic tradition of learning. The *Essence*, after all, is a history of the world beginning with Creation, and for the early section of the work Âli utilized as sources not only histories and popular cosmological works, but also Qur'ânic exegesis, mystical works (particularly those of Ibn ʿArabî), and their commentaries.[28]

Âli's difficulties in establishing a single comprehensive stance, his vac-

[27] COUNSEL, I, 80 (trans.), 181 (text).

[28] KA, I, 17-19, 54-57.

illations between a Rumi and a *medrese* viewpoint, stem directly, in a symbolic and psychological sense, from the *kanun-şeri'at* dilemma. Âli was unable to propose an institutional solution to the problem that faced the Ottoman sultans from Fatih Mehmed on: how could imperial authority be established, and an Islamic empire centralized, without compromising the moral authority of the universal, egalitarian *şeri'at* and its representatives, the traditionally decentralized and politically independent ulema? Âli could only suggest that the resolution of the dilemma lay in the conscience, ability, and learning of the monarch himself, who should ideally embody both administrative acumen and a sincere commitment to religion and religious ideals. Yet even in Âli's solution there is an element of paradox. The same Fatih Sultan Mehmed who expanded the Ottoman *medrese* system and encouraged scholarship utilized that system to control the ulema and to turn them into government functionaries. It was also he who made the royal household the center of government through the *devşirme*, which Âli so admired, and made the Ottoman state into an Ottoman empire with the imperial concerns that gave birth to the promulgation of Empire-wide *kanun*. Indeed, some of the manifestations of "decline" about which Âli complains—such as the corruption of the ulema or the prevalence of vezirs of Christian background—were direct results of institutional innovations that the Conqueror made in order to create an imperial system. Although he assigned great value to creativity and literary experimentation, Âli in his later years remained something of a conservative. For him, the limits of acceptable institutional change were defined by his vision of what the Ottoman Empire had been in the middle of the sixteenth century. Âli's attitude toward education is a case in point. Although the time of transformation of Ottoman education is difficult to pinpoint with precision, it appears clear that until the middle of the sixteenth century full education was only the traditional Islamic one associated with the *medrese*. However, elements of the *medrese* curriculum were incorporated into the Palace education system, and therefore even such *devşirme* products as Lutfi Paşa were able to make claims to scholarship despite their lack of formal *medrese* training.[29] Later in the sixteenth century the bureaucracy underwent a similar professionalization, or Ottomanization, providing specialized professional training that presupposed or incorporated a certain core of the education previously available only in the *medrese*. Âli's views on Lutfi Paşa's scholarship, and on the quality of professional bureaucrats, show that he was unable to accept these developments, which might be termed the Ottomanization of education. For Âli, true learning meant only the *medrese*.

It is fascinating to trace Âli's relative consciousness of his value sys-

[29] On the Palace education system, see İnalcık, "Ghulâm," EI^2.

tems through the course of his life. Early on, Âli the young Ottoman and candidate for judicial office was thoroughly committed to an emergent belles-lettres mode solidly grounded in the Arabo-Persian literary tradition cultivated by the ulema. In mid-career Âli the bureaucrat became more concerned with specifically Ottoman, regional themes: *kanun*, administration, warfare, and mores. Finally, late in life Âli became an historian who took it upon himself to trace the development of his own society and its ideals, and to view it within the larger context of the history of the Islamic world as a whole. Two aspects of this latter development are particularly noteworthy. One is an increasing Ottoman focus in both themes and use of language, illustrated in such works as the *Etiquette of Salons, Tables of Delicacies, Conditions of Cairo*, and the Ottoman portion of the *Essence of History*. The other is a growing preoccupation with the non-Ottoman past and associated religious traditions, exemplified by the *Ascending Stair of Holy War, Adornment of Men, Beauties of Polite Observance*, the pre-Ottoman portion of the *Essence*, and Âli's extended contemplation of the poetry of Ḥâfiẓ and ʿUmar Khayyâm. Âli was personally embittered and disenchanted with his own society, to whose youthful ideals he had yet committed his entire life and effort. He became hypercritical, but was also well read and quite intelligent, and it was the combination of these factors that made him a prolific and capable historian. Late in his life he had perceived that the Ottoman experiment had failed, gone sour. What should have been better than what had gone before was not. It contained the seeds of its own downfall, just as was the case with his own erratic career and impatient personality.

Âli's recognition of fundamental disappointment, of the disparity between ideal and reality, effected among other things the relative detachment that made him an effective historian. It also produced a kind of cultural and temporal schizophrenia, or breakdown into discrete segments. Âli could become now the objective historian, now the fervent admirer of Ottoman accomplishments, now the stern voice of the *ilmiye*. This phenomenon can even be perceived in Âli's escapist longings for the non-Ottoman past. In the last eight years of his life, as he wrote the *Essence of History*, the Rumi product of a frontier society found gratification in immersion in Anatolian folk traditions and saint-worship, while the *medrese* graduate yearned for escape to Iran, the historical locus and symbolic embodiment of high Islamic literary and courtly traditions.

ELEVEN

THE TURKIC AND MONGOL HERITAGE

THE POST-CALIPHAL POLITICAL ORDER

PRIOR to the Mongol invasions of the thirteenth century, the political life of the Islamic world was dominated by the theory, if only rarely the reality, of the universal Muslim caliphate. The caliphal institution represented the sole legitimate locus of political authority in the Islamic domains; it symbolized the moral unity of the community of believers and the integral universality of the *şeri'at*. Regional dynasties and institutions like the Selcuk sultanate ultimately derived such legitimacy as they possessed from caliphal dispensation, and from recognition of the ultimate paramountcy of the *şeri'at* and its protector, the caliph. When the non-Muslim Mongols conquered Baghdad and put an end to the Abbasid caliphate in 1258, they not only destroyed the old order, but also introduced radically alien elements into the political life of the Islamic world. The Mongol İlhans and the Turkic tribal elements that accompanied them or were assimilated into the Mongol order formed a military elite whose notions of political order, law, and social justice were informed not by sedentary Islamic values, but by the nomadic traditions of the steppe.

First, the Mongols replaced the ideal of the universal caliphate with their own universalist ideology, which held that divine dispensation to rule the world, including both nomadic and sedentary peoples, was given to Cengiz (Chingis) Han and his descendants. The Cengiz Hanid house constituted the paramount clan of a vast nomadic confederation; Cengiz Hanid prestige was such that it endured as a principle of political legitimacy in portions of the Eurasian steppe, such as the Crimea, throughout the eighteenth century. After the dissolution of the İlhanid state in the mid-fourteenth century, another steppe tradition of universal hegemony, that of the Oğuz Turks, increasingly came to rival Cengiz Hanid ideology in those parts of the Islamic world held by Türkmen tribal confederations such as the Karakoyunlu and Akkoyunlu of Azerbaycan and Iran.[1]

[1] The major characteristics of steppe traditions of hegemony are outlined by Zeki Velidi Togan, *Umumi Türk Tarihine Giriş*, I (Istanbul, 1946), 100, 106.

New political and social institutions, as well as steppe ideologies, accompanied the invaders. Society was split into a military aristocracy and a tax-paying subject class, a division that initially mirrored the ethnic distinction between the nomadic invaders and the sedentary population. Muslim subjects lived according to the *şeri'at*, while the conquerors, even after their conversion to Islam, regulated their affairs according to their own legal codes, Cengiz Hanid *yasa* and Turkic *töre (törü)*. These expressed Central Asian concepts of impersonal justice, and derived their authority from clan custom and formal proclamation by the head, more usually the founder, of the nomadic state. *Yasa* and *töre* governed such matters as treatment of the subject population, succession within the paramount clan, and its relationship with affiliated clans. Steppe notions of land ownership, according to which all conquered territories belonged to the ruling family and were to be disbursed to relatives and confederates as the head of state saw fit, radically altered the modes of land use that prevailed in the Islamic domains before the Mongol incursions.[2]

From the mid-fourteenth century, when the Mongol world order completely collapsed, until the early sixteenth century, the political life of the greater part of the Islamic world was characterized by the struggle of a variety of successor states, including surviving remnants of the Cengiz Hanid dispensation, to fill the void. The majority of these were either ethnically or culturally Turkic, and politically nomadic. They were also Muslim, and this period of roughly one and a half centuries is marked by a process of amalgamation between the political ideals of the steppe and the sedentary values and institutions of the Irano-Islamic high cultural traditions to which the conquerors had fallen heir by confession. The process was not an easy one, for the two sets of values, broadly considered, were on certain points antithetical. A ruler in the steppe tradition, who had the power to make law and owned, theoretically, nearly all of his dominions, had far more absolute authority than the caliph who could only uphold and submit to God's law, and was to respect private property.

This same period saw a great deal of experimentation with varieties of political ideology that in large measure reflected the progressive steppe-Islamic synthesis. In the fifteenth century, for example, the Ottomans attempted to capitalize on both religious sentiment and steppe traditions of hegemony by at once invoking the prestige conferred by success in *gaza* warfare against non-Muslims and claiming Oğuz descent. The Safavis, by contrast, relied upon the military support of confederations of Türkmen groups, but based their explicit claims to legitimacy on being *seyyid*s, de-

[2] Togan, *Giriş*, pp. 106-10, 277-85; İnalcık, *Ottoman Empire*, pp. 65-69; İnalcık, "Veraset," pp. 82-85.

scendants of the Prophet, and upon their spiritual prestige as hereditary heads of the Safavi order. Down to the early part of the sixteenth century the majority of these ideological experiments, those of the Ottomans included, must be viewed as attempts to find a basis upon which to establish universalistic claims. The ideal of universal dominion was an expectation generated, albeit in different forms, by Islamic and steppe traditions alike, and the recent Cengiz Hanid precedent, and the more remote caliphal one, showed that the ideal could become a reality. Furthermore, as the Mongol successor polities battled each other for territory and prestige, it became clear that only claims to universal dispensation, whether in the nomadic or the Islamic mold, could justify the conquest of other Muslims and establish the moral as well as political superiority of one state over another. By the end of the sixteenth century the rivalry of the Mongol successor states reached a plateau that would have been unthinkable in the fifteenth century: the Islamic world was divided into the four regional empires of the Ottomans, Safavis, Özbeks, and Tîmûrid Mughals, the borders between which were, with certain temporary exceptions, fixed and acknowledged. This is the broad historical context within which the Ottoman state was born, expanded, and became an empire. We may now turn to an examination of the place of the Ottoman Empire in the post-caliphal world, and of Âli's analysis of these three and one-half centuries of Islamic history.

THE STEPPE HERITAGE

IN CERTAIN aspects of origin and structure, the Ottoman Empire in the sixteenth century and the other major Islamic polities that were contemporary with it, had much in common with the Mongol and Tîmûrid states. The Ottomans had sprung from a nomadic background and had built a polity based on conquest and confederation under a paramount clan.[3] Ottoman succession practice through the middle of the sixteenth century,[4] diplomatic practice,[5] recognition of the Cengiz Hanid legitimacy of the Crimean and Özbek *hans*, and promulgation of a dynastic law code separate from the Islamic *şeri'at* all suggest that the Ottomans for some time adhered to the political traditions of the steppe at the same time that they created a new regional

[3] On Ottoman nomadism, and the inclusive character of early Ottoman tribalism, see Rudi Paul Lindner, *Nomads and Ottomans in Medieval Anatolia* (Bloomington, Indiana, 1983), pp. 1-38. For a discussion of the formative influence of the political norms of the steppe on pre-Mongol Muslim states (Selcuk, Zangid, and Ayyûbid), see Humphreys, *Saladin*, pp. 66-75. On the prestige that Cengiz Hanid traditions enjoyed in the Mamluk dominions, see A. N. Poliak, "The Influence of Chîngîz-Khân's Yâsâ upon the General Organization of the Mamlûk State," BSOAS 10 (1939-42): 862-76.

[4] İnalcık, "Veraset," pp. 85-89.

[5] R. Rahmeti Arat, "Fatih Sultan Mehmed'in Yarlığı," TM 6 (1936-39): 285-322.

Islamic polity. Like Tîmûr, the Ottomans attempted to reconcile their Islamic identity with their nomadic origins and political traditions through the creation of a religiously based ideology in the form of the *gazi* ideal. In the cultural sphere the Ottomans owed much to the Tîmûrids, and, probably, to the Mongols, though this latter influence is at the moment less easy to document. There are also marked contrasts between the Ottomans and their predecessors.

The Ottomans developed and maintained a highly centralized regional state, and, after 1555 at the latest, made no universalist claims. Cengiz Han and Tîmûr, by contrast, established universal empires that fragmented rapidly after their founders' deaths. Furthermore, Ottoman legitimacy was very weak from the standpoint of both Islamic and nomadic political tradition; the caliphate from which they could have extracted religious sanction was effectively dead, and they were neither *seyyid*s, nor Cengiz Hanid, nor even members of a major branch of the Oğuz. Their success, in fact, owed far more to efficiency than to ideology.

What was the nature of the Ottoman heritage from the steppe, and how did educated Ottomans like Âli perceive it? The first part of this question can be addressed only in very general terms for the purposes of this study; the problem of the extent to which the Ottomans can be viewed as nomads who preserved something of their Central Asian background has provoked considerable scholarly controversy.[6] The Tîmûrid influence upon Ottoman civilization is direct and well documented. Tîmûr himself challenged and dismantled the first Ottoman empire; later, the scholars and literary language of the Tîmûrid domains played an essential role in the development of Ottoman culture. Âli refers constantly to the Tîmûrid court of Ḥusayn Bâyqarâ as a model of cultural greatness and political wisdom. Mongol influences are more difficult to trace, but recent research has begun to bring a number of connections to light.[7] For present purposes it is sufficient to point out ways in which Âli demonstrates an awareness of the importance of the specific Mongol, and more general Central Asian, legacy to the sixteenth-century Islamic world. Âli attached great importance to the prestige and political legitimacy of dynasties of Cengiz Hanid descent; he almost invariably

[6] For examples, see Paul Wittek, *The Rise of the Ottoman Empire* (London, 1938); Fuad Köprülü, *Les Origines de l'empire Ottoman* (Paris, 1935), translated into Turkish, with a new preface, as *Osmanlı Devletinin Kuruluşu* (Ankara, 1972); Lindner, *Nomads*.

[7] Colin Heywood has recently begun a study of the importance of Mongol models for the development of Ottoman chancery formulae (oral communication, August 1979). It is also highly probable that such late Mongol administrative manuals as the *Risâleh-i Falakîyeh* (ed. W. Hinz, Wiesbaden, 1952) had an impact on Ottoman statecraft. Mr. Boyd Johnson, under the supervision of Professors John Woods and Halil İnalcık of the University of Chicago, has undertaken a doctoral dissertation that will deal with administrative centralization under the last three İlhans. Mr. Johnson's research should illuminate the nature of the Mongol precedents for Ottoman administrative practice.

appended a citation of their illustrious genealogy to any mention of the Özbek and Crimean *hans*. Even though the latter were Ottoman vassals, Âli still referred to them in his own time as legal sovereigns in their own right.[8] In the final portion of the *Essence of History* Âli gives a tantalizing hint of perpetuation of contact with the Turkish nomadic past by citing a saying on courage and cowardice "in the language of Oğuz."[9]

Âli's sensitivity to the impact of the steppe upon the political traditions of the world in which the Ottoman Empire arose is shown nowhere more clearly than in his explication of his own mode of historiography. While he intends here to outline the nature of political life in the post-Mongol Islamic world, he also utilizes the Mongol and Tîmûrid precedents as standards against which to measure the success of the Ottoman experiment.

Âli opens the Ottoman portion of the *Essence* with a listing of the four great Islamic states and their sovereigns in the year A.H. 1000/1591-92. His exposition may be paraphrased thus: the Ottomans of Anatolia and Rumeli, which together form the state of Rum, have ruled for three hundred years and are known for their zeal for religion and for the justice of their laws. The current ruler, Sultan Murad, is the twelfth of the dynasty. Iran is ruled from its capital of Qazvin by Shâh ʿAbbâs, seventh of the Safavi dynasty of Ardabil, which has held power for nearly one hundred years. In Transoxiana the legal ruler is the Özbek ʿAbdullâh Khân, who rules from his appanage seat of Samarkand and who is the twelfth descendant of Abu'l-khayr Khân. The Özbeks have ruled for one hundred and fifty years. Finally, the Tîmûrid Jalâl al-dîn Akbar, fifth (sic) in his line, holds sway in India, and is famed for his generosity. The Tîmûrids have possessed dynastic legitimacy for two hundred years. Âli places the four regional empires on a level of parity, each having its own geographical sphere of influence and dynastic history. The political force of dynastic identity is shown by the fact that Âli also lists the Cengizid Giray *hans* of the Crimea and the Meccan *şerifs* of the line of Abu Numayy as legitimate sovereigns, despite their vassalage to the Ottomans.[10]

[8] FUSUL, *fasls* 23 and 24, 68b-75b; KA, IV/3, 18-19. Âli describes the Crimean *han* Mehmed Giray, whom he met in the course of the Şirvan campaign, in the following words in KA, Murad/Third Vezirate of Sinan Paşa, Nur 3409, 409b-410a: "The respected *han*, of a line of *hans* who, for thirty or forty generations, from father to son, have been the glorious and exalted possessors of the rights of coinage and prayer [*sikke ve hutbe*] which inhere in conquering monarchs." Âli also designates the Giray *hans* of the Crimea as sovereign rulers in the unique Leiden recension of the KA (4a). On the importance of Cengiz Hanid genealogy and nomadic traditions of political legitimacy in the Islamic world of the fourteenth and fifteenth centuries, see John E. Woods, *The Aqquyunlu: Clan, Confederation, Empire* (Minneapolis, 1976), pp. 5-6.

[9] KA, Mehmed/Fourth Vezirate of Sinan Paşa, Halet Ef. 598, 433a (cf. AB, p. 79).

[10] KA, V, 6-7, supplemented by MS Leiden, 4a. Interestingly enough, Âli designates Samarkand the *kürsi*, "seat," of Transoxiana, since it was in fact an appanage seat in the nomad tradition rather than the capital (*pây-i taht*) of a politically sedentarized state, such as Istanbul or Qazvin. On the appanage system, see Martin B. Dickson, "Shâh Ṭahmâsb and the Ûzbeks"

All four independent states fall into a larger category of Âli's historical scheme. In the general introduction to the *Essence* Âli explains that the work has been arranged in four volumes or Pillars (*rükn*). The first deals with Creation, geography, and the history of the world until the appearance of the Prophet. The second deals with Islamic history in the period of "Arab" dominion through the end of the Abbasid caliphate.[11] The third volume is consecrated to the history of the "Turks and Tatars":

Herein is comprised the tale of the Tatar people,
And all that concerns the affairs of the Oğuz.
The Tîmûrid dynasty and Cengizid house,
Those sharp-headed plunderers,
Have all been described in this volume,
From the start of the story to its end;
From this garden, like a moist blossom,
Bloomed those praiseworthy ones who are the Ottoman House.[12]

The history of the empires contemporary with that of the Ottomans occurs in this third volume. Finally, Âli devoted the fourth Pillar to Ottoman history. This he undertook with the stated intention of producing a more accurate, comprehensive, and critical history of the Ottoman house than any other historian.[13] In beginning this task, however, Âli re-emphasized that from an historical perspective the Ottomans, in terms of origins and political identity, must properly be classed with the Turks and Mongols.[14] We will return to the question of what distinguishes the Ottomans among other polities of similar background; for the moment it is sufficient to note that Âli identifies the Ottomans as part of the post-Mongol Islamic historical context, which was dominated as much by nomadic traditions of government

(Ph.D. dissertation, Princeton University, 1958), pp. 32-37. It should be noted that Âli's dynastic counts differ from those of other historians; such counts vary according to who is considered an official sovereign and founder of dynastic power. ʿAbbâs, for example, was the fifth Safavi shah, if one begins with Ismâʿîl I; Âli must have included the father and grandfather of Ismâʿîl I, Ḥaydar and Junayd, in his reckoning. Similarly, Akbar was the grandson of Babur, the founder of Tîmûrid power in India. Babur's own grandfather, Abû Saʿîd Mîrzâ, to whom Âli appears to trace Akbar's lineage, was the great-grandson of Tîmûr. The Özbek ʿAbdullâh II was actually the eleventh Abu'l-khayrid *han*.

[11] KA, I, 13-14.

[12] KA, I, 15. The printed version of the third Pillar (KA, IV) does not precisely conform to this arrangement, and is undoubtedly based upon a defective manuscript, for it lacks many important entries such as the histories of Cengiz Han, the İlhans, the Tîmûrids before Bâyqarâ, and others. These missing sections, together with the history of the Giray *hans*, are found in at least two manuscripts of this section of the KA, MSS Hazine 1358 (251b-256a) and Revan 1123 (285a-292a). These accounts were written in 1598-99/1007 (Hazine 1358, 254b), and are virtually identical with the corresponding chapters of FUSUL (*fasl*s 4, 12, 15, 18), with only a few changes made in order to accommodate the different contexts.

[13] KA, I, 15.

[14] Quoted above, chapter 10, note 2.

and Cengizid, Tîmûrid, and Türkmen ideologies as by the Islam of the sedentarized population.

THE HIERARCHY OF SOVEREIGNTY

IN THE beginning of the fourth volume of the *Essence*, Âli pursues the comparative contextual considerations raised by his identification of a post-caliphal Turco-Mongol complex in an examination of the political terminology then current in all four of the Muslim empires. The most general term for the sovereign head (*hutbe ve sikke sahibi*) of a large territorial state or empire in the Islamic mold is the Persian *padişah* or "emperor"; this is the word Âli applies generically to the Ottoman, Safavi, Mughal, and Özbek heads of state. Another title in use in the sixteenth century was an Islamic one, *sultan*, which had its origins in the caliphal order; the sultanate was established in the eleventh century in order to legitimize the caliph's delegation of all his temporary authority to the Selcuk Tuğrul Beğ. *Shâh* invoked pre-Islamic Iranian traditions of kingship and universal dominion, being the title applied to the Sasanian and Achaemaenid emperors; in the Islamic context *shâh* also had folk-mystical associations, particularly in Shi'i circles, for it was a common mode of reference to either a Sufi master or the first imam Ali. Finally, Cengiz Hanid and Oğuz prestige had given currency to the title *han*, from *ka'an*, the title given to the universal ruler in steppe tradition. Âli's ruminations on the terminology of sovereignty current in his own time are as follows. Although the same Arabic and Persian vocabulary is available to and in use in all four states, usage differs significantly. For example, the title *sultan* is applied in Rum only to the sovereign ruler (*sikke ve hutbe sahibi, padişah*) and to royal princesses, while in Iran the same term signifies a provincial governor equivalent to a *sancak beği*. The Mughal Tîmûrid rulers are also titled *sultan*. In Iran the sovereign is styled *shâh*, and in Transoxiana and the Kıpçak steppe he is called *han*. International usage is yet more complex; the sultan of Rum is called by non-Ottomans *padişah* or *hünkâr* (from Persian *khudâvandigâr*, "lord, emperor," a title favored by the Mongol İlhans). Âli's point is that from the standpoint of regional sovereignty all of these terms are equivalent in the function and status they denote.[15] However, Âli continues, given that the notion of a multiplicity of regional sovereigns is accepted, these monarchs themselves may be categorized according to two other designations: *mü'eyyed min ınd Allah*, "succored by God," and *sahib-kıran*, "master of an auspicious conjunction." The former term denotes a sovereign never de-

[15] KA, V, 125-26. On the Ottoman sultan's use of these titles, see H. İnalcık, "Padişah," İA.

feated in battle, and three Ottoman sultans achieved this standing: the Conqueror, Selim I, and Süleyman. *Sahib-kıran* signifies a world conqueror who establishes a universal dominion. According to Âli, the world has seen only three of these—Alexander, Cengiz Han, and Tîmûr. Selim I, had he lived beyond the eighth year of his reign, might have become a *sahib-kıran*.[16]

Universal sovereignty, in this typology, is the highest form of kingship, the legitimacy of which cannot be denied because such striking success gives tangible evidence of God's will.[17] Âli devoted a chapter of the *Tables* to the nature of the sovereignty of nonuniversal monarchs.[18] The rulers of his own time, Âli states, acquire the status of *zill Allah*, "shadow of God," solely from their diligent observance of the *şeri'at*. This title, redolent of memories of the universal Muslim caliphate and suggestive of divine sanction for rule within the Islamic context, became particularly popular among post-Mongol commentators on government, who sought to reconcile the reality of the political dominance of steppe peoples with the sedentary Islamic ideal of a divinely ordained social order exemplified by the *şeri'at* and symbolized, in pre-Mongol times, by the caliphate. Âli here shows himself to be completely in tune with the theoretical political tenor of his times.[19] Nonuniversal rulers are of two sorts:

[16] KA, V, 16-17. That this categorization is not peculiar to Âli is indicated by the attempt of Za'im Mehmed (fl. 1578/985), author of another universal history, to justify the popular designation of Selim I as *sahib-kıran*. In the course of this discourse, which occurs at the beginning of his account of Selim's reign, Za'im Mehmed also refers to the *mü'eyyed min ınd Allah*, though his use of these terms is less precise than that of Âli (*Câmi'üt-tevârîh*, MS Fatih 3406, ff. 255a-b).

[17] On the Central Asian origins of the notion that military success demonstrates divine favor (*te'yid-i ilâhi*) and good fortune (*kut, baht*), see İnalcık, "Veraset," pp. 72-80. The theme of divine support for military victory is, of course, also Qur'ânic; see *Qur'ân* 8 (*al-Anfâl*), and especially 3:13 (*Âl ʿImrân*): "God supports with his aid whom he wills; in this there is a warning for those with eyes to see." *(Wa Allâhu yu'ayyidu bi-naṣrihi man yashâ'; inna fî dhâlika la-ʿibratan li-ûlî al-abṣâr.)*

[18] The following discussion of political legitimacy is based on MEVA'İD, pp. 68-73.

[19] See A.K.S. Lambton, "Islamic Political Thought," in *The Legacy of Islam*, 2nd ed., eds. J. Schacht and C. E. Bosworth (Oxford, 1974), pp. 404-24, and Woods, *Aqquyunlu*, pp. 114-19. Woods traces the devices used in Akkoyunlu ideology under Uzun Ḥasan to legitimize the new empire on religious as well as tribal grounds, and signals the importance of the scholar Jalâl al-dîn Davânî (d. 1503/908) in the process of reconciling Islamic ideals with the realities of political life in the Mongol-Türkmen period. It was Davânî who, in his famous ethics treatise, the *Akhlâq-i Jalâlî* (Lucknow 1283/1879), decisively formulated the doctrine of the post-Mongol imamate that could legitimately be claimed by any Muslim monarch, regardless of descent, who demonstrated devotion to protection of the *şeri'at*. Davânî's work was read and interpreted in Ottoman domains, most notably by Kınalızade Ali Çelebi, who expanded Davânî's *Akhlâq* in his own Ottoman Turkish *Ahlak-ı 'Ala'i*. The views of these two important theoreticians and adaptors of the Islamic philosophical tradition on the *ẓill Allâh*, while not precisely the same (Kınalızade refers to the absolute ruler of the philosophers as the "true caliph" rather than "imam"), are quite similar; see Davânî, *Akhlâq*, p. 235; Kınalızade, *Ahlak*, Book II, pp. 75-76; Fleischer, "Royal Authority," pp. 206-207, 219. Fażl Allâh b. Rûzbihân Khunjî (d. 1521/927), a student of Davânî who ended his career in Özbek service, discussed

1. Hereditary rulers, qualified by inheritance and descent to rule in a specific region.

2. Those who take power by force of arms, and whose right to rule is indicated simply by their success, which demonstrates that they are possessed of divine favor (*mü'eyyed min ınd Allah*). Such rulers are termed *sahib-i zuhur*, "the manifest one." Âli's use of the term in this and other contexts shows clearly that it signifies in its most neutral sense an eponym or dynastic founder. The Ottoman Osman was a *sahib-i zuhur*, while Tîmûr was both *sahib-i zuhur* and *sahib-kıran*. Âli goes on to explain in the *Tables* that the designation *sahib-i zuhur* (or *sahib-zuhur*) is equally applicable to anyone attempting to establish sovereignty by force, including bandits and rebels. The fundamental difference between these latter and legitimate monarchs is relative success. Âli cites the Samanids, Selcuks, Sasanians, and Abbasids as examples of hereditary rulers overthrown by "manifest ones," to which group the Ottomans pertain by implication. The difference between the two categories is, of course, a purely chronological one; once a *sahib-i zuhur* has established a legitimate state and dynasty, his successors rule by right of heredity (*haseb-i neseb*).[20] More precisely, what distinguishes the Ottomans from bandits, Âli says, is their political sagacity, justice, adherence to the *şeri'at*, and of course the absence of a more legitimate candidate as head of state.

Two types of situations allow the overthrow of an established sovereign or dynasty by a rebel. The first is that in which the reigning monarch is unjust, corrupt, and oppressive, and has lost the loyalty of both subjects and military. Then the people are justified in supporting a rival claimant, whatever his lineage, who in comparative terms will be a better sovereign. It then becomes incumbent upon the rebel to revolt. The second instance, related to the first, is that of an established dynasty that allows itself to decline, a process Âli views as part of an inherent dynastic tendency against which

the post-Mongol imamate in more strictly juristic, but equally pragmatic, terms; see the summary of A.K.S. Lambton, *State and Government in Medieval Islam* (Oxford, 1981), pp. 178-200. It is also of interest to note that one religious concept of which Uzun Ḥasan made use, that of the Renewer of Religion (*mujaddid*) who is to appear at the beginning of each Islamic century, was also invoked, albeit in rather offhand fashion, by Âli, who termed the Ottoman eponym, Osman, the Renewer of the 8th/14th century (KA, V, 25). For a summary of the lore of the Renewer and an analysis of its importance in the sixteenth (Muslim tenth) century, see Ignaz Goldziher, "Zur Charakteristik Ǵelâl ud-dîn Sujûṭî's und seiner literarischen Thätigkeit," *Sitzungsberichte der Kaiserlichen Akademie der Wissenschaften. Philosophisch-Historische Klasse* 69 (1871): 7-28, expanded by Erika Glassen, "Krisenbewusstsein und Heilserwartung in der islamischen Welt zu Beginn der Neuzeit," *Die islamische Welt zwischen Mittelalter und Neuzeit: Festschrift für Hans Robert Roemer*, eds. U. Haarmann and P. Bachmann (Beirut, 1979), pp. 167-79.

[20] In describing the depredations of Celâli rebels and would-be sovereigns, Âli notes that they are usually the chiefs (*başbuğ*) of Türkmen tribal groups (*etrâkün boy beğleri*), and that they generally attempt to claim some sort of genealogical legitimacy, in the form of descent either from the Prophet or from an old dynastic family (MEVA'İD, pp. 70-71).

vigilant monarchs must guard. The longer a dynasty endures, the more its scions tend to take their hereditary authority for granted; they acquire wealth, abandon themselves to worldly pleasures and debauchery, and forget their responsibilities to look after the order of their state and the welfare of their subjects. The signs of such decline are corruption and bribery in the state, debauchery of the monarch, and growing influence of the women of the harem in political affairs. Such events signal a dynasty's abandonment of mandate to rule; the ruler has become a tyrant and the dynastic mandate itself, expressed in dynastic custom and law (*kanun*) has fallen by the wayside. This is a sign that the dynasty has run its allotted course and may be overthrown and replaced by another:

> [Then] the count of months and years decreed from the beginning of Eternity for the ruling lineage has been fulfilled and finished; that is to say that the scions and descendants that are to appear from that illustrious race have reached their end and are at the point of extinction. This is the manner in which the Samanids, Selcuks, Sasanians, Abbasids and all the other majestic lines of sovereigns were separated from the glory of government . . . [verse]
>
> [When] an oppressive ruler gains control of the realm
> Its laws and justice [*kanun*] are utterly destroyed.[21]

Although Âli cites historically remote dynastic examples here to strengthen his argument, his point is clear. The Ottomans, in historical perspective, are no different than other dynasties, and are subject to the same processes unless they take care to remain faithful to their mandate, i.e., *kanun*. Âli drives the point home poetically, saying that a state has two treasuries. One is money—silver and gold—the other its subjects. The latter, whose loyalty must be won and kept by justice, is the more important; if the human treasure is neglected, the monetary one will necessarily pass to another.[22]

Âli's overall perspective may be summarized thus: effective, efficient, and just government is ultimately of greater importance than hereditary legitimacy. The candidate for sovereignty best qualified by lineage is not necessarily the best monarch; true kingship and legitimate rule are better demonstrated by acts than by invocation of theory, a concept that Âli extends in

[21] MEVA'İD, p. 72.

[22] MEVA'İD, pp. 72-73. Âli is forever conscious of the relevance of history to the Ottoman situation. For example, in his outline of the Mongol successor states in the *Seasons*, Âli praises the Jalâyirid Sulṭân-(Shaykh) Uvays for his patronage of scholars and for his lack of ostentation. Âli says that although Uvays collected much money in tribute and taxes from low-level state functionaries, he did not hoard it or spend it on luxurious palaces, as was done in Âli's own time. Rather, he expended his gains on patronage, knowing that having works of learning dedicated to him would perpetuate his name far more effectively than buildings constructed for his own pleasure (FUSUL, *fasl* 15, 46a-b).

modified form to pre-Mongol political theory as well. Of the contest between ʿAlî b. Abî Ṭâlib and Muʿâwiya over the caliphate, for example, Âli says that all were agreed that ʿAlî was the rightful and best qualified candidate. Muʿâwiya, however, was more active and forceful, and thereby gained the caliphate. ʿAlî effectively brought about his own downfall by being too moral and too unworldly to listen to practical counsel and deal forcefully with the situation. From this incident, Âli states, proceeded the distinction between caliphate and emirate. Caliphate referred to government by the rightful ruler of the Muslim community, while an emir was a lesser candidate able to seize and maintain sovereignty by force of will and effective action.[23]

TWO CASE STUDIES: HÜLEGÜ HAN AND AMÎR TÎMÛR

ÂLI's application of his rationalization of the nature of sovereignty and political legitimacy in the post-Mongol Islamic world, a rationalization heavily informed by the Ottoman example, is illustrated most clearly in his discussions of the Mongol İlhanid and Tîmûrid states.[24] In the case of Cengiz Han, Âli frankly admits that the early history of Mongol dominion presents grave problems for Muslim historians. Cengiz was a world conqueror, a *sahib-kıran*, but he was also a non-Muslim, as was his grandson Hülegü; and it was Hülegü who in 1258 annihilated the five-hundred-year-old Abbasid caliphate that symbolized the unity of the Muslim oekumene and the universality of the *şeri'at*. The difficulty of this situation for the historian is clear: how to admit the legitimacy of the universal dispensation of the nomadic, non-Muslim Cengizids when, for the Muslim, the only legal form of universal dominion is that of the Islamic community and its revealed law. Although the specific issue of divine sanction for the Mongol conquest is avoided, such sanction is implicit in the fact of its occurrence. Âli solves the problem by comparing Hülegü and Mustaʿṣim, the last Abbasid caliph, on a nonsectarian basis. His conclusion is that Mongol military success, Mongol justice, and Mongol zeal to patronize learning and culture made the Cengizids more worthy and effectual sovereigns than the irresponsible, ignorant, and morally corrupt scions of the Muslim Abbasid house. Hülegü, for example, cherished and acquired the loyalty of scholars such as Naṣîr al-dîn Ṭûsî, whom Mustaʿṣim, in his ignorance, had insulted and alienated. Ṭûsî became Hülegü's loyal advisor; Mustaʿṣim thus prepared his own destruction and justified it. Âli stresses the legitimating importance of the prin-

[23] FUSUL, *fasl* 1, 8a-10b. For parallels with Ibn Khaldûn, see my "Royal Authority," pp. 205, 208.

[24] The following discussion of Âli's treatment of the Cengizids is based upon the relevant portions of the KA (IV/1, 210-18) and the FUSUL (*fasl*s 4 and 12, 15a-20b, 35a-38a).

ciple of universal justice, which the Mongols implemented in the form of *yasa*, the dynastic law promulgated by Cengiz Han to regulate the affairs of the nomad ruling elite. This stress is hardly fortuitous, for Âli specifically equates *yasa* with Ottoman *kanun*, and the context makes it clear that such secular promulgations, rooted in Central Asian political traditions, symbolize dynastic prestige and constitute a tangible sign of a legitimate mandate to rule. When the Grand Han Mönke heard of the sorry state of the Abbasid domains and of the Abbasid notables' alienation from the caliph, he sent Hülegü to secure Mustaʿṣim's submission with the words, "If he resists you, plunder and destroy his lands, in accordance with the *kanun* of Cengiz Han."[25] Such linking of Ottoman and Mongol traditions is not coincidental. It bespeaks an awareness of communality of political tradition, and it also addresses the Ottomans' political status, for they had very little in the ideological sphere to legitimate their rule beyond *kanun*. The sum of Âli's analysis of the significance of the Mongol destruction of the caliphate is that just kingship is not necessarily dependent upon Islamic identity, and that a non-Muslim monarch coming from a political environment completely divorced from Islamic tradition may in fact be a better and more legitimate sovereign than a Muslim one. In short, Âli separates the concepts of government and religious law, and distinguishes Islamic doctrinal theory from government in practice. Âli displays the same religious open-mindedness and commitment to law and order in a section of the *Essence* which deals with Sinan Paşa's Austrian campaigns. Âli compares the strict discipline maintained in the Hapsburg armies with the anarchy and depradations of the Janissary Corps, and finds the Christian officers superior to the Muslim ones.[26]

Tîmûr presents Âli with a somewhat different but no less intriguing case.[27] Like Cengiz, Tîmûr was *sahib-kıran*, but unlike the former he was a Muslim and therefore had to be judged by somewhat different standards. Tîmûr had dismembered the first short-lived Ottoman Empire when he defeated Yıldırım Bayezid at the battle of Ankara in 1402. For this reason, Âli notes, he was usually dealt with very harshly by Ottoman historians. Âli, with his broader historical perspective, takes self-conscious exception to this partisan judgment and explains the necessity of historical objectivity:

> The historian ʿArabshâh [Ibn ʿArabshâh] wrote a vicious and malicious account of Tîmûr, while the historian Mîrkhvând exaggerated his praise of Tîmûr because he wrote in the time of Sultân-Ḥusayn Mîrzâ Bâyqarâ, of Tîmûr's line. But the historians of Rum have villified Tî-

[25] FUSUL, 17b.

[26] KA, Mehmed/Fourth Vezirate of Sinan Paşa, Halet Efendi 598, 434a.

[27] The following discussion of Âli's treatment of Tîmûr is based on KA, V, 81-105, esp. 101-105.

mûr unjustly and eulogized Sultan Bayezid in their writings. I have told the truth; in all I have written myself I have been veracious and objective, and whatever I have taken from others I have quoted fully, without omission. I say this because there is no greater fault in an historian than that he should conceal the truth of a matter, and that he should choose to praise or condemn someone out of ulterior personal motives. The reader should know that I have not indulged in partisanship or axe-grinding, and those who know the truth understand that I have not invented or lied.[28]

Bayezid, in Âli's view, should have submitted to Tîmûr as a vassal. Âli gives two sets of reasons for this judgment, one based on the ideology of kingship and the other upon religion. First, Tîmûr was a world conqueror and therefore superior in status to the sultan of Rum, a mere regional ruler. Tîmûr also observed royal protocol strictly, acting courteously and correctly in his dealings with Bayezid. The Ottoman, by contrast, behaved arrogantly and churlishly, going so far in violation of diplomatic practice as to insult, and threaten the lives of, Tîmûr's ambassadors. These affronts to his stature justified Tîmûr's invasion of Anatolia, and Bayezid should have submitted to the world conqueror. Âli's second reason is that Tîmûr was in fact a better Muslim monarch than Bayezid, for part of his motivation for conquest was restoration of the political and religious unity of the Islamic world. Bayezid had allowed the *şer'i* judicial establishment of his dominions to become corrupt, and had thereby permitted justice and the paramountcy of the *şeri'at* to lapse. As a conscientious Muslim, as well as a *sahib-kıran*, Tîmûr was right to conquer the Ottoman domains, for he reformed the judicial system, dismissing and replacing corrupt judges.[29] Tîmûr thus combined the ideals of a sovereign mandated to establish a universal polity, in the Cengiz Hanid tradition, with the Islamic ideal of universal regard for the *şeri'at* enforced by a social and political unification of the Muslim world.[30] The essence of Âli's exposition can be summarized in three points:

1. Legitimate sovereignty rests as much upon observance of regal prac-

[28] KA, V, 103; cf. Atsız's romanization of this passage, AB, p. 7.

[29] Complaints about the corruption of judges appear to have been voiced first, and most vociferously, in the reign of Bayezid I. Later historiographical tradition credits him with the innovation of fixing the fees that judges were to receive for their services. The measure was ostensibly intended to prevent impoverished judges from seeking bribes, but fifteenth-and sixteenth-century historians, concerned with what they saw as judicial venality in their own time, saw in Bayezid's legalization of transaction fees the beginnings of institutionalized "corruption" of the learned class. See KA, V, 104-105; Lutfi Paşa, *Tevarih-i Âl-i Osman*, ed. Âli (Istanbul, 1925), pp. 46-48; Heyd, *Studies*, p. 212; and my "Islamic Ideals and Ottoman Realities."

[30] For a detailed account of the diplomatics of the confrontation between Bayezid and Tîmûr which gives special attention to the participants' invocation of Mongol, Türkmen, Rum Selcuk, and Islamic *gazi* legitimating principles, see M. H. Yınanç, "Bayezid I," İA.

tice and recognition of the obligations and responsibilities of kingship as upon force; justice and propriety must be strictly maintained.

2. The monarch who happens to be a Muslim is obliged to uphold the *şeri'at* and observance of its spirit as well as its letter.

3. The universal "orthodox" Muslim monarch is superior in status to the regional *gazi* warrior for the faith.

ANALYSIS

WE HAVE established that Âli was keenly aware of a Turco-Mongol political tradition which was as significant in the formation of his own polity as Islamic confession, and have examined his concept of the separability of sovereignty from Islam. We must now look at what Âli's statements on Mongol and Tîmûrid history in the Islamic context can tell us about the Ottoman self-image and historical consciousness in the sixteenth century.

Âli's observations on the nature of sovereignty in the post-caliphal Islamic world give striking substantiation to the views of a number of modern scholars, most notably Martin Dickson, Marshall Hodgson, and John Woods.[31] These hold that the ideal of a universal Islamic empire effectively died in 1258 with the Mongol conquest of Baghdad, and that subsequent universalist claims, and indeed most political experiments, were based on a nomadic Central Asian tradition of hegemony separate from, but not necessarily antithetical to, the "classical" sedentary Islamic pattern of government. Âli's division of Islamic history into Arab/caliphal and Turco-Mongol/post-caliphal periods, and his sensitivity to Cengiz Hanid and Tîmûrid prestige, show that this too was Âli's perception. The concept of a universal caliphate was indeed a dead letter by the fifteenth-sixteenth centuries; although the title "caliph" was used in diplomatic correspondence throughout this period, it signified nothing more than "Muslim sovereign."

In origin the major post-Mongol polities of the Islamic world began as tribal confederations whose claims to political legitimacy were founded on genealogical or political association with the dominant Cengiz Hanid and Türkmen Oğuz traditions of hegemony; Tîmûr began his career of conquest claiming authority in the name of the Cengiz Hanid Çagatay *han*s, and the Akkoyunlu dispensation rested upon the paramount clan's theoretical descent from Oğuz Han. As these polities stabilized and centralized, high

[31] Hodgson, *Venture*, II, 386-410, 428-36; III, 18-133. Hodgson's exposition of the post-caliphal situation, in its general lines, owes much to the views of Martin Dickson, as Hodgson repeatedly acknowledges. In his own presentation Hodgson suffers from a surprisingly strident antipathy toward what he perceives as Turkic nomadic militarism, a perception probably rooted in his firm Quakerism. John Woods gives a more succinct and detailed analsis of post-Mongol political life based on the Akkoyunlu example in *Aqquyunlu*, pp. 1-6, 114-23. Professor Dickson's seminars in Islamic history at Princeton University provided much of the inspiration for Professor Woods's exposition, and for my own.

Irano-Islamic ideals of sovereignty and statecraft amalgamated with the traditions of the steppe to produce a variety of syntheses that found both ideological and institutional expression. Through the fourteenth and fifteenth centuries such syntheses were experimental and fragile; Tîmûr could lay claim to being the protector of Cengiz Hanid hegemony or Sunni or Shi'i Islam, depending upon his audience, but his empire did not have the institutional or ideological stability to survive its founder by many years. By the mid-sixteenth century, however, the steppe-Islamic synthesis had taken definitive form. The ideal of any form of universal empire had virtually expired with establishment and consolidation of the four regional empires, Ottoman, Özbek, Safavi, and Tîmûrid-Mughal, all of them Muslim and all of them Turkic. By the end of the century, Âli states clearly, all four states recognized the political parity and geographical sphere of influence of the others. Universalistic claims and confederational forms of military organization were abandoned in favor of regional centralization and cultivation of a specific dynastic tradition that incorporated a conception of the sovereign as a protector of both religion and state. In the Ottoman case it was *kanun*, issued by the *padişahs* of the line of Osman, which made explicit this conception and gave the ruling house legitimacy. And it was *kanun*, dynastic law modeled on an idealized *yasa* and integrated with Islamic law, which represented the most enduring and powerful legacy of the steppe to the Ottoman Empire.[32]

In the fifteenth century the Ottomans, too, experimented with ideology. Of all the major post-caliphal states, the Ottomans had the weakest claim to political legitimacy as formulated by dominant Turco-Mongol ideals, and early Ottoman historiography reflects the variety of solutions to the problem which were attempted. The dynasty and its adherents, conscious of the force of Akkoyunlu claims to descent from Oğuz Han through his grandson Bayındır Han,[33] manipulated Ottoman and Oğuz genealogy in order to invoke Türkmen political traditions. As regional rulers, they attempted to de-

[32] The prestige that the *yasa*, or the conception of *yasa*, maintained into the early sixteenth century when the regional empires were being formed is illustrated by the observation made by Babur, the founder of the Indo-Tîmurîd empire, when he described his meeting with other Tîmûrid princes in Herat in 1506 in an effort to organize the defense of the Tîmûrid domains against the Özbek Şibani Han: "Our forefathers through a long space of time had obeyed the Chîngîz-tûrâ (ordinance), doing nothing opposed to it, whether in assembly or Court, in sittings-down or risings-up. Though it has not Divine authority so that a man obeys it of necessity, still good rules of conduct must be obeyed by whomsoever they are left; just in the same way that, if a forefather have done ill, his ill must be changed for good." (Annette Susannah Beveridge, trans., *The Babur-nama in English* [London, 1969, repr.], pp. 298-99.) This passage also expresses an awareness of the potential conflicts that observance of the *yasa* may have presented the Muslim rulers of the Turkic empires. For a recent summary, see Mansura Haider, "The Mongol Traditions and Their Survival in Central Asia (XIV-XV Centuries)," *Central Asiatic Journal* 28/1-2 (1984): 57-79.

[33] Cf. Woods, *Aqquyunlu*, pp. 38-41. Âli himself calls the Akkoyunlu rulers "the Bayındır sovereigns" (*selâtîn-i Bâyındırîye*) (KA, Selim I/7, Fatih 4225, 211b).

pict themselves as successors to the Selcuk sultans of Rum, whose dispensation at any rate pertained to the pre-Mongol caliphal order, and whose rule was associated with Irano-Islamic high cultural traditions in Anatolia. Finally, Ottoman historians elevated *gaza*, holy warfare against non-Muslims, from the level of a pious concept to that of a political principle that legitimized an otherwise purely pragmatic situation of border warfare.[34] The *gazi* ideal had by this time already gained a firm foothold in the lore of Muslim Türkmen tribal groups; rich in associations with popular mysticism, the syncretistic, "low" religious culture of the marches, and the loose solidarity of confederated tribal freebooters, the *gaza* concept represented yet another coalescence of nomadic and Islamic tradition equally far removed from steppe notions of aristocracy and from the Islam of the *medrese*. In the fifteenth and early sixteenth centuries such ideologies were no more exclusive or fixed than were the borders of the empire; stable regional empires represented the status quo only later in the sixteenth century. Although most of the ideologies current in a variety of forms at the time were intended to legitimize regional dominion, they also presupposed, in theory, universalistic ideals. Certainly Fatih Mehmed, Selim I, and possibly Süleyman adopted goals of conquest predicated upon the notion that a dominion approximating the universal could and should be established. While *gazi* prestige was useful in prosecuting the conquest of non-Muslim territories, it could only tenuously and dangerously be utilized to justify the conquest of Muslim principalities, as Yıldırım Bayezid discovered. To go further, *gaza* might serve to justify such conquest, but would not serve to win the allegiance of the Muslim Türkmen of Anatolia to a sultan with universalistic pretensions. To effect such allegiance the Ottomans would need to employ different ideological strategies, such as Oğuz genealogy, or, in the case of Selim I, Sunni religious sensibility, until such time as the Ottoman dynastic tradition itself acquired sufficient prestige to command allegiance and justify conquest and rule. In the Ottoman schema this occurred with Süleyman, whose particular prestige derived from his conquests and from his concern for universal justice in the form of *kanun*.

Writing at least a century after the *Tevarih-i Âl-i Osman* writers who sought to answer the Ottoman need for legitimacy through appeals to *gazi*,

[34] The classic examination of Ottoman experimentation with legitimizing ideologies, and exposition of the "*gazi* thesis," is Paul Wittek's *The Rise of the Ottoman Empire*. See also Woods, *Aqquyunlu*, Appendix A, pp. 186-96, for a detailed analysis of Oğuz genealogical traditions. Wittek, whose work has had considerable impact on subsequent studies of early Ottoman history, underestimates the political sophistication of nomadic polities and exaggerates the extent to which the Ottomans of the early fifteenth century were fervent Muslims removed from the political environment of the steppe and from Türkmen Oğuz tradition. He does not take seriously Ottoman manipulation of Oğuz genealogy, viewing it rather as a kind of nostalgic exercise. Consequently, Wittek overstates the ideological significance of the *gazi* ideal, taking it as the cornerstone of a universalist ideology rather than one of a number of ideological devices available for use depending upon audience and purpose.

Türkmen, and Selcuk-succession motifs, Âli both implicitly and explicitly acknowledged the weakness of such attempts to establish an ideological basis for the Ottoman state. Indeed, in his own time they were irrelevant. From the historical perspective Âli admits that neither genealogy nor religion was sufficient to legitimize early Ottoman universalist pretensions. He also acknowledges that universal dominion can no longer be entertained as an ideal of Ottoman sovereignty. Âli does, however, elaborate an alternative justification for Ottoman regional sovereignty. This justification is not totally explicit; it rather emerges as the set of assumptions that underlie Âli's treatment of Mongol, Tîmûrid, and Ottoman sovereignty.

In his discussion of Hülegü's destruction of the Abbasid caliphate, Âli indicates that just kingship is not necessarily dependent upon or coterminous with Islamic confession, and that the interests of a polity might be better served by an able and strong non-Muslim ruler than by an incompetent Muslim one. Analogously, a rebel against an established hereditary dynasty may have a more compelling right to rule if he is more just and capable than the latter. This notion presupposes that government can be separated from religion, and that the *şeri'at* remains in force to guide the acts of individual believing Muslims and their communities. Maintenance of order, control, and political stability is the proper province of government. This is best achieved, once political control has been established, by promulgation of a dynastic law that ensures justice and fair administration. Such a law derives its authority solely from the prestige and equity of the promulgator. Divine sanction for the ruler and his law may be presumed only insofar as his political success bespeaks God's favor and assistance, a conception which in this context is probably rooted in Central Asian political traditions. In the post-caliphal Islamic world, in which Turkic rulers were also Muslims bound to observe the *şeri'at*, the situation becomes more complex. These monarchs must be both good rulers and good Muslims, paying heed to the obligations of kingship made explicit in dynastic law at the same time that they uphold the spirit, if not the letter, of the *şeri'at*. Âli presents a concept of two forms, or two spheres, of justice—Ottoman *kanun* and Islamic *şeri'at*—which, coupled with strong central authority, must constitute the primary legitimizing principles in Ottoman political theory.[35]

[35] The importance of the Mongol model, and of the promotion of an Ottoman ideology of justice, for establishing dynastic legitimacy is most succinctly expressed in the introduction to the Ottoman portion of the *Iskendername* of Ahmedi (d. 1413):

> Though so many histories have been composed, / Still, my heart was at once moved: / "More words," whispered Inspiration; / What choice is there but to complete [the histories]? / Those rulers who have passed before, / Their conditions and deeds have been related. / Some were unbelievers, some tyrants; / The fate of all was grief, no more, no less. / First, the justice of the Mongol sultans; / Hear now the explanation of how it was. / They did not do as did Cengiz Han, / Who made it [justice], to the people, distinct from injustice. / They were oppressors; but by means of his [Cengiz Han's] law [*kanun*] / They did

Of the ruling dynasties of the four great regional empires, the Ottomans alone had neither a genealogical mandate for sovereignty, as the Özbeks and Tîmûrid Mughuls did, nor a religious one, as was the case with the Safavis. While tacitly admitting that this is so, Âli also displays his natural pro-Ottoman bias by presenting the case against the absolute validity and universal applicability of ideologies based upon either lineage or religion. He instead offers a regionally defined concept of sovereignty in which he stresses the supreme importance of royal justice that goes beyond or supplements the *şeri'at*. That Âli should do so is hardly surprising in light of the Ottoman situation. The *şeri'at* was a given in all Muslim lands; what the Ottomans lacked in lineage they made up for in active promotion of a dynastic tradition based upon justice. Commitment to justice was necessarily made as explicit as possible and associated with Ottomanism by means of *kanun*. In addition to giving expression and form to the Ottoman imperial tradition as it grew, *kanun* was in a very real sense fundamental to the establishment of the imperial state, for it provided the means whereby the dynasty consolidated and centralized a dominion comprising widely disparate territories, ethnic groups, and regional administrative traditions.

A strong central authority, in the person of the sultan, was key to the maintenance of a continuity and balance between *kanun* and *şeri'at*, which in theory pertained to separate domains of social and political life, but in practice could collide. *Şeri'at* was universal, immutable, divinely revealed, and hence spiritually supreme, while *kanun* was regional, amendable, and

---

not bathe their hands in the people's blood. / When injustice [*zulm*] is performed in the name of law [*kanun*], / A just leader [*adl beği*] easily comes forth for that people. / In those words [i.e., *kanun*] there is little deficiency; / Let us now do away with any faults [that remain]. / Since all of those oppressors have been named, / Let us now bring to mind all the just as well. / Let us name, from start to finish, those *beğs* [i.e., the Ottomans] / Who were both Muslims and just rulers. / The task of all of them was fighting the infidels; / What they ate and wore was lawful to them. / Let us bring the first [i.e., the oppressors] to an end with the latter [i.e., the just]; / With the latter let the former be finished. / I'll write you a book of Holy War [*gazavatname*]! / Hear it, or tell me your objections. / Don't say, "The *gazis* came last, what right have they?" / Don't say, "They're lesser, why have they come [to rule]?" / Who comes later, and remains, is better than his predecessors; / The thoughtful know the truth of what I say.

I follow the text found in an anonymous *Tevarih-i Âl-i Osman* formerly owned by Tayyıb Gökbilgin (photocopy, pp. 4-5). This *Anonymous* is substantially the same as that of Friedrich Giese (*Die altosmanischen anonymen Chroniken in Text und Übersetzung* (I, Breslau, 1922; II, Leipzig, 1925), except that it is incomplete and contains (pp. 243-46) an interpolation of several folios not found in Giese (I, 83-84) that identifies the writer (*kâtib ül-huruf*) as one Mehmed b. Elvân. The text of Ahmedi's opening found in this copy, however, is closer to that given by Nihad Sami Banarlı in "Ahmedi ve *Dasitan-ı Mülûk-i Âl-i Osmân*," TM 6 (1936-39): 111, than to the text of Giese (I, 1; II, 5-6).

For chronologically intermediate evidence of the significance of justice for Ottoman legitimacy, note Şehzade Korkud's refutation of the Ottoman Empire's international renown for the equity and effectiveness of its laws, cited in my "Islamic Ideals and Ottoman Realities."

created by human reason, and for that very reason was often of greater immediate relevance to the life of the Ottoman polity than the *şeri'at*. Only the wisdom of the ruler, whose duty it was to protect both religion and state, could keep the one from overshadowing the other. Therefore, the ideal ruler had to combine within himself the political sagacity and worldly wisdom of the administrator, the humanism and learning of the scholar, and the spiritual understanding and breadth of mind of the mystic or philosopher. In short, he had to approximate the Perfect Man, who could operate in all spheres of life. Only thus could he know how to deal with a situation affecting the entire state, and, if a given action involved a seeming violation of the *şeri'at*, be able to obey the spirit of the law while bending its precise strictures. It is not surprising that Âli should single out the reign of Sultan Süleyman Kanuni, who did so much to consolidate Empire-wide *kanun* legislation and legitimize it by reconciling it with the Holy Law, as a high point of imperial development.[36] It was this ruler whom Âli's mentor Kınalızade described as a philosopher-king who integrated rational and revealed law, the prime examples of which he cites as being Cengiz Hanid *yasa* and *şeri'at*, respectively. Invoking philosophical principles as a means to effect the intellectual synthesis of steppe and Islam, the jurist Kınalızade credited Süleyman with having established Utopia, the Virtuous City (*medine-i fazile*), throughout his dominions.[37] This consciousness of a dual heritage, of the significance of the Cengiz Hanid model, and of the utility, for Ottoman legitimists, of reconciling the disparities through an appeal to Platonic political theory, had deep roots in Ottoman intellectual culture. In the late fifteenth century Tursun Beğ, who like Kınalızade based his formulations of social theory on the *Ethics* of Naṣîr al-dîn Ṭûsî, wrote:

> If this Regulation is imposed by Divine Wisdom . . . [and] provides for happiness in the Two Worlds [this one and the next] the philosophers call it the Divine Ordinance, and the one who establishes it the Lawgiver. The men of the Holy Law call it the *şeri'at*, and the one who establishes it the *şâri'*, who is the Prophet. But, should the Regulation not be of this stature, but rather only a product of Reason [established] for the order of the visible world, such as, for example, [the law of] Cengiz Han, then they attribute it to its [proper] cause and call it sul-

[36] See especially KA, MS Leiden, 5a (ed. and trans. into Dutch by Schmidt, "Verantwoording"), and MEVA'İD, *passim*, where the practice of Süleyman's time, by and large and despite Âli's criticisms of that ruler, is taken as canonical.

[37] Kınalızade, *Ahlak*, Book II, pp. 105-106. Kınalızade treats politics in a manner that foreshadows Âli's approach, and differs from that of his (Kınalızade's) two primary authorities, Ṭûsî and Davânî, in that he makes frequent and conscious use of relatively recent historical example. Kınalızade stresses that historical comparison between the Ottoman house and earlier Islamic dynasties clearly points up the greater justice and efficacy, and by implication equal legitimacy, of the former. See, for examples, *Ahlak*, Book II, pp. 112-27, esp. p. 126.

tanic ordinance and imperial *yasak* [=*yasa*] [*siyâset-i sultani ve yasağ-ı padişahi*], which in our usage they call *örf*. Whichever [of the two forms of law] might be in effect, its preservation requires the existence of a sovereign. It is not necessary that there be a prophetic Lawgiver in each age. For Divine Decree, for example the religion of Islam, is sufficient to all people for the ordering of the visible and invisible world; there is no need for another prophet. But it is necessary that there be a sovereign at all times, for he has the full authority, in every era and age, to institute and implement these measures in accordance with the public interest. If his authority should be ended, men cannot live together as they should; indeed, all [people] may be destroyed, and that [divine] order too will perish.[38]

Âli used an analogous approach to solve the problem of Ottoman legitimacy, which as a conscientious universal historian he had to confront. He first dissociated religious and political principles and then reunited them in the form of two parallel modes of justice, the one embodying the dynastic mandate, the other expressing the Islamic character of the state. Both together manifested the Ottoman commitment to universal equity. This same concept of universal justice, religious and secular, allowed Âli to link Ottoman hegemony to the dominant Turco-Mongol tradition while it also enabled him to discount the ultimate importance of genealogical legitimating principles. The triad of *şeri'at, kanun*, and sultan, which Âli posited as the cardinal elements of Ottoman identity and legitimacy, represents the historian's elaboration of the principles to which the Ottoman class owed its allegiance: Religion, State, and the Ottoman Way.[39]

[38] Tursun Beğ, *Târîh-i Ebü'l-Feth*, ed. Tulum, pp. 12-13. Since Tursun Beğ and Ḳınalızade elsewhere follow Ṭûsî closely, it is significant in this context to note that they, like Âli, go yet further in discounting the importance of what Ṭûsî declares to be the first of seven qualities required of the proper sovereign: distinguished lineage, followed, in order, by high aspiration, firm opinion and acumen, determination, endurance, affluence, and upright assistants (Naṣîr al-dîn Ṭûsî, *The Nasirean Ethics*, trans. G. M. Wickens [London, 1964], pp. 227-28). To be sure, at the end of his discourse Ṭûsî says, "Of these qualities, good descent is not necessary, great though its effect may be." Tursun Beğ (p. 17) writes: "No one [ruler] can be worthy of praise or be justly proud unless it is by reason of possessing all or some of these four virtues [wisdom, courage, honesty, and justice]. Those who take pride in their descent and lineage [can only] do so because they have fathers and ancestors who were known for these virtues." Ḳınalızade, following Davânî, reduces royal lineage to the position of seventh requirement and states that this is the only one of the seven that is not absolutely necessary (*Ahlak*, Book II, pp. 126-27). Ḳınalızade does make a token case for the regal character of the Ottoman house, but he can muster only the authority of a few lines of rhetorical praise for the lineage of Fatih Mehmed, which the poet and mystic Jâmî included in a famous letter he sent to the Conqueror: "If one were to trace origins back to Adam/[One would find that] your forebears were all enthroned and crowned."

[39] Thomas, *Naima*, p. 121.

TWELVE

THE REIGN OF MURAD III

INTRODUCTION

ALI WAS NOT a theoretical historian in the sense that he began from explicit principles or models of historical development. His expressed methodology, in those sections of his work in which he generalizes, is presented as inductive rather than deductive. To be sure, certain assumptions about the nature of authority and structure of society do inform Âli's evaluation of events. These premises are primarily implicit, and are articulated only in the context of observation of historical events and patterns. In terms of presentation, Âli derives his general principles from analysis of history before applying those principles to interpretation of his subject matter. This is not to imply that Âli was a sort of early positivist, but rather that he strove to achieve an historical objectivity within the context of the social, religious, and psychological presuppositions that were part of his society. His interpretation of history, for example, represented by the *Seasons of Sovereignty*, followed the detailed chronicling of dynastic histories found in the *Essence*, which was largely completed by the time the *Seasons* was undertaken. This formally inductive approach to history is an aspect, or perhaps outgrowth, of the pragmatic, problem-solving orientation evidenced in the *Counsel*, in which Âli first displayed a concern with the history of his own time, and with which his evolution from littérateur to historian began. By the time Âli undertook the writing of the *Essence*, at the very end of his life, this evolution was complete.

Âli's treatment of the reign of Murad III is, for several reasons, a highly appropriate focus for an examination of Âli's aims and methods of historical analysis. Murad reigned for most of Âli's full adulthood, and Âli had some degree of personal involvement with many of the major personalities and events of this reign. The years of Murad's rule, 1574-95, also corresponded to the period during which Âli experienced the greatest professional disaster and disappointment. Âli's history of this era, therefore, represents a test of the historian's ability to gain perspective on events that were not only recent but traumatic.

This portion of the *Essence* is also, at least circumstantially, a more demonstrably individual product than other parts of the work. For events occurring later than the middle of the sixteenth century, when Celalzade and Ramazanzade completed their histories, Âli had no comprehensive source or formal model on which to base his structuring of information. Not only did he have to cull his own basic data for subsequent years from very diverse sources, but he was also freed from the influence of precedent or established format for the representation of events. He himself had to select the most significant occurrences and present them within the annalistic framework to which he formally adhered. We shall now, therefore, analyze Âli's treatment of the reign of Murad III as a case study in the historiographical method of a premodern historian. We must begin with a summary of a large portion of the *Essence of History* which delineates Âli's own arrangement of material. This summary necessarily repeats, but with a different purpose, some information already included in the biographical portion of our study.

One caveat must attend this examination. Âli treated the reign of Murad III at the very end of the *Essence* and at the very end of his life, during the years of 1596-98. This portion of the history is incomplete, and does not contain the usual biographies of notables following the events of the reign, although Âli states that he intended to write this section, in keeping with the format he adopted.[1] Haste and preoccupation, as well as Âli's historical sensibilities, had an impact on the structure of Âli's representation of the Ottoman Empire of Murad's time.

SUMMARY OF EVENTS

ÂLI begins his account of the reign with an introduction and proceeds to relate thirty-eight Events, which elsewhere in the *Essence* are normally arranged in chronological order. The annalistic rubrics break off after the thirty-eighth Event, giving way to "Third Grand Vezirate of Sinan Paşa," "Conquest of Komran (Komárno)," "Hungarian Wars" (spanning the last days of Murad and the early portion of Mehmed's reign), and "Death of Murad." The entire reign occupies some 139 large folios, or about one-third of MS Nuruosmaniye 3409, which begins with the accession of Süleyman. The following summary of portions of this section will illustrate Âli's approach to contemporary history and the degree to which he manipulated the annalistic form for his own purposes. Folio references are to the manuscript cited above.

1. *Introduction* (288a-293a): The Introduction focuses on the sultan, his family, and his closest confidants. Âli stresses the sultan's initial attachment to his official wife Safiye Hatun, and his later devotion to the pleasures of

[1] KA, Murad/Introduction, Nur 3409, 291a (dated 1005), 292a (dated 1007); Murad/Death, Nur 3409, 419a.

the concubines provided him by his sister İsmihan and his mother Nurbanu, who sought by these means to combat Safiye's influence over Murad. Murad's greatest fault was his cupidity, which Âli suggests was reinforced by a desire to store riches against the upheaval predicted by astrologers for the millennium. Âli portrays Murad as being possessed of contradictory character traits; he inclined toward the unworldly ethic of the dervish, as his poetry showed, but he also loved wealth. Âli lists the names and analyzes the influence of those closest to the sovereign: his confidants Şemsi and Doğancı Mehmed Paşas, his tutor Sa'düddin, the Palace Overseer Gazanfer Ağa, and the Mistress Housekeeper Canfeda Hatun. The latter two, Âli notes, represented the rapidly growing influence of the Harem. Âli closes the introduction with the observation that Murad's first words after his accession were "I am hungry." This presaged a period of famine and poverty, the like of which had never been experienced since the establishment of the Empire.

2. *Event 1* (292a): "The disorder of the age and perturbations of space and time which appeared, one by one, after this ruler's accession, and which proved to be the cause of the disruption and degeneration of the order of most of the world." Şemsi Paşa wished to unseat Sokollu, and was at Murad's side constantly. He encouraged Murad to accept petitions and complaints about maladministration each time they rode out together. This led to a flood of uncontrolled complaints, which were then laid to Sokollu's account. Responsible rulers, Âli says, employ spies to report on the reliability of such accusations, which might be untrue and malicious. Murad did not do this, but rather took them at face value out of a misguided and naive desire to see justice done. He thus abdicated responsibility and allowed witch hunts to take place with increasing frequency. Murad effectively allowed the credibility and authority of government to disintegrate.

3. *Event 2* (293a-b): "The disorder of the innovative proliferation of Royal Rescripts." Previous rulers had not used the Royal Rescript extensively; the written approval of the grand vezir (*buyruldu*) was sufficient for most appointments. Murad required that he see and sign most documents of appointment, except for those dealing with initial and supplementary *timar* grants. This innovation had two negative effects: the grand vezirs lost authority and their customary independence of action, and the eunuchs and concubines of the harem were able to begin controlling and selling appointments by virtue of their proximity to the sultan.

4. *Event 3* (292b-294a): Baki's exile through the calumnies of his rival Mu'allimzade. Soon after Murad's accession, the *Sahn* professor Mu'allimzade, hoping to be promoted to the Süleymaniye, organized a clever campaign to bring his rival for the post, Baki, into disfavor. He succeeded, and Baki was exiled from Istanbul, though the beleaguered Sokollu

later intervened to restore him to favor. Âli takes this as a symbolic event that set a trend for *ilmiye* life in Murad's time; while earlier sultans had patronized and helped the most able and learned, Murad allowed them to be exiled. Mu'allimzade was so poor a scholar that he could not continue in a teaching career; he was made chancellor, in which position he also failed.

5. *Event 4* (294a-295a): The excessive influence of Murad's depraved, avaricious, and heretical Sufi master, Şeyh Şüca'. Âli elaborates on Şüca's vile character and base origins, despite which Murad clung to him fervently until the sheikh's death. Even great ulema and vezirs were dependent upon Şeyh Şüca's goodwill. The Jewish Duke of Naxos, Josef Nasi, gained influence by virtue of his position as Şüca's personal wine supplier.

6. *Event 5* (295a-296b): "Şemsi Paşa's appointment as companion, and his satanic corruption of the Imperial Person by encouraging him to accept bribes." Âli asserts that, in his attempts to check and destroy the authority of Sokollu Mehmed Paşa, Şemsi Paşa accused him of taking bribes on a large scale without passing any of the proceeds to the sultan. Şemsi appealed to Murad's cupidity and convinced him to become the primary recipient of graft money in the Empire, through the intermediacy of the Queen Mother and the Palace Overseer. Şemsi Paşa told Âli that he himself had thus taken revenge for the Ottomans' displacement of his own family, the İsfendiyaroğulları. Âli supposedly incurred Şemsi's wrath for replying that this was hardly surprising, since the İsfendiyaroğulları claimed descent from Khâlid b. al-Walîd, who had first introduced the practice of bribery in the early Muslim community. Finally, Âli says,

> The Ottoman state's disintegration appeared from that day forth. At that time, in addition to the Inner and Outer Treasuries, even the treasury of Yedi Kule was filled to the brim. As soon as bribery began, even such great treasuries as these were emptied; the governors, *timar*-holders, and *za'ims* became poverty-stricken, the peasants and subjects dispersed and fled, and all at once the prosperous lands of Rum headed for ruin.

7. *Event 6* (296b): After the death of Josef Nasi (1583) the three ranking financial officers of the Empire—the treasurer, Okçuzade Mehmed; the finance director of Anatolia, Muhyi Efendi; and the director of the Second Branch, Sinan Efendi—were ordered to register his estate. They were later accused of stealing from it and were all dismissed, two of them, Okçuzade and Sinan, suffering torture and confiscation.[2]

[2] Âli dates this event to 1583/991. SELANİKİ, p. 169, assigns it to the previous year and does not specify the nature of the charges brought against the three, except to say that they were held guilty of graft. Selâniki also states that Sinan Efendi was *Anadolu defterdarı* and that one Ahmed Efendi was *şıkk-ı sani defterdarı*.

8. *Event 7* (296-298a): Decline in the value of the currency and subsequent economic chaos. In recent times the practices of clipping and counterfeiting had become rampant, and government officials had contributed to the fall in the value of currency by decreasing the silver content of newly minted *akçe*. After a statistical exposition of this practice, Âli states that by 1582/990 the official proportion of *akçe* to gold pieces, sixty to one, rose to sixty-five or seventy to one. At the instigation of crafty financial officials, Murad sought to save money in the payment of Palace troops by establishing a new official rate of one hundred twenty to the florin, this cutting in half the real income of all functionaries whose stipends were calculated in *akçe*.[3] Immediately, prices doubled and government price controls disappeared. The *Beğlerbeği* Incident of 1589, which further destroyed order and the authority of government, proceeded directly from the rapid decline in currency value. The Palace troops refused to accept payment in severely debased coin, which had in turn been part of a tax payment accepted only because the grand vezir had been bribed to turn a blind eye to its poor quality. Literally and figuratively, the dynasty's prestige fell with its coin.

9. *Event 8* (298b-299b): Death of Arab Ahmed Paşa—incomplete.

10. *Event 9* (298b-299b): The conspiracy to strip the incumbent grand vezir, Sokollu Mehmed Paşa, of his powers. The coterie gathered around the newly enthroned Murad, comprised of Hoca Sa'düddin, Şemsi Paşa, Üveys Çelebi, and Şeyh Şüca', attempted to discredit Sokollu and, if possible, have him killed. Sokollu replied in kind, instituting plots against his enemies, who nevertheless succeeded in removing many of Sokollu's protégés from office, depriving them of stipends and confiscating their property. Sokollu, who had virtually controlled the Empire and government for eight years, lost considerable authority, prestige, and support.

11. *Event 10*, Introduction (299b-300b): Formulation of plans to launch the Şirvan campaign, and the appearance of the great comet of 1577. Since the comet was traveling from west to east, it was popularly interpreted to portend war and Ottoman victory over the Safavis. No one thought, Âli says, that it also presaged the destruction of Rum as well, through ten years of warfare, poverty, bankruptcy, and destruction of the land.

12. *Events 10-38* (300b-399b): Straightforward chronological account of the major events of Murad's reign.

13. *Third Grand Vezirate of Sinan Paşa* (399b-415a): After two years of exile from office, Sinan Paşa began his third term as grand vezir in January 1593/Rebi' II 1001. Âli divides this section equally between the Austrian wars, in which Sinan embroiled the Empire in order to aggrandize his own

[3] Cf. Mustafa Akdağ, *Türk Halkının Dirlik ve Düzenlik Kavgası (Celâli İsyanları)* (Ankara, 1975), pp. 36-41.

position, and the innumerable character defects of the man Âli felt had almost single-handedly completed the destruction of the state. According to Âli, Sinan was arrogant, foolish, cowardly, and absolutely committed to acquiring personal power. He fomented factionalism and encouraged violence within the political system. The war he insisted upon starting cost many lives, destroyed military morale and discipline, and was ruinously expensive. In order to drive home the message that at this point the Empire had lost its ideals and was on the brink of ruin, Âli cites the story of one Mustafa Çavuş, who had been captured by the Hapsburgs and after his release reported to the sultan on the state of the enemy's resources. Mustafa Çavuş said that the Christians had four things no longer found in the Ottoman domains, and particularly in the army: justice and genuine care for the welfare of the populace, more-than-adequate provisions, abundant funds to pay the soldiery, and brave soldiers and able officers who maintained discipline.[4]

14. *Revolt of the Tributary Territories of Moldavia, Wallachia, and Transylvania in 1594-95/1003* (415a-417a): Âli states that under Murad the appointed administrators (*voyvoda*s) of these territories came to be changed yearly. The reason for this was that the new appointee gave monetary gifts to the sultan, vezirs, and Porte functionaries sent officially to install him. Frequent changes of *voyvoda*s therefore meant full treasuries and pockets, and the practice became customary. The result was disorder and oppression of the peasants by debt-ridden short-term *voyvoda*s. Since the time of Süleyman, Âli says, Moldavia had lost one-third of its population, and Wallachia over two-thirds, many former inhabitants having fled to Hungarian territory. Under such conditions rebellion is natural; Âli's sympathies are with the oppressed peasantry, and he blames maladministration, greed, and the sultan's irresponsibility for these events. To make matters worse, the personal rivalry of Sinan Paşa and Ferhad Paşa hindered serious attempts to control the rebellions.

15. *Death of Sultan Murad in 1595*/1003 (417a-419b): Murad's character, birth and death dates, and the execution by the new sultan, Mehmed, of his nineteen brothers, in accordance with Ottoman dynastic law. Âli evokes the apocalyptic air of the court in Murad's last days, and comments on the sultan's lack of foresight and responsibility: by giving in to his lust for women, he left an excessive number of male offspring who would have to be killed at his death.

16. *The Official Şehnameci*s (419b-422a): Âli begins this section with a capsule version of the cultural history of Rum. He divides Ottoman history into two phases: (1) 1300-1453, when Ottoman dominion was limited to certain portions of Anatolia and Rumeli, and (2) 1453 to the present, when

[4] KA, Nur 3409, 407a-408a.

the Empire's borders were much expanded both east and west. During the first period the Ottoman sultans possessed no great learning themselves, but prized and cultivated the educated. Fatih Mehmed set a new style; unlike his predecessors, he was a well-educated and cultivated man. Hearing of the fabled court of Ḥusayn Bâyqarâ, Fatih set out to emulate and rival the Tîmûrid in both personal scholarship and patronage of famous scholars. In this the Conqueror was encouraged by his vezir, Mahmud Paşa, and Fatih's successors and their statesmen continued to give patronage of learning a very high priority. With the accession of Selim II, however, this pattern changed because Harem functionaries gained a certain amount of control over appointments that had previously been the province of the grand vezir. These were more interested in riches than in learning, and began to sell posts to the highest bidder rather than see that they were given to the most worthy candidate. Under Murad the *kanun* that forbade inhabitants of the Harem to have contact with the world outside the Palace was allowed to lapse, and these began to set up independent establishments. This enabled Harem officials to extend their political influence even to *ilmiye* appointments. These developments served to politicize the learned class and lower its standards of accomplishment, and to render Palace secrets the stuff of common gossip.[5]

Âli quotes a poem of Mevlana Feridi, which relates this development to all the disorders plaguing the Empire. Corruption, poor education, disruption of the military, the decline of the *ilmiye*, and the relaxation of the restriction on marriage for Janissaries all proceeded from the sultan's neglect of affairs of state. In effect, Âli says, learning and literature had become bureaucratized. Patrons were no longer interested in learning, or sufficiently learned themselves to be so. While literary patronage was expected of them, they performed it perfunctorily, as if conducting a transaction, without caring for actual quality. So it was that the office of court *şehname*-writer, established by Süleyman, came to be perpetuated in Selim's time. Knowing that a royal poet and atelier were necessary for the prestige of the state, Selim and Murad simply sought to have the post filled like a vacant *timar* slot, without caring for the quality of the incumbent. All but the first *şehnameci*, Âli says, degraded the office.

17. *Remaining Events of Sinan Paşa's Third Grand Vezirate* (422a-426b): Sinan remained in office for slightly over three weeks after Murad's death. This section is devoted to three subjects. The first is the rivalry between Sa'düddin and Bustanzade for Sultan Mehmed's favor and for control of the *ilmiye* establishment. With the help of the Queen Mother, Sa'düddin eventually won out. The scandals that this bickering occasioned, Âli says, introduced severe disorder into the very beginning of the new sultan's reign

[5] Cf. KA, MS Leiden, 5b.

and caused his name to be cursed from the outset. Âli next expatiates on the universal hatred among poets for Sinan Paşa, who had no interest in literature. Finally, Âli deals with the unfortunate predominance of lowborn Iranians and Iranian Turks, which began in Murad's time. Because of the excessive favor shown to such undesirables, the sultan's proper servitors, his *kul*s, suffered deprivation and injustice.

ANALYSIS

ÂLI clearly conceived of this portion of the *Essence* as a whole, and endeavored to structure it as such in accordance with his own vision of history. To some extent historiographical unity can be said to be a function of the nature of the chronicle format, which dictated division of dynastic history into individual reigns. Nevertheless, the preceding summary shows that the significance of Murad's reign as a thematic whole transcends a purely chronological unity. It was a period vividly marked by abrupt and catastrophic change, and it was upon the hydra-headed manifestations of this phenomenon that Âli focused his attention in an attempt to comprehend and explain it historically.

Let us look again at the opening portion of Âli's account of Murad's reign. Âli begins with an examination of the sultan, his character, and the personal and environmental influences upon him. Here Âli adheres to a rather formal style of presentation, listing the sultan's confidants and giving biographical details without judgmental commentary. The important fact is that Âli documents the presence around the monarch of strong personalities possessed of great influence, who by implication helped to shape Murad's rule. Âli also evokes the harem environment, fraught with intrigue. No such listing of major personal influences occurs in the introduction to any other reign in the *Essence*; Âli's purpose, conscious or otherwise, is to establish the presence of the harem and of a clique gathered around the royal person as part of the new political environment, which is implicitly contrasted with that which obtained in the reigns of earlier sultans. Âli saves his explicit judgment for Murad, whose weakness is shown by his inability to control his appetites. Finally, Âli symbolically links Murad's character with the upheavals and degeneration which, in Âli's view, were the distinguishing feature of the entire reign and that of his successor. Âli seeks the beginnings, if not the precise causes, of the Ottoman situation of 1597 in the events of 1574.

Âli pursues this process of symbolic association in the first ten Events. These are not in strict chronological order, but jump back and forth across the first twelve years of Murad's rule. Using the Event rubric, Âli in fact seeks to isolate and identify what he perceives as the major problems of the period, the separate symptoms of a massive degeneration that might have become apparent later but which Âli identifies as beginning with Murad's accession. These are, in order: the sultan's irresponsibility and susceptibility to pernicious influences; destruction of veziral authority and of respect for government; politicization of *ilmiye* life and decline of learning; Murad's inability to distinguish between true and false spirituality; corruption at the highest levels of government; the unfortunate prominence and moral corruption of the financial service; inflation and economic crisis; military disorder; corruption of administrative morality; growing factionalism; and protracted and useless warfare.

Some of these presentations, such as that on coinage, are very specific and historically analyze discrete phenomena. Others, such as the exile of Baki, the prominence of Şeyh Şüca', and the dismissal of the financial officers, are, rather, symbolic of associated patterns. Âli could not relate causally all manifestations of what he saw as decline, although he worked hard to trace individual trends; but his representation of these phenomena reflects their association and interrelatedness in his own perception.

Having established these themes in his introductory section, Âli returns to them constantly throughout the remainder of the *Essence*. By the end of the section on Murad's reign the historian has become thoroughly problem-oriented, as in the *Counsel*. His description of Murad's death and the circumstances surrounding it is, except for its apocalyptic tone, almost incidental to his anxiety to identify and analyze problems that emerged in Murad's time and continued into the reign of Mehmed. For Âli these were trends which threatened to destroy completely the fabric of state and society, and which no simple change of administration in itself could reverse. True, Âli's personal grievance against Sinan Paşa had much to do with the great amount of space he devoted to the grand vezir and his pernicious acts. At the same time, the historian argues that the persistent return of Sinan, even after repeated dismissal and disgrace, to the highest office in the land constituted a sorry statement on Ottoman administrative standards, royal judgment, and the nature of the appointment process. Furthermore, Âli pointed to the effects of Sinan's ambition and successive appointments: factionalism, military disintegration, political instability, warfare, and economic disruption.

One theme, one thread, binds the elements of Âli's discourse: the indivisible authority and ultimate responsibility of the ruler, with whose person and character the ideals of post-Mongol statecraft identified the state and its fortunes.[6] Soon after finishing his *Essence* account of the reign of Murad III, or perhaps as he was completing it, Âli articulated his conception of the na-

[6] See İnalcık, *Ottoman Empire*, pp. 47-48, 65-69; Hodgson, *Venture*, II, 400-410; and chapter 11 above.

ture of kingship and its duties in the *Seasons*, which he dedicated to Murad's son, Mehmed. Âli's exposition reveals his debt to the lore of statecraft adumbrated by such earlier theoreticians as Tursun Beğ and Kınalızade; it also shows how much further he has gone in elaborating and systematizing received political wisdom and in linking it practically to serious historical study:

1) God has appointed sovereigns on earth and has charged them to rule justly. He has given them kings, vezirs, generals, and judges to guide them in what they do not know.
2) They must consult the ulema and those experienced in administration.
3) They must keep their counselors and retainers separate from the common folk, and must not allow the latter into government or raise them to high position.
4) The sovereign's retainers must maintain the same distinction in their selection of their own servitors.[7]

The security and stability of the realm can only be maintained by the ruler when he meets the following conditions:

1) He must make himself universally beloved for his justice.
2) He must employ disinterested and learned counselors, especially the ones acquainted with historical science.
3) He must not be angered when these speak the truth, and must ignore the counsel of self-interested parties.
4) He must familiarize himself with the most intimate details of administration and of social conditions in his realm, so that he may make informed judgments. He should not allow the lowly to become wealthy, nor the worthy to be poor.
5) He must employ spies to report on the true nature of events in all parts of the state, and more spies to control the spies.
6) He must keep abreast of events in the capital, and particularly inform himself about the affairs of the major figures of state.[8]

Having thus established the absolute responsibility of the sovereign for

[7] FUSUL, Introduction, 1b-2a. With this and the following section, compare Tursun Beğ, *Târîh-i Ebü'l-Feth*, ed. Tulum, pp. 10-15 (on the necessity of the sovereign); pp. 16-18 (on the absolute necessity of justice, divine and temporal, as the counterweight to absolute royal authority); pp. 18-21 (on the requirement of patience and forebearance in the sovereign); pp. 22-23 (on the requirement of honesty); pp. 23-26 (on the requirement of wisdom and gratitude to God); pp. 26-28 (on the requirement of generosity to soldiers and servitors and attentiveness to their needs, whereby loyalty is won and preserved); pp. 28-29 (on the requirement of seeking the company of ulema and holy men); pp. 29-30 (on attaining happiness in both worlds). Âli presents a vision of the good ruler that is, if anything, more pragmatic and more absolutist than that of Tursun Beğ, who in his history sought to instruct Sultan Bayezid II (often called *veli*, "the Saint") in ways to avoid the difficulties that the authoritarian policies of Bayezid's father, the Conqueror, had caused.

[8] FUSUL, Introduction, 2a-3a.

the condition of the state, Âli goes on in the *Seasons* to exhort Sultan Mehmed to fulfill his regal obligations and put right the disastrous situation of the Empire. He holds the sultan to be innocent of active wrongdoing because no one, except Âli, will tell him of the corruption and injustice of which those to whom his authority has been delegated are guilty; but he must now begin to take his duty seriously.[9] Âli rephrased and redirected these precepts one year later in the *Tables of Delicacies*, where he states that good and enduring sovereignty requires more than lineage, justice, and strict adherence to *kanun*. A ruler, Âli says, must ensure the loyalty of the military and of the learned hierarchy by making sure that the former is paid, the latter patronized and cultivated, and the sensibilities of both scrupulously regarded. He must also be aware of all that transpires in his realm.[10]

Âli's enunciation, in these late moralistic works, of the principles of sovereignty characteristic of what Marshall Hodgson has aptly termed "the military patronage state"[11] has clear implications for the interpretation of his historiographical purpose and method. Âli's treatment of the reign of Murad III resembles a case study, the historical ground in which Âli's conceptions of kingship and statecraft are imbedded, and against which they are displayed. Given an identification between the health of the state and the strength of sovereign authority, a recounting of growing disorder and of corruption and incompetence at high levels of government becomes, of necessity, a documentation of the breakdown of the monarch's will and sense of responsibility. This logic clearly played a part in Âli's mode of discourse, for he portrays Murad as the microcosm of the state. He shows Murad as a ruler in whose character both laudable and reprehensible influences conflicted and frequently canceled each other out. In a similar fashion, the state still retained its basic structure and preserved successful institutions that were, according to Âli, later perverted by self-interest, dishonesty, and neglect. It is important to note, however, that except in certain instances of policy decision, Âli does not perceive the relationship between microcosm and macrocosm to be a strictly causal one; as often as not the connection is indirect, psychological, or symbolic, a function of the moral dimension of historical process.

For all his attempts to view history comprehensively and analytically, Âli of necessity made use of the traditional political lore that was available to him, such as the Circle of Equity, the Medical Analogy, and the conception of cyclical dynastic decline. In this sense, despite his mode of presentation, he was no more inductive or "scientific" than was Ibn Khaldûn, to whom

[9] FUSUL, Introduction, 4b-5a.
[10] MEVA'İD, pp. 68-73.
[11] Hodgson, *Venture*, II, 400-410.

he may be likened.[12] But such models did not limit his analysis or method of representation any more than did the established chronicle format. Âli did not see himself as the kind of historian who subordinates historical fact to theory held a priori, and his historiography possesses a strongly pragmatic streak. It was the cataclysmic character of the era over which Murad presided that forced Âli to test and apply, and in some measure to elaborate and recast, the political philosophy of his age. His conviction that he had a mission to analyze the causes of disorder and to make an intellectual, didactic contribution to the salvation of the Empire is clearly displayed in the last portion of the *Essence*. Not only did Âli, in his old age, devote increasing attention to contemporary problems and to the threats they posed for the newly enthroned Mehmed, but he also expended great energy in trying to bring them to the sultan's attention. Âli was so convinced of danger and decline, or so overconfident, that he did not hesitate to speak frankly and harshly of Mehmed's recently deceased father.[13] The devices Âli used were literary, conventional where appropriate, and innovative, but not radically so, where an established framework was inadequate. For this reason Âli's theoretical statements, explicit or implicit, cannot be taken at face value, or classified as typical or idiosyncratic, until they are evaluated in practice, in the historical and historiographical context he provides. Although Âli dwelt in the *Seasons of Sovereignty*, for example, on the cyclical rise and fall of dynastic states, in intent and practice he did not view the schema as wholly deterministic, or Ottoman decline as inevitable. His interest was in the identification of problems and their solutions, which he saw to lie primarily in adherence to the principles of *şeri'at* and *kanun* enforced by a strong and able sovereign.

This observation could imply a simplistic determinism of its own, whereby a weak sultan would necessarily produce social and political degeneration. To see such an equation in the *Essence* account of the reign of Murad III would be to do injustice to Âli's historical sensibility. Whatever the nature of his declared absolute ideals, Âli did not apply them absolutely; he was far too fascinated by people, events, and the processes of which they were a part to do so. Even in discussing phenomena that he categorizes as part of the disorder of the late sixteenth century, Âli demonstrates a comparative and relativistic sense, and an ability to suspend absolute judgment. For example, while Âli traces the beginnings of pernicious harem influence in political and cultural life to the accession of Selim II, he elsewhere praises Selim himself as a patron of literature and protector of *kanun*, though he was not a ruler of Süleyman's stature.[14] Selim fulfilled at least

[12] Fleischer, "Royal Authority," 199-203, 213.

[13] See chapter 5, note 37.

[14] See chapter 1, note 71; chapter 4, note 106; chapter 10, note 13.

part of his duty as sovereign by maintaining able and responsible deputies, primarily Sokollu Mehmed Paşa, who kept the state in order. Âli's treatment of Sokollu in various contexts presents another fascinating instance of the historian's multifaceted perception. In the *Counsel* and the *Essence* Âli ventured to criticize Sokollu Mehmed Paşa, because he practiced nepotism on a scale that purportedly surpassed anything that had occurred in Süleyman's time, and also because he acquired powers of authority that were theoretically reserved for the sultan. But in these same works Âli tempered his criticisms with the observation that at least most of Sokollu's protégés were in fact able and worthy people.[15] Âli distinguished between individuals and institutions; the decline of the authority of the grand veziral office, itself the reflection and bulwark of royal authority, and the fall of Sokollu himself, however richly deserved on moral grounds, both contributed significantly to the decline of the state. To Âli, the iron hand of Sokollu Mehmed Paşa was preferable to the factionalism and disintegration of authority that followed his loss of favor and eventual murder under Murad.

This example raises another issue central to understanding Âli's approach to history. Âli was extremely interested in human personality, as the lengthy biographical portions of the *Essence* show, and he devoted much space to analysis of the character and personal quirks of the major figures of the day. It may be that this becomes particularly apparent in his treatment of Murad's reign because Âli was then personally acquainted with many of the primary participants in the political life of the Empire. For him, history was a matter of individual personalities as much as of institutions, wars, and momentous events; historical processes were not faceless, but could be directed by individual acts. Hence, Âli could approve of Sokollu's appointment to the grand vezirate, in the absence of a strong sultan, but deplore Sinan Paşa's long, if intermittent, tenure in office, because of the difference in the moral qualities of the two. Sokollu, like Sinan Paşa, manipulated rival factions, such as those of Lala Mustafa Paşa and Sinan Paşa. The difference was that Sokollu's actions maintained the integrity of the grand vezir's authority and, as long as that authority rested with Sokollu, served to keep the office above factional dispute. Sokollu could serve both himself and the state; Sinan Paşa, on the other hand, subordinated all interests to his own, and made the highest office in the land the object and center of factional violence, thereby demeaning it and perverting its purpose.

Âli took a very personal view of the history of his times, which is hardly surprising. It was, in a very immediate sense, his own history. Fascinated as he was by concrete events and their causes and results on the one hand, and by the horrifying general apocalypse he perceived around him on the

[15] See chapter 7, note 6.

other, Âli attempted to combine, reconcile, and thereby comprehend both the specifics of the history of his own time and the generalities of the laws governing human societies. He sought to understand a vast historical fabric, that of the Ottoman civilization of which he was a part. It was, however, a fabric composed of many elements, social, political, cultural, moral, historical, and human. Âli's approach, as an historian, was to examine the segments of that unity, each of which presented a different aspect in different contexts; hence, he concerned himself variously with institutions, individuals, economics, morality, and spirituality, as well as with political history.

Underneath this diversity lay a presumption of the unity, or rather interrelatedness, of all these phenomena, a sense dictated by the Ottoman ideals with which Âli had grown up and which he had worked so hard to fulfill. Âli applied this unitative sense to his writing of history in the form of an implicit concept of balance between all elements, tangible and intangible, of social and political life, a balance that is the historiographer's version of the Circle of Equity. Âli expressed this notion in the *Seasons* by means of an economic metaphor referring to market imbalance: "The order of the world has been destroyed; men can neither enforce the ordinances of rulers, nor maintain the true daily price [of goods]."[16] According to the value system which informs Âli's political commentary (like that of Ibn Khaldûn), the natural tendency of human beings is to seek their own interests, but a wise ruler can, through his exercise of authority, curb this tendency and make it serve the state. Other factors can also play a role in maintaining social justice and stability. Sokollu had more power than was right for him to possess, but the temptation to abuse his authority was tempered by education and a moral sense that prevented him from transgressing the spirit of Ottoman ideals of statecraft. Furthermore, his own strength and commitment to the state, though these too were part of his self-interest, compensated for Sultan Selim's disinterest in political affairs. Âli was keenly aware of the checks, balances, and relativism that inhere in the notion of a unitary system.

Another, perhaps more pointed, example of Âli's historical perspective and view of causality is provided by his repeated references to fiscal chaos and attendant moral decline throughout the Empire, which Âli relates to the situation of the religious establishment. While in the introduction to Murad's reign he presents specific financial problems as the product of official policy and the depravity of financial officers, he elsewhere cites poverty and inflation as factors contributing to moral chaos.[17] These two references, together with many others of similar tone, show that Âli saw the late-six-

[16] FUSUL, Introduction, 5a.

[17] See chapter 5, note 62.

teenth-century financial crisis as both fostering and fostered by erosion of moral standards. This view is perfectly congruent with an historical approach based upon a holistic notion of unitary balance, in which indirect relationship between events is as significant as direct causality.

It may be that Âli, in his efforts to understand how his times and society could become so unbalanced, can be seen by historians of our own age to have described "symptoms rather than causes." Modern historians have a perspective of four hundred years and access to sources that reveal, in the context of the financial crisis, causes in the form of a population explosion, new trade patterns, and influxes of Peruvian silver.[18] Mustafa Âli lived at the end of the sixteenth century and disposed of resources that were, materially and geographically, far more limited, yet he documented the history of his polity and analyzed its problems with a comprehensiveness, vigor, and insight that commanded the respect of the generations of Ottomans who read his history after his death. For this, and for the ineluctable quality of his accomplishment, he deserves our respect as well.

[18] İnalcık, *Ottoman Empire*, pp. 45-52.

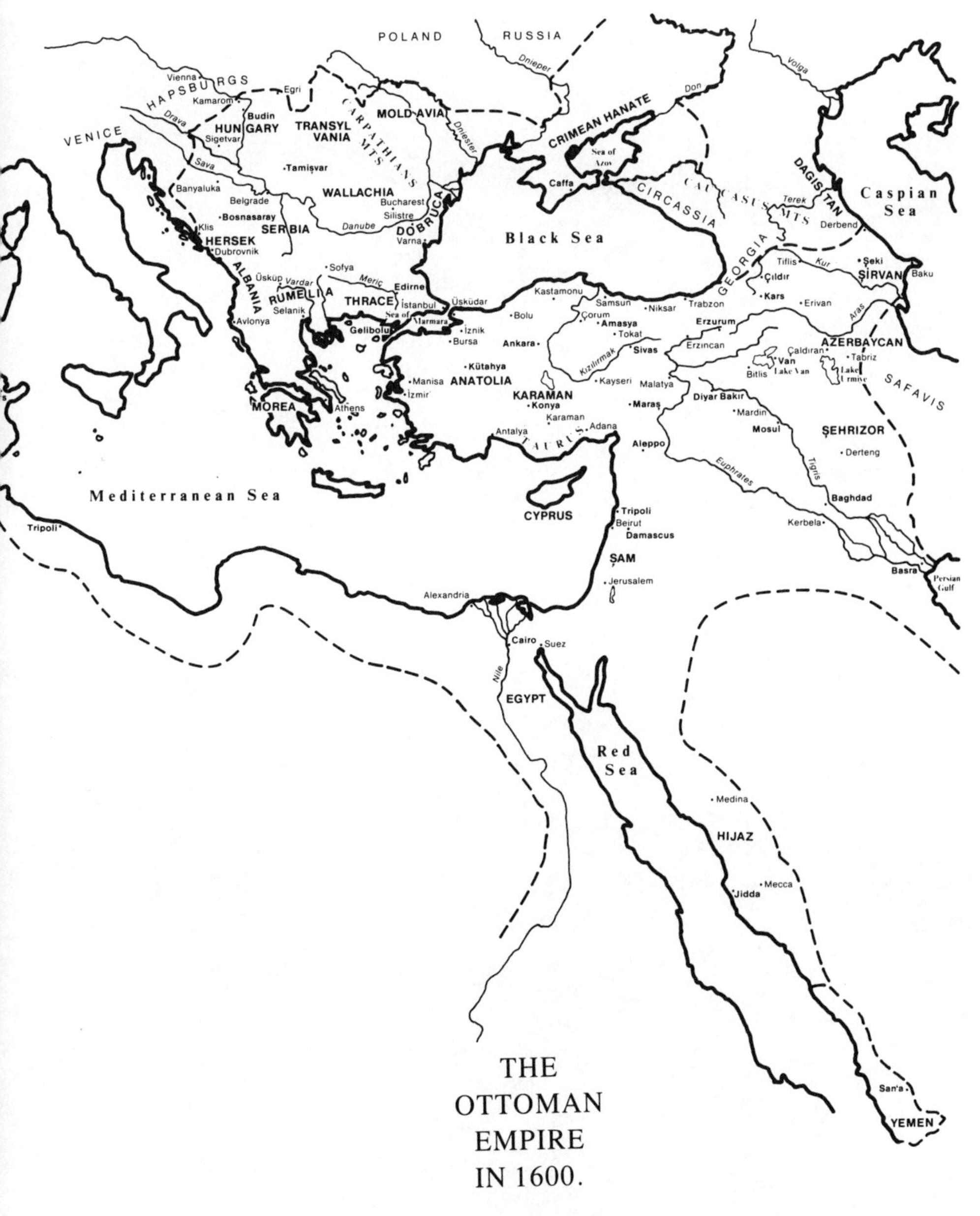

THE
OTTOMAN
EMPIRE
IN 1600.

APPENDIX A

THE STRUCTURE OF THE OTTOMAN FINANCIAL ESTABLISHMENT IN THE SIXTEENTH CENTURY

THE ORIGINS of the Ottoman financial bureaucracy are still somewhat mysterious. The title *defterdar* ("keeper of the register"), used to designate a financial official, appears to derive from İlhanid usage. In the Ottoman context the term in this form is attested in the *Kanunname* of the Conqueror, in which reference is made to a "chief *defterdar*" (*başdefterdar*) and at least two other *defterdar*s. The *başdefterdar* was also known as *Rumeli defterdarı*. The first financial official to be appointed at the Ottoman court, perhaps in the time of the Conqueror or even earlier, the *Rumeli defterdarı* was originally charged with supervising the imperial *hass* income from the Rumelian provinces and with keeping the accounts of the treasury. As the Ottoman financial establishment grew, the *defterdar* of Rumeli became the general supervisor of all imperial finances, the treasurer, and served on the Imperial Council. Although he worked under the direction of the grand vezir, the treasurer had independent authority to authorize and account for all expenditures or withdrawals from the treasury.[1]

By the end of the reign of the Conqueror a second central financial office had appeared, the *defterdarlık* of Anatolia. The *Anadolu defterdarı* also served on the Imperial Council and supervised the financial administration of imperial holdings in the Anatolian provinces. Shortly after Selim I's conquest of Eastern Anatolia and Syria, a third office was added to the Empire's financial structure in order to administer the fiscal affairs of the new provinces. The incumbent of this position, the *Arab ve Acem defterdarı*, resided in Aleppo. Between 1544 and 1573 this *defterdarlık* began to be broken up into smaller finance directorships (*defterdarlık*) attached to the treasuries of major provinces such as Diyar Bakır, Aleppo, and Erzurum. In some important newly acquired provinces such as Budin (Buda, conquered 1541), which became a major frontier staging area, independent treasuries appear to have been established almost immediately. In some cases, such as that of Egypt, these directorates seem to have evolved from the function of supervision of imperial finances (*nezaret-i emval*) at the provincial level, which, in the 1540s and 1550s before the formal constitution of independent treasuries and directorates, was bestowed variously, on a more or less annual basis, on either provincial governors or, more commonly, other mem-

[1] Uzunçarşılı, *Merkez*, pp. 325-27; Matuz, *Kanzleiwesen*, pp. 57-59; B. Lewis, "Defterdar," EI².

bers of the military-administrative class specifically assigned to the task. The finance directors of provinces (*hazine defterdarı, mal defterdarı*) were called *kenar defterdarları*, "*defterdars* of the periphery," to distinguish them from the *defterdars* of the Porte. Early in Süleyman's reign a third *defterdarlık* of the Porte was established, the *şıkk-ı sani* or "second branch," which dealt with the collection and accounting of treasury revenues gathered in and around Istanbul. Yet another *defterdarlık* of the Porte, the *şıkk-ı salis*, "third branch," was created in about 1585 in order to deal with imperial income from the Danube region, but it was abolished shortly after its establishment.[2]

In the late sixteenth century the ranking of the central financial offices of the Ottoman Empire was as follows:[3]

1. *Başdefterdar (Rumeli defterdarı, baş kalem)*
2. *Andolu defterdarı* (also called *orta*, "middle")
3. *Şıkk-ı sani defterdarı*

In the normal course of promotion during this period, the treasurer (*başdefterdar*) would become a *sancak beği* or governor-general, and be succeeded in his office by the *Anadolu defterdarı*. The latter's place would be taken by the *şıkk-ı sani defterdarı*, whose vacant post would be filled by either the secretary-in-chief (*re'isülküttab*) or one of the more important provincial *defterdars*.

It is difficult to establish how many full provincial treasuries, and corresponding finance directorships, were in existence at any given time in the late sixteenth century; their number shifted with the tide of conquest, loss, and administrative reorganization. Ayn-ı Ali, writing in 1607, listed twelve of thirty-two provinces as having independent treasuries and *defterdars*, and he did not include the finance directors of Rumelia, Anatolia, or Egypt in this count.[4] Âli mentions at least two other full provincial finance directorships not cited by Ayn-ı Ali, those of Rum (Si-

[2] The standard and very summary treatments of these developments are Uzunçarşılı, *Merkez*, pp. 328-31, and Matuz, *Kanzleiwesen*, p. 58. Uzunçarşılı's chronology for the establishment of financial offices has been amended on the basis of the following documents. In his introduction to Tursun Beğ, *Târîh-i Ebü'l-Feth*, p. xvii, Mertol Tulum adduces evidence showing that the Anatolian directorate was established in the time of the Conqueror rather than in that of Bayezid, as Uzunçarşılı implies. The second branch was already in existence in 1524/930, according to a state budget published by Halil Sahillioğlu ("1524-1525 Osmanlı Bütçesi," İÜİFM, 41/1-4, [1983], 417, 435). The earliest extant *mühimme* register, TKS Arşivi E 12321, which dates from 1544-45/951, shows that already at that time there was a *mal defterdarı* in Baghdad (doc. 209), in Diyar Bakır (docs. 39, 50), and in Budin (docs. 155, 228). The provincial *nezaret-i emval* is frequently attested in the appointment registers from the reign of Süleyman, which I have used together with narrative materials as the basis for a detailed study, now in progress, of the evolution and rapid expansion of the central and provincial financial establishments. In the current context it is worthwhile to note that the so-called *History of Rüstem Paşa*, under the year 1547/953-54, refers to the *nezaret-i emval* of Egypt, to the *defterdarlık* of Budin, and to a third *defterdarlık* of the Porte (Ludwig Forrer, ed. and trans., *Die osmanische Chronik des Rustem Pascha* [Leipzig, 1923], pp. 144-45). This reference also attests instances of a phenomenon revealed by the early appointment registers: the regular promotion of *defterdars* (*pace* Röhrborn) to *sancak* governments.

[3] This is the order given in KPT 246, p. 29, dated July-August 1585/Şa'ban 993.

[4] Ayn-ı Ali, pp. 11-37.

vas) and Şirvan, the latter no longer a province in 1607.[5] Other evidence refers to finance directorships established during the sixteenth century (Yemen, Lahsa, Gence, Egri, and Basra), which later appear to have disappeared.[6]

To some extent provincial finance directorships appear to have been ranked according to their order of establishment.[7] Aleppo, for example, retained its prestige as the oldest treasury center outside of the capital, and the *defterdar* of Aleppo was the highest-ranking provincial finance director next to that of Egypt, whose circumstances were in any case quite different because of Egypt's special status among the provinces of the Empire. The financial apparatus established in any given province depended upon its importance and upon whether the *timar* system was in effect. *Salyane* provinces such as Egypt, in which the *timar* system was not applied, had *defterdars* who supervised the collection and disbursal of imperial revenues.[8] In provinces in which the *timar* system was applied, but which had no treasury of their own, two financial officials were appointed by the Porte: the *defter kedhüdası* regulated the distribution of *zeâmets*, and the *timar defterdarı* looked after the allocation of *timars*. These two officials were probably responsible to the registrar (*defter emini*), who had general supervision of the disposition of *miri* lands and those granted under the *timar* system.[9] In such provinces, the general supervision of all aspects of imperial finance in the region (*nezaret*) rested with the governor-general. A *timar defterdarı*, when promoted, would become a *defter kedhüdası*, and the latter was eligible for elevation to a finance directorship (*hazine, mal defterdarlığı*). The *mal defterdarları* (i.e., financial officials who dealt with actual revenues rather than with land allocation) were the chief financial officials of provinces that had both a provincial treasury and the *timar* system. While the provincial finance directors supervised the activities of their two chief subordinates, the *defter kedhüdası* and *timar defterdarı*, they were more immediately concerned with the collection of taxes, keeping regular accounts, controlling the provincial treasury, paying provincial administrative expenses, and sending the required yearly revenue remittance (*irsaliye*) to the central treasury, which they represented. The *mal defterdarları* worked under the *başdefterdar*.

The financial and military branches of provincial government were theoretically separate; the *mal defterdarı* of a province was responsible directly to the treasury and to the *başdefterdar*, who was the sultan's personal financial official, while the governor-general answered to the grand vezir, who administered the Empire as the sultan's agent. The independence of the spheres of authority of the grand vezir and treasurer was mirrored on the provincial level. The purpose of this separation of powers was to ensure that powerful governors or vezirs did not abuse their positions to the detriment of the treasury or of the taxpaying subjects. In some provinces, however, governors-general were granted general supervisory powers over the finance

[5] See chapters 3 and 4, and Uzunçarşılı, *Merkez*, p. 230.
[6] Röhrborn, "Emanzipation," pp. 128-29; Matuz, *Kanzleiwesen*, p. 42 (Basra).
[7] Uzunçarşılı, *Merkez*, pp. 328-31; Matuz, *Kanzleiwesen*, p. 58.
[8] For examples, see Ayn-ı Ali, pp. 8-10.
[9] Uzunçarşılı, *Merkez*, pp. 96-98; Pakalın, *Tarih Deyimleri*, I, 418-20.

director, which enabled rapacious governors to interfere in financial matters. Such supervision was also given to governors-general on a temporary basis if a finance director died or was dismissed, so that the provincial fisc might not become disordered before the arrival of a replacement. Financial supervision could also be a permanent part of a governor-general's duties if his province's independent treasury was abolished.[10]

[10] İnalcık, *Ottoman Empire*, pp. 117-18.

APPENDIX B

CHRONOLOGY

28 April 1541/2 Muharrem 948 Mustafa Âli born in Gelibolu (Gallipoli).

ca. late 1556/963-64 Âli moves from Gelibolu to Istanbul in order to seek admission to an imperial *medrese*.

1560-61/968 Âli completes training for a religious career at the *medrese* of the Conqueror; travels to the court of Prince Selim at Konya and presents his first work, *Mihr u Mah*; Prince Selim offers post as chancery secretary, Âli accepts.

1561-62/969 Selim's court moves to Kütahya; Âli completes *Tuhfet ül-uşşak*.

1562-63/970 Âli travels to Istanbul but fails to win patronage from Sultan Süleyman; returns to Kütahya and presents *Mihr u Vefa*, which fails.

1563/970 Âli travels to Aleppo to become the confidential secretary of the governor-general, Lala Mustafa Paşa; both men move to Damascus later the same year, when Lala Mustafa is transferred to the government of that province. Soon after arrival Âli meets Kınalızade Âli Çelebi and begins *Enis ül-kulub*.

1566/974 Sultan Süleyman dies on campaign at Sigetvar; his son Selim ascends the throne as Selim II, "the Sot."

1567/975 Âli compiles his first *divan*.

1568/976 In the spring Âli and Lala Mustafa Paşa move to Cairo to prepare for the Yemen campaign Lala Mustafa Paşa is to command. In August, Lala Mustafa Paşa is dismissed and replaced by Sinan Paşa, and he and Âli return to Damascus for an official investigation. Lala Mustafa Paşa returns to Istanbul in October while Âli travels overland and takes refuge at the Manisa court of Prince Murad b. Selim, where he completes and presents *Nadir ül-maharib*.

1569/977 Âli moves to Murad's summer court at Bozdağ and writes *Rahat ün-nüfus* by commission. By September he returns to Istanbul.

1570/977-78 Âli completes *Heft Meclis* and is assigned to Klis in Dalmatia, where he serves the *sancak beği* Gazi Ferhad Beğ.

1574/982 By the end of the year Âli and Ferhad Beğ have been transferred to Banyaluka in Bosnia, of which *sancak* Ferhad had become governor. Selim II dies; following the accession of his son Murad III to the sultanate Âli formally compiles and dedicates his first *divan, Vâridat ül-enika*.

1575/982-83 Âli produces *Zübdet üt-tevarih* for Ferhad Beğ, and in the spring travels to Istanbul to personally present an accession ode to the new sultan; failing to gain royal patronage, he returns to Bosnia, where he now has a 60,000-*akçe zeâmet*.

1576-77/984 Âli's son Fazlullah is born.

1577/985 By the spring Âli resigns his *zeâmet* and returns permanently to Istanbul; later he completes *Hilyet ür-rical*, by royal commission.

1578/985 Âli is appointed secretary to Lala Mustafa Paşa, field marshal of the Şirvan campaign.

1578/986 The Ottoman army leaves Istanbul for the Caucasus (April/Safer). By October Âli has been appointed *timar*-registrar (*timar defterdarı*) of Aleppo. Winter in Erzurum.

1579/987 Second winter in Erzurum. Sokollu Mehmed Paşa is assassinated and Lala Mustafa Paşa is recalled to Istanbul.

1580/988 Sinan Paşa made *serdar* and then grand vezir; Lala Mustafa Paşa dies. Âli completes *Nusretname*, begins *Fursatname* by order of new field marshal Sinan Paşa, and goes to Aleppo for the winter.

1581/989 Âli spends campaign season in Van and returns to Aleppo for the winter. Closes his first *divan, Vâridat ül-enika*, and begins collecting his second, *Lâyihat ül-hakika*; writes bulk of *Nushat üs-selâtin*.

1582/990 Âli commissions an illuminated copy of *Nusretname*, and in the summer is ordered to write a letter of congratulations on the occasion of the circumcision of Prince Mehmed. Âli seeks the help of acquaintances at court to secure transfer out of the *timar*-registry of Aleppo.

1583/991 In the spring Âli resigns his post and travels to Istanbul. *Nusretname* is presented at court, and Âli is appointed to oversee production of the imperial edition.

1584/992 Early in the year Âli writes *opera minora* for Murad (*Câmi' ül-kemâlât, Tâli' üs-selâtin, Nükât ül-kal*). In September the newly appointed grand vezir, Özdemiroğlu Osman Paşa, has Âli appointed finance director of Erzurum, to which city he travels in October.

1585/993 In August, Özdemiroğlu reaches Erzurum, and Âli is transferred to the finance directorship of Baghdad. Soon after his arrival there at the end of the year, Âli learns of his dismissal and of the death of Özdemiroğlu.

1586/994 Âli leaves Baghdad in midsummer to return to Istanbul, where he hopes to have the treasurer, Üveys Paşa, secure for him a finance directorship of the Porte; but he finds no position waiting for him upon his arrival in November.

1587/995 Âli seeks help from Gazanfer Ağa, Hoca Sa'düddin, and Doğancı Mehmed Paşa; writes *Ferâ'id ül-vilâde, Mir'ât ül-avâlim, Menakıb-ı hünerve-*

ran, and *Kavâ'id ül-mecâlis*, and presents *Nushat üs-selâtin*; closes correspondence collection, *Menşe' ül-inşa*.

1588/996 In February, Âli is appointed to the finance directorship of Sivas, and he travels there in the spring. Over the following winter and spring he composes *Nevâdir ül-hikem* and *Mirkat ül-cihad*.

1589/997 In the spring Âli learns he has been dismissed from his post, and returns to Istanbul soon after the *Beğlerbeği* Incident. He remains unemployed and begins to immerse himself in Sufi piety.

1589-90/998 Âli completes treatise on mysticism, *Riyaz üs-sâlikin*, which he had abandoned nearly thirty years earlier.

1590-91/999 Reduced to having to sell his possessions in order to maintain his household without an income, Âli attempts unsuccessfully to ingratiate himself with Grand Vezir Koca Sinan Paşa.

1591/1000 In the first month of the new millennium Âli closes his second *divan*, *Lâyihat ül-hakika*.

1591-92/1000 In midwinter Âli begins his *magnum opus*, *Künh ül-ahbar*. He also composes the Persian *Majmaʿ al-baḥrayn* at the suggestion of his pupil Nef'i.

1592/1000-1001 In mid-July, Âli is appointed secretary of the Janissary Corps by the new grand vezir, Siyavuş Paşa. Four months later he is dismissed, but soon thereafter he is appointed registrar of the Imperial Council (*defter emini*).

1593/1001 One month after Sinan Paşa's third appointment as grand vezir, at the end of January, Âli is dismissed from the Registry on charges of dishonesty. In the spring Âli spends several months in retreat in Gelibolu, where he composes *Sadef-i sad güher* and *Gül-i sad berg*.

1593/1002 Âli returns to Istanbul, still unemployed. He compiles *Sübhat ül-ebdâl* and begins *Badîʿ al-ruqûm*, while continuing work on the *Künh*.

1594/1003 With the help of Hoca Sa'düddin and Gazanfer Ağa, Âli attempts to gain the favor of Koca Sinan Paşa. In December, Sultan Murad reappoints him secretary of the Janissary Corps.

1595/1003 In January, Sultan Murad dies and his son Mehmed III ascends the throne. Âli resigns as secretary of the Janissaries and receives provisional appointment as finance director of Egypt. However, this appointment is revoked and he is instead made *sancak* governor of Amasya and finance director of Sivas (Rum). He arrives in Amasya in August, and soon thereafter the finance directorship of Rum is abolished.

1596/1004-1005 Âli is transferred to the *sancak* government of Kayseri, dismissed, and then restored to his post. Koca Sinan Paşa dies during his fifth term as grand vezir, and Âli seeks appointment to the chancellorship from his successor, Damad İbrahim Paşa. Âli writes *Mahâsin ül-âdâb* and dedicates it to

Sultan Mehmed and Grand Vezir İbrahim Paşa. By fall Âli has been dismissed and returns to Istanbul, where he continues to work on the *Künh*.

1597-98/1005-1007 In Istanbul Âli puts himself under the protection of Gazanfer Ağa and addresses pleas to Sultan Mehmed to make him chancellor or to give him a governor-generalship. Disappointed, he asks to be allowed to retire to Mecca. In late 1598 he completes *Fusûl-i hall ve akd* and dedicates it to the sultan and Queen Mother Safiye.

1599/1007-1008 In the spring Âli is appointed governor-general of Damascus but loses the post when he delays his arrival there in order to perform the pilgrimage. Instead he is made trustee and *sancak beği* of Jidda. He spends much of the summer and fall in Cairo, where he composes *Hâlât ül-Kahire*, dedicated to Gazanfer Ağa, and puts an end to the *Künh*. Late in the year he travels to Jidda and begins *Mevâ'id ün-nefâ'is*, which he completes in Mecca while visiting the Holy Places.

1600/1008 Âli dies in Jidda.

GLOSSARY

Note: Definitions are given according to sixteenth-century usage.

Ağa "Lord," "Master"; title used for a ranking servant of the imperial household, especially:
1. One of the eunuchs of the harem such as the *kapı ağası*, chief white eunuch and Palace overseer, and the *kızlar ağası*, chief black eunuch in charge of the women of the harem.
2. Pages of the Privy Chamber
3. Commanders of the Janissary Corps and of the six Palace cavalry units. Collectively these officers, together with a number of other Outer Service commanders, were known as Ağas of the Stirrup (*üzengi ağaları*), since they rode with the sultan on campaign.

Akçe Asper; the silver coin denomination in which all salaries and stipends were calculated.

Âlim Singular of ulema (q.v.).

Askeri "Military"; designation for the nontaxpaying Ottoman military-administrative establishment, and by extension applied to all those associated with government, including judges and scholars.

Bâb üs-sa'âdet ağası See *kapı ağası*.

Bahname Sex manual.

Bakaya (pl. of *bakiye*) Tax arrears.

Başdefterdar *Defterdar* of Rumeli; see *defterdar*.

Beğ "Military commander"; a title applied in the sixteenth century to military administrators of district governor (*sancak beği*, q.v.) rank; to bureaucrats considered to have attained such rank; to the hereditary ruler of an independent or autonomous principality.

Beğlerbeği Governor-general; administrator and military commander of the forces of a province (*vilâyet*, q.v.).

Beğlerbeğilik State of being a governor-general; government of a province (*vilâyet*, q.v.), its income, or the province itself.

Beğlik State of being a *beğ*; a district (*sancak*, q.v.) government.

Bektaşi Sufi *tarikat* (q.v.) organized to propagate the teachings of Hacı Bektaş (fl. second half of 13th century), esoteric, Shi'i (*imami*), and syncretic in rite. The Janissary Corps (q.v.) were, almost invariably, Bektaşi adherents.

Berat Letter of patent, certificate of grant, for a *timar*-holder.

Beytülmal The state or communal treasury (from Arabic, *bayt al-mâl al-muslimîn*); lands and properties over which the state was accorded rights by law. See also *hazine*.

Birun Outer Palace; those services associated with the Outer Palace (Outside Service).

Bölük, bölük halkı One of the six standing mounted units of the Palace military establishment, as opposed to the provincial *timar*-holding cavalry.

Buyruldu Grand vezir's written approval of an order.

Cebelü Armed retainer supported and equipped by a *timar*-holding *sipahi* (q.v.).

Celâli A rebel in the Anatolian provinces in the sixteenth century.

Chancellor See *nişancı*.

Cönk Memorabilia album.

Council See *divan*.

Çelebi A title of respect applied in the sixteenth century to
1. Men born into the upper levels of the *askeri* class, such as members of the *müteferrika* (q.v.) corps.
2. Men distinguished by learning and rank, such as ranking bureaucrats and judges.

Chief jurisconsult See *seyhülislam*.

Çıkma ''Ascent'' or ''departure''; the graduation process whereby the *kul*s (q.v.) in training in the Palace services were either ''sent out'' to military posts or promoted within the Palace ranks.

Dahil medreseleri See *medrese*.

Danişmend An advanced *medrese* (q.v.) student; more technically, a *Sahn* (q.v.) student.

Defter Register; log book.

Defter emini Registrar; the official in charge of the Registry (*defterhane-i âmire*), where all transactions in imperial lands and revenues were recorded.

Defter kedhüdası Provincial officer in charge of overseeing the *zeâmet* (q.v.) registers (also called *timar kedhüdası*), superior of the *timar defterdarı*, subordinate to the *mal defterdarı* (see *defterdar*).

Defterdar Finance director; an official serving at either the imperial court, a princely one, or in a province. The title applied to three categories of functionaries:
1. *Defterdar*s of the Porte, those of Rumeli, Anatolia, the East, and the Second Branch. The finance director of Rumeli was the treasurer, the chief financial officer of the Empire (*başdefterdar*).

2. Finance directors and representatives of the central treasury in major provinces, the imperial finances of which they oversaw (*hazine defterdarı, mal defterdarı*).
3. Registrars of *timars* in each *vilâyet* (*timar defterdarı*), subordinate to both the *defter kedhüdası* and the *mal defterdarı*.

Defterdarlık Office of a *defterdar*.

Defterhane Imperial Registry for lands and taxes at the Palace.

Der-i sa'adet "Gate of Felicity"; the Sublime Porte; the imperial Palace, seat of Ottoman government.

Devatdar (*divitdar*) Ink-keeper.

Devşirme Ottoman levy on non-Muslim subjects, from whom they recruited boys who were enslaved, converted, and trained for military or administrative service. The term is also used to describe the slaves so recruited.

Dirlük "Living"; assignment of salary or prebend, as well as the office attached to the income.

Divan 1. Council, at the imperial or provincial level; the central policy-making and executive mechanism of government.
2. Collection of verse by a poet, arranged according to rhyme scheme and genre or form.

Divan-i hümayun Imperial Council, presided over by the grand vezir.

Divan kâtibi Chancery secretary, scribe of the Council (also called *kâtib-i divan*).

Ecnebi "Foreigner," officeholder who has not attained his position through one of the accepted channels of birth, training and service.

Efendi "Lord," a title of respect accorded nonmilitary men, particularly members of the scribal or learned professions.

Ehl-i ilm See Men of Learning.

Ehl-i kalem See Men of the Pen.

Ehl-i seyf See Men of the Sword.

Elite Corps See *müteferrika*.

Emanet Trusteeship, office of *emin* (q.v.).

Emin Trustee, particularly of an imperial revenue source, such as a *mukata'a* (q.v.).

Enderun The Inner Palace, or one of the services associated with it (Inner Service).

Eskilik Seniority in a career path.

Ferman Imperial order, edict.

Fethname Official victory announcement, including an account of the battle.

Field marshal See *serdar*.

Finance director See *defterdar* (*hazine, mal*).

Gaza Holy warfare to expand the domains of Islam.

Gazel A short lyric poem (''sonnet'').

Gazi ''Warrior for the faith''; esp. of Anatolian Türkmen; one engaged in conquering non-Muslim territories, or fighting non-Muslims in march zones.

Gedük Authorization or designation to fill a military or bureaucratic post (sometimes upon a vacancy); acknowledgment of seniority within a career line.

Governor-general See *beğlerbeği*.

Grand vezir See *sadrazam*.

Hâkim Hereditary governor of a *sancak*, with some autonomy; vassal prince.

Halife ''Successor,'' ''lieutenant,'' as the caliphs who followed the Prophet Muhammad. In a Sufi brotherhood, an advanced initiate and lieutenant of the head of the lodge (*şeyh, post-nişin*, q.v.), authorized to propagate the teachings of the *tarikat* (q.v.).

Halveti Sufi order particularly favored in Istanbul and the rest of the Ottoman Empire in the late fifteenth and sixteenth centuries.

Han Khan, from Turco-Mongol *qa'an*; title assumed by the universal ruler in nomad tradition and retained by all Cengizid rulers.

Harem The private portion of a household establishment, forbidden to outsiders; when used in capitalized form in reference to the Palace household, it is synonymous with *enderun* (q.v.).

Haric medreseleri See *medrese*.

Haric vezirleri See *vezir*.

Hasodabaşı Chief of the sultan's Privy Chamber.

Hass Land revenue grant valued at 100,000 *akçe* or more per annum, attached to high administrative office in provincial or central government as a salary for the incumbent. *Hass* grants were also made to high-ranking retirees and to members of the imperial family.

Hatib Preacher; member of the ulema assigned to a mosque and authorized to deliver the Friday communal sermon (*hutbe*) and to lead Friday prayer.

Hatt-i hümayun Imperial rescript.

Hazine ''Treasury'' of the state, divided into the inner (*enderun*) treasury, located in the Harem and considered a reserve against depletion of the outer (*birun, taşra*) treasury, the state treasury proper called the *hazine-i âmire*. *Hazine* also applied to the provincial treasuries of funds due the central government.

Hoca-ı sultani Sultan's tutor in the religious sciences.

Hurufi Member of an extremist, esoteric sect founded by Faḍl Allâh of Astarâbâd (d. 1394/796), a central point of whose teachings was the mystical significance of the letters of the alphabet (*huruf*).

İcazet Certificate of mastery of a text and permission to teach it, issued to *medrese* students by individual teachers.

İlmiye The religious learned establishment; the educational and judicial organization of the *ulema*, the Men of Learning; the learned professions, comprising *kadı*s (q.v.), *müderris*es (q.v.), and *müfti*s (q.v.).

İltizam "Tax-farming"; appointment by contract whereby the appointee promises to remit a specified amount of tax revenues for a specified period, sometimes in advance of assuming his post.

İmam 1. That member of the community (among Sunni Muslims) who leads communal prayer, or the member of the ulema, attached to a mosque, authorized to lead prayer and supervise mosque affairs. Also used as a title for a great religious teacher.
2. ʿAlî b. Abî Ṭâlib or one of his eleven descendants, who for *imami* (Twelver) Shi'is were the repositories of all exoteric and esoteric religious truth. Also revered by Sunnis in the fifteenth and sixteeth centuries.

İmam-ı sultani Personal *imam* (q.v.) of the sultan.

İmaret Hospice; charitable complex established by endowment (*vakıf*, q.v.) for the good of the community.

Imperial Council See *divan-ı hümayun*.

Inner Service See *enderun*

Inner *Medrese*s See *medrese*.

Intendant of *zeâmet* holders See *defter kedhüdası*.

İntisab "Connections"; patronage relationship carrying many of the rights and obligations of family relationship.

İrfan Esoteric mystical knowledge or understanding.

İrsaliye Tax remittance, due from the provincial government to the central treasury, usually submitted annually.

Janissary See *yeniçeri*.

Judge See *kadı*.

Kadı Judge, appointed from the ulema to adjudicate according to the Holy Law (*şeri'at*, q.v.), but also, under Ottoman rule, administering dynastic law (*kanun*, q.v.). Provincial *kadı*s also had administrative charge of a *kaza* (q.v.); their salaries ranged from 20 *akçe* per day in the smallest towns to 500 in the most important cities, to each of which a judge was assigned.

Kadıasker One of the two chief military judges (from Arabo-Persian *qâżi-yi ʿaskar*) of Rumeli and Anatolia. Until the end of the reign of Süleyman, when the *şeyhülislam* (q.v.) acquired supervisory control over the entire *ilmiye* (q.v.) hierarchy, these two officials had charge of all pedagogical and judicial appointments in their respective regions.

Kâhya kadın See *kedbanu-yi harem*.

Ka'immakam *Locum tenens*; one appointed to discharge the duties of a post during the temporary absence of the incumbent.

Kalem 1. "Pen"; financial or chancery bureau of the central or provincial bureaucracy.
2. In bureaucratic slang, a *timar* (q.v.) assignment.

Kalemiye The bureaucratic career; bureaucratic organization, consisting of chancery and financial branches.

Kanun Dynastic law, promulgated by the sultan under the discretionary authority (*örf*, q.v.) accorded the ruler by the *şeri'at* (q.v.). Justified as a support and supplement to the Holy Law, *kanun* was composed of both customary usage and decree, and governed matters ranging from court ceremonial and salaries to regional tax practices. *Kanun* also symbolized the dynastic commitment to justice.

Kanunname Dynastic legal code, formal codification of *kanun*. *Kanunnames* were both general, governing Empire-wide practice, and specific, laying out the tax structures of particular districts and provinces.

Kapı ağası Chief white eunuch and overseer of the Palace, *major domo*; see also *ağa*.

Kapıcı "Gate-keeper"; the *kapıcı* corps acted as Palace bailiffs and guards.

Kasaba Provincial market town, seat of a *kadı* (q.v.).

Kâtib Secretary, scribe. See also *divan kâtibi*.

Kaza Subdistrict of a *sancak* (q.v.), assigned to a *kadı* (q.v.).

Kedbanu-yi harem Mistress Housekeeper of the privy apartments of the Palace, in charge of training the female Harem staff under the *valide sultan* (q.v.).

Kedhüda Steward, intendant, agent, especially of a *paşa* (q.v.).

Kitâbet Scribal service.

Kızılbaş "Red head"; the Türkmen supporters of the Shi'i Safavi cause, organized in *oymak*s (q.v.), who continued to dominate the Safavi military administration throughout the sixteenth century. The insignia of their adherence to the Safavi *tarikat* (q.v.) was the red "crown" on which their twelve-gored turbans were wrapped.

Kul 1. "Slave," especially of the sultan, recruited through the *devşirme* (q.v.).
2. Any servant of the dynasty, slave or free.

Lala Tutor of a prince assigned to provincial government and gubernatorial regent during the minority of the prince. *Lala*s were usually selected from the district (*sancak*) governors' ranks.

Mahlas Nom de plume of a poet.

Maliye Financial branch, and attendant service, of the central and provincial bureaucracies.

Matbah Imperial Kitchen, presided over by the *matbah emini*, the Keeper of the Kitchen.

Mecmu'a Literary scrapbook, collection of assorted works in a single volume.

Medrese Institution of higher learning for the religious sciences, built and endowed as a part of a mosque complex. *Medrese*s were categorized according to curricular level and the daily salary in *akçe* (q.v.) of their professors, the pinnacle of the system being the imperial institutions found mostly in Istanbul, the professors of which earned 50-100 *akçe*. At the 50-*akçe* level the *medrese*s were divided into "outer" (*haric*) and "inner" (*dahil*) categories, the latter being more prestigious.

Mekteb Primary school, in which the elements of Arabic were taught.

Melâmi Dervish, member of a Sufi *tarikat* (q.v.) in which the prescriptions of formal religion, or of outward piety, were ignored or purposely neglected.

Men of Learning See *ilmiye*.

Men of the Pen See *kalemiye*.

Men of the Sword See *seyfiye*.

Mensub Protégé or member of a prominent man's household.

Mevlâ Also *menlâ*; "molla," "master," a title of respect (Arabic *mawlâ*) accorded men of religion, usually of the ulema. Also, *kadı* (q.v.) of a major provincial capital.

Mevlevi Member of a Sufi *tarikat* (q.v.), centered at Konya, organized by the followers of Mawlânâ (Mevlana) Jalâl al-dîn Rûmî (d. 1273), author of the Persian *Masnavî*; music and rhythmic dance are central to the rites of the Mevlevi, also known as the "Whirling Dervishes."

Mevleviyet Quality of being a *mevla* (q.v.); judgeship of a major provincial capital.

Military See *askeri*.

Military judge See *kadıasker*.

Mirahur Equerry.

Mirahur-ı kebir Chief equerry of the Palace.

Miri "Imperial," especially state lands and revenues.

Mir-i alem "Standard bearer"; the Palace official in charge of the care of the horse-tail standard and pennants carried before the sultan.

Mistress Housekeeper See *kedbanu-yi harem*.

Müderris Teacher, professor in a *medrese* (q.v.).

Mü'eyyed min ind Allah "Succored by God"; sovereign never defeated in battle.

Müfti Jurisconsult, specialist in Islamic law.

Muhafaza Garrison or protection assignment made in absence of a governor or governor-general.

Muhafaza beği Garrison commander of the Citadel in Cairo equivalent to a *sancak beği* (q.v.).

Muhafız Garrison commander, assigned to protect a *sancak* (q.v.) or *vilâyet* (q.v.) in the absence of the incumbent.

Mukata'a A source of state revenue (customs, mines, etc.) farmed out to individuals for a specified number of years.

Mülâzemet Status of *mülâzim* (q.v.)

Mülâzim *Medrese* (q.v.) graduate admitted to candidacy for an *ilmiye* (q.v.) position when a suitable beginning teaching or judicial post should become available. Such designations were restricted in number, and would only be made by the sultan or one of the ranking members of the *ilmiye* (q.v.).

Münşe'at Collections of correspondence, used to provide examples of styles and forms of address.

Müşahere-horan Recipients of direct monthly stipends from the treasury, usually members of the Palace retinue and special guests, such as foreign princes.

Musahib Royal companion; intimate and confidant of the sultan or prince. At the Palace in Istanbul this was a formal office.

Müsta'idd 1. Advanced *medrese* (q.v.) student at one of the imperial mosque schools.
2. One prepared and qualified for designation as *mülâzim* (q.v.).

Müteferrika "Elite"; a designation bestowed upon individuals of distinguished lineage and upon ulema associated with the court. Such designation could be honorific or could carry a salary. There was also an elite cavalry corps of the Porte, staffed by the children of distinguished Ottomans, known by this name.

Nakşbendi A Sufi *tarikat* (q.v.) of *melâmi* (q.v.) character established in Central Asia by the followers of Muḥammad Naqshband (d. 1389/791); enjoyed great popularity in the Ottoman domains in the sixteenth century.

Nazire Parallel verse, "imitation" of a known poem.

Nevruz Vernal new year, March 10-11 (Julian), March 21-22 (Gregorian).

Nezaret Supervision of financial affairs of a province, occasionally vested in governors-general rather than the independent finance director (*mal defterdarı*, q.v.) of a province.

Nişancı Chancellor. Chief of the imperial chancery, also responsible for inscribing the sultan's *tuğra* (q.v.) on documents. The chancellor was also the chief codifier and overseer of *kanun* (q.v.) legislation.

Nüzül emini Army supply master.

Örf (*ʿurf*) 1) Custom, customary law.
2) The discretionary prerogatives of the sovereign to legislate in matters not covered by the *şeri'at* (q.v.) to which *kanun* (q.v.) assimilated.

Örfi (*ʿurfi*) Pertaining to *örf* (q.v.).

Outer medreses See *medrese*.

Oymak Tribe (loosely), esp. of the nomadizing Türkmen who supported the Safavi cause.

Padişah Emperor, sovereign ruler (Persian); in Ottoman usage, a generic term for ruler of a regional empire.

Palace *Saray*, composed of *enderun* (q.v.) and *birun* (q.v.). The residence of the sultan in Istanbul and seat of government; also the center of education and training for the most promising *devşirme* (q.v.) recruits.

Palace Cavalry See *bölük halkı*.

Paşa Title accorded military administrators of the rank of governor-general or vezir, or to bureaucrats attaining *beğlerbeğilik* (q.v.).

Paşazade Son of a *paşa* (q.v.).

Paye Honorific rank.

Pir 1. Advanced mystic and spiritual guide to an individual.
2. Head of a *tarikat* (q.v.).

Pişkeş "Tribute"; a gift, usually of money, given to the grand vezir by a new appointee to office. In the late sixteenth century this courteous custom began to be seen as a form of bribery.

Pence Official signature of a vezir or campaign commander.

Post-nişin Head of a *tekke* (q.v.), seated on the sheepskin spread for him during dervish rites.

Queen Mother See *valide sultan*.

Re'âyâ "Flock"; the taxpaying subjects, Muslim and non-Muslim, including peasants, artisans, and merchants.

Registrar See *defter emini*.

Registry See *defterhane*.

Re'isülküttab Secretary-in-chief of the Imperial Council, director of the chancery under the *nişancı* (q.v.).

Rum The Ottoman domains in Rumelia and Anatolia, particularly those areas that formed the core of the Empire before the conquests of Selim I.

Rüşvet Bribe money, corruption, the practice of graft.

Rütbe Rank joined to appropriate function, as opposed to purely honorific rank (see *paye*).

Sadaret-i uzma See *sadrazamlık*.

Sadrazam Grand vezir; chief minister, the first in rank of the vezirs of the Dome (q.v.). The *sadrazam* presided over the Imperial Council and was the sultan's absolute deputy in all military, administrative, and judicial matters.

Sadrazamlık Rank of office of *sadrazam* (q.v.).

Sahib-keramât "Master of blessings"; miracle-working mystic or holy man.

Sahib-kıran "Master of an auspicious conjunction"; title accorded universal conquerors.

Sahib-i zuhur "Manifest one"; dynastic founder or eponym, founder of a state.

Sahn Short for *Sahn-ı seman* (q.v.).

Sahn-ı seman The eight specialized schools at the *medrese*-mosque complex of the Conqueror Mehmed II in Istanbul, which until the completion of the *Süleymaniye* in the mid-sixteenth century represented the pinnacle of the Ottoman university system.

Salyane 1. Salary, "yearly remittance."
2. Designation for a province in which the *timar* system was not in effect, and where officials of the central government were paid by yearly salary.

Sancak "Standard"; the district or provincial unit upon which Ottoman administration was based. Several *sancaks*, each governed by a *sancak beği*, together made up a *vilâyet* (q.v.) or *beğlerbeğilik* (q.v.).

Sancak beği Governor, military administrator of a *sancak* (q.v.).

Second Branch See *şıkk-ı sani*.

Secretary-in-chief See *re'isülküttab*.

Serdar Field marshal; campaign commander.

Seyfiye "Men of the Sword"; the military class or establishment, or the military-administrative career.

Shi'i "Partisan" of the family of the Prophet, i.e., the *imams* (q.v.) descended from the first *imam* ʿAlî b. Abî Ṭâlib and his wife Fâṭima, the daughter of Muḥammad, in whose line Shi'is consider ultimate religious and legitimate political authority for the Muslim community to inhere. Twelver or Imami Shi'ism, which the Safavis made their state religion, holds that the last (twelfth) *imam* occultated in the ninth century; the return of the Hidden Imam will inaugurate the millennium.

Silahdar 1. Sultan's personal weapon bearer, the highest-ranking page of the Harem after the *hasodabaşı* (q.v.).
2. Name of one of the Palace cavalry units (see *bölük halkı*).

Simürg A fabulous, griffinlike bird said to inhabit the Alburz mountains in Iran.

Sipahi 1. Member of the provincial cavalry, supported by a *timar* (q.v.) grant.
2. Name of one of the Palace cavalry units, the Sipahis of the Porte (see *bölük halkı*).

Standard Bearer See *mir-i alem*.

Subaşı A provincial administrator, usually a *za'im* (q.v.), under the *sancak beği* (q.v.). The *subaşı* commanded the *sipahi*s (q.v.) of his district (often a *kaza*, q.v.) and preserved order there in peacetime.

Sufi Generic designation for Muslim mystics; probably derived from the coarse woolen (Arabic, *ṣûf*) cloaks worn by the early dervishes.

Sultan The Islamic title, signifying "temporal power," most commonly accorded the Ottoman ruler; originally used in the eleventh century as the title of the figure to whom the caliph delegated his military and administrative authority.

Sunni One of the majority of the Muslim community, those who accept the legitimacy of all of the first four caliphs, the validity of communal consensus as a principle of law, and the formulations of the *şeri'at* enshrined in the four legal rites (Ḥanafî, Mâlikî, Shâfiʿî, and Ḥanbalî). The Ottoman state formally adhered to the Ḥanafî rite.

Şehnâmeci A court appointment established by Sultan Süleyman in the mid-sixteenth century which became the almost exclusive preserve of Iranian Türkmen. The *şehnameci* was to compose historical panegyric for the Ottoman house in Persian verse and in the metrical and narrative form of Firdawsî's *Shâhnâme*. In the late sixteenth century the *şehnamecis* began to compose Turkish verse and prose.

Şehnâmegû See *şehnâmeci*.

Şehzade "Shah-born," i.e., royal prince.

Şeri'at The Holy Law of Islam, governing public as well as private morality, by which the entire Muslim community was obliged to live. Its bases, for Sunnis, are Qur'ânic revelation, Prophetic Tradition, communal consensus, and analogical reasoning.

Şerif 1. Descendant of the Prophet.
2. Of Mecca; *şerif*s of the line of Abû Numayy who ruled the Hijaz as sovereign dynasts under Ottoman suzerainty.

Şeyh 1. *Pir* (q.v.), accomplished mystic and a spiritual master or guide.
2. Sheikh, elder, head of a Sufi *tarikat* (q.v.) or lodge (see *tekke*).

Şeyhülislam Chief jurisconsult or *müfti* (q.v.) of the Ottoman Empire, responsible to the sultan. From the middle of the sixteenth century the *şeyhülislam* also controlled the entire *ilmiye* (q.v.) hierarchy.

Şıkk-ı sani "Second branch," third finance directorate of the Porte, headed by a *defterdar* (q.v.) responsible for imperial properties in and around Istanbul.

Şıkk-ı sani defterdarı See *şıkk-ı sani*.

Talib-i ilm "Seeker of knowledge," student at early or intermediate stages of *medrese* (q.v.) education. Also occurs as pl., *talebe*.

Tarih 1. Annalistic history or chronicle.
2. Chronogram.
3. Date.

Tarikat "Path"; a Sufi (q.v.) brotherhood or order, organized either according to a particular mystical posture or style of ceremonial or practice (for example, Halveti) or according to the teachings and practice of a particular mystical guide, revered by later generations as the founder of the "Path" (for example, Mevlevi).

Tarik-i ilm "Path of Learning"; see *ilmiye*.

Tarik-i kitabet "Path of scribal service"; see *kalemiye*.

Teftiş-i âmm Comprehensive official investigation of charges brought against an Ottoman official.

Tekke Lodge of a particular *tarikat* (q.v.), including residential, educational, and ceremonial areas, supported by *vakıf* (q.v.).

Terakki Merit increment to salary or *timar* (q.v.).

Tezkere 1. Memorandum, especially from a *beğlerbeği* (q.v.), recommending a *timar* (q.v.) grant.
2. A biographical compendium and anthology, usually of poets (*tezkere-i şu'ara*).

Tezkereci 1. Secretary of the Imperial Council.
2. Council secretary and administrative assistant to a *beğlerbeği* (q.v.).

Timar A grant of agricultural revenue from a specified portion of state lands, worth less than 20,000 *akçe*, made to a *sipahi* (q.v.) in return for military service and police duty in the area assigned. The *timar* system of usufruct grants was the economic support of the provincial cavalry and the primary mechanism whereby most Ottoman administrators were paid.

Timar defterdarı Registrar of *timars* for a *vilâyet* (q.v.), the third-ranked representative of the central treasury in the province after the *defter kedhüdası (timar kedhüdası)* (q.v.) and *hazine (mal) defterdarı* (q.v.).

Timar kedhüdası See *defter kedhüdası*.

Timar-registrar See *defterdar*.

Töre (törü) In Turco-Mongol tradition, tribal law, largely composed of custom but modified and codified by the edicts of great rulers.

Treasurer See *defterdar*.

Treasury See *beytülmal, hazine*.

Tuğra Imperial signature-seal, an elaborate design inscribed by the *nişancı* (q.v.).

Ulema Men of learning, scholars, especially of the religious sciences. The most accomplished ulema held religious positions as *kadı*s (q.v.)., *müfti*s (q.v.), and *müderris*es (q.v.). Scholarly status, however, was fundamentally conferred by education and consensus among the learned, rather than by formal appointment.

Vakıf Mortmain endowment by an individual of a revenue usually derived from immovable property. The endowment was to establish and maintain in perpetuity a pious public foundation; mosques, *medrese*s, hospitals, fountains, and other public and charitable institutions were provided for by *vakıf*. *Vakıf* properties were theoretically inviolable and indivisible, and so family foundations enabled some, especially the sultan's *kul*s (q.v.), to circumvent Islamic inheritance laws.

Valide sultan Queen Mother, mother of the reigning sultan and ruler of the women's portion of the Harem.

Vezir Minister of state, advisor to the sultan chosen from the most senior and able of the sultan's *kul*s (q.v.), performing military as well as administrative duties. Vezirs were of two types:
1. Vezirs of the Dome (*kubbe vezirleri*). These were members of the Imperial Council, ranked by seniority; the first vezir was the grand vezir or *sadrazam* (q.v.). During the reign of Selim II the number of these rose from four to seven.
2. "Outer" vezirs (*haric vezirleri*), *beğlerbeği*s (q.v.) or *serdar*s (q.v.) of particular prominence who were accorded veziral status without being given a seat on the Imperial Council.

Vezirs of the Dome See *vezir*.

Vilâyet Large province made up of a number of *sancaks* (q.v.); also called *eyâlet* and *beğlerbeğilik* (q.v.). The *vilâyet* was governed by a *beğlerbeği* (q.v.).

Voyvoda 1. Administrator appointed to a tributary territory.
2. Administrator of a *mukata'a* (q.v.) (17th century).

Yasa Mongol law code promulgated by, or in the name of, Cengiz Han. The *yasa* was to guide the actions of the conquering nomad elite, and constituted a sign of the universal mandate of the dynasty; akin to *töre* (q.v.), and the prototype of Ottoman *kanun* (q.v.).

Yeniçeri Janissary, literally ''new soldier.'' The Janissary Corps, recruited largely through the *devşirme* (q.v.), was the standing infantry force of the Porte.

Yeniçeri ağası Head of the Janissary Corps; see *ağa*.

Zâviye Lodge or convent of a *tarikat* (q.v.); could also function as a hospice.

Za'im Holder of a *zeâmet* (q.v.), sometimes carrying additional duties as *subaşı* (q.v.).

Zeâmet (ze'âmet) A *timar* (q.v.) grant valued between 20,000 and 99,999 *akçe* (q.v.) held by a *za'im*.

Zill Allah ''Shadow of God,'' a title applied particularly in post-Mongol times to Muslim rulers. The *zill Allah* acquired this status solely through diligent protection and enforcement of the *şeri'at* (q.v.).

BIBLIOGRAPHY

DICTIONARIES, BIBLIOGRAPHIES, ENCYCLOPEDIAS, CATALOGUES

Atsız, Nihal. *Âli bibliyografyası*. Istanbul, 1968.

Babinger, Franz. *Die Geschichtsschreiber der Osmanen und ihre Werke*. Leipzig, 1927.

Bregel', Yuri E., rev. and trans. *Persidskaya Literatura (Persian Literature)*, by C. A. Storey. 3 vols. Moscow, 1972.

Brockelmann, Carl. *Geschichte der arabischen Literatur*. 2nd ed., 2 vols. Leiden, 1943-49; suppl., 3 vols. Leiden, 1937-42.

Danişmend, İsmail Hami. *İzahlı Osmanlı Tarihi Kronolojisi*. 5 vols. Istanbul, 1971.

Encyclopaedia Iranica. Ed. Ehsan Yarshater. London, Boston, and Henley, 1982–.

Encyclopaedia of Islam. 1st ed. Eds. M. T. Houtsma, T. W. Arnold, R. Basset, et al. 4 vols. and suppl. Leiden and London, 1912-42.

Encyclopaedia of Islam. 2nd ed. Eds. H.A.R. Gibb, J. H. Kramers, E. Levi-Provençal, et al. 4 vols. Leiden and London, 1954-.

Götz, Manfred. *Verzeichnis der orientalischen Handschriften in Deutschland*. Vol. 13, part 4, *Türkische Handschriften*. Wiesbaden, 1979.

İslâm Ansiklopedisi. 12 vols. Istanbul, 1940-78.

Karatay, Fehmi Edhem. *Topkapı Sarayı Müzesi Kütüphanesi, Türkçe Yazmalar Kataloğu*. 2 vols. Istanbul, 1961.

Levend, Agâh Sırrı. *Türk Edebiyatı Tarihi*. Vol. 1. Ankara, 1973.

Pakalın, M. Zeki. *Tarih Deyimleri ve Terimleri*. 3 vols. Istanbul, 1946-54.

Redhouse, Sir James. *Turkish-English Lexicon*. Istanbul, 1890.

Rieu, Charles. *Catalogue of the Turkish Manuscripts in the British Museum*. London, 1888.

Sertoğlu, Midhat. *Muhteva Bakımından Başvekâlet Arşivi*. Ankara, 1955.

Sohrweide, Hanna. *Verzeichnis der orientalischen Handschriften in Deutschland*. Vol. 13, part 5, *Türkische Handschriften*. Wiesbaden, 1981.

Storey, C. A. *Persian Literature: A Bio-bibliographical Survey*. 2 vols. London, 1970 (repr.).

PRIMARY SOURCES

Works by Âli

Badîʿ al-ruqûm. SK. MS Kadızade Mehmed 429, 82b-123a.

Câmi' ül-buhur der mecâlis-i sûr. TKS. MS Bağdat Köşkü 203.

Câmi' ül-kemâlât. SK. MS Reşid Efendi 1146, 50b-78b.
Divan [completed A.H. 975].
(1) MS Ali Emiri Efendi Türkçe Manzum 271.
(2) MS DKM Majâmî' Turkîya 25.
Divan [completed A.H. 1008]. MS İÜ Türkçe 768.
Ferâ'id ül-vilâde. MS İÜ Türkçe Mecmua 3543, 28b-32a.
Fursatname. MS Berlin, Preussische Staatsbibliothek, MS or. oct. 2927.
Fusul-i hall ve akd fi usul-i harc ve nakd.
(1) MS Ali Emiri Efendi Tarih 245.
(2) MS Nuruosmaniye 3300.
(3) MS Gökbilgin, dated 7 Zulka'de 1147, Erzurum [photocopy].
Gül-i sad berg. MS Ali Emiri Efendi Türkçe Manzum 978, pp. 286-90.
Hâlât ül-Kahire min el-âdât iz-zâhire. Ed. and trans. Andreas Tietze. *Muṣṭafâ ʿÂlî's Description of Cairo of 1599*. Vienna, 1975.
Heft Meclis. Istanbul, 1898-99/1316.
Hilyet ür-rical.
(1) SK. MS Reşid Efendi 1146, 1b-46b.
(2) TKS. MS Revan Köşkü 465.
Hulasat ül-ahvâl.
(1) Tietze, Andreas, ed. and trans. "The Poet as Critique of Society: A 16th-Century Ottoman Poem." *Turcica* 9/1 (1977): 120-60.
(2) "Postscript." *Turcica* 11 (1979): 205-209.
İstidâname. John R. Walsh, "Müverrih Âli'nin bir İstidânamesi." TM 13 (1958): 131-40.
Kavâ'id ül-mecâlis.
(1) SK. MS Reşid Efendi 1146, 119b-142a.
(2) Ms İÜ Türkçe 3951.
Künh ül-ahbar.
(1) *Künh ül-ahbar*. 5 vols. Istanbul, 1861-69/1277-85. This printed edition comprises the first three *rükn*s of the *Künh* and part of the fourth, ending in 1453. Vol. IV is divided into three parts, each separately paginated.
(2) *Rükn* 3.
(a) TKS. MS Hazine 1358.
(b) TKS. MS Revan Köşkü 1123.
(3) *Rükn* 4, Ottoman History.
(a) SK. MS Nuruosmaniye 3409 [1520-97].
(b) SK. MS Halet Efendi 598 [1520-97].
(c) SK. MS Fatih 4225.
(d) SK. MS Esad Efendi 2162.
(e) MS Nuruosmaniye 3406.
(f) MS University of Leiden, Cod. 288 Warner.
Layihat ül-hakika. MS DKM Adab Turkî 21, 1b-156a.
Mahâsin ül-âdâb.

(1) MS Nuruosmaniye 3668.
(2) MS Nuruosmaniye 4224.
Menakıb-ı hünerveran. Ed. İbnülemin Mahmud Kemâl (İnal). Istanbul, 1926.
Menşe' ül-inşa. MS Velieddin 1916, 183b.-282a.
Mevâ'id ün-nefâ'is fi kavâ'id il-mecâlis.
(1) M. Cavid Baysun, ed. *Mevâ'idü'n-nefâ'is fî ḳavâʿidi'l-mecâlis*. Istanbul, 1956.
(2) Gökyay, Orhan Şaik, trans. *Görgü ve Toplum Kuralları Üzerinde Ziyafet Sofraları*. 2 vols. Istanbul, 1978.
(3) Yener, Cemil, trans. *Mevâ'idü'n-nefâ'is fî kavâ'idi'l-mecâlis*. Istanbul, 1975.
Mihr u mah. SK. MS İsmihan 342.
Mir'ât ül-avâlim. SK. MS Reşid Efendi 1146, 80b-101b.
Mirkat ül-cihad.
(1) TKS. MS Revan Köşkü 364.
(2) MS Millet-Genel Kütüphanesi, Raşid Efendi 678.
Nadir ül-maharib.
(1) MS DKM Majâmîʿ Turkîya 2, 1b-66b.
(2) TKS. MS Revan Köşkü 1290, 1b-25a.
Nevâdir ül-hikem. MS İÜ Türkçe 1846, 2b-28b.
Nükât ül-kal fi tazmin il-makal. SK. MS Reşid Efendi 1146, 113b-116b.
Nushat üs-selâtin.
(1) Tietze, Andreas, ed. and trans. *Muṣṭafâ ʿÂlî's Counsel for Sultans of 1581*. 2 vols. Vienna, 1978-82.
(2) SK. MS Husrev Paşa 311.
(3) TKS. MS Revan Köşkü 406.
Nusretname.
(1) TKS. MS Hazine 1365.
(2) MS British Museum Add. 22,011.
Rahat ün-nüfus. SK. MS Şehid Ali Paşa 2014.
Riyaz üs-sâlikin. MS Velieddin 1916, 5b-106b.
Sadef-i sad güher. MS Ali Emiri Efendi Türkçe Manzum 978, pp. 233-85.
Sübhat ül-ebdal. MS Ali Emiri Efendi Türkçe Manzum 978, pp. 292-303.
Tâli' üs-selâtin. SK MS Reşid Efendi 1146, 102b-108b.
Tuhfet ül-uşşak. SK. MS Abdullah Çelebi 277.
Vakıfname.
(1) İÜ Türkçe Mecmua 3543, 90b-105a.
(2) MENŞE, 243a-244a, 244a-244b.
Vâridat ül-enika.
(1) SK. MS Hamidiye 1107.
(2) MS DKM Adab Turkî 21, 157a-330b.
(3) MS İÜ Türkçe 695.
Zübdet üt-tevarih.

(1) SK. MS Reşid Efendi 663.
(2) TKS. MS Hazine 1330.

Biographical, Bibliographical, and Epigraphic Sources

Ahdi, Ahmed Çelebi. *Gülşen üş-şu'ara*. SK. MS Halet Efendi Eki 107.

Ali Mınık. *Al-ʿIqd al-manẓûm fî dhikr afâḍil al-Rûm*. Beirut, 1975.

Âşık Çelebi. *Meşâʿir üş-Şuʿarâ*. Ed. G. M. Meredith-Owens. Gibb Memorial Series, n.s. 24. London, 1971.

Ayvansarayi, Hafiz Hüseyin. *Hadikat ül-cevâmi'*. 2 vols. Istanbul, 1865/1281.

Beyani, Şeyh Mustafa. *Tezkere*. MS İÜ Halis Efendi 2568.

Beygu, Abdurrahim Şerif. *Erzurum. Tarihi. Anıtları. Kitabeleri*. Istanbul, 1936.

Bursalı Mehmed Tahir. *Osmanlı mü'ellifleri*. 3 vols. Istanbul, 1914-24/1333-42.

Kâtib Çelebi. *Keşf el-ẓunûn*. Eds. Şerafettin Yaltkaya and Rifat Bilge. 2 vols. Istanbul, 1941-43.

Kınalızade, Hasan Çelebi. *Tezkeret üş-şu'ara*. 2 vols. Ed. İbrahim Kutluk. Ankara, 1978-81.

Konyalı, İbrahim Hakkı. *Abideleri ve Kitabeleri ile Erzurum Tarihi*. Istanbul, 1960.

Laoust, Henri, ed. and trans. *Les Gouverneurs de Damas sous les mamlouks et les premiers ottomans (658-1156/1260-1744). Traduction des annales d'Ibn Ṭulûn et d'Ibn Ğumʿa*. Damascus, 1952.

Latifi. *Tezkeret üş-şu'ara*. Istanbul, 1314.

Mustakimzade, Süleyman Sa'düddin. *Devhat ül-meşâyih*. Istanbul, n.d.; reprint ed., Istanbul, 1980.

———. *Tuhfe-i hattatin*. Ed. İbnülemin Mahmud Kemâl (İnal). Istanbul, 1928.

Nev'izade Ata'i. *Hada'ik ül-haka'ik fi tekmilet iş-şaka'ik*. Istanbul, 1851-52/1268.

Riyazi, Mehmed. *Riyaz üş-şu'ara*. MS Millet-Genel Kütüphanesi 765.

Sehi. *Heşt Bihişt*. Ed. Günay Kut. Cambridge, Mass., 1978.

Şemsüddin Sami. *Kamus ül-a'lam*. 6 vols. Istanbul, 1889-98.

Süreyya, Mehmed. *Sicill-i osmani*. 4 vols. Istanbul, 1890-97/1308-15.

Taşköprüzade Ahmed. *Al-Shaqâ'iq al-nuʿmânîya*. Beirut, 1978.

Yazdî, Quṭb al-dîn. "Risâle-i dar târîkh-i khaṭṭ va naqqâshî." Ed. Khadîv-Jam. *Sukhan* 17, nos. 6-7 (1967/1346): 666-76.

Zâkir Şükri Efendi. *Die Istanbuler Derwisch-Konvente und ihre Scheiche* (*Mecmu'a-ı tekaya*). Eds. Mehmet Serhan Tayşi and Klaus Kreiser. Freiburg, 1980.

Narrative and Literary Sources, Advice Literature

Akhisari, Hasan el-Kâfi.
(1) *Usûl ül-hikem fi nizâm il-âlem*. SK. MS Düğümlü Baba 438, ff. 1-67.
(2) Mehmet İpşirli, "Hasan Kâfî el-Akhisarî ve Devlet Düzenine ait Eseri *Usûlü'l-hikem fî Nizâmi'l-Âlem*," *Tarih Enstitüsü Dergisi* 10-11 (1979-80): 239-78.

Atsız, Nihal, ed. and trans. *Osmanlı Tarihleri, I*. Istanbul, 1949.

Beveridge, Annette Susannah, ed. and trans. *The Babur-nama in English*. London, 1922 (repr., 1969).

Davânî, Jalâl al-dîn. *Akhlâq-i Jalâlî*. Lahore, 1879/1296.
Evliya Çelebi. *Seyahatname*. 10 vols. Istanbul, 1896-1938.
Forrer, Ludwig, ed. and trans. *Die osmanische Chronik des Rustem Pascha*. Leipzig, 1923.
Giese, Friedrich. *Die altosmanischen anonymen Chroniken in Text und Übersetzung*. 2 vols. Breslau, 1922; Leipzig, 1925.
Kâtib Çelebi. *Mizan ül-hakk*.
(1) *Mizan ül-hakk*. Istanbul, 1863-64/1280.
(2) Geoffrey Lewis, trans. *The Balance of Truth*. London, 1957.
———. *Destûr ül-amel li ıslah il-halel*. Istanbul, 1863/1280.
Kınalızade Ali Çelebi. *Ahlak-ı Ala'i*. Bulaq, 1833/1248.
Kitab-ı Müstetab. Ed. Yaşar Yücel. Ankara, 1974.
Kitâbu Mesâlihi'l-Müslimîn ve Menâfi'i'l-Mü'minîn. 2 vols. Ed. Yaşar Yücel. Ankara, 1980-81.
Koçi Beğ. *Risale*. Ed. Ali Kemâli Aksüt. Istanbul, 1939.
Korkud b. Bayezid, Şehzade. *Daʿwat al-nafs al-ṭâliḥa ilâ al-aʿmâl al-ṣâliḥa*. MS Gökbilgin (microfilm).
Lutfi Paşa. *Tevarih-i Âl-i Osman*. Ed. Âli. Istanbul, 1925.
Na'ima. *Tarih*. 6 vols. Istanbul, 1864-66/1281-83.
Peçevi (Peçuyi) İbrahim Paşa. *Tarih*. 2 vols. Istanbul, 1864-66/1281-83.
Sa'düddin. *Tâc üt-tevârîh*. 2 vols. Istanbul, 1863/1280.
Selâniki, Mustafa. *Tarih*.
(1) *Tarih*. Istanbul, 1281; repr. ed. Freiburg, 1970 [to A.H. 1000].
(2) MS Gökbilgin (photocopy).
Târîh Ṣâḥib Giray Hân (Histoire de Sahib Giray, Khan de Crimée de 1532 à 1551). Ed. and trans. D. Özalp Gökbilgin. Ankara, 1973.
Tevârîh-i Âl-i Osmân. MS Gökbilgin. Photocopy.
Tschudi, Rudolf, ed. and trans. *Das Âṣafnâme des Luṭfî Pascha*. Berlin, 1910.
Tursun Beğ. *Tarih-i Ebülfeth*.
(1) *Târîh-i Ebü'l-Feth*. Ed. Mertol Tulum. Istanbul, 1977.
(2) İnalcık, Halil, and Rhoads Murphey, eds. and trans. *The History of Mehmed the Conqueror*. Minneapolis and Chicago, 1978.
Ṭûsî, Naṣîr al-dîn. *The Nasirean Ethics*. Trans. G. M. Wickens. London, 1964.
Woodhead, Christine. *Taʿlîkî-zâde's Şehnâme-i hümâyûn: A History of the Ottoman Campaign into Hungary, 1593-94*. Freiburg, 1983.
Yahya Bey. *Divan*. Ed. Mehmed Çavuşoğlu. Istanbul, 1977.
Za'im Mehmed. *Câmi' üt-tevarih*. MS Fatih 3406.

Miscellanea and Collections

Mecmua. SK. MS Halet Efendi Eki 245.
Mecmua. MS Türk Tarih Kurumu Kütüphanesi Mecmua 231.
Mecmua. MS Berlin, Preussische Staatsbibliothek MS or. fol. 3332.
Mecmua. MS İÜ Türkçe Mecmua 3543.
Mecmua. SK. MS Esad Efendi 3436.

Kanun Codes

Ayn-ı Ali Efendi. *Kavanin-i Âl-i Osman*. Istanbul, 1863/1280.

Mehmed Ârif, ed. *Kanunname-i Âl-i Osman*. TOEM, suppl. 2. Istanbul, 1911/1329 [*Kanunname* of Süleyman].

———. *Kanunname-i Âl-i Osman*. TOEM, suppl. 3. Istanbul, 1912/1330 [*Kanunname* of Fatih Mehmed].

Archival Sources

(1) BBA, Ru'us Defterleri.
  (a) KPT 218
  (b) KPT 236
  (c) KPT 237
  (d) KPT 238
  (e) KPT 246
  (f) KPT 285
(2) BBA, Maliyeden Müdevver Defterleri.
  (a) Maliyeden Müdevver 426
  (b) Maliyeden Müdevver 559
  (c) Maliyeden Müdevver 7118
  (d) Maliyeden Müdevver 7164
  (e) Maliyeden Müdevver 17881
(3) BBA, Mühimme Defterleri.
  (a) MD 2
  (b) MD 4
  (c) MD 20
  (d) MD 22
  (e) MD 23
  (f) MD 24
  (g) MD 32
  (h) MD 50
  (i) MD 51
  (j) MD 58
  (k) MD 59
  (l) MD 60
  (m) MD 73
  (n) MD 74
(4) TKS Arşivi
  (a) D9614
  (b) E12321

SECONDARY SOURCES

Akdağ, Mustafa. *Türk Halkının Dirlik ve Düzenlik Kavgası (Celâli İsyanları)*. Ankara, 1975.

Akün, Ömer Faruk. ''Sürûri.'' İA.

Alderson, A. D. *The Structure of the Ottoman Dynasty*. Oxford, 1956.

Algar, Hamid. ''The Naqshbandî Order: A Preliminary Survey of Its History and Significance.'' *Studia Islamica* 44 (1976): 123-52.

''ʿÂlî.'' *Küçük Türk-İslam Ansiklopedisi*. Fasc. 1. Istanbul, 1974.

Arat, R. Rahmeti. ''Fatih Sultan Mehmed'in Yarlığı.'' TM 6 (1936-39): 285-322.

Âsım, Necib. ''Osmanlı tarih-nüvisleri ve müverrihleri.'' TOEM (1909/1327): 425-35.

Atsız, Bedriye. ''Das Albanerbild der Türken nach osmanischen Chroniken des 15.-16. Jahrhunderts.'' *Münchner Zeitschrift für Balkankunde* 1 (1978): 15-25.

Babinger, Franz. *Mehmed the Conqueror and His Time*. Trans. Ralph Manheim, ed. William Hickman. Princeton, 1978.

Bacqué-Grammont, Jean-Louis. ''Notes et documents sur Divane Hüsrev Paşa.'' *Rocznik Orientalistczny* 41/4 (1979): 21-55.

Banarlı, Nihat Sami. "Ahmedi ve *Dâsitân-i Tevârîh-i Âl-i Osmân*." TM 6 (1936-39): 49-135.

Barkan, Ömer Lutfi. "H. 933-934 (M. 1527-1528) Mali Yılına âit bir Bütçe Örneği." İÜİFM 15 (1953-54): 251-329.

———. "954-955 (1547-1548) Mali Yılına âit bir Osmanlı Bütçesi." İÜİFM 19 (1957-58): 219-76.

Baysun, M. Cavid. "Ebüssuʿûd Efendi." İA.

———. "Müverrih Âli'nin Meva'id ün-nefâ'is fî kavâʿid il-mecâlis'i Hakkında." *Tarih Dergisi* 2/1 (1950): 389-400.

Birnbaum, Eleazar. "The Date of ʿÂlî's Turkish Mesnevi *Mihr u Mâh*." BSOAS 23 (1960): 138-39.

Boratav, Pertev Naili. "Türklerde Hızır." İA.

Browne, Edward Granville. *A Literary History of Persia*. 4 vols. Cambridge, Eng., 1969.

Brunschvig, R. "ʿAbd." EI².

Çetin, Nihad. "Latifi." İA.

Chittick, William C. "Sulṭân Burhân al-Dîn's Sufi Correspondence." WZKM 73 (1981): 33-46.

Dickson, Martin B. "Shâh Ṭahmâsb and the Ûzbeks (The Duel for Khurasan with ʿUbayd Khân: 930-946/1524-1540)." Ph.D. dissertation, Princeton University, 1958.

———. and Stuart Cary Welch. *The Houghton Shahnameh*. 2 vols. Cambridge, Mass., 1981.

Dilger, Konrad. *Untersuchungen zur Geschichte des osmanischen Hofzeremoniells im 15. und 16. Jahrhundert*. Munich, 1967.

Erünsal, İsmail. "Taci-zade Ca'fer Çelebi, as Poet and Statesman." *Boğaziçi Üniversitesi Dergisi: Beşeri Bilimler* 6 (1978): 123-48.

———. *The Life and Works of Tâcî-zâde Caʿfer Çelebi, with a Critical Edition of his Divan*. Istanbul, 1983.

"Firişte-oğlu." İA.

Fleischer, Cornell H. "Alqâs Mîrzâ Ṣafavî." *Encyclopaedia Iranica*.

———. "Bedlîsî, Edrîs." *Encyclopaedia Iranica*.

———. "From Şehzade Korkud to Mustafa Âli: Cultural Origins of the Ottoman *Nasihatname*." Paper presented at Third International Congress on the Economic and Social History of Turkey, Princeton, 1983.

———. "Gelibolulu Mustafa Âli Efendi, 1541-1600: A Study in Ottoman Historical Consciousness." Ph.D. dissertation, Princeton University, 1982.

———. "Islamic Ideals and Ottoman Realities: The *Kitab Daʿwat al-Nafs* of Prince Korkud, Son of Sultan Bayezid II" (forthcoming).

———. "Mustafâ ʿÂlî's *Curious Bits of Wisdom*." WZKM (1986).

———. "Royal Authority, Dynastic Cyclism, and 'Ibn Khaldûnism' in Sixteenth-Century Ottoman Letters." *Journal of Asian and African Studies* 18/3-4 (1983):198-220.

Flemming, Barbara. "Der *Ǧâmiʿ ül-meknûnât*: Eine Quelle ʿÂlî's aus der Zeit Sultan Süleymâns.'' *Studien zur Geschichte und Kultur des vorderen Orients. Festschrift für Bertold Spuler zum 70. Geburtstag*, pp. 79-92. Leiden, 1981.

Gibb, Sir Hamilton A. R. ''Târîkh.'' In *Studies on the Civilization of Islam*, pp. 108-37. Eds. Stanford J. Shaw and William R. Polk. Boston, 1962.

Giese, Friedrich. ''Einleitung zu meiner Textausgabe der altosmanischen anonymen Chroniken *Tewârîḫ-i âl-i ʿosmân*.'' MOG 1/2-3 (1922): 49-75.

Glassen, Erika. ''Krisenbewusstsein und Heilserwartung in der islamischen Welt zu Beginn der Neuzeit.'' *Die Islamische Welt zwischen Mittelalter und Neuzeit. Festschrift für Hans Robert Roemer zum 65. Geburtstag*, pp. 167-79. Beirut, 1979.

Gökbilgin, M. Tayyıb. ''Celâl-zâde.'' İA.

———. ''Cığala-zâde.'' İA.

———. ''Kanuni Sultan Süleyman Devri Müesseseler ve Teşkilatına Işık Tutan Bursa Şer'iye Sicillerinden Örnekler.'' *İsmail Hakkı Uzunçarşılı'ya Armağan*, pp. 91-112. Ankara, 1976.

———. ''Korkud.'' İA.

———. ''Mehmed III.'' İA.

———. ''Mehmed Paşa, Sokollu.'' İA.

———. ''Nişancı.'' İA.

Goldziher, Ignaz. ''Zur Charakteristik Ǵelâl al-dîn Sujûṭî's und seiner literarischen Thätigkeit.'' *Sitzungsberichte der Kaiserlichen Akademie der Wissenschaften. Philosophische-historische Klasse* 69 (1971): 7-28.

Gölpınarlı, Abdülbaki. *Hurufilik Metinleri Kataloğu*. Ankara, 1973.

Hammer, Joseph von. *Geschichte des osmanischen Reiches*. 10 vols. Pesth [Budapest], 1827-35.

Hardy, Peter. *Historians of Medieval India: Studies in Indo-Muslim Historical Writing*. London, 1969 (repr. Westport, 1982).

Hayder, Mansura. ''The Mongol Traditions and Their Survival in Central Asia (XIV-XV Centuries).'' *Central Asiatic Journal* 28/1-2 (1984): 57-79.

Heyd, Uriel. *Studies in Old Ottoman Criminal Law*. Ed. V. L. Ménage. Oxford, 1973.

Heywood, Colin. Review of *Muṣṭafâ ʿÂlî's Description of Cairo of 1599*. Ed. and trans. Andreas Tietze. BSOAS 40/2 (1977): 392-95.

Hodgson, M.G.S. *The Venture of Islam*. 3 vols. Chicago, 1974.

Humphreys, R. Stephen. *From Saladin to the Mongols: The Ayyubids of Damascus, 1193-1260*. Albany, 1977.

İbnülemin Mahmud Kemâl (İnal). Introduction to *Menakıb-ı hünerveran* by Âli. Istanbul, 1926.

İnalcık, Halil. ''Djizya.'' EI².

———. *Fatih Devri Üzerinde Tetkikler ve Vesikalar, I*. Ankara, 1954.

———. ''Ghulâm.'' EI².

———. ''Military and Fiscal Transformation in the Ottoman Empire, 1600-1700.'' *Archivum Ottomanicum* 6 (1980): 283-337.

———. ''Örf.'' İA.

———. ''Osmanlı Hukukuna Giriş.'' SBFD 13/2 (1958): 102-26.

———. "Osmanlı-Rus Rekabetinin Menşei ve Don-Volga Kanali Teşebbüsü." *Belleten* 8 (1944): 349-402.

———. "Osmanlılarda Saltanat Veraseti." SBFD 14.1 (1959): 69-94.

———. *The Ottoman Empire: The Classical Age, 1300-1600*. Trans. C. Imber and N. Itzkowitz. New York, 1973.

———. "Ottoman Methods of Conquest." *Studia Islamica* 2 (1954): 104-29.

———. "Padişah." İA.

———. "Re'is ül-küttâb." İA.

———. "The Rise of Ottoman Historiography." In *Historians of the Middle East*, pp. 152-67. Eds. B. L. Lewis and P. M. Holt. London, 1962.

———. "Suleiman the Lawgiver and Ottoman Law." *Archivum Ottomanicum* 1 (1969): 105-38.

Itzkowitz, Norman. *Ottoman Empire and Islamic Tradition*. New York, 1972.

Kappert, Petra. *Geschichte Sulṭân Süleymân Ḳânûnîs von 1520 bis 1557*. Wiesbaden, 1981.

Karahan, Abdülkadir. "Âli'nin bilinmeyen bir Eseri: *Mecmau'l-Bahreyn*." *V. Türk Tarih Kongresi. Tebliğler*, pp. 329-40. Ankara, 1960.

———. "Nev'i." İA.

Kırzıoğlu, M. Fahrettin. *Osmanlıların Kafkas-Ellerini Fethi (1450-1590)*. Ankara, 1976.

Kissling, Hans Joachim. "Aus der Geschichte des Chalvetijje-Ordens." ZDMG 103 (1953): 232-89.

———. "Zur Geschichte des Derwischordens der Bajramijje." *Südostforschungen* 15 (1956): 237-68.

Köprülü, Mehmed Fuad. "Baki." İA.

———. *Les Origines de l'empire ottoman*. Paris, 1935.

———. *Türk Edebiyatı Tarihi*. 2nd ed. Istanbul, 1980.

Kortantamer, Tunca. *Leben und Weltbild des altosmanischen Dichters Ahmedi unter besonderer Berücksichtigung seines Dîwâns*. Freiburg, 1973.

Kortepeter, Carl Max. *Ottoman Imperialism during the Reformation: Europe and the Caucasus*. New York, 1972.

Kunt, İ. Metin. "Ethnic-Regional (*Cins*) Solidarity in the Seventeenth-Century Ottoman Establishment." IJMES 5 (1974): 233-39.

———. "Kulların Kulları." *Boğaziçi Üniversitesi Dergisi: Beşeri Bilimler* 3 (1975): 27-42.

———. *Sancaktan Eyalete: 1550-1650 Arasında Osmanlı Ümerası ve İl İdaresi*. Istanbul, 1978.

———. *The Sultan's Servants: The Transformation of Ottoman Provincial Government, 1550-1650*. New York, 1983.

Kurat, Akdes Nimet. "The Turkish Expedition to Astrakhan in 1569 and the Problem of the Don-Volga Canal." *Slavonic and East European Review* 40 (1960): 1-23.

Kütükoğlu, Bekir. *Kâtib Çelebi "Fezlekesinin" Kaynakları*. Istanbul, 1974.

———. "Murad III." İA.

———. *Osmanlı-İran Siyasi Münasebetleri, 1578-90. Istanbul, 1962.*

Lambton, A.K.S. "Islamic Political Thought." In *The Legacy of Islam*, 2nd ed., pp. 404-27. Eds. J. Schacht and C. E. Bosworth. Oxford, 1974.

———. *State and Government in Medieval Islam*. Oxford, 1981.

Levend, Agâh Sırrı. *Ali Şir Nevai*. 4 vols. Ankara, 1965-68.

Lewis, Bernard. "Defterdar." EI[2].

———. "Bayt al-mâl (Ottoman)." EI[2].

Lindner, Rudi Paul. *Nomads and Ottomans in Medieval Anatolia*. Bloomington, Indiana, 1983.

Majer, Hans Georg. "Die Kritik an den Ulema in den osmanischen politischen Traktaten des 16.-18. Jahrhunderts." In *Social and Economic History of Turkey*, pp. 147-55. Eds. Osman Okyar and Halil İnalcık. Ankara, 1980.

———. "Sozialgeschichtliche Probleme um Ulema und Derwische im osmanischen Reich." In *I. Milletler Arası Türkoloji Kongresi (Istanbul, 15-20 X. 1973). Tebliğler*, vol. 1, pp. 218-33. Istanbul, 1979.

Mantran, Robert, and Karl Süssheim. "ʿÂlî." EI[2].

Matuz, Josef. *Das Kanzleiwesen des Sultan Süleymans des Prächtigen*. Wiesbaden, 1974.

Mélikoff, Irène. *La Geste de Melik Danişmend*. 2 vols. Paris, 1960.

Ménage, V. L. "The Beginnings of Ottoman Historiography." In *Historians of the Middle East*, pp. 168-79. Eds. B. L. Lewis and P. M. Holt. London, 1962.

———. "Bidlîsî, Idrîs." EI[2].

———. "Devshirme." EI[2].

———. "Edirneli Rûhî'ye Atfedilen Osmanlı Tarihinden İki Parça." *Ord. Prof. İsmail Hakkı Uzunçarşılı'ya Armağan*, pp. 311-312. Ankara, 1976.

———. "Kemâl Pasha-zâde." EI[2].

———. *Neshrî's History of the Ottomans: The Sources and Development of the Text*. London, 1964.

———. "Seven Documents from the Reign of Mehmed II." In *Documents from Islamic Chanceries*, pp. 81-118. Ed. S. M. Stein. Oxford, 1965.

———. "Some Notes on the Devshirme." BSOAS 29 (1966): 64-78.

Minorsky, Vladimir. "Tât." EI[1].

Murphey, Rhoads. "The Veliüddin Telhis: Notes on the Sources and Interrelations between Koçi Bey and Contemporary Writers of Advice to Kings." *Belleten* 43 (1979): 547-71.

Orhonlu, Cengiz. *Habeş Eyaleti*. Istanbul, 1974.

———. "Khazîne." EI[2].

Özergin, M. K. "Rûhî." İA.

Parmaksızoğlu, İsmet. "İbrahim Paşa, Damad." İA.

Pellat, Charles, trans. *Le Livre de la Couronne*. Paris, 1954.

Petry, Carl F. *The Civilian Elite of Cairo in the Later Middle Ages*. Princeton, 1981.

Poliak, A. N. "The Influence of Chingîz-Khân's Yâsâ Upon the General Organization of the Mamlûk State." BSOAS 10 (1939-42): 862-76.

Repp, Richard. "Some Observations on the Development of the Ottoman Learned Hierarchy." In *Scholars, Saints, and Sufis*, pp. 17-32. Ed. Nikki R. Keddie. Berkeley, 1972.

Röhrborn, Klaus. "Die Emanzipation der Finanzbürokratie im osmanischen Reich (Ende 16. Jahrhundert)." ZDMG 122 (1972): 118-39.

———. *Untersuchungen zur osmanischen Verwaltungsgeschichte*. Berlin, 1973.

Rosenthal, Franz. *A History of Muslim Historiography*. Leiden, 1952.

Šabanovič, Hazim. *Bosanski Pašaluk*. Sarajevo, 1959.

Sahillioğlu, Halil. "1524-1525 Osmanlı Bütçesi." İÜİFM 41/1-4 (1983): 415-52.

Schmidt, Jan. "De 'Verantwoording' in het Leidse Handschrift van de *Künhü'l-ahbar*." *Doctoraal-scriptie*, University of Leiden, 1983.

Schwarz, Klaus. "Eine Herrscherurkunde Sultân Murâd II fûr den Wesir Fażlullâh." *Journal of Turkish Studies* 5 (1983): 45-60.

Seif, Theodor. "Der Abschnitt über die Osmanen in Šükrüllâh's persischer Universalgeschichte." MOG 21-2 (1925): 63-128.

Sohrweide, Hanna. "Das *Enîs el-Qulûb*, ein verschollenes Werk des Historikers Muṣṭafâ ʿÂlî." In *VIII. Turk Tarih Kongresi (Ankara, 11-15 Ekim 1976). Kongreye Sunulan Bildiriler*, vol. II, pp. 983-91, 3 vols. Ankara, 1981.

———. "Dichter und Gelehrte aus dem Osten im osmanischen Reich." *Der Islam* 46 (1970): 263-302.

———. "Gelehrte Scheiche und sufische ʿUlemâ im osmanischen Reich." In *Studien zur Geschichte und Kultur des vorderen Orients. Festschrift für Bertold Spuler zum 70. Geburtstag*, pp. 375-86. Leiden, 1981.

Sümer, Faruk. *Oğuzlar (Türkmenler): Tarihleri, Boy Teşkilatı, Destanları*. Rev. 3d ed. Istanbul, 1980.

Süssheim, Karl. "ʿÂlî." EI[1].

Taeschner, Franz. "ʿÂshik-Pasha-zâde." EI[2].

Thomas, Lewis V. *A Study of Naima*. Ed. Norman Itzkowitz. New York, 1972.

Tietze, Andreas. "Muṣṭafâ ʿÂlî of Gallipoli's Prose Style." *Archivum Ottomanicum* 5 (1973): 297-319.

———. "Muṣṭafâ ʿÂlî on Luxury and the Status Symbols of Ottoman Gentlemen." In *Studia Turcologica Memoriae Alexii Bombaci Dicata*, pp. 577-90. Naples, 1982.

Togan, Zeki Velidi. "Câmi." İA.

———. *Umumi Türk Tarihine Giriş*. Istanbul, 1946.

Turan, Şerafettin. *Kanuni'nin Oğlu Şehzade Bayezid Vak'ası*. Ankara, 1961.

———. "Lala Mustafa Paşa Hakkında Notlar ve Vesikalar." *Belleten* 22 (1958): 551-93.

———. "Ramazân-zâde." İA.

———. "Sa'd-ed-Dîn." İA.

———. "Sinan Pasa, Koca." İA.

Uzunçarşılı, İsmail Hakkı. *Mekke-i Mükerreme Emirleri*. Ankara, 1972.

———. *Osmanlı Devletinin İlmiye Teşkilatı*. Ankara, 1965.

———. *Osmanlı Devletinin Merkez ve Bahriye Teşkilatı*. Ankara, 1948.

———. *Osmanlı Devleti Teşkilatından Kapukulu Ocakları*. 2 vols. Ankara, 1943-44.

———. *Osmanlı Devletinin Saray Teşkilatı*. Ankara, 1945.

Waldman, Marilyn Robinson. *Toward a Theory of Historical Narrative: A Case Study in Perso-Islamicate Historiography*. Columbus, Ohio, 1980.

Walsh, John R. "The Historiography of Ottoman-Safavi Relations in the Sixteenth Century." *In Historians of the Middle East*, pp. 197-211. Eds. B. L. Lewis and P. M. Holt. London, 1962.

Wensinck, A. J. "Hızır." İA.

Wittek, Paul. *The Rise of the Ottoman Empire*. London, 1938.

Woodhead, Christine. "An Experiment in Official Historiography: The Post of *Şehnâmeci* in the Ottoman Empire." WZKM 75 (1983): 157-82.

———. "From Scribe to Littérateur: The Career of a Sixteenth-Century Ottoman *Kâtib*." *Bulletin of the British Society for Middle East Studies* 9 (1982): 55-74.

Woods, John E. *The Aqquyunlu: Clan, Confederation, Empire*. Minneapolis, 1976.

Yazıcı, Tahsin. "Fetih'ten Sonra İstanbul'da İlk Halveti Şeyhleri: Çelebi Muhammad Cemâleddin, Sünbül Sinan ve Merkez Efendi." *İstanbul Enstitüsü Dergisi* 2 (1956): 87-113.

Yınanç, Mükrimin Halil. "Bayezid I." İA.

Yurdaydın, Hüseyin G., ed. *Beyân-ı Menâzil-i Sefer-i ʿIrâḳeyn-i Sulṭân Süleymân Hân*, by Naṣûhü' s-Silâḥî (Maṭraḳçi). Ankara, 1976.

INDEX

ʿAbbâs, Shâh, Safavi, 277
Abbasids, 273; destruction of caliphate, 283-84
Abdi (ʿAbdî), poet, 31
Abdülgani b. Emirşah (ʿAbdülġanî b. Emîrşâh), *kadıasker* of Anatolia, 128n
ʿAbdullâh Khân, Özbek, 277, 278n
Abdullah Kırimî (ʿAbdullâh Ḳirîmî), calligrapher, 123n
Abdülmuhyi Paşa. *See* Muhyi Çelebi
Abu'l-khayr Khân, Özbek, 277
Abû Numayy, *şerif* of Mecca, 185n, 277
Abûbakr Mîrzâ, Şirvanşah, 78n
Acem (Iran), as cultural zone, 30, 142n, 154, 158
Acem Menla Ağa (ʿAcem Menlâ), *müteferrika*, 49, 51
acemi, 154, 157-58
acemi ocağı, 21n
adaletname, 198
Adana, *sancak*, seat of Ramazanoğulları, 41
Adornment of Men (Âli). See *Hilyet ür-rical*
Affection and Fidelity (Âli). See *Mihr u vefa*
ağa, rank and promotion of, 193
Ahdi (ʿAhdî), poet and anthologist, 24, 123, 251
ahlak (ethics), 100
Ahlak-ı Ala'i (*Aḫlâḳ-ı ʿAlâ'î*), by Kınalızade, 43, 100, 262n, 291n
Ahmed Beğ (Aḥmed), *sancak beği* of Maʿarra, relative of Sinan Paşa, 88n
Ahmed Çelebi, Lalezarzade (Lâlezârzâde Aḥmed), finance director of Erzurum, 85-86, 86n, 104
Ahmed Efendi (Aḥmed), finance director of Baghdad, 122
Ahmed b. Abdullah (Aḥmed b. ʿAbdullâh), father of Âli, 13-16, 20, 23
Ahmed b. Ruhullah Ensari (Aḥmed b. Rûḥullâh el-Enṣârî), *kadıasker* of Rumeli, 128n
Ahmed Paşa (Aḥmed), governor-general of Damascus, 180
Ahmed Paşa, Gedük (Gedük Aḥmed), grand vezir to Mehmed II, 186
Ahmed Paşa, Kara (Ḳara Aḥmed), grand vezir to Süleyman I, 259
Ahmed Paşa, Semiz (Semiz Aḥmed), grand vezir to Murad III, 85, 87
Ahmed Paşa b. Çerkes İskender Paşa (Aḥmed), governor-general of Aleppo, 90, 99, 104
Ahmed-i Da'i (Aḥmed-i Dâʿî), historian, 250
Ahmedi (Aḥmedî), historian, 250, 289n
Akbar, Sulṭân Jalâl al-dîn, Tîmûrid, 277, 278n
Akhisari (Aḳḥiṣârî, Ḥasan el-kâfî), *nasihat* author, 102
Akhlâq-i Jalâlî (Davânî), 100n, 280n
Akhlâq-i Nâṣirî (Ṭûsî), 100n, 292n
Akkoyunlu, 273, 286-87
Akli (ʿAḳlî), poet, 157
Aksaray, *sancak*, 163
Akşemsüddin (Aḳşemsüddîn), Bayrami sheikh, 167
Albanians, ethnicity and solidarity, 16n, 157, 164-65, 165n. *See also* ethnicity
Aleppo: *vilâyet*, administrative conditions in, 104, 112; artists in, 106; *defterdarlık* of, 109, 113, 115, 311-13. *See also* Âli: career
Alexander, as universal ruler, 280
Ali Çelebi. *See* Kınalızade
Ali Çelebi (ʿAlî), author of *Hümayunname*, 43
Ali Kuşçi (ʿAlî Ḳûşçî), scholar, 158
ʿAlî b. Abî Ṭâlib, Imam, 279, 283
Ali Mınık (ʿAlî Mınıḳ), scholar and biographer, 251, 251n
Ali Kuşçi (ʿAlî Ḳûşçî), scholar, 158
ʿAlî b. Abî Ṭâlib, Imam, 279, 283
Ali Mınık (ʿAlî Mınıḳ), scholar and biographer, 251, 251n
Âli, Mustafa (Muṣṭafâ ʿÂlî)
  appointments and dismissals
    appointed: campaign secretary to Lala Mustafa Paşa, 75; chancery secretary to Ferhad Beğ, Klis, 58-59; chancery secretary to Lala Mustafa Paşa, 42; chancery secretary to Prince Selim II, 35; *defter emini*, 144; finance director of Baghdad, 117-18; finance director of Erzurum, 115; finance director of Sivas, 129; governor-general of Damascus, 180; imperial atelier, to, 110; *sancak beği* and *emin* of Jidda, 180; *sancak beği* of Amasya and finance di-

Âli, Mustafa (*cont.*)
rector of Sivas, 161; *sancak beği* of Kayseri, 163; *timar defterdarı* of Aleppo, 82, 82n; *yeniçeri kâtibi*, 143, 151
dismissed: as *defter emini*, 146; as finance director of Baghdad, 118; as finance director of Sivas, 162; as governor-general of Damascus, 180; as *sancak beği* of Kayseri, 168; as *yeniçeri kâtibi*, 144
career: in Aleppo, as *timar* registrar, 89-108; leaves Aleppo, seeks court post, 109; in Anatolia, central, 131-33, 161-68; in Baghdad, 103, 120-24; in Bosnia, in service of Ferhad Beğ, 60-69; leaves Bosnia for Istanbul, 70; in Damascus, 42-48, 50; in Egypt, 48-51, 181-83; in Erzurum on campaign, 84-87; in Erzurum as finance director, 115-17; in Gallipoli, 13, 21-25, 147-48; in Hijaz, 183-87; in Istanbul, 25-34, 55, 70, 109, 124, 133, 148, 168; in Istanbul, unemployed, 55, 70-75, 109-10, 124-29, 133-43, 148-51, 168-80; in Istanbul, as *yeniçeri kâtibi* and *defter emini*, 143-47; in Konya and Kütahya, in chancery of Prince Selim II, 34-39; in Manisa, at court of Prince Murad III, 54-55; in Mecca, as pilgrim, 185; in Şirvan and eastern Anatolia, 80-89
compared, with that of peers, 66-67, 113-15, 149-50, 155, 158, 162, 172
educational: early, in Gallipoli, 21-25; in Istanbul, 25-34
ilmiye, 25-29, 32-33, 34-35, 67, 150
maliye, 84, 103, 109-10, 113, 115, 137, 144, 152
personal life: birth, 13, 13n; childhood and adolescence, 13-24; death, 187, 187n; endowment of books, 128; endowment of fountain, at Kerbela, 124; ethnic origins, 15-16; family, 16-21 (*see also* Ahmed b. Abdullah, Derviş Çelebi, Faz lullah, Ibniyamin, Mehmed b. Ahmed, Şeyh Muslihüddin Mustafa); household, 70, 137-39; languages, 22, 110n; marriage, 70; pen name, adopts, 24; son, birth of, 70. *See also* Appendix B, 315-18
personality
ideals and values: evolution of, 272; *kanun* and, 93-94, 102, 113-14, 158, 161-62, 173-74, 228-30; moral and cultural, 269-72; summarized, 186
identities: critic of Ottoman society, 101-103, 127-28, 136, 177-79, 181-82, 185-86; historian, 100-103, 173-75, 235-37, 241-42, 247-49, 288-90, 293-94; informer, 99, 147; *kanun* expert, 8, 94-99, 169, 174-75, 192, 198; poet, 24, 31, 37-38, 44-45, 63, 140, 142, 153
interest: in Anatolian folklore, 131-32, 166-68; in book illumination, 105-106, 110-11; in calligraphy, 123; in Caucasian folklore, 80; in dreams, interpretation of, 151
piety: Âli rejects, 145n; millennial, 135-37; Sufi, 23, 42, 131-32, 135-37, 166-68; *tarikat* affiliations, 136
self-identification: as *gazi*, 65; as historian, 140-41, 242-49, 272, 284-85; with *ilmiye*, 36, 94, 100, 115, 128-29, 149, 160, 175, 258, 270; with Ottoman state, 191, 253, 269, 272; as poet, 45, 63, 67, 142, 146n, 148, 153, 170, 171; with Rum, 141, 154-55, 166-68, 254, 270-72; as scholar, 70-71, 75-76, 80, 128-29, 138-39, 149-50, 155, 169; as servitor of Ottoman dynasty, 186; as social outcast, 88-89, 113, 129, 138-40, 147; summarizes life to age fifty, 137
sexuality, 23, 45
relations with individuals and groups: Âşık Çelebi, 63-64; Azmi Efendi, 91; Baki, 31n, 31-32, 171; Bali Efendi, 57-58, 61, 133n, 149; Celalzade, 30-31; Dal Mehmed Çelebi, 81-82, 251; Doğancı Mehmed Paşa, 125, 126-27, 133; Ferhad Paşa, 60, 66-69; Feridun Ahmed, 66; Gazanfer Ağa, 110, 125, 126, 170-72, 175, 180; Hadim Hasan Paşa, 175; Halvetis, 57-58; Hamze Çelebi, 91-92, 117, 172-73; Hasan Paşa b. Sokollu Mehmed Paşa, 86n; Husrev Paşa, 87, 107, 108n; İbrahim Paşa, Damad, 99n, 109, 117, 133n, 165-66, 171; dedicates *Mahâsin ül-âdâb* to İbrahim Paşa, Damad, 170; Kınalızade Ali Çelebi, 43, 43n; Kınalızade Hasan Çelebi, 43, 43n, 116; Lala Mustafa Paşa, 39-40, 46, 54, 61-62, 80, 86-88, 107; Lam Ali Çelebi, 172-73; Mehmed, brother, 44, 137; Mehmed III, 152-54, 161-62, 172, 175, 178-79, 184-86, 303; dedicates *Mahâsin ül-âdâb* to Mehmed III, 170 (*see also* Âli: views); Mehmed Paşa, Boyalı, 91; Mehmed Paşa, Sokollu, 58-59, 66-67, 86 (*see also* Âli: views); Murad III, 54-55, 69, 75, 111-13, 127, 135, 144-45, 151-52; Âli seeks favor

from Murad III, for poets, 148; Âli seeks favor from favorites of Murad III, 74-75; dedicates *divan* to Murad III, 68 (*see also* Âli: views); Mustafa Paşa, Sokollu, 65-66; Nakşbendis, 57, 132n; Nef'i, 141; Osman Paşa, Özdemiroğlu, 51, 81, 107, 114-15, 117, 129; Piri Paşa Ramazanoğlu, 41; poets in Baghdad, 123; poets in Bosnia, 63-64; poets in Istanbul, 31-32, 56, 146; poets in Kütahya, 37-39; Ramazanzade, 30-31; Sa'düddin, 74, 92, 108-109, 125, 127, 150-51, 177, 180; Selâniki, 130-31; Selim II, Prince, 34-35, 40, 67 (*see also* Âli: views); Şemsi Paşa, 56, 74-75; Şemsüddin Ahmed, teacher, 28-29; Şeyh Şüca', 74-75; Sinan Paşa, 51, 88-89, 88n, 108, 135, 137, 146, 150-51 (*see also* Âli: views); Sirri, 116; Süleyman I, 38-39 (*see also* Âli: views); Sürûri, teacher, 28-29; ulema, endorsed by, 128; Üveys Paşa, 99n, 104, 107, 109, 124; Yahya Beğ, 63-64; Zirek Ağa, 112n. *See also* individual names in main index

seeks: chancellorship, 91-95, 110, 125, 145, 165, 172, 174-75, 228-29; finance directorship, provincial (Aleppo) 112, (Aleppo, Egypt) 113, 125, (Damascus) 130, (Egypt) 153; finance directorship, of the Porte, 125; governor-generalship, 162, 166, 171, 174, (Aleppo) 172, (Aleppo, Basra) 125, (Egypt) 183; Imperial Council appointment, 108; *kalemiye* appointment, 67, 113; loans, 91n; Palace appointment, 153; permission for pilgrimage, 131-32; retirement, 176; *sancak* governorship, 169; secretariat, 113, 125; treasurership, 113

views and attitudes

historical past: decline, 139, 176-77, 230-31, 258, 267, 271, 299-305; dynastic cyclism, 177-78, 304; education, *medrese*, 271; empires, regional, 277-83; "golden age," 89, 101, 140-41, 153, 226-27, 254-57, 259-60, 263, 266; historiographical method, 272, 284-85, 304-306; Rum, cultural history of, 254-57, 298-99

individuals: Bayezid I, 284-86; Bayezid II, 139, 205; Lala Mustafa Paşa, 46, 50, 85-86, 89n; Mehmed II, 139, 141, 153, 174, 178, 263-64, 280; Mehmed Paşa, Sokollu, 48, 56, 86, 305-306; Murad III, character of, 103, 205, 294-95, 300-301; Murad III, reign of, 153-59, 293-306; Selim I, 139, 153, 280; Selim II, 38, 40, 56, 259, 304; Sinan Paşa, 51, 88-89, 108, 164-65, 297-98, 299-300, 301, 305; Süleyman I, 153, 174, 280; Tîmûr, 284-86. *See also* Âli: relations with individuals

kanun, 226-28, 230, 261-71; and *şeri'at*, 270-71

Ottoman governmental careers, 158-59, 201-13, 224-31; *devşirme*, 255-57; *ilmiye*, 202-205, 227-28, 230, 266-68, 270; *kalemiye*, 96-97, 174-75, 204-207, 224-29; *maliye*, 174-75, 201-204, 207, 212-13, 228-29; meritocracy in, 96-97, 134, 158, 171, 173-75; nepotism in, 56, 86, 97-98, 202, 208-209, 259, 305; *seyfiye*, 67, 201-204, 206-10, 229-30; specific offices: financial officials, 228-29; *şehnamecis*, 248-49, 298-99; vezirs, 96, 170, 258, 266

religious culture and institutions: Islam, 257-61, 263-66, 270-71; millennium, 138-42; *şeri'at*, 261-71; Sufism, 135-37

society: ethnicity in, 155-59, 165n, 254-57; language and culture in, 70-71, 141-42, 253-57, 270-72; social morality in, 63, 143, 306-307

sovereignty: 279-86, duties of, 302-303; ideal qualities for, 264-65; and legitimacy, dynastic, 285-92; Turco-Mongol legacy to theories of, 276-79, 283-84, 289-91; universal, 285, 287

works

apocalyptic themes in, 134-35, 137

composed: *Badî' al-ruqûm*, 142; *Câmi' ül-buhur der mecâlis-i sûr*, 106-107; *Câmi' ül-kemâlât*, 111; *divans*, 44-45, 68, 140, 170 (see also *Layihat ül-hakika; Vâridat ül-enika*); *Enis ül-kulub*, 43; *Ferâ'id ül-vilâde*, 126; *fethname*, for Osman Paşa, 114n; *fethname*, for Sinan Paşa, 151; *Fursatname*, 89; *Fusul-i hall ve akd fi usul-i harc ve nakd*, 177-79, 177n; *Gül-i sad berg*, 148; *Hâlât ül-Kahire min el-âdât iz-zâhire*, 179, 182-84; *Heft meclis*, 58, 240; *Hilyet ür-rical*, 75; *Hulasat ül-ahvâl*, 134n; *Kavâ'id ül-mecâlis*, 127-28; *Kırk hadis*, 171; *Künh ül-ahbar* (begun) 140-41, (introduction to) 148, (dedication of) 165-66n, 169; *Layihat ül-hakika*, 13n, (begun) 90, (completed) 138-39; *Mahâsin ül-âdâb*, 166; *Majma' al-baḥreyn*, 141-42; *Menakıb-ı*

Âli, Mustafa (*cont.*)
hünerveran, 105, 127; *Menşe' ül-inşa*, 129; *Mevâ'id ün-nefâ'is fi kavâ'id il-mecâlis*, 181-82, 184-86; *Mihr u mah*, 22n, 34; *Mihr u vefa*, 39; *Mir'at ül-avâlim*, 126; *Mirkat ül-cihad*, 132-33; *Nadir ül-maharib*, 22n, 44, 240; *Nevâdir ül-hikem*, 131; *Nükat ül-kal fi tazmin il-makal*, 111; *Nushat üs-selâtin*, 58n, 95-99; *Nusretname* (completed) 89, (production of) 110; *Rahat ün-nüfus*, 55; *Riyaz üs-sâlikin* (begun) 42, (completed) 135; *Sadef-i sad güher*, 13, 147-48; *Sübhaı ül-ebdal*, 148; *Tâli' üs-selâtin*, 111; *Tuhfet ül-uşşak*, 37; *Vâridat ül-enika*, 68, (completed) 90; *Zübdet üt-tevarih*, 69-70, 70n. *See also* names in main index
style: early, 45; in *inşa*, 113, 45; in poetry, early, 23-24, 45; simplified, 179-80
symbolic representation in, 300-303
translations: *Ayyuhâ al-walad* (Ghazâlî), 61; *Faṣl al-khiṭâb* (Khvâjeh Muḥammad Pârsâ), 75; *Ishrâq al-tawârîkh* (Qâḍî ʿAḍud al-dîn), 69; *Rujûʿ al-shaykh ilâ ṣabâh* (Tifâshî), 55
Ali Paşa, Elvendoğlu (Elvendoğlı ʿAlî), governor-general of Damascus, 121, 122
Ali Paşa, Kapudan (Ḳapûdân ʿAlî), 158n
ʿAlî Shîr Navâ'î. *See* Navâ'î
ʿAlqamî, Abbasid vezir, 237
Amasya: Ottoman cultural center, 167; Peace of, 77-79, 84; *sancak*, 161
Anadolu defterdarı. See *defterdar*
Anatolia: *defterdarlık* of, see *defterdar*; *vilâyet*, conditions in, 161-63. *See also* Âli: career
apprenticeship, financial, 222-23
Arabic, in educational curriculum, 21
Arabs, 154
Arab ve Acem defterdarlığı. See *defterdar*
Ârif Ali (ʿÂrif ʿAlî), author of *Danişmendname*, 132
Ârif Çelebi. *See* Ârifî
Ârifî (Fatḥullâh ʿÂrif), *şehnameci*, 30, 155, 239n
Aristotle, 262
artisans, imperial, 111
Artists' Exploits (Âli). See *Menakıb-ı hünerveran*
Âsafi. *See* Dal Mehmed Çelebi
Asafname (*Âṣafnâme*), by Lutfi Paşa, 100-101
Ascending Ladder of Holy War (Âli). See *Mirkat ül-cihad*
Âşık Çelebi (ʿÂşıḳ), poet and anthologist, 63, 251. *See also* Âli: relations with individuals
Âşıkpaşazade (Âşıḳpaşazâde), historian, 235, 238, 247
askeri (class), 64; defined, 5-7; formation of, 256-57; infiltration of, 20, 153-59; structure of, 212, 213, 223. See also *ilmiye; kalemiye; kul;* Palace; *seyfiye*
astrology, 151-52
Ata'ullah Efendi (ʿAṭâ'ullâh), tutor to Selim II, 53
Avvad Keşçi Memi (ʿAvvâd Keşçî Memî), companion to Prince Selim II, 38n
Aya Sofya, mosque, 151
Ayas Paşa (Ayâs), brother of Sinan Paşa, 48
Ayn-ı Ali Efendi (ʿAyn-ı ʿAlî), 193, 312
ʿAyshî, calligrapher, 123n
Ayyuhâ al-walad (Ghazâlî), 61. *See also* Âli: works
Azerbaycan, cultural prestige of, 154
Aziz Efendi b. Hoca Sa'düddin (ʿAzîz), 139n
Azmi Efendi (ʿAzmî), tutor to Mehmed III, 91

Babur (Bâbur), Tîmûrid, 287n
Badîʿ al-ruqûm (Âli), 142
Baghdad: cultural life in, 123; *defterdarlık* of, 119, 226, 312n; *vilâyet*, administrative conditions in, 117n, 120-22, 156. *See also* Âli: career
Baha'üddin Efendi (Bahâ'üddîn), *kadıasker* of Rumeli, 128n
Bahjat al-tavârîkh (Şükrullah), 240, 255
Baki (Bâḳî), poet and *kadıasker*, 137n, 142, 145, 171; death of, 187n; early career of, 31-33; judicial appointments of, 128, 153; peers of, 149-50; political alliances of, 160-61, 176, 295. *See also* Âli: relations with individuals
Bâli Çelebi, Münşi. *See* Firuz
Bali Efendi (Sarhoş Bâlî, Cevherî), Halveti sheikh, 57-58, 61, 133n, 149
Bali Efendi, Sofyalı (Şofyalı Bâlî), Halveti sheikh, 58n
Banyaluka, *sancak* seat of Ferhad Beğ, 66
Barbaro, Venetian bailo, 56
başdefterdar. *See* treasurer; *defterdar: Rumeli*
başkâtib, 37
Basra, *defterdarlık* of, 313
Bayezid, Prince (Şehzâde Bâyezîd b. Sulṭân

Süleymân), 34, 78; at war with brother Selim II, 48, 259
Bayezid I, Sultan (Sulṭân Bâyezîd b. Sulṭân Murâd, Yıldırım), 284-85
Bayezid II, Sultan (Sulṭân Bâyezîd b. Sulṭân Meḥmed): bureaucracy of, 215-16; patron of historiography, 139, 205, 238-39, 248; protector of *şeri'at*, 266. *See also* Âli: views
Bâyqarâ, Sulṭân-Ḥusayn, Tîmûrid, 71, 169, 186; symbolic significance of, 141
Bayrami (Bayrâmî) Sufi order, 136, 166-67
Beauties of Polite Observance (Âli). See *Mahâsin ül-âdâb*
beğ, title, 204, 207-208
beğlerbeği: defined, 60; fiscal authority of, 119-21, 313-14, (abused) 104; promotion of, 47, 192-93. See also *hass;* provincial government
Beğlerbeği Incident, 133, 297
Bidlîsî, İdrîs, historian, 52n, 194, 239, 248
birun, 194, 209. *See also* Palace
Blossoms of a Hundred Leaves (Âli). See *Gül-i sad berg*
bölük halkı, 152, 155; rebellions of, 156
Book of Opportunity (Âli). See *Fursatname*
Book of Victory (Âli). See *Nusretname*
Bosnasaray (Sarajevo), 64
Bosnia: *sancak*, 60-68; *vilâyet*, 60n. *See also* Âli: career
Bosnians, ethnicity and solidarity, 16n, 157, 165n. *See also* ethnicity
Boyalı Mehmed Paşa. *See* Mehmed Paşa, Boyalı
Bozdağ, summer court of Prince Murad III, 55
Bozok, *sancak*, 166
bribery (*rüşvet*), 62, 96, 98, 259. *See also* corruption; gifts
Budin (Budun, Buda): *vilayet*, 65; *defterdarlık* of, 311
bureaucracy, Ottoman. See *kalemiye; maliye*
Burhân 'Alî (Burhân al-dîn 'Alî), Şirvanşah, 78n
Bursa, *medreses* of, 25, 26
Bustanzade Efendi (Bustânzâde), *kadıasker* of Rumeli, *şeyhülislam*, 128n, 150, 153, 176; rivalry with Sa'düddin, 159-61, 299

Ca'fer Ağa (Ca'fer), *yeniçeri ağası*, 57
Ca'fer Beğ (Ca'fer), brother of Gazanfer Ağa, 53, 72
Cağaloğlu Sinan Paşa (Cağalazâde Yûsuf Sinân), grand vezir to Mehmed III, 166n, 169, 169n, 170-72, 180
Çagatay Turkish (language). *See* Turkish
caliphate, Abbasid. *See* Abbasids
Câmi' ül-buhur der mecâlis-i sûr (Câmi' ül-buḥûr der mecâlis-i sûr), by Âli, 106-107
Câmi' ül-kemâlât (Câmi' ül-kemâlât), by Âli, 111
Câmi' ül-meknunat (Câmi' ül-meknûnât), by Mevlana İsa, 248
Câmi' üt-tevârîh (Câmi' üt-tevârîh), by Za'im Mehmed, 280n
Canfeda Hatun (Cânfedâ), 72-73, 295. See also *kedbanu-yi harem*
career paths, Ottoman: disruption of, 158, 225-26; integrity of, 201-13; interrelationship of, 7, 113, 196-97, 212-13; structure of, 125-26, 162, 192-213. *See also* Âli: views; *ecnebi*; household; *ilmiye; kalemiye; maliye*; Palace; seniority; *seyfiye*
Carnal Souls' Comfort (Âli). See *Rahat ün-nüfus*
Caucasus: Ottoman conquest of, 80; Ottoman policy in, 76-77
çavuş, 20, 21n, 119
çebelü, 59
Celal Beğ (Celâl, Celâlî), poet and companion to Prince Selim II, 38n, 45, 52, 53
Celâli rebellions, 161, 163, 166
Celalzade Mustafa Çelebi (Celâlzâde Muṣṭafâ, Ḳoca Nişâncı), chancellor, 30-31, 36, 94, 94n, 204, 227, 248; as codifier of *kanun*, 218; as historian, 236, 241-42. *See also* Âli: relations with individuals
Çelebi Mehmed (Meḥmed), *kadıasker* of Rumeli, 128n
Celili (Celîlî), poet, 45
Cenabi, Mustafa (Muṣṭafâ Cenâbî), historian, 241
Cengiz Han: ideological significance of, 273, 275-77; as universal ruler, 280, 283. *See also* Mongols
Çepni, Türkmen, 156
Cerrah Mehmed Paşa (Cerrâḥ Meḥmed), vezir to Murad III, 133; mosque of, 148n
Çeşmi (Çeşmî), Âli's first pen name, 24
Cevheri. *See* Bali Efendi
Cezerizade Safi Çelebi (Cezerîzâde Şâfî, Ḳoca Ḳâsım Paşa), chancellor, treasurer to Bayezid II, 215

chancellor: as authority on *kanun*, 92-95, 220, 227-28; career path of, 214-21; history of office, 30, 93n, 129n; at princely court, 38n; promotion of, 192-93, 203; symbolic significance of, 174-75, 204. *See also* Âli: views
chief jurisconsult. See *şeyhülislam*
Chingis Khân. *See* Cengiz Han
Choicest of Histories (Âli). See *Zübdet üt-tevarih*
Cihadname (Cihâdnâme), by Safi, 90n
çıkma, 83, 193-94
Circle of Equity, 262, 270, 303, 306
circumcision, of Ottoman princes, 106-107
Çivizade (Çivîzâde), *şeyhülislam*, 128n, 139n
cizye, defined, 62
companion, royal. See *musahib*
Conditions of Cairo Concerning her Actual Customs (Âli). See *Hâlât ül-Kahire min el-âdât iz-zâhire*
Confluence of the Two Seas (Âli). See *Majmaʿ al-baḥreyn*
Conqueror, the. *See* Mehmed II, Sultan
corruption, governmental, 85-86, 104, 108, 120-21, 153, 175, 178, 296. *See also* bribery
Counsel for Sultans (Âli). See *Nushat üs-selâtin*
Crimea, hans of, 275, 277. *See also* Devlet Giray; Mehmed Giray; Sahib Giray
Cübni Sinan. *See* Sinan
Curios of the Lovers (Âli). See *Tuhfet ül-uşşak*
Curious Bits of Wisdom (Âli). See *Nevâdir ül-hikem*
currency, devaluation of, 98, 133, 297

dahil. See *medrese*: hierarchy
Dal Mehmed Çelebi (Dâl Meḥmed, Âṣafî), poet, governor-general of Şirvan, 81-82, 251
Damad İbrahim Paşa. *See* İbrahim Paşa, Damad
Damascus, *vilâyet*, 40, 42-43, 48, 121. *See also* Âli: career; Lala Mustafa Paşa
danişmend, 27-29
Danişmendname (Dânişmendnâme), by İbn Alâ and Ârif Ali, 132
Darülhadis. *See* Süleymaniye
Darüşşifa. *See* Süleymaniye
Davânî, Jalâl al-dîn (*Akhlâq-i Jalâlî*), 100n, 262, 280n
Dâvûd Khân, ruler of Tiflis, 80
decline: dynastic, 282; Islamic, 140-41; Ottoman ideology of, 101-103, 154, 182. *See also* Âli: views
defter, 61, 65; defined, 62
defterdar, 175; abuse of authority by, 104; *Anadolu defterdarı*, 98, 311-13; *Arab ve Acem defterdarlığı*, 113n, 311; in archival usage, 117n; defined, 311; of Porte (see *Anadolu defterdarı; Arab ve Acem defterdarlığı; Rumeli defterdarı; şıkk-ı salis defterdarı; şıkk-ı sani defterdarı*); at princely court, 37; promotion of, 192-93, 203, 220n, 312; provincial, duties of, 82-83, 312-14 (*see also* Aleppo; Baghdad; Basra; Budin; Diyar Bakır; Egri; Egypt; Erzurum; Gence; Lahsa; Rum [Sivas]; Şirvan; Yemen); *Rumeli defterdarı*, 215, 311-12 (*see also* treasurer); *şıkk-ı salis defterdarı*, 312; *şıkk-ı sani defterdarı*, 73, 98, 219, 296, 312; *timar defterdarı* (see *timar*)
defter emini, 98, 144-45, 214, 216, 313
defterhane, 145. See also *defter emini*
defter kedhüdası, 82, 113, 313
Demirkapı. *See* Derbend
Derbend, history of, 80
Derviş Çelebi (Dervîş), great-uncle of Âli, 17-18, 20, 25, 28
devatdar, 219
Devlet Giray Han (Devlet Girây), Crimean han, 52n
devşirme, 6, 15, 19, 46, 154-56, 173, 193, 221, 255-56. See also *askeri; kul*; Palace
Dickson, Martin, 286
dirlük, 208
divan (council), provincial, 42
divan (poetry collection): Âli's first, 44-45 (see also *Vâridât ül-enika*); Âli's second (see *Layihat ül-hakika*); Âli's third, 140, 170; defined, 44
Divane İbrahim Paşa. *See* İbrahim Paşa, Divane
Divan-ı hümayun. *See* Imperial Council
Diyar Bakır: *defterdarlık* of, 311; *vilâyet*, administrative irregularities in, 104
Doğancı Mehmed Paşa. *See* Mehmed Paşa, Doğancı
dreams, 151
Dukakin, *beğs*, 223

Ebülfazl Mehmed b. İdrîs-i Bidlîsî (Ebülfazl Meḥmed), treasurer to Selim II, 250
Ebu Nümeyy. *See* Abû Numayy
Ebüssu'ud Efendi (Ebüssuʿûd), *şeyhülislam*, 21, 28, 136, 160, 227
ecnebi, 153, 154n, 158, 158n, 178, 207.

See also *askeri; kul*
Edirne, *medreses* of, 25-26
education, Ottoman: by apprenticeship, 222-23; *medrese*, 21, 24-29, 224-25, 258-60, 271; Palace, 158, 196, 209, 222-25, 271. *See also* Âli: views; *mekteb; medrese; müderris*
efendi, title, 204
Eflatun-ı Şirvani (Eflâṭûn-ı Şîrvânî), *şehnameci*, 155, 239n
Egri: campaign of, 166, 169; *defterdarlık* of, 313
Egri Abdizade (Egri ʿAbdîzâde), chancellor, treasurer to Süleyman I, 204, 206, 215, 217
Egypt: condition of, 182-83; *defterdarlık* of, 113, 115, 312-13, 312n; *sancak beğis* of, 203, 207; *vilâyet*, administration of, 48-50, 205, 207. *See also* Âli: career
ehl-i kalem. See *kalemiye*
Ehli (Ehlî), poet, 137n
Elegant Inspirations (Âli). See *Vâridat ül-enika*
Elite Corps. See *müteferrika*
Elvendoğlu Ali Paşa. *See* Ali Paşa, Elvendoğlu
emanet, 116n. See also *emin*
Embellishment of Inscriptions (Âli). See *Badîʿ al-ruqûm*
emin, 180. See also *emanet*
Emir-i Buhari Tekkesi (Istanbul), 17, 17n, 29
enderun, 193, 208. *See also* Palace
Enis ül-kulub (Enîs ül-ḳulûb), by Âli, 43
Erlau. *See* Egri
Erzurum: *defterdarlık* of, 311; *vilâyet*, 40, 81, 84, 115, 117n. *See also* Âli: career
eskilik. *See* seniority
Essence of History (Âli). See *Künh ül-ahbar*
ethnicity, in Ottoman Empire, 156-59, 165n, 254-58. *See also* Albanians; Bosnians; Hungarians; Iranians; Kurds; Türkmens
Etiquette of Salons (Âli). See *Kavâʾid ül-mecâlis*
Evrenos Beğ, *imaret* of, 61
examination system, Âli's proposals for, 134-35, 173
exile, internal, 51, 64

factionalism, 268; under Mehmed III, 98, 159-61, 164-66, 176; under Murad III, 71-74, 76-77, 98, 133, 160, 297, 305; under Selim II, 52-53, 72
Faṣl al-khiṭâb (Khvâjeh Muḥammad Pârsâ), 75. *See also* Âli: works
Fatḥullah ʿÂrif Çelebi. *See* ʿÂrifî
Fatih, quarter (Istanbul), 139; *medrese*, 26. See also *Sahn-ı seman*
Fatih Sultan Mehmed. *See* Mehmed II, Sultan
Fazli (Fażlî), poet and secretary to Selim II, 37, 38n, 45
Fazlullah (Fażlullâh), son of Âli, 70
Fehmi (Fehmî), poet, son of Kınalızade Ali Çelebi, 44n, 157n, 244
Fenarizade Ahmed Çelebi (Fenârîzâde Aḥmed), chancellor, treasurer to Mehmed II and Bayezid II, 215
Ferâʾid ül-vilâde (Âli), 126
Ferhad Paşa (Ferhâd), grand vezir to Murad III and Mehmed III, 143, 156, 159, 161, 164; rivalry with Sinan Paşa, 298
Ferhad Paşa (Ġâzî Ferhâd Beğ), 54, 58, 60-61, 66-67, 67n, 69. *See also* Âli: relations with individuals
Feridi (Ferîdî), poet, 299
Feridun Ahmed (Ferîdûn Aḥmed), *reʾisülküttab*, chancellor, 66, 73, 97, 196, 206, 221, 224. *See also* Âli: relations with individuals
ferman, 27, 51n
fethname: for Osman Paşa (Âli), 114n; for Sinan Paşa (Âli), 151
Feylesufzade Ahmed Çelebi (Feylesûfzâde Aḥmed), chancellor, treasurer to Bayezid II, 215
Figani (Fiġânî), poet, 106n
finance director. See *defterdar*
financial administration. See *defterdar; maliye*
Firdawsî, poet, 30, 142, 169
Firuz, Münşi Bâli Çelebi (Fîrûz Münşiʾ Bâlî), tutor and chancellor to Prince Selim II, 38n
fodla, 152n
Fountainhead of Composition (Âli). See *Menşeʾ ül-inşa*
Fünûni Sami Beğ (Fünûnî Sâmî), poet to Prince Selim II, 38n
Fursatname (Furṣatnâme), by Âli, 89
Fusul-i hall ve akd fi usul-i harc ve nakd (Fuṣûl-i ḥall ve ʿaḳd fî uṣûl-i harc ve naḳd), by Âli: compared to *Künh ül-ahbar*, 237, 293; composed, 177-79; political theory in, 302-304, 306

Gatherer of Perfections (Âli). See *Câmiʾ ül-kemâlât*
Gathering of the Seas on the Scenes of the Celebration (Âli). See *Câmiʾ ül-buhur der mecâlis-i sûr*

gaza, ideology of, 65, 274-76, 288. *See also* Âli: personality
Gazalgüveği Mustafa Beğ (Ġazalgüveği Muṣṭafâ), *sancak beği* of Egypt, 49; executed, 51
Gazanfer Ağa (Ġażanfer), *bab üs-sa 'âdet ağası:* early career of, 72; as patron of Âli, 110, 125-26, 130, 132n, 150, 168n, 170-72, 177, 180, 182-84; political alliances of, 73, 114, 169, 295. *See also* Âli: relations with individuals
gazi. See *gaza*
gedük, 156
Gedük Ahmed Paşa. *See* Ahmed Paşa, Gedük
Gelibolu (Gallipoli), provincial center, 13, 16, 16n, 17, 147. *See also* Âli: career
Gence, *defterdarlık* of, 313
Genci (Gencî), poet of Gallipoli, 16n
Georgia, Ottoman occupation of, 84
gifts, social and political function of, 62, 120-21, 152
Göğüszade Mustafa Çelebi (Göğüszâde Muṣṭafâ), *defterdar* of Şirvan, 81n
"golden age," 101, 139, 200, 263, 268; of Süleyman I, 226-27, 266. *See also* Âli: views
governor-general. See *beğlerbeği*
Göynük, 166
grand vezir. *See* vezir
Gül-i sad berg (Gül-i ṣad berg), by Âli, 148
Gülabi Beğ (Gülâbî), companion to Prince Selim II, 38n
Güllizade Mehmed Beğ (Güllizâde Meḥmed), *sancak beği* of Beyşehir, 49, 86
Gülşen üş-şu 'ara (Gülşen üş-şu ʿarâ), by Ahdi, 24n
gypsies, 156

Habeş, *vilâyet*, 181
Habib-i Hamidi (Ḥabîb-i Ḥamîdî), scholar, 21
Hacı Bayram (Ḥâcî Bayrâm), saint, 167
Hacı Bektaş (Ḥâcî Bektâş), saint, 167
Hacı İbrahim Efendi (Ḥâcî İbrâhîm), treasurer to Murad III, 97, 108
Haçova, battle of, 169
Hadim Hasan Paşa. *See* Hasan Paşa, Hadim
Ḥâfiẓ, Shîrâzî, poet, 141, 147
Hafız-ı leng (Ḥâfıẓ-ı leng), poet of Gallipoli, 23
Hâlât ül-Kahire min el-âdât iz-zâhire (Ḥâlât ül-Ḳâhire min el-ʿâdât iẓ-ẓâhire), by Âli, 179, 182-84, 203-208
halife, 17
Halveti (Halvetî), Sufi order, in Istanbul, 57. *See also* Âli: relations with individuals and groups
Hamzavi (Ḥamzavî), historian, 250
Hamze Çelebi (Ḥamze Beğ, Paşa), *re 'isülküttab*, chancellor, 91-92, 97, 117, 172, 196, 221, 224, 229n. *See also* Âli: relations with individuals
han, title, 279
hanekah, 20n
Hapsburgs, Ottoman campaigns against, 98, 150-51, 166, 297-98
harac, defined, 62
harem. *See* Palace
haric. See *medrese*
Hasan Ağa, Yemişçi (Yemişçi Ḥasan), *yeniçeri ağası*, 165n
Hasan Baba (Ḥasan Bâbâ), saint, 167
Hasan Çelebi. *See* Kınalızade Hasan
Hasan b. Ebi Nümeyy (Ḥasan), *şerif* of Mecca, 185
Hasan Paşa, Hadim (Ḫâdim Ḥasan), grand vezir to Mehmed III, 160, 168n, 175, 176
Hasan Paşa b. Sokollu Mehmed Paşa (Ḥasan), 86n, 116
Hasan Paşa, Sa'atçi (Sâʿatçi Ḥasan), governor-general of Diyar Bakır, 151
Haseki Sultan, mosque and *medrese* (Istanbul), 28
Hasht Bihisht (Bidlîsî), 239, 248
hasodabaşı, 72
hass, 83n, 181n; defined, 60
Hatemi (Ḥâtemî), poet to Prince Selim II, 37, 37n, 38n, 137n
hatib, 17, 18
Hâtifî, poet, 142
hatt-ı hümayun, 75, 119, 295
Hayali Beğ (Hayâlî), poet, 25n, 30, 31, 45
Haydar, Nakkaş. *See* Nakkaş Haydar
Hayreti (Ḥayretî), poet, 45
hazine defterdarı. See *defterdar*: provincial
Hearts' Familiar (Âli). See *Enis ül-kulub*
Heft Meclis (Âli), 58, 240
Hijaz, under Ottoman rule, 181. *See also* Âli: career
Hilyet ür-rical (Ḥilyet ür-ricâl), by Âli, 75
historiography, Ottoman, development of, 155, 238-45
Hızır (Ḥıżr), saint, 167
Hızır Paşa (Ḫıżr), governor-general of Egypt, 184
hoca, title, 13-14
hoca-ı sultani, 53, 160n
Hoca Sa'düddin. *See* Sa'düddin
Hocazade, Bokyedi Re'is (Ḫvâcezâde Po-

ḫyedi Re'îs), companion to Prince Selīm II, 38n
Hocazade Mehmed Çelebi (Ḫvâcezâde Meḥmed), chancellor and treasurer to Selim I, 215
Hodgson, Marshall, 286, 303
Holy Law. See *şeri'at*
household: imperial, 18, 20n, 172, 173; of *paşas*, 42, 83; of princes, 33-39; system, 19, 208-10, 225. *See also* Palace
Hubbi Hatun (Ḥubbî), companion to Selim II, 53
Hubbi Ömer Beğ b. Hayali (Ḥubbî ʿÖmer), 30
Hükmi (Ḥükmî), poet of Gallipoli, 16n
Hulasat ül-ahval (Hulâṣat ül-aḥvâl), by Âli, 134n
Hülegü, İlhan, 283
Hümayunname (Hümâyûnnâme), by Ali Çelebi, 43
Hünername (Hünernâme), by Seyyid Lokman, 106n
Hungarians, ethnicity of, 157. *See also* ethnicity
hünkâr, title, 279
hünkâr imamı. See *imam-ı sultanî*
Hurrem Sultan (Hurrem), wife of Süleyman I, 258-59
Ḥusayn Bâyqarâ. *See* Bâyqarâ, Sulṭân-Ḥusayn
Ḥusayn b. ʿAlî b. Abî Ṭâlib, Imam, 148
Hüseyin Beğ, Tütünsüz (Tütünsüz Ḥuseyn), *lala* to Prince Selim II, 39, 53n
Husrev Paşa (Ḫusrev), governor-general: of Baghdad, 119, 121; of Damascus, 180; of Erzurum, 107, 108n; of Van, 82n, 87

İbadi (ʿIbâdî), poet, 23
İbn Alâ (İbn ʿAlâ'), author of *Danişmendname*, 132
Ibn ʿArabshâh, historian, 250, 284
Ibn al-Athîr, historian, 240
Ibn Khaldûn, 283n, 303, 306
İbniyamin b. Ahmed (İbnyâmin Çavuş), brother of Âli, 20, 21n, 132n, 137
İbrahim (İbrâhîm), poet of Gallipoli, 16n
İbrahim Efendi, Hacı. *See* Hacı İbrahim
Ibrâhîm Khân Turkmân, Safavi ambassador, 79n, 116
İbrahim Paşa, Damad (Dâmâd İbrâhîm): governor-general of Egypt, 109, 117; grand vezir, 164-66, 169-71; vezir, 99n, 108n, 121, 133, 160. *See also* Âli: relations with individuals
İbrahim Paşa, Divane (Dîvâne İbrâhîm), brother of Canfeda Hatun, 72
İbrahim Paşa (İbrâhîm, Frenk), grand vezir to Süleyman I, 94n
icazet, 29
İdrîs-i Bidlîsî. *See* Bidlîsî
illumination, of books, 105-106, 110-12
ilmiye: as part of *askeri* class, 19-20; bureaucratization of, 267-68, 299; career, 7, 34-36, 115, 129; controlled by Sa'düddin, 72; *cursus honorum* of, 26-27; entrance to, 32-33; factionalization of, 160-61; intellectual orientation of, 100; *intisab* in, 27-29; *kalemiye*, relationship to, 227; lower echelons of, 17; seniority in, 32-33; *seyfiye*, relationship to, 195-97; subordinated to sultan, 264-67; symbolic significance of, 260-61; under Murad III, 296. *See also* Âli: views; ulema
iltizam, 62, 119-21, 125, 130; defined, 98-99
İlyas (İlyâs), saint, 167
imam, 17
imam-ı sultani, 18
Imperial Council: personnel and structure of, 47, 81, 194, 196, 203, 207, 210, 214, 217, 311; attacked by Janissaries, 133
imperial kitchen. See *matbah*
India, 172. *See also* Timûrids
information, circulation of, 107, 112n, 238
inkıraz. *See* decline
Inner Palace. See *enderun*
Inner Services. See *enderun*
inşa, 43, 113
Intimations of Truth (Âli). See *Layihat ül-hakika*
intisab, 19-20, 27-29, 209-10
Iran, 172. *See also* Safavis
Iranians, preferment of, 154-59. *See also* ethnicity
irsaliye, 104, 119, 313
İsa, Mevlana (ʿİsâ), author of *Câmi' ül-meknunat*, 247
İsfendiyaroğlu. *See* Şemsi Ahmed Paşa
Ishrâq al-tawârîkh (Qâḍî ʿAḍud al-dîn), 69. *See also* Âli: works
İskender Paşa (İskender), governor-general of Van, 97n
Islam: under Mongols, 274; in Ottoman Empire, 257-71; under Timûr, 285
Ismâʿîl II, Shâh, Safavi, 77-79
İsmail Çelebi, Taczade (Tâczâde İsmâʿîl), 85-86
İsmihan (İsmîḫân), sister of Murad III, 295

Istanbul: as educational center, 25-26, 263-64; Jewish quarter of, burns, 56-57; plague and fires in, 134. *See also* Âli: career

Jâḥiẓ, 166
Jâmî, Persian poet, 70, 169
Janissary Corps, 19, 21n, 144, 152; indiscipline of, 178; members of in trade, 161; riots, 133. See also *yeniçeri*
Jidda, *sancak*, 180, 181, 183, 184
judge. See *kadı*
Jurjânî, Sayyid Sharîf, scholar, 260
justice, in Ottoman political theory, 289-92, 302-303
Juveynî, ʿAṭâʾ Malik, historian, 240

kadı, 17; appointment and promotion of, 26, 193, 195-96, 202-204, 207, 211; corruption of, 202, 285n. See also *ilmiye*
kadıasker, 26, 32, 160, 196. See also *ilmiye*
Kadızade (Kâḍîzâde), *kadıasker* of Rumeli, 74
kâhya kadın. See *kedbanu-yi harem*
kalem: bureau, 66; slang for *timar*, 62n
kalemiye: defined, 7; expansion of, 126, 175, 214-22, 225-26; hierarchy of, 113; military ranks in, 196-97; recruitment to, 204-207, 223-24; relationship of, to other careers, 35-36, 95, 213. *See also* Âli: views and attitudes; career paths: Ottoman
Kâmi (Kâmî), *kadı* of Edirne, poet, 56, 57n
Kansuh Gavri (Qânṣûḥ Ghawrî), Mamlûk sultan, 49
kanun: career paths defined by, 92-93, 108, 113, 145, 155, 192-97, 211, 225-27; defined, 192; as dynastic ideology, 139, 165, 174, 178, 182, 282, 287; evolution of, 198-200, 212; governing *ilmiye*, 26, 32; interpretation of, 226-28; in *Künh ül-ahbar* (Âli), 169, 173; legitimation of, 218, 227-28; in *Nushat üs-selâtin* (Âli), 173; in Ottoman political theory, 290-92; as parallel to *yasa*, 284; relationship of, to *şeriʾat*, 100, 261-71. *See also* Âli: views
kanun-consciousness, 8, 102, 158. *See also* Âli: views; *kanun*
Kanuni. *See* Süleyman I, Sultan
Kanunname (Ḳânûnnâme), of Mehmed II: Âli's usue of, 174, 247; nature of, 197-200; promotion prescribed by, 192-93, 196-97, 202, 204, 211-12, 214-15, 220, 311
kapı ağaları, promotion of, 193
kapıcı, 86
kapıkulu. See *bölük halkı*
Kara Ahmed Paşa. *See* Ahmed Paşa, Kara
Kara Üveys Çelebi. *See* Üveys Paşa
Karakoyunlu, 273
Karaman, *vilâyet*, 163
Karamani Mehmed Efendi. *See* Mehmed Efendi, Karamani
Kars, reconstruction of fortress, 84
Kasımi (Ḳâsımî), poet to Prince Selim II, 38n
Kasım Paşa, quarter (Istanbul), 29
Kassabzade-yi Nabi (Ḳaṣṣâbzâde-yi Nâbî), companion to Prince Selim II, 38n
Kâtib Çelebi, *nasihat* author, 102
Kâtibî, poet, 142
Kavâʾid ül-mecâlis (Ḳavâʿid ül-mecâlis), by Âli, 127-28
kaza, 26, 62
kedbanu-yi harem, 72
Kemalpaşazade (Kemâlpaşazâde), historian, 239, 248
kenar defterdarı. See *defterdar*: provincial
Kerbela, Âli's foundation in, 124
Khudâbandeh, Shâh Muḥammad, Safavi, 79, 84
Khusraw-i Dihlavî (*Maṭlaʿ al-anvâr*), 37
Khvâjeh Muḥammad Pârsâ (*Faṣl al-khiṭâb*), 75
Khvândamîr, historian, 250
Kınalızade Ali Çelebi (Ḳınalızâde ʿAlî), *kadı* and *ahlak* author, 56, 227, 262; *Ahlak-ı Alaʾi* of, 100-101, 280n; compared to Ṭûsî, 292n; in Damascus, mentor to Âli, 43; on duties of sovereign, 302; on Ottoman legitimacy, 291. *See also* Âli: relations with individuals
Kınalızade Hasan Çelebi b. Ali Çelebi (Ḳınalızâde Ḥasan), author of *Tezkeret üş-şuʾara*, 43-44, 116, 251. *See also* Âli: relations with individuals
Kırk hadis (Ḳırḳ ḥadîs̱), by Âli, 171
Kırşehir, *sancak*, 163
Kitab-i müstetab (*Kitâb-i müsteṭâb*), 102, 156
Kitâb al-tâj (Jâḥiẓ), 166
Kızıl Ahmedlü. *See* Şemsi Ahmed Paşa
Kızılbaş, 77-79, 82, 84, 157
Klis, *sancak*, 58, 60n. *See also* Âli: career
Koca Sinan. *See* Sinan Paşa
Koçi Beğ (Ḳoçî), *nasihat* author, 102
Konya, *sancak* seat of Prince Selim II, 34. *See also* Âli: career
Korkud, Prince (Şehzâde Ḳorḳud b. Sulṭân Bâyezîd), 266-68, 290n
Köse Mustafa (Muṣṭafâ), steward of Lala

Mustafa Paşa, 42, 49, 118n
Küçük Sinan Beğ (Sinân), *sancak beği* of Egypt, 223
kul, 6, 15, 15n, 16, 19, 21n, 33, 83, 115, 155, 193-95, 208-209, 223, 225, 255-56, 300; *müşterâ*, 14. See also *askeri; devşirme*; household
Künh ül-ahbar (Künh ül-ahbâr), by Âli: begun, 140-41; conceptual structure of, 278, 293, 300-306; dating of, 173n, 245; dedication of, 165n, 169, 236; didactic purpose of, 242-47, 301-305; *Fusul-i hall ve akd fi usul-i harc ve nakd*, compared to, 237, 278n; introduction to, 148; *kanun*, as exposition of, 173, 229; Murad III's reign, summarized in, 293-300; organizational innovations in, 237; preoccupation of Âli with, 140-43, 153, 176-77, 181; sources of, 41, 44, 80, 174, 247-52; status in Ottoman letters of, 7-8; structure of, 245-47; style of, 235-37, 246; *Tarih* of Selâniki, compared to, 130-31
Kunt, İ. Metin, 195, 209
Kurd Beğ b. Divane Husrev Paşa (Ḳurd), companion to Prince Selim II, 38n
Kurd Paşa (Ḳurd), governor-general of Egypt, 157n
Kurds, 119, 124, 154, 156-57. *See also* ethnicity
Kütahya, *sancak* seat of Prince Selim II, 34, 37-39
Kuyruklu Yıldız Mehmed Beğ. *See* Mehmed Beğ, Kuyruklu Yıldız

Lahsa, *defterdarlık* of, 313
lala, 33, 39
Lala Mustafa Paşa (Lala Muṣṭafâ), 87; appointed field marshal (Cyprus expedition) 55, (Şirvan campaign) 76, 79-85, (Yemen campaign) 47-50; appointed governor-general (Aleppo) 40, (Damascus) 40, 42, (Erzurum) 40; appointed vezir (second) 85-88, (third) 76, (sixth) 53; character of, assessed by Âli, 89n; death of, 88-89; dismissed (Şirvan campaign) 85, (Yemen campaign) 50-52; endowments of, in Erzurum, 40n; family of, *see* Kurd Beğ b. Divane Husrev Paşa; Mehmed Beğ b. Lala Mustafa Paşa; Mehmed Paşa; political alliances of, (Özdemiroğlu Osman Paşa) 107, (Palace) 73, (Mehmed Paşa, Sokollu) 47-48, 50, 53, 57, 76, 79, (Sinan Paşa, rivalry with) 48-50, 79, 85, 87; Prince Selim II, *lala* to, 39; protégés, (corruption of) 85-86, (purged) 88; related to Sokollu Mehmed Paşa, 46; seeks grand vezirate, 46, 87; as source for Âli's history, 44; steward of, 118n; war of princes Selim and Bayezid, role in, 48. *See also* Âli: relations with individuals; Âli: views
Lalezar Mehmed. *See* Mehmed Çelebi, Lalezar
Lalezarzade. *See* Ahmed Çelebi, Lalezarzade
Lam Ali Çelebi (Lâm ʿAlî), chancellor to Mehmed III, 172-73, 224
Lari, Muslihüddin (Muṣliḥüddîn Lârî), historian, 158, 241, 250
Latifi (Laṭîfî), poet, anthologist, 23, 251
law. See *kanun; örf; şeriʾat; yasa*
Lawgiver, the. *See* Süleyman I, Sultan
Layihat ül-hakika (Lâyiḥât ül-ḥaḳîḳa), by Âli: discovered, 13n; begun, 90; completed, 138-39
literacy. *See* education
Lokman, Seyyid. *See* Seyyid Lokman
Lustre of a Hundred Jewels (Âli). See *Sadef-i sad güher*
Lutfi Beğzade (Luṭfî Beğzâde), *kadı* of Edirne, 128n
Lutfi Paşa (Luṭfî), grand vezir to Süleyman I, 165n, 271; *Âsafname* of, 100-101; *Tevarih-i Âl-i Osman* of, 240, 250

maʾcun, 143
Mahâsin ül-âdâb (Maḥâsin ül-âdâb), by Âli: composed, 166; dedicated, 170
mahlas, 24
Mahmud Çelebi (Maḥmûd), of Salonika, 63
Mahmud Efendi (Maḥmûd), treasurer to Murad III, 133
Mahmud Efendi, Muʾallimzade. *See* Muʾallimzade Mahmud Efendi
Mahmud Paşa (Maḥmûd), vezir to Mehmed II, 178, 240; as patron, 299
Majmaʿ al-baḥreyn (Âli), 141-42
Makali-yi sani (Maḳâlî-yi ṣânî), poet to Prince Selim II, 38n
mal defterdarı. See *defterdar*: provincial
maliye: ethnicity in, 159n; expansion and professionalization of, 214-22, 225-26; structure of, 82-83, 311-14. *See also* Âli: views
Malkoç Beğ (Malḳoç), *sancak beği* of Bosnia, 65
Maqṣûd Khân, Safavi governor of Tabriz, 90n

Ma'ruf Efendi (Maʿrûf), tutor to Sinan Paşa, 146
matbah, 146
Maṭlaʿ al-anvâr (Khusraw-i Dihlavî), 37
Matrakçı Nasuh (Maṭraḳçı Naṣûḥ), 240
Mecca, under Ottoman rule, 185, 277. *See also* Âli: career
Mecdi (Mecdî), poet, 137n
meclis (pl. *mecâlis*), 22, 127
mecmu'a, 107
Medhi (Medḥî), poet of Gallipoli, 16n
Medical Analogy, 244, 303
medrese, 6-7, 17, 100; hierarchy of institutions, 21, 24-29, 32, 263-64; significance of, for *kalemiye* service, 36, 94-95, 175, 217-19, 221, 225. *See also* education; *ilmiye*; *müderris*
Mehmed, brother of Âli. *See* Mehmed b. Ahmed
Mehmed II, Sultan, Conquer (Sulṭân Meḥmed b. Sulṭân Murâd, Fâtiḥ): bureaucracy of, 215-16; as imperial founder and universal ruler, 141, 199, 271, 288; *Kanunname* of, 197-200; as patron, 299; as patron of religion, 139, 186, 260, 263-64; symbolic significance of, 153, 174, 178. *See also* Âli: views
Mehmed III, Sultan (Sulṭân Meḥmed b. Sulṭân Murâd): accession of, 151-53; cultural orientation of, 179-80, 268; Egri campaign, leads, 166; exhorted by Âli, 303; influenced by mother, 177; as prince, 55, 91, 109, 106-107. *See also* Âli: relations with individuals; factionalism
Mehmed Ağa (Meḥmed), *yeniçeri ağası*, 165n
Mehmed Beğ b. Lala Mustafa Paşa (Meḥmed), 49
Mehmed Beğ, Kuyruklu Yıldız (Ḳuyruḳlı Yıldız Meḥmed), *sancak beği* of Egypt, 49; executed, 51
Mehmed Çelebi, Lalezar (Lâlezâr Meḥmed), treasurer to Selim II and Murad III, 73, 85, 86n, 97
Mehmed Efendi, Karamani (Ḳaramânî Meḥmed), scholar, 149
Mehmed Giray Han (Meḥmed Girây), Crimean han, 84, 114
Mehmed b. Ahmed (Meḥmed), brother of Âli, 20, 20n, 21, 44, 137
Mehmed Paşa, Boyalı (Boyalı Meḥmed, Ḳara Nişâncı), chancellor to Murad III, 91, 97, 219n, 221
Mehmed Paşa, Cerrah. *See* Cerrah Mehmed Paşa
Mehmed Paşa, Doğancı (Doğancı Meḥmed), vezir and companion to Murad III, 118, 125-27, 133, 184, 295. *See also* Âli: relations with individuals
Mehmed Paşa (Meḥmed), relative of Lala Mustafa Paşa, governor-general of Erzurum, 88n
Mehmed Paşa b. Sinan Paşa (Meḥmed), governor-general of Rumeli, 137n, 151, 164
Mehmed Paşa, Şerif. *See* Şerif Mehmed Paşa
Mehmed Paşa, Sokollu (Ṣoḳollı Meḥmed): controls appointments, 55-56; death of, 85, 89; *devşirme* utilized by, 46; dismisses Derviş Çelebi, 18; family of, 46, 58 (*see also* Hasan Paşa b. Sokollu Mehmed; Mustafa Paşa, Sokollu); Lala Mustafa Paşa, relationship with, 47-48, 50, 53; Murad III, companions of, oppose, 71-74; nepotism of, 86, 165n, 259; Özdemiroğlu Osman Paşa, relationship with, 51; *pir* of, 57; political troubles of, 295-97; rivalries of, 71-74, 76, 79, 97; Selim II, courtiers of, oppose, 52-53; Selim II, Sokollu intimidates, 56. *See also* Âli: relations with individuals
Mehmed, Prince (Şehzâde Meḥmed b. Sulṭân Süleymân), tomb and mosque of, Istanbul. *See* Şehzade Cami'i
Mehmed Paşa, Ramazanzade. *See* Ramazanzade Mehmed Paşa
mekteb, 21, 223
Melami (Melâmî), Sufis, 136, 166-67
Men of Learning. See *ilmiye*
Men of the Pen. See *kalemiye*
Men of the Sword. See *seyfiye*
Menakıb-ı hünerveran (Menâḳıb-ı hünerverân), by Âli, 105, 127; sources of, 123
Menşe' ül-inşa (Menşe' ül-inşâ'), by Âli, 129
Merdi (Merdî), poet to Prince Selim (II), 38n
meritocracy. *See* Âli: views
Meşa'ir üş-şu'ara (Meşâʿir üş-şuʿarâ), by Âşık Çelebi, 63, 251
Mesihi (Mesîḥî), poet, 45
Mevâ'id ün-nefâ'is fi kavâ'id il-mecâlis (Mevâ'id ün-nefâ'is fî ḳavâʿid il-mecâlis), by Âli: composed, 181-82, 184-86; on kalemiye, 204-205, 227; on sovereignty, 303; style of, 179
mevleviyet, 114, 129
Mezőkeresztes. *See* Haçova
Mihr u mah (Mihr u mâh), by Âli, 22n, 34

Mihr u vefa (Mihr u vefâ), by Âli, 39; presented to Prince Murad III, 54
Mihr u vefa (Mihr u vefâ), by Mustafa Çelebi, 39
mıklacı, 207
military judge. See *kadıasker*
millennium: approach of, 103n, 134-35; significance of, 178, 138, 244-45; signs of, 112, 126. *See also* Âli: personality
Mîr ʿAlî Shîr. *See* Navâʾî
mirahor, 37, 57
Mirʾat ül-avâlim (Mirʾât ül-ʿavâlim), by Âli, 126
Mirek Çelebi (Mîrek), companion to Prince Selim II, 38n
miri, 104
Mirkat ül-cihad (Mirḳât ül-cihâd), by Âli, 132-33
Mîrkhvând, historian, 240
Mirror of the Worlds (Âli). See *Mir'at ül-avâlim*
mirrors for princes, 99-100, 166
Mirza-Ali Beğ (Mîrzâ-ʿAlî), *sancak beği* of Pasin, 86
Misali (Mis̱âlî), poet, 137n
Moldavis, revolt of, 298
Mongols: influence of, on Ottomans, 276-79; political legacy of, 273-75, 286-87. *See also* Cengiz Han
Mönke, grand han, 284
Mosul, *sancak*, 119, 124
Mu'allimzade Mahmud Efendi (Muʿallimzâde Maḥmûd), chancellor to Murad III, 218, 295-96
Muʿâwiya, Umayyad caliph, 283
Mücmil üt-tûmâr (Mücmil üt-ṭûmâr), by Seyyid Lokman, 105
Müdami (Müdâmî), poet of Gallipoli, 16n
müderris, 17, 18n, 26; promotion to chancellorship of, 193. See also *ilmiye; medrese*
müʾeyyed min ınd Allah, title, 279, 281
müfti. See *şeyhülislam*
Mughals. *See* Tîmûrids
muhafaza beğleri, 203, 207
Muḥammad Khudâbandeh. *See* Khudâbandeh
Muḥammad Raḥîm-i Mashhadî, calligrapher, 123n
Muḥammad Riżâ Tabrîzî, calligrapher, 123n
Muhibbi (Muḥibbî), poet, 31
mühimme, 98, 104
Muḥtasham-i Kâshânî, poet, 142
Muhyi Çelebi (ʿAbdülmuḥyî Paşa), *Anadolu defterdarı* and chancellor to Murad III, 97, 196, 221, 296
mujaddid, 281n
mukataʾa, 116n, 224n
mülâzemet, 26, 32-34, 36-37; abuses of, 160n
mülâzim. See *mülâzemet*
mültezim. See *iltizam*
münşeʾat, 107, 129
Murad III, Sultan (Sulṭân Murâd b. Sulṭân Selim): accepts bribes, 70-71, 259, 295, 296; accession of, 67-68; chancellors of, 196; companions of, 71-74; cultural orientation of, 268; eastern problem, causes, 154-59; illness and death of, 151-52, 298; as patron, 18, 105, 109, 127, 144-45, 184, 231, 299; as prince at Manisa, 37, 54-55; reign evaluated by Âli, 96, 153, 205; Şeyh Şücaʾ, devotion to, 296; Sufism, interest in, 75, 103, 111-13, 126; symbolic significance of, 277, 300-301; vezirs, dismisses, 133. *See also* Âli: relations with individuals; Âli: views; factionalism
müşâhere-horan, 218n
musahib, 38, 135; duties of, 74, 75n, 159n. *See also* Murad III: companions of; Selim II: companions of
Muslihüddin, Lari. *See* Lari
Muslihüddin, Nurüddinzade. *See* Nurüddinzade
Muslihüddin Mustafa. *See* Şeyh Muslihüddin Mustafa
Mustafa Çavuş (Muṣṭafâ), prisoner of Hapsburgs, 298
Mustafa Çelebi (Muṣṭafâ), author of *Mihr u vefa*, 39
Mustafa Çelebi, Tanbur-nevaz Şeyhzade, Adanalı (Ṭanbûr-nevâz Şeyhzâde Muṣṭafâ), companion to Prince Selim II, 38n
Mustafa b. Abdülcelil (Muṣṭafâ b. ʿAbdücelîl), calligrapher, 110n
Mustafa Paşa, Lala. *See* Lala Mustafa Paşa
Mustafa Paşa, Sokollu (Soḳollı Muṣṭafâ), governor-general of Budin, 66, 73. *See also* Âli: relations with individuals
Mustafa, Prince (Şehzâde Muṣṭafâ b. Sulṭân Süleymân), 222, 258-59; execution of, 63
müstaʾidd, 27n, 29, 31-32
Mustaʿṣim, Abbasid caliph, 283-84
müteferrika, 36, 36n, 194. See also bölük halkı

Nadir ül-maharib (*Nâdir ül-maḥârib*), by Âli, 22n, 44, 141, 240; completed, 54; style of, 179, 235-36

Nahj al-maslûk fî siyâsat al-mulûk (ʿAbd al-raḥmân al-Shayzarî), 95n
Na'ima (Naʿîmâ), historian, 102, 238
Nakkaş Haydar (Naḳḳâş Ḥaydar, Nigârî), companion to Prince Selim II, 38n
Nakşbendi (Naḳşbendî), Sufi order, in Istanbul, 17, 29, 57, 132n. *See also* Âli: relations with individuals and groups
narcotics, 28. See also *ma'cun*
Nasi, Josef, duke of Naxos, 296
nasihatname, 8, 101, 102, 156, 226. *See also* "golden age"; *Nushat üs-selâtin*
Naṣîr al-dîn Ṭûsî. *See* Ṭûsî, Naṣîr al-dîn
Nasuh Ağa (Naṣûḥ), eunuch, 108
Navâ'î, Mîr ʿAlî Shîr, scholar, poet, 70, 169, 186
Necati (Necâtî), poet, 45
Nef'i (Nefʿî), poet, 141
nepotism. *See* Âli: views; Mehmed Paşa, Sokollu
Neşri (Neşrî), historian, 235, 238, 247
Nevâdir ül-hikem (Nevâdir ül-ḥikem), by Âli, 129n, 131, 134, 141
Nevbaharzade (Nevbahârzâde), *şıkk-ı sani defterdarı*, 219
Nev'i (Nevʿî), scholar and poet, 137n, 142, 149-50, 149n, 153
nezaret, 103, 120, 162n, 313
nezaret-i emval, 311-12
Nigâri. *See* Nakkaş Haydar
Niğde, *sancak*, 163
Nihani. *See* Turak Çelebi
nişancı, nişancılık. *See* chancellor
Niẓâm al-dîn Shâmî. *See* Shâmî, Niẓâm al-dîn
Nogays, 115
Nükat ül-kal fi tazmin il-makal (Nükât ül-ḳâl fî tażmîn il-maḳâl), by Âli, 111
numerology, 112, 152
Nurbanu (Nûrbânû), mother of Murad III, 72-73, 295
Nurüddinzade Muslihüddin (Nûrüddînzâde Muşliḥüddîn), Halveti sheikh, 57-58
Nushat üs-selâtin (Nuṣḥat üs-selâṭîn), by Âli: analyzed, 96-103; on careers, 202-203, 206; composed, 95-99; dates in, 58n; presented to Murad III, 129; prototypes of, 99-101; significance of, 8, 101-103, 228, 238, 293; veracity of, 103-105
Nusretname (Nuṣretnâme), by Âli: completed, 89; illumination of, 105; imperial edition of, 110-11; style of, 235, 240
Nutki (Nuṭḳî), *şehnameci*, 239n, 249

Oğuz, ideology of, 273-76, 278-79, 288n
Okçuzade Mehmed Paşa (Oḳçızâde Meḥmed), treasurer to Murad III, 82n, 97-98, 107n, 108, 296
Okçuzade Şah Mehmed Efendi (Oḳçızâde Şâh Meḥmed), chancellor to Mehmed III, 97-98
Ömer Beğ (ʿÖmer), *sancak beği* of Trabzon, 87
örf, 292; in Ottoman Empire, 260-67. See also *kanun*
Osman (ʿOs̱mân), court translator in Aleppo, 99n, 104
Osman (ʿOs̱mân Ġâzî): as *mujaddid*, 281n; as Ottoman eponym, 5, 281
Osman Paşa, Özdemiroğlu (Özdemüroğlı ʿOs̱mân): appointed governor-general, (of Ṣanʿâ) 49, (of Şirvan) 81, 107; appointed grand vezir, 114, 121; besieged in Derbend, 84; campaigns of, (Tabriz) 115-17, (Yemen) 50-51; death of, 118; as patron of Âli, 51, 81, 107, 107n, 115, 119, 129; Sokollu Mehmed Paşa expels, 51. *See also* Âli: relations with individuals
Osmanlı. *See* Ottoman
Osmanşah Beğ (ʿOs̱mânşâh), *sancak beği* of Bosnia, 66n
Ottoman dynasty: ideological experimentation of, 274-76, 286-89; origins of, 5, 278; succession practice of, 33-34, 152. *See also* Âli: views
Ottoman Empire: education in *see* education; historiography in, 105, 242-44, 247; origins and evolution of, 254-57, 298-99; political theory in, 289-92, 302-303 (*see also* justice; sovereign); relations: in Caucasus, 76-77, with Hapsburgs, 98, 150-51, 166, 297-98, with Safavis, 76-79, 98, 115-16; social structure of, 5-7. *See also* Âli: personality; Âli: views
Ottoman Turkish (language). *See* Turkish
Outer Palace. See *birun*
Outer Services. See *birun*
Outside Services. See *birun*
oymak. *See* Kızılbaş
Özbeks, 275-77, 279, 290
Özdemiroğlu Osman Paşa. *See* Osman Paşa, Özdemiroğlu

padişah, title, 279
Palace: cavalry (see *bölük halkı*); class, 95, 196-97, 208-213; education, *see* education: Palace; harem, influence of, 159, 176-77, 282, 295, 299; service, importance of, 208-10; slaves, in *kalemiye*, 204-205. See also *birun; enderun*; fac-

tionalism; household; *kul*
Path of Learning. See *ilmiye*
Path of Scribal Service. See *kalemiye*
patronage, literary and scholarly, 30, 67, 126, 137-38, 162, 170-71, 182, 186, 231, 260, 264. See also *intisab*
pâye, 196
Peace of Amasya. *See* Amasya, Peace of
Peçevi İbrahim Paşa (Peçuyî İbrâhîm), historian, 54, 54n, 144; style of, 236
Perfect Man, 291
Persian (language), 21-22; at Ottoman court, 30, 155, 239
pir, 20n, 57
Piri Paşa (Pîrî), vezir of Selim I, 206-207
Piri Paşa, Ramazanoğlu (Ramażânoğlı Pîrî), heriditary *sancak beği* of Adana, 41
pişkeş, 120-21
poetry, in Ottoman society, 22-24, 30, 37-39
post-nişin, title, 17n, 20n
professionalization, of bureaucracy. See *kalemiye; maliye*
provincial government: administration of, 59-60, 82-83, 210, 312-14; hierarchy of, 226, 313; in wartime, 118-23, 162-63. See also *beğlerbeği; defterdar; hass; sancak; timar; vilâyet*

Qara Valî Beg, Ûstâjlû, Safavi ambassador, 79n
Qâsim ʿAlî Tabrîzî, calligrapher, 123n
Queen Mother. See *valide sultan*

Raab, fortress of, 150
Rahat ün-nüfus (Râḥat ün-nüfûs), by Âli, 55
Rahmi (Raḥmî), poet, 142
Ramazanoğlu, Piri Paşa. *See* Piri Paşa
Ramazanzade Mehmed Paşa (Ramażânzâde Meḥmed, Küçük Nişâncı), chancellor to Süleyman I, 30-31, 36, 94, 204, 215, 217; as historian, 240-42
Rarity of Warriors (Âli). See *Nadir ül-maharib*
Rashîd al-dîn, historian, 240
Raziye Hatun (Rażîye), companion to Murad III, 72
re'âyâ, 5-7, 15, 18-20; infiltrate *askeri*, 156-59
regional empires, Muslim, 275, 277-79, 287-88. *See also* Ottoman Empire; Özbeks; Safavis; Tîmûrids
registrar, of Imperial Council. See *defter emini*
re'isülküttab: duties of, 113, 214, 214n; at princely court, 37; promotion of, 193, 220, 228, 312. See also *kalemiye*
retirement, from government service, 139, 153
rical ül-gayb, 168
rind-meşreb, 23
Risâleh-i Bâbîyeh (Yûsuf Sinân al-dîn), 80n
Riyaz üs-salikin (Riyâż üs-sâlikîn), by Âli, 42, 135
Röhrborn, Klaus, 201, 220, 221
Ruhi (Rûḥî), poet, 31, 123
Ruhi (Rûḥî), historian, 247
Rujûʿ al-shaykh ilâ şahâh (Tifâshî), 55. *See also* Âli: works
Rum (Ottoman dominions): as cultural zone, 24, 142n, 158; Islam in, 254-60; *sipahis* of, 156-57. *See also* Âli: views
Rum (Sivas), *vilâyet, defterdarlık* of, 157-58, 162, 226, 312-13. *See also* Âli: career; *defterdar*
Rumeli defterdarı. See *defterdar*
Rümuzi (Rümûzî), poet, 31
Rüstem Paşa, grand vezir to Süleyman I, 39, 64, 94n, 222, 258-59; chronicle of, 240; mosque and medrese of (Istanbul), 28-29
rüşvet. *See* bribery
rütbe, 196
ru'us, 98, 104
ruznamçe-i hümayun, 32

Sa'atçi Hasan Paşa. *See* Hasan Paşa, Sa'atçi
Sadef-i sad güher (Ṣadef-i ṣad güher), by Âli, 13, 147-48
Sa'düddin, Hoca Efendi (Ḫvâce Saʿdüddîn), tutor to Murad III and Mehmed III: Âli seeks favor from, 74, 92, 108-109, 125; appointed *şeyhülislam*, 176; Bustanzade, rivalry with, 159-61, 299; controls *ilmiye*, 72; death of, 184; as historian, 236, 241, 248; opposes Sokollu Mehmed Paşa, 72, 297; as patron of Âli, 126-27, 150-51; peers of, 149-50; political allies of, 169, 177, 180, 295; role in campaigns, (Egri) 166, (Şirvan) 76, 87. *See also* Âli: relations with individuals
Safavis: dynasty, 277-79, 287; ideology of, 274-75, 290; relations of, with the Ottomans, 76-79, 98, 115-16. *See also* regional empires
Safi (Ṣâfî), author of *Cihadname*, 90n
Safi, Mustafa (Muṣṭafâ Ṣâfî), 90n
Safiye Hatun (Ṣafîye), mother of Mehmed III, 176-77, 294
Sahib Giray Han (Ṣâḥib Girây), Crimean han, 52n
sahib-i zuhur, title, 281

sahib-kıran, title, 279-80, 281, 283, 285
Sahn-ı seman, 26-27, 29, 32, 34
Sâ'i (Sâʿî), poet, 137n
Saints' Rosary (Âli). See *Sübhat ül-ebdal*
Salmân-i Sâvajî, poet, 142
salyane, 114n, 181n, 313
Şamhal, ruler of Dağıstan, 78n; as source for *Künh ül-ahbar*, 80
Sâmî Şeyhzade Mehmed Çelebi (Sâmî Şeyhzâde Meḥmed), companion to Prince Selim II, 38n
Ṣanʿâ, capital of Yemen, 47
sancak; defined, 33-34. *See also* provincial government; *sancak beği*
sancak beği: appointment of, 119, 162-63, 172, 192-93; defined, 60, 279; of Egypt, 203, 207. *See also* provincial government; *sancak*
Şani (Şânî), poet, 64
Sarı Rami (Ṣaru Râmî), poet to Prince Selim II, 38n
Seasons of Sovereignty on the Principles of Critical Expenditure (Âli). See *Fusul-i hall ve akd fi usul-i harc ve nakd*
Şecâ'atname (Şecâʿatnâme), by Âsafi, 82
Second Branch. See *defterdar: şıkk-ı sani*
secretariat. See *re'isülküttab*
secretary-in-chief. See *re'isülküttab*
Seekers' Bower (Âli). See *Riyaz üs-sâlikin*
Sehi (Sehî), anthologist, 251
şehir oğlanı, 223
şehnameci, 30, 105, 155, 239-40, 248-49, 298-99
şehnamegûy. See *şehnameci*
Şehzade Cami'i (Istanbul), 18, 25
Selâniki, Mustafa (Muṣṭafâ Selânîkî), historian, 98, 155, 244; compared to Âli, 160n, 130-31; style of, 236; views on *kanun* of, 102, 200, 226. *See also* Âli: relations with individuals
Selim I. Sultan (Sulṭân Selîm b. Sultân Bâyezîd): bureaucracy of, 206, 215-17; conquests of, 52n, 199, 311; cultural orientation of, 268; symbolic significance of, 139, 153; as universal ruler, 280, 288. *See also* Âli: views
Selim II, Sultan (Sulṭân Selîm b. Sulṭân Süleyman): accession of, 46; chancellors of, 196; companions of, 38n, 52-53; death of, 67; decline, role in Ottoman, 259; Lala Mustafa Paşa, relations with, 48, 53, 56; Kütahya, princely court at, 33-40, 94; as patron, 38, 40, 142n, 231, 299, 304-305; war with brother Bayezid, 34, 48, 78. *See also* Âli: relations with individuals; Âli: views; factionalism
Selimname (*Selîmnâme*), by Şükri, 251
Semiz Ahmed Paşa. *See* Ahmed Paşà, Semiz
Şemsi Ahmed Paşa (Ḳızıl Aḥmedlü Şemsî Aḥmed, İsfendiyâroğlı), companion to Selim II and Murad III, 56, 74-75; bribes Murad III, 259, 296; opposes Sokollu Mehmed Paşa, 71-75, 295, 297. *See also* Âli: relations with individuals
Şemsi Efendi (Şemsî), tutor to Selim II, 53
Şemsüddin Ahmed b. Ebüssu'ud (Şemsüddin Aḥmed), scholar, 28-29
seniority, 92, 114-15, 125, 131, 162, 173, 206, 219
serdar, 47, 118
Şeref Han, Bidlisi (Şeref Ḫân Bidlîsî), 82n
şeri'at: under Mongol rule, 274, 280; in Ottoman Empire, 28, 260-67, 285; relationship to *kanun*, 174, 192, 227, 261-71, 289-92; as revealed law, 291; universality of, 93, 220, 273. *See also* Âli: views; *şeyhülislam*
şerif, of Mecca, 185, 277
Şerif Mehmed Paşa (Şerîf Meḥmed), treasurer, governor-general of Egypt, 97, 157, 157n
Seven Scenes (Âli). See *Heft Meclis*
sexual mores, 63, 127, 256n
seyfiye: defined, 7, 194; relationship to *ilmiye* and *kalemiye*, 195-97. *See also* career paths: Ottoman
şeyh, title, 20n
Şeyh Abdürrahman (Şeyḫ ʿAbdürraḥmân), saint, 167
Şeyh Bali Efendi. *See* Bali Efendi
Şeyh Husrev (Ḫusrev), Bektaşi sheikh, 92
Şeyh Muslihüddin Mustafa (Muṣliḥüddîn Musṭafâ), Nakşbendi sheikh, greatgrandfather of Âli, 17, 20, 29, 57
Şeyh Parmak (Şeyḫ Parmaḳ), saint, 167
Şeyh Ramazan (Şeyḫ Ramażân), Haveti sheikh, 57
Şeyh Şüca' (Şeyḫ Şücâʿüddîn), *pir* of Murad III, 72, 74-75, 296; opposes Sokollu Mehmed Paşa, 297. *See also* Âli: relations with individuals; Murad III
Şeyh Şüca'üddin. *See* Şeyh Şüca'
Şeyhi Efendi (Şeyḫî), *şeyhülislam*, 128n
şeyhülislam authority of, 160n; compared to chancellor, 93, 95, 218; defined, 26, 28. See also *şeri'at*
Seyyid Ahmed Buhari (Seyyid Aḥmed Buḫârî), Nakşbendi sheikh, 17
Seyyid Lokman (Seyyid Loḳmân), *şehnameci*, 105, 105n, 155, 239, 239n, 249, 249n

shâh, title, 279
Shâh ʿAbbâs, Safavi. *See* ʿAbbâs
Shâh Ṭahmâsb, Safavi. *See* Ṭahmâsb
Shâmî, Niẓâm al-dîn, historian, 250
Sharaf al-dîn Shîrvânî, scholar, 142
Sharaf al-dîn Yazdî, historian, 250
Shaykh Muṭahhar, Zaydî Shiʾi imam, 47
Shayzarî, ʿAbd al-raḥmân (*Nahj al-maslûk fî siyâsat al-mulûk*), 95n
Shiʾi, 77, 157
Shîrvânî, Sharaf al-din. *See* Sharaf al-dîn Shîrvânî
shrines, visitation of, 136
Sıdkî (Şıdḳî), poet of Gallipoli, 16n
Sigetvar, campaign of, 58
Şihabi (Şihâbî), poet, 250
şıkk-ı salis. See *defterdar*
şıkk-ı sani. See *defterdar*
Sinan, Cübni (Cübnî Sinân), finance director of Aleppo, 109
Sinan Efendi (Sinân), *şıkk-ı sani defterdarı* to Murad III, 296
Sinan Halife (Sinân Ḫalîfe), grammarian of Gallipoli, 21
Sinan Paşa. *See* Cağaloğlu Sinan Paşa
Sinan Paşa, Koca (Ḳoca Sinân): Ali's complaints about, 135; appointed field marshal, (Şirvan campaign) 85, (Yemen campaign) 50; appointed governor-general, (Aleppo) 48, (Egypt) 48-51; appointed to grand vezirate, (first) 87, (second) 133, (third) 146, (fourth and fifth) 297-98; appointed seventh vezir of the Dome, 54n; Austrian campaign of, 150-51, 297-98; character and ethnicity of, 164; contest with Lala Mustafa Paşa, 49-51; death of, 163-65; dismissed, (first grand vezirate) 108, (Şirvan campaign) 79, (third grand vezirate) 159; in the east, 89; family of, *see* Ahmed Beğ, Ayas Paşa, Mehmed Paşa b. Sinan Paşa; Gazanfer Ağa, relations with, 150; Hoca Saʾdüddin, relations with, 150; as patron, 137, 157n, 300; rivalries of, 160; tutor of, 146. *See also* Âli: relations with individuals; Âli: views
sipahi, 6, 19, 178, 181n; defined, 59. *See also* Rum (Ottoman dominions); *timar*
Sirri (Sirrî), poet, 31, 116
Şirvan: campaign, 76-85; culutural prestige of, 155; *defterdarlık* of, 313; Ottoman administration of, 81; Ottoman occupation of threatened, 84
Şirvanşah, dynasty, 78n. *See also* Abûbakr Mîrzâ; Burhân ʿAlî
Sivas. *See* Rum: *vilâyet*
Siyavuş Paşa (Siyâvuş), grand vezir to Murad III: governor-general of Rumeli, 53n; grand vezirate, first, 108, 114, 133; grand vezirate, second, 143-44; *yeniçeri ağası*, 57
slave. See *kul, devşirme*
Sokollu Hasan Paşa. *See* Hasan Paşa, Sokollu
Sokollu Mehmed Paşa. *See* Mehmed Paşa, Sokollu
Sokollu Mustafa Paşa. *See* Mustafa Paşa, Sokollu
sovereign: duties of, 290-92; as microcosm, 303-304; typology of, 279-87; universal, 273-75. *See also* Âli: views; Circle of Equity; Justice; Medical Analogy; Ottoman Empire
Sübhat ül-ebdal (Sübḥat ül-ebdâl), by Âli, 148
Subtleties of Discourse on the Quotation of Speech (Âli). See *Nükat ül-kal fi tazmin il-makal*
Şücaʾüddin. *See* Şeyh Şücaʾ
Sufi orders. See *tarikat*
Sührab (Sührâb), *sancak beği* of Derteng, 119, 121, 124, 210
Şükri (Şükrî), author of *Selimname*, 251
Şükrullah (Şükrullâh), author of *Bahjat al-tavârîkh*, 240, 250, 255
Süleyman (Süleymân), finance director of Baghdad, 121-22
Süleyman I, Sultan, Lawgiver (Sulṭân Süleymân b. Sulṭân Selîm, Ḳânûnî): appoints Derviş Çelebi imam, 18; bureaucracy of, 214, 218-19; court and patronage of, 30, 33, 231, 239; death of, at Sigetvar, 46-47; defines *ecnebi*, 158n; generation of, 89; "golden age" of, 101, 226-27, 266; idealized by Âli, 153; as Lawgiver, 199, 262, 288, 291; Prince Mustafa, executes, 258-59; promotion policy of, 173; rebuffs Âli, 39; symbolic significance of, 174; as universal ruler, 288; vezirs of, 150; war between sons, Selim and Bayezid, 34. *See also* Âli: relations with individuals; Âli: views
Süleyman Paşa b. Kubad Paşa (Süleymân), governor-general of Baghdad, 119, 121
Süleymaniye, mosque and *medrese*, 26-27, 32
sultan, title, 279
Sulṭân-Ḥusayn Bâyqarâ. *See* Bâyqarâ
Sultana (Sulṭâna), tavern girl, 23
Sultans' Ascendant (Âli). See *Tâliʾ üs-selâtin*

Summary of Circumstances (Âli). See *Hulasat ül-ahvâl*
Sun and the Moon (Âli). See *Mihr u mah*
Sun'i (Ṣunʿî), poet of Gallipoli, 16n, 23
Sunnis, of Şirvan, 77
Süruri (Sürûrî), scholar, 28-29

Tab'i (Ṭabʿî, Şânî), poet of Gallipoli, 16n
Tabakat ül-memalik fi derecat il-mesalik (Ṭabaḳât ül-memâlik fî derecât il-mesâlik), by Celalzade, 31, 248
Tables of Delicacies (Âli). See *Mevâ'id ün-nefâ'is fi kavâ'id il-mecâlis*
Tabriz, Ottoman occupation of, 115, 118
Tac Beğ. *See* Tacizade Ca'fer Çelebi
Tacizade Ca'fer Çelebi (Tâcîzâde Caʿfer), chancellor to Bayezid II and Selim I, 172, 205
Tac üt-tevarih (Tâc üt-tevâriḫ), by Sa'düd din, 72, 241, 248
Taczade. *See* Ismail Çelebi, Taczade
Ṭahmâsb, Shâh, Safavi, 34, 77-78, 123
talebe (*talib-i ilm*), 27n
Tâli' üs-selâtin (Ṭâliʿ üs-selâṭîn), by Âli, 111
Ta'likizade (Taʿlîḳîzâde), *şehnameci*, 154n, 155, 239n, 249
Tarih-i nişancı (Târiḫ-i nişâncı), by Ramazanzade, 31, 248
tarik-i ilm. See *ilmiye*
tarik-i kitabet. See *kalemiye*
tarikat, 17-18, 20n, 29, 57, 136. *See also* Bayrami; Halveti; Nakşbendi
Tarzi (Ṭarzî), poet, 123
Taşköprüzade (Taşköprizâde), scholar and biographer, 251, 251n
Tat, 156
tekke, 17, 20n
tetimme. See *Sahn-ı seman*
Tevarih-i Âl-i Osman (Tevâriḫ-i Âl-i ʿOs̱mân), 238, 240-41, 250, 290n
tezkereci, 81, 81n, 214
Tezkere-i şu'ara (Teẕkere-i şuʿarâ), by Latifi, 23n
Tezkeret üş-şu'ara (Teẕkeret üş-şuʿarâ), by Kınalızade Hasan, 43
Third Branch. See *defterdar*: *şıkk-ı salis*
Tietze, Andreas, 100
Tifâshî (*Rujûʿ al-shaykh ilâ şabâh*), 55
Tiflis, Ottoman occupation of, 80, 84
timar: defterdarı, duties of, 82, 313; *kedhüdası* (see *defter kedhüdası*); qualifications for, 156; system, 19, 59-60, 83n; system, abuse of, 99, 104. See also *dirlük*
Timûr, 276, 280, 284-87
Timûrids, of India, 275-77, 279, 287, 290. *See also* regional empires
Tiraşi (Tirâşî), poet of Gallipoli, 16n
Ṭoqmaq Khân, Safavi governor of Erivan, 84
töre (törü), 274
Transylvania, revolt of, 298
treasurer: compared to chancellor, 95, 113, 228, 311-12; office of, 215-21. See also *defterdar: Rumeli*
treasury, provincial. See *defterdar*
tuğra, defined, 51, 93. *See also* chancellor
Tuğrul Beğ (Ṭuġrıl), Selcuk, 279
Tuhfet ül-uşşak (Tuḥfet ül-ʿuşşâḳ), by Âli, 37
Turak Çelebi (Ṭuraḳ, Nihânî), *defterdar* of Prince Selim II, as patron, 37, 38, 38n
Turkish (language): Çagatay, 22; Oğuz, 277; Ottoman, 22-24, 30, 149, 179, 236, 238-39, 248-49
Türkmens: ethnicity of, 76, 154-57; Kızılbaş, 77, 78; *şehnameci*s from among, 105, 105n, 274, 279. *See also* ethnicity
Tursun Beğ (Ṭûrsun), historian, 217n, 221n; compared to Ṭûsî, 227n, 291, 292n; on duties of sovereign, 302
Ṭûsî, Naṣîr al-dîn (*Akhlâq-i Nâṣirî*), 100n, 227n, 291; advisor to Hülegü, 237, 283-84; on sovereignty, 292n
Tütünsüz Hüseyin Beğ. *See* Hüseyin Beğ

ulema: in *kalemiye*, 204-205, 217-19, 221; in *seyfiye*, 193, 225, 260. *See also* Âli: views; factionalism: *ilmiye; kalemiye; medrese*
Ulvi (ʿUlvî), poet, 37, 38n
Ümmi Sinan (Ümmî Sinân), dervish, 72
Unique Pearls on the Birth (Âli). See *Ferâ'id ül-vilâde*
ʿurf. See *örf*
Üsküp (Skopje), 63
Üveys Çelebi. *See* Üveys Paşa
Üveys Paşa (Ḳara Üveys, Çelebî), treasurer to Murad III: as Âli's patron, 106n, 107, 108n, 109; appointed governor-general, (Aleppo) 99, 104, (Damascus) 121, (Egypt) 126; career summarized, 194, 204; early career of, 73; opposes Sokollu Mehmed Paşa, 297; as treasurer, 97, 124, 206. *See also* Âli: relations with individuals

Va'iz-i Firaki (Vâʿiẓ-i Firâḳî), poet to Prince Selim II, 38n
vak'anüvis, 237-38

vakıf, 17, 20n, 124, 128
valide sultan, 72, 175, 180
Valîjân Tabrîzî, painter, 106
Van, fortress, repaired, 115-16
Vardar Yenicesi, poets of, 30-31
Vâridat ül-enika (Vâridât ül-enîḳa), by Âli, 44, 68, 68n, 70, 74n, 90
Vaṣṣâf, historian, 240
vezir: appointment of, 193-94, 197; categories of, 47; grand, financial authority of, 311. *See also* Âli: views
vilâyet, 33; appointments to, 119-21. See also *beğlerbeği*; hass; provincial government

Wallachia, revolt of, 298
Wittek, Paul, 288n
Woods, John E., 286, 286n

Yahya Beğ (Yaḥyâ), poet, 63-64, 142, 222-23. *See also* Âli: relations with individuals *yasa*, 274, 284, 287, 291-92
Yazdî, Sharaf al-dîn. *See* Sharaf al-dîn Yazdî
Yazdî, Quṭb al-dîn, calligrapher, 123
Yazıcızade, Ahmed (Aḥmed Yazıcızâde), Bayrami poet, 16
Yazıcızade, Mehmed (Meḥmed Yazıcızâde), Bayrami poet, 16, 167
Yemen: *defterdarlık* of, 313; Ottoman campaign in, 46-52
Yemişçi Hasan Ağa. *See* Hasan Ağa, Yemişçi
yeniçeri: ağası, promotion of, 57, 193; *kâtibi*, 143, 144, 144n, 152. *See also* Janissary Corps
Yûsuf Sinân al-dîn (*Risâleh-i Bâbiyeh*), 80n

Ẓahîr-i Faryâbî, poet, 142
za'im, duties and status of, 83, 156, 209
Za'im Mehmed (Za'îm Meḥmed), historian, 280n
Zati (Ẕâtî), poet, 45
zeâmet, 65; defined, 59-60, 83n
zill Allah, title, 280
Zirek Ağa (Zîrek), eunuch, 112n
Zireki (Zîrekî), poet, 42n
Zübdet üt-tevarih (Zübdet üt-tevârîh), by Âli: composed, 69; rededicated, 70, 70n
Zuhuri (Ẓuhûrî), poet of Gallipoli, 16n
Zvornik, 64

Library of Congress Cataloging-in-Publication Data

Fleischer, Cornell H., 1950-
Bureaucrat and intellectual in the Ottoman empire.

(Princeton studies on the Near East)
Bibliography: p.
Includes index.
1. Âlî, Mustafi bin Ahmet, 1541-1599. 2. Historians—Turkey—Biography.
3. Turkey—Politics and government.
4. Turkey—Officials and employees.
I. Title. II. Series.

DR438.9.A45F44 1986 956.1′01 85-43277
ISBN 0-691-05464-9